T0260075

Smart and Sustainable Intelligent Systems

Scrivener Publishing
100 Cummings Center, Suite 541J
Beverly, MA 01915-6106

Sustainable Computing and Optimization

The objective of the series is to bring together the global research scholars, experts, and scientists in the research areas of sustainable computing and optimization from all over the world to share their knowledge and experiences on current research achievements in these fields. The series aims to provide a golden opportunity for the global research community to share their novel research results, findings, and innovations to a wide range of readers. Data is everywhere and continuing to grow massively, which has created a huge demand for qualified experts who can uncover valuable insights from the data. The series will promote sustainable computing and optimization methodologies in order to solve real life problems mainly from engineering and management systems domains. The series will mainly focus on the real-life problems, which can suitably be handled through these paradigms.

Submission to the series:

Dr. Prasenjit Chatterjee
Department of Mechanical Engineering,
MCKV Institute of Engineering, Howrah - 711204, West Bengal, India
E-mail: dr.prasenjitchatterjee6@gmail.com

Dr. Morteza Yazdani
Department of Management, Universidad Loyola Andalucia, Seville, Spain
E-mail: morteza_yazdani21@yahoo.com

Dr. Dilbagh Panchal
Department of Industrial and Production Engineering,
Dr. B. R. Ambedkar National Institute of Technology (NIT) Jalandhar, Punjab, India
E-mail: panchald@nitj.ac.in

Publishers at Scrivener
Martin Scrivener (martin@scrivenerpublishing.com)
Phillip Carmical (pcarmical@scrivenerpublishing.com)

Smart and Sustainable Intelligent Systems

Edited by

Namita Gupta
Prasenjit Chatterjee and
Tanupriya Choudhury

Scrivener
Publishing

WILEY

This edition first published 2021 by John Wiley & Sons, Inc., 111 River Street, Hoboken, NJ 07030, USA and Scrivener Publishing LLC, 100 Cummings Center, Suite 541J, Beverly, MA 01915, USA
© 2021 Scrivener Publishing LLC
For more information about Scrivener publications please visit www.scrivenerpublishing.com.

Wiley Global Headquarters
111 River Street, Hoboken, NJ 07030, USA

For details of our global editorial offices, customer services, and more information about Wiley prod-ucts visit us at www.wiley.com.

Limit of Liability/Disclaimer of Warranty
While the publisher and authors have used their best efforts in preparing this work, they make no representations or warranties with respect to the accuracy or completeness of the contents of this work and specifically disclaim all warranties, including without limitation any implied warranties of merchant-ability or fitness for a particular purpose. No warranty may be created or extended by sales representatives, written sales materials, or promotional statements for this work. The fact that an organization, website, or product is referred to in this work as a citation and/or potential source of further information does not mean that the publisher and authors endorse the information or services the organization, website, or product may provide or recommendations it may make. This work is sold with the understanding that the publisher is not engaged in rendering professional services. The advice and strategies contained herein may not be suitable for your situation. You should consult with a specialist where appropriate. Neither the publisher nor authors shall be liable for any loss of profit or any other commercial damages, including but not limited to special, incidental, consequential, or other damages. Further, readers should be aware that websites listed in this work may have changed or disappeared between when this work was written and when it is read.

Library of Congress Cataloging-in-Publication Data

ISBN 978-1-119-75058-1

Cover image: Pixabay.Com
Cover design by Russell Richardson and Farzil Kidwai

Set in size of 11pt and Minion Pro by Manila Typesetting Company, Makati, Philippines

Dedication

Prof. Namita Gupta would like to dedicate this book to her husband Mr. Arvind Goyal and her sons Anish Goyal and Ansh Goyal for their patience and support. She expresses extreme gratitude to Dr N. K. Garg (Founder and Chief Advisor, MATES), Prof. Neelam Sharma (Director MAIT) and Prof. S. S. Deswal (Dean Academics, MAIT) for their valuable guidance and encouragement.

Dr. Prasenjit Chatterjee would like to dedicate this book to his late grandparents, father Late Dipak Kumar Chatterjee, his mother Mrs. Kalyani Chatterjee, beloved wife Amrita and his little angel Aheli.

Dr. Tanupriya Choudhury would like to dedicate this book to his late grandparents, his father Sri Mrigendra Choudhury, his mother Mrs. Minakshi Choudhury, beloved wife Rituparna and his son Rajrup and his respected guides, his research collaborators, friends, scholars, most beloved students and colleagues.

Contents

Part 4: Communication and Networks   373

Preface

This book covers emerging computational and knowledge transfer approaches, optimizing solutions in varied disciplines of science, technology and healthcare. The idea behind compiling this work is to familiarize researchers, academicians, industry persons and students with various applications of intelligent techniques for producing sustainable, cost-effective and robust solutions of frequently encountered complex, real-world problems in engineering and science disciplines.

The chapters include the list of topics that spans all the areas of smart intelligent systems and computing such as: Data Mining with Soft Computing, Evolutionary Computing, Quantum Computing, Expert Systems, Next Generation Communication, Blockchain and Trust Management, Intelligent Biometrics, Multi-Valued Logical Systems, Cloud Computing and security etc. An extensive list of bibliographic references at the end of each chapter guides the reader to probe further into application area of interest to him/her.

Organization of the Book

The complete book is organized into 36 Chapters. A brief description of each of the chapters is presented as follows:

Chapter 1 proposes to improve the residual block architecture to define a modified residual dense block with the addition of the batch-normalization layer and secondly & improvised the Perceptual loss function according to our GAN. After these two changes, the authors introduce a new GAN based architecture for the Single Image Super-Resolution task for higher up-sampling levels.

Chapter 2 proposes a solution to google landmark recognition challenge 2019 hosted on Kaggle and an intuition for facilitating a tour guide recommender engine and visualization using method attempts to predict landmarks using CNN, pre-trained with VGG16 neural network used with transfer learning from ImageNet.

Chapter 3 suggests that Neural Network Models specifically CNN performed way better than other models with some fine-tuning for classification of 200 species of birds with an accuracy of 86.5%.

Chapter 4 proposes the use of Advance Image Processing Techniques and OpenCV functions to detect lanes on a public road along with calculating the radius of curvature of the lane and vehicle position in respect to the road lane i.e. central offset. In this paper, the front facing camera on the hood of the car is used for recording the video of the road in front of the car and feeding that video in the algorithm for better predictions of the road area. Used techniques like Search from Prior and Sliding window to create a more efficient and accurate algorithm better than previous approaches.

Chapter 5 proposes a methodology to detect human and animated faces in real time video and images. The facial expression would then be classified six basic emotions- happy, surprise, fear, anger, sad, disgust and a neutral face.

Chapter 6 proposes a system that does not segment the input of images, but rather the layers extract relevant features from the scanned images fed as input. Compared with previous systems for handwritten text recognition, the given architecture is end-to-end trainable and does not require different components to be trained separately. It naturally handles sequences in random lengths, involving no horizontal scale normalization or character segmentation. The model is smaller yet effective, thus, more practical for application in real-world scenarios.

Chapter 7 presents a machine learning modelled system able to analyse the image of an automobile captured by a camera, detect the registration plate and identify the registration number of the automobile. The algorithm also accepts live feed videos and pre-recorded videos, which are broken into frames. This system was made to solve security problems which exist in residential buildings, societies, parking areas and other institutions and areas where the pre-existing security systems cannot be installed.

Chapter 8 presents the finding of the best algorithm that can be used to predict the disease or chances that the disease can occur in the person.

Chapter 9 build a model which is combination of CNN model classification problem (to predict whether the subject has brain tumor or not) & Computer Vision problem (to automate the process of brain cropping from MRI scans). VGG-16 model architecture is used for feature extraction, which along with other features is fed as input to an Artificial Neural Network classifier through transfer learning. Binary Classifier classifies the input images as either 0 (No tumor) or 1 (Tumor exists).

Chapter 10 discusses the challenges faced in understanding the gestures of deaf and mute people in India and identified the need for a proper translator arises.

Chapter 11 designs a heterogeneous 3-Dimensional mesh (or network) to co-train 3 dimensional medical images dataset so as to make a series of pre-trained classifiers.

Chapter 12 explores a simpler approach to recommender systems that are fairly easy to use for small scale e- retail websites.

Chapter 13 discusses the recommendations to users on the basis of various user preferences while interacting with a social media platform, such as the gender, age, number of meetups, the skills and ratings of user profiles, image quality. All are taken into consideration to provide the ultimate user recommendation possible to make the software more relevant and user centric with recommendations strictly based on the way a given user interacts with the platform.

Chapter 14 discusses and compares the various machine learning algorithms applied to predict the literacy rate of various states.

Chapter 15 discusses an approach for video to video translation using various poses generated in the frames of video for translation. The approach makes use of Pose Generation Convolutional Neural Network to synthesize arbitrary poses from source videos and train the pix2pix - DCGAN which is a conditional generative adversarial network consisting of multi scale discriminator and generator for target video frames generation. It uses PatchGAN loss, VGG loss and Feature Matching Loss function for improving and optimizing models. The presented approach provides compelling results of the generated DCGAN model with the discriminator loss of 0.0003 and generator loss of 5.8206.

Chapter 16 compares different classification and boosting algorithms like Count Vectorizer with xG Gradient Boosting, TF-IDF Vectorizer with xG Gradient Boosting, Logistic Regression, and Random Forest.

Chapter 17 discusses development of traditional pixel-based methods and ends with the evolution of the latest object-based change detection techniques. LANDSAT and PALSAR images are used to represent the changes developed in the land use/land cover using pixel-based and object-based approaches.

Chapter 18 presents a study of four different machine learning algorithms namely J48, JRip, Random Forest and Naive Bayes, to detect three types of bad smells God Class, Long Method and Feature Envy. The results demonstrated that the machine learning algorithms achieved high accuracy with the validation method of 10-fold cross-validation.

Chapter 19 discusses the work done by the different researchers for identification of the negation's cues and their scope. Chapter is organized according to the different feature selection methods employed and how different researchers contributed to this.

Chapter 20 describes the methodology and experimental setup used for the generation and development of bilingual speech corpus. Continuous and spontaneous (discrete) speech samples from both languages are collected on different mobile phones in a real-time environment, unlike studio environments. A brief comparative study of 18 readily available multilingual speech corpus developed for Indian languages is made against the proposed corpus. An annotation scheme is discussed to carry out further study how the recognition rate varies on the basis of language, device, text, and utterance.

Chapter 21 focuses on building an Intelligent Intrusion Detection System utilizing a blend of Nature Inspired Heuristics and Automated Machine Learning. The study applies Evolutionary Algorithms for feature selection as well as Hyperparameter Optimization. Moreover, the research explores Bayesian Search for Neural Architecture Search to estimate the ideal architecture of an artificial neural network (ANN).

Chapter 22 introduces the concept of distributed ownership of any digital asset (NFT) amongst many people in the form of percentage shares. Distributed NFT (dNFT), holds the properties of NFTs as well as it can be traded in the form of percentage shares as in real world. Each digital asset in this model is validated by the validators who act as a trust entity in the system. Hence, it is authentic, verifiable and acts as real market place for all types of digital assets.

Chapter 23 compares 5 most popular blockchain platforms on the basis of 21 different attributes concluded with a summary of different platforms and some suggestions for most commonly and widely used blockchain platforms.

Chapter 24 discusses how the installation of smart bins will contribute towards an enhanced waste management system that will create a circular economy coupled with evolving production and consumption behavior while minimizing the environmental impact.

Chapter 25 discusses the structure of IDS; different types of intrusion detection techniques and various types of attacks and compare various intrusion detection systems based on techniques used, various parameters of detection performance and their use in different domains.

Chapter 26 features increasing demand for green communication technology in telecom and IT industry for better energy efficiency.

Chapter 27 discusses the integration of IoT with cloud, edge and fog computing; challenges associated with it and its applications.

Chapter 28 discusses the importance of privacy in telecommunication systems, the cheap adversary actions taken to generate a social profile, targets a vulnerability in GSM mobile architecture using open source software and software-defined radio, and discusses the awareness of the existing vulnerabilities among the public. It also predicts the security awareness rating for colleges using ridge regression and binary classification.

In Chapter 29, a novel Consumer Oriented Trust Model in E-Commerce is discussed. Proposed model has divided into five levels with five components.

Chapter 30 discusses various data mining techniques that can be used for making profitable business management decisions.

Chapter 31 categorizes data deduplication techniques applied on stored data in distributed computing condition to provide security when database size expands. In this study the authors elaborated the coordinating procedures of scrambled information and open difficulties for information deduplication.

Chapter 32 proposes an approach towards procedural generation of music which can be used by a person without any musical knowledge. This can be used to create recreational music according to a person's disposition. It can also be used in professional capacity to make music of different genres by content creators, game developers, animators and/or musicians to quickly create music loops, ambient/background sounds, gameplay music or even film scores with an interface providing control over each parameter to generate limitless variations.

Chapter 33 presents an approach that tackles photographs which have been morphed by using Photoshop alone using a neural network trained on real face images and their fake counterparts which have been manually generated by us using automation in Photoshop.

Chapter 34 presents review of various SQL injection approaches with the methods available to counter these attacks.

Chapter 35 discusses Futuristic Communication technology, Smart Energy Communication, Ubiquitous Communication and how Green technology sustainably affect environment and human life.

Chapter 36 includes survey on three types of cloud services: Software-as-a-Service (SaaS), Platform-as-a-Service (PaaS) and Infrastructure-as-a service (IaaS).

The Editors are grateful to the many chapter contributors, acknowledged international authorities in their respective fields, whose contributions constitute the substance of this book. They have made time in their very busy lives to devote attention to the generation of their exceptional manuscripts. Appreciation is expressed to Mr Alok Sharma, Mr Anupam Kumar, Mr Ashish Sharma, Dr Pooja Gupta, Ms Ruchi Goel, Mr Yogesh Sharma and Dr Farzil Kidwai for helping in the manuscripts review process.

Acknowledgement

The editors express their sincere gratitude to all the chapter authors who contributed their time and expertise to this book.

The editors also wish to acknowledge the valuable contributions of all the reviewers who extended their supports for improvement of quality, coherence, and content presentation of chapters.

The editors express their gratitude and sincere thanks to Scrivener Publishing for providing such a great opportunity and extending cooperation and support in every facet.

Last but not the least, the editors are extremely thankful to all readers and look forward to receive constructive feedback and suggestions.

Part 1

MACHINE LEARNING AND ITS APPLICATION

Single Image Super-Resolution Using GANs for High-Upscaling Factors

Harshit Singhal*, Aman Kumar, Shubham Khandelwal, Anupam Kumar and Mini Agarwal

Maharaja Agrasen Institute Of Technology, Guru Gobind Singh Indraprastha University, Dwarka, New Delhi, India

Abstract

Some state-of-the-art networks have solved the problem of recovering photorealistic features up to a certain level of up-sampling factor, basically up-to a factor of 4× in the task of Single Image Super-Resolution, but recovering fine and photorealistic features in up-sampling factors of 8× and above still remains unsolved. To solve this problem, we studied some components of SRGAN and came up with some improvements in these networks. Firstly, we propose to improve the residual block architecture to define a modified residual dense block with the addition of the batch-normalization layer and secondly, we improvised the Perceptual loss function according to our GAN. After these two changes, we introduce a new GAN-based architecture for the Single Image Super-Resolution task for higher up-sampling levels.

Keywords: Super resolution, 8× upsampling, GANs, higher upsampling, higher upscaling, dense block for upsampling, realistic super resolution, single image upsampling

1.1 Introduction

Image Super Resolution is one of the problems in Computer Science which has numerous applications. Single Image Super Resolution is the problem which is defined as converting a Low-Resolution Image into a High-Resolution Image without losing the Quality of the image and still capturing fine photo-realistic textures. The applications of this class of problem are in the field of medical science [1], in Digital Image Processing [2] and in various other fields [3, 4] are of great importance.

A very practical example of Image Super resolution is what we see in movies and shows where someone zooms into a picture and the quality improves and detail appears as shown in Figure 1.1. A very interesting use case of this is imagine transferring a picture on a network where you are sending 128 × 128 resolution image where 1,024 × 1,024 image is needed. It would also be beneficial in many other areas e.g., medical applications, aerospace, etc.

---

*Corresponding author: harshitsinghal33@gmail.com

Namita Gupta, Prasenjit Chatterjee and Tanupriya Choudhury (eds.) Smart and Sustainable Intelligent Systems, (3–16)

Figure 1.1 Low resolution–high resolution.

The approach we are trying is to solve this problem using GANs. Since traditional algorithm-based upscaling methods usually do not capture the finer details, humanly, this task is lengthy and too much time-consuming.

Obviously, on applying a degradation method available in the industry, we can acquire the Low-Resolution Image from the High-Resolution Image. Yet, would we be able to do the reverse? Of course, we can in an ideal situation if we know the method which was used to degrade the image in the first place, by applying its opposite to the LR picture, we can regenerate the HR picture. Problem in most cases is that we are just provided the Low-Resolution image and we are expected to upgrade it without knowing the source of the image, since we do not know the source of image, we can't find the degradation method used and can't recover the High-resolution image.

The task of single image super resolution is also a very ill-posed problem due to multiple possible outputs for the same low-resolution image. Since in low resolution images a lot of information is lost, for example if we have a low-resolution image which needs to be converted to 8× up sampling factor, then a single pixel in low resolution image corresponds to 16 pixels in the higher resolution image. So basically a 64-pixel information is compressed and degraded to a single pixel. This information needs to be generated for which various methods including interpolation techniques [5, 6] were used. But they did not result in regenerating the higher resolution image in desired manner which led to the use of Deep Learning based methodologies for solving this problem. Good results were obtained when Convolutional Neural Networks were used for this task [7, 8], but the use of Convolutional Neural Networks were not able to regenerate the fine textural details. This is where supervised learning approach were unable to properly solve this problem. Then the unsupervised learning based approach like GANs came into picture with the evolution of SRGAN [9] which was among the first GANs-based super resolution solution.

With detailed study of SRGAN, our work reflects how the basic structure of SRGAN can be modified to get better performance in the task of super resolution. Here in this work we will focus on how Residual Block architecture in SRGAN is modified and in accordance to it how generator is modified to get better results for 8× up sampling factors.

1.2   Methodology

1.2.1   Architecture Details

1. Generator Architecture: The task of Single Image Super Resolution involves providing only a Single Low-Resolution Image (denoted by I_{LR}) and generating a High-Resolution image output (denoted as I_{OHR}). In the following work, we describe a GANs generator network which helps to obtain photo-realistic features in I_{OHR} which is very identical to the Ground Truth High-Resolution Image (denoted as I_{GHR}).

   The previous work on super resolution task involves SRGAN [9], which has a very good Generator and Discriminator network architecture. Some works on SRGAN modified the Residual Block Architecture to get better building block for the Generator of SRGAN like in Ref. [10].

   The architecture shown in Figure 1.2 is a representation of how I_{LR} can be converted to High Resolution Image by a factor of 8×.

   The network consists of a Input layer which takes the I_{LR} as the input, this Input layer is followed by a convolution layer having Kernel/Filter size equals to 9 and the number of kernels equals to 64 which is denoted by K9 and N64 respectively. The Activation layer following the convolution layer is Parametric Rectified Linear Unit. The PReLU activation is used through-out the generator network (expect output layer) as it is an advanced activation function which is able to learn the leakage coefficient during network training. Following this layer is another convolution layer having kernel size equals to 3 and the number of filters equals to 64 followed by PReLU activation. (The network from Input Layer till the output of current PReLU layer is referred to as Pre-Modified Residual Dense Block Part). Then follows the Modified Residual Dense Block which is a modification of the Residual Dense Block defined in RDN [14]. Since the Residual Dense Block in RDN is engineered according the Supervised Training concept, we modified this Residual dense block to fit our GANs-based Unsupervised problem. The Modified residual dense blocks applied are 16 in number. Next comes the Post-Modified Residual Dense Block Part which focuses on Upsampling. This part includes a Convolution layer with kernel size 3 and 64 number of kernels, following which is a batch normalization layer followed by Element wise sum with the output Pre-Modified Residual Dense Block. Moving forward is Upsampling Block which

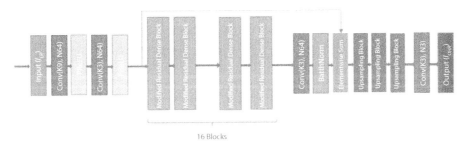

Figure 1.2 Generator network.

is same as that of SRGAN, but here Upsampling is done using TensorFlow's depth_to_space layer rather than using a Pre-trained Pixel Shuffler.

Each Upsampling block provides a 2× Upsampling factor, if the scale factor is set to 2. So to obtain 8× Upsampling, 3 Upsampling Blocks are used. Different levels of Upsampling can be obtained by changing the number of Upsampling blocks and changing the scale factor. After the Upsampling blocks follow the last convolution layer, having filter size 3 and number of kernels equals to 3 get an RGB image. This layer is followed by the tanh activation function layer which forms the output layer.

2. Structure of Modified Residual Dense Block: The modified residual dense block is shown in Figure 1.3. The evolution of state-of-art network due to small structures like Residual Blocks and Dense Blocks are storming the Deep Neural Networks. The integration of these two blocks have led to different structures like RRDB in [10].

We modified the combination of the Residual Dense Block in RDN [14] according to the GAN generator and resulted in the above architecture. This modified residual dense block has convolution layer with K3 and N64 followed by batch normalization followed by PReLU. Such 3 structures are connected in series, with input of each convolution being the concatenation of the input modified residual dense block and the output of each activation layer preceding it. The last part of this block has convolution with input as concatenation of outputs of previous activation layer in the same block and the input to the block. This follows a batch normalization layer and then the output of the block is the element-wise sum of last preceding batch normalization layer and the input of the modified residual dense block.

3. Discriminator: The Discriminator used in this network is same that of the SRGAN Figure 1.4 except that the batch normalization's momentum is set to default value.

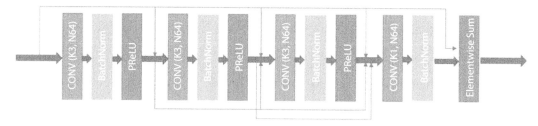

Figure 1.3 Structure of modified residual dense block.

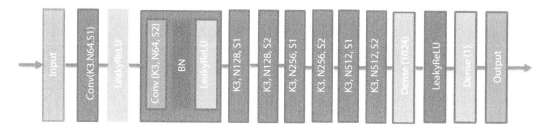

Figure 1.4 Discriminator network.

1.2.2 Loss Function

The loss function used for training is a modification of the Perceptual Loss function, which is a combination of Content loss and Adversarial loss. The Adversarial loss gives a weight of 10-3 to the discriminator loss, but in out implementation, the weight of this loss is increased to 10^{-2}.

1.3 Experiments

1.3.1 Environment Details

Training a Generative Adversarial Network requires high computation power. Due to the limited resources we trained our network on Google Collab GPU environment having 1× Tesla K80 GPU with 12 GB of GDDR5 VRAM.

1.3.2 Training Dataset Details

The training dataset used is DIV2K (DIVerse 2K) open source dataset consisting of 800 training examples of different resolution.

Our implementation consisted of 16 px ∗ 16 px Low Resolution images which are converted to 128 px ∗ 128 px High Resolution Images. Since the dataset had High Resolution Images of different sizes, the High Resolution training set was created by taking the center crop of the original images. The corresponding low resolution images are generated using OpenCV's bi-cubic interpolation technique.

The result analysis is done on PSNR(Peak Signal to Noise Ratio) for the generated images over the whole images without cropping 4 px wide strip unlike SRGAN.

1.3.3 Training Parameters

The training of GAN require separate training of Generator and Discriminator, so we trained the generator and discriminator alternately 1 epoch each, so the GAN's 1 epoch included 1 epoch training of Discriminator followed by 1 epoch training of Generator [26].

In our implementation the Batch Normalization momentum is kept to default configuration of 0.99 (rather than 0.8 as in SRGAN). Due to the resource constraints we presented the results of 1,500 epoch training, but the usual training requires around 10^5 epochs for best results. So to do the comparative analysis we trained the SRGAN model with its default configuration up to 1,500 epochs.

The optimizer used is Adam Optimizer with learning rate of 10^{-4} which is same across generator and discriminator and while keeping the value of beta_1 and beta_2 to the default values.

The context loss is calculated against the 9th layer of the VGG19 network, Pretrained on ImageNet Dataset which provides better feature extraction. The batch-size in our experimentation is kept 16 (should be kept above 12 for proper training of Batch Norm Layer).

1.4 Experiments

We compared our model trained for 1,500 epochs on DIV2K datasets for 8× Upsampling rate. For comparison, we present the Qualitative Results upon the public benchmark dataset which include: SET5 [27], SET14 [28] and BSD100 [29] in Table 1.1.

The qualitative results in Table 1.1 show that our GAN network with Modified Residual Dense Block outperform the state-of-the-art SRGAN architecture.

The results from Figure 1.5 represent how well our model converges on the training dataset.

The results from Figures 1.6, 1.7, and 1.8 are visual representations of the results on public test datasets SET5, SET14 and BSD100 respectively.

Table 1.1 PSRN comparison between SGRAN and our network for different datasets for 8× Upsampling rate.

Data Source	SRGAN	Ours
DIV2K	17.37	21.46
SET5	15.18	19.67
SET14	14.77	18.07
BSD100	15.54	18.12

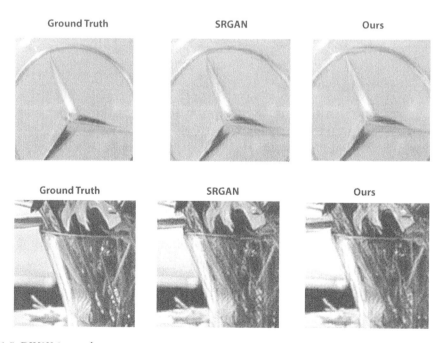

Figure 1.5 DIV2K 8× results.

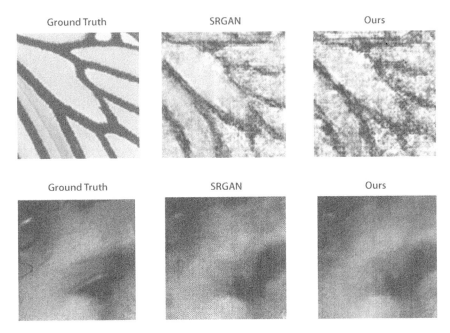

Figure 1.6 SET5 8× SR results.

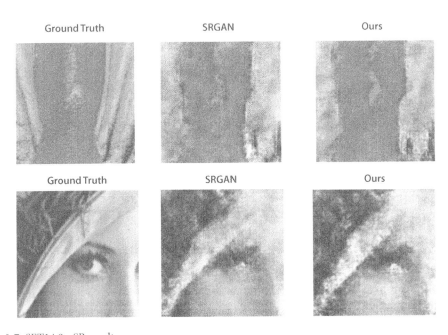

Figure 1.7 SET14 8× SR results.

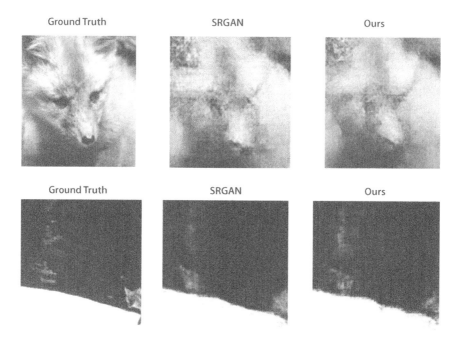

Figure 1.8 BSD100 8× SR results.

1.5   Conclusions

In this paper we discussed how the basic building unit *Residual Block* of the SRGAN network can be modified. We have finally presented a better substitute for residual block which was not able to extract local deep features by describing Modified Residual Dense Block architecture for GANs based approach which significantly improved the qualitative results measured in terms of Peak Signal to Noise Ratio. We have also presented how the generator architecture and the perceptual loss function adapts to the change in residual block. We also described how different level of Upsampling can be achieved by playing the Upsampling Block.

Thus, we finally conclude that our Modified Residual Dense Block architecture for GANs based approach outclass the basic SRGAN architecture to reconstruct the photo realistic high-resolution images for 8× Upsampling.

1.6   Related Work

Super Resolution GAN [9] was the first unsupervised learning based approach to solve the problem of image super resolution. Their work focused on defining a better loss function for proper training of super resolution task. Their work proposed the definition of Perceptual loss function which now is widely used loss function for super resolution in case of using GANs approach. Another contribution made by this paper is the development of a fine Generator and Discriminator network. The Generator is based on the Residual Block structure which provided great success to this architecture. To produce higher resolution images it applies combination of both deep network and an adversary network.

ESRGAN (Enhanced SRGAN) introduced by Wang [10] was an improvement over the SRGAN. Their work talked about changing the structure of Residual Block into a Residual in Residual Dense Block(RRDB) and removing Batch-Normalization layers from the whole network to get improved results. Another contribution made by their work included using a Realistic Discriminator [11] instead of the discriminator defined in Standard GAN. This Realistic Discriminator would be used to classify if the input is Realistic or not which was an improvement over fake or not fake discriminator approach for the standard GAN. Which means their discriminator is dealing with whether image is more realistic than other image which is done by adding real world detail while also maintain their original texture. This is advanced version of SRGAN discriminator which deals with only real and fake image.

Another work by Wang [12] was the development of Deep Spatial Feature Transform Network known as SFT-GAN. Their work included development of SFT layer which could be trained end to end with Super Resolution Networks. This SFT layer modified the feature of the middle layers. They demonstrated their work by using this SFT layer in the Residual Blocks of the SRGAN leading to the development of SFT-GAN.

In spite of the fact that incredible steps have been made, texture recovery in SR stays an open issue. Creating realistic textures which are more reliable to the inherent class is difficult. They suggest that the outcomes acquired by utilizing perceptual and adversarial losses (without earlier) do add fine subtleties to the remade HR images. Without more grounded earlier data, existing techniques battle in recognizing the LR patches and reestablishing normal and realistic surfaces consequently. In this paper, they thought that the prior category classification, which portrays the semantic class of a district in a picture (e.g., sky, building, plant), is critical for compelling the conceivable arrangement space in SR. We demonstrate the effectiveness of categorical prior using the same example in Figure 1.1. Specifically, we try to restore the visually ambiguous plant and building pairs using two different CNN models, each of which is specially trained on a plant dataset and a building dataset. It is observed that generating realistic textures faithful to the inherent class can be better achieved by selecting the accurate class specific model.

The major problem arrives when there are multiple regions of alike classes and magnitude appears together in a single image. As of now no work has been done to choose categories to obtain and use in the reconstruction process. This experiment uses this option and tries to prove that segmenting maps is a great choice to summaries high category priors to very small i.e., up to pixel level. The rest of the question is to identify a formula to form factors of texture generation in a Super Resolute network which has been conditioned on segmentation maps. If they train a separate Super Resolute model for every class that is semantic, it is neither scalable not efficient to scale. Merging Low Resolution images with these segmentation maps for inputs or joining with segmenting maps with some middle depth functions don't make a good use to it.

Also, in their wok, they came up with a new methodology which they called as Spatial Feature Transform (SFT) that is able to change the nature of a Super Resolute Network, just via changing the characteristics of some middle layers of the network. More precisely, a Spatial Feature Transform layer is based on probability of semantic segmentation maps.

It generates a duo of parameters to use affine changes spatially on the characteristic maps of the network.

Zhang's [13] work was the development of Deep Residual Channel Attenuation Networks (RCAN). RCAN consisted of Residual in Residual Structure, forming deep nets with skip connections which are obtained from far previous layers. Channel wise feature rescaling is done using CAN.

Modification of Residual Block is proposed by many state-of-the-art architectures. One of which is RDN. Residual Dense Network by Zhang [14] proposed a Residual Dense Block which is a combination of two best known structures: Residual Block and Dense Block. This block was used to extract local features. Using Residual Dense Block and Global Residual Learning RDN network was able to complete with some of the state-of-the-art networks.

Wang presented a survey on Super Resolution [15]. In this paper different stages of up-sampling were discussed. In the Pre-Upsampling Super Resolution the Low Resolution image is Up-sampled in early stages of the network and then post Upsampling network works to refine the up-sampled Image as done in Ref. [16]. Networks with post-Upsampling works exactly opposite to pre-Upsampling network. Progressing Upsampling networks as in Ref. [17] focused on learning and refining in small steps rather than doing all the Upsampling at once.

Upsampling stands as the main component of the Super Resolution task. This Upsampling can be both learnable and non-learnable. Learnable Upsampling are becoming more and more popular with Transpose Convolution which works the opposite of Convolution operation or does de-convolution [18]. Sub-pixel Layer [19] is another end to end learnable Upsampling technique which changes channels by reshaping them.

Among GAN-based techniques another state-of-the-art network is WGAN by Arjovsky [20], which provides steps to improve model stability and prevent the model from collapsing and provides direction to train a proper GAN. EDSR [21] by B. Lim, improves the residual block structure by removing Batch Normalization layer which makes the learning of the network computationally expensive.

Delving Deep into Rectifiers [22] introduced learnable activation and improved initialization from previous models which helped in reducing the risk of Model Overfitting.

Texture synthesis using CNN, introduced by Gatys [23], described approaches to generate texture by resampling techniques, in this manner they minimized feature space error and improves the visual quality.

Image net classification with deep convolution neural network [24], works on large data set to minimize the over-fitting problem, optimize the cost of 2D convolution network to handle a huge data set.

Preventing CO-adaption of feature detectors [25] describes the method to prevent over fitting by dropping random features of the images.

The residual block talked in the above papers was actually a very important building block of deep convolutional neural networks and was discussed with the discovery of ResNet architecture in Ref. [30]. This block lays the foundation of the basic building block of the base line architecture for Super Resolution which is SRGAN. The SRGAN's generator is powerful due to the its building block being the residual block modified according to the requirement. The property of residual block that it powers the deep neural networks is that it solves the problem of vanishing gradients. As the network depth grows it is harder for the initial layers of the network to get trained as the gradients diminishes upon reaching the starting layer. Thus the layers getting trained properly are the one which are present near the output layer. The ResNet architecture solved this problem by introducing the skip connections which helps in the training of the initial layers of the network. This thing also powers the SRGAN architecture as the generator is quite complex and in order to train all the layers global and local residual connections are provided.

Huang in Ref. [31] introduced a more powerful variation of residual block known as Dense Block in Dense Net architecture. The dense block is variation of residual block as in it not only includes the skip connection from one layer preceding the current layer, rather it takes into account the output of all the layers into the current layer. So we will be having multiple skip connections to the current layer, all the features from the skip connections are concatenated and results in a power network. This dense block architecture also helps in solving the vanishing gradients problem as discussed in Ref. [30]. This block also supports the feature propagation to the farther layers and feature reuse. One of the major advantage of this block is that it helps in reducing the total number of parameters of the model, as one dense block can do the work of multiple convolution layers all together. Thus enabling less dense networks and supports easy training. Most of the current state of the art networks also use dense block as the basic building block. This block can also support the super resolution task as discussed in the methodology section.

Multi-grained Attention Networks for Single Image Super-Resolution [32] and Deep Convolutional Neural Networks (CNN) have attracted incredible consideration in image super-resolution (SR). As of late, visual consideration component, which exploits both of the element significance and relevant prompts, has been acquainted with image SR and ends up being powerful to improve CNN-based SR performance. In this paper, they make a careful examination on the consideration components in an SR model and shed light on how straight forward and viable enhancements for these thoughts improve the condition of state-of-the-arts. They further propose a bound together methodology called "multi-grained consideration systems (MGAN)" which completely exploits the benefits of multi-scale and attention mechanisms in SR tasks. In Their strategy, the significance of every neuron is figured by its encompassing areas in a multi-grained style and afterwards is utilized to adaptively re-scale the element reactions. All the more significantly, the "channel consideration" and "spatial consideration" procedures in past strategies can be basically considered as two extraordinary instances of their technique. They additionally acquaint multiscale dense connection which extracts the picture highlights at numerous scales and catches the highlights of various layers through dense skip associations. In comparison with other state-of-the-art SR methods, their method shows the superiority in terms of both accuracy and model size.

References

1. Sano, Y., Mori, T., Goto, T., Hirano, S., Funahashi, K., Super-Resolution Method and Its Application to Medical Image Processing. *IEEE 6th Global Conference on Consumer Electronics*, pp. 1–2, 2017.
2. Singh, A. and Sindhu, J.S., Super-resolution Applications in Modern Digital Image Processing. *Int. J. Comput. Appl.*, 150, 2, 975–8887, 2016.

3. Yue, L. and Shen, H., Image Super-Resolution: The Techniques, Applications, and Future. *Signal Process.*, 128, 389–408, 2016.

4. Zou, W.W.W. and Yuen, P.C., Very Low Resolution Face Recognition Problem. *IEEE Transactions on Image Processing: A Publication of the IEEE Signal Processing Society*, vol. 21, no. 1, pp. 327–367, 2012. PubMed.

5. Gavade, A. and Sane, P., Super Resolution Image Reconstruction by Using Bicubic Interpolation, and others, Ed., *ATEES 2014 National Conference Elsevier Science and Technology Publications*, p. 204, 2013.

6. Rukundo, O. and Cao, H., Nearest Neighbor Value Interpolation. *Int. J. Adv. Comput. Sci. Appl.*, 3, 4, 25, 2012.

7. Kim, J., Lee, J.K., Lee, K.M., Accurate image super-resolution using very deep convolutional networks, in: *2016 IEEE Conference on Computer Vision and Pattern Recognition (CVPR)*, pp. 1646–1654, Las Vegas, NV, 2016.

8. Dong, C., Learning a Deep Convolutional Network for Image Super-Resolution. *Computer Vision—ECCV 2014*, D.F. *et al.*, Ed. Springer Link, pp. 184–99, 2014.

9. Ledig, C., Photo-Realistic Single Image Super-Resolution Using a Generative Adversarial Network, Cs, *arXiv e-prints,* 1609.04802, 2017. arXiv.org.

10. Wang, X., ESRGAN: Enhanced Super-Resolution Generative Adversarial Networks. *The European Conference on Computer Vision Workshops (ECCVW)*, arXiv e-prints, arXiv:1609.04802, 2018, Sept. 2018.

11. Jolicoeur-Martineau, A., The Relativistic Discriminator: A Key Element Missing from Standard GAN, Cs, *ArXiv*, abs/1807.00734, Sept. 2019. arXiv.org.

12. Wang, X., Recovering Realistic Texture in Image Super-Resolution by Deep Spatial Feature Transform. *IEEE Conference on Computer Vision and Pattern Recognition (CVPR)*, 2018.

13. Zhang, Y., Li, K., Li, K., Wang, L., Zhong, B., Fu, Y., Image Super-Resolution Using Very Deep Residual Channel Attention Networks. *ECCV*, 2018.

14. Zhang, Y., Tian, Y., Kong, Y., Zhong, B., Fu, Y., Residual Dense Network for Image SuperResolution. *CVPR*, 2018.

15. Wang, Z., Chen, J., Hoi, S.C., Deep Learning for Image Super-Resolution: A Survey, in: *IEEE Transactions on Pattern Analysis and Machine Intelligence*, 2019, https://arxiv.org/abs/1902.06068.

16. Dong, C., Loy, C.C., He, K., Tang, X., Learning a deep convolutional network for image super-resolution. *ECCV*, 2014.

17. Wang, Y., Perazzi, F., Mcwilliams, B., Sorkine-Hornung, A., Sorkine-Hornung, O., Schroers, C., A fully progressive ap- proach to single-image super-resolution. *CVPRW*, 2018.

18. Zeiler, M.D., Krishnan, D., Taylor, G.W., Fergus, R., Deconvolutional Networks. *IEEE Computer Society Conference on Computer Vision and Pattern Recognition*, 2010.

19. Rueckert, D. and Wang, Z., Real-time single image and video super-resolution using an efficient sub-pixel convolutional neural network. *CVPR*, 2016.

20. Bottou, L., Arjovsky, M., Chintala, S., Wasserstein, G.A.N., *arXiv e-prints*, arXiv:1701.07875, ArXiv, 2017. arXiv.org.

21. Lim, B., Son, S., Kim, H., Nah, S., Lee, K.M., Enhanced Deep Residual Networks for Single Image Super-Resolution, in: *2017 IEEE Conference on Computer Vision and Pattern Recognition Workshops (CVPRW), arXiv.org*, 1132–1140, 2017.

22. He, K., Zhang, X., Ren, S., Sun, J., Delving Deep into Rectifiers: Surpassing Human-Level Performance on ImageNet Classification, in: *2015 IEEE International Conference on Computer Vision (ICCV) ArXiv*, 1026–1034, 2015.

23. Gatys, L.A., Ecker, A.S., Bethge, M., Texture Synthesis Using Convolutional Neural Networks, *ArXiv*, abs/1505.07376, 2015. Cs, q-Bio.

24. Krizhevsky, A., ImageNet Classification with Deep Convolutional Neural Networks. *Adv. Neural Inf. Process. Syst.*, 25, 1097–1105, 2012.

25. Hinton, G.E., Improving Neural Networks by Preventing Co-Adaptation of Feature Detectors, *ArXiv*, abs/1207.0580, 2012.

26. Goodfellow, I.J., Generative Adversarial Networks, *Cs*, abs/1406.2661, 2014.

27. Bevilacqua, M., Roumy, A., Guillemot, C., Alberi-Morel, M.L., Low-complexity single-image super-resolution based on nonnegative neighbor embedding. *BMVC*, 2012.

28. Zeyde, Elad, M., Protter, M., On single image scale-up using sparse-representations. *Curves and Surfaces*, pp. 711–730, 2012.

29. Segmented natural images and its application to evaluating seg- mentation algorithms and measuring ecological statistics. *IEEE International Conference on Computer Vision (ICCV)*, vol. 2, pp. 416–423, 2001.

30. He, K. *et al.*, Deep Residual Learning for Image Recognition. *2016 IEEE Conference on Computer Vision and Pattern Recognition (CVPR)*, *ArXiv:1512.03385 [Cs]*, 770–778, Dec. 2015. *arXiv.org*, http://arxiv.org/abs/1512.03385.

31. Huang, G. *et al.*, Densely Connected Convolutional Networks. *2017 IEEE Conference on Computer Vision and Pattern Recognition (CVPR)*, *ArXiv:1608.06993 [Cs]*, 2261–2269, Jan. 2017. *arXiv.org*, http://arxiv.org/abs/1608.06993.

32. Wu, H. *et al.*, Multi-Grained Attention Networks for Single Image Super-Resolution, *ArXiv:1909.11937 [Cs, Eess]*, abs/1909.11937, Sept. 2019. *arXiv.org*, http://arxiv.org/abs/1909.11937.

Landmark Recognition Using VGG16 Training

Ruchi Jha, Prerna Jain, Sandeep Tayal and Ashish Sharma*

Maharaja Agrasen Institute of Technology, PSP Area, Rohini, Delhi, India

Abstract

The paper proposes a solution to Google landmark recognition challenge 2019 hosted on Kaggle and an intuition for facilitating a tour guide recommender engine and visualization. Too often while surfing our photos from last trip we stumble upon a few which leave us clueless about the castle or the river behind us. A landmark recognition engine can be the best anodyne. The challenge comprised a huge and vast dataset classified into sheer amount of predictions. With the presence of ample amount of "junk" images, broken links and images with multi-class predictions, our method attempts to predict landmarks using CNN, pre-trained with VGG16 neural network used with transfer learning from ImageNet.

Keywords: Convolutional neural network, deep learning, neural network, VGG16, deep local features, landmark retrieval, landmark recognition, image classification

2.1 Introduction

Landmark recognition is a problem of extreme classification centering on instance level recognition rather than entity-based classification of an input image such as rivers or cars. This problem is the follow up of series of challenges part of which are Landmark Recognition challenge and Landmark Retrieval challenge. The training data comprised of over 1.2 million images classified across 15k labels having one landmark per image and the testing data consisting of 117, 703 images labeled with zero or more landmarks. The release of datasets such as ImageNet (ILSVRC), Open Images (ECCV 2018) and COCO dataset (COCO challenges of 2018) have fostered great advancements in autonomous and unsupervised detection of underlying patterns across a plethora of labels, annotated or otherwise.

The second in the series of this challenge, Google-Landmarks-v2, a larger dataset including over 5 million images classified into over 200 thousand different images comprising of two new competitions (Landmark recognition and retrieval challenges 2019). The evaluation is done using Global Average Precision (GAP) metric taking confidence score for each landmark label predicted into consideration. The procedures and dataset construction deviate from conventional image classification and deals with both popular and not so popular

---

Corresponding author: ashish@mait.ac.in

Namita Gupta, Prasenjit Chatterjee and Tanupriya Choudhury (eds.) Smart and Sustainable Intelligent Systems, (17–40)

landmarks despite less training data available regardless the size and annotation of datasets. Due to the immovability of the landmarks, whose features are visually entrenched, the variations are only due to augmentation in height, width, different angles, brightness, zoom, shear, rotation, occlusion, illumination, etc., requiring our solution to be incisive against the existing entity-based recognition. Such an engine aims to bring a multitude of useful recognition and recommender applications. Figure 2.1 shows a few examples of sample images of database. First, it can provide for a richer database for unpopular landmarks boosting tourism prospects in and around that region. Second, a local feature spatial matching (achieved using DeLF) and geometric verification can facilitate a meticulous application for unsupervised geo-tagging of both images and videos. Third, a large part of data availability is through Wikimedia commons and user-clicked images obtained from different platforms (bloggers, tourist guides, *et al.*), the challenge of indefinite storage and sharing of images is valuable for our research.

Deep Local Features attempts to be especially useful for huge-scale object level recognition. It represents the semantic local features which can show geometrical proximity to other images which eventually makes us conclude the similarity between the objects and hence, the classification. The DELF models have already been pre-trained on the google dataset for landmark recognition—1. To build such a vast recognition application, the following issues, however, need to be taken on: (a) the training set consist of data having only

Figure 2.1 Examples of sample images of database.

one landmark, whereas the testing data is supposedly having a huge number of IDs having zero landmarks; (b) the images in the data are in the form of URL links which are subject to changes over the time and many others are inherently broken/damaged; (c) efficiency and accuracy of a huge scale engine requires a large storage space and mostly resizing of images, making it adamantly challenging.

2.2   Related Work

Datasets: This section describes the standard datasets used for evaluation of image retrieval and recognition techniques, the detailed description of landmark dataset, Deep Local Features (DeLF), ImageNet dataset (VGG16 model) and other renowned image recognition challenges providing valuable datasets. Figure 2.2 shows the landmark collection of Indian monuments.

2.2.1   ImageNet Classification

The ImageNet Large Scale Visual Recognition Challenge (ILSVRC) is a prominent yearly computer vision competition based on the open-sourced ImageNet dataset. This dataset represents a hierarchical structure just as Wordnet dataset (only nouns). It is a collection of multitudes of human annotated images which has led to state of art algorithms and techniques modelled for deep learning and image processing. The dataset comprises of around 14 million images (in the form of URLs precluding any kind of direct distribution)

Figure 2.2 Landmark collection of Indian monuments.

distinguished across 21k groups or classes and over 1 million images annotated with bonded boxes, created and maintained by research groups at various American Universities. Jia Deng *et al.* [2] have demonstrated the usefulness of ImageNet through applications in object recognition, image classification and automatic object clustering and the development of data resource by leveraging Amazon Mechanical Turk. Karen Simonyan *et al.* [35] open-sourced their winning models and trained weights (coming to be known as ImageNet pre-trained weights) as VGG model in Keras as two, VGG16 and VGG19 facilitating various parameters such as weights, classes, input_sensor, input_shape, etc. Alex Krizhevsky *et al.* [3] have been able to achieve top-1 and top-5 error rates of 37.5 and 17.0% respectively using deep convolutional network and a curated "dropout" method of regularization to reduce overfitting. They have established a drop of 2% in top-1 performance of the model on removal of any of the intermediate middle layers from the deep network. Both the VGG models help loading and preparing images and making and interpreting predictions through preponderance of labels with top probabilities. The VGG models using Keras have been first used in our solution to make predictions of present categories and pre-training the CNN model for further predictions. The model has been impeccably able to capture generic features form the images and made it a prior choice as a model for transfer learning process. Olga Russakovsky *et al.* [1, 4] have discussed a detailed collection of ground truth human annotations and have highlighted advancements in state-of-art accuracy from ILSVRC 2010 to ILSVRC 2014.

Kaiming He *et al.* [5] proposed rectified activation units neural networks for image classification from advancements of two, Parametric rectified linear unit (PReLU) that generalizes the conventional rectified units, and a meticulous initialization method that incisively considers the rectifier nonlinearities. It efficiently managed to achieve 4.94% top-5 test error on the ImageNet 2012 recognition challenge and a 26% comparative improvement over the winning ILSVRC 2014 submission and also claimed to be have achieved an ascendancy in all human level performances in the dataset.

Mohammad Rastegari *et al.* [6] have been able to propose efficient approximations to traditional neural networks using Binary-Weighed-Nets and XNOR-Networks. Filters have been appropriated with binary values leading to 32× memory saving and XNOR-networks have approximated convolutions using binary operations. These methods have outperformed the codes in more than 16% in top-1 accuracy.

Daniel Kuettel *et al.* [7] suggested an iterative and continuous segmentation to follow the further segmentation of new images occurring at both image level and class level and estimation of new probabilities of a pixel to be prominent. Experimented over 577 classes across 500k labels, the model was able to efficiently scale the hierarchical skeleton.

Dimitrios Marmanis *et al.* [8] learned a regressor capable of delivering 92.4% accuracy leveraging CNNs, deep learning models over two stage pre-trained classification. Thomas Deselaers and Vittorio Ferrari [9] have proposed an incisive analysis to determine semantic similarity built on distance function between training variables mapped through ImageNet classification and have demonstrated its outperformance at places. Leon Yao and John Miller [10] have successfully trained a pittance of image data consisting around 10k images over 200 distinct classes achieving a testing set error rate of 56.7%.

Xundong Wu *et al.* [31] created an architecture for neural networks based on Binarized Neural Networks trained on ILSVRC2012. ImageNet classification job.

Behavior of weights parameterized during the training was analyzed and the observations were used to obtain the proper learning rates. The suggested neural network had more than normal channels than regular networks at initial stages and usual at later layers. An 80% accuracy was obtained on the network. Following the binary network for all layers of BNN implemented in CIFAR-10 dataset, a regular weight convolutional layer was used for first layer of network. Against the synaptic weights used during the training stage of a usual BNN network, the extra units are removed at the output layer stage. These have been named binary synapses with internal/hidden features [32]. They were able to train a 13-layer network and obtain an 80% accuracy rate. Adding more layers to the network might cause a network overfitting contrast to the network better performance. To overcome this, a network distillation was used where a multilayer pretrained net was used to generate easily applied targets. Combined soft and usual targets were found to be significantly improving the performance of network. The results showed a proper an effective combination of architectural neural network and training strategies could drastically change and improve results. The distillation factor and the parameter tweaking are promising to improve network efficiency.

Minyoung Huh *et al.* [33] have enunciated about the reasons behind significantly improved performance of ImageNet while implementing transfer learning on the neural networks. The factors and features studied in the proposed reasons are size of examples dataset, number of classes and count of images per class. The pre-trained CNN was implemented on subsets of the ImageNet dataset and the transfer learning efficiency has been computed against various tasks. They have submitted the causes of using ImageNet classification used as a pre-training in many image classification techniques for CNN networks.

Several impressive results have been obtained in many classification tasks after having used the ImageNet pre-classification as illustrated in Figure 2.3 AlexNet-ImageNet classification with CNN, with some people arguing the presence of 1,000 class labels as providing an impressive hierarchy of generalizable features and the others arguing the presence of equally proportioned images per class. A number of factors have been consequently investigated in their findings such as the number of limited pre-trained ImageNet classification examples that might be deemed sufficient for running the transfer learning of our intended dataset. Along with the number of classes required for a sufficiently efficient transfer learning. Given the same limitation of resources for pre-training the images, which of classes or

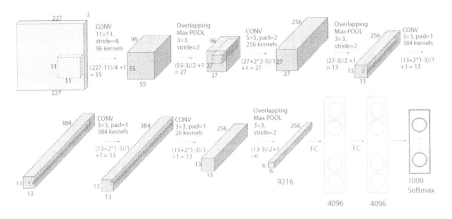

Figure 2.3 AlexNet–ImageNet classification with CNN.

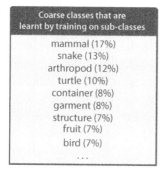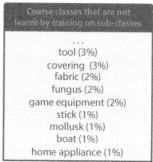

Coarse classes that are learnt by training on sub-classes	Coarse classes that are not learnt by training on sub-classes
mammal (17%)	...
snake (13%)	tool (3%)
arthropod (12%)	covering (3%)
turtle (10%)	fabric (2%)
container (8%)	fungus (2%)
garment (8%)	game equipment (2%)
structure (7%)	stick (1%)
fruit (7%)	mollusk (1%)
bird (7%)	boat (1%)
...	home appliance (1%)

Figure 2.4 Contrast shown in the difference between the number of class labels used [33].

number of images per class should be tweaked. What amount of data is deemed helpful in the context of training the image classification?

And lastly, how importance of fine-tuned analysis for learning good features for transfer leaning. Following this a useful discussion has also been done on the stage at which the pre-training must be halted to prevent overfitting and what layers should be used at the preliminary stages.

Any applied ImageNet classifier requires a differentiation between 1,000 labels few of which are extremely fine-tuned, which is even starkly contrasting to most human abilities to perceive the images into classified labels. The question about whether a huge number of fine graining of recognition of images is required in the first place. Their study showed that when only 127 classes are used, fine grain classification is only about 15% degraded as compared to the earlier unaltered case. The variation can be seen in Figure 2.4 which displays the contrast in the difference between the number of class labels used.

The paper has been successfully able to realize the effect of training data on transfer features and quality of ImageNet pre-trained features on transfer learning. It got insights about the fact the programmers might have been overestimating the amount of training data and class labels required. The CNN training features do not require an enormous data and other models if trained on bigger data might still even not be close to the ImageNet results.

2.2.2 Deep Local Features

DeLF (DEep Local Features) utilizes convolutional neural networks to train with instance level annotations to determine semantically corresponding local features. A descriptor that is supposed to be a trivial description of images or its contents, videos or the algorithms and modules/techniques curating such descriptions involving brightness, texture, elevation, color and so on is efficiently matched using Deep Local Features. DeLF finds immense applications in object detection in general and product, features and patent places detection in particular. Huge advances in key point selection have been also proposed using descriptor learning method introduced by Hyeonwoo Noh, André Araujo *et al.* [11]. The image retrieval technique mentioned in the approach have stressed on the detection of semantically approximate features. It mainly has described a large scale image descriptor and retrieval system based on a convolutional neural network. CNN based local feature has then been introduced which is primarily trained with convolutional neural network under weak supervision. Exactly this new descriptor is referred to as DELF descriptor. The retrieval system proposed under the research has been primarily based on dense local feature extraction, key selections and reducing the dimensions. The former has been proposed through complete convolutional network, along with classification loss. The FCN were used to handle scale changes and the features are localized based on their receptive fields. An idea of not using the densely corrected features and rather a subset of the extracted ones has been put forth. This has been referred to as advanced key-point selection. The huge part of incongruous images is essentially eliminated, enabling the technique to only focus the pre-training on relevant dat images. The aforementioned weak supervision has been referred to response of the performance to straightaway relevance scores. The score function designed for the job of weak supervision is that of a 2-layer convolutional network with softplus activation. The descriptors and the trained model are both learned with landmark IDs based level images only. The pipeline achieves both pre-training of model by encoding a higher level semantics in the feature map, and learning to select discriminative features for the classification task. The dimensionality reduction in this prominent research has been done through PCA reduced to a 40 point vector, which is a good contrast with resizing and differentiation. The clustering done by KNN and KD-tree brings a local optimized product optimizer. DELF significantly outperforms the other algorithms and feature extractors as it searches for similarity within local regions. This helps finding similar object with different positioning, inclination, viewpoint and clutter as the same image. The descriptor also has proven in their research to be better performing in objects of small size and aspect ratio. Besides modest developments in varied sized datasets [12, 13], its efficiency remains highly challenged by visual hindrances such as occlusion, rotation, illumination and viewpoint variations.

The images used in the curation of Deep Local features are from various places across the world associated with each annotations and GPS coordinates. Most of the images in the dataset are focused on landmark IDs making the global descriptors perform well but the images with variations in occlusion, viewing angles, cluttered images collected from community repositories need to be particularly taken care of due to what is called "distractors". They play a supposedly important role in deciding if the algorithm is robust enough to find useful mappings between images.

CNN based local features have been proposed for instance level mapping models [14–16]. But these techniques are not found to be specifically optimizing for image retrieval due to lack of ability to detect meaningful features and show limited robustness. Many image recognition problems incorporate deep neural networks based visual attention including entity detection [17], image auto annotation [18], visual Q/As [19], etc. The algorithms in DeLF annotation are broadly based on Ref. [20]. A DeLF feature extraction is done by incorporating a fully convolutional network (FCN) taken from ResNet50 model [21] constructed by an image pyramid. The feature locus of the receptive field used the pixel coordinates of centre. Attention-based key point selection is the methodology of selective extraction of subset of features important for both efficiency and accuracy.

Artem Babenko and Victor Lempitksy [34] have recognized the deep convolutional CNNs to be very useful for extracting features from any image of any given size and ratio. The constructed convolutional features are used to produce a global image descriptor for image retrieval. An extensive comparison of deep convolutional features and SIFTs have been done to form a new global image descriptor to avoid the not so required embedding steps and to explore design choices suitable for the descriptor. In the involved experiments, the features, just like other transfer learning procedures, are calculated by inputting the image through a pre-trained model of deep convolutional network. The deep features are supposedly more efficient as they are have been iterated through a massive amount of data of images in a supervised environment. They finally evaluated the performance of these descriptors and compared the performances with other aggregation algorithms through four popular different datasets. The Fisher vectors have been first fed with a PCS-resized 32 dimensions vector before final embedding. The paper gave us prominent insights about the benefits of feature descriptor and a comparison with other similar algorithms. Figure 2.5 illustrates the Network architectures used for training of DeLF models. A proper and useful analysis of aggregation strategies performed tells us about the numerous advantages of deep local features global descriptor over the traditional algorithms. The aggregation methods used were Fisher vectors and triangulation embedding.

Deep aggregation of 3D geometric variables for 3D retrieval has been proposed by Takahiko Furuya [21] that is able to devise a detailed geometry of a 3D model with minimal changes to 3D rotation of local 3D regions with these features accumulated into feature as per 3D model. They learned about the ascendancy of aggregation-of-local-features approach and also the shortcomings of 3D-DCNN model missing sensitive geometric features due to their discrete shapes into fine 3D analogue of pixels. It proposed a novel deep neural network that was inclusive of both movement invariant features and its accumulation in single deep skeleton.

Deep networks trained on local inputs as feature extractors have been proposed in Ref. [22], which are furthered into global features to ultimately map onto global variables in training data. The feature mapping between two images recognized according to the threshold can be seen in Figure 2.6. The experimental results showed that simple appropriation on the scarce sampled features have been beneficial. Video labels are supposedly large and expensive to retrieve the annotations as compared to images. Feeding the training or testing variables into any model demands space and resources unheard of. Uneconomical labeling of videos hampers the collection, appropriation as well as storage of an annotated dataset. They proposed to common practices in image classification and the training and testing data have noisy as well as incorrect labels.

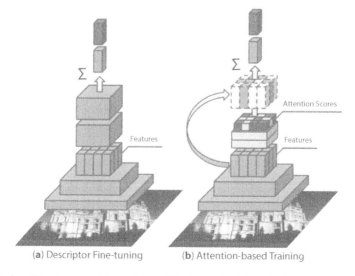

(a) Descriptor Fine-tuning   (b) Attention-based Training

Figure 2.5 Network architectures used for training of DeLF models (from [11]).

Figure 2.6 Feature mapping between two images recognized according to the threshold.

2.2.3 VGG Architecture

Convolutional neural networks have been a part and parcel of computer vision tasks such as image classification which predicts which of the 1,000 entity classes the image belongs to. VGG model was open-sourced by the Visual Geometry Group at Oxford as a winning solution to ImageNet classification. The model has been open-sourced in Keras library of python and provides freely available model weights and facilitated pre-training of the data-set. VGG released two CNN models called VGG16 and VGG19 layer model to be easily loaded using Keras library and facilitates varying parameters to pre-train the model as per convenience. Figure 2.7 depicts the VGG CNN hierarchy.

The images were taken largely from web and annotated by users using Amazon's Mechanical Turk crowd sourcing tool mostly containing variable resolution making them down sampled to 256 × 256 sizes. The input to the convolutional neural networks is fixed at 224 × 224 RGB image followed by spatial and max-pooling. The image goes through a sequence of convolutional layers having filters with short receptive field. The fully connected are followed by a max-pooled layer with unvaried configuration across fully connected layers.

The intermediate layers are supposedly associated with rectification non-linearity (ReLU). We also learned about how Local Response Normalization (LRN) leads to increased memory, space and computation time without any performance improvements. The two VGG16 and VGG19 models only differ in middle weight layers a6 or 19. The expansion of convolutional layers is small, starting at 6 and increasing by a factor of 2 till it reached 512.

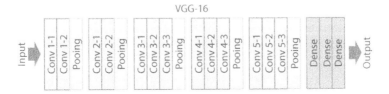

Figure 2.7 VGG CNN hierarchy.

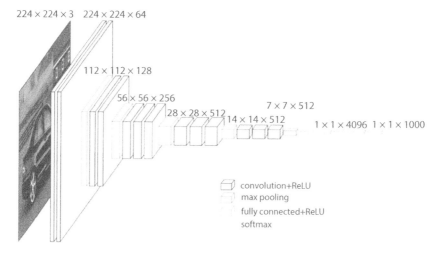

Figure 2.8 VGG architecture consisting of 2 ReLU and 1 soft max pooling having images of resolution 22 × 224.

The VGG architecture consisting of 2 ReLU and 1 soft max pooling having images of resolution 22 x 224 can be seen in Figure 2.8. VGG16 can be of immense usage in many deep learning image classification problems but are preferred on smaller and definite datasets. It outperforms the traditional models used in previous ILSVRC challenges. It faces many challenges regarding speed of training and the huge size of network architecture and its deployment over cloud-platforms.

2.3 Proposed Solution

This section describes our approach in detail and the sequences involved and modules used.

2.3.1 Revisiting Datasets

The recognition challenge training dataset consists of 1,225,029 images classified across 14,951 classes besides the testing dataset comprising of 117,703 images. With training data strictly having one landmark ID per image, the testing data primarily have large count of images with no landmarks. Figure 2.9 shows a few of the sample database images. This vast dataset is found to be deviant from conventional datasets pertaining to the sheer amount of classes the images are classified into. The second version of the Google Landmarks dataset also comes with two challenges called Recognition and Image retrieval. As Yan-Tao Zheng *et al.* [23] have proposed the process of appropriation of this huge scale dataset consisting of discernible and well-documented and annotated landmark images across the tourist places by primarily exploring various sources on the internet such as Wikimedia commons, photo sharing websites such as picasa.google.com, now defunct panoramio data, tourist guides, bloggers and so on. Much of this data source consists of geo-tagged data along with human annotations availing much instincts into both foreground and background and surroundings. The landmark IDs have been determined with the help of the names in annotations

Figure 2.9 Sample database images.

and extent to which a photograph is famous in landmarks is found by the number of users uploading or visiting the place in general, for e.g. Eiffel Tower vs an unpopular castle or river in the backdrop. The source of geo-tagged data has a unique ID, GPS coordinates, textual suggestions and uploader/user ID. With a huge number of classes present to be classified into, most of the classes have only image belonging to it, which poses a challenge to patience and computation efficiency due to too few images per class. Figure 2.10 shows a few of the sample query images with some having zero landmarks. The collection of images has been accounted as a partial list from the user uploaded images and their viewpoint. The landmarks and places are perceptive and subjective to user collecting it, that people belonging to different demography perceive differently and caption or describe it differently. Some other sources have also been surfed to compliment this list such as the social networking

Figure 2.10 Sample query images.

sites, wikitravel.com, and the travelling communities having constant inflow of good quality human annotated pictures. The challenge of mining legitimate landmark images out of the huge amount of noisy and cluttered images have been efficiently tackled with developed object recognition methods such as in [24, 25]. This work establishes visual clustering on the junk image dataset and assuming the dense structures to be legit landmark IDs with are then authenticated with the names and annotations mentioned in the images. The indefinite amount of images in the data sources thus obtained have been effectively computed by leveraging parallel databases, efficient clustering algorithms and KD tree index mapping. The algorithm suggested by Ref. [23] applies clustering on photos' GPS and as a result obtain several other landmarks with semantic similarity. The consequent visual clustering performed on this cluttered dataset then results in true landmarks mined. The landmark IDs are then processed according to the textual suggestions provide by the photographer or uploader. For the travel documents made available via HTML documents by travel bloggers, *et al.*, entity extraction takes place by semantic clues embedded in the hierarchy of the document. The textual associated data is then used to perform google search to generate a fresh junk data out of which true landmarks are generated based on complementing visual clustering. The images considered non-photographic against the photographic images are discarded using suitable classifiers.

2.3.1.1   Data Pre-Processing

Evidently the training as well as test classes consists of class imbalance and lesser correlation in the data together with variably large sized and "junk" images. This step comprises of mostly the transformation of raw and unprocessed images in the data sources to a viable and executable format to be able to feed to the machine learning models developed or trained all along. The immense dataset required huge computational power and an efficient database system to set the whole process up. The images resulting in huge space consuming due to higher resolution of the images and we learned that model training was much easier and faster on smaller resolution images compared to otherwise. The download of images of any variant of sizes of images took more or less the same time, the major time-consuming task for the regressor was of opening of the URL links and subsequent downloading. For the ease of faster computation, it was decided to work on images of resolution 96 × 96 rather than full raw sizes acquired.

For a pilot run on the complete dataset, it was viable to choose a platform for running the intensive modules such as Amazon Web Services (AWS) or Google Cloud Platform (GCP).

The data pre-processing step starts with the distribution of classes on chosen 2,000 classes (1,000–2,999 in our case).These IDs were not Landmark IDs but class labels. The training and testing images in the form of URL links comprise of all kinds of authentic as well as "junk" values and broken links. The class distribution is found to be shrunk across 2,000 image labels as suggested by utilizing Matplotlib and pyplot in python modules. Figure 2.11 shows the plot between the number of classes and number of images in original dataset.

The rationale for convenient resizing of images have been served by changing the links having s/{} (most of which were s/1,600) to suitable s/224 or others as per requirement,

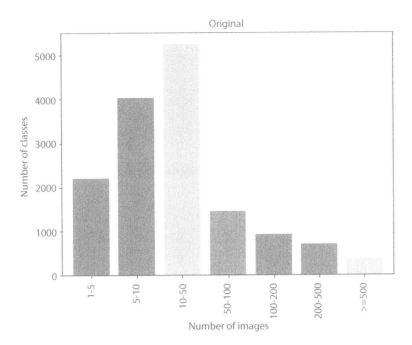

Figure 2.11 Distribution of images in original dataset.

following [26]. The resized images to a target size of 96 × 96 were essentially downloaded in a shorter time by scripting a complete overwriting. Figure 2.12 shows the distribution of data in resized dataset.

Given test images were consisted of mostly "junk" images and broken links and most of the testing class folders not containing single landmark, a separate hold out data had to formed out of the training set only for our evaluation. About 1% of images from each class made out a holdout set. Train-validation split was executed on remaining 99% data. 1/5th of which were labeled as validation set and the rest as training set, comprising almost 80% of the entire data, not tampering with the final results at much extent. Test set finally comprised of 128,600 variables, 31,145 in validation set and 1,160 in data test. This data distribution was an essential part of the pre-processing step as it accounted for acknowledging most of the class labels available across the entire dataset of Google-Landmarks-v2. The images after splitting of the data frames were prerequisites for fetching the images into the folders. The appropriate folders created had distribution according to the class sampling done at the rudimentary stages of the data pre-processing. Ref. [27] suggested removal of classes with no more than 3 images per class (comprising of a total of 53,435 fine-tuned images). This was certainly substituted as per satisfactory non-corrupt files downloaded earlier which had file size lesser than or equal to 1,000 bytes. The images possessing this identity were conveniently and incisively discarded.

The train and validation data are placed in a suitable directory format to be able to be used with Keras library and effectively train or pre-train the models.

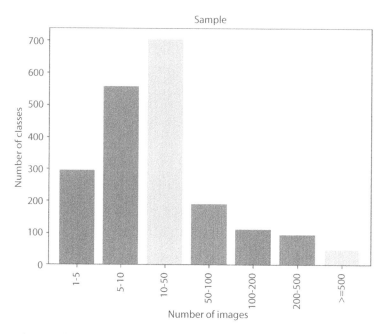

Figure 2.12 Distribution of data in resized dataset.

The classes having sparse image distribution in the corresponding folders did not contribute substantially to validation dataset. Absence of image folders in this case created problems which was taken on by creating empty folders for those class labels. This happened majorly due to 20% split done for holding validation data (contributing less than 1 with 1/5th of 4). We find further learning prospects to improve our performances int this respect.

The landmark candidates as discussed in Ref. [23] supposedly have images varying with only the angles, purview shifts, zoom, shearing, rotation, cluttering, occlusion and so on. Similar variations happened to be found in the test data as well. We have incisively explored and looked up to perform image augmentation to perform these variations in the system and be able to use directly as input to the deep network and make it viable for eyeballing the images and parameterize based on accuracy resulting after model training.

2.3.1.2   Model Training

A VGG19 CNN architecture is supposed to be a heavy architecture and is distributed with multiple layers at middle intermediate levels, as compared to VGG16 architecture. Training VGG16 is hence, chosen for a time efficient and viable for this classification problem. Figure 2.13 illustrates the VGG16 architecture. The model training begins with pre-training on Google ImageNet weights to predict landmarks. These weights, appropriately parameterized in the model of our choice for transfer learning, has been able to capture most of the features from our images and predict the classes these

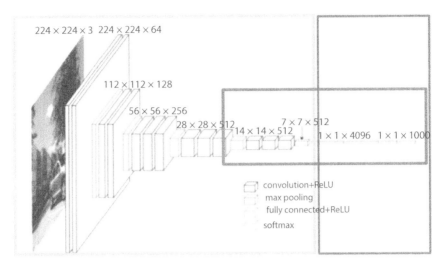

224 × 224 × 3 224 × 224 × 64

112 × 112 × 128

56 × 56 × 256

28 × 28 × 512

14 × 14 × 512

7 × 7 × 512

1 × 1 × 4096 1 × 1 × 1000

convolution+ReLU
max pooling
fully connected+ReLU
softmax

Figure 2.13 VGG16 architecture.

images belong to with the preponderance of different probabilities. After referring to previous works regarding best practices of transfer learning, an additional step for initialising the weights on prior three layers were also added on the entire network. The model finally had 2 ReLU activation and 1 softmax pooling and compiled to make the network learn for images besides ImageNet images. The variables for parameters in the complied model were optimizers, hyperparameters, batch-length and epoch counts. The VGG16 architecture is taken upto the last convolutional layer and added fully connected layers over the sequencing layers, which if done otherwise would force us to use a fixed size for the model (224 × 224, the initial formatting). The number of layers with weights while training the data are changed while proceeding.

The results and the added "dropout" layers are tested in subsequent runs. The finest efficiency is found to have been achieved by 2 ReLU and 1 soft max pooling and ImageNet weights complimenting at the bottom layers.

Optimizers inject in a split architecture with s simplistic lucrative configuration. As suggested by Matt Settles and Bart Rylander [28], the vectors are differentiated into even sub vectors each separately optimized in its own swarm. Following which a plain "attractor" is fed into each swarm. Varied optimizers such as SGD, etc. are used to further in the direction of improving accuracy. No particular rate of learning has served for all kinds of optimizers. The time to train invariably rises with increasing data size and more or less of learning rate values work equally well on huge datasets as well. The hyperparameters needed to be tuned are mostly leaning rates, iterative counts, momentum and point of decay. Adam supposedly works fine with regressors with varied learning rate for gradient descent problems, as also have been suggestive in Refs. [28, 30]. A reference to this article about hyperparameters has been of great importance [29]. Further image augmentation done reveals that a peculiar angle for rigid landmarks, that of 15–30 angle yields appreciating accuracy values.

Aggregation of images into batches has to be done in to instances. One for augmenting images to feature vectors for VGG16 layers causing the number of images in all three datasets to be a multiple of this created batch size. Second was during the model training which further leads to a trade-off between training time and the accuracy score. The batch size in these cases has to be made keeping in mind memory and CPU constraints of the system. Figure 2.14 shows the different optimizers used. The projections of various optimizers have been shown.

The model trained with VGG16 architecture is expected to give accuracy of 75–80% on validation set. But this threshold can be effectively varied commensurate with varying parameters instead of moving onto other models such as Inception or Resnet.

The validation accuracy as promising as it seems, still poses a challenge of large number of images in testing data lacking correlation with each other. Most of these images are not even landmarks pertaining to the photos uploaded by users without any popular background. This misleads the neural network largely as it predicts all the images with in a range of confidence scores as one of the classes, even the one having no landmarks. This problem is resolved by Deep Local Features as already discussed above. In a DeLF architecture, the feature with the highest score is selected and the features of query image passed through are matched against the images present in the database, done through Random sample Consensus and deciding over the inliers present. The threshold point of the DeLF is determined and supplied by the user. This threshold number of features decides if an image is a landmark or no landmark and effectively changes with resolution of images. The higher the resolution, easier it is to decide the threshold. This process of sending the images through DeLF is done after the predictions are made by neural network and the query input image is tested against the database images. There arise three cases of possibilities, (a) matching features more than threshold; (b) matching features lesser than threshold; (c) no matching features. Figure 2.15 depicts a suitable selected threshold helps which helps in finding the apposite matching of common features.

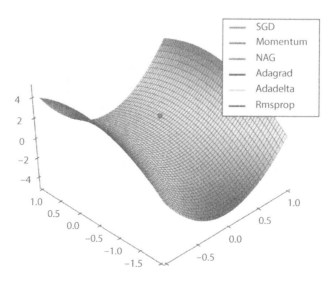

Figure 2.14 Different optimizers used. Projections of various optimizers have been shown.

47 Matched Features
Same Landmark

21 Matched Features
Different Landmarks

0 Matched Features
Unrelated Images

Figure 2.15 A suitable selected threshold helps in finding the apposite matching of common features.

2.4   Results and Conclusions

We demonstrate the results of trained models of VGG16 and the predictions of the existing datasets and its extensions. For this experiment we compared the probabilities of various categories predicted. We assumed the final predictive class based on the entity with maximum probability vis-à-vis top 3 entities. The predicted probabilities shown by in built VGG16 ImageNet trained weights on Keras also reveal that ImageNet weights have been easily able to capture the features. The predictions of images are in the form of prediction label, entity class and their predicted probability as shown in the listed outputs. Figure 2.16 illustrates the photo being predicted as cliff with probability 0.489, and cliff_dwelling as 0.1790. Figure 2.17 has been predicted as castle with probability 0.86, and as monastery as 0.077. Figure 2.18 has been predicted as megalith with probability as 0.913, and as cliff with probability 0.04 and thatch as 0.67. Figure 2.19 has been predicted as church with probability 0.82. Figure 2.20 has been predicted as tower

Figure 2.16 Predicted as cliff with probability 0.489, cliff_dwelling as 0.1790.

Figure 2.17 Predicted as castle with probability 0.86, as monastery as 0.077.

Figure 2.18 Predicted as megalith with probability as 0.913, as cliff with probability 0.04 and thatch as 0.67.

Figure 2.19 Predicted as church with probability 0.82.

Figure 2.20 Predicted as tower with probability 0.79.

with probability 0.79. Figure 2.21 has been predicted as stupa with probability 0.18, as palace with probability 0.15 and as shield with probability 0.04.

We presented a model trained with CNN pre-trained with VGG16 as well as in built Keras function prediction using ImageNet weights. We have learnt about the various resources that can be utilized for efficient computation power like most other cloud platforms. The immense emergence of landmark based tourism has inspired many researchers to build an earth-scale landmark recognition engine. The engine incorporates a huge number of training landmarks and labels to be classified into. The experiments substantiate a fair accuracy can be promised with a large dataset too. We have learnt about Deep Local features and its incorporation into a location based classification regressor that learns with weak supervisor using image-level labels only. We have also acknowledged some of the shortcomings that made the project more challenging like the pilot run of the model on a smaller dataset, tensorflow usage on GPU and removal of distractors. Another aspect of a landmark recognition still remains open that is the multilingual annotation of the described images. The only language use during the appropriation of the dataset id English. Most of the world tourism thrives on indigenous languages and cultures of people. Multilingual processing would be beneficial in collecting more landmarks widely popular across the world.

Figure 2.21 Predicted as stupa with probability 0.18, as palace with probability 0.15 and as shield with probability 0.04.

2.5   Discussions

Image recognition can be used to make predictions of everything ranging from movement patterns, traffic signs and even medical diagnosis primarily using Convolutional Neural Network which is the one of the most popular models for image processing. The landmark recognition is only a subset problem for large scale recognitions. The researches into the field can be vastly expanded to useful recommender systems for both image recognition and user usage predictions and visits to certain places.

As a future scope of the project, various optimization algorithms can be employed to pace the performance of convolutional neural network. The running of transfer learning algorithm on the given requires huge computational resources such as space and memory requirements. Those can be achieved by Google Cloud Platform and AWS. A quantum optimization technique can very well be applied on the CNN pre-training to optimize the performance and for faster results.

References

1. Russakovsky, O., Deng, J., Su, H., Krause, J., Satheesh, S., Ma, S., Berg, A.C., Imagenet large scale visual recognition challenge. *Int. J. Comput. Vis.*, 115, 3, 211–252, 2015.
2. Deng, J., Dong, W., Socher, R., Li, L., Li, K., Fei-Fei, L., ImageNet: A large-scale hierarchical image database. *2009 IEEE Conference on Computer Vision and Pattern Recognition, Miami, FL*, pp. 248–255, 2009.
3. Krizhevsky, A., Sutskever, I., Hinton, G.E., Imagenet classification with deep convolutional neural networks. *Adv. Neural Inf. Process. Syst.*, 1, 1097–1105, 2012.

4. Bailer, C., Finckh, M., Lensch, H.P.A., Scale Robust Multi View Stereo, in: *Computer Vision – ECCV 2012. ECCV 2012. Lecture Notes in Computer Science*, vol. 7574, A. Fitzgibbon, S. Lazebnik, P. Perona, Y. Sato, C. Schmid (Eds.), Springer, Berlin, Heidelberg, 2012.

5. He, K., Zhang, X., Ren, S., Sun, J., Delving deep into rectifiers: Surpassing human-level performance on Imagenet classification. *Proceedings of the IEEE International Conference on Computer Vision*, pp. 1026–1034, 2015.

6. Rastegari, M., Ordonez, V., Redmon, J., Farhadi, A., Xnor-net: Imagenet classification using binary convolutional neural networks. *European conference on computer vision*, Springer, Cham., pp. 525–542, October 2016.

7. Kuettel, D., Guillaumin, M., Ferrari, V., Segmentation Propagation in ImageNet, in: *Computer Vision–ECCV 2012. ECCV 2012. Lecture Notes in Computer Science*, vol. 7578, A. Fitzgibbon, S. Lazebnik, P. Perona, Y. Sato, C. Schmid (Eds.), Springer, Berlin, Heidelberg, 2012.

8. Marmanis, D., Datcu, M., Esch, T., Stilla, U., Deep Learning Earth Observation Classification Using ImageNet Pretrained Networks. *IEEE Geosci. Remote S.*, 13, 1, 105–109, 2016.

9. Deselaers, T. and Ferrari, V., Visual and semantic similarity in ImageNet. *CVPR 2011*, Providence, RI, pp. 1777–1784, 2011.

10. Yao, L., Miller, J.M., Stanford, *Tiny ImageNet Classification with Convolutional Neural Networks*, CS 231n, Stanford, 2015.

11. Noh, H., Araujo, A., Sim, J., Weyand, T., Han, B., Large-scale image retrieval with attentive deep local features. *Proceedings of the IEEE International Conference on Computer Vision*, pp. 3456–3465, 2017.

12. Philbin, J., Chum, O., Isard, M., Sivic, J., Zisserman, A., Object retrieval with large vocabularies and fast spatial matching. *2007 IEEE Conference on Computer Vision and Pattern Recognition, Minneapolis, MN*, pp. 1–8, 2007.

13. Philbin, J., Chum, O., Isard, M., Sivic, J., Zisserman, A., Lost in quantization: Improving particular object retrieval in large scale image databases. *2008 IEEE Conference on Computer Vision and Pattern Recognition, Anchorage, AK*, pp. 1–8, 2008.

14. Han, X., Leung, T., Jia, Y., Sukthankar, R., Berg, A.C., MatchNet: Unifying Feature and Metric Learning for Patch-Based Matching. *Proc. CVPR*, 2015.

15. Zagoruyko, S. and Komodakis, N., Learning to compare image patches via convolutional neural networks. *Proceedings of the IEEE Conference on Computer Vision and Pattern Recognition*, pp. 4353–4361, 2015.

16. Yi, K.M., Trulls, E., Lepetit, V., Fua, P., Lift: Learned invariant feature transform. *European Conference on Computer Vision*, Springer, Cham., pp. 467–483, 2016, October.

17. Zhou, B., Khosla, A., Lapedriza, A., Oliva, A., Torralba, A., Learning deep features for discriminative localization. *Proceedings of the IEEE conference on computer vision and pattern recognition*, pp. 2921–2929, 2016.

18. Hong, S., Noh, H., Han, B., Cortes, C., Lawrence, N.D., Lee, D.D., Sugiyama, M., Garnett, R. (Eds.), *Decoupled Deep Neural Network for Semi-supervised Semantic Segmentation Advances in Neural Information Processing Systems 28*, pp. 1495–1503, Curran Associates, Inc, MIT Press, Cambridge, MA, United States, 2015.

19. Xu, K., Ba, J., Kiros, R., Cho, K., Courville, A., Salakhudinov, R., Bengio, Y., Show, attend and tell: Neural image caption generation with visual attention. *International Conference on Machine Learning*, pp. 2048–2057, June 2015.

20. Zheng, Y.-T., Zhao, M., Song, Y., Adam, H., Buddemeier, U., Bissacco, A., Brucher, F., Chua, T.-S., Neven, H., Tour the World: Building a Web-Scale Landmark Recognition Engine, pp. 1085–1092, In Proc. CVPR, 2009.

21. Furuya, T. and Ohbuchi., R., Deep Aggregation of Local 3D Geometric Features for 3D Model Retrieval. *Proceedings of the British Machine Vision Conference (BMVC)*, R.C. Wilson, E. R. Hancock and W.A. P. Smith, editors, BMVA Press, pp. 121.1–121.12, September 2016.

22. Lan, Z., Zhu, Y., Hauptmann, A., Newsam, S., Deep Local Video Feature for Action Recognition. 1219–1225, 2017. 10.1109/CVPRW.2017.161.

23. Dugas, C., Bengio, Y., Bélisle, F., Nadeau, C., Garcia, R., Leen, T.K., Dietterich, T.G., Tresp, V. (Eds.), Incorporating Second-Order Functional Knowledge for Better Option Pricing. *Advances in Neural Information Processing Systems*, vol. 13. pp. 472–478, MIT Press, MIT Press, Cambridge, MA, United States, 2001.

24. Lowe, D.G., Object recognition from local scale-invariant features. *Proceedings of the seventh IEEE international conference on computer vision*, vol. 2, IEEE, pp. 1150–1157, 1999, September.

25. Sivic, and Zisserman, Video Google: a text retrieval approach to object matching in videos. *Proceedings Ninth IEEE International Conference on Computer Vision*, Nice, France, vol. 2, pp. 1470–1477, 2003.

26. https://www.kaggle.com/lyakaap/fast-resized-image-download-python-3

27. Gu, Y. and Li, C., Team JL Solution to Google Landmark Recognition 2019. ArXiv, 2019. abs/1906.11874.

28. Settles, M. and Rylander, B., Neural Network Learning using Particle Swarm Optimizers. *Adv. Inf. Sci. Soft Comput.*, 224–226, 2002.

29. https://www.freecodecamp.org/news/how-to-pick-the-best-learning-rate-for-your-machine-learning-project-9c28865039a8/

30. Sculley, D. and Brodley, C.E., Compression and machine learning: A new perspective on feature space vectors. *Data Compression Conference (DCC'06)*, IEEE, pp. 332–341, 2006, March.

31. Wu, X., Wu, Y., Zhao, Y., Binarized neural networks on the Imagenet classification task, arXiv, 2016. preprint arXiv:1604.03058.

32. Baldassi, C., Braunstein, A., Brunel, N. *et al.*, Efficient supervised learning in networks with binary synapses. *BMC Neurosci.*, 8, S13, 2007. https://doi.org/10.1186/1471-2202-8-S2-S13.

33. Huh, M., Agrawal, P., Efros, A.A., What makes ImageNet good for transfer learning? arXiv, 2016. preprint arXiv:1608.08614.

34. Babenko, A. and Lempitsky, V., Aggregating deep convolutional features for image retrieval, arXiv, 2015. preprint arXiv:1510.07493.

35. Simonyan, K. and Zisserman, A., Very deep convolutional networks for large-scale image recognition, arXiv, 2014. preprint arXiv:1409.1556.

A Comparison of Different Techniques Used for Classification of Bird Species From Images

Sourabh Kumar*, Vatsal Dhoundiyal†, Nishant Raj‡ and Neha Sharma§

Department of Computer Science Engineering, Dr. Akhilesh Das Gupta Institute of Technology and Management, Delhi, India

Abstract

Identifying birds is a difficult task that even the biologist fails to identify the correct species of the bird with the naked eye and is even more difficult for the beginners. So, to help the biologists and naïve people identify the bird species correctly, we have compared the techniques used in the past for Bird Species Classification from images. The paper shows that Neural Network Models specifically CNN performed way better than other models with some fine-tuning for classification of 200 species of birds with an 86.5% accuracy.

Keywords: Machine learning, deep learning, image classification, bird classification, neural network, biologists, comparison

3.1 Introduction

Mother Nature's diversity is unmatched and the world is full of varieties of flora and fauna. One such majestic creature are birds, which gave us the inspiration to fly and nature's biggest and best example of aerodynamics. But with so many species currently available in world sometimes even the most famous biologists and ornithologists can't recognize all and some birds lead to dispute between various personalities. Bird identification hence, has become a challenging task for both humans and computer.

Bird Species Classification can be done by both Acoustic and Visual Features. A lot of research has been put into classifying the birds based on the vocal data of birds and has attained a much higher accuracy in classifying on the new testing data.

Classifying the birds based on only the visual features is a large hurdle to cross due to the involvement of the background and also the noise in the foreground of the image. Due to this, there is still ongoing research in this field and researchers have achieved a decent accuracy rate in classifying on the basis of visual features. Many researches have been done

---

Corresponding author: sourabh99967780@gmail.com

Corresponding author: vatsaldh98@gmail.com

Corresponding author: nishantraj515@gmail.com

Corresponding author: nehash2689@gmail.com

Namita Gupta, Prasenjit Chatterjee and Tanupriya Choudhury (eds.) Smart and Sustainable Intelligent Systems, (41–50)
© 2021 Scrivener Publishing LLC

based on different techniques for the classification of birds ranging from simple raw classification to the fine-grained classification of the images.

Our aim is to combine the knowledge of all those researches and analyze the result of different techniques for the classification. The techniques used in the research papers include Machine Learning, Deep Learning and Hybrid Approaches so to attain the maximum accuracy. Many Machine Learning models and approaches have been experimented varying on the type of features they extract from the image with the use of some image processing techniques. Some of the machine learning models used are Support Vector Machines, KNN and Decision Tree Classifier.

There has been done many Deep Learning Experiments too involving mostly CNNs and extraction of various other features like Color, Beak size, etc. Some researches involved use of pretrained CNNs like AlexNet, ImageNet and ResNet for feature classification.

All these techniques and combination have varying dataset usage and testing accuracies. We will try to reach at the best method for classification of Bird Species Classification and fine-grained Image Classification.

We have used Python 3.7 based Jupyter notebook on anaconda framework having conda 4.8.1 for analysis and simulation work. For plotting the statistics, we have used Matplotlib, Seaborn, Numpy and Pandas in Python library.

3.2   CUB_200_2011 Birds Dataset

Mostly used dataset is the CUB_200_2011 dataset as shown in Figure 3.1 which contains 200 species of birds with 40–60 images of each giving a total of 11,788 images of bird of varying dimensions and scenarios. There are 15 Part locations, 312 Binary attributes and 1 Bounding Box per image. Some of the images in this dataset are also present in ImageNet [1].

3.3   Machine Learning Approaches

In this section, we will be analyzing the datasets, Machine Learning techniques and features used for classification of Bird Species. Prior to analyzing the techniques and features, an intro to the technology is essential.

Machine Learning is the technology that provides the computer with the ability to learn just like humans and adapt according to the environment. ML is one of the most exciting technologies that one would have ever come across. Computers can learn to make sentence, recognize images, generate music, etc. with the help of Machine Learning.

The learning process proceeds in 4 phases i.e. Data Collection, Data Pre-processing, Data fitting in the model and the last phase is the Prediction Phase.

In Data Collection, the data is collected from various sources and that could be raw i.e. having many null entries, wrong entries and ambiguous entries also. For this comparison, the data is collected from Caltech. Precisely, the data is CUB_200_2011 Birds Dataset (Figure 3.1).

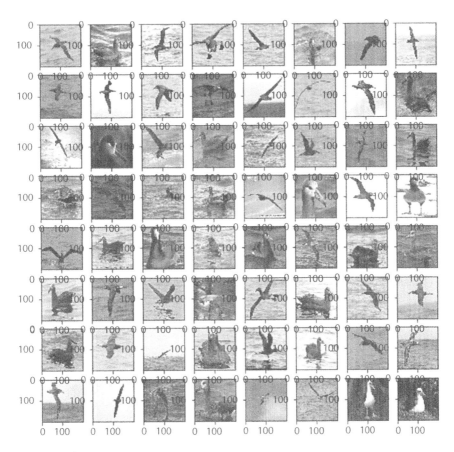

Figure 3.1 Snippet of CLUB_200_2011.

The data pre-processing has different stages i.e. Data Cleaning, dealing with NAN entries and handling faulty entries. The NAN value can be dealt with by either replacing the NAN entries with the average of that column or could be replaced by some static entries. If none of the above is suitable, we can remove the rows containing NAN entries. Filling NAN entries with some other value could either improve our accuracy of training or decrease it depending on what it is replaced with. But, deleting the NAN entries will result in data loss and could lead to underfitting of data in model which hits negatively to the accuracy. The libraries that could be very useful for this purpose are Numpy and Pandas in python.

Numpy is a library provided by python for preforming scientific calculations over arrays and number and Numpy arrays are faster in iterations and performing calculations over the whole array.

Pandas is also a python library providing the capability to represent data in a tabular format and process the data easily. Pandas converts the data into a dataframe that is easy to view and alter by iteration or direct access by various functions such as .iloc(), .loc(), etc.

Data fitting can be done in various different ways i.e. a model could be made or taken from Sklearn (a python library providing different Machine Learning Algorithms and model selection techniques) and data could be fitted in that model for training purpose. Sklearn also provides function to split the data for training and testing purpose. Different Machine Learning Models provided by Sklearn are Linear Regression, Logistic Regression, K Nearest Neighbours, etc. Every model object has a .fit() function to fit the data for training purpose.

The last stage is the prediction which is also provided by the model object, predict() function to predict the output of the testing data. The score of the prediction can further be calculated using the score() function provided by the model itself.

Machine Learning models like SVM (Support Vector Machine), Decision Tree, KNN (K-Nearest Neighbors), Naive Bayes tend to change a simple line and change the slope of the line at various places so as to fit the line in such a way that the data points are separated from each other based one different classes or categories and find a pattern to generalize over it.

For the Classification of Images, the models that could be used are SVM, Decision Trees, Naïve Bayes, Logistic Regression, K-Nearest Neighbors Classifier, Random Forests and Softmax Regression.

Bird Species Classification is a tough set of images to classify. Hence, the models that have been used by researchers in the past are Support Vector Machines, Decision Tree Classifies, K-Nearest Neighbors Classifier and Softmax Regression with some additional feature extraction techniques like Principal Component Analysis, Hierarchal Subset Learning, etc.

The datasets that is used for classification by most researchers is Caltech UCD-200-2011 Dataset that consists of 200 different species of birds with 40–60 images of each species that counts to around 12k images of the birds.

The different machine learning approaches with different features used are:

3.3.1   Softmax Regression

Softmax Regression is a multiclass classification that is generalized over Logistic Regression assuming that the classes are mutually exclusive unlike Logistic Regression which is a binary classification. In this, the Sigmoid function used in Logistic Regression is replace with Softmax function.

Softmax Regression has been used for classification based on 2 categories: with Specific Classes and with Broad Classes. Specific Classes means that all the birds are having different classes and Broad Classes refers to categorising the similar kind of bird into a broad class.

The results obtained on applying the above-mentioned techniques taken from Ref. [2] are mentioned in Table 3.1.

Table 3.1 Accuracy on Softmax Regression.

Method Used	No. of Bird Species Used	Testing Accuracy
Softmax Regression with Specific Classes	200	54%
Softmax Regression with Broad Classes	200	70%

3.3.2   Support Vector Machine

A support vector machine (SVM) is a supervised machine learning model that uses classification algorithms for two-group classification problems. After giving an SVM model set of labeled training data for each category, they're able to categorize new text.

Support Vector Machines is one of the most popular techniques used for fine-grained image classification and bird species classification used by the researchers in the past along with some fine tuning or addition of some extra features and feature extraction techniques.

Researcher have used Color of the birds as a feature, color spaces based on mean, standard deviation and skewness of each plane, Different Color spaces such as RGB (Red Green Blue), HSV (Hue Saturation Value) and YUV (luma, blue minus luma, red minus luma). Some researchers have also found some other features such as Beak to eye length, etc.

Certain experiments have been done using Support Vector Machines in different combinations and the results are very promising.

When SVM is used with Image Processing and RGB color features on 200 species of birds, we get an accuracy of 9% [2]. When SVM is used with 9 color-based features of mean, standard and skewness of each plane on 2 species, we get a 98.33% accuracy [3]. When One-vs-most classifier (SVM) is used on 500 species, we achieve an 82.4% accuracy [4].

A Decision tree when used with SVM and taking beak length as a feature and using different color spaces on 15 bird species, we achieve different accuracies. With RGB color space, an accuracy of 75.28% can be achieved, with HSV as a color space, we get a 73.28% accuracy and with YUV color space, we get an 83.87% accuracy [5].

Focussing on the acoustic features, if it is used with SVM Classifier on 46 species, we get an accuracy of 94.5% [6] and when SVM is used with KNN on color features on 200 species, an accuracy of 75% can be achieved [7].

SVM Classifier can perform very much accurate even when the dataset if larger as in One—vs—most classifier with 500 species.

3.3.3   K-Means Clustering

K-Means Clustering algorithm is an unsupervised machine learning algorithm and it is used to cluster the data into different groups based on the mean distance of the data points from each other.

There has been an experiment done using Collaborative K-Means Clustering on Bird Species Classification but the dataset used is the Ponce and the Indian Birds Dataset, both containing 6 species each. The testing results are gathered from Ref. [8] and clustered into Table 3.2.

Table 3.2 Accuracy on different K-Means Clustering on different datasets.

Method Used	No. of Bird Species used	Accuracy
Collaborative K-Means Clustering on Ponce dataset	6	88.1%
Collaborative K-Means Clustering on Indian Birds Dataset	6	89.9%

3.4   Deep Learning Approaches

In this section, we will be analyzing the datasets Deep Learning techniques used and features used for classification of Bird Species. Prior to analyzing the techniques and features, an intro to the technology is essential.

Deep Learning is a subset of Machine Learning with the involvement of a neural network rather than a conventional mathematical line to classify the data into different classes. Neural Network serve as a brain to the model which has some weights and biases to adjust to fit a mathematical model to the data. Deep Learning techniques include CNN Convolutional Neural Network, RNN (Recurrent Neural Network), LSTM (Long Short-Term Memory), etc.

Out of the above-mentioned techniques, the most famous techniques used for classification of images is Convolutional Neural Network (CNN). CNN has proven to be state-of-the-art model to be used for Image Classification. There are different types of CNN available such as R-CNN, RA-CNN, DCNN, etc. which enhances the performance of the existing CNN depending on the type of data.

3.4.1   CNN

CNN (Convolutional Neural Network) are majorly used for Image Classification in Deep Learning and it is one of the best techniques for Image Classification. CNN can also be used for Object Detection, Face Recognition, etc. This project also involves a major use of CNN in classifying the birds to their respective classes. In CNN, there are various layers involved i.e. the Convolution Layer, Hidden Layer, Dense Layer, Flatten and Output Layer.

An image goes through a CNN network, the computer sees the image and tries to classify it from certain categories. e.g. Ships, Humans, Cats, Dogs, etc. The image is an array of pixels on which the computer depends on the image resolution. Based on the image resolution, it will see h × w × d (h = Height, w = Width, d = Dimension).

Convolution layer is the first layer to extract features from an input image. Convolution layer does the work of resizing the image preserving the previous relationship in the image. It creates a small box of pixels that goes over the image sequentially and process that square or set of pixels and apply some mathematical operations to produce a single value from all those values that represent the same relationship. Hence, it reduces the size of the image by preserving relationship. Different Kernels are used as Mathematical Operations to reduce those set to pixels to a single value. The most commonly used operation is the average of all the values. Convolution of an image with different filters can perform operations such as edge detection, blur and sharpen by applying filters.

3.4.2   RNN

RNN are the Recurrent Neural Networks. As its name suggests, it is an intelligent combination of Neural Networks and Recursion in programming. Recurrent Neural Networks are also used for Image Classification and Natural Language Processing.

Recurrent Neural Networks are a little bit different than the conventional Neural Networks in a way that RNN feed the output of Network to the input for further training making a loop which keeps the model an always learning phase or continuous learning state and hence increasing the accuracy progressively. In summary, in a vanilla neural network, a fixed size input vector is transformed into a fixed size output vector. Such a network becomes "recurrent" when you repeatedly apply the transformations to a series of given input and produce a series of output vectors. There is no pre-set limitation to the size of the vector. And, in addition to generating the output which is a function of the input and hidden state, we update the hidden sate itself based on the input and use it in processing the next input.

Most of the researchers working on Bird Species Identification of Fine-grained Image Classification have used the Caltech UCD-200-2011 dataset which consists of 200 species of birds with a total of 12k images of birds and as a neural network to perform better need more data to be trained on. Hence, every deep learning technique utilizes all the species available in the dataset i.e. 200.

For Bird Species Classification, mostly CNN has been used with some finetuning or with some feature extractor involving a machine learning model such as KNN which enhances the performance of CNN Network. Many pretrained CNN Models have also been used such as the AlexNet, ImageNet, and Inception models such as Inception V1, Inception V2, Inception V3 and lately Inception V4 with ResNet.

3.4.3   InceptionV3

InceptionV3 is a widely used Image recognition model created by Google that is trained on a large number of images and classification is done accordingly. It is the 3rd variation of deep Learning Convolutional Architectures having 48 layers and 1,000 classes of images. You can always take a pretrained inceptionV3 model and add some more layers of your own to classify the images in your dataset accordingly using Transfer Learning. The images in the inceptionV3 model are of dimension (299 by 299). You can use the InceptionV3 model from the Cloud Platform using Machine Learning API.

3.4.4   ImageNet

ImageNet is a CNN model that has been trained on a million of images to classify them according and has some bird images too which can be fine-tuned to perform better on the bird species classification. For e.g. some layers of AlexNet could be changed to work on the Bird Species Classification Dataset.

The different CNN models that past researchers have used are Bilinear CNN, RA-CNN (Recurrent Attention CNN), CNN with hierarchical subset Learning, DCNN (Deep CNN), CNN with Staged Training in Low and High Res Images, etc. Due to fact that Neural Networks perform far better in many situations than normal machine leaning models, CNN have performed significantly better and the results that are obtained from Refs. [9–15] are given in Table 3.3.

We started plotting the data on the graph as shown in Figure 3.2 and found that Multi-Attention CNN performed the best in case of Bird Species Classification.

Table 3.3 Testing Results of Different CNN Techniques.

Method	Accuracy
Bilinear CNN with Deep Dictionary Learning	84.6%
RA-CNN with RAM Localization	79.77%
Hierarchical Subset Learning CNN	72.7%
DCNN with Foreground Fischer Vector	86%
CNN with Staged Training	55.3%
Multi-Attention CNN	86.5%
Recurrent Attention CNN	82.4%

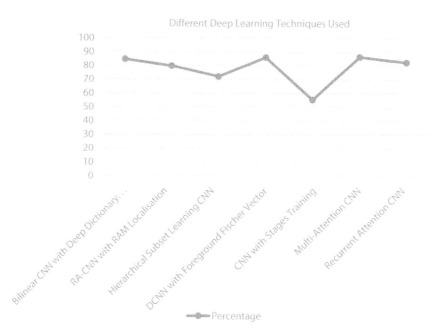

Figure 3.2 Analysis of different deep learning techniques.

3.5   Conclusion

From the above analysis, we can come to a conclusion that Machine Learning Models like SVM can perform better in only a certain condition a fixed set of datasets. It is not well suited for any kind of fine-grained classification. On the other hand, Neural Networks can perform better than general machine learning algorithms for fine-grained image classification. When a CNN is slightly fine-tuned for the dataset, it can produce impressive results even on the whole 200 species and can reach an accuracy of up to 86.5% which is commendable.

Hence, we conclude that if a pretrained CNN is combined with some fine tuning produces the best classification results.

3.6   Conclusion and Future Scope

This comparison of different techniques provided with the insight on which technique to work on and extend the work further to improve it. It also helped in identifying the future of Bird Species Identification by Image Classification. This classification could be combined with acoustic features of birds to increase the accuracy. When achieving a respectable accuracy, this could be deployed over web to make a web app that will take image of birds as input and classify them and also provide information about the bird by fetching from Wiki data or other sources. An android or IOS app could also be made that would be must user friendly as they would be able to capture the image of birds from camera and classify them in real time. The app will also provide information about the bird and further details on its origin, geographic features, etc. This would be a real time use of the model which could be deployed with the help of Tensorflow.js which will be much faster than the conventional Tensorflow model.

References

1. Welinder, P., Branson, S., Mita, T., Wah, C., Schroff, F., Belongie, S., Perona, P., *Caltech-UCSD Birds 200*, California Institute of Technology. CNS-TR-2010-001, 2010.

2. Alter, Anne L. and Wang, K., An Exploration of Computer Vision Techniques for Bird Species Classification. 2017.

3. Roslan, R., Nazery, N.A., Jamil, N., Hamzah, R., Color-based bird image classification using Support Vector Machine. *2017 IEEE 6th Global Conference on Consumer Electronics (GCCE)*, Nagoya, pp. 1–5, 2017.

4. Berg, T., Liu, J., Lee, S.W., Alexander, M.L., Jacobs, D.W., Belhumeur, P.N., Birdsnap: Large-Scale Fine-Grained Visual Categorization of Birds. *2014 IEEE Conference on Computer Vision and Pattern Recognition*, Columbus, OH, pp. 2019–2026, 2014.

5. Qiao, B., Zhou, Z., Yang, H., Cao, J., Bird species recognition based on SVM classifier and decision tree. *2017 First International Conference on Electronics Instrumentation & Information Systems (EIIS)*, Harbin, pp. 1–4, 2017.

6. Nanni, L., Costa, Y.M.G., Lucio, D.R., Silla, C.N., Brahnam, S., Combining Visual and Acoustic Features for Bird Species Classification. *2016 IEEE 28th International Conference on Tools with Artificial Intelligence (ICTAI)*, San Jose, CA, pp. 396–401, 2016.

7. Marini, A., Facon, J., Koerich, A.L., Bird Species Classification Based on Color Features. *2013 IEEE International Conference on Systems, Man, and Cybernetics*, Manchester, pp. 4336–4341, 2013.

8. Chakraborti, T., McCane, B., Mills, S., Pal, U., Fine-grained Collaborative K-Means Clustering. *2018 International Conference on Image and Vision Computing New Zealand (IVCNZ)*, Auckland, New Zealand, pp. 1–6, 2018.

9. Srinivas, M., Lin, Y., Liao, H.M., Deep dictionary learning for fine-grained image classification. *2017 IEEE International Conference on Image Processing (ICIP)*, Beijing, pp. 835–839, 2017.

10. Semeniuta, S. and Barth, E., Image classification with recurrent attention models. *2016 IEEE Symposium Series on Computational Intelligence (SSCI)*, Athens, pp. 1–7, 2016.

11. Ge, Z., McCool, C., Sanderson, C., Bewley, A., Chen, Z., Corke, P., Fine-grained bird species recognition via hierarchical subset learning. *2015 IEEE International Conference on Image Processing (ICIP)*, Quebec City, QC, pp. 561–565, 2015.

12. Pan, Y., Xia, Y., Shen, D., Foreground Fisher Vector: Encoding Class-Relevant Foreground to Improve Image Classification. *IEEE Trans. Image Process.*, 28, 10, 4716–4729, Oct. 2019.

13. Peng, X., Hoffman, J., Yu, S.X., Saenko, K., Fine-to-coarse knowledge transfer for low-res image classification. *2016 IEEE International Conference on Image Processing (ICIP)*, Phoenix, AZ, pp. 3683–3687, 2016.

14. Zheng, H., Fu, J., Mei, T., Luo, J., Learning Multi-attention Convolutional Neural Network for Fine-Grained Image Recognition. *2017 IEEE International Conference on Computer Vision (ICCV)*, Venice, pp. 5219–5227, 2017.

15. Fu, J., Zheng, H., Mei, T., Look Closer to See Better: Recurrent Attention Convolutional Neural Network for Fine-Grained Image Recognition. *2017 IEEE Conference on Computer Vision and Pattern Recognition (CVPR)*, Honolulu, HI, pp. 4476–4484, 2017.

Road Lane Detection Using Advanced Image Processing Techniques

Prateek Sawhney* and Varun Goel

B.Tech. Information Technology, MAIT, G.G.S.I.P.U, Rohini, New Delhi, India

Abstract

Self-Driving Cars are no longer the talks of Science fiction. Ever since the DARPA challenge, significant research in the field of autonomous vehicles has been carried out. Various companies are working in this field of research. Various driving support systems are now available these days like lane assist, park assist, etc. These functions are called ADAS or Advanced Driver Assistance Systems. Lane Assistance is basically lane detection i.e. assisting the drivers in recognizing lane lines in front of the car in adverse road conditions. Lane detection is one of the most important tasks required for the successful working of autonomous vehicles or self-driving cars. Detecting Lane Lines is a challenging task because of the different road conditions while driving. In view of this attribute, this paper proposes the use of Advance Image Processing Techniques and OpenCV functions to detect lanes on a public road along with calculating the radius of curvature of the lane and vehicle position in respect to the road lane i.e. central offset. In this paper, the front facing camera on the hood of the car is used for recording the video of the road in front of the car and feeding that video in the algorithm for better predictions of the road area. Used techniques like Search from Prior and Sliding window to create a more efficient and accurate algorithm better than previous approaches.

Keywords: Computer vision, image warping, sliding window approach, camera calibration, perspective transform, autonomous vehicles, self driving cars, lane detection

4.1 Introduction

Identifying lanes of the road is a very common task that a human driver performs. This is important to keep the vehicle in the constraints of the lane. This is also a very critical task for an autonomous vehicle to perform. People can find lane lines on the road fairly easily, even in a wide variety of conditions.

*Corresponding author: Prateek.sawhney97@gmail.com

Namita Gupta, Prasenjit Chatterjee and Tanupriya Choudhury (eds.) Smart and Sustainable Intelligent Systems, (51–72)
© 2021 Scrivener Publishing LLC

Unless there is snow covering the ground, extremely heavy rainfall, the road is very dirty or in disrepair, we can mostly tell where we are supposed to go, assuming the lines are actually marked. Computers, on the other hand, do not find this easy [1]. Shadows, glare, small changes in the color of the road, slight obstruction of the line are all things that people can generally still handle, but a computer may struggle mightily with.

The goal is to design a pipeline using advance image processing techniques to make this task easy for computers. In this paper, we proposed the approach for identifying lane lines in the input video from the car. The input video is recorded from the camera which is located on the hood of the car. Further, we used Camera Calibration, Image Warping and Perspective Transformation for bird's eye view and converted the images into Binary threshold. In this research, we proposed the idea of "Search from Prior" i.e. using the detected lane lines information from the current frame and using that information to detect road lane lines into future frames after a high confidence detection in the current frame. Also, we calculated the Radius of Curvature of the road and Central Offset of the vehicle on the road.

4.2 Related Work

In the paper [2], the authors use a novel adaptive soft voting scheme using high-confidence voters established upon a local voting region to detect road boundaries in a single image. J.G. Kul *et al.* [3] use Hough transform for fast lane detection and tracking. In the paper [4], the authors use enhanced Hough transformation to attain straight-track road lane detection. In the paper [5], research is done on lane detection using Machine Vision. A. Goel [6] presents a review of different lane-detection techniques in practice. G. Kaur and D. Kumar [7] present a comprehensive review of challenges in lane detection. Most of the prevailing road lane detection mechanisms are based on normal Hough transformation which mainly focuses on detecting lines in an image and report low accuracy on curved roads.

In this paper, instead of blindly searching for road lanes in each frame of video, we provided the current detected road lane information to the algorithm to search for the position of road lane lines in subsequent frames of the input after high confidence detection in the current frame. This makes our pipeline better than the previous applied approaches.

4.3 Proposed Approach

In this paper, we used OpenCV, a library of real-time Computer Vision functions. The visual display of the lane boundaries is detected irrespective of the road texture, brightness, contrast, curves, etc.

We also used Image Warping and Sliding Window approach to find and plot the lane lines and also determined the real curvature of the lane and vehicle position with respect to center.

4.4   Analysis

4.4.1   Dataset

The test video contains 50 s of northbound footage through the S-curves along the Junipero Serra Freeway near Woodside Glens, USA. The video begins just before Exit 27, in a gentle left turn of 914-meter radius followed by a straight section of about 360 m (indicated by the dashed red line above). The straight 04 of 18 terminates at the end of a bridge (over Farm Hill Boulevard) followed by a slow right turn of 1,037 m radius. Just after the halfway point through this turn is another bridge (over Cañada Road). The video ends as the road straightens out of the turn. Average speed over this distance is 114 km/h (or 71.4 mph). Although lighting conditions appear to be ideal with high-contrast pavement markings, there are incongruous anomalies near the bridges. These include abrupt road-surface color shifts from dark- to light-gray, sporadic cast shadows from vegetation, and several vehicle/camera-pitch bounces caused by the uneven road surface at the approach slabs.

Various test images were extracted out of the video and used for analysis in various stages of the pipeline. All of the images in their raw form i.e. distorted images taken from the camera on the hood of the car are depicted below as Figure 4.1, Figure 4.2, Figure 4.3 and Figure 4.4.

Figure 4.1 Test Image-1.

Figure 4.2 Test Image-2.

Figure 4.3 Test Image-3.

Figure 4.4 Test Image-4.

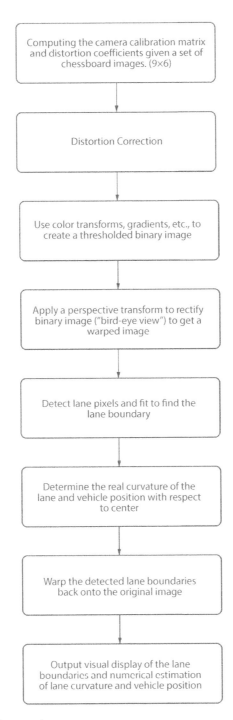

Figure 4.5 Overall methodology used.

4.4.2 Camera Calibration and Distortion Correction

The first step in the pipeline as shown in Figure 4.5 is to undistort the camera. Some distorted images of a 9 × 6 chessboard are taken. The task is to find the Chessboard corners and plot them. For this, after loading the images we calibrate the camera using Open CV [8] functions. The captured 2-dimensional image from a camera lens isn't perfect because of the physical properties of the lens. There are image distortions that change the relative size and shape of the object in the image. Due to this, some objects appear farther or closer than they actually are. These distortions are corrected in the first step of the pipeline. Figure 4.6 shows the image before distortion correction and Figure 4.7 shows the image after distortion correction. All the distortion information is collected from chessboard images because chessboards have regular high contrast patterns. Figure 4.8, Figure 4.9, Figure 4.10 and Figure 4.11 illustrates the camera calibration performed on chessboard images.

Figure 4.6 Original image of chewssboard.

Figure 4.7 Distortion corrected image of chessboard.

Figure 4.8 Camera calibration performed on chessboard image (example-1).

Figure 4.9 Camera calibration performed on chessboard image (example-2).

Figure 4.10 Camera calibration performed on chessboard image (example-3).

Figure 4.11 Camera calibration performed on chessboard image (example-4).

To approximate the camera's field of view and focal length, if the corrected video is displayed full-screen on a 24" monitor and viewed closely from a distance of 10 in., the vehicles in other lanes appear to be correctly shaped. Figure 4.12 shows an original image on which distortion correction is applied. This explains the apparent pincushion distortion when viewed from a greater distance, where the vehicle shapes begin to elongate (Most notable in the white car in the "corrected" image below as shown in Figure 4.13).

Figure 4.12 Original image.

Figure 4.13 Distortion corrected image.

4.4.3   Threshold Binary Image

Detecting edges around trees or cars is easy because these lines can be mostly filtered out by applying a mask to the image and essentially cropping out the area outside of the lane lines. It's most important that we reliably detect different colors of lane lines under varying degrees of daylight and shadow. So, that our self-driving car does not become blind in extreme daylight hours or under the shadow of a tree. We performed gradient threshold and color threshold individually and then created a binary combination of these two images to map out where either the color or gradient thresholds were met as shown in Figure 4.14, Figure 4.15, Figure 4.16, Figure 4.17, Figure 4.18 and Figure 4.19.

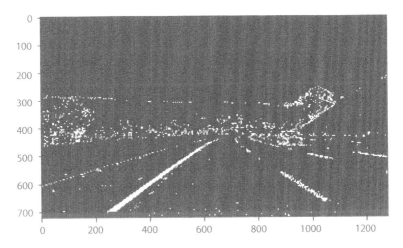

Figure 4.14 Binary image of road scene (example-1).

Figure 4.15 Binary image of road scene (example-2).

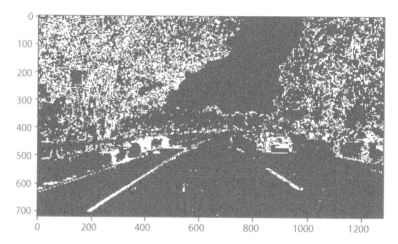

Figure 4.16 Binary image of road scene (example-3).

Figure 4.17 Binary image of road scene (example-4).

Figure 4.18 Binary image of road scene (example-5).

Figure 4.19 Binary image of road scene (example-6).

4.4.4   Perspective Transform

Perspective Transform [9] is the Bird's eye view for Lane images. We want to look at the lanes from the top and have a clear picture about their curves. To determine the perspective, transform into an overhead view, four corners of a lane were pinpointed on a straight segment of the road. We made a function wrapper which takes in the Binary Warped Image and return the perspective transform using *cv2.getPerspectiveTransform()* and *cv2.warpPerspective()* functions. The results are shown below in Figure 4.20, Figure 4.21, Figure 4.22, Figure 4.23, Figure 4.24 and Figure 4.25.

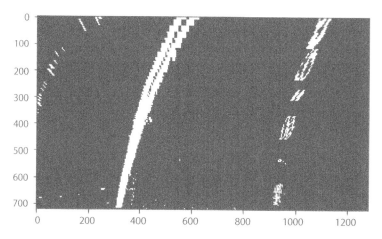

Figure 4.20 Warped image of road (example-1).

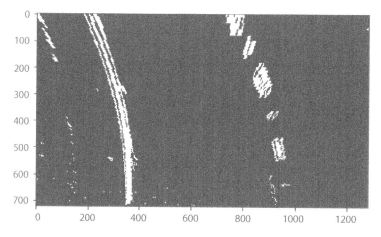

Figure 4.21 Warped image of road (example-2).

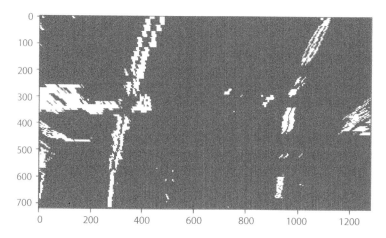

Figure 4.22 Warped image of road (example-3).

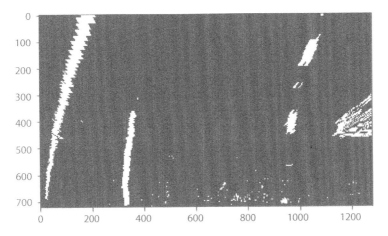

Figure 4.23 Warped image of road (example-4).

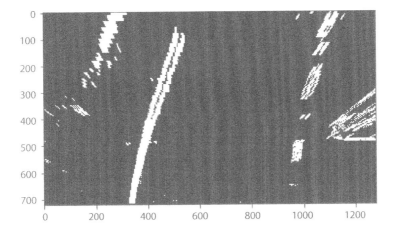

Figure 4.24 Warped image of road (example-5).

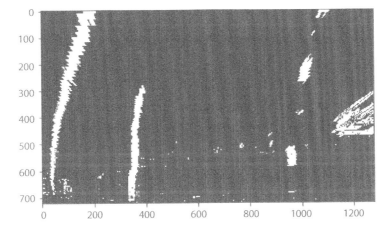

Figure 4.25 Warped image of road (example-6).

4.4.5   Finding the Lane Lines—Sliding Window

Once we got the Perspective Transform of the binary warped images, we first used sliding window [10] to plot the lane lines and fitted a polynomial using fit_polynomial function in OpenCV. Later on, we used the Search from Prior technique and fitted a more accurate polynomial through the perspective transformed images as shown in Figure 4.26, Figure 4.27, Figure 4.28, Figure 4.29 and Figure 4.30.

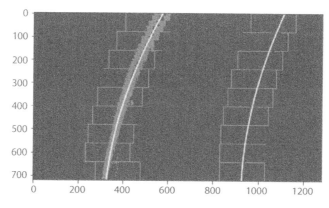

Figure 4.26 Sliding window illustration 1.

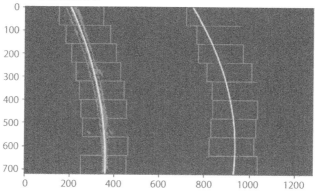

Figure 4.27 Sliding window illustration 2.

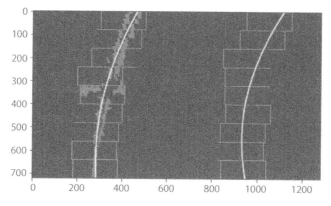

Figure 4.28 Sliding window illustration 3.

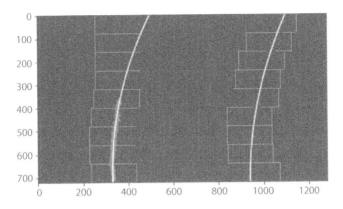

Figure 4.29 Sliding window illustration 4.

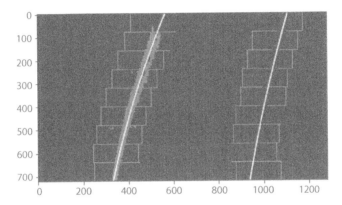

Figure 4.30 Sliding window illustration 5.

Further, detecting lane lines in a video frame, finding them in the next frame is easy because their position doesn't change to a large extent. Our task is to fit a new polynomial to all the pixels extracted from a close vicinity of the previous detection as shown in Figure 4.31, Figure 4.32, Figure 4.33, Figure 4.34 and Figure 4.35.

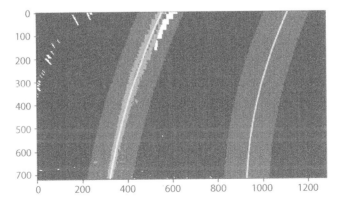

Figure 4.31 Search from sliding window illustration 1.

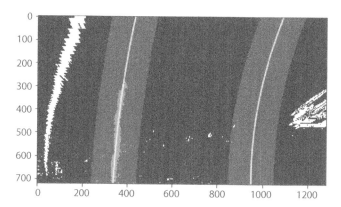

Figure 4.32 Search from sliding window illustration 2.

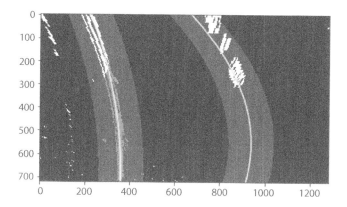

Figure 4.33 Search from sliding window illustration 3.

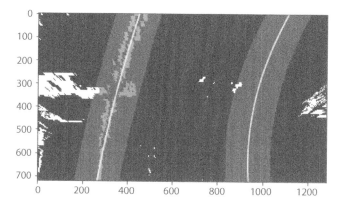

Figure 4.34 Search from sliding window illustration 4.

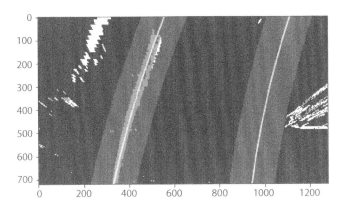

Figure 4.35 Search from sliding window illustration 5.

4.4.6   Radius of Curvature and Central Offset

For calculating the radius of curvature and the position of the vehicle with respect to center, we made a function and used left_lane_inds and right_lane_inds for performing the task of returning curvature and offset. We used the function *fit_poly* which returns left_fitx, right_fitx, ploty to calculate the real radius of curvature and offset.

4.5   Annotation

The input video is processed using MoviePy [11] and each frame of the video is fed into the *process_image* function to output the lane detected and also the radius of curvature and center offset is depicted on each frame of the image as shown in Figure 4.36 and Figure 4.37.

Figure 4.36 Lane area drawn without information.

Figure 4.37 Lane area drawn with radius of curvature and central offset.

4.6   Illustrations

Various examples illustrating the detected road lane area under situations like intense sunlight, shadow, etc. are depicted below in Figure 4.38, Figure 4.39, Figure 4.40, Figure 4.41 and Figure 4.42.

Figure 4.38 Example-1 (straight road).

Figure 4.39 Example-2 (intense sunlight).

Figure 4.40 Example-3 (low light).

Figure 4.41 Example-4.

Figure 4.42 Example-5 (shadow of trees on road area).

4.7   Results and Discussions

The pipeline is successful in drawing the lane area over the road with the radius of curvature and center offset clearly plotted and changing their values in the video.

We followed an approach to not just search blindly for the lane lines in each frame of video, but rather, after have high-confidence detection, we used that to inform the search for the position of the lines in subsequent frames of video. For example, if a polynomial fit was found to be robust in the previous frame, then rather than search the entire next frame for the lines, just a window around the previous detection could be searched. This improves speed and provides a more robust method for rejecting outliers.

4.8   Conclusion and Future Work

The pipeline fails when the road curves a lot and there is a sudden change in the direction like the roads in hilly areas. Some measures could be taken so as to adjust the pipeline so that it also draws lane areas over the roads of hilly areas as well i.e. where there are a lot of curves.

References

1. Cario, G., Casavola, A., Lupia, M., Lane Detection and Tracking Problems in Lane Departure Warning Systems, in: *Computer Vision and Imaging in Intelligent Transportation Systems*, Loce, R.P., Bala, R., Trivedi, M. (Eds.), 2017.
2. Kong, H., Audibert, J., Ponce, J., General Road Detection From a Single Image. *IEEE Trans. Image Process.*, 19, 8, 2211–2220, Aug. 2010.
3. Kuk, J.G., An, J.H., Ki, H., Cho, N.I., Fast lane detection & tracking based on Hough transform with reduced memory requirement. *13th International IEEE Conference on Intelligent Transportation Systems*, Funchal, pp. 1344–1349, 2010.
4. Wei, X., Zhang, Z., Chai, Z., Feng, W., Research on Lane Detection and Tracking Algorithm Based on Improved Hough Transform. *2018 IEEE International Conference of Intelligent Robotic and Control Engineering (IRCE)*, Lanzhou, pp. 275–279, 2018.
5. Yang, X., Gao, D., Duan, J., Yang, L., Research on Lane Detection Based on Machine Vision. *Proceedings of the 2011 International Conference on Informatics, Cybernetics, and Computer Engineering (ICCE2011) November 19–20, 2011*, Advances in Intelligent and Soft Computing, vol 110, Jiang, L. (eds.), Melbourne, Australia, Springer, Berlin, Heidelberg, 2011.
6. Goel, A., Lane Detection Techniques—A Review. *Int. J. Comput. Sci. Mob. Comput.*, 3, 2, 596–602, February—2014.
7. Kaur, G. and Kumar, D., Lane Detection Techniques: A Review. *Int. J. Comput. Appl.*, 112, 10, 0975–8887, pp. 4-6, February 2015.
8. Li, Q., Chen, L., Li, M., Shaw, S., Nüchter, A., A Sensor-Fusion Drivable-Region and Lane-Detection System for Autonomous Vehicle Navigation in Challenging Road Scenarios. *IEEE Trans. Veh. Technol.*, 63, 2, 540–555, Feb. 2014.

9. Aly, M., Real time detection of lane markers in urban streets, in: *2008 IEEE Intelligent Vehicles Symposium*, Eindhoven, pp. 7–12, 2008.

10. Yoo, H., Yang, U., Sohn, K., Gradient-enhancing conversion for illumination-robust lane detection. *IEEE Trans. Intell. Transp. Syst.*, 14, 3, 1083–1094, Sep. 2013.

11. Sun, T.-Y., Tsai, S.-J., Chan, V., HIS color model based lane-marking detection. *Proc. IEEE Intelligent Transportation Systems Conference*, Toronto, Ont., pp. 1168–1172, 2006.

Facial Expression Recognition in Real Time Using Convolutional Neural Network

Vashi Dhankar* and Anu Rathee

Maharaja Agrasen Institute of Technology, PSP Area, Rohini, Delhi, India

Abstract

Facial expressions are highly important in the way that most emotions and meaning in a conversation are depicted through one's facial expressions. In the evolving field of human computer interaction and image processing the problem of face and emotion recognition is still a tricky one. Human emotions are hard to detect automatically at a fast changing rate for e.g. in a video, surveillance footage, etc. The human face is high-dimensional object which hence needs a sophisticated method for its focal points detection and the classification of these features. The combination of these features depicts different things in different people. Hence facial expression detection task is complex as it differs from person to person. In this paper we will be using a methodology to detect human and animated faces in real time video and images. The facial expression would then be classified 6 basic emotions—happy, surprise, fear, anger, sad, disgust and a neutral face.

Keywords: Facial expression recognition (FER), transfer learning, VGG16, real time, convolution neural networks (CNN)

5.1 Introduction

Our aim can be simplified as detection of human face in real time video and find out the probability of seven basic emotions i.e. anger, neutral, disgust, fear, happy, sadness and surprise.

This model is trained to detect emotion in real time video primarily but using the same mechanism it gives accurate results for still images as well. In both cases the human face image is given to the model. It works by m aking predictions on the image fed to it, taken by it using any frame in time. Using Haar cascade the face is detected. Haar cascade looks for several features in an image like line, edge, center-surround features. Using a sliding window these features are applied as it passes through the image. It uses AdaBoost algorithm for selecting the most relevant features. The image is grayscale, cropped and resized for better and fast prediction to 350 * 350. The model we made will make use of transfer learning, where we will use a pertained model VGG-16 which is a deep learning model

---

**Corresponding author:* vashi.dhankar1998@gmail.com

Namita Gupta, Prasenjit Chatterjee and Tanupriya Choudhury (eds.) *Smart and Sustainable Intelligent Systems,* (73–90)

used for image processing task. On top of that we will be creating our own architecture of CNN which has a total of 5 layers which will test and train bottleneck features obtained from VGG-16. This is done because creating and training a CNN is a computational heavy and may not give desired results. The VGG-16 model creates Bottleneck features for the test and train set for both set of images i.e. human and animated images. The VGG-16 model has 5 convolution blocks with different number of filters in each block. It consists of max-pooling, convolution and among others. The model is trained on both human and animated images. This enables the model to detect human as well as animated agents. This was done because we wanted to fine tune the model. An extra of 8,000 images e.g. Figure 5.1 FERG-DB were taken with the approx. 1,500 human images e.g. Figure 5.2 CK++ dataset. This was not enough to make a good model. We use this combined dataset to model and ultimately do the predictions.

Figure 5.1 Samples of animated agents from FERG-DB.

Figure 5.2 Sample images from CK++ dataset.

5.1.1 Need of Study

Facial Expression Recognition (FER) is a continuously growing space in machine learning with new algorithms also being used from deep learning to improve results. This area which combines human–computer-interaction (HCI) and emotion computing is exponentially growing due to its immense applications. Hence a lot of focus in current times is to develop machines that can detect and discriminate human emotions in real time. But even with major breakthroughs this is a complicated domain as so much so depends on the human subject. The facial expressions are complex, and these complexities vary from person to person and with different expressions [4].

Face to face communication has lot variables when it comes to understanding them. Since it's a real time process, the correct decision needs to be deciphered with minimum latency while being accurate also.

5.2 Related Work

Convolutional Neural Networks (CNNs) are currently the most widely used neural network for image recognition and classification. The fully connected layers at the end of the CNN are crucial, making them the go-to model for image classification. CNN follows a hierarchical model, with the last layer being the most important. This is because they contain most of the dense parameters in a CNN. Our CNN model is trained on still images using VGG16 for transfer learning. VGG16 [1] contains approximately 95% of all its parameters in their last fully connected layers.

One of the many ways to model a CNN for FER is the Time-Delayed 3D-Convolutional Neural Network model as demonstrated in Ref. [10]. The training sample consists of progression of the facial images, forming a series of part to present expressions. A training sample will be labeled according to the emotion label on the most recent image out of total n images. Hence the main idea can be stated as—capturing the expressions one by one as they lead up to a final emotion.

A similar model to Time-delay model is the Convolutional LSTM neural network. It combines the fundamentals of both CNN and RNN. Convolutional [5] neural network uses a feature detector, which is $n * n$ matrix called the kernel. A convolution/feature map is generated after this operation. Recurrent NNs (RNNs) on the other hand has internal memory so they can memorize previous inputs. This [15–18] makes them a better option for handling sequential data than CNN. The sequence and time context is what differentiates these two models from each other. The Time-delay model, takes the context from a single face within the video clip i.e. the comparison subject remains same, whereas ConvolutionLstmNN uses still images, having no relation with one another. There is not necessarily any difference as seen in Figure 5.3.

Recent models such as Inception V3 [2] was also analyzed. By using a global average pooling operation the amount of parameters in last layers can also be reduced greatly. New research in CNNs has discovered a modern efficient architecture such as Xception [3]. It's successful as it is based on two very strongly supported assumptions. These are residual models and second depth wise separable convolutions. Figure 5.4(b) Depth-wise separable convolutions are efficient due to their different technique. They reduce the amount of

Figure 5.3 Training set for convolutional long short term memory neural net.

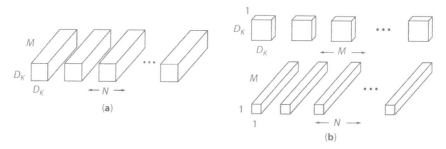

Figure 5.4 (a) Standard convolution. (b) Depth wise convolution.

parameters by separating the processes of feature extraction and combination within a convolutional layer.

Using square hinged loss [6] state of the art models have been trained on different face expressions dataset. A model can achieve a very high accuracy such as 71% [7] using very high number of parameters. In detecting macro-facial expressions the face of the person captured can have different pose, lighting angles, background conditions and settings. Many of these concerns are addressed in Ref. [8] which presents a deep analytical overview of techniques like DBN (Deep Belief Network), Auto Encoders and RNN (Recurrent Neural Network). R. Ginne *et al.* [9] also presented a survey on CNN based FER techniques.

5.3   Methodology

The FER model has the following steps as seen in Figure 5.5. We will be using CK+ dataset and animated images from the FERG-DB. The dataset is divided for human and animated images and further divided into 7 folders one for each emotions. The divided data frames will be combined for training, but for testing we will keep the human and animated images separate.

- The first step is to import the necessary libraries like Numpy, Pandas, Seaborn, Glob, cv2, etc.
- The dataset for each emotion is loaded and then the images are pre-processed as follows.
- Grayscaling—Grayscaling is the process of converting a colored image input into an image whose pixel value depends on the intensity of light on the image. Grayscaling is done as colored images are difficult to process by an algorithm.

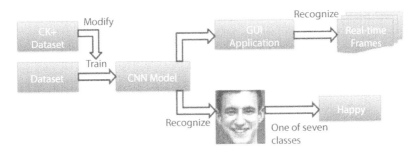

Figure 5.5 A pictorial representation of the methodology which is elaborated below.

- Next the image is cropped and then resizing is done. The image is resized to remove the unnecessary parts of the image. This reduces the memory required and increases computation speed.
- Detect faces using OpenCv Haar Cascade.
- The steps are performed for both the datasets. The distribution of class labels is then visualized across all the sets

5.3.1 Applying Transfer Learning using VGG-16

In the process of convolution between two functions the shape of one function is modified by the other. The result of convolution express how that shape is modified. This process while being efficient is computation heavy as the number of hyper parameters increase. These hyper-parameters depend on the size of the dataset. Our dataset comprising of FERG-DB and CK++ dataset is of relatively big size. This leads to a big computation and time overhead. Therefore we will use a CNN that is already trained on a standard images dataset and modify some of its layers as per our dataset. This is the concept of transfer learning and it will highly reduce our overheads.

Transfer learning is a concept which can solve the problem of training a deep neural network for a large dataset [19]. We don't need to build our custom model from scratch instead we use leverage previous learnings. Popular pre-trained CNN models for image processing are VGG-16, VGG-19, GoogLeNet (e.g. InceptionV3) and Residual Network (e.g. ResNet50). We can use them as starting points of our custom neural network. We can do this by training them on our data and ultimately get the features for our images.

The last layer in CNN is the fully connected layer. To [20–21] customize the model we remove this layer and the pre-trained weights in that layer. But the original network before the fully connected network is frozen so that, when the training is start on the new data set, only the newly added FC network is trained. Here the input to the FC network is called the bottleneck features.

They represent the activation map from the last conv. layer in the network. Hence with frozen weights in the main network, we will get to use the pre-trained weights to get important feature activations as bottleneck features into our newly added FC network, and now this new FC network (trained on our data) gives us the required inference as per training.

For training our model we are using VGG-16. Out of 16 layers convolution operation is applied in 13 layers. The [22–24] Keras API is used to import this model. Using model.predict() function we have to provide the input one at a time. The output features are stored in a numpy array.

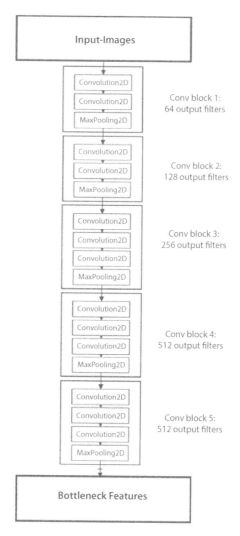

Figure 5.6 VGG-16 bottleneck features.

5.3.2 Modeling and Training

After the bottle-neck features are obtained from the transfer learning model the next step is to create a model on top of VGG-16 as coded in Figure 5.7. This takes place of the fully connected layer in VGG-16.

After this a Multi-Class Log-Loss/Cross-Entropy layer is also added. The final combined model is as follows:

- Sequential()—A sequential model is an simplistic and efficient way of building a convolutional model layer by layer. It gradually creates layer on top of one another.
- model.add(Dropout())—Dropout is used to prevent and reduce overfitting. Overfitting occurs when large dataset is utilized for a large neural net. Dropout is a technique where randomly selected neurons are ignored during the training. They are "dropped out" randomly. This reduces overfitting.

```
In [3]:  no_of_classes = 7

In [30]:  #model architecture
          def model(input_shape):
              model = Sequential()

              model.add(Dense(512, activation='relu', input_dim = input_shape))
              model.add(Dropout(0.1))

              model.add(Dense(256, activation='relu'))

              model.add(Dense(128, activation='relu'))
              model.add(BatchNormalization())

              model.add(Dense(64, activation='relu'))
              model.add(Dense(output_dim = no_of_classes, activation='softmax'))

              return model
```

Figure 5.7 Model architecture overview.

- model.add(Conv2D())—This creates a 2D Convolutional layer which gives a tensor as the output. As the name suggests this layer does convolution i.e. change the shape of one function as per the second function. Generally a kernel of size 3 * 3 is used to create the activation map. ReLu is used as the activation function. It's one of the most popular activation function. Its output is zero for negative values functions and positive value for positive valued functions.
- model.add(BatchNormalization())—The normalization process is done so that the input output of previous layer is in a specific range. The Input to the next layer should not be scattered, hence batch normalization is used.
- model.add(Dense())—The Dense layer is used for dimensionality update. It takes N dimension vector as an input and the dense layers do matrix vector multiplication on it. The output is an m dimensional vector on which rotation, translation and scaling is applied for transformation.

The architecture consists of 5 dense layers, all of which are fully connected. Each of them consists of relu activation units [25–27]. The number of units in the first one is 512, 256 activation units in the second, 128 activation units in the third and 64 in the fourth layer. The rectifier is an activation function defined as the positive part of its argument:

$$f(x) = x+ =\max(0,x) \tag{5.1}$$

The last layer is the output layer (fifth layer), it consists of 7 softmax units. Softmax unit is used to make the resultant value lie between 0 and 1. It's a generalization of logistic function that squashes a k-dimensional vector of arbitrary relative values to a k dimensional vector of real values. Simply put it can be understood as multi-class log loss [28, 30]. Probability values corresponding to seven classes will be generated by it and their combined sum is equal to 1.

Mathematically the softmax function is shown below, where z is a vector of the inputs to the output layer (if you have 10 output units, then there are 10 elements in z). And again, j indexes the output units, so j = 1, 2, ..., K.

$$\sigma(z)_j = \frac{e^{zj}}{\sum\limits_{k=1}^{k} e^{zk}} \tag{5.2}$$

The result is then fed as the input to the final cross-entropy function which minimizes loss through back-propagation. To understand cross entropy function assume that a neuron with several input variables, x1, x2, x3 and so on, corresponding weights w1,w2,w3 and so on and with a bias b, as shown in Figure 5.8.

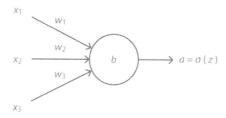

Figure 5.8 A neuron with variable inputs, corresponding weights and outputs.

The output of the neuron is a = σ(z), where z = Σjwjxj + b is the weighted sum of the inputs. The cross entropy function for this neuron is defined by Equation (5.1)

$$C = -\frac{1}{n}\sum_{x} \dot{c}\dot{c}\ (1-y)\ln(1-a)]$$

(5.3)

Where n is the total number of items in training data and the sum is over all training inputs, x and y is the corresponding output. All these mathematical functions are used in CNN layers described in the VGG-16 model in Figure 5.6.

5.4   Results

We ran our model till 200 epochs. The model was run for both human and animated agents. The results are described below. The graph for epochs vs loss (Figure 5.9) and the graph for epochs vs accuracy (Figure 5.10) describes our model results.

Loss	Result percentage Epoch 1	Result percentage Epoch 2
CK++ dataset	2.45	0.04
FERG-DB	2.21	0.01

Accuracy	Result percentage Epoch 1	Result percentage Epoch 2
CK++ dataset	17	93
FERG-DB	19	97.7

The Confusion, Figure 5.11 Recall Figure 5.12 and precision matrix Figure 5.13 for the test set are plotted as follows:

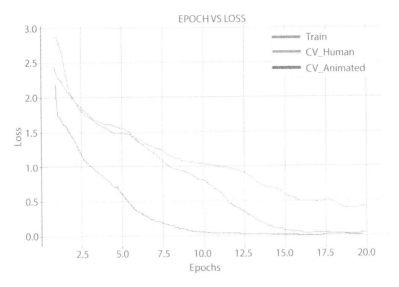

Figure 5.9 The losses were reduced from 1st epoch to 200th epoch.

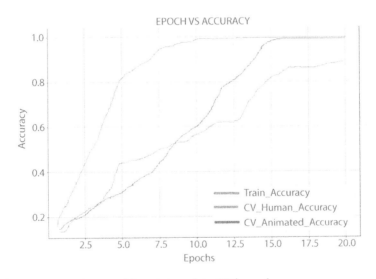

Figure 5.10 The accuracy was increased from 1st epoch to 200th epoch.

For testing in real time video, similar steps are followed in pre-processing of images and then the model is trained. The steps taken are as follows:

1. First the image is captured from any instance of the video and then converted into grayscale.
2. It is then cropped and resized. For accurate, fast processing the size of image is kept to 350 * 350 and then image is saved.
3. For the saved gray-scale image we use Haar cascade of OpenCV to detect the face.
4. Processed image is read then cropped-resized and finally reshaped and normalized.

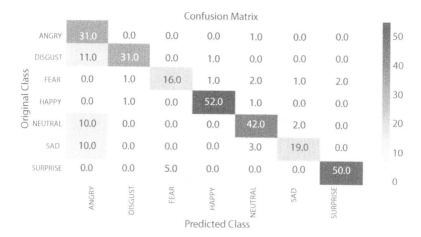

Figure 5.11 Confusion matrix.

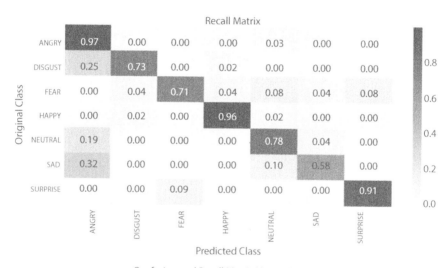

Figure 5.12 Recall matrix.

5. The next step then is of transfer learning where the processed image is fed to the VGG-16 model to obtain the bottleneck features.
6. Then for the last layers we will use our own CNN model to do the emotions classification.

For facilitating learning of complex shapes and spontaneous visuals more number of hidden layers is needed. CNN needs 3 to 8 convolutional layers followed by pooling layers. Pooling layers are essential for shortening the training time and overcome overfitting.

But some researchers [11, 12] follow a different approach where one pooling layer follows after two consecutive convolutional layer. By doing this the model is learning more through repetition and then decreasing the number of parameters using pooling layer. As

Precision Matrix

Original Class	ANGRY	DISGUST	FEAR	HAPPY	NEUTRAL	SAD	SURPRISE
ANGRY	0.52	0.00	0.00	0.00	0.02	0.00	0.00
DISGUST	0.17	0.91	0.00	0.02	0.00	0.00	0.00
FEAR	0.00	0.03	0.76	0.02	0.04	0.05	0.04
HAPPY	0.00	0.03	0.00	0.96	0.02	0.00	0.00
NEUTRAL	0.16	0.00	0.00	0.00	0.87	0.10	0.00
SAD	0.16	0.00	0.00	0.00	0.06	0.85	0.00
SURPRISE	0.00	0.00	0.23	0.00	0.00	0.00	0.95

Predicted Class

Figure 5.13 Precision matrix.

the number of layers increase the problem of large number of hyper-parameters needs to be handled. For this, Z. Yu *et al.* [13] used the dropout technique [14]. This is done in the dropout layer where random neurons are dropped to introduce randomness in the model which is helpful in reducing the risk of overfitting of model.

The CNN model is tested in real time by creating a Qt5 GUI application. This application is loaded with our CNN model. The webcam is then activated which displays the user's image and detect the probability of each expression The probability for all the seven emotions are given for the user in real time (Figures 5.14–5.20).

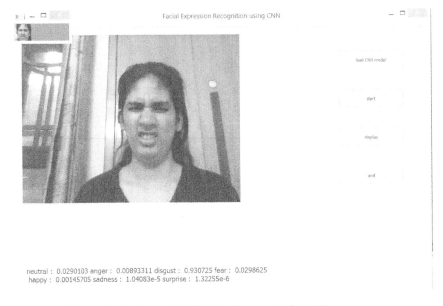

neutral : 0.0290103 anger : 0.00893311 disgust : 0.930725 fear : 0.0298625
happy : 0.00145705 sadness : 1.04083e-5 surprise : 1.32255e-6

Figure 5.14 The model gives the highest probability for disgust, which is 0.93.

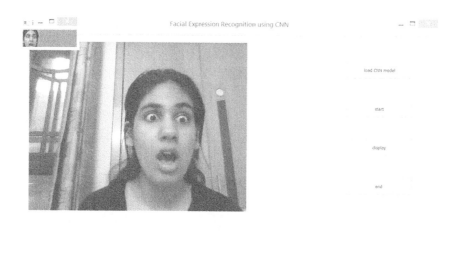

neutral : 3.18436e-6 anger : 9.60903e-13 disgust : 1.05692e-9 fear : 6.94592e-6
happy : 5.27918e-12 sadness : 0.000131958 surprise : 0.999858

Figure 5.15 Here the expression detected is surprise as it has the highest probability of 0.9998.

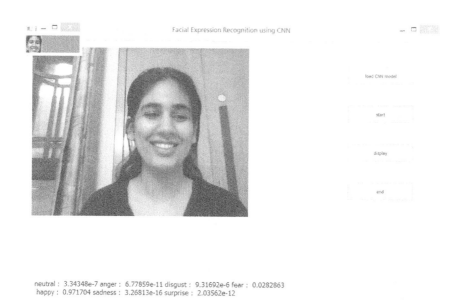

neutral : 3.34348e-7 anger : 6.77859e-11 disgust : 9.31692e-6 fear : 0.0282863
happy : 0.971704 sadness : 3.26813e-16 surprise : 2.03562e-12

Figure 5.16 Here the expression with the highest probability is happy with a probability of 0.971.

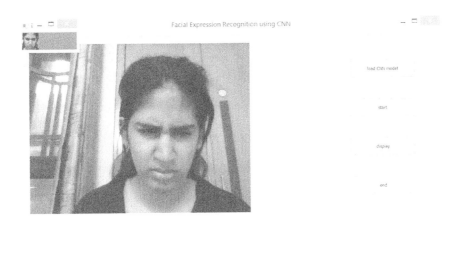

neutral : 0.0326247 anger : 0.844263 disgust : 0.122264 fear : 0.000724401
happy : 9.73151e-5 sadness : 2.66752e-5 surprise : 3.9354e-8

Figure 5.17 The image predicts this as a mix of anger and disgust which is rightly so, with a higher probability of anger as 0.844.

neutral : 0.744663 anger : 1.84724e-5 disgust : 3.59538e-5 fear : 0.100243
happy : 2.67411e-7 sadness : 0.060866 surprise : 0.0941726

Figure 5.18 Neutral has the highest probability i.e. 0.744.

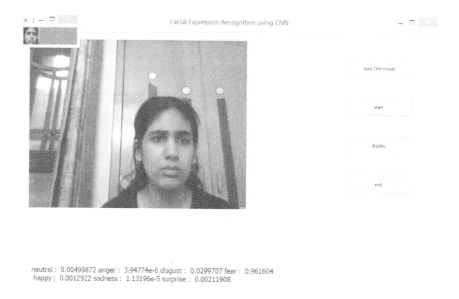

neutral : 0.00499872 anger : 3.94774e-6 disgust : 0.0299707 fear : 0.961604
happy : 0.0012922 sadness : 1.13196e-5 surprise : 0.00211908

Figure 5.19 The predicted expression is fear with probability of 0.961.

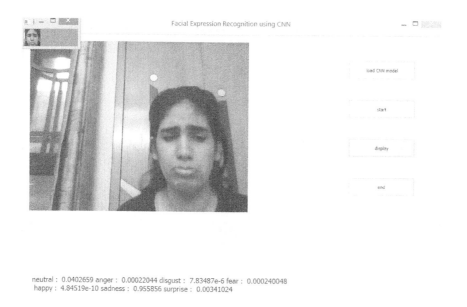

neutral : 0.0402659 anger : 0.00022044 disgust : 7.83487e-6 fear : 0.000240048
happy : 4.84519e-10 sadness : 0.955856 surprise : 0.00341024

Figure 5.20 The predicted expression is sadness with probability of 0.955.

5.5 Conclusion and Future Scope

In conclusion we were successful in implementing transfer learning and using custom CNN to predict the real time macro expressions with high accuracy and least latency possible in both. We achieved an accuracy of 82.43% on human images. This was possible by using a large dataset comprising of humans as well as animated images [29].

We have also successfully overcome the problem of overfitting using data augmentation. Data augmentation is also used by [15–18] to solve the same issue i.e. minimizing problem of overfitting. In conclusion we can say the following about the result and the architecture of the model:

- To achieve the best results and to incorporate more emotions and expressions in the probability of result more human images can be used. Having more variance in these images will provide more accuracy.
- For Frontal face images a CNN which is concise having less number of hidden layers and hyper parameters works the best.
- A more complex CNN is preferred for giving real time results with minimum latency. The complex CNN with its more layers and parameters will increase accuracy
- We can also fine tune last 2 or 3 convolution blocks of VGG-16 layer as it not only updates the architecture but also restrains the CNN nodes to learn new object classes.

To achieve an accuracy greater than 95% on real world images and in real time a few changes can be made for e.g. fine tuning hyper-parameters like number of hidden units and learning rate, but this will require more time and computation power. This [31] is primarily designing our own CNN. But this will require a large dataset with up to 75k images and diverse dataset also with each image resolution higher than $400 * 400$.

References

1. Simonyan, K. and Zisserman, A., Very deep convolutional, Networks for large-scale image recognition, Vol.1, pp. 2–3 arXiv preprint arXiv:1409.1556, 2014.
2. Szegedy, C., Vanhoucke, V., Ioffe, S., Shlens, J., Wojna, Z., Rethinking the inception architecture for computervision, in: *Proceedings of the IEEE Conference on Computer Vision and Pattern Recognition*, pp. 2818–2826, 2016.
3. Chollet, F., "Xception: Deep Learning with Depthwise Separable Convolutions." 2017 IEEE Conference on Computer Vision and Pattern Recognition (CVPR) (2017): 1800–1807.
4. He, K., Zhang, X., Ren, S., Sun, J., Deep residual learning for image recognition, in: *Proceedings of the IEEE Conference on Computer Vision and Pattern Recognition*, pp. 770–778, 2016.
5. Howard, A.G. *et al.*, MobileNets: Efficient Convolutional Neural Networks for Mobile Vision Applications, Vol 1, pp. 6–7, 2017, CoRR, abs/1704.04861, 2017.
6. Yichuan Tang, Deep Learning using Support Vector Machines, CoRR, abs/1306.0239, pp. 167–169, 2013.
7. Goodfellow, Ian J. *et al.* Challenges in representation learning: A report on three machine learning contests. *J. Intrl. Neural Network Soc.*, 64 (2015): 59–63.
8. Shan Li and Weihong Deng, Deep Facial Expression Recognition: {A} Survey, CoRR, abs/1804.08348, pp. 9–11, 2018.
9. Ginne, R. and Jariwala, K., Facial Expression Recognition using CNN: A Survey. *Int. J. Adv. Electron. Comput. Sci.*, pp. 10–11, 5, 3, 2018. https://arxiv.org/abs/1802.09386

10. Meng, H., Bianchi-Berthouze, N., Deng, Y., Cheng, J., Cosmas, J.P., Time-Delay Neural Network for Continuous Emotional Dimension Prediction From Facial Expression Sequences. *IEEE Trans. Cybern.*, 46, 4, 916–929, 2016.

11. Chen, X., Yang, X., Wang, M., Zou, J., Convolution Neural Network for Automatic Facial Expression Recognition. *International Conference on Applied System Innovation (ICASI)*, pp. 814–817, 2017.

12. Liu, K., Zhang, M., Pan, Z., Facial Expression Recognition with CNN Ensemble. *2016 International Conference on Cyberworlds (CW)*, pp. 163–166, 2016.

13. Yu, Z. and Zhang, C., Image based Static Facial Expression Recognition with Multiple Deep Network Learning. *Proceedings of the 2015 ACM on International Conference on Multimodal Interaction*, pp. 435–442, 2015.

14. Srivastava, N., Hinton, G., Krizhevsky, A., Sutskever, I., Salakhutdinov, R., Dropout: A simple way to prevent neuranetworks from overfitting. *J. Mach. Learn. Res.*, 15, 1, 1929–1958, 2014.

15. Lopes, A.T., de Aguiar, A.F.D.S.E., O-Santos, T., Facial Expression Recognition with Convolutional Neural Networks: Coping with Few Data and the Training Sample Order. *Pattern Recognit.*, pp. 67-68, 2018.

16. Lopes, A.T., de Aguiar, A.F.D.S.E., O-Santos, T., Facial Expression Recognition with Convolutional Neural Networks: Coping with Few Data and the Training Sample Order. *Pattern Recognit.*, 70–71, 2017.

17. Yang, S., Luo, P., Loy, C.C., Tang, X., Faceness-Net: Face Detection through Deep Facial Part Responses. *IEEE Trans. Pattern Anal. Mach. Intell.*, 40, 8, 1845–1859, 2017.

18. Biao, Y., Jinmeng, C., Rongrong, N., Yuyu, Z., Facial Expression Recognition using Weighted Mixture Deep Neural Network Based on Double-channel Facial Images. *IEEE Access*, 6, 4630–4640, 2018.

19. Simonyan, K. and Zisserman, A., Two-stream convolutional networks for action recognition in videos, in: *Proc. Int. Conf. Neural Inf. Process. Syst.*, Montreal, QC, Canada, pp. 568–576, 2014.

20. Jiang, N. and Wang, L., Quantum image scaling using nearest neighbor interpolation. *Quantum Inf. Process.*, 14, 5, 1559–1571, May. 2015.

21. Hinton, G.E. and Salakhutdinov, R.R., Reducing the dimensionality of data with neural networks. *Science*, 313, 5786, 504–507, 2006.

22. Shan, C., Gong, S., Mcowan, P.W., Robust facial expression recognition using local binary patterns, in: *Proceedings of the IEEE International Conference on Image Processing*, 2005.

23. Kumar, P., Happy, S.L., Routray, A., A real-time robust facial expression recognition system using hog features, in: *Proceedings of the International Conference on Computing, Analytics and Security Trends*, pp. 289–293, 2017.

24. Liu, M., Li, S., Shan, S., Chen, X., Au-aware deep networks for facial expression recognition, in: *Proceedings of the IEEE International Conference and Workshops on Automatic Face and Gesture Recognition*, pp. 1–6, 2013.

25. Poursaberi, A., Noubari, H.A., Gavrilova, M., Yanushkevich, S.N., Gauss–Laguerre wavelet textural feature fusion with geometrical information for facial expression identification. *EURASIP J. Image Video Process.*, 1, 1–13, 2012-17, 2012.

26. Ghimire, D., Jeong, S., Yoon, S., Choi, J., Lee, J., Facial expression recognition based on region specific appearance and geometric features, in: *Proceedings of the Tenth International Conference on Digital Information Management*, pp. 142–147, 2016.

27. Zhalehpour, S., Onder, O., Akhtar, Z., Erdem, C.E., BAUM-1: A spontaneous audio-visual face database of affective and mental states. *IEEE Trans. Affective Comput.*, 8, 3, 300–313, Jul./Sep. 2016.

28. Zhang, S., Zhang, S., Huang, T., Gao, W., Tian, Q., Learning affective features with a hybrid deep model for audio–visual emotion recognition. *IEEE Trans. Circuits Syst. Video Technol.*, 28, 10, 3030–3043, Oct. 2018.

29. Aneja, D., Colburn, A., Faigin, G., Shapiro, L., Mones, B., Modeling stylized character expressions *via* deep learning, in: *Asian Conference on Computer Vision*, Springer, Cham, pp. 136–153, 2016.

30. Zhao, H., Liu, Q., Yang, Y., Transfer learning with ensemble of multiple feature representations. *2018 IEEE 16th International Conference on Software Engineering Research, Management and Applications (SERA)*, IEEE, 2018.

31. Feutry, C., Piantanida, P., Bengio, Y., Duhamel, P., Learning Anonymized Representations with Adversarial Neural Networks. vol. 3. pp. 5–6, 2018, https://arxiv.org/abs/1802.09386.

6

Feature Extraction and Image Recognition of Cursive Handwritten English Words Using Neural Network and IAM Off-Line Database

Arushi Sharma* and Shikha Gupta

Maharaja Agrasen Institute of Technology, PSP Area, Rohini, Delhi, India

Abstract

The Neural Network implementation of cursive handwritten English words, in this paper, aims to convert an individual handwritten word to digital format. The Neural Network consists of layers of Convolutional Neural Network (CNN), Recurrent Neural Network (RNN) and Connectionist Temporal Classification (CTC), which can be trained on the CPU. The system proposed does not segment the input, but rather the layers extract relevant features from the scanned images fed as input. Compared with previous systems for handwritten text recognition, the given architecture is end-to-end trainable and does not require different components to be trained separately. It naturally handles sequences in random lengths, involving no horizontal scale normalization or character segmentation. The model is smaller yet effective, thus, more practical for application in real-world scenarios.

Keywords: Feature extraction, deep learning, IAM off-line database, image recognition, image pre-processing, handwriting recognition, character-probability matrix

6.1 Introduction

Handwriting recognition (HWR) is the task of receiving and interpreting comprehensible handwritten input from various sources. HWR methods are categorized as off-line and on-line. While offline handwriting recognition is the identification of handwritten text obtained from scanned images, online HWR recognizes text that originates from devices like a personal digital assistant (PDA). The two methods primarily differ in their sources of feature extraction. The data obtained by Offline handwriting recognition is regarded as a static representation of handwriting. Some of the traditional techniques involved in this process are: character extraction, character recognition and feature extraction. Common imperfections are associated with Character extraction. The most frequent is when connected

---

Corresponding author: arushiuma1997@gmail.com

Namita Gupta, Prasenjit Chatterjee and Tanupriya Choudhury (eds.) Smart and Sustainable Intelligent Systems, (91–102)

Figure 6.1 Illustration of HTR: A digital text is outputted by the HTR system for an image containing text.

characters are returned as a single sub-image consisting of both characters. This causes a significant problem in the recognition phase. Yet there are a number of algorithms that can reduce the risk of connected characters. Feature extraction works like neural network recognizers. However, programmers must manually decide on the properties they identify as prime. This method gives the recognizer the deciding power in terms of which properties to be used in identification. Yet any system using this approach requires considerably more time in development than a neural network because the process of learning the properties was not automatic. Offline handwriting recognition is more popular among researchers because as compared to the on-line technique, it's difficult to implement. The difficulties include the cursive nature of handwriting, dissimilar shape and size of each character, and extensive vocabularies. Figure 6.1 shows an illustration of HTR. It shows the digital text as output for a scanned image containing text as input. Handwriting differs widely from one author to other. It also varies from instance to instance for one particular author. While modern neural networks show decent performance at HWR, available training data is often insufficient to capture the above-mentioned variations. As a result, this paper introduces a more robust technique to model the differences using Deep Learning networks for automated handwriting recognition (HWR) [1]. The proposed approach in this paper seeks to translate individual cursive handwritten words to a digital form. It is a minimalistic Neural Network implementation of handwritten text recognition using a Neural Network layers of Convolutional Neural Network (CNN), Recurrent Neural Network (RNN) and Connectionist Temporal Classification (CTC) [14, 15].

6.1.1 Scope of Discussion

This paper focuses on the classifier, its parameters, pre-processing methods for the input and a text postprocessing method for the output. The investigated classifier builds on Neural Networks. Only Offline HTR is discussed because images of handwritten text serve as input. Document analysis methods to detect the text on a page or to segment a page into lines is not discussed. The model can input images of size 128×32 and can output a maximum of 32 characters. So, it is possible to recognize one to two words. It is, however, not possible to detect longer sentences because of the small input and output size. The proposed approach makes use of ANNs. Multiple Convolution Network Layers (CNNs) are trained to extract relevant features from the input image. These layers output 1-D or a 2-D feature map (or sequence) which handed over to Recurrent Neural Network layers (RNNs). The RNN propagates information through the sequence. Afterwards, the output of RNN is mapped onto a matrix which contains a score for each character per sequence. As the ANN is trained according to a specific coding scheme, a decoding algorithm should be applied to the RNN output to get the final text. Training and decoding from this matrix are done by the Connectionist Temporal Classification (CTC). Decoding can take advantage of Language Model (LM) [16]. There are two reasons for pre-processing: making the problem easier for the classifier and (on-the-fly) data augmentation. One of the notable contributions of this paper is an implicit word segmentation based on the decoding algorithm for the RNN output.

This paper is organized in the following sections: In Section 6.2 the work done earlier by the researchers is defined. Section 6.3 introduces the methodology used to implement the proposed HTR system. This section introduces the dataset and the evaluation metric used to evaluate the proposed model. It also discusses in detail the pre-processing method and the implementation and training procedure used. The method of implementation and training uses CNN, RNN and CTC and is discussed in this section along with sample examples from the IAM dataset. Section 6.4 presents the results of the performed experiments on the model followed by Section 6.5 which concludes the paper.

6.2   Literature Survey

6.2.1   Early Scanners and the Digital Age

Handwritten text recognition began with the classification of digits for postal mail. Postal readers by Jacob Rabinows combined scanning equipment and logic for identifying monospaced fonts [2]. Allum *et al.* brought further development by creating an innovatory scanner that was flexible enough to accommodate variations in the text [3]. Ray Kurzweil invented the first prominent Optical Character Recognition software in 1974 which allowed recognition of any font [4]. This software made use of pattern matching. It compared bitmaps of the template character with those of the read character and contrasted the two of them to discern with which character was the read character in close proximity with. The shortcoming of this software was that it was sensitive to variations in size and the distinctions between each individual's way of writing. As part of further improvement, OCR technology began to make use of feature extraction instead of templating. For every character, the software would find out features like zoning, geometric moments and projection histograms [5].

6.2.2   Machine Learning

Lecun *et al.* stressed on using a gradient-based learning technique using machine learning models [9]. The subsequent eminent upgrade in producing high OCR accuracies was the implementation of the Hidden Markov Model for performing Optical Character Recognition.

This approach uses letters as a state, thus permitting the character's context to be taken into consideration while finding out the succeeding hidden variable [7]. This led to better accuracy compared to both feature extraction methods and the Naive Bayes technique [6]. The primary downside was the manual extraction of features as this required prior information about the language. This approach also did not accommodate the complexity and variety of handwriting. Ng *et al.* applied Convolution Neural Networks to the problem of taking text found in the wild and recognized text within the image [8]. Where conventional methods are based on segmenting discrete characters for recognition, latest techniques focus on identifying all the characters in a segmented text line. Specifically they concentrate on machine learning techniques that are able to memorize visual features, away from the limited feature engineering used previously. State-of-the-art techniques utilize convolutional networks to draw out visual features over a handful of overlapping windows of an image of text line, which an RNN uses to produce probabilities of a character.

6.3   Methodology

The proposed system makes use of ANNs. The data flow diagram of the proposed system is shown in Figure 6.2. Multiple Convolution Network Layers (CNNs) are trained to extract appropriate features from the input image. These layers output 1-D or a 2-D feature map (or sequence) which is handed over to Recurrent Neural Network layers (RNNs). The RNN propagates information through the sequence. Afterwards, the output of RNN is mapped onto a matrix which contains a score for each character per sequence. As the ANN is trained according to a specific coding scheme, a decoding algorithm should be applied to the RNN output to get the final text. Training and decoding from this matrix are done by the Connectionist Temporal Classification (CTC). Decoding can take advantage of Language Model (LM) [10]. There are two reasons for pre-processing: making the problem easier for the classifier and (on-the-fly) data augmentation. One of the notable contributions of this paper is an implicit word segmentation based on the decoding algorithm for the RNN output.

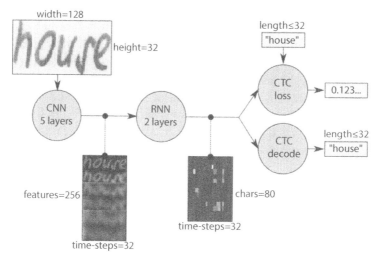

Figure 6.2 Outline of the neural network operations and the flow of data through it.

The Neural Network can be viewed more formally as a function which maps a matrix (an image) M of size W×H to a sequence of characters (c1, c2, …) with a length between 0 and L. Words or texts not present in the training data can also be identified as the text-recognition takes place on character-level.

$$NN:M \rightarrow C1, C2, …, Cn$$

$$W \times H \quad 0 \leq n \leq L$$

Equation 6.1: The Neural Network written as a mathematical function which maps an image to a character sequence.

6.3.1   Dataset

The primary resource for training the handwriting recognizer was the IAM Handwriting Dataset [11]. This dataset contains the handwritten text from over 600 writers, contributing to 5,500+ sentences. The words are then segmented and manual verification is carried out thereafter; metadata associated with form labels is included in XML files. The source text is built on the Lancaster-Oslo/Bergen (LOB) corpus, consisting of full English sentences and a total of over 1 million words. The dataset also contains over 1,000 forms by nearly 400 different writers. This dataset, given its size and quality, tends to aid many handwriting-recognition tasks and thus has been used as the training, validation, and test data for this model. Also, in deep learning, datasets of large sizes are required (deep learning models need a minimum of 105 training examples to be in a position to perform well, notwithstanding transfer learning). This dataset containing over 100K+ words met those requirements. Generally, it is used to classify writers according to their writing styles. A traditional way of solving such a problem is extracting features like spacing between letters and curvatures and feeding them into Support Vector Machines. To solve this problem by Deep learning using Keras and Tensorflow, the full IAM Handwriting Dataset, is not needed. Some authentic subset that can be used for training such as a subset of images by the top 50 persons who contributed the most towards the dataset is sufficient. This dataset contains images of each handwritten sentence with the dash-separated filename format. The first field represents the test code, second the writer id, third passage id, and fourth the sentence id. The database contains a collection of unconstrained handwritten text. This text can be scanned at a resolution of 300 dpi and saved as PNG images with 256 gray levels.

Figure 6.3. provides samples of a completed form, a line of text and some extracted words. All sentences and extracted words are available for download as PNG files. The corresponding XML meta-information is provided in the image files. An automatic segmentation scheme is used to extract words from pages of scanned text. The extracted words are then verified manually. All word, line and form images are provided as PNG files. Variety of estimated parameters from the pre-processing and segmentation information form part of form label files. These label files are contained within the image files as metadata in the

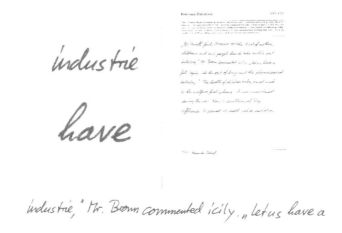

Figure 6.3 Sample images containing text from IAM database.

XML file format (DTD). The IAM Database is divided into a total of five datasets: one training, one testing, and two validation sets. Each writer has contributed to one of these sets only as the lines of text are mutually exclusive for all data sets.

6.3.2   Evaluation Metric

The most common error measures for HTR are Character Error Rate (CER) and Word Error Rate (WER). CER is calculated by counting the number of edit operations to transfer the recognized text into the ground truth text, divided by the length of the ground truth text (see Equation (6.2)). For WER, the text is split into a sequence of words. This word sequence can then be used to calculate the WER just as a character sequence is used to calculate the CER. Both CER and WER can take on values greater than100% if the number of edit operations exceeds the ground truth length. As an example the CER and WER of the recognized text "Hxllo World" with the ground truth text "Hello World" is calculated. The character edit-distance is 1, the length of the ground truth text is 11, therefore CER = 1/11. For WER the unique words are written to a table with unique identifiers yieldingw1 = "Hxllo", w2 = "Hello", w3 = "World". Then, each word is replaced by its identifier from the table, so the two strings become"w1w3" and "w2w3". The word edit-distance is1, the ground truth length is 2, therefore WER = 1/2.

$$CER = \frac{insertions + deletions + substitutions}{length\,(\text{GT})}$$

Equation 6.2: Character Error Rate.

6.3.3   Pre-Processing

Generally, the images from the dataset do not have the exact size of 128 × 32. Therefore, resizing is done for each image (without distortion) until they are either 128 in width or 32 in height. Then, the images are copied into a white target of size 128 × 32. This method is shown in Figure 6.4. Finally, the grey-values of the images are normalized, which streamlines the task for the Neural Network [12]. Instead of aligning the images to the left or by resizing the images randomly, data augmentation can easily be integrated by replicating the images at random positions.

Firstly, it is important to pre-process the input image such that it looks like a sample from IAM. For that, it should be cropped Figure 6.5 shows the pre-processing steps. Firstly, the image should be cropped. Next, its contrast should be increased. Now, the model gives a much better output: "tello", in Figure 6.5. This is almost correct. If the lines are thickened by applying a morphological operation, the model is finally able to recognize the correct text: "Hello."

Figure 6.4 Left: Arbitrary sized image from the dataset scaled to fit the target size of 128 × 32. The empty part of the target image is filled with white color.

Cropping can be performed with a word-segmentation algorithm like the one given by N. Srimal and R. Manmatha [13]. The python code can be used to increase the contrast and apply the morphological operation. Pre-processing is not suitable in certain situations like when new data samples include characters not contained in the IAM dataset (e.g., ö, ä, ü, …). The pre-trained model cannot recognize these. The same is true when the writing style is entirely different from IAM (e.g. machine-printed text), or the background contains noise that cannot be removed by pre-processing (e.g. cross-section paper). In such cases, training the model on the new data makes sense. We need image-text pairs that have to be converted into an IAM-compatible.

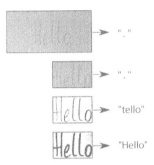

Figure 6.5 Pre-processing steps and the recognized text for each of them.

6.3.4   Implementation and Training

Convolutional Neural Network (CNN): The image given as input is given to the CNN layers. These layers extract pertinent features from the image. Three critical operations correspond to each layer. First is the convolution operation, in which filter kernels of size 5×5 and 3×3 are applied in the first two and last three layers respectively. Second is the non-linear RELU function. Finally, image regions and outputs are summarized by a pooling layer. The height of the image is downscaled by two in every layer. Channels (feature maps) are included so that the size of the output sequence is 32×256.

Recurrent Neural Network (RNN): RNN circulates relevant information through the feature sequence, which has 256 features per time-step. Instead of vanilla RNN, the well-known Long Short-Term Memory (LSTM) is used [19]. LSTM is a well-known implementation of RNN which is capable of spreading information through greater distances and provide better characteristics for training. The output sequence for RNN is mapped to a matrix of 32×80. There are a total of 80 entries for each of the 32 time-steps. 79 different characters are present in the IAM dataset. Further, an extra character is needed for the CTC operation.

Connectionist Temporal Classification (CTC): While training the Neural Network, the CTC computes the loss value from the given output matrix from RNN and the ground truth text. The CTC is given the output matrix while inferring, and it decodes the given matrix into the final text.

Both the ground truth text and the recognized text can be of a maximum length of 32 characters. The Neural Network is trained using the mean loss values of the batch elements. The output is then fed into an optimizer.

6.4   Results

The proposed Neural Network correctly recognizes 85% of the words from the IAM dataset. The average validation character error rate (CER) of the model is 10.624916%. The output after every step is as follows.

6.4.1   CNN Output

A sequence length of 32 is outputted by the CNN layers. Each entry contains 256 features The output of CNN Layers is shown in Figure 6.6. RNN layers further process these features. However, some of them show a large correlation with properties of the input image like a great degree of correlation with duplicate characters (e.g. "tt"), or with other specific properties of characters like loops (as contained in handwritten "e"s).

6.4.2   RNN Output

Figure 6.7 depicts a visualization of the RNN output matrix for the image with the word "little". The matrix shown in the graph on the top consists of the characters' scores, with the last entry of CTC blank label. Other entries that are part of the matrix are: "! #&'() *+,. /0123456789: ABCDEFGHIJKLMNOPQRSTUVWXYZabcdefghijklmnopqrstuvwxyz". Generally, the characters are predicted to be exactly at the position they appear in the image. However, this is fine, as the CTC operation does not pay attention to absolute positions. It is segmentation-free. The text can be easily decoded from the graph on the bottom displaying

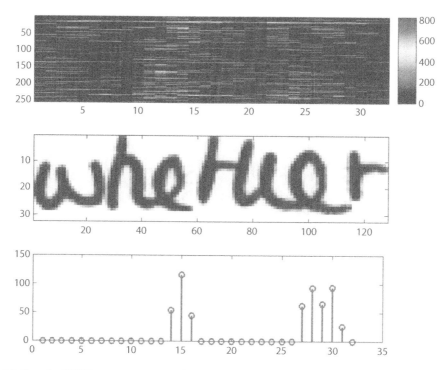

Figure 6.6 Top: the CNN layers compute 256 features per time-step. Middle: input image. Bottom: plot of the 32nd feature, containing a great degree of correlation with the occurrence of the character "e" in the image.

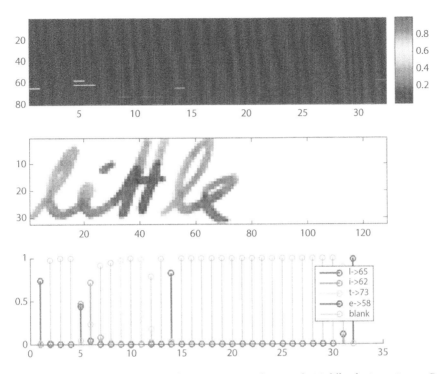

Figure 6.7 Top: output matrix of the layers of Recurrent Neural Network. Middle: the input image. Bottom: Probabilities for the characters of the word "little" and the CTC blank label.

the CTC blank label and scores for the characters of the word in the image: "l", "i", "t", "e". The most credible characters from each time-step are taken. They form the so-called best path. Repetitive characters are thrown away and finally all blanks: "l---ii--t-t--l-...-e" → "l---i--t-t--l-...-e" → "little".

6.4.3 Model Analysis

Figure 6.8 shows how the probability of the ground-truth text changes with the text shifting to the right. As all training images from the IAM dataset are left-aligned, the model is

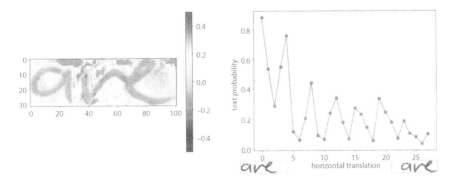

Figure 6.8 Analysis of the model with ground truth value: 'are'.

not translation invariant. Adding data augmentation can improve the translation invariance of the model as it uses random text-alignments.

6.5   Conclusion and Future Work

A neural network is discussed in the paper, which can recognize text in images. It consists of 5 Convolutional Neural Network and 2 Recurrent layers and outputs a character-probability matrix. This matrix is either used for Connectionist Temporal Classification (CTC) loss calculation or CTC decoding. The model is tested on IAM Offline database. To have a more robust model, and improve the accuracy, further pre-processing methods to simplify the task of the classifier can be included. One promising method is to remove the slope of the text, which results in text lying approximately horizontal direction. This also enables tighter cropping of the text-lines, which yields larger text in the input images. More variability can be added to the data using augmentation methods [18]. Token passing or word beam search decoding can be used to constrain the output to dictionary words [17]. If the recognized word is not present in a dictionary, a search can be carried out for the most similar one. The model can input images of size 128×32 and can output a maximum of 32 characters. Thus, it is possible to recognize one to two words. It is, however, not possible to detect longer sentences because of the small input and output size. There are two ways to handle this:

6.5.1   Image Pre-Processing

If there are significant gaps between words or small gaps between characters of a word, then a word-segmentation technique like the one proposed by N. Srimal and R. Manmatha can be used [13]. The segmented words, as in Figure 6.9, can then be fed to the model.

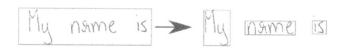

Figure 6.9 Word-segmentation.

6.5.2   Extend the Model to Fit Text-Lines

There are situations in which word-segmentation can prove to be complicated. Punctuation marks written next to a word are difficult to segment. So, it can be a cursive writing style. The model can be extended such that the input can fit larger images, and the output can fit longer character strings.

6.5.3   Integrate Word Beam Search Decoding

It is feasible to use word beam search decoding [17]. Using this method of decoding, words are restricted to those present in a dictionary, but random symbols, characters (punctuation

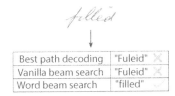

Best path decoding	"Fuleid"
Vanilla beam search	"Fuleid"
Word beam search	"filled"

Figure 6.10 Word beam search coding.

marks) or numerals can still be identified. Figure 6.10 shows a sample word for which word beam search decoding is able to identify the accurate text.

References

1. Balci, B., Saadati, D., Shiferaw, D., Handwritten text recognition using deep learning, in: *CS231n: Convolutional Neural Networks for Visual Recognition*, Stanford University, California, US, Course Project Report, Spring, 2017.

2. Jacob, R. and Holt, A.W., Control Data Corp, 1966. *Reading system with dictionary look-up*. U.S. Patent 3,259,883., July 5, 1966.

3. Allum, D.R., Johns, F.S. and Clysdale, D.G., Canada Post Corp, *Mail encoding and processing system*. U.S. Patent 5,420,403, 1995.

4. Kleiner, A., A Description Of The Kurzweil Reading Machine And A Status Report, *Bulletin of prosthetics research*, Cambridge, United States, 1977.

5. Trier, Ø.D., Jain, A.K. and Taxt, T., Feature extraction methods for character recognition-a survey. *Pattern recognition*, 29(4), pp. 641-662, 1996.

6. Kurzweil Computer Products: http://www.kurzweiltech.com/kcp.html.

7. Bunke, H., Roth, M., Schukat-Talamazzini, E.G., Off-line cursive handwriting recognition using hidden Markov models. *Pattern Recognit.*, 28.9, 1399–1413, 1995.

8. Socher, R., Huval, B., Bath, B., Manning, C.D. and Ng, A., Convolutional-recursive deep learning for 3d object classification. *Advances in neural information processing systems*, 25, pp. 656-664, 2012.

9. LeCun, Y., Bottou, L., Bengio, Y. and Haffner, P., Gradient-based learning applied to document recognition. *Proceedings of the IEEE*, 86(11), pp. 2278-2324, 1998.

10. Mikolov, T. *et al.*, Recurrent neural network based language model. *Eleventh Annual Conference of the International Speech Communication Association*, 2010.

11. Marti, U.-V. and Bunke, H., The IAM-database: an English sentence database for offline handwriting recognition. *Int. J. Doc. Anal. Recogn.*, 5.1, 39–46, 2002.

12. Perwej, Y. and Chaturvedi, A., Neural networks for handwritten English alphabet recognition, *International Journal of Computer Applications* (0975 – 8887), 7, 1–5, 2011.

13. Manmatha, R. and Srimal, N., Scale space technique for word segmentation in handwritten documents. *International Conference on Scale-Space Theories in Computer vision*, Springer, Berlin, Heidelberg, 1999.

14. Lakhani, P. *et al.*, Hello world deep learning in medical imaging. *J. Digit. Imaging*, 31.3, 283–289, 2018.

15. Graves, A. *et al.*, Connectionist temporal classification: labelling unsegmented sequence data with recurrent neural networks. *Proceedings of the 23rd International Conference on Machine Learning*, 2006.

16. How many words are there in the English language?, https://en.oxforddictionaries.com/explore/howmany-words-are-there-in-the-english-language.

17. Scheidl, H., Fiel, S., Sablatnig, R., Word beam search: A connectionist temporal classification decoding algorithm. *2018 16th International Conference on Frontiers in Handwriting Recognition (ICFHR)*, IEEE, 2018.

18. Convolutional Neural Network Benchmarks: https://github.com/jcjohnson/cnn-benchmarks.

19. Kozielski, M., Doetsch, P. and Ney, H., Improvements in rwth's system for off-line handwriting recognition, *12th International Conference on Document Analysis and Recognition* pp. 935-939. IEEE, August, 2013.

7

License Plate Recognition System Using Machine Learning

Ratan Gupta[1]*, Arpan Gupta[2], Amit Kumar[2], Rachna Jain[1] and Preeti Nagrath[1]

[1]Computer Science and Engineering, Bharati Vidyapeeth's College of Engineering, New Delhi, India
[2]Information Technology, Bharati Vidyapeeth's College of Engineering, New Delhi, India

Abstract

This paper presents a machine learning modeled system able to analyze the image of an automobile captured by a camera, detect the registration plate and identify the registration number of the automobile. The algorithm also accepts live feed videos and pre-recorded videos, which are broken into frames. This system was made to solve security problems which exist in residential buildings, societies, parking areas and other institutions and areas where the pre-existing security systems cannot be installed (due to reasons such as low budget, high maintenance required by complex security systems, etc.). This paper presents the procedure and various parameters used for the training of SVC algorithms on a set of images and videos for efficient and automated object recognition.

The accuracies for the 4-fold cross validation were 96.07, 99.01, 97.05 and 100%.

Keywords: License plate recognition, SVC, cross validation, CCA, OpenCV, character segmentation, image segmentation, security, automated security system

7.1 Introduction

From the last few years, Car License Plate Recognition (CLPR) has been a very famous research concept in the image processing domain. License Plate Recognition (LPR) assists in the identification of automobiles entering a house or building, together with its land and outbuildings. Thus, License Plate Recognition is a dire need in nations where security systems are still in development. With the heavy increase in traffic on roads everywhere, there is a need for smart traffic management and control systems which can detect, identify and track vehicles [11].

A license plate recognition system which detects, identifies and assists in tracking a vehicle in real-time is important and a very challenging task [14].

**Corresponding author*: ratan10@outlook.com

Namita Gupta, Prasenjit Chatterjee and Tanupriya Choudhury (eds.) Smart and Sustainable Intelligent Systems, (103–114)
© 2021 Scrivener Publishing LLC

Connected Component Labeling (CCA) helps us to group and label connected regions in the foreground. A pixel is deemed to be connected to another if they both have the same value and adjacent to each other. Blob extraction is generally performed on the binary image [22].

OpenCV is a library of programming functions mainly aimed at real-time computer vision. Through this library we can easily convert video and real time data into frames for processing and can also be converted into arrays or lists for training the machine learning model for prediction [18].

As the license plate detection and recognition are two distinct processes, these two processes have been studied separately. Many techniques and algorithms have been developed and applied on detection and recognition. In our algorithm, we have performed detection and recognition of license plates on automobiles. Concepts from the upcoming fields of image processing and various other domains were applied for more accuracy; however, room for improvement still exists. In the age where the cost of hardware devices is plummeting, computing speed is increasing exponentially and the omnipresent nature of embedded devices, we can find new and improved solutions. Additionally, every nation has its own license plate numbering system, with specific fonts, sizes, colors and characters. License plates also differ from state to state in a country [16].

Certain modules and concepts of Image Processing [2] were used to detect the license plate of a car. Images, videos and live feed can be used.

For the recognition of characters of the license plate, we used a dataset containing the letters A to Z (except O and I) [17] and numbers 0 to 9. Each character contained multiple images so as to achieve greater accuracy.

We train our model on Support Vector Classifier (SVC) which is a part of Support Vector Machine (SVM) which is a part of supervised machine learning.

The SVM module (SVC, NuSVC, etc.) contains the libsvm library and supports different kernels while LinearSVC supports a linear kernel. So: SVC(kernel = 'linear').

The advantages of support vector machines are:

- Effectual in high dimensional spaces.
- Effectual in instances where the number of samples is less than the number of dimensions.
- Training points subset is used in the decision function (support vectors), which makes the process memory efficient.
- Versatile: different kernel functions can be defined for the decision function. Common kernels exist, but custom kernels can also be specified.

This paper is divided into seven sections. The first section is the Introduction which is followed by a brief section explaining Machine Learning as Section two. The third section is Related Work and mentions all the papers and projects similar to ours. The fourth section explains the various Classification Models in machine learning. The fifth section is Proposed Work and Methodology where our work on this project is explained in detail. The sixth and seventh sections are Result and Conclusion respectively. We conclude the paper with References.

7.1.1   Machine Learning

Machine Learning is the science and art of programming computers so they can learn from data. Here is a slightly more general definition: "It is the field of study that gives computers the ability to learn without being explicitly programmed."—Arthur Samuel, 1959.

A more engineering-oriented approach: "A computer program is said to learn from experience E with respect to some task T and some performance measure P, if it's performance on T, as measured by P, improves with experience E."—Tom Mitchell, 1997.

Machine Learning aims at building the right models using the right features that achieve the right tasks. In aspect, features refer to a language in which we describe the relevant objects of our domain, be the email or complex organic molecules. Features play such an important role in machine learning as we do not have to go back to the domain object after the suitable representation of features. A task is an abstract representation of a problem we want to solve regarding those domain objects: the most common form of these is classifying them into two or more classes. Many of these tasks can be represented as a mapping from data points to outputs. This mapping or model is itself produced as the output of a machine learning algorithm applied to the training data, there is a wide variety of models to choose from. No matter what variety of machine learning models you may encounter, you will find that they are designed to solve one of only a small number of tasks and use only a few different types of features. One could say that machine learning gets its diversity from its models and unity from its tasks and features.

To summarize, Machine Learning is great for:

- Problems for which existing solutions require a lot of hand-tuning or long lists of rules: one Machine Learning algorithm can often simplify code and perform better.
- Complex problems for which there is no good solution at all using a traditional approach: the best Machine Learning techniques can find a solution.
- Fluctuating environments: a Machine Learning system can adapt to new data.
- Getting insights about complex problems and large amounts of data.

7.2   Related Work

License plate detection can be divided into two parts. First, locating the position of the license (registration) plate and second, segmentation of the characters of the license plate to predict the license plate number.

Shan [7] used a combination of vertical pixel projection and edge detection was used in the development of a license plate detection program.

RGB images were segmented by mean shift algorithm into probable regions and then classified into two categories that were 'plate' or 'not a plate'. Loumos [10], used low resolution video frames for the application of AdaBoost algorithm. License plate was located using the series of frames extracted by the video.

To locate the license plate a distinct approach was used. Jia [15], instead of applying the features of the algorithm they tried to find all the character-like regions in the processed image. So a region based initiative is used for detection. If a combination of characters is identified, then we can assume that the license plate is located in the image.

For detecting number plates of different countries Ankush [21] presented, improved segmentation algorithm. The number plate segmentation algorithm is a four-step procedure including median filtering, adaptive thresholding, component labeling and region growing and segmentation and normalization to remove noise, for binarization of image, to label the pixel according to color value and to segment the plate of 15×15 pixel size. The authors used Otsu's method for image binarization in the adaptive thresholding process.

To locate Chinese number plates Wu and Li [27] proposed a method to find horizontal and vertical differences, to find the exact rectangle with vehicle number. The authors converted vehicle images into grayscale and then applied automatic binarization using MATLAB. Any further details regarding number plate detection algorithms are not mentioned in this paper. The authors claim to have an average recognition rate of 0.8 s.

In Ref. [13], statistical methods and the edge detection of the shapes have been used to find plaque location.

Disadvantages of this approach are that, firstly, only one plate is extracted from an image. Secondly, the extraction of plate from images with complex backgrounds is quite difficult.

In Ref. [1] instead of using conventional gradient filters, Porikli computed a matrix of low level pixel wise features within a given image window. This method captures both statistical and special properties. They used integral image based data propagation techniques to accelerate the covariance matrix extraction.

In Refs. [3, 9] they used, multilayer perceptron strategy which consists of many classifications of one image using multiple adjusted window grids. This grid will determine whether the pixel belongs to the license plate or not. To increase the efficiency of this system he used morphological operations.

7.3   Classification Models

In machine learning and statistics, classification is a supervised learning approach in which the computer program learns from the data input given to it and then uses this learning to classify new observations. This data set may simply be bi-class (like identifying whether the person is male or female or that the mail is spam or non-spam) or it may be multi-class too. Some examples of classification problems are speech recognition, handwriting recognition, biometric identification, document classification, etc.

Here we have some of the types of classification algorithms in Machine Learning:

1. Logistic Regression
2. Decision Trees
3. Random Forest
4. K Means Clustering
5. Support Vector Machines.

7.3.1   Logistic Regression

Logistic Regression (also called Logit Regression) is commonly used to estimate the probability that an instance belongs to a particular class. If the estimated probability is greater than 50%, then the model predicts that the instance belongs to that class (called the positive class, labeled "1"), or else it predicts that it does not (i.e., it belongs to the negative class, labeled "0"). This makes it a binary classifier.

7.3.2   Decision Trees

Decision trees are versatile machine learning algorithms that can perform both classification and regression tasks, and even multi output tasks. They are very powerful algorithms, capable of fitting complex datasets. They are also the fundamental components of random forest classification. Decision trees make very few assumptions about the training data. To avoid overfitting of the training data, we need to restrict the decision tree's freedom during the training. This process is known by regularization. Through this we can restrict the depth of the decision tree.

7.3.3   Random Forest

Random forest is an ensemble of decision trees generally trained via the bagging method, typically with max_samples set to the size of the training set. The random forest algorithm introduces extra randomness when growing trees, instead of searching for the very best feature when splitting a node, it searches for the best feature among a random subset of features. This results in a greater tree diversity which trades a higher bias for a lower variance, generally yielding an overall better model.

7.3.4   K Means Clustering

Clustering is the task of identifying similar instances and assigning them to clusters, i.e., groups of similar instances. Anomaly detection is particularly useful in detecting defects in manufacturing, or for fraud detection. Cluster is: it really depends on the context, and different algorithms will capture different kinds of clusters.

The K-Means algorithm is a simple algorithm capable of clustering this kind of dataset very quickly and efficiently, often in just a few iterations. Despite its many merits, most notably being fast and scalable, K-Means is not perfect. As we saw, it is necessary to run the algorithm several times to avoid sub-optimal solutions, plus you need to specify the number of clusters, which can be quite a hassle. Moreover, K-Means does not behave very well when the clusters have varying sizes, different densities, or non-spherical shapes.

7.3.5   Support Vector Machines

A Support Vector Machine (SVM) is a very powerful and versatile Machine Learning model, capable of performing linear or nonlinear classification, regression, and even outlier detection [20]. SVMs are particularly well suited for classification of complex but small or medium sized datasets.

There are two types of SVM classifications:

1. Linear Classification
2. Nonlinear Classification.

7.3.5.1   Linear Classification

Linear SVM is the newest extremely fast machine learning (data mining) algorithm for solving multiclass classification problems from ultra large data sets that implements an original proprietary version of a cutting plane algorithm for designing a linear support vector machine. LinearSVM is a linearly scalable routine meaning that it creates an SVM model in a CPU time which scales linearly with the size of the training data set. Our comparisons with other known SVM models clearly show its superior performance when high accuracy is required.

7.3.5.2   Nonlinear Classification

Although linear SVM classifiers are efficient and work surprisingly well in many cases, many datasets are not even close to being linearly separable. One approach to handling nonlinear datasets is to add more features, such as polynomial features in some cases that can result in a linearly separable dataset.

Adding polynomial features is simple to implement and can work great with all sorts of Machine Learning algorithms (not just SVMs), but at a low polynomial degree it cannot deal with very complex datasets, and with a high polynomial degree it creates a huge number of features, making the model too slow.

Fortunately, when using SVMs you can apply an almost miraculous mathematical technique called the kernel trick. It makes it possible to get the same result as if you added many polynomial features, even with very high degree polynomials, without actually having to add them. So there is no combinatorial explosion of the number of features since you don't actually add any features.

Out of all the models suitable for classification in Machine Learning, SVM model was the one chosen for its advantages as mentioned in Section 1, Introduction of this paper.

7.4   Proposed Work and Methodology

License Plate Detection using Machine Learning can be achieved by using OpenCV through which we can convert the video files into frames and then determine the height and width of the number plate [23]. Segmentation is performed on the image to determine the characters for recognition [10]. Training of the image datasets is done. Dataset contains multiple images of the digits from 0 to 9 and alphabet from A to Z. We apply the trained model on the SVC algorithm. Now prediction for all the characters from the license plate is done.

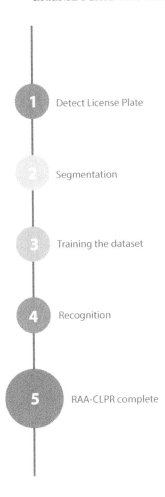

We divide our work into 4 segments :

1. Detect License Plate
2. Segmentation
3. Training
4. Prediction and Recognition.

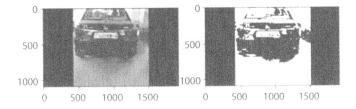

Figure 7.1 Grayscale and binary images.

Figure 7.1 are grayscale and binary images that have been converted from the original image which was a frame extracted from a video by OpenCV [25].

7.4.1　Detect License Plate

For detection of license plates we use OpenCV to capture a video and convert it into frames for image processing [4]. For good accuracy of detection we convert our colored image into binary image pixels whose range is between 0 and 255. To recognize the plate as shown in Figure 7.2 we assume the location of the plate by specifying the coordinates and matching it with the probable coordinate and finally detecting the location of the license plate [19]. We make two assumptions for determining the location of the license plate [6, 24]. Through Matplotlib we measure the dimensions of the image so as to make the assumptions. Two assumptions were as follows:

1. Height of the license plate should be between 5 and 15% of the image.
2. Width of the license plate should be between 35 and 60% of the image.

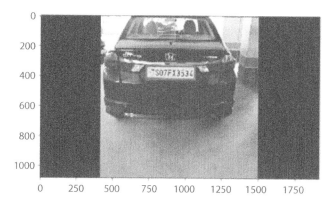

Figure 7.2 Honda after detection.

7.4.2　Segmentation

In segmentation, we identify each character of the license plate as shown in Figure 7.3 and store it in a list. In this section we invert the binary image into white and black pixels to increase the accuracy of our detection [5]. We store the characters of the license plate in the specific order in which they are written. Each character has its own index for easy access. Segmentation can also be done by using pytesseract but here we are using regionprops library in Matplotlib to determine the characters as it is much simpler to determine [8].

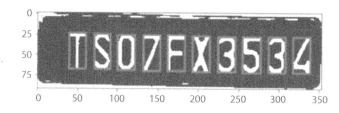

Figure 7.3 License plate characters being extracted individually.

7.4.3   Training the Model

In training we have the image dataset of all the digits and alphabets which contains multiple images and train our dataset on SVC model of machine learning to classify the characters in the license plate with the trained model. We train our model with Cross Validation technique whose output is shown in Figure 7.4 and use 4 folds for training and testing. Then we fit the trained and tested models using SVC. The SVC model is used because of its linearity and can easily classify the characters and its accuracy is better than any other model.

```
Cross Validation Result for  4  -fold
[ 96.07843137  99.01960784  97.05882353 100.
```

Figure 7.4 Accuracy of the 4-fold Cross Validation Model.

7.4.4   Prediction and Recognition

We read each character of the license plate one at a time and detect the registration number. We load the trained model and loop our code for every character for recognition [12, 26].

The output is as shown in Figure 7.5.

```
Predicted license plate
FTS07FX3534
License plate
FTS07FX3534

Each character of the license plate shown individually
['F']
['T']
['S']
['0']
['7']
['F']
['X']
['3']
['5']
['3']
['4']

Indexes according to the image axes
0
39
69
99
130
160
191
221
252
282
313
```

Figure 7.5 Final output.

7.5   Result

The accuracy for the 4-fold cross validation performed while training the dataset were 96.07, 99.01, 97.05 and 100%.

The predicted license plate was found to be exactly the same as the license plate of the car as shown in Figure 7.6.

```
Predicted license plate
FTS07FX3534
License plate
FTS07FX3534
```

Figure 7.6 Predicted versus determined number plate.

7.6   Conclusion

The machine learning algorithm with custom training was found to be very successful in predicting the license plate or registration number of a vehicle. SVC classifier proved to be a very good algorithm for object character recognition. Custom Training also showed an accuracy of around 97%. This model can be used for various security purposes.

A fair amount of study has been conducted on the detection and identification of license plates. A number of researchers have tackled the problem in various ways and have come up with different solutions for this task. Every technique or solution or algorithm has many benefits and drawbacks. Additionally, every nation has its own license plate numbering system, with specific fonts, sizes, colors and characters. License plates also differ from state to state in a country.

RAA-CLPR can be used to detect and recognize any license plate of any car all around the world.

The proposed approach has been tested on multiple images and videos. A relatively high accuracy has been obtained which shows the efficiency of this approach.

7.7   Future Scope

Taking into consideration the high accuracy of the model, it is well suited to be used as an ANPR security system in residential buildings, offices, complexes, educational institutes, etc. Integrated on a Raspberry Pi along with a security camera, this model will work as an automated security system, modifying the job description of security guards in residential buildings and offering them a better pay by enhancing their skill set.

References

1. Porikli, F. and Kocak, T., Robust License Plate Detection using Covariance Descriptor in a Neural Network Framework, in: *IEEE International Conference on Video and Signal Based Surveillance (AVSS 2006)*, p. 107, 2006.

2. Gonzalez, R.C. and Woods, R.E., *Digital Image Processing*, 3rd Edn., p. 954, Prentice Hall, Upper Saddle River, NJ.

3. Carrera, L., Mora, M., Gonzalez, J., Aravena, F., License plate detection using neural networks, in: *International Work-Conference on Artificial Neural Networks*, Springer, Berlin, Heidelberg, pp. 1248–1255, 2009, June.

4. Lim, J.S., *Two-dimensional Signal and Image Processing*, 1st Edn., p. 694, Prentice Hall, Englewood Cliffs, 1990.

5. Otsu, N., A threshold selection method from gray-level histograms. *IEEE Trans. Syst. Man Cybern.*, 9, 62–66, 1979.

6. Sarfraz, M., Ahmed, M.J., Ghazi, S.A., Saudi Arabian license plate recognition system. *Proceedings of the International Conference on Geometric Modeling and Graphics, Jul. 16-18*, IEEE Xplore Press, Saudi Arabia, pp. 36–41, 2003.

7. Shan, B., License plate character segmentation and recognition based on RBF neural networks. *Proceedings of the 2nd International Workshop on Education Technology and Computer Science, Mar. 6-7*, IEEE Xplore Press, Wuhan, pp. 86–89, 2010.

8. Soille, P., *Morphological Image Analysis: Principles and Applications*, 2nd Edn., p. 391, Springer, Berlin, 2003.

9. Wang, W., License plate recognition algorithm based on radial basis function neural networks. *Proceedings of the International Symposium on Intelligent Ubiquitous Computing and Education, May 15-16*, IEEE Xplore Press, Chengdu, pp. 38–41, 2009.

10. Anagnostopoulos, C., Anagnostopoulos, I., Loumos, V., Kayafas, E., License plate-recognition from still images and video sequences: a survey. *IEEE Trans. Intell. Transp. Syst.*, 9, 3, 377–391, 2008.

11. Anagnostopoulos, C., Anagnostopoulos, I., Loumos, V., Kayafas, E., A license plate-recognition algorithm for intelligent transportation system applications. *IEEE Trans. Intell. Transp. Syst.*, 7, 3, 377–392, 2006.

12. Cano, J., Perz-Cortes, J.C. *et al.*, Vehicle license plate segmentation in natural images, in: *Lecture Notes on Computer Science*, vol. 2652, F.J. Perales (Ed.), pp. 142–149, Springer, New York, 2003.

13. Chacon, M.I. and Zimmerman, A., License plate location based on a dynamic PCNN scheme, in: *Proceedings of the Int. Joint Conf. on Neural Netw.*, vol. 2, pp. 1195–1200, 2003.

14. Chang, S.L., Chen, L.S., Chung, Y.C., Chen, S.W., Automatic license plate recognition. *IEEE Trans. Intell. Transp. Syst.*, 5, 1, 42–53, 2004.

15. Jia, W., Zhang, H., He, X., Region-based license plate detection. *J. Netw. Comput. Appl.*, 30, 4, 1324–1333, 2007.

16. Jiao, J., Ye, Q., Huang, Q., A configurable method for multi-style license plate recognition. *Pattern Recognit.*, 42, 3, 358–369, 2009.

17. Matas, J. and Zimmermann, K., Unconstrained licence plate and text localization and recognition, in: *Proceedings of the IEEE Int. Conf. on Intell. Transp. Syst.*, 2005.

18. Suresh, K.V., Kumar, G., Rajagopalan, A.N., Superresolution of license plates in real traffic videos. *IEEE Trans. Intell. Transp. Syst.*, 8, 321–331, 2007.

19. Zheng, D., Zhao, Y., Wang, J., An efficient method of license plate location. *Pattern Recognit. Lett.*, 26, 15, 2431–2438, 2005.

20. Kim, K., Jung, K., Kim, J.H., Color Texture-Based Object Detection: An Application to License Plate Localization, in: *SVM 2002*, LNCS, vol. 2388, S.-W. Lee and A. Verri (Eds.), p. 293, Springer, Heidelberg, 2002.

21. Roy, A. and Ghoshal, D., Number Plate Recognition for use in different countries using an improved segmentation, 2011, March, https://www.researchgate.net/publication/261267320_Number_Plate_Recognition_for_use_in_different_countries_using_an_improved_segmentation.

22. Clark, P. and Mirmehdi, M., Finding Text Regions using Localised Measures. *Proceedings of the 11th British Machine Vision Conference*, pp. 675–684, 2000.

23. https://docs.opencv.org/2.4/doc/tutorials/tutorials.html.

24. Gonzalez, R.C. and Woods, R.E., *Digital Image Processing*, 2d ed., Prentice Hall, Englewood Cliffs, NY, 2002.

25. Parisi, R., Di Claudio, E.D., Lucarelli, G., Orlandi, G., Car Plate Recognition by Neural Networks and Image Processing. *Proceedings of the 1998 IEEE International Symposium on Circuits and Systems*, pp. 195–198, 1998.

26. Remus, B., License Plate Recognition System. *Proceedings of the 3rd International Conference in Information, Communications and Signal Processing*, pp. 203–206, 2001.

27. Wu, H. and Li, B., License plate recognition system, 2011, August, https://www.researchgate.net/publication/261037230_License_plate_recognition_system.

Prediction of Disease Using Machine Learning Algorithms

Annu Dhankhar* and Shashank Jain

B.M. Institute of Engineering & Technology, Ans Sonipat, India

Abstract

Medical Analysis is a field of vast research and there has been a huge requirement for the creation of a particular algorithm by which any disease on the basis of its feature sets or its symptoms can be detected. This Research paper tries to find the best algorithm that can be used to predict the disease or chances that the disease can occur in the person. This Research paper tries to find the best algorithm for heart attack prediction and breast cancer detection using various machine learning approaches from the datasets obtained from UCI Machine Learning Repository.

Keywords: Medical analyzer, machine learning, decision tree classifier, random forest classifier, support vector machines, K means clustering algorithm

8.1 Introduction

In the field of medical analysis, there has been a huge demand for determining or predicting the disease that the person has been suffering through before the actual occurring of disease by just knowing its symptoms. With the help of certain analysis and by using certain prediction and classification strategies [15] we can determine the actual disease that the person can suffer through in the future. Machine Learning [18] is the field by which a machine can predict certain outcomes without being explicitly programmed by using certain strategies and classification techniques. With the help of vast technology such as machine learning we can justify the correlations that exist between the data, with the help of machine learning technologies and using its algorithm.

I have prepared different types of classifiers [19] for certain diseases by which we can predict whether the person is suffering from certain disease or chances that he can suffer from that particular disease for which classifier is created.

With the help of various classification techniques such as Naive Bayes Classifiers [16], Neural Network Classifier [17], Random Forest Classifier according to their predictive analysis I have prepared classifiers for diseases such as heart attack and Breast Cancer as these diseases are the region of primary concern having high chances of their

---

Corresponding author: annudhankhar13@gmail.com

Namita Gupta, Prasenjit Chatterjee and Tanupriya Choudhury (eds.) Smart and Sustainable Intelligent Systems, (115–126)
© 2021 Scrivener Publishing LLC

occurrences, thereby performed analysis that which classifier would be the best suited for finding particular disease. With the help of UCI machine learning repository [7] extracted the datasets for heart disease [4] and breast cancer disease prediction [5] which are used for the analysis which algorithm is more preferable for prediction of these diseases. These datasets are rich in its vastness by which one can easily analyze the diseases of the person by the help of certain common parameters used to analyze those diseases [1, 3, 6, 10, 12, 14].

8.2   Datasets and Evaluation Methodology

This is the general flow (Figure 8.1) of Machine Learning algorithms that I had used to analyze the datasets and the perform the analysis on the datasets to gather the results and determining the best possible algorithm for both the dataset and then testing out the algorithm to gather the results this involves Data Gathering process in which the data is gathered from the source which is the datasets in the .csv format and then after the processing the dataset by doing scaling and preprocessing according to the required analysis by the model if required and then splitting the data to determine what should be the appropriate training and testing set of the data to perform analysis on the data to get the required results that can be used for analysis. After that we train several different algorithms on the training set and after gathering the certain weight matrices we find the correlations in the algorithm then the last step involves determining the best possible results using Confusion Matrix is

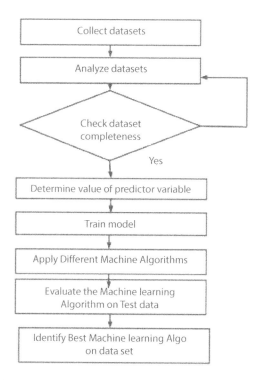

Figure 8.1 Evaluation process.

used the following format to get the value of results and it's immediate predictions are gathered using that and then after getting the results best possible model with the best possible accuracy is determined.

8.2.1 Datasets

These datasets due to their vastness in multiple attributes of features for better analysis of the disease is taken from the UCI Machine Learning Repository [7] which can be further used to analyze the performance of the algorithms on the diseases.

Dataset for Heart Attack Prediction is taken from UCI repository for heart disease dataset [4] which consists of various independent variables or features for prediction of the disease (Figure 8.2).

Parameters such as age, sex, cp, trestbps, cholestrol, fasting blood sugar, restecg, maximum heart rate achieved ,exercise induced agina, oldpeak, slope, number of major vessels (0–3) colored by flourosopy and thal are used for prediction of the number which is either 1 or 0 on the basis of the results where 1 indicates that the person has a heart attack and 0 indicates the person did not have a heart attack which can be used for prediction of the chances that the person can suffer from heart attack.

In this heart disease detection dataset (Figure 8.3) we have used the ratio of training to testing as 80:20 as the size chosen for the training size in 80% and testing size is about 20% of the whole dataset to be used to analyze the data values.

For breast cancer detection another dataset is taken from machine learning UCI Repository. In this breast cancer, Wisconsin data [5] is taken from the repository for analyzing breast cancer.

Certain parameters that are used to perform analysis are diagnosis, radius mean, texture_mean, perimeter_mean, area_mean, smoothness_mean, compactness_mean, concavity_mean, concave points_mean, symmetry_mean, fractal_dimension_mean, radius_se, texture_se, perimeter_se, area_se, smoothness_se, compactness_se, concavity_se, concave-points_se, symmetry_se, fractal_dimensio n_se, radius_worst, texture_worst, perimeter_worst,

```
In [6]: df.head()
Out[6]:
```

	age	sex	cp	trestbps	chol	fbs	restecg	thalach	exang	oldpeak	slope	ca	thal	target
0	63	1	3	145	233	1	0	150	0	2.3	0	0	1	1
1	37	1	2	130	250	0	1	187	0	3.5	0	0	2	1
2	41	0	1	130	204	0	0	172	0	1.4	2	0	2	1
3	56	1	1	120	236	0	1	178	0	0.8	2	0	2	1
4	57	0	0	120	354	0	1	163	1	0.6	2	0	2	1

Figure 8.2 Heart disease detection dataset features.

```
X_train,X_test,y_train,y_test=train_test_split(X,y,test_size=0.2)

X_test.shape
(61, 13)

X_train.shape
(242, 13)
```

Figure 8.3 Heart disease detection dataset training to testing.

```
In [2]:  df=pd.read_csv("./dataset_breast_cancer/data.csv")
```

```
In [6]:  df.head()
Out[6]:
```

	id	diagnosis	radius_mean	texture_mean	perimeter_mean	area_mean	smoothness_mean	compactness_mean	c
0	842302	M	17.99	10.38	122.80	1001.0	0.11840	0.27760	
1	842517	M	20.57	17.77	132.90	1326.0	0.08474	0.07864	
2	84300903	M	19.69	21.25	130.00	1203.0	0.10960	0.15990	
3	84348301	M	11.42	20.38	77.58	386.1	0.14250	0.28390	
4	84358402	M	20.29	14.34	135.10	1297.0	0.10030	0.13280	

5 rows × 33 columns

Figure 8.4 Breast cancer detection dataset.

```
In [13]:  X_train,X_test,y_train,y_test=train_test_split(X,y,test_size=0.2)
```

```
In [27]:  X_train.shape
Out[27]:  (455, 30)
```

```
In [28]:  y_test.shape
Out[28]:  (114,)
```

Figure 8.5 Breast cancer detection dataset training to testing.

area_worst, smoothness_worst, compactness_w orst, concavity_worst, concavepoints_worst, symmetry_worst, fractal_dimension_worst. Here diagnosis is used as the dependent variable for performing analysis which type of cancer either benign or malign exists in a person (Figure 8.4).

In his dataset we have used the ratio of training to testing as 80:20 as the size chosen for the training size in 80% and testing size is about 20% of the whole dataset to be used to analyze the data values (Figure 8.5).

8.3 Algorithms Used

Algorithms such as Decision Tree Classifier, Random Forest Classifier, Support Vector Machines, K Nearest Neighbors are used [20, 26] for performing the analysis to analyze the gathered data and then getting the accuracy of the data according to the data our model being trained upon [21, 30–32].

8.3.1 Decision Tree Classifier

Decision Trees is the supervised machine learning algorithm which consists of a series of decisions along with their consequences used to perform analysis.

In this I have used Gridsearchcv algorithm [9] which is used to do some random analysis on the data by using the brute force method in which we supply some certain values or different values of hyperparameters which after tuning can give the best possible results to perform certain analysis [8, 29].

Figure 8.6 Confusion matrix for decision tree.

```
In [21]: from sklearn.tree import DecisionTreeClassifier

         /home/shashank/anaconda3/lib/python3.6/importlib/_bootstrap.py:219: RuntimeWarning: numpy.dtype size changed, may i
         ndicate binary incompatibility. Expected 96, got 88
           return f(*args, **kwds)

In [22]: classifier1=DecisionTreeClassifier()

In [23]: classifier1.fit(X_train,y_train)

Out[23]: DecisionTreeClassifier(class_weight=None, criterion='gini', max_depth=None,
                     max_features=None, max_leaf_nodes=None,
                     min_impurity_decrease=0.0, min_impurity_split=None,
                     min_samples_leaf=1, min_samples_split=2,
                     min_weight_fraction_leaf=0.0, presort=False, random_state=None,
                     splitter='best')

In [24]: y_pred=classifier1.predict(X_test)

In [25]: from sklearn.metrics import confusion_matrix

In [26]: cm=confusion_matrix(y_test,y_pred)

In [27]: cm

Out[27]: array([[42,  3],
                [ 5, 64]])
```

Figure 8.7 Confusion matrix for decision tree.

Thereafter performing the analysis gives the result as depth of the tree as 8 this means 8 the level of depth of the tree is required in order to make certain decisions used in analysis and leaf nodes required for heart disease are 20.

For Heart Disease Dataset (Figure 8.6)

For Breast Cancer Dataset (Figure 8.7)

8.3.2   Random Forest Classifier

Random forest classifier is the supervised machine learning classifier which aims to use the method of ensemble learning which signifies the fact of reiterating the same algorithm multiple times in order to achieve some desired results. By using the Grid Search Algorithm [9] for analyzing which hyper parameter is best suited for analyzing the data thereby obtaining 37 estimators which are required for analyzing the data. Similarly for breast cancer detection the number of estimators that is obtained is 10 for giving us the required data.

For Heart Disease Dataset (Figure 8.8)

```
In [71]:  classifier.fit(X_train,y_train)
Out[71]:  RandomForestClassifier(bootstrap=True, class_weight=None, criterion='gini',
                     max_depth=None, max_features='auto', max_leaf_nodes=None,
                     min_impurity_decrease=0.0, min_impurity_split=None,
                     min_samples_leaf=1, min_samples_split=2,
                     min_weight_fraction_leaf=0.0, n_estimators=37, n_jobs=1,
                     oob_score=False, random_state=None, verbose=0,
                     warm_start=False)

In [ ]:

In [72]:  y_pred=classifier.predict(X_test)

In [73]:  cm=confusion_matrix(y_test,y_pred)

In [74]:  cm
Out[74]:  array([[27,  4],
                 [ 2, 28]])
```

Figure 8.8 Confusion matrix for random forest classification.

For Breast Cancer Dataset (Figure 8.9)

```
In [52]:  classifier=RandomForestClassifier()

In [53]:  classifier.fit(X_train,y_train)
Out[53]:  RandomForestClassifier(bootstrap=True, class_weight=None, criterion='gini',
                     max_depth=None, max_features='auto', max_leaf_nodes=None,
                     min_impurity_decrease=0.0, min_impurity_split=None,
                     min_samples_leaf=1, min_samples_split=2,
                     min_weight_fraction_leaf=0.0, n_estimators=10, n_jobs=1,
                     oob_score=False, random_state=None, verbose=0,
                     warm_start=False)

In [54]:  y_pred=classifier.predict(X_test)

In [ ]:

In [56]:  from sklearn.metrics import confusion_matrix

In [57]:  cm=confusion_matrix(y_test,y_pred)

In [58]:  cm
Out[58]:  array([[47,  2],
                 [ 2, 63]])
```

Figure 8.9 Confusion matrix for random forest classification.

8.3.3   Support Vector Machines

In this algorithm we try to maximize the distance between two hyperplanes by finding the two nearest points in the plane, thereby finding the hyperplane which can be used to classify the classes for performing the analysis of the model. For heart attack dataset best parameter obtained after performing grid search are C = 100, gamma = 0.0001, kernel = rbf.

Similarly for breast cancer dataset the best parameter obtained after performing grid search are C = 1,000, gamma = 0.0001, kernel = rbf are used [11, 22–25, 27, 28].

For Heart Disease Dataset (Figure 8.10)

```
In [115]: grid.best_estimator_
Out[115]: SVC(C=100, cache_size=200, class_weight=None, coef0=0.0,
              decision_function_shape='ovr', degree=3, gamma=0.0001, kernel='rbf',
              max_iter=-1, probability=False, random_state=None, shrinking=True,
              tol=0.001, verbose=False)

In [16]: y_pred=grid.predict(X_test)

In [18]: from sklearn.metrics import confusion_matrix

In [20]: cm=confusion_matrix(y_test,y_pred)

In [21]: cm
Out[21]: array([[14, 14],
                [ 1, 32]])
```

Figure 8.10 Confusion matrix for SVC.

For Breast Cancer Dataset (Figure 8.11)

```
In [28]: grid.best_estimator_
Out[29]: SVC(C=1000, cache_size=200, class_weight=None, coef0=0.0,
              decision_function_shape='ovr', degree=3, gamma=0.0001, kernel='rbf',
              max_iter=-1, probability=False, random_state=None, shrinking=True,
              tol=0.001, verbose=False)

In [29]: y_pred=grid.predict(X_test)

In [31]: from sklearn.metrics import confusion_matrix

In [32]: cm=confusion_matrix(y_test,y_pred)

In [33]: cm
Out[33]: array([[39,  3],
                [ 1, 71]])
```

Figure 8.11 Confusion matrix for SVC.

8.3.4   K Nearest Neighbors

KNN involves finding the results whether the particular newly entered point belongs to which class and on the basis of that analysis by using the nearest neighboring pairs to determine whether the newly entered point belongs to which class and for that model learns the correlation between existing data points to analyze which data is more accurate and then by determining the data certain values for these points are known and according to the minimum distance between the plausible pairs then accurate pairs are suggested to minimize the distance to predict the neighboring pairs and classifying the data accordingly.

For Heart Disease Dataset (Figure 8.12)

```
In [21]: grid.best_params_
Out[21]: {'leaf_size': 30, 'n_neighbors': 9}

In [22]: y_pred=grid.predict(X_test)

In [23]: from sklearn.metrics import confusion_matrix

In [25]: cm=confusion_matrix(y_test,y_pred)

In [26]: cm
Out[26]: array([[16, 12],
                [11, 22]])

In [28]: (16+22)/(51)
```

Figure 8.12 Confusion matrix for KNN.

For Breast Cancer Dataset (Figure 8.13)

```
                ICU] leaf_size=30, n_neighbors=9
In [21]:  grid.best_params_
Out[21]:  {'leaf_size': 30, 'n_neighbors': 6}

In [22]:  y_pred=grid.predict(X_test)

In [23]:  from sklearn.metrics import confusion_matrix

In [24]:  cm=confusion_matrix(y_test,y_pred)

In [25]:  cm
Out[25]:  array([[47,  4],
                 [ 1, 62]])

In [26]:  (47+62)/(47+4+62+1)
Out[26]:  0.9561403508771193

In [ ]:
```

Figure 8.13 Confusion matrix for KNN.

Table 8.1 Confusion matrix obtained using UCI machine learning repository data to perform the analysis.

S. No.	Disease To Be Analyzed	Classifier Used	Classifier Used	Confusion Matrix (TN)	Confusion Matrix (FP)	Confusion Matrix (FN)	Accuracy Obtained
1	Heart Attack Prediction	Decision Tree Classifier	23	27	8	3	88%
2	Heart Attack Prediction	Random Forest Classifier	27	28	4	2	90%
3	Heart Attack Prediction	Support Vector Machines	14	32	14	1	75.5%
4	Heart Attack Prediction	K-Nearest Neighbor	16	22	12	11	74.50%
5	Breast Cancer Prediction	Random Forest classifier	47	63	2	2	96%
6	Breast Cancer Prediction	Decision Tree Classifier	44	61	5	4	92%
7	Breast Cancer Prediction	Support Vector Machines	39	71	3	1	96.49%
8	Breast Cancer Prediction	K-Nearest Neighbors	47	62	4	1	95.6%

8.4   Results

As from the above analysis (Table 8.1) for our model being trained on UCI Machine Learning Repository having around 303 rows or 303 persons have been analyzed in this data according to their occurrence of any heart attack problems or not.

Confusion Matrix [2] is used to perform analysis on the data. As confusion matrix tells about the prediction of certain results which perform analysis on the basis of predicted and actual results, thereby categorizing as True Positive, False Positive, True Negative, False Negative for performing the analysis on the data. These values tell about the accurate prediction of these results.

We can see that the best model for analyzing the data is Random Forest Classification, where we have used 37 estimators to perform analysis on the data. Having the true positive value as 27 which tells the prediction for correctness, true negative value as 28 which tells for the false correct prediction results, False positive as 4 which are wrong results obtained for correct values, False Negative as 2 which are wrong results obtained for incorrect values.

And thereby obtaining the accuracy [13] of 90% which means we can predict whether the person is suffering from heart disease or not.

The second analysis is done on Breast cancer prediction which is done by UCI Machine Learning Repository. Our model is trained on around 569 rows.

We have used Confusion matrix [2] for analyzing our data. Having the true positive value as 39 which tells the prediction for correctness ,true negative value as 71 which tells for the false correct prediction results, False positive as 3 which are wrong results obtained for correct values, False Negative as 1 which are wrong results obtained for incorrect values.

So the best model from the above analysis as Support Vector Machines in which we performed our analysis using 2 clusters giving us the accuracy about 96.49% i.e. the person having breast cancer will be detected 96.49% correctly.

8.5   Conclusion

From the above analysis we can conclude that machine learning is one of the best solutions which can be used in the field of medical analysis for predicting the chances of a person being suffering from a particular disease or not. Thereby, leading to the conclusion that the best algorithm for prediction of heart disease of the person correlated on the UCI machine learning repository can be done using Random Forest Classification algorithm which is the best measure to perform analysis.

Similarly one of the best algorithms for breast cancer detection correlated on UCI machine learning repository can be done using Support Vector Machines.

References

1. Guimarães, W.W., Pinto, C.L.N., Nobre, C.N., Zárate, L.E., The Relevance of Upstream and Downstream Regions of mRNA in the Prediction of Translation Initiation Site of the Protein. *Bioinformatics and Bioengineering (BIBE) 2017 IEEE 17th International Conference on*, pp. 112–118, 2017.

2. Ting, K.M., Confusion Matrix, in: *Encyclopedia of Machine Learning and Data Mining*, C. Sammut and G.I. Webb (Eds.), Springer, Boston, MA, 2017.

3. Duda, R.O., Hart, P.E., Stork, D.G., *Pattern Classification*, 2nd edition, Wiley, New York, 2001. Another popular text is Statistical Pattern Recognition, Second Edition. Andrew R. Webb, John Wiley & Sons, Ltd. 2002.

4. Detrano, R., Janosi, A., Steinbrunn, W., Pfisterer, M., Schmid, J., Sandhu, S., Guppy, K., Lee, S., Froelicher, V., International application of a new probability algorithm for the diagnosis of coronary artery disease. *Am. J. Cardiol.*, 64, 304–310, 1989.

5. Huang, K., Yang, H., King, I., Lyu, M.R., Chan, L., Biased Minimax Probability Machine for Medical Diagnosis. *AMAI*, 2004.

6. Gennari, J.H., Langley, P., Fisher, D., Models of incremental concept formation. *Artif. Intell.*, 40, 11–61, 1989.

7. Street, W.N., Wolberg, W.H., Mangasarian, O.L., Nuclear feature extraction for breast tumor diagnosis. *IS&T/SPIE 1993 International Symposium on Electronic Imaging: Science and Technology*, San Jose, CA, vol. 1905, pp. 861–870, 1993.

8. Sharma, H. and Kumar, S., A Survey on Decision Tree Algorithms of Classification in Data Mining. *Int. J. Sci. Res.*, 5, 4, 2094–2097, 2016.

9. Rossi, A.L.D. and de Carvalho, A.C.P., Bio-inspired Optimization Techniques for SVM Parameter Tuning, in: *10th Brazilian Symposium on Neural Networks, 2008. SBRN '08. Presented at the 10th Brazilian Symposium on Neural Networks, 2008. SBRN '08*, pp. 57–62, 2008.

10. Amit, Y., Blanchard, G., Wilder, K., *Multiple randomized classifiers: MRCL Technical Report*, Department of Statistics, University of Chicago, USA, 1999.

11. Drucker, H., Burges, C.J.C., Kaufman, L., Smola, A., Vapnik, V., Support vector regression machines, in: *Proceedings of the 9th International Conference on Neural Information Processing Systems*, Denver, CO, USA, pp. 155–161, 3–5 December 1996.

12. Srinivas, K., Rani, B.K., Govrdhan, A., Applications of Data Mining Techniques in Healthcare and Prediction of Heart Attacks. *Int. J. Comput. Sci. Eng. (IJCSE)*, 2, 2, 250–255, 2010.

13. Bailey, T. and Jain, A., A note on distance-weighted k-nearest neighbor rules. *IEEE Trans. Syst. Man Cybern.*, 8, 311–313, 1978.

14. Mosa, A.S.M. and Yoo, I., Lincoln Sheets. *BMC Med. Inform. Decis. Mak.*, 12, 67, 2012, Published online 2012.

15. Kaviani, P. and Dhotre, S., Short Survey on Naive Bayes Algorithm. *Int. J. Adv. Res. Comput. Sci. Manage.*, 4, 11, 115, 2017.

16. Prasanna, P. and Rao, Dr., Text classification using artificial neural networks. *Int. J. Eng. Technol. (UAE)*, 7, 603–606, 2018.

17. Tan, C.F., Wahidin, L.S., Khalil, S.N., Tamaldin, N., Hu, J., Rauterberg, M., The application of expert system: A review of research and applications. *ARPN J. Eng. Appl. Sci.*, 11, 2448–2453, 2016.

18. Akinsola, J.E.T., Supervised Machine Learning Algorithms: Classification and Comparison. *Int. J. Comput. Trends Technol. (IJCTT)*, 48, 128–138, 2017.

19. Fabris, F., de Magalhaes, J.P., Freitas, A., A review of supervised machine learning applied to ageing research. *Biogerontology*, 18, 2017.

20. Khanam, M., Mahboob, T., Imtiaz, W., Ghafoor, H., Sehar, R., A Survey on Unsupervised Machine Learning Algorithms for Automation, Classification and Maintenance. *Int. J. Comput. Appl.*, 119, 34–39, 2015.

21. Muthuvel, M., Sivaraju, D., Ramamoorthy, G., Analysis of Heart Disease Prediction using Various Machine Learning Techniques, in: *Conference: International Conference on Artificial Intelligence, Smart Grid and Smart City Applications, (AISGSC 2019)*, PSG College of Technology, Coimbatore, 2019.

22. Kumar, B.S., Adaptive Personalized Clinical Decision Support System Using Effective Data Mining Algorithms. *J. Netw. Commun. Emerg. Technol. (JNCET)*, 8, 1, 2017, www. jncet.org8.1.

23. Alansary, A., Oktay, O., Li, Y., Le Folgoc, L., Hou, B., Vaillant, G., Kamnitsas, K., Vlontzos, A., Glocker, B., Kainz, B., Rueckert, D., Evaluating Reinforcement LearningAgents for Anatomical Landmark Detection. *Med. Image Anal.*, 53, 156–164, 2019.

24. Birkhead, G.S., Klompas, M., Shah, N.R., Uses of electronic health records for public health surveillance to advance public health. *Annu. Rev. Public Health*, 36, 345–359, 2015.

25. Chen, H., Ni, D., Qin, J., Li, S., Yang, X., Wang, T., Heng, P.A., Standard planelocalization in fetal ultrasound *via* domain transferred deep neural networks. *IEEE J. Biomed. Health Inf.*, 19, 5, 1627–1636, 2015.

26. Jo, T., Nho, K., Saykin, A.J., Deep Learning in Alzheimer's Disease: Diagnostic Classification and Prognostic Prediction Using Neuroimaging Data. *Front. Aging Neurosci.*, 2019, https://doi. org/10.3389/fnagi.2019.00220.

27. Basole, R.C., Braunstein, M.L., Sun, J., Data and Analytics Challenges for a Learning Healthcare System. *ACM J. Data Inf. Qual.*, 6, 2–3, July 2015.

28. Archenaa, J. and Mary Anita, E.A., A Survey Of Big Data Analytics in Healthcare and Government. *2nd International Symposium on Big Data and Cloud Computing (ISBCC'15)*, 2015.

29. Solanas, A., Casino, F., Batista, E., Rallo, R., Trends and Challenges in Smart Healthcare Research: A Journey from Data to Wisdom. *IEEE*, 2017.

30. Rahman, F., Application of Big-Data in Healthcare Analytics—Prospects and Challenges. *IEEE*, 2017.

31. Asri, H., Mousannif, H., Al Moatassime, H., Noel, T., Big Data in Healthcare: Challenges and Opportunities. *IEEE*, 2015.

32. Yadav, P., Steinbach, M., Kumar, V., Simon, G., Mining Electronic Health Records (EHRs): A Survey. *ACM Comput. Surv.*, 50, 6, January 2018.

Part 2

DEEP LEARNING AND ITS APPLICATION

9

Brain Tumor Prediction by Binary Classification Using VGG-16

Vaibhav Singh*, Sarthak Sharma, Shubham Goel, Shivay Lamba and Neetu Garg

Department of Computer Science and Engineering, Maharaja Agrasen Institute of Technology (GGSIPU), Rohini Sector 22, Delhi, India

Abstract

A brain tumor is basically the abnormal growth of the cells in the brain. Talking at ground level, two types of tumors are there: benign and cancerous (malignant) tumors. Cancerous tumors can be developed in the brain which are called primary tumors and also other tumors are there as well known as brain metastasis tumors which spread from elsewhere. Many symptoms can be produced by the tumors which solely depend upon the brain's respective part involved. Symptoms can be problems with vision, vomiting, headaches, seizures and mental changes. One may experience difficulty in walking, speaking or with other sensations. As the disease progresses, unconsciousness may occur. The main purpose of this project was to build a CNN model that would classify if the subject has a tumor or not based on MRI scan using deep learning. We used the VGG-16 model architecture and weights to train the model for this binary problem. This project is a combination of CNN model classification problem (to predict whether the subject has brain tumor or not) & Computer Vision problem (to automate the process of brain cropping from MRI scans). VGG16 for feature extraction, which along with other features is fed as input to an Artificial Neural Network [1] classifier through transfer learning. Binary Classifier is a proposed model that classifies the input images as either 0 (No tumor) or 1 (Tumor exists). The final accuracy is much higher than 50% baseline (random guess) and it can be improvised by using a large number of trained images and through hyper parameters tuning. The system achieved 90% accuracy on test set and 86% accuracy on validation set. By experimental results performed on the different images [2], it is clear that the analysis for the brain tumor detection is fast and accurate when compared with the manual detection performed by clinical experts or the radiologists. The various performance factors also indicate that the proposed algorithm provides better results.

Keywords: Deep learning, machine learning, MRI, VGG16, CNN, malignant, benign

Corresponding author: singh.vaibhav32@gmail.com

Namita Gupta, Prasenjit Chatterjee and Tanupriya Choudhury (eds.) Smart and Sustainable Intelligent Systems, (129–138)
© 2021 Scrivener Publishing LLC

9.1   Introduction

Intracranial tumor also known as a brain tumor is an unwanted, abnormal mass of tissue in which large numbers of cells grow and multiply in an uncontrollable fashion. Tumors can be of different types and can have different features and thus have different treatment processes too. In a ground level, tumors basically are of two types i.e. Metastatic tumor and Primary tumor. Primary brain tumor occurs in the brain and stays there while the metastatic leads to cancer in later stages. Segmentation [3] of Brain tumor is very popular and common for the treatment of the tumor. A large amount of Brain Magnetic Resonance is being used for the automatic division of its stimulation. Many techniques have been proposed to segment the tumor. GLCM (Gray-Level Co-Occurrence Matrix) is used for texture segmentation. GLCM is used for the extraction of the optimum features from MRI images. Over the years there has been a significant improvement in the techniques for the evaluation of the tumors. Though, we have diagnosing tools. Unfortunately, we have not reached the stage to cure brain tumors but we are moving a few steps forward to reach our ultimate goal. MRI which stands for Magnetic Resonance Imaging is a technique to diagnose brain tumors and to monitor their treatment. For high quality imaging we are using MRI scans as brain tumor can be easily identified by these scans. They are helpful in locating and finding the parts of the tumor easily. Presently all the techniques used are through human interpretation which may lead to false results. Machine based identification and evaluation can make it easier and clear when compared to manual methods. Tumor-growth modeling provides a way to deal with tumors previously missing from the thing during registration. For this, two different tumor-growth models have been compared. While a simplified tumor growth model offered an advantage in computation speed, a more sophisticated tumor building model showed a better ability to provide more original and meaningful segmentation [4]. Both approaches have been summed into a common framework for analyzing tumor-bearing brain images, which typically uses all image data available in clinics. This segmentation framework paves the way for better evaluation, analysis, identification, treatment planning, and surveillance in radiotherapy.

9.2   Existing Methodology

The main aim of this project is to build a CNN model that would classify whether the subject has tumor or not based on MRI scan (Figure 9.1). VGG-16 model architecture along with the weights are used to train the binary problem. One of the metrics used is Accuracy to measure the model performance which can be defined as:

Accuracy = (Number of correctly predicted images / Total number of tested images) * 100.

9.2.1   Dataset Description

Image data that has been used consist of MRI scans of two classes:

NO—means no tumor, encoded as 0

YES—means tumor, encoded as 1.

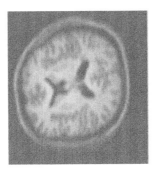

Figure 9.1 MRI original image.

9.2.2   Data Import and Preprocessing

This process is used to enhance the chances of detecting the suspicious region in an MRI image. Finer details of the image are enhanced and noise is removed from the respective images. MRI images (Figure 9.2) when corrupted with noise reduces the accuracy of the image.

For normalization (Figure 9.3) method first step is to crop out the brain from the images by finding the extreme points in contours with OpenCV.

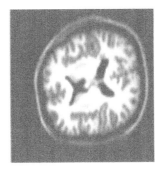

Figure 9.2 MRI enhanced image.

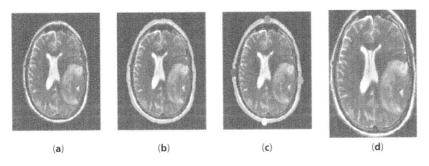

| (a) | (b) | (c) | (d) |

Figure 9.3 (a) Original image. (b) Contour. (c) Extreme points. (d) Cropped image.

9.3   Augmentation

Augmentation methods (Figure 9.4, Figure 9.5, Figure 9.6 & Figure 9.7) are used to artificially increase the size and quality of the dataset. They help in solving overfitting problems and enhance the model's generalization ability during training.

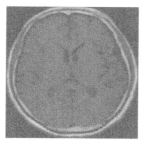

Figure 9.4 Original image.

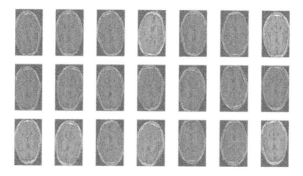

Figure 9.5 Augmented images.

Tumor : NO

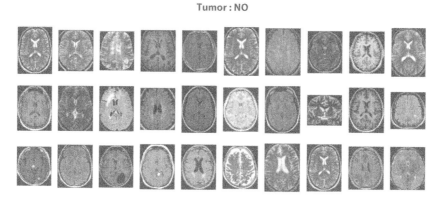

Figure 9.6 Cropped images labelled with NO Tumor.

Tumor : YES

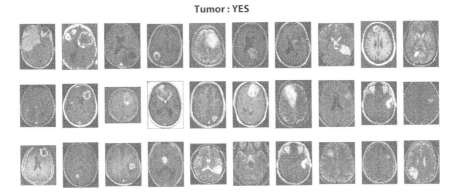

Figure 9.7 Cropped images labelled with YES Tumor.

9.3.1   For CNN Model

Images which are of different size variants are converted to the same specific size. Biggest contour in the image is extracted and subsequently the extreme points of contour. Finally, the image is cropped so that extreme points lie closest to the edges.

9.3.2   For VGG 16 Model

Images are resized to 224,224 as they are of different length and width. Image pixels are normalized by dividing it by 255.

9.4   Models Used

9.4.1   CNN Model

CNN [5] model has been created from scratch. Relu function is being used as the activation function. In addition to that convolution, max pooling layers as well as Adam optimizer has been used. Finally, Sigmoid function is used as the softmax function after the fully connected layer. First convolution layer uses max-pool of size $2 * 2$ and 32 filters of size $3 * 3$. Same specification is again used by the 2nd layer. After this the first dense layer uses Relu as the activation function and second dense layer uses Sigmoid function.

9.4.2   VGG 16 Model

It's a convolutional neural network [6] that is trained on more than a million images, they are from the ImageNet database. 224 by 224 [7] is an input size of the respective network. An approach called Transfer Learning [8] is also used.

9.4.2.1   Pre-Trained Model Approach

A model which is pre trained is chosen from available models. Large and challenging data-sets are released by many research institutes that are included in the pool of respective models. Pre-trained models [9] are used as a starting point for a model on the second task which involves all parts of the model. Model should be tuned in order to adapt to the input output pair data available for the given task. It's a better technique than fine-tuning in which we tweak the parameters of the network which is already trained so that it adopts to the new task.

Very generous features are learned by the initial layers. Going to higher levels of the network, the layer tends to learn patterns which are more relevant to the work for which it is trained. Initial layers are kept intact for fine tuning and later layers are retrained. Network is freezed upto the second last convolution block, after which it is restrained.

9.5   Results

The data used here is a set of MRI images of the brain tumor which are divided into train, validate and test data sets. Validate dataset is used to check for the overfitting. It is used during the model training to adjust hyper parameters. Taking the help of test data set required convolution neural network and is applied to get the final model performance [10]. The model performance are followed here:

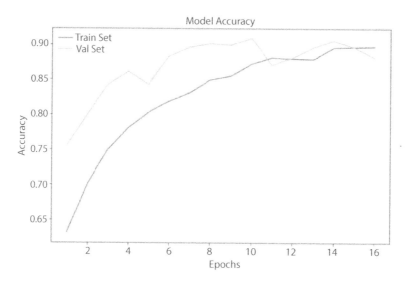

Figure 9.8 Accuracy curve for CNN model.

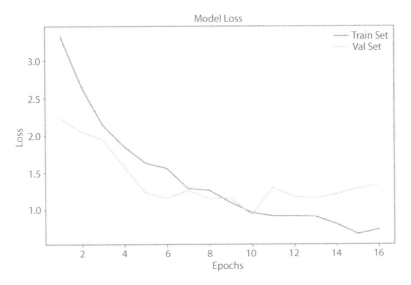

Figure 9.9 Loss curve for CNN model.

The above two figures are basically the graph showing the model accuracy (Figure 9.8) and model loss (Figure 9.9) respectively. System achieved an accuracy of about 90% is obtained by the system on the test dataset and 86% accuracy on the validation set.

Confusion matrix (Figure 9.10) shown below is used to describe the performance of a classifier on a set of test data for which the true values are known.

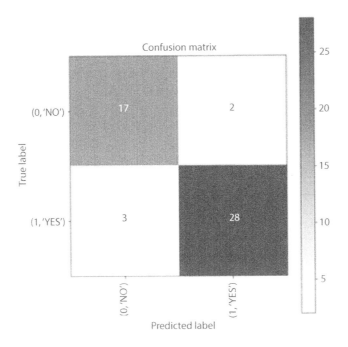

Figure 9.10 Confusion matrix for CNN.

It is used to measure the metrics Recall and Precision for the model:

1. Recall
   = 28 / (28 + 3)
   Result obtained = 90%
2. Precision
   = 28 / (28 + 2)
   Result obtained = 93%

9.6   Comparison

The performance of the fine-tuned VGG 16 model is way better than the customized CNN model. One of the major reasons behind this is that the pre-trained model on ImageNet seems to be better at identifying high level features like edges, patterns, etc. This model is good at understanding certain feature representation, which can be used again thereby helping in faster convergence. Figure 9.11 represents the graphical comparison of the performance of the two models.

9.7   Conclusion and Future Scope

This paper has almost the best overlook in context to the [11] class of MRI-based brain tumor segmentation techniques. This project is a summation of CNN model classification problem and Computer Vision problem. The final model accuracy is much higher than 50% baseline. It could be further increased by model hyper parameters tuning or larger number of train images. The motivation behind this process is to provide a fundamental judgement on identification, tumor checking, treatment and also giving strong outcomes inside a sensible calculation time. It is prominent that the computation strategies for resolving the biological problems, especially problems related to medical imaging, can be fast and cost

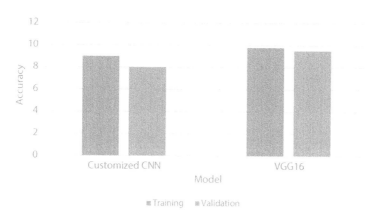

Figure 9.11 Comparison performance of CNN and VGG16.

effective. The current model focuses out that deep learning, CNN particularly has an excellent feature extraction mechanism which is far better than the traditional way of extracting features in terms of time and efficiency. Further, it is noticed that the transfer learning gives better accuracy and therefore the proposed model contains the transfer learning concepts.

From the experimental results performed on various images, it is clear that the analysis is faster and accurate to detect brain tumors than manual detection performed by radiologists or clinical experts. Various performance factors also indicate that the proposed algorithm provides better results. Although the model is quite accurate, the accuracy can be further enhanced by the use of large data sets [12].

In future work, to improve the accuracy of the classification of the present work, we plan to investigate the selective scheme of the classifier by combining more than one classifier and feature selection techniques. A bigger dataset can lead to the improvement of the performance of the model. Better feature extraction strategies, pre-processing of data images are needed to be worked upon in order to get better results.

Although the proposed model performance outshone the existing model by giving 90% accuracy on the test dataset and 86% accuracy on the validated dataset, there is still scope for improvement in terms of increasing the accuracy in future.

References

1. Mahmud, M., Kaiser, M.S., Hussain, A., Vassanelli, S., Applications of deep learning and reinforcement learning to biological data. *IEEE Trans. Neural Networks Learn. Syst.*, 29, 6, 2063–2079, 2018.

2. Liu, J., Pan, Y., Li, M., Chen, Z., Tang, L., Lu, C., Wang, J., Applications of deep learning to MRI images: A survey. *Big Data Min. Anal.*, 1, 1, 1–18, 2018.

3. Menze, B.H., Jakab, A., Bauer, S., Kalpathy-Cramer, J., Farahani, K., Kirby, J., Lanczi, L., The multimodal brain tumor image segmentation benchmark (BRATS). *IEEE Trans. Med. Imaging*, 34, 10, 1993–2024, 2015.

4. Bakas, S., Akbari, H., Sotiras, A., Bilello, M., Rozycki, M., Kirby, J.S., Davatzikos, C., Advancing the cancer genome atlas glioma MRI collections with expert segmentation labels and radiomic features. *Sci. Data*, 4, 170117, 2017.

5. Chato, L. and Latifi, S., Machine learning and deep learning techniques to predict overall survival of brain tumor patients using MRI images, in: *2017 IEEE 17th International Conference on Bioinformatics and Bioengineering (BIBE)*, IEEE, pp. 9–14, 2017.

6. Wang, X., Yang, W., Weinreb, J., Han, J., Li, Q., Kong, X., Wang, L., Searching for prostate cancer by fully automated magnetic resonance imaging classification: deep learning versus non-deep learning. *Sci. Rep.*, 7, 1, 15415, 2017.

7. van Grinsven, M.J., van Ginneken, B., Hoyng, C.B., Theelen, T., Sánchez, C.I., Fast convolutional neural network training using selective data sampling: Application to hemorrhage detection in color fundus images. *IEEE Trans. Med. Imaging*, 35, 1273–1284, 2016.

8. Paul, R., Hawkins, S.H., Balagurunathan, Y., Schabath, M.B., Gillies, R.J., Hall, L.O., Goldgof, D.B., Deep feature transfer learning in combination with traditional features predicts survival among patients with lung adenocarcinoma. *Tomography*, 2, 4, 388, 2016.

9. Ari, A. and Hanbay, D., Deep learning based brain tumor classification and detection system. *Turk. J. Elec. Eng. Comp. Sci.*, 26, 5, 2275–2286, 2018.

10. Nie, D., Zhang, H., Adeli, E., Liu, L., Shen, D., 3D deep learning for multi-modal imaging-guided survival time prediction of brain tumor patients, in: *International Conference on Medical Image Computing and Computer-Assisted Intervention*, Springer, Cham, pp. 212–220, 2016.
11. Pratt, H., Coenen, F., Broadbent, D.M., Harding, S.P., Zheng, Y., Convolutional neural networks for diabetic retinopathy. *Procedia Comput. Sci.*, 90, 200–205, 2016.
12. Burke, H.B., Goodman, P.H., Rosen, D.B., Henson, D.E., Weinstein, J.N., Harrell, F.E., Jr., Bostwick, D.G., Artificial neural networks improve the accuracy of cancer survival prediction. *Cancer*, 79, 4, 857–862, 1997.

10

Study of Gesture-Based Communication Translator by Deep Learning Technique

Rishabh Agarwal, Shubham Bansal*, Abhinav Aggarwal, Neetu Garg and Akanksha Kochhar

Maharaja Agrasen Institute of Technology, New Delhi, India

Abstract

According to a survey conducted by the Department of Empowerment of Persons with Disabilities, about one million people in India are suffering from hearing and speaking problems. The concerns faced by the mute and deaf people in India can be classified into groups like social networks, behavioral enigmas, communication, and safety affairs. They face a lot of complications while conversing face to face. So, these people mostly use gestures for interaction and communication purposes. However, they feel that it is quite challenging for an average human to understand and perceive these gesticulations. Hence, a need for a proper translator arises. But if we look at the facts and numbers of trained individuals who understand these signs are less in number. Also, if people suffering from these handicaps are not inculcated at an early age, it becomes tough for them to learn and adapt these techniques in the later stages of their lives.

It is believed that in the upcoming future, intelligent agents will magnify human capabilities in several fields. Artificial intelligence is the power to manifest intelligence by devices or software. Artificial Intelligence is becoming a big field in computer science, as it has enhanced human life in many areas. Study in the field of artificial intelligence has given rise to the rapidly growing technology known as an expert system. Artificial intelligence and big data have disruptively changed the industry, as the barriers of its implementation (cost, computing power, open-source platforms, etc.) disappear. All these successful applications of AI and its sub-branches look possible to solve the problems faced by the deaf and mute individuals in India, which can be solved using Deep Learning in a very Cost-Effective Approach.

Keywords: Deep learning, image processing, human computer interaction, convolutional neural network, computer vision, template matching, image classification, supervised learning

10.1 Introduction

Gesture-based communication is a different type of conversation that mostly goes ignored. The conversion process of signs into a spoken or written language is often called 'interpretation,' the role that an interpreter performs is equivalent to that of a translator for a human

---

Corresponding author: bansalshubham51@gmail.com

Namita Gupta, Prasenjit Chatterjee and Tanupriya Choudhury (eds.) Smart and Sustainable Intelligent Systems, (139–150)
© 2021 Scrivener Publishing LLC

speech. In this project, we study the Indian Sign Language, which is practiced in India. Twenty-six gestures are corresponding to the 26 alphabets.

Deaf and Mute individuals are usually withheld of good conversation with other souls in our society. It has been observed that there are only a few people that are able to perceive the gestures formed by these people. Mute and deaf individuals are not able to communicate like normal people; hence, they depend upon this gesture-based translator for communication.

The mute and deaf community uses this gesture-based language as the principal medium for conversation. This language also has its vocabulary and grammar but uses signs and gestures for communication. The dilemma starts when the deaf and mute community attempt to converse with other people while using this gesture-based language. These situations happen as healthy people are not able to understand these signs and gestures. Hence, deaf and mute individuals are only able to converse with their deaf and mute community and their family. Nowadays, this type of translator and interpreter are recognized and accepted worldwide.

In this era, when technology has bloomed, gesture-based technology is a necessity for the deaf and mute community. The researchers are finding and innovating for the same and are having success in bringing out the results. Many innovative and mind-blowing

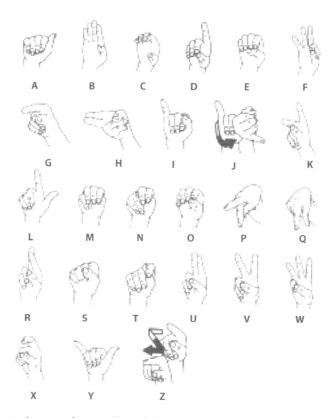

Figure 10.1 Indian sign language finger spelling alphabet.

products are developing for recognition of speech. But unfortunately, there has been no useful product in the current world market. We want to build an interactive and exciting gesture-based translator for deaf and mute people to communicate. Signs are the information that is exchanged without any verbal speech. Researchers researching visual interpretation and image processing are very much interested in this type of project.

We aim to create a Human–Computer Interaction (HCI) that understands the gestures and signs illustrated in Figure 10.1, used for communication by the deaf and mute community. This project needs many modern, sophisticated, and advanced algorithms for the programming of these signs and gestures into low-level language that machines can interpret. Image Processing, Template Creation, and Template matching will be the key features that will be concentrated and worked on this project.

For this project, we have used the data set from University of California Irwine's Machine Learning Database. We have chosen over 58,000 images of English Alphabets Gestures with each Alphabet Gesture containing 2,000 different images. This amount of data has been used in order to achieve good accuracy as well as efficiency in order to recognize the gestures made. Initially we were thinking of using Logistic Regression for the classification problem but ended up using Deep Learning with convolutional neural networks for best results.

10.2 Literature Review

In recent years, convolutional neural networks have been contributing significantly towards the image recognition areas and have been an enormous success in terms of accuracy and implement ability. The focus has been more on just image pixels like the specific characteristics of every image. Every image is considered as a unique frame to extract data from. With the help of image processing, the process is made much more accessible by generating original gravity and motion outlines for each and every gesture [1].

The utilization of depth-sensing technology is quickly gaining an edge over other techniques that aim to work on the same area due to its exceptional accuracy and reliability. Development of Custom-Designed color gloves also has been providing significant contributions to the fields of recognition and feature extraction by making specific gestural units simple to classify and identify [3].

However, methods of automatic gesture recognition were not able to utilize the full potential of Depth-Sensing Technology as it was not available as abundantly and universally as it is nowadays. Older works were based on fundamental camera technology to create datasets of pixelated images without depth or contours knowledge. Nonetheless, efforts at using convolutional networks to manage and classify images of American Sign language had some success [2], with the help of pre-trained GoogLeNet architecture.

Roel Verschaeren proposes a CNN model [7] that recognizes a set of 50 different signs in the Flemish Sign Language with an error of 2.5%, using the Microsoft Kinect.

Unfortunately, this work is limited in the sense that it considers only a single person in a fixed environment.

In an American Language recognition system is presented with a vocabulary of 30 words. They constructed appearance-based representations and a hand tracking system to be classified with a hidden Markov model (HMM). An error rate of 10.91% is achieved on the RWTH-BOSTON-50 database [8].

Pigou *et al.*'s application of CNN's to classify 20 Italian gestures from the ChaLearn 2014 Looking at People gesture spotting competition. They use a Microsoft Kinect on full body images of people performing the gestures and achieve a cross-validation accuracy of 91.7%. As in the case with the aforementioned 3-D glove, the Kinect allows capture of depth features, which aids significantly in classifying ASL signs [4].

Singha and Das obtained accuracy of 96% on 10 classes for images of gestures of one hand using Karhunen–Loeve Transforms. These translate and rotate the axes to establish a new coordinate system based on the variance of the data. This transformation is applied after using a skin filter, hand cropping and edge detection on the images. They use a linear classifier to distinguish between hand gestures including thumbs up, index finger pointing left and right, and numbers [5].

Christopher and Xu developed a glove-based gesture recognition system based on Hidden Markov Models (HMM). CyberGlove is used to recognize gestures from sign language alphabet. Hidden Markov Models can interactively recognize gestures and perform online learning of new gestures. It can also update its model of a gesture iteratively with each example it recognizes. This system can be used to make cooperation between robots and humans easier in applications such as teleoperation and programming [6].

10.3   The Proposed Recognition System

In this section, we discuss the proposed recognition system.

The proposed system briefly elaborates the working of our model and briefly depicts our approach towards solving the problem. It is important that the steps depicted in the proposed system are operated in the order of their depiction in Figure 10.2. We have carefully divided our problem into four different steps. Gesture-Based Recognition System consists of the following steps:

1. Image Acquisition.
2. Pre-processing.
3. Classification and recognition.
4. Post-processing.

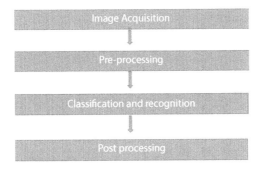

Figure 10.2 Block diagram of proposed system.

10.3.1   Image Acquisition

In Image acquisition, the real-time image of hand gesture is acquired by the recognition system as input. There must be ample of light in the background in order for the recognition system to correctly acquire the image. Hence the machine should be calibrated beforehand according to the background lighting conditions using the initial calibration track bar as shown in Figure 10.3. In our project we have also introduced a calibration system that will help the user or the individual to modify the Hue Saturation Value in accordance to the background lighting. The user can set the lower and higher values for Hue Saturation Value via the final calibration track bar illustrated in Figure 10.4. This image is obtained through a digital camera or any other suitable digital input device.

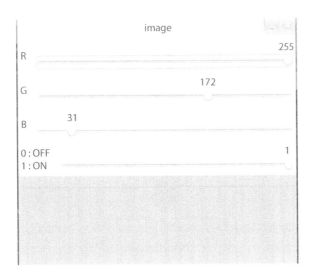

Figure 10.3 Initial calibration track bar.

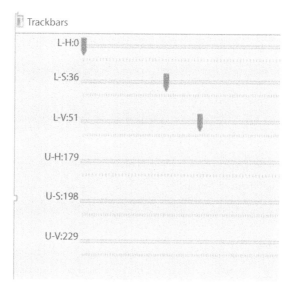

Figure 10.4 Final calibration track bar.

The input image which we will feed to the machine learning model would be taken live by the user as shown in Figure 10.5. The user has to take the image by launching the application, adjusting the calibration settings as per his environment and then making the hand gestures (as per the official Indian Sign Language guide) into the green box which will crop the input image and do all the pre-processing work.

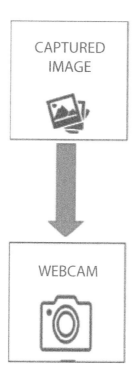

Figure 10.5 Image capturing technique.

10.3.2   Pre-Processing

Preprocessing is a series of operations executed on the captured gestures used as an input image. It enhances the input image and makes it suitable for further processing. To produce the dataset, images corresponding to each gesture were captured, using background-subtraction techniques, we excluded the backgrounds from each image as shown in Figure 10.6. Initially, we divided the dataset into two sets that are one for training and the other for testing purposes; the project efficiency was noted to be high. Nonetheless, when we used datasets of two separate origins, i.e., testing on ours and training on the premade and in reverse, the project efficiency was reduced. Hence as using datasets from two independent sources did not give us accurate results; therefore, we used premade datasets for our signs to train the model network.

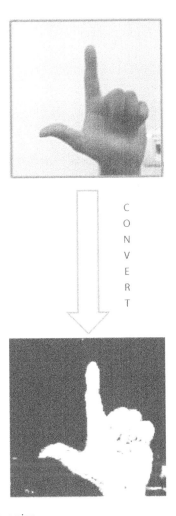

Figure 10.6 RGB to HSV image conversion.

10.3.3 Classification and Recognition

The converted image is now passed through the Convolutional Neural Network shown in Figure 10.7 to match with the character/alphabet, referring to the gesture in the cropped image.

The image matching or template matching is done with the help of pixel values of an image which is matched while the image is sent into the convolutional neural networks.

The Flatten Layer which is usually present at the end of the network, converts the two dimensional array of pixel values into a single array which is in turn sent to Dense and Dropout Layers before producing the final output.

The Dropout layers help to prevent overfitting.

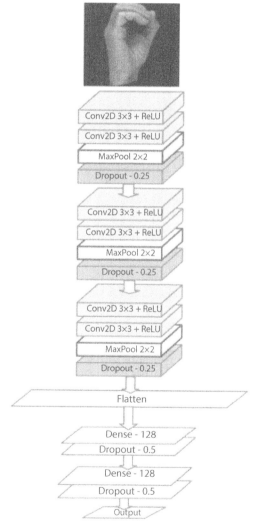

Figure 10.7 Neural network architecture.

The last layer of our Convolutional Neural Network contains 26 neurons because of the 26 different characters in the English alphabet. Once the image is passed on to the neural networks, that is, the orientation of the image pixels, it matches the character referring to it and displays it on the screen. The whole process has been depicted in Figure 10.8.

10.3.4 Post-Processing

The fact that communication is not done just by using a single character/alphabets but through words and sentences. So, to make it possible, we added a crucial feature in this process. If the user wants to make a word from the character, they need to press the 'p' key on their keyboard when the matching character displays on the screen as it stacks up the alphabet to its previous character. This key is sufficient to make a complete word, but for making a complete sentence, we need to add space between the words. For that 'w' key will be pressed after stacking up the last character of the previous and before the first character for the next word is added.

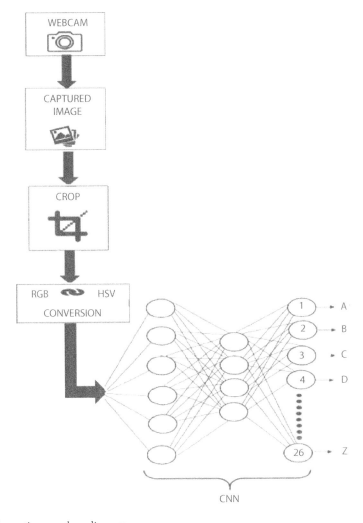

Figure 10.8 Schematic procedure diagram.

Further adding an extra feature, when the sentence/word is complete and read by the second person 'n' key, will be used to clear the text for the next word/sentence.

10.4   Result and Discussion

The dialects and gestures in sign language differ from country to country and region-wise. Thus, to showcase an example of the formation of words through the dataset of 26 characters, we have formed some non-standard gestures and words of our own, which can be used in general conversation and prototyping.

The Training model was found to have an accuracy of 99.17%, and value losses are 4.03% as depicted in Figure 10.9. The accuracy increased as we increased our datasets. We used 58,000 data for our English Alphabet Gestures from University of California Irwine's Machine Learning Database.

```
369ms/step - loss: 0.7301 - acc: 0.7683 - val_loss: 0.1626 - val_acc: 0.9663
362ms/step - loss: 0.1913 - acc: 0.9353 - val_loss: 0.1488 - val_acc: 0.9701
361ms/step - loss: 0.1299 - acc: 0.9547 - val_loss: 0.0938 - val_acc: 0.9811
361ms/step - loss: 0.0956 - acc: 0.9671 - val_loss: 0.0817 - val_acc: 0.9905
358ms/step - loss: 0.0816 - acc: 0.9718 - val_loss: 0.1114 - val_acc: 0.9879
360ms/step - loss: 0.0653 - acc: 0.9784 - val_loss: 0.0958 - val_acc: 0.9877
360ms/step - loss: 0.0611 - acc: 0.9800 - val_loss: 0.0333 - val_acc: 0.9931
358ms/step - loss: 0.0550 - acc: 0.9815 - val_loss: 0.0403 - val_acc: 0.9917
```

Figure 10.9 Efficiency of training model.

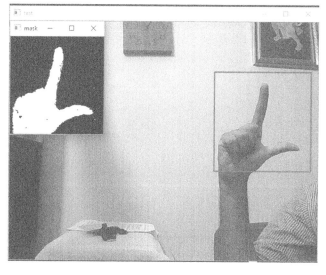

Figure 10.10 Recognition of letter 'L'.

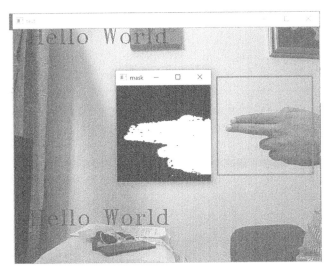

Figure 10.11 Formation of the sentence 'Hello World'.

Letter 'L' was successfully recognized in real-time as seen in Figure 10.10 using convolution neural networks. Input Image was matched against numerous templates of all the alphabets before showing the desired result.

The phrase 'Hello World' was constructed letter by letter as shown in Figure 10.11. The gesture of each alphabet in the phrase was provided, recognized, and eventually stacked up to mold a word resulting in the formation of a meaningful sentence. These sentences can be used to construct a definitive communication process.

10.5   Conclusion

Gesture based communication translator allows us to overcome the shortcomings faced by deaf and mute people while communicating with others without crossing the budget barrier. Our Project automatically comprehends, recognizes and translates gestures into universally understandable language.

We have tried to understand the need for Deaf and Dumb people and devise a solution best suitable for them. The outcome of our research and hard work is that we have developed a prototype of a system utilizing computer vision and machine learning, which can very cost-effectively fulfill the need for an external costly Human translator.

Moreover, our research has also shown us ways how this can be integrated into various current technologies like video calling and accessibility-based applications to empower the idea of ease of access further.

10.6   Future Work

There were many factors and ideas which we took in our sight while starting developing this project and this project can be extended for all those other usages like the prototype utilizes human inputs as callbacks to build sentences. In the future, this can be converted to an automatic system by making the system learn the required time a person needs to show a symbol correctly. By understanding this, we can calculate resolution time and trigger automatic callbacks accordingly. The reverse communication channel can be built quickly to convert the natural language to sign language.

The Real use of this research is in the integration of this technology with currently working technologies and empower ease of access. It can be utilized with applications like video chats, speech recognition, etc. to give a differently-abled citizen a chance to get mixed with the mainstream.

References

1. Agarwal, A. and Thakur, M., Sign Language Recognition using Microsoft Kinect, in: *IEEE International Conference on Contemporary Computing*, 2013.
2. Garcia, B. and Viesca, S., Real-time American Sign Language Recognition with Convolutional Neural Networks, in: *Convolutional Neural Networks for Visual Recognition at Stanford University*, 2016.
3. Dong, C., Leu, M.C., Yin, Z., American Sign Language Alphabet Recognition Using Microsoft Kinect, in: *IEEE International Conference on Computer Vision and Pattern Recognition Workshops*, 2015.
4. Pigou, L. *et al.*, Sign Language Recognition Using Convolutional Neural Networks. *European Conference on Computer Vision*, 6–12 September 2014.
5. Singha, J. and Das, K., Hand Gesture Recognition Based on Karhunen-Loeve Transform. *Mobile and Embedded Technology International Conference (MECON)*, India, pp. 365–371, January 17–18, 2013.
6. Christopher, L. and Xu, Y., *Online Interactive Learning of Gestures for Human Robot Interfaces*, Carnegie Mellon University, The Robotics Institute, Pittsburgh, Pennsylvania, USA, 1996.
7. Verschaeren, R., *Automatische herkenning van gebaren met de microsoft kinect*, Ghent University, Ghent, Belgium, 2012
8. Szegedy, C., Liu, W., Jia, Y. *et al.*, Going deeper with convolutions, in: *Proceedings of the Computer Vision And Pattern Recognition (CVPR)*, Boston, MA, USA, June 2015.

11

Transfer Learning for 3-Dimensional Medical Image Analysis

Sanket Singh*, Sarthak Jain, Akshit Khanna, Anupam Kumar and Ashish Sharma

Maharaja Agrasen Institute of Technology, New Delhi, India

Abstract

The accuracy of deep learning models is significantly affected by the size of training data available. Models pre-trained from massive dataset speed up training convergence and betters the performance of the model. Similarly, tools based on high volume datasets are necessary for the development of deep learning in machine learning in 3-Dimensional medical images. Nonetheless, it is very difficult to build a large enough dataset because of the difficulty of data acquisition and annotation in 3-Dimensional medical imaging. We accumulate the dataset from considerable challenges to build 3D Seg-8 dataset with varied modalities, targeted organs, and pathologies. To extract three-dimension (3-Dimensional) features, we design a heterogeneous 3-Dimensional mesh (or network) to co-train our dataset so as to make a series of pre-trained classifiers. Experiments show that our model can further the training convergence twice as compared with model pre-trained on Kinetics dataset, and about tentuple in comparison with training from scratch as well as attain accuracy in the range of 3 to 20%. Transferring our model on a state-the-of-art DenseASPP segmentation network, in case of a single model, we achieve 94.6%.

Keywords: Pretrain, multisite, keras, NIfTI, epochs

11.1 Introduction

Approaches based on large volumes of data like deep convolutional neural networks (DCNN), etc. have recently achieved globally acceptable standards and cutting-edge performances on different computer vision tasks such as semantic, image classification, object detection, segmentation, etc. One of the crucial factors contributing to this success is the massive abundance of training data available with detailed labels and annotations. In the medical image's domain, however, finding or building a sufficiently large 3-Dimensional dataset is extremely challenging due to the invasive nature of some medical imaging modalities (like CT, MRI), the lengthened imaging duration along with the laborious annotation in these images. As a result, there is a need for large-scale 3-Dimensional medical images

---

*Corresponding author: singhsanket143@gmail.com

Namita Gupta, Prasenjit Chatterjee and Tanupriya Choudhury (eds.) Smart and Sustainable Intelligent Systems, (151–172)
© 2021 Scrivener Publishing LLC

training data that is available to the public as an open source for them to train future base-line 3-Dimensional DCNNs [1].

To avert the menial performance caused by training new networks from bottom up using the limited amount of data available, certain solutions have been proposed involving converting 3-Dimensional data to 2D and use pre-existing well-defined pre-trained models from ImageNet [2]. Even though this solution results in better accuracy than building from scratch, there still remains a large distance due to the neglected spatial information of 3-Dimensional images. Other solutions worked on taking the 3-Dimensional spatial information into account available in the Kinetics dataset. However, the information gathered by the spatial video data and the 3-Dimensional image data is still very different leaving a strong bias for learning a 3-Dimensional image network in the medical domain transferred from natural scenic videos [3].

Our project is an encode–decode Classification network that is heterogeneously trained to extract general medical multi-dimensional features. It is a deep learning image classifier model that uses CNN technology [4, 5]. To train our classifier we will need a large dataset of medical images with significant annotations. We accumulate this dataset from numerous medical challenges to create a dataset from different medical imaging modalities [6]. Our aim is to create a general open to all backbone network which can later be used in transfer learning creating models for other medical tasks to achieve better performance than training from scratch.

11.2   Literature Survey

11.2.1   Deep Learning

Image classifiers now-a-days are used in numerous applications and for a vast number of purposes. The abundance of data has helped in the booming of DCNN and other deep learning models to make accurate and precise classifiers. Deep learning is part of a broader family of machine learning methods based on artificial neural networks. Deep learning models are directly proportional to the amount of data available as input. Deep learning has evolved hand-in-hand with the digital era, which has brought about an explosion of data in all forms and from every region of the world. This data, known simply as big data. However, what should be known is that deep learning requires much more data than a traditional machine learning algorithm (Figure 11.1) [7].

It is an artificial intelligence feature that mimics or enacts the functioning of the human brain in how it formulates and processes data by finding out linking patterns for making common knowledge best decisions. Deep learning is a subset of machine learning in artificial intelligence (AI) that has networks capable of learning unsupervised from data that is unstructured or unlabeled. Also known as deep neural learning or deep neural network [8, 9].

Deep learning is considered the most eye catching and noise making tech subject under the current environment (Figure 11.2). Big corporations along with uprising new companies and startups are all looking for opportunities in this field. 'The Economist' says that

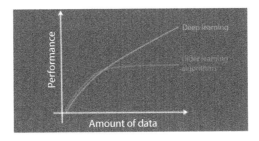

Figure 11.1 Deep learning vs Classical learning. Courtesy—towardsdatascience.com.

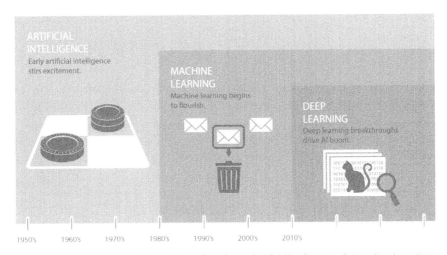

Figure 11.2 Evolution of deep learning. Courtesy—Nvidia.

'data is the new oil' in the 21st Century. It can be assumed that data is the raw undug oil, then DBs and warehouses will work as drilling rigs that searches the required data from sources and fill up the internet [10]. Deep Learning in this case can be thought of as the oil refinery that converts available oil to the useful and resourceful end product. This makes deep learning essential as a construct in the data-driven future where everything created will result in new data and which will result in further creation.

11.2.2 Transfer Learning

We have used the ResNet model to build our classifier upon. By applying transfer learning we acquired features and parameters from a pre-trained ResNet model which will give us an advantage over training from scratch (Figure 11.3).

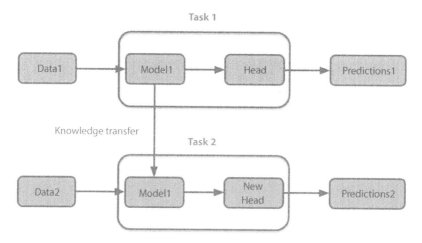

Figure 11.3 Transfer learning. Courtesy—topbots.com.

During the initial phase we train the network and all its parameters on a huge dataset, model is learned. Transfer learning helps create a classifier on our own built upon a pre-existing network so that all its features and parameters can be used. Here we have a classifier in its different weights [11, 12]. The basic idea behind ResNet is introducing a so-called "identity shortcut connection" that misses a layer or more known as null layers. Stacking identity mappings (layers that don't do anything) together should not result in deteriorating the network performance. It simply states that the deeper model with more layers should not give a training error higher than its shallower models [13].

It refers to a highly used ability of the deep learning field in which previously created and trained classifiers and models act as the beginning point on artificial intelligence instead of starting from scratch with no previous knowledge. They provide significant leaps in training due to its knowledge on related tasks. It makes our model act more like the human brain.

11.2.3   PyTorch and Keras (Our Libraries)

The classifier is built in the PyTorch library. PyTorch library is a scientific computing package based on python, targeted at 2 distinct groups—A replacement for NumPy library to use the advantages and strengths of GPUs. PyTorch was chosen over other libraries because pre-trained weights of ResNet models were only available in PyTorch.

PyTorch allows us to easily build ResNet models. It enables automation capabilities for managing the distribution of resources, running experiments, logging data and tracking models. It helps in scaling in our ResNet projects. It is highly compatible with ResNet but still it is complex and less user friendly. *Keras* on the other hand is a high-level neural networks API, written in Python. Keras is able to run on top of Theano, CNTK, and even TensorFlow. It was developed with a focus user friendliness, modularity, and extensibility. It supports both convolutional networks and recurrent networks and runs seamlessly on CPU and GPU.

Figure 11.4 PyTorch and Keras. Courtesy—keras.com, pytorch.org.

The project depends on study of documentation of 'PyTorch' and 'Keras' (Figure 11.4) and to gather important methods and tools provided by them to execute our program. We also required a GPU for processing which we used from the free and open 'Google Colab' editor. The project requires an understanding of convolution neural networks (CNN) and specifically ResNet model and how it functions. We need to implement these concepts to create a classifier suitable for our needs based on transfer learning. We took notice of the importance of neuroimage classification in the medical field. We looked for similar projects available online and their applications. We have created a project which takes care of certain problems previously faced while analysing medical images. This project used already available theories to implement a transfer learning model which provides better accuracy and precision in the case of lack of available training data. We established a general backbone network that can be transferred to other medical tasks to gain better performance and accuracy than acquired while training from scratch.

11.3   Related Works

Image classifiers now-a-days are used in numerous applications and for a vast number of purposes. The abundance of data has helped in the booming of DCNN and other deep learning models to make accurate and precise classifiers. Deep learning is part of a broader family of machine learning methods based on artificial neural networks. Deep learning models are directly proportional to the amount of data available as input. Our project is centered on the field of medical neuroimages which are obtained from imaging techniques like MRIs and CT scans. Although the machine learning is very prominent in the field of medicine but there is still a lack of training data as the images produced from above mentioned methods are scarce in number and are not readily available with their own features and parameters. This project works on the fields of machine learning and neural networks. It establishes a method which allows medical scanning and predictions to be accurate even with lack of data to train a classifier. It is exceedingly difficult to construct an adequately large 3-Dimensional dataset due to the invasive nature of some photographic modalities (like CT, MRI), and their stretched imaging duration. We will work on this problem in the following way—the first phase is to collect the data and

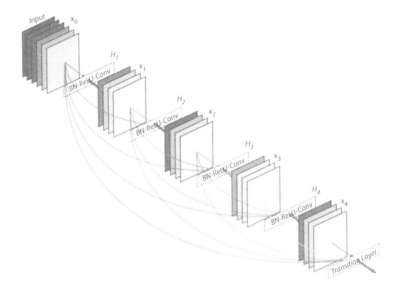

Figure 11.5 Skip connections in ResNet. Courtesy—towardsdatascience.com.

understand it. We have used ADNI data and their labels provided and processed it. It provides us with neuroimages of brains suffering from Alzheimer's disease as provided from MRI scans. We studied what Alzheimer's is and what are its classifications. It exists in three forms—MCI (Mild cognitive impairment), CN (cognitively normal), and AD (advanced dementia) [14–16]. The different labels were available to us and were used to make a feature set to implement classification (Figure 11.5).

We have used the ResNet model to build our classifier upon. By applying transfer learning we acquired features and parameters from a pre-trained ResNet model which will give us an advantage over training from scratch.

During the initial phase we train the network and all its parameters on a huge dataset, model is learned. Transfer learning helps create a classifier on our own built upon a pre-existing network so that all its features and parameters can be used. Here we have a classifier in its different weights. The basic idea behind ResNet is introducing a so-called "identity shortcut connection" that misses a layer or more identified as null layers. Stacking identity mappings (layers that do nothing) together should not consequence in deteriorating the neural network performance. It simply concludes that the deeper model with more layers should not give a training error higher than its shallower models.

11.3.1 Convolution Neural Network

CNN is the first neural network that we are using to extract high-level features from the frames of a video in order to decrease the complexity of the data available. We are also utilising a pre-trained neural network model to apply the technique of transfer learning. This is because current object recognition classifiers consider hundreds of parameters and could go on for long durations until fully trained. Is the person suffering from Alzheimer's Disease? Class of Alzheimer—AD, CN, MCI.

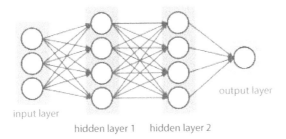

Figure 11.6 CNN layers. Courtesy—towardsdatascience.com.

To solve the above-mentioned problem, we are using a combination of computer vision and supervised machine learning techniques would be utilized which would create phenomenal results in the detection of the activities and their categorization. We have used two Different Neural Networks. One is the Convolutional Neural Network (CNN) and the other one is Transfer Learning (Figure 11.6).

11.3.2 Transfer Learning

Transfer learning is a machine learning technique where the knowledge learned in one or more already available sources is transferred or distributed and used to improvise the learning of a related target task. While most algorithms are constructed to address some particular tasks, the development of these algorithms that allow transfer learning is a new-age topic gaining interest among the machine-learning community. In transfer learning, you can leverage knowledge (features, weights, etc.) from previously trained models to tackle problems like having less data for the newer task and even for training newer models. It focuses on storing knowledge gained while solving one problem and applying it to a different but related problem. Here are the steps to apply transfer learning (Figure 11.7):

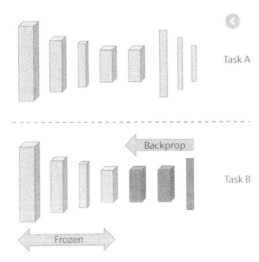

Figure 11.7 Layer condition for transfer learning. Courtesy—paperswithcode.com/task/transfer-learning.

1. First, you delete what's known as the "loss output" layer, which is the final layer used to make predictions, and replace it with a new loss output layer for horse prediction. This loss output layer is a fine-tuning node for determining how training penalizes deviations from the labeled data and the predicted output.
2. Next, you would take your smaller dataset for horses and train it on the entire 50-layer neural network or the last few layers or just the loss layer alone. By applying these transfer learning techniques, your output on the new CNN will be horse identification.

We propose a neural network aiming for 3-Dimensional multi-domain medical data, able to derive general three dimensional features even when there is a large inconsistency of data domain distribution. We transfer our model to three new 3-Dimensional medical image models. We proved the performance, effectiveness and accuracy with the help of comprehensive experiments.

The need for Transfer Learning for 3-Dimensional Medical Image Analysis is mentioned below:

- Since patients are suffering from Alzheimer's but there wasn't any model that could classify patients and tell them that if they're suffering then of which type with this high accuracy.
- There is a need to show in which frame and which parts of it contain the unusual activity which aids the faster judgment of that unusual activity being abnormal or suspicious.
- With encounters occurring often, and with an increasing trend of people suffering from Alzheimer's are not getting diagnosed, a smart system that can instantly alert the medical authorities of a probable patient in its early stage is vital in ensuring the safety of the people and our loved ones.
- There is no model which can work on 3-Dimensional images and provide such high accuracy.
- Our project "Transfer Learning for 3-Dimensional Medical Image Analysis" is unique among the other existing projects which detect Alzheimer's and its type.
- Our project works flawlessly on PyTorch.
- Our project works on batches of 3-Dimensional images of Brain scan.
- We also provide the 2-step classification for the disease.
- Our project signifies such high accuracy.
- It has been trained from scratch that provides us the trust in its working.

It can be further used to detect other diseases by using this approach on other training set of the other diseases of human body parts.

11.4   Dataset

11.4.1   Previously Used Dataset

Alzheimer's Disease Neuroimaging Initiative (ADNI) is a medical collection consisting of brain scans and images acquired from different medical image modalities. The main aim of ADNI is to improve clinical trials all around the world and lead to the treatment and prevention of Alzheimer's disease (AD). ADNI is a multisite cooperative study which bands together expertise and funding from the private as well as the public sector. Researchers present at over 63 sites in North America record the progression of AD in humans and how it acts in the brain with the help of neuroimaging, genetic biological markers, and biochemical.

ADNI has made a worldwide impact, after developing a convention of standard law and rules to allow easy relation and comparison of results from multiple sites. Also, due to its data-sharing policy making it openly available for all and not just qualified professionals and researchers globally. Statistics today show that over 1,000 scientific publications have cited ADNI data.

11.4.2   Data Acquiring

The first phase of any project is to acquire data related to the project, so that some observations can be done on the data to get an idea of the work process to follow to achieve the goal. Experts have a difficult challenge to improve the accuracy of a machine learning model with the amount of resources they have. Even after all the effort of, changing algorithms and optimizing the solution, if the accuracy does not change for the better then there is a necessary need for DATA. Data gathered from multiple sources is lengthy and difficult. Data acquisition uplifts your model's accuracy (Figure 11.8).

We used ADNI (Alzheimer's Disease Neuroimaging Initiative) dataset for our purposes. It is a warehouse of medical images which helps our concerns. Moreover it is open source (Figure 11.9).

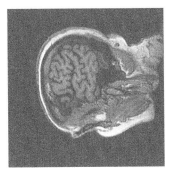

Figure 11.8 ADNI dataset image.

Figure 11.9 Computable data around the globe. Courtesy—promptcloud.com.

11.4.3   Cleaning the Data

The data that is acquired from various sources needs to be cleaned, i.e. that suppose if some images are not of any use discarding them, discarding null values in a table, using algorithms to make the text in some manner which the model can understand. And more such processes to get the data into the shape that can be used as an input to our model. For each 3-Dimensional image we are using 50 middlemost planes in order to get as many feature rich images as possible. Inconsistent and false data bring about incorrect conclusions. Therefore, cleaning your data and the quality of cleaning has a high impact on the quality of the results.

11.4.4   Understanding the Data

The ADNI connects researchers and scholars with data to study as they work to determine the progression of Alzheimer's disease (AD). ADNI collects, validates and utilizes data, including MRI and PET scan images, genetics, cognitive tests, CSF and blood markers as determiners of the disease. Research resources and dataset from the North American ADNI study are available on their webpage, including Alzheimer's disease patients, mild cognitive impairment subjects, and elderly controls (Figure 11.10).

It is a multisite research that aims to refine clinical trials for the prevention from Alzheimer's disease and treatment of Alzheimer's patients. The data provided by ADNI is in the form of nii files. The NII file type refers to the NIfTI-1 Data Format given by Neuroimaging Informatics Technology Initiative. NIfTI-1 is a special version of the commonly used ANALYZE 7.5 file format. It is therefore still very much compatible with the

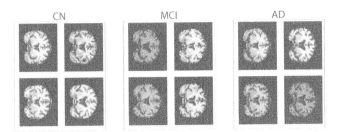

Figure 11.10 Alzheimer classification.

older programs that still use the ANALYZE 7.5 file format. NIfTI-1 basically is ANALYZE 7.5 with a changed and upgraded header. It uses the empty space in the header to add many more new attributes. The primary goal of NIfTI is to provide informatics utility tools related to neuroimaging. It is a new Analyze-style data format to facilitate inter-operation of functional MRI data analysis software packages (Figure 11.11).

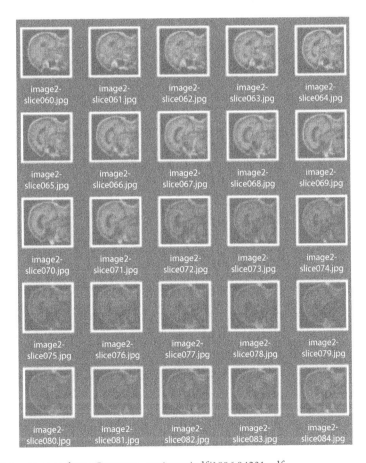

Figure 11.11 Dataset image slices. Courtesy—arxiv.org/pdf/1906.04231.pdf.

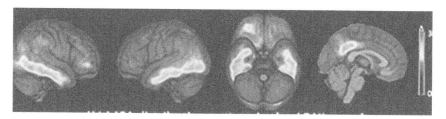

Figure 11.12 Distribution pattern in ADNI sample.

11.5 Description of the Dataset

The dataset contains 329 3-Dimensional Neural images from which we extracted 50 planes per image that evaluates to 16,450 2D images from ADNI dataset. The following image shows the 2D plane images extracted out of the dataset.

The following images (Figure 11.12) were processed into Numpy arrays and visualized using Matplotlib library. For each image we have a set of labels i.e. Image Data ID, Subject, Group, Sex, Age, Visit, Modality, Description, Type, Acq Date, Format, Downloaded. We extracted out important features in order to pass then to the designed Deep learning mode. For each 2D plane image we set the height of the image as 192 and width as 160 in order to pass a uniform image set to the corresponding model. Out of the 329 3-Dimensional images 250 3-Dimensional images were taken as training set and the rest as testing set.

11.6 Architecture

Transfer learning for 3-Dimensional medical image analysis consists of an architecture based on convolutional neural networks (Figure 11.13).

- The first deep learning model is convolutional, with the purpose of drawing out high-level features from the image dataset and lowering the complexity of the input. We utilised a pre-trained model called ResNet (Figure 11.14). We used this model to implement the process of transfer learning. Modern recognition networks have millions of parameters and can take huge time to completely train a dataset. Transfer learning is a technique that optimizes

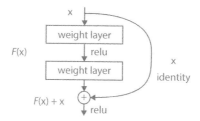

Figure 11.13 Building block of ResNet. Courtesy—towardsdatascience.com.

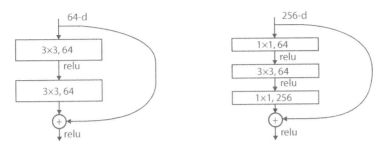

Figure 11.14 Building block of ResNet with cardinality. Courtesy—towardsdatascience.com.

a ton of this task by taking a fully trained model for a set of categories like MedicalNet and retrains from the existing weights for new classes.

- Selection of appropriate Batch Normalization and Average Pooling Layer—Batch normalization is a process for improvising the speed, performance, accuracy and consistency of artificial networks. It is used to normalize the incoming value by varying and scaling the activations. While the result of batch normalization is noticeable, the reasons behind its success remain disputed. Batch normalization was first suggested to solve the problem of internal covariate shift. While the training stage of networks, as the variables of the preceding layers change, the distribution of inputs to the current layer variates accordingly, such that the present layer needs to constantly readjust to newer distributions. This issue is especially critical for deep neural networks, because tiny changes in shallower hidden layers will be amplified as they move forward within the network, resulting in effective shifts in deeper hidden layers. Therefore, the way of batch normalization is recommended to decrease these unwanted shifts to expedite training and to generate more reliable neural models. Although batch normalization has become the chosen way due to its immense strengths, the functioning mechanism of the process is not yet clear. Researchers show that internal covariate shift has not decreased notably by batch normalization, despite general opinion. Some scholars attribute the good results to smoothing the objective method, while others suggest that length-direction decoupling is the phenomenon backing its effectiveness (Figure 11.15).

- The Adam optimization algorithm is an extension to stochastic gradient descent algorithm which has lately seen wider adoption for deep learning applications in CV and NLP. Adam is an optimization algorithm that can be used in place of the general stochastic gradient descent algorithm to amend network weights iteratively based on training dataset. Adam is different from general stochastic gradient descent, which maintains a uniquely valued learning rate (called alpha) for all weight updates and the learning rate remains the same during training. Specifically, the procedure calculates an exponential moving mean of the gradient and the squared gradient, and the parameters beta 1 and beta 2 control the decay rates of these dynamic averages. The initial value of the dynamic averages and beta 1 and beta 2 are closer to 1.0 (always recommended) resulting in a bias of moment approximates towards zero. This bias is overcome by first solving the biased estimates before then finding bias-corrected estimates (Figure 11.16).

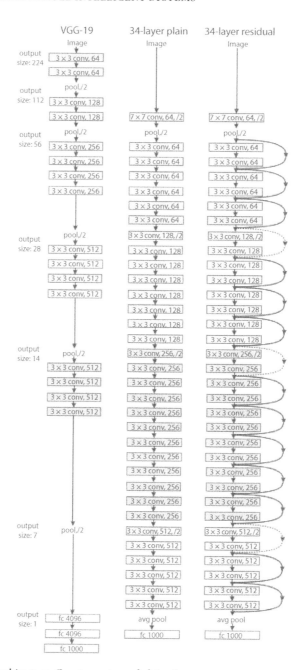

Figure 11.15 ResNet architecture. Courtesy—towardsdatascience.com.

- Multi-task learning and concept drift and is not exclusively an area of study for deep learning. Nevertheless, transfer learning is popular in deep learning given the enormous resources required to train deep learning models or the large and challenging datasets on which deep learning models are trained. Transfer learning only works in deep learning if the model features learned from the first task are general.

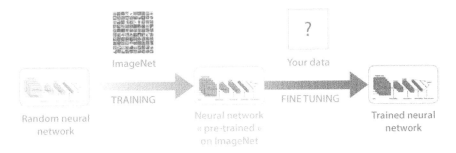

Figure 11.16 Down-sampling is performed. Courtesy— cv-foundation.org

layer name	output size	18-layer	34-layer	50-layer	101-layer	152-layer
conv1	122 × 112	7 × 7, 64, stride 2				
		3 × 3, max pool, stride 2				
conv2_x	56 × 56	$\begin{bmatrix} 3 \times 3, 64 \\ 3 \times 3, 64 \end{bmatrix} \times 2$	$\begin{bmatrix} 3 \times 3, 64 \\ 3 \times 3, 64 \end{bmatrix} \times 3$	$\begin{bmatrix} 1 \times 1, 64 \\ 3 \times 3, 64 \\ 1 \times 1, 256 \end{bmatrix} \times 3$	$\begin{bmatrix} 1 \times 1, 64 \\ 3 \times 3, 64 \\ 1 \times 1, 256 \end{bmatrix} \times 3$	$\begin{bmatrix} 1 \times 1, 64 \\ 3 \times 3, 64 \\ 1 \times 1, 256 \end{bmatrix} \times 3$
conv3_x	28 × 28	$\begin{bmatrix} 3 \times 3, 128 \\ 3 \times 3, 128 \end{bmatrix} \times 2$	$\begin{bmatrix} 3 \times 3, 128 \\ 3 \times 3, 128 \end{bmatrix} \times 4$	$\begin{bmatrix} 1 \times 1, 128 \\ 3 \times 3, 128 \\ 1 \times 1, 512 \end{bmatrix} \times 4$	$\begin{bmatrix} 1 \times 1, 128 \\ 3 \times 3, 128 \\ 1 \times 1, 512 \end{bmatrix} \times 4$	$\begin{bmatrix} 1 \times 1, 128 \\ 3 \times 3, 128 \\ 1 \times 1, 512 \end{bmatrix} \times 8$
conv4_x	14 × 14	$\begin{bmatrix} 3 \times 3, 256 \\ 3 \times 3, 256 \end{bmatrix} \times 2$	$\begin{bmatrix} 3 \times 3, 256 \\ 3 \times 3, 256 \end{bmatrix} \times 6$	$\begin{bmatrix} 1 \times 1, 256 \\ 3 \times 3, 256 \\ 1 \times 1, 1024 \end{bmatrix} \times 6$	$\begin{bmatrix} 1 \times 1, 256 \\ 3 \times 3, 256 \\ 1 \times 1, 1024 \end{bmatrix} \times 23$	$\begin{bmatrix} 1 \times 1, 256 \\ 3 \times 3, 256 \\ 1 \times 1, 1024 \end{bmatrix} \times 36$
conv5_x	7 × 7	$\begin{bmatrix} 3 \times 3, 512 \\ 3 \times 3, 512 \end{bmatrix} \times 2$	$\begin{bmatrix} 3 \times 3, 512 \\ 3 \times 3, 512 \end{bmatrix} \times 3$	$\begin{bmatrix} 1 \times 1, 512 \\ 3 \times 3, 512 \\ 1 \times 1, 2048 \end{bmatrix} \times 3$	$\begin{bmatrix} 1 \times 1, 512 \\ 3 \times 3, 512 \\ 1 \times 1, 2048 \end{bmatrix} \times 3$	$\begin{bmatrix} 1 \times 1, 512 \\ 3 \times 3, 512 \\ 1 \times 1, 2048 \end{bmatrix} \times 3$
	1 × 1	average pool, 1000-d fc, softmax				
FLOPs		1.8×10^9	3.6×10^9	3.8×10^9	7.6×10^9	11.3×10^9

Figure 11.17 Compete transfer learning architecture. Courtesy—medium.com by conv31, conv41, and conv51.

Transfer learning (Figure 11.17) is a deep learning technique where a model trained on one task is re-purposed on a second related task. Transfer learning is an optimization that allows rapid progress or improved performance when modeling the second task. Transfer learning is related to problems such as:

11.7 Proposed Model

Training the model Training our neural network model in PyTorch requires a more experimental approach than if we use Keras because Keras is more modular and easy. The main process loops over and calculates all of the epochs and on each epoch we iterate via the train DataLoader. We then yield one batch of data and targets which we pass through our model. At the end of training of every batch, loss is calculated, backpropagate the loss gradients w.r.t. the model parameters, and then update the parameters with the optimizer. The back-propagation and parameter update step is done manually.

PyTorch allows us to easily build ResNet models. It enables automation capabilities for managing the distribution of resources, running experiments, logging data and tracking models. It helps in scaling in our ResNet projects. It is highly compatible with ResNet but still it is complex and less user friendly. Keras on the other hand is an advanced networks

API, written in Python. It was developed with a focus user friendliness, modularity, and extensibility. It supports both convolutional networks and recurrent networks and runs seamlessly on CPU and GPU (Figure 11.18).

The project depends on study of documentation of 'PyTorch' and 'Keras' and to gather important methods and tools provided by them to execute our program. We also required a GPU for processing which we used from the free and open 'Google Colab' editor. The project requires an understanding of convolution neural networks (CNN) and specifically ResNet model and how it functions. We need to implement these concepts to create a classifier suitable for our needs based on transfer learning.

Currently the pre-trained model weights for the 3D ResNet for different architectures like 50, 152, etc. are available with the library of PyTorch. So, the base training of the transfer learning is done in PyTorch with the pre-trained weights. We took in notice the importance of neuroimage classification in the medical field. We looked for similar projects available online and their applications. We have created a project which takes care of certain problems previously faced while analysing medical images. This project used already available theories to implement a transfer learning model which provides better accuracy and precision in the case of lack of available training data. Our aim is to create a generic backbone neural network which can later be used in transfer learning creating models for various medical functions to achieve higher performance and accuracy than acquired while training from scratch.

For the project the base architecture used in the neural network is the residual network of the ResNets. The main purpose to use the Residual networks is to overcome the problem of saturation in accuracy of Simple Neural Network.

To solve the problem, instead of learning a direct mapping of x => y with a function G(x) (A few stacked non-linear layers).

Let us define the residual function using $F(x) = G(x) — x$, which can be reframed into $G(x) = F(x) + x$, where $F(x)$ and x represents the stacked non-linear layers and the identity function (input = output) respectively. If we consider identity function mapping optimal, we can easily push the residuals to zero $(F(x) = 0)$ than to fit an identity mapping (x, input = output) by a stack of non-linear layers. In simple language it is very easy to come up with a solution like $F(x) = 0$ rather than $F(x) = x$ using a stack of non-linear CNN layers as a function (Think about it). So, this function $F(x)$ is what the authors called Residual function.

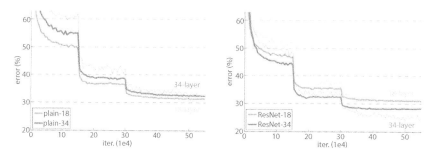

Figure 11.18 Training Error (Left: plain networks of 18 and 34 layers. Right: ResNets of 18 and 34 layers). Courtesy—cv-foundation.org

11.7.1   Model 1

ResNet-50 is a convolutional neural network that is 50 layers deep. The model used was a pre-trained model which was originally trained on the medical-net dataset. Being a 3D ResNet model it is capable of handling 3D medical images. The output layer of the ResNet-152 CNN has three neurons which are used to classify the entire dataset into 3 categories i.e. MCI (Mild Cognitive Impairment), CN (Cognitively Normal) and AD (Alzheimer's Disease). There are 329 3-Dimensional images and each image contains 50 planes of 2D images. The optimizer and loss function used for training this model are Adam and categorical_crossentropy loss.

11.7.2   Model 2

To overcome the imperfections caused due to overfitting in model 1, we trained a transfer learning based ResNet-101 CNN model. ResNet-101 is a convolutional neural network that is 101 layers deep. The last classifier layer was changed in order to classify 3 classes. Adam optimizer along with Cross Entropy loss was used to train this model along with the learning rate as 0.003, with a batch size of 10 and 25 epochs. The testing accuracy was improved to 51% and loss was reduced to 22.8.

11.7.3   Model 3

Model 3 is designed to reduce overfitting to a considerable level.

The transfer learning model was changed from ResNet-101 to 152. ResNet-152 is a convolutional neural network that is 152 layers deep Moreover, the optimizer for model 3 is changed to Adam with the learning rate of 0.001 and number of epochs to 40.

Figures 11.19, 11.20 and 11.21 show that changing the model and updating the configurations improved the accuracy of the model.

11.8   Results and Discussion

Mathematical Understanding of Transfer Learning Model—The fundamental steps to train a Transfer Learning model can be described as following:

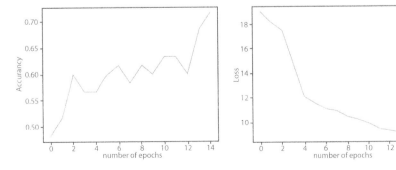

Figure 11.19 Accuracy and loss of model 1.

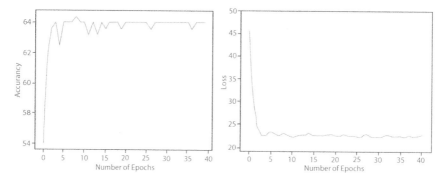

Figure 11.20 Accuracy and loss of model 2.

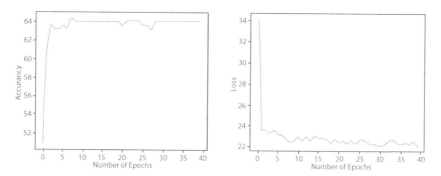

Figure 11.21 Accuracy and loss of model 3.

- Process the neural images in order to extract 2D planes out of them.
- Load a pre-trained 3-Dimensional ResNet Model compatible to the framework.
- Mark the requires_grad property to false in order to stop the gradient update of the body of the model.
- Update the head of the model depending on the problem
- Train the model with different epochs and learning rate. The performance comparision of the trained models has been represented in Table 11.1.

Table 11.1 Performance results comparison.

PERFORMANCE COMPARISON OF ALL MODELS					
	train_loss	**train_acc**	**test_loss**	**test_acc**	**epochs** .
Model 1	9.4	70.1	9.52	46.2	15
Model 2	26.7	55.6	22.83	50	25
Model 3	22.18	64	22.9	70.5	40

11.8.1   Coding the Model

The coding of this classifier was accomplished with the help of Google Colab as it provides a concurrent programming and modular approach.

- A pretrained model of ResNet was used which was initially trained on Kinetics dataset. Kinetics dataset serves as an efficient way to teach a basic model.
- The model available is only compatible to PyTorch. The model is available in the form of files with .pth extension and hence makes PyTorch a necessary library for manipulation.
- Update the ResNet class according to the trained model. We use the ResNet with appropriate weights and then pre-process it to make it compatible with our learning model.

In Fine-tuning, that is the only thing we need to do whereas in Feature Extraction we need to freeze the weight.

Update the head of the model by updating the model.fc parameter in order to update the head of the model so that we can use this new information as a starting point and would not need to train from scratch.

In ResNet152, the last layer is a fully-connected layer with 1,000 neurons. Since we are doing binary classification we will alter the final layer to have three neurons.

CNN are classified and trained with the help of stochastic gradient descent function. They are therefore associated with a loss function which is established while designing and configuration of a model. The choice of loss function is very important. Loss function ensures that the accuracy can reach its peak. Optimizing the loss function to get better results if possible—As the neural networks make use of loss functions so we should make use of exact optimizers and loss functions for better results.

11.9   Conclusion

We are proposing a transfer learning approach to determine Alzheimer's in patients on the basis of their medical MRI images of the patient. Because of the complexities of these true to life brain scans, application of ordinary dataset alone is not always the best option for anomaly detection. We have attempted to exploit both MRI and CT Scans. We train a general model of classification using CNN on the ADNI dataset mainly focusing on real-world MRI scans w of different types of Alzheimer's. To validate the suggested approach, preliminary results on this dataset are shown which prove that our proposed approach performs significantly better than baseline methods.

11.10   Future Scope

The classifier can be extended and gain more precision with more layers and with increase in input data. New and different CNNs can be used to gain better accuracy. Using the ResNet model ensures that optimal accuracy can be obtained with minimum complexity. We train a general model of classification using CNN on the ADNI dataset mainly focusing on real-world MRI scans w of different types of Alzheimer's. The classifier is hence easier and highly portable. DCNN and other models are highly dependent on training data but this project provides a way to allow medical image analysis even though data for such purposes is very scarce. Many recent approaches like GANs have found a way to bypass the need of abundance of data or high quantity big data.

This project builds on that idea and establishes a backbone to a new series of networks that can understand the information even with the amount of data being fairly less. This tool could be used to create further models of high accuracy working flexibly with low amounts of data. The same can be used in other fields of CV which have low dataset to begin with.

The new ideas and technologies in the field of machine learning should be focused less on data and more on achieving human-like networks. The new age requires data to be more secured but security in its highest standards will be ensured by machines that think like humans.

Acknowledgement

The authors feel immense gratitude towards our esteemed mentor Mr. Anupam Kumar (Assistant Professor, CSE Department, MAIT Delhi) and want to express our sincere thanks for his valuable guidance, help and constant encouragement for completing this project. His meaningful suggestions through this entire work and collaborative attitude are sincerely acknowledged.

We are also grateful to our teachers Dr. Namita Gupta (HOD, CSE) for her assistance and constant guidance. We further would like to express our indebtedness to our individual parents and other family members whose blessings and support always helped us when faced with difficulties and challenges.

References

1. Mohammadi, S., Perina, A., Kiani, H., Vittorio, M., Angry crowds: Detecting violent events in videos, in: *ECCV*, 2016.
2. Xu, D., Ricci, E., Yan, Y., Song, J., Sebe, N., Learning deep representations of appearance and motion for anomalous event detection, in: *BMVC*, 2015.
3. Wu, S., Moore, B.E., Shah, M.M., Chaotic invariants of lagrangian particle trajectories for anomaly detection in crowded scenes, in: *CVPR*, 2010.
4. Cui, X., Liu, Q., Gao, M., Metaxas, D.N., Abnormal detection using interaction energy potentials, in: *CVPR*, 2011.
5. Anti, B. and Ommer, B., Video parsing for abnormality detection, in: *ICCV*, 2011.
6. Hospedales, T., Gong, S., Xiang, T., A Markov clustering topic model for mining behaviour in video, in: *ICCV*, 2009.
7. Zhu, Y., Nayak, I.M., Roy-Chowdhury, A.K., Context aware activity recognition and anomaly detection in video, in: *IEEE Journal of Selected Topics in Signal Processing*, 2013.
8. Kratz, L. and Nishino, K., Anomaly detection in extremely crowded scenes using spatio-temporal motion pattern models, in: *CVPR*, 2009.

9. Lu, C., Shi, J., Jia, J., Abnormal event detection at 150 fps in Matlab, in: *ICCV*, 2013.

10. Mehran, I.R., Oyama, A., Shah, M., Abnormal crowd behavior detection using social force models, in: *CVPR*, 2009.

11. Saleemi, I., Shafique, K., Shah, M., Probabilistic modeling of scene dynamics for applications in visual surveillance. *TPAMI*, 31, 8, 1472–1485, 2009.

12. Zhao, B., Fei-Fei, L., Xing, E.P., Online detection of unusual events in videos *via* dynamic sparse coding, in: *CVPR*, 2011.

13. Hasan, M., Choi, J., Neumann, J., Roy-Chowdhury, A.K., Davis, L.S., Learning temporal regularity in video sequences, in: *CVPR*, June 2016.

14. Datta, A., Shah, M., Da Vitoria Lobo, N., Person-on person violence detection in video data, in: *ICPR*, 2002.

15. Karpathy, A., Toderici, G., Shetty, S., Leung, T., Sukthankar, R., Fei-Fei, L., Large-scale video classification with convolutional neural networks, in: *CVPR*, 2014.

16. Tran, D., Bourdev, L., Fergus, R., Torresani, L., Paluri, M., Learning spatiotemporal features with 3 Dimensional convolutional networks, in: *ICCV*, 2015.

12

A Study on Recommender Systems

Agrima Mehandiratta*, Pooja Gupta and Alok Kumar Sharma

Maharaja Agrasen Institute of Technology, New Delhi, India

Abstract

In today's world, where we have an abundance of data collected over the years, Machine Learning aims to put this data to use. This data can be used to train machines to accurately predict the behavioral patterns of users, thus making many processes automated. This project explores one such specimen being implemented in the field of e-commerce today: Recommender system. As shopping moves from the physical to the online world, providing products to customers according to personal preferences becomes a bigger challenge. Recommender systems are the solution to this problem. Most recommender systems in practice today use complex characteristics to improve performance and results. However, in this exposition, we explored a simpler approach to recommender systems that are fairly easy to use for small scale e-retail websites. Further, we tried and tested small variations in the data set and compared their performances, therefore, obtaining the best performing algorithm.

Keywords: Machine learning, recommender system, collaborative recommender, content-based recommender system, e-commerce

12.1 Introduction

Today, the world is amidst a transformation as each process is being digitized. All fields are using technology for their betterment. As the e-commerce industry accepts this process of digitization and automation; shopping is moving from the physical to the online world. Customers now have thousands of products to choose from. Thus, providing products to customers according to personal preferences becomes a bigger challenge. Recommender systems are the solution to this problem.

Recommender systems are algorithms that attempt to predict products that users might like based on some information provided. Most existing recommender systems in use today apply content based or collaborative techniques or hybrid methods that merge both algorithms.

---

*Corresponding author: agrima.mehandiratta@gmail.com

Namita Gupta, Prasenjit Chatterjee and Tanupriya Choudhury (eds.) Smart and Sustainable Intelligent Systems, (173–180)

Collaborative filtering is considered to be the most successful technique in use today, it works by identifying previous customers whose interests were similar to those of a given customer and recommending products to the given customer that were liked by previous customers [1]. However, two major problems associated with it are scalability and sparseness.

In their paper, Joeran *et al.* have evaluated a large number of recommender systems and reached the conclusion that it is very difficult to determine which recommender systems have the best performance. They conclude that a key reason for this is that the means to evaluate the performance do not exist [2]. However, there has been advancement in performance evaluation metrics of machine learning models since 2003.

In Ref. [3], Sita *et al.* have studied the moderating effect of product attributes and consumer reviews on the efficacy of a collaborative filtering recommender system on an e-commerce site and the impact of several different recommender algorithms, commonly used in e-commerce and online services, on sales volume and diversity. They further state that building recommender systems takes hard work as well as extensive experience in the field of artificial intelligence.

It can be observed that the advanced knowledge required to develop recommender systems from scratch is inhibiting small scale online businesses from accepting such technology. Thus, there is a need to develop a user-friendly recommender system that small scale e-retailers may use without hiring people with extensive experience in the field of artificial intelligence.

This paper explores a fairly simple and easy-to-use recommender system that is achieved by comparison and performance analysis of various combinations of data as well as features to finally select the best performing system. To achieve this we make use of the collaborative based method. Additionally, we also explore the performance of popularity based recommender systems.

This simple recommender system due to its ease of understanding can be used by small and upcoming e-retail websites that do not have the budget to hire machine learning experts yet want to take advantage of machine-learning to improve their business.

The outline of this article is as follows: Section 2 explores the background of the paper, Section 3 explores the methodology and application of the algorithm on the data set, Section 4 presents the results and analysis while Section 5 contains the conclusion of the paper.

12.2   Background

A recommendation system is a decision maker strategy for e-commerce environments. It provides the recommendations to the users which makes it easy to purchase items on e-commerce sites. It helps to reduce the transaction cost in an online shopping environment as well proves to improve the decision making process and quality [4]. Recommender systems can be classified primarily into three types: Popularity, Content and Collaborative-based. They have been discussed below.

12.2.1   Popularity-Based

These systems are the ones that consider popularity of an article to generate recommendations. They rely on the assumption that users are mainly interested in items and tags with similar popularity to those they already own. These systems reach a good tradeoff between algorithmic complexity and the level of personalization of recommended items [5].

12.2.2   Content-Based

These systems check the response of user according to the content he/she search for, from that recommender system easily know the user response [6]. For example, a user who frequently watches movies of comedy genre will be recommended comedy movies by the system.

12.2.3   Collaborative Systems

They recommend an item to the user based on the people with similar tastes and preferences have liked in the past [7]. The main basis for collaborative filtering recommendations is the user's opinion [1].

For example, let us assume users A and B are similar; if user A purchases products P and Q while user B purchases products P, Q and R; the system will recommend product R to user B as well.

To decide whether users are similar, we evaluate either of the following:

- Pearson Correlation Coefficient—Pearson's coefficient mirrors the level of direct relationship between two factors, i.e. the degree to which the factors are connected [8]. Similarity between x and y can be calculated using the given formula—

$$\frac{\sum (x-\bar{x})(y-\bar{y})}{\sqrt{\sum (x-\bar{x})^2(y-\bar{y})^2}}$$

- Cosine Similarity Coefficient—It simply measures the value cosine of the angle between two vectors. The coefficient can be calculated by the given formula—

$$\frac{\sum (x)(y)}{\sqrt{\sum (x)^2(y)^2}}$$

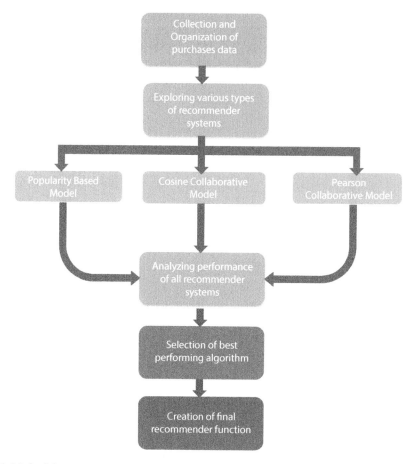

Figure 12.1 Methodology.

12.3   Methodology

The basic methodology of this paper has been illustrated in Figure 12.1. As the main motive of this paper is to make a fairly accurate recommender system that is easy-to-use even for people who are not experts in the field, we use a simple data set. The description of the data set is as given below.

The data set contains a list of IDs of purchased products along with the respective customer identification numbers. There is also a separate list of customer identification numbers.

- Number of instances: 62,000
- Number of attributes: 2
- Missing Values: N/A

12.3.1   Input Parameters

After creation of all the recommendation functions, they are passed the input parameters so that results may be produced. The input parameters as applied can be observed in Table 12.1.

Table 12.1 Input parameters.

Algorithm	Model	Input parameters	Value
Popularity Based	Popularity	Customer ID	Integer
		Product ID	Integer
		No. of purchases	Integer
Collaborative based	Cosine	Customer ID	Integer
		Product ID	Integer
		No. of purchases (binary)	Binary (0 if not purchased, 1 if purchased)
	Cosine with Binary Data	Customer ID	Integer
		Product ID	Integer
		No. of purchases (binary)	Binary (0 if not purchased, 1 if purchased)
	Pearson	Customer ID	Integer
		Product ID	Integer
		No. of purchases	Integer
	Pearson with Binary Data	Customer ID	Integer
		Product ID	Integer
		No. of purchases (binary)	Binary (0 if not purchased, 1 if purchased)

12.3.2   Implementation

To choose the best performing algorithm, various combinations of algorithms are implemented so that the best performing model can be chosen. The application of all models was done on the data set using python programming language. Standard libraries such as NumPy, MatplotLib, Pandas, Scikit and Turicreate were used. The following models were implemented on the data set—

- Popularity-based Algorithm
- Collaborative-based Algorithm with Cosine similarity
- Collaborative-based Algorithm with Pearson similarity

Since scalability is a limitation faced by collaborative filtering, to overcome the same we tried using purchase count in binary form. Thus, the number of purchases was represented in two forms—

- Purchase count (the number of items of given product ID purchased by customer)
- Binary Purchase count (1 if number of items of given product ID purchased is >=1 and 0 if no products were purchased).

Thus, five different combinations of the above models and data sets were implemented and then evaluated so that the best one can be selected. The combinations are as shown below—

- Popularity-Based
- Cosine Model with purchase count
- Cosine Model with binary purchase count
- Pearson Model with purchase count
- Pearson Model with binary purchase count.

12.3.3   Performance Measures

The performance metrics used to evaluate the systems are as shown below—

- Precision—This is the measure of all relevant instances out of all predicted instances [9] and is calculated as follows—

$$\frac{TP}{TP+FP}$$

Here True Positive is abbreviated as TP, True Negatives as TN and False Negative as FN.

- Recall—This measures the ability of a model to select instances of a certain class from a given data set [10]. It is also called sensitivity. The formula for recall is as given below.

$$\frac{TP}{TP+FN}$$

- RMS Error—This stands for root mean square error and is used to measure the difference between predicted and observed values of the model.

12.4   Results and Discussion

Upon implementation of all the five combinations on the selected data set, we obtain the output. The values of mean precision and mean recall obtained for recommending 5 products to a user can be observed in Table 12.2.

Table 12.2 Mean precision and recall.

Algorithm	Model	Mean precision	Mean recall
Popularity based	Popularity	0.0061	0.0159
Collaborative based	Cosine	0.0383	0.1067
	Cosine with Binary Data	0.0336	0.0905
	Pearson	0.0383	0.1061
	Pearson with Binary Data	0.0335	0.0904

The RMS Error for each of the implemented algorithms is represented in Figure 12.2.

Upon studying the popularity-based model it was observed that it predicts the same n most popular products to all customers thus no personalized recommendations are provided. Moreover, it had lower values of precision and recall and thus, high value of RMS error.

On the other hand, the collaborative method using binary purchase count has better results, due to personalized recommendations for each customer. Since keeping record is easier in binary form as size of the data set increases and it does not compromise on performance; it is best to keep record of purchase count in binary form. It is also observed that the cosine similarity model has a lower value of RMS error as compared to Pearson similarity. Thus, out of the five-implemented algorithms, using Cosine Similarity based Collaborative algorithm along with binary purchase data is the best choice.

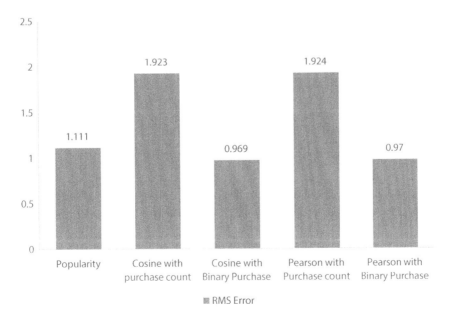

Figure 12.2 RMS error.

12.5   Conclusions and Future Scope

The aim of this study was to obtain a simple and easy-to-use recommender algorithm that can be used without expert knowledge on the subject. Such an algorithm would provide upcoming e-retail businesses a chance to enhance their sales with personalized predictions without having to spend excess funds to hire experts. Upon comparative performance analysis of all algorithms used, it is observed that the Cosine Similarity model that is a Collaborative recommender algorithm provides the most accurate predictions. Moreover, it is also advised to store the purchase count of each product in binary form. As the data set increases in size over time, storing the data in binary form would make it easier to handle and process without substantially decreasing the accuracy of the results. Future endeavors could be aimed at creating user friendly and simple applications that enable small businesses to use recommender systems. These applications could provide generic recommender systems based on the profile of the e-retail business. There is vast scope in the progression of use of recommender systems as e-commerce and e-retail spreads to all parts of the world.

References

1. Sohail, S., Siddiqui, J., Ali, R., Product Recommendation Techniques for Ecommerce—past, present and future. *Ijarcet*, 1, 219–225, 2012.
2. Docear, J.B., Docear, S.L., Docear, M.G., Gipp, B., Breitinger, C., Numberger, A., Research paper recommender system evaluation: A quantitative Literary Survey. *Proceedings of the International Workshop on the reproducibility and replication in recommender systems evaluation*, 2003.
3. Sita, P. and Yeruva, S., Recommendation System in Sales—An Online Shopping/Suggesting Friend. *Int. J. Comput. Math. Sci.*, 7, 2, 2018.
4. Bajpai, V. and Yadav, Y., Survey Paper On Dynamic Recommendation System For Ecommerce. *Intnl. J. Advan. Research Com. Sci.*, 9, 1, 774–777, 2018.
5. Arnaboldi, V., Campana, M., Delmastro, F., Pagani, E., PLIERS: a Popularity-Based Recommender System for Content Dissemination in Online Social Networks, SAC, pp. 671–673, 2016.
6. Kaur, J., Bedi, R., Gupta, S.K., Product Recommendation Systems a Comprehensive Review. *Int. J. Comput. Sci. Eng., IJCSE*, 6, 1192–1195, 2018.
7. Jonnalagedda, N. and Gauch, S., *Personalized News Recommendation Using Twitter, WI-IAT*, pp. 21–25, IEEE, Atlanta, GA, USA, 2013.
8. Senthilkumar, M., Calculating the User-item Similarity using Pearson's and Cosine Correlation. *ICEI*, 2017.
9. Mehandiratta, A., Vij, N., Khanna, A., Gupta, P., Gupta, A., Prediction of Celiac Disease Using Machine-Learning Techniques. *ICICC Springer Nature*, Chap. 59, 2020.
10. Janardhanan, P., Heena, L., Sabika, F., Effectiveness of support vector machines in medical data mining. *J. Comm. Softw. Syst.*, 11, 25–30, 2015, https://doi.org/10.24138/jcomss.v11i1.114.

13

Comparing Various Machine Learning Algorithms for User Recommendations Systems

Rahul Garg, Shivay Lamba* and Sachin Garg

Department of Information Technology, Maharaja Agrasen Institute of Technology (GGSIPU), Rohini, Delhi, India

Abstract

Recommending users on the basis of various user preferences while interacting with a social media platform, such as the gender, age, number of meetups, the skills and ratings of user profiles, image quality. All are taken into consideration to provide the ultimate user recommendation possible to make the software more relevant and user centric with recommendations strictly based on the way a given user interacts with the platform. Several machine learning algorithms have been used such as Neural Networks, random forests, linear regression to compare which provides the best possible recommendations for a user. Specifically, a weighted social interaction network is first mapped to represent the interactions among social users according to the gathered information about historical user behavior.

Keywords: Machine learning, neural networks, random forests, user recommendations, linear regression, normalization, XGboost, Ada boost

13.1 Introduction

The effort is to make the ultimate recommendation system for a user on a given social platform. Understanding each and every user interaction with the platform and then coming up with user recommendations depending upon this understanding of the user behavior can provide with the much required and accurate recommendations.

The first and foremost thing is to understand how the user interacts with the platform. Based on the user's search patterns, the recommendation engine takes into account the user behavior and uses that in its final results to calculate the recommendation scores.

The users on the platform register themselves with their skill sets and mention what specific skill set they are looking for, this way they get recommendation for that particular skill set.

*Corresponding author: lakshaylamba123@gmail.com

Namita Gupta, Prasenjit Chatterjee and Tanupriya Choudhury (eds.) Smart and Sustainable Intelligent Systems, (181–190)

13.2   Related Works

A lot of the related work has been using the Facebook Recommendation system using collaborative filtering to recommend users based on common interests. But it doesn't take into account the user history or user behavior into account and this is what differentiates this with the model.

Netflix uses an algorithm to save every user's information in vector form [1]. The vector contains the past history and behavior of the user, for example. The movies were liked or disliked by the user and the ratings given to various shows. The vector is called the profile vector. All information related to movies is put in another vector called the item vector. This item vector has the details of every movie, like genre, cast, etc.

13.3   Methods and Materials

We discuss various types of data filtration techniques:

13.3.1   Content-Based Filtering

This algorithm recommends items similar to the ones which a user has used and liked in the past [7]. The content-based filtering algorithm is used to find the cosine of angle between the profile and item vector, i.e. cosine similarity. Let's suppose A is the profile vector and B is the item vector, then the cosine similarity between A & B is calculated as:

$$sim(A, B) = cos\ cos(\emptyset) = A.B/||A||||B|| \tag{13.1}$$

13.3.2   Collaborative Filtering

The collaborative filtering algorithm uses the Behavior of the user for recommending items. It is one of the most frequently used algorithms in recommendation systems since it doesn't depend on further or any additional information.

13.3.3   User–User Collaborative Filtering

The collaborative filtering algorithm uses the Behavior of the user for recommending items. It is one of the most frequently used algorithms in recommendation systems since it doesn't depend on further or any additional information [5]. The prediction of an item for a user u is known by calculating the weighted sum of the user ratings given by the other users to an item i.

$$P_{u,i} = \frac{\sum (r_{v,i} * s_{u,v})}{\sum s_{u,v}} \tag{13.2}$$

13.3.4   Item–Item Collaborative Filtering

In Item–Item Collaborative algorithm, we calculate the similarities between each pair of items. The algorithm works similar to the user–user collaborative filtering with slight changes—we take the weighted sum of ratings of "item-neighbors", instead of taking the weighted sum of ratings of "user-neighbors". The prediction is given as:

$$P_{u,i} = \frac{\sum (r_{v,i} * s_{u,v})}{\sum s_{u,v}}$$

(13.3)

There is going to be a comparison of different machine learning model techniques to see which one gives the most efficient recommendation possible.

13.3.5   Random Forest Algorithm

Random Forest Algorithm: Random forest as is an ensemble of un-pruned regression or classification trees, activated from bootstrap samples of the training data, adopting random feature selection in the tree imitation process [2]. The prediction is made by accumulating the predictions of the ensemble by superiority voting for classification. It returns generalization error rate and is more potent to noise. Still, similar to most classifiers, RF may also suffer from the curse of learning from an intensely imbalanced training data set. Since it is constructed to mitigate the overall error rate, it will tend to focus more on the prediction efficiency of the majority class, which repeatedly results in poor accuracy for the minority class.

$$ni_j = w_j C_j = w_{left(j)} C_{left(j)} - w_{right(j)} C_{right(j)}$$

(13.4)

13.3.6   Neural Networks

Neural Networks: Neural networks are group of algorithms, based and modeled loosely after the human brain, that are designed to recognize patterns similar to a human brain [11]. Just like the human brain interprets sensory data through nerve endings, neural network interprets this as a kind of machine perception or labeling or clustering raw input [17]. The patterns which are recognized is usually numerical and contained in vectors, into real world data for example images, sound, text or time series, must be transcribed and translated to be used as the resultant.

$$S_t \to 1 : input \to input + w_t \{w_t > 0 : input \uparrow, excitation\ w_t < 0 : input \downarrow, inhibition$$

(13.5)

13.3.7   ADA Boost Classifier

ADA Boost Classifier: ADA-boost classifier algorithm is used to group together weak classifier algorithms to form strong classifier algorithm [3]. A single algorithm is bound to classify the objects poorly in most scenarios. But if a combination of multiple classifiers is taken which has selection of training set at every iteration and assigned the right amount of weight in final iteration, can result in a good score of accuracy for the classifier.

$$MME_{emp}^{(j)} = \frac{\sum_{i=1}^{N} \widehat{w_i I(y_i \neq h_j(x_i))}}{\sum_{i=1}^{N} w_i} \tag{13.6}$$

13.3.8   XGBoost Classifier

XGBoost Classifier: For every booster object, predict function could only be called from one given thread [13]. If there is a need to run the prediction using multiple threads, then the xgb.copy () function should be called in order to make copies of the model object and then the prediction function needs to be called.

$$L^{(t)} = \sum_{i=1}^{n} l\left(y_i, \hat{y}_i^{(t-1)} + f_t(x_i)\right) + \Omega(f_t) \tag{13.7}$$

13.3.9   Trees

Tree: The tree algorithm is used to deal with classification problems and regression problems [16]. Random trees is an algorithm which is an ensemble of tree predictors called a random forest.

The classification algorithm is bound to performs as follows: Random trees classifier for input takes the feature vector, then it categories it with individual trees in the random forest, gives output as the class label receiving the most number of favorable votes [12]. In the site of a regression algorithm, the classifier model's response is calculated as the average of all the responses over all the trees in the random forest. In random tree algorithm we see that all the trees in the forest are to be trained with the same parameters but have different training sets. The original training set is used to create these sets and adopt the basic bootstrap procedure and for each given training set, we randomly choose the same number of vectors as that are there in the initial given set. These vectors are to be chosen with replacement and can be seen:

$$IG(A,S) = H(S) - \sum_{i \in T} p(t)H(t) \tag{13.8}$$

Here,
- H(S)—Entropy of set S
- T—The subsets created from splitting set S by attribute A

- p(t)—The proportion of the number of elements in t to the number of elements in set S
- H(t)—Entropy of subset T.

13.3.10   Regression

Regression Model: The relation between any two variables by fitting a linear equation to the given observed data [4]. One of the given variables is considered to be an explanatory variable, and the other is considered to be a dependent variable [14]. The most frequent methodology for fitting a regression line is by using the method of least-squares. The method of least-squares is used to calculate the best-fitting line for the given observed data which involves the minimizing of the sum of the squares of the vertical deviations from every data point to the line. There are no cancellations between positive and negative values, because the deviations are first squared, and then they are

$$a = \frac{\left(\sum y\right)\left(\sum x^2\right) - \left(\sum x\right)\left(\sum xy\right)}{n\left(\sum x^2\right) - \left(\sum x\right)^2}$$

$$b = \frac{n\left(\sum xy\right) - \left(\sum x\right)\left(\sum y\right)}{n\left(\sum x^2\right) - \left(\sum x\right)^2} \tag{13.9}$$

13.3.11   Dataset Description

Dataset Description: The dataset (refer Figure 13.1) contains the various parameters of users such as age, gender, profile completion, ranking, and number of connections.

13.4   Experiment Results and Discussion

We have shown the distribution of the various parameters being used in the dataset [15]. Normalization is defined as a technique which is regularly used and applied as a part of data composition and preparation for algorithms of machine learning. The main aim of normalization is to be able to alter the values of numeric columns in the given dataset to a common

	Age	DistanceFromHome	Gender	job_title	skillRating	no_of_connections	PersonalRating	ActiveHours	image_quality	no_of_meetups	profile_comple
0	41	1	0	Sales Executive	4	5993	3	26	319	2	
1	49	8	1	Research Scientist	2	5130	4	11	112	18	
2	37	2	1	Laboratory Technician	3	2090	3	30	281	13	
3	33	3	0	Research Scientist	3	2909	3	37	330	10	
4	27	2	1	Laboratory Technician	2	3468	3	31	282	11	
5	32	2	1	Laboratory Technician	4	3068	3	29	349	11	
6	59	3	0	Laboratory Technician	1	2670	4	43	131	4	

Figure 13.1 Dataset of user experience.

scale, so that there is no distortion of the differences in the ranges of values. For the various machine learning algorithms, each and every dataset may not require normalization. It is mainly required only when the features have alternating and different ranges. In the given training data (refer Figure 13.2), there is a need to normalize the dataset (refer Figure 13.3).

We have used different machine learning models and compared their accuracy. The table shown gives a good view of the performance of the various machine learning techniques utilized (refer Table 13.1).

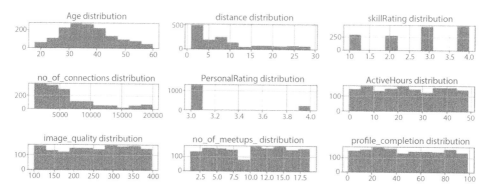

Figure 13.2 Data distribution vs frequency.

	Age	male	female	PersonalRating	no_of_connections	profile_completion	skillRating
0	0.446350	0	1	−0.426230	−0.108350	1.343744	1.153254
1	1.322365	1	0	2.346151	−0.291719	1.768228	−0.660853
2	0.008343	1	0	−0.426230	−0.937654	1.768228	0.246200
3	−0.429664	0	1	−0.426230	−0.763634	−0.637184	0.246200
4	−1.086676	1	0	−0.426230	−0.644858	0.954633	−0.660853
...	...	...	...	...	...	...	...
1465	−0.101159	1	0	−0.426230	−0.835451	0.990007	1.153254
1466	0.227347	1	0	−0.426230	0.741140	0.141038	−1.567907
1467	−1.086676	1	0	2.346151	−0.076690	−1.556901	−0.660853
1468	1.322365	1	0	−0.426230	−0.236474	−1.025380	−0.660853
1469	−0.320163	1	0	−0.426230	−0.445978	1.697481	0.246200

Figure 13.3 Normalized data set.

Table 13.1 Accuracy of different models being used.

Model	Accuracy
Linear Regression	0.0062
Tree	50
Neural Network	51
Neural Network 5 Layer	52
ADA Boost	64
XGB Boost	72

In the neural network approach (refer Figure 13.4) that was applied with 3 hidden layers: We run through epochs and see the trend of this data for both accuracy and loss curve for the model (refer Figure 13.5):

Model : "model_1"

Layer (type)	Output Shape	Param #
input_1 (InputLayer)	(None, 7)	0
dense_1 (Dense)	(None, 16)	128
dense_2 (Dense)	(None, 128)	2176
dense_3 (Dense)	(None, 32)	4128
dense_4 (Dense)	(None, 2)	66
activation_1 (Activation)	(None, 2)	0

Total params : 6,498
Trainable params : 6,498
Non-trainable params : 0

Figure 13.4 Keras multilayer perceptron model.

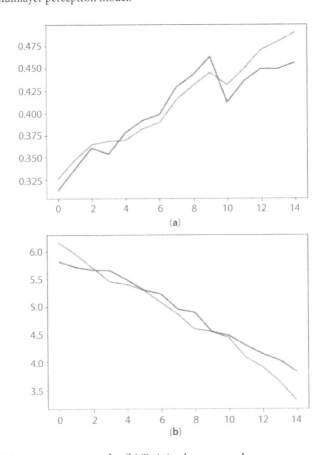

Figure 13.5 (a) Training accuracy vs. epochs. (b) Training loss vs. epochs.

Despite seeing the graph, the accuracy of the model is only 53%. Since the dataset has around 2,000 entries the neural networks don't give high accuracy as the model moves towards overfitting for less quantity of data being available [19].

XGB Boost which is an algorithm for classification is giving the most promising results.

The low accuracy for most of the algorithms is given on the basis of the unstructured data and highly depends on the huge load of data needed to have to improve accuracy of any model.

Simple models like [20] Linear Regressions or Tree clearly fail in such cases since the user can look at profiles on various parameters and even multivariate linear regression fails, because of these parameters.

The diagram (refer Figure 13.6) clearly shows why the performance of XGBoost has the best result, as its training time is also lesser as compared to other models.

Another table (refer Table 13.2) showing how much the data fit to the model has also been shown.

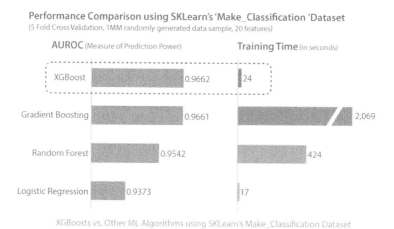

Figure 13.6 XG boost vs different machine learning algorithms.

Table 13.2 Fitting accuracy of the models being used.

Model	Accuracy
Linear Regression	<5%
Tree	97
Neural Network 3 Layer	70
Neural Network 5 Layer	75
ADA Boost	94
XGB Boost	99

For the various algorithms that we are using the above table showcases how much input training data is actually fitting to the data. Since our problem is a classification problem, we can clearly see that the simple models like Regression don't work and are not able to fit any data.

But other techniques like Decision trees, ADA Boost [18], XGBoost give higher degree of fitting and most of the test and train data aligns with the model.

Therefore even in fitting of the data, this gives us better results as compared to the other algorithms.

We must also choose the right configuration of the algorithm for a dataset by tuning the hyper-parameters. Furthermore, there are several other considerations for choosing the winning algorithm such as computational complexity, explain ability, and ease of implementation.

The data used here is a set of MRI images of the brain tumor which are divided into train, validate and test data sets. Validate dataset is used to check for overfitting. It is used during the model training to adjust hyper parameters. Taking the help of a test data set requires convolution neural networks and is applied to get the final model performance. The model performance is followed here:

13.5   Future Enhancements

XG Boost Algorithm accuracy can be further enhanced by adding these features:

Regularization: Results in penalization of higher complexity models through the regularization techniques such as LASSO (L1) and Ridge (L2) which is used to prevent overfitting.

Sparsity Awareness: XGBoost algorithm natively allows various scant feature set for input values by automatically understanding the best missing value which depends upon the training loss and it handles various categories of sparsity patterns in the data more effectively and efficiently.

Weighted Quantile Sketch: XGBoost algorithm engages the frequently used weighted and distributed Quantile Sketch algorithm which effectively finds the most optimal split points among the given weighted datasets.

Cross-validation: The XGBoost Algorithm has with built-in incorporation of the cross-validation method at every iteration, removing the need to explicitly define the search and to specify what is the exact number of boosting iterations that are required in a single run.

13.6   Conclusion

By comparing different machine learning models we get the best method to classify the various feature sets and get recommendations feeding it with a number of parameters we can get more customized recommendations which not only just depend upon the actual content, but also how the interaction of

The system is being handled by the user. This makes the network very personalized for each and every user.

References

1. DataMafia, *The next big thing in data*, DataMafia, 2019, [Online]. Available: https://datamafia2.wordpress.com/.

2. machinelearningmastery, *machinelearningmastery*, 2017, [Online]. Available: https://machinelearningmastery.om/bagging-and-random-forest-ensemble-algorithms-for-machine-learning.

3. Patel, S., *Medium.com*, Medium.com, 2017, [Online]. Available: https://medium.com/machine-learning-101/https-medium-com-savanpatel-chapter-6-adaboost-classifier-b945f330af06.

4. https://statistics.yale.edu/, https://statistics.yale.edu/, Yale.edu, 2015. [Online]. Available: https://statistics.yale.edu/.

5. Giacomo, D., Gianluca, M., Andrea, P., Karin, P., Job Recommendation From Semantic Similarity of LinkedIn Users' Skills, in: *Conference: 5th International Conference on Pattern Recognition Applications and Methods (ICPRAM)*, Bologna, 2016.

6. semanticscholar, *semanticscholar*, 2016, [Online]. Available: https://pdfs.semanticscholar.org/959b/6d911898ac04dcc7.

7. analyticsvidhya, *analyticsvidhya*, analyticsvidhya, 2018, [Online]. Available: https://www.analyticsvidhya.com/blog/2018/06/comprehensive-data-science-machine-learning-interview-guide/.

8. Sanjeevi, M., *medium.com*, medium.com, 2019, [Online]. Available: https://medium.com/deep-math-machine-learning-ai.

9. Jung, H., *towardsdatascience*, towardsdatascience, 2018, [Online]. Available: https://towardsdatascience.com/adaboost-for-dummies-breaking-down-the-math-and-its-equations-into-simple-terms-87f439757dcf.

10. Morde, V., *towardsdatascience*, towardsdatascience, 2019, [Online]. Available: https://towardsdatascience.com/https-medium-com-vishalmorde-xgboost-algorithm-long-she-may-rein-edd9f99be63d.

11. http://www.sageorb.com/, http://www.sageorb.com/, http://www.sageorb.com/, 2019. [Online]. Available: http://www.sageorb.com/.

12. http://docs.opencv.org, http://docs.opencv.org/, http://docs.opencv.org/, 2018. [Online]. Available: http://docs.opencv.org/.

13. http://buildmedia.readthedocs.org/, http://buildmedia.readthedocs.org/, http://buildmedia.readthedocs.org/, 2018. [Online]. Available: http://buildmedia.readthedocs.org/.

14. Gupta, M., *geeksforgeeks*, geeksforgeeks, 2017, [Online]. Available: https://www.geeksforgeeks.org/ml-linear-regression/.

15. Jaitley, U., *medium.com*, medium.com, 2018, [Online]. Available: https://medium.com/@urvashilluniya/why-data-normalization-is-necessary-for-machine-learning-models-681b65a05029.

16. Gupta, S., *Hackerearth*, Hackerearth, 2018, [Online]. Available: https://www.hackerearth.com/practice/machine-learning/machine-learning-algorithms/ml-decision-tree/tutorial/.

17. Chen, J., *investopedia*, investopedia, 2019, [Online]. Available: https://www.investopedia.com/terms/n/neuralnetwork.asp.

18. Brownlee, J., *machinelearningmastery*, machinelearningmastery, 2016, [Online]. Available: https://machinelearningmastery.com/develop-first-xgboost-model-python-scikit-learn/.

19. Andew, B., https://beamandrew.github.io/deeplearning/2017/06/04/deep_learning_works.html, https://beamandrew.github.io/deeplearning/2017/06/04/deep_learning_works.html, 2017. [Online]. Available: https://beamandrew.github.io/deeplearning/2017/06/04/deep_learning_works.html.

20. Epstein, F., *quora*, quora, 2018, [Online]. Available: https://www.quora.com/What-does-linear-regression-fail-at.

Indian Literacy Analysis Using Machine Learning Algorithms

Shubhi Jain, Sakshi Bindal, Ruchi Goel* and Gaurav Aggarwal

Maharaja Agrasen Institute of Technology, Delhi, India

Abstract

Indian Literacy Rate Analysis Dashboard is a project that utilizes data analysis and visualization along with machine learning models for prediction of outcome, all integrated together and displayed on a web app. The dashboard consists of a well visualized data released by Human Resource Development (HRD) department on literacy rate of India in different states and districts along with features that constitute towards the present education status of that particular area. A well visualized data will contribute towards a better understanding of current condition of edification in various areas and the final accrued result will adjunct towards the measures that can be taken to improvise a state and in-turn overall literacy rate of the country. Data analysis makes use of mathematical libraries like Scikit-learn and Numpy which are open source libraries providing various features like data visualization and analysis. Predictions will be done by regression models and neural networks. Regression algorithms are used to find the relationship and interdependence between variables using a set of statistical processes to predict the further unknown values. It consists of several techniques for modeling and analyzing various features, and is used to derive the relationship between the dependent variable and one or more independent variables. With the help of an Artificial Neural Network (ANN) which is similar to the biological nervous systems, deep learning of the relationships and underlying trends are identified and used to predict the new values. Various machine learning algorithms have been applied to predict the literacy rate of various states and the outcomes of each algorithm have been compared for accurate results.

Keywords: Indian literacy rate analysis, literacy rate, machine learning, ensemble learning, feature selection, data visualization

14.1 Introduction

Literacy rate of a country plays a major role in various factors like the economy of the country, the GDP growth rate and difficulties in understanding social issues. Education

---

*Corresponding author: ruchigoel@mait.ac.in

Namita Gupta, Prasenjit Chatterjee and Tanupriya Choudhury (eds.) Smart and Sustainable Intelligent Systems, (191–204)
© 2021 Scrivener Publishing LLC

attainment and literacy levels are important indicators of development in a developing nation like India as they are a quick indicator of the people, their quality of life and their way of living, awareness level and also level of skill that people possess. Health parameters are also affected since better literacy and educational level lead to better health awareness and thus, have a positive impact on people's health. Education provides a person with the ability to think rationally and take decisions in the welfare of the society. The more the people of a country are literate, the more is the ability of a nation to grow. Illiteracy only leads to more problems and affects all arenas of life. Those with low literacy skills face a number of problems and are more likely to live in poverty. They face an increasing number of health issues because they are unable to understand and read instructions on medicines or prescription labels, and grow isolated in the fast-changing technological world which is heavily dependent on computers. Education parameters have a high weightage in the Human Development Index. The current literacy rate in India is only 74.04% and despite all the government programs not very high increment in the rate has been observed. There can be many factors which cannot be directly noticed by us but plays a great part in affecting the literacy rate. Education and accessibility of schools plays an important factor in determining the literacy rate of any region, especially in rural areas. In 2006–2007, a major reason for low literacy rate was poor sanitation and shortage of classrooms. In Central and Northern India, 59% of the schools did not have clean water for drinking and 89% did not have toilets [2]. The basic literacy instruction dispensed by barely qualified para teachers in approximately 600,000 urban slums and villages is free and compulsory education [3]. There is a shortage of teachers in India with an average student teacher ratio of 4:2. From 1951 to 2002, it has been found that the expenditure allocated to education was not above 4.3% of GDP despite the target of 6% set by the Kothari Commission [5] which further complicates the literacy problem in India.

Severe caste disparity also plays a crucial role in illiteracy [3]. Discrimination of lower caste is a big reason behind high dropout rates and low enrollment rates. Various organizations like NFH (National Family Health) and NSS (The National Sample Survey Organisation) collected data of children who are completing primary school in India and found the percentage to be only 37.7 and 36.8 respectively [6]. Also the Prime Minister of India said that "only 47 out of 100 children enrolled in class I reach class VIII, putting the dropout rate at 52.78%" [4]. It was found in a study that at least 35 million, and possibly around 60 million children of age 6–14 years are not studying in school [3]. Also another reason for low literacy rate is the large proportion of illiterate females is another reason and inequality based on gender differences resulted in female literacy rates being lower at 65.46% than that of their male counterparts at 82.14% [7]. Females are discouraged to pursue formal education and encouraged to work in agricultural farms as the latter requires no formal schooling [8]. Only about 2% of girls are into both agriculture work and schooling [8].

Kerala has achieved a remarkable literacy rate of 93.91% while the Indian literacy rate stands at a much lower 74.04% [9] with Bihar at the bottom with a literacy rate of 63.82% [10]. The total literacy movement in Kerala was first initiated in the late 80's at Ernakulam District and Kottayam Municipality. Several other social indicators of Kerala and Bihar are correlated with these rates, such as life expectancy at birth, infant mortality per 1,000 live births, birth rate per 1,000 people and death rate per 1,000 people. Needless to say, Bihar performs poorly as compared to Kerala in these aspects. Bihar has a higher death rate than Kerala at 7.9 while the latter being at 6.4. Bihar also has a lower life expectancy than Kerala by almost 6 years for males and 10 years for females [11]. The figures clearly show that Kerala is performing great as far as literacy is concerned while Bihar is still fighting to achieve a considerable literacy rate. The high literacy rate of Kerala is worth an applause and if other states try to accelerate their pace to achieve a high literacy rate, India's growth as a developing nation would ramp up steadily.

Although all census after 1881 have reported a rising trend of literacy in the country, it has almost always been offset by the rate of growth of population. The 2001–2011 decade is the second census period when the number of Indian illiterates reduced by 31,196,847 people, indicating towards the literacy growth rate outstripped the population growth rate [12]. 70% of the country's illiterate population is from states like Uttar Pradesh, Bihar, Madhya Pradesh, Rajasthan, Andhra Pradesh (including Telangana) and West Bengal [13]. Approximately half of all the Indian illiterates (48.12%) are in the states of Rajasthan, Uttar Pradesh, Bihar, Madhya Pradesh, Jharkhand and Chhattisgarh [13]. Many states in India are just below or above and a few states are at the top and bottom of the national average.

Therefore, since literacy plays such an important role in the growth of a nation, adequate steps should be taken to promote education amongst the citizens of the country. Community schools should be encouraged so that more and more children are able to access education from an early age. Public schools and local co-operative schools can also be set up. Social service institutions and contribution of NGO's can help in promoting the same. Tax benefits to companies providing CSR funds in the field of education can be given. Also, many poor families who do not have access to education should be made aware about the benefits of sending their children to school rather than employing them in the family business for the purpose of earning money. Modern and innovative methods adhering to the latest trends and technology should be adopted to make children develop interest. The government of India has taken various steps to increase the literacy rate and shall continue to do so. However, a collective effort from the side of the citizens as well as the government will only make the condition of the country better.

14.2 Related Work

Venkatanarayana [14] did a comprehensive research on the latest trends for Indian literacy rates. He compared the data from various states and age demographics and provided projection models to predict the year by which India will achieve nationwide adult literacy standards. He took 2008 as the base year for the projection models. He divided the models into 5 variants each with a different assumption. The projection models in his work predict that India will not reach 100% adult literacy even by the year 2050. The best estimate of adult literacy by 2050 will be 91%.

Swati Jain, Nitin Mishra *et al.* [15] in their research paper tried to forecast the literacy rate of the state of Chhattisgarh. They use logistic curve methods to predict the population growth in Chhattisgarh and feed the projections to a multiple regression model to predict the literacy rates over 1961–2011. They also compared their findings with the widely accepted GALP model used to predict the literacy rates.

Tarun Verma, Sweety Raj, Mohammad Asif Khan and Palak Modi [16], in their research paper have provided some solution approaches for analyzing the literacy data. Pre-existing solutions along with the Weka tool are used to define the region wise literacy rates, on national as well as international level. Input to the tool is given in the form of data that is to be analyzed and output is produced in the form of a decision tree which is easily understandable.

Augustus Wali, Epiphanie Kagoyire, Pacifique Icygingeneye [17], have provided in their research paper a mathematical model (logistic equation) to model the population growth of the people of Uganda.

Asur and Huberman [18], in their paper have demonstrated how social media content can be used to predict real-world outcomes. They have forecasted the box-office revenues for movies from Twitter.com showing that a simple model built from the rate at which tweets are created about particular topics can outperform market-based predictors. They further demonstrated how sentiments extracted from Twitter can be utilized to improve the forecasting power of social media.

Dr. R. Ravichandran in their paper "A Study on Population Projection using the Logistic Curve method in Time series analysis with reference to India Indian Journal of Applied Research, Vol.III, Issue.V, May 2013" [19] have showed that population projection is the numerical outcomes of a particular set of assumption could be various types as long as they are related to the population changes. In their method they have selected three points of the Logistic growth curve in Time series analysis and have used it as a model for population growth. Their paper concluded that the long-term population projection gives accurate results.

Sandra Silva Lustosa, Ana Cristina Guarinello, Ana Paula Berberian, Gisele Aparecida de Athayde Massi, Daniel Vieira da Silva in their paper "Analysis of the literacy practices of entering and graduating students from a higher education institution: case report" [20] characterize and analyze the quality of the practices and the level of literacy, as well as the possibilities of texts reading and comprehension, present in the daily academic and extra academic life of entering and graduating students from a Brazilian university. For the analysis, they have adopted a qualitative and quantitative approach. They observed that although the texts presented belong to primary genres, students got incorrect answers and were not conducive to the education level in which they are enrolled.

The review article "Academic boredom, engagement and the achievement of undergraduate students at university: a review and synthesis of relevant literature" by John G Sharp, Jane C Sharp, Emma Young focuses on academic boredom which is a negative and deactivating achievement-related emotion known to impact usually adversely on student engagement and performance and hence becomes a reason to drop out from school or a reason for their poor performance. This also contributes to the low literacy rate of a place.

14.3   Solution Approaches

Following are the steps that were used in approaching the analysis of the data.

1. Preparation Of Dataset
2. Data Visualization and analysis
3. Prediction using various trained machine learning models.

14.3.1   Preparation of Dataset

Data preprocessing is a procedure in data mining that includes transforming crude, raw data into a comprehensible format. Data obtained from the real-world is frequently inadequate, conflicting, and lacking in certain behaviors, and contains numerous blunders. This real world data can't be directly used for predictions of any kind. Thus, there is a strong need to convert this unprocessed, unstructured data into a structured, clean format which is easily understandable and can be fed into the machine learning models.

Data preprocessing is essentially important for resolving such conflicts. It includes cleaning, integration, and various data reduction approaches. All these techniques aim to solve different kinds of problems which are present in the data.

The following steps are undertaken during preprocessing:

Data Cleaning: Raw Data is generally filled with bogus and ambiguous data which compiles up to form unclean noisy data overall. There is a need for the cleaning of such data. Inconsistencies such as various outliers which are present in data are removed. These outliers can accumulate due to human error in measuring the value, or a wrong entry in the data file.

Real world data does not always guarantee the complete data, and thus it is highly possible that there are some missing values. They can lead to wrong predictions. Thus they are either dropped or are filled with a suitable calculated guess using various present techniques.

Data Integration: Generally data is collected not from one source, instead from multiple sources. Data from these various sources needs to be integrated into one combined source.

As it is possible there are differences between these sources, like using different methods or scales to measure the value. This all must be resolved before merging the data into one concrete dataset. This includes passing data through various transformers to normalize the data into one prescribed values range. This ensures that data remains consistent through all dimensions.

14.3.2   Data Reduction

With so much historical data present, generally data contains so much dimension that causes for the model to learn from it. It causes overfitting to the data and poor optimization of the learning.

Thus data need be reduced in dimensions to produce a summarized version of data for better understanding and analysis. This step helps to present a reduced form of data in a data warehouse. This includes using techniques like Linear Discriminant Analysis (LDA) and Principal Component Analysis (PCA) to reduce the dimension without losing the important aspects of data at the same time.

14.3.3   Data Visualization

After producing concrete, clean and structured data, the next step is to visualize the data to gain the insight of the data. Data visualization is a vital step to analyze the data from its visual representation.

It presents the visual aspect of the data and helps us to know data visually apart from the numerical values present. As the data had a spatial aspect as a dimension, visualizing the data in a spatial graph tends to present a much more sophisticated way to understand the data.

Statistical and informational graphics, plots, charts and other tools are used for data visualization to understand the information in a clear and efficient manner. In order to encode numerical data the dots, lines and bars are used, to visually communicate a quantitative message.

Data visualization helps the user to view data from different perspectives and analyze it completely for further reason and evidence. Complex data can be visualized easily since data visualization makes it more understandable and usable. It helps in understanding causality and making comparisons.

14.3.4   Prediction Models

After cleaning and visualizing the data, the next step is to select and train an appropriate machine learning model that can produce good estimations of the target variable, here Literacy Rate.

As per the data present, some of the basic choices are:

1. K Nearest Neighbors (KNN)
2. ElasticNet Regression
3. Artificial Neural Networks
4. Random Forest.

These were trained separately and tested using various accuracy metrics to find out the best model present. These are built using libraries like sklearn and Keras API from TensorFlow to get the most optimized model.

14.3.4.1   KNN (K-Nearest Neighbors)

K Nearest Neighbors or KNN is an algorithm that is used for both regression and classification tasks. It exploits the concept of feature to predict new values of the data points by the similarity of the 'k' closest present data points. It is based on the fact that the close points depict much more correlation among them than the points that are far away.

The prediction is based on the closeness of the data point to the training points. The closer the new point is to an existing point, it matches more to the existing point. Thus a State which shares various parameters like closeness in infrastructure, GDP of state, laws, and geometric closeness will act as better predictors for the new values.

14.3.4.2   ElasticNet Regression

ElasticNet Regression is a statistical regression technique that uses the concept of both ridge and lasso regression, or L1 and L2 regularization. Regularization is the process which shrinks the various coefficients of the model to 0. It is done so to reduce the complexity of the model to avoid overfitting and to make the model generalize well over new data. Regularization also helps the model selection to a simpler model which makes it pretty efficient.

It incorporates the goodness of both L1 and L2 regularization. As lasso, it removes the weak variables while as ridge, it reduces them to zero without completely eliminating them from the model. Thus the trade-off between the Lasso and Ridge regularization is controlled by a parameter named as Alpha. Alpha parameter decides the overall nature of ElasticNet function with Lasso and Ridge functionalities.

14.3.4.3 *Artificial Neural Networks*

Artificial Neural Networks or generally known as ANN are the deep learning models which are inspired from the working of the human brain, with neuron nodes interconnected like a web. It has thousands of artificial neurons, which are interconnected. Data flows through each neuron through this connection. These neurons consist of input and output units. Like the Human Brain, they are activated or controlled by some non-linear activation functions like sigmoid, tanh or other version of Relu.

For training, several passes of training data are passed through the model. This helps the model to learn the values of various weights and biases values. This completes the forward propagation step. After the output is produced, loss value is calculated which is a measure of how well our model is learning, The network compares the output obtained with the actual output and the difference is calculated. This difference is then propagated back through back-propagation algorithm, it readjusts the various weights and biases using an optimizer function which are generally a version of Gradient Descent like Stochastic Gradient Descent or ADAM.

It is repeated until the difference between the actual and desired outcome produces the lowest possible error.

14.3.4.4 *Random Forest*

Random Forest is one of the ensemble learning methods. Several base models are combined together in an ensemble model in order to produce one of the optimal predictive models. For both classification and regression problems random forest can be used.

They work on the principle of ensemble learning from the various decision trees that made up the entire forest. Any prediction is evaluated from the collective results from individual trees and then taking mode or mean of the results.

They are generally used to reduce the over fitting problem which is usually caused by using a single decision tree for the modeling. A Random Forest Model is somewhat similar to Bagging.

14.4 Proposed Approach

Following steps were used:

- Collecting previous year data from MHRD website: Data included state wise segregation of literacy rate, number of school going students, number of private and government schools, etc.
- Cleaning and structuring the relevant data: All the inaccurate, inconsistent and incomplete data points were recognized so that the quality of the dataset

can be improved and all the inconsistencies were removed by correcting the detected errors and omitting the inaccurate data. Also, the attributes which were incomplete but played a major role in deriving the result were completed by putting random values (in the range of the pre-existing values in the attribute) or the average value of the attribute.

- Missing values were imputed in the data using several clustering techniques.
- Plotting heat maps and removing highly correlated features: Heat Maps are used in order to see how much an attribute correlates or is dependent on each other. Such features which do not have a great impact on the concerned attribute (which is to be predicted) need to be removed.
- Using Feature Selection method, dimensionality of the dataset is reduced: As the dataset used for the research had several attributes out of which many attributes had no significance and did not contribute anything or much to the prediction, such features were removed from the dataset and the features which played a major role in deriving the result were kept in the dataset.
- Training and evaluating different models : Several Models such as
  - K Nearest Neighbors,
  - ElasticNet Regression
  - Artificial Neural Networks
  - Random Forest
  were trained and were evaluated.
- Applying selected model and tuning the hyper parameters further to obtain a better model.
- Using the developed model to predict results: These results are state wise predictions of literacy rate taking account several selected features.

ElasticNet regression was chosen as it provided the best accuracy and fits best to the given dataset. Hyperparameter tuning fine tunes the model to give highly accurate results. The loss function used here was Regression Loss (14.1).

$$min\left(\|Y - X\theta\|_2^2 + \lambda_1 \|\theta\|_1 + \lambda_2 \|\theta\|_2^2\right) \qquad (14.1)$$

ElasticNet Regression Loss

Where
  Y: Actual Y value
  X: Predicted Value
  Alpha1: Lasso Regression Penalty
  Alpha2: Ridge Regression Penalty.

Lower the loss, lower is the difference between the true values and our predicted values. This makes our prediction more reliable.

14.5   Result Analysis

Various algorithms have been applied to the dataset to predict the literacy rate. Based on the results, the accuracy of the algorithms has been compared. The results obtained after training the various models to the dataset are discussed in this section. The accuracy of the prediction is evaluated by using the following algorithms: K Nearest Neighbors (KNN), ElasticNet Regression, Random Forests and Artificial Neural Network (ANN) getting the accuracy as 91.21, 99.83, 87.08 and 98.87% respectively as shown in Figure 14.1.

As it is a problem of regression, loss was the metric used to calculate the accuracy. Decreasing this loss results in better accuracy of the model. It was calculated using Equation (14.2):

$$1 - (\Sigma(|\,Y\ actual - Y\ predict\,| \div Y\ actual)) \tag{14.2}$$

Loss Function

Where
  Y actual: Actual literacy rate
  Y predicted: Predicted literacy rate.

In our effort, we have tried to predict the Literacy Rates of each state using a reduced set of features. There are a lot of features which are redundant in nature, or indirectly not useful for the model. Thus, such features only increase the complexity of the model and may lead to incorrect or misleading results. Hence, we plotted heat maps to find the correlated features and select the reduced set among them (Figure 14.2).

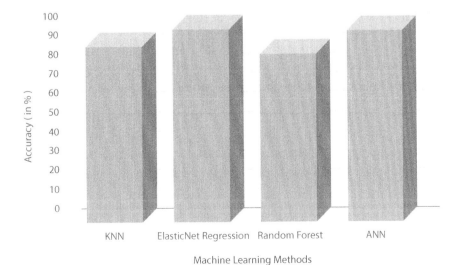

Figure 14.1 Accuracy (in %) obtained by different machine learning models.

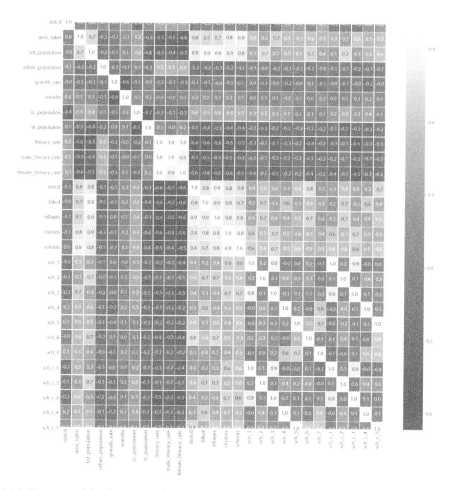

Figure 14.2 Heat map of the dataset correlation.

Heat maps helped in visualizing the data in an efficient manner and deriving useful conclusions. Some observations that we obtained are:

- Kerala tops the literacy rate ranking among all states with 91.5%.
- Bihar ranked the least among all states with 63%.
- Literacy rate varies from 63 to 91.5%.

The following figure demonstrates the predicted literacy rate in percentage for each state of India.

Some observations from the given graph (Figure 14.3) are:

- Mizoram, Lakshadweep and Kerala are the only three regions with a literacy rate of 90% and above.
- Literacy rate is higher than 60% in each state of India.
- States like Bihar, Jammu and Kashmir, Rajasthan and Uttar Pradesh are lacking in terms of literacy with almost one third of the population being illiterate.

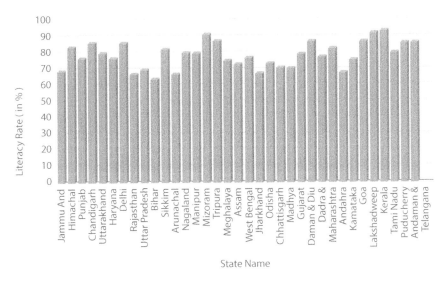

Figure 14.3 Literacy rate (in %) for each state of India.

Bihar holds the lowest position in terms of literacy when compared to other states in India. A large number of people do not have access to education, thus creating a crisis in the state's education system. The following graph depicts the age wise distribution of people attending educational institutes in Bihar. The dotted line demonstrates the national average of people attending educational institutions.

From the given graph (Figure 14.4), the following conclusions can be drawn:

- A gradual decline can be observed in the percentage of people attending educational institutions in the late teen years and in the early twenties. This signifies that a very small number of people are going for higher studies in Bihar.

Kerala has the highest literacy rate when compared to other states in India. The following graph depicts the age wise distribution of people attending educational institutes in Kerala. The dotted line demonstrates the national average of people attending educational institutions.

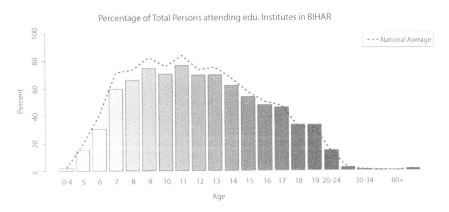

Figure 14.4 Age distribution of Bihar.

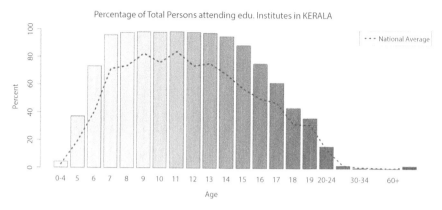

Figure 14.5 Age distribution of Kerala.

As seen in Figure 14.5, the following conclusions can be drawn:

- It can be clearly observed that the percentage of people attending educational institutions in Kerala is much higher than the national average for all age groups.
- A maximum number of students are attending educational institutions in Kerala.
- Almost 100% of students are attending school upto the age of 15.

14.6 Conclusion and Future Scope

14.6.1 Conclusion

So from the above research we can conclude that in India, the highest literacy rate was found to be of Kerala which was 91.5% and the lowest was of Bihar which is 63 %. It was also found that the states with literacy rate more than 905 were:

1. Kerala
2. Lakshadweep
3. Mizoram.

On categorizing regionally North has the least literacy rate followed by West, East and South with the highest literacy rate. Literacy rate predicted using several Machine Learning models gives results very close to the rate given by the census of India. Among the Various Models ElasticNet Regression provided the best accuracy of 99.83%. Table 14.1 depicts the accuracies of various models that have been used during the research.

14.6.2 Future Scope

- The scope of the project can be further extended by the simple application of our platform by any government or non-government organizations to

Table 14.1 Accuracy obtained by applying different Machine Learning Models on the dataset.

Machine Learning Models	Accuracy (in %)
KNN	91.21
ElasticNet Regression	99.83
Random Forest	87.08
ANN	98.87

understand not only education but other major sectors like health, crime, jobs in a similar way.

- With the help of the time series model, we can predict the literacy rate in future and can also derive the factors which had the major significance in the increment or decrement of the literacy rate. This can be done using LSTMs (Long Short Term Memory Networks) by feeding the network with real time information on what all measures are being taken in order to increase the literacy rate.
- A model can also be used to analyze what all schemes could have the maximum impact on the literacy rate and what all schemes could fail in the future.
- A similar model can be used to promote girl child education by diving into the roots of the problem and predicting the major factors that are responsible for hampering girl child education in various states.

References

1. Educating India, in: *Source: Scribd*, Retrieved 15 September 2011, https://en.wikipedia.org/wiki/Literacy_in_India.
2. Basu, K. and Suma Latha, P., Women Literacy and Development. 3, 8, August Special Issue—2014, https://www.worldwidejournals.com/global-journal-for-research-analysis-GJRA/recent_issues_pdf/2014/August/August_2014_1565183374_170.pdf, 29 November 2004.
3. *The Challenges for India's Education System (PDF)*, Chatham House, https://www.chathamhouse.org/sites/default/files/public/Research/Asia/bpindiaeducation.pdf, Retrieved 15 September 2011.
4. *Global campaign for education—more teachers needed*, UNICEF India, Retrieved 15 September 2011.
5. *Primary Education in India: Key Problems*, Dise, http://www.dise.in/Downloads/Use%20of%20Dise%20Data/Ajay%20Deshpande,Sayan%20Mitra.pdf, Retrieved 15 September 2011.
6. *Social Exclusion of Scheduled Caste Children from Primary Education in India*, UNICEF, http://www.unicef.org/files/Social_Exclusion_of_Scheduled_Caste_Children_from_Primary_Education_in_India.pdf, Retrieved 15 September 2011.
7. India's Literacy Panorama, *Education for all in India*, https://educationforallinindia.com/page172.html, Retrieved 15 September 2011.
8. *Gender Inequalities and Demographic Behaviour*, Snap3, http://snap3.uas.mx/RECURSO1/unfpa/data/docs/unpf0022.pdf, Retrieved 15 September 2011.

9. *Tripura beats Kerala in literacy*, The Times of India, 8 September 2013, https://timesofindia.indi-atimes.com/home/education/news/Tripura-beats-Kerala-in-literacy/articleshow/22416019.cms.

10. Nayar, K.R. and Kumar, A., Health Analysis—Kerala and Bihar: A Comparison. *Yojana*, 49, SSRN 1354541, The inter-sectoral action needs to be recognized for achieving any health improvement in Bihar, July 2005.

11. *Census 2011: Provisional Population Tools*, The Hindu, Chennai, India, March 31, 2011.

12. *Literacy Rate on the Rise, 11th Plan Targets 80%*, The India Post, 4 September 2008, retrieved 28 November 2009, In all the States and Union Territories the male literacy rate except Bihar (59.68%) is now over 60%, http://www.theindiapost.com/2008/09/04/literacy-rate-on-the-rise-11th-plan-targets-80/.

13. Venkatanarayana, M., *When Will India Achieve Universal Adult Literacy: Status and Prospects*, MPRA, 49, Paper No. 48061, July 2013, https://www.ijser.org/researchpaper/Literacy-Rate-Analysis.pdf.

14. Jain, S. and Mishra, N., Forecasting Of Literacy Rate Using Statistical And Data Mining Methods. *Int. J. Adv. Comput. Eng. Networking*, 3, 8, August 2015.

15. Verma, T., Raj, S., Khan, M.A., Modi, P., Literacy Rate Analysis. *Int. J. Sci. Eng. Res.*, 3, 7, July-2012, http://www.ijser.org.

16. Wali, A., Kagoyire, E., Icyingeneye, P., Mathematical Modeling of UgandaPopulation Growth. *Appl. Math. Sci.*, 6, 84, 4155–4168, 2012.

17. Asur, S. and Huberman, B.A., Predicting the Future with Social Media. *IEEE/WIC/ACM International Conference on Web Intelligence and Intelligent Agent Technology*, Washington, DC, USA, vol. 01, pp. 492–499, 2010.

18. Ravichandrran, R., A Study on Population Projection using the Logistic Curve method in Time series analysis with reference to India. *Indian J. Appl. Res.*, 3, May 2013.

19. Lustosa, S.S., Guarinello, A.C., Berberian, A.P., de Athayde Massi, G.A., da Silva, D.V., Analysis of the literacy practices of entering and graduating students from a higher education institution, July-August 2016, CEFAC - Associacao Institucional em Saude e Educacao.

20. Sharp, J.G., Sharp, J.C., Young, E., Academic boredom, engagement and the achievement of undergraduate students at university: A review and synthesis of relevant literature. *Res. Pap. Educ.*, 35, 2, 144–184, 2020.

Motion Transfer in Videos using Deep Convolutional Generative Adversarial Networks

Savitoj Singh, Bittoo Aggarwal, Vipin Bhardwaj and Anupam Kumar*

Maharaja Agrasen Institute of Technology, Guru Gobind Singh Indraprastha University, New Delhi, Delhi, India

Abstract

Motion Transfer has a wide variety of applications such as creating motion synchronized videos in film industries and video making apps. The research paper presents a novel approach for motion transfer from a source video to the target person. This approach focuses on video to video translation using various poses generated in the frames of video for translation. The approach makes use of Pose Generation Convolutional Neural Network to synthesize arbitrary poses from source videos and train the pix2pix–DCGAN which is a conditional generative adversarial network consisting of multi scale discriminator and generator for target video frames generation. It uses PatchGAN loss, VGG loss and Feature Matching Loss function for improving and optimizing models. The presented approach provides compelling results of the generated DCGAN model with the discriminator loss of 0.0003 and generator loss of 5.8206.

Keywords: Generative adversarial networks, convolutional neural network, pose detection and estimation, video to video translation, motion transfer

15.1 Introduction

Motion transfer between two video subjects is transferring body posture of one video subject to another. It has a wide variety of applications in film industries. It can be used for synthesizing synchronized dancing videos or action sequences. Another widely used application is generating realistic-looking videos and images for photo editing software. Motion transfer between source and target video subjects is a tricky process which focuses on translating body posture, facial expressions and source subjects pose to the target subject while generating a constant streamlined motion forming a video.

In this paper, we present a novel approach for motion translation between source and target videos. The goal is to impose poses of the source subject onto the target subject. To achieve this, we propose an end to end approach using Deep Convolutional Generative Adversarial Networks (DCGAN) for generating high quality motion translated images. Our aim is to translate the hand, legs and body posture of the source in the first image to that in the target

---

Corresponding author: anupamkumar@mait.ac.in

Namita Gupta, Prasenjit Chatterjee and Tanupriya Choudhury (eds.) Smart and Sustainable Intelligent Systems, (205–214)
© 2021 Scrivener Publishing LLC

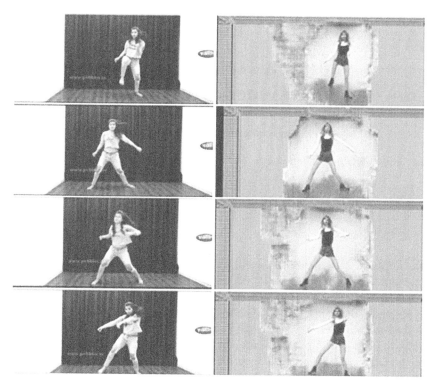

Figure 15.1 Motion translation from source to target.

as shown in Figure 15.1. Due to the lack of output images of the target in various different poses it is impossible to perform this task of motion transfer through supervised learning techniques. Generative Adversarial Networks is used for generating unsupervised images of the source. Although this technique helps in the realistic motion transferring, it is susceptible to complex background, different object sizes and scales, lighting, clarity and various noises in the image. The approach is also vulnerable to problems like multiple subjects in the source video performing multiple different actions and position of the target in the generated frames.

The dataset used for training the DCGAN is a video in which the target object is doing body movements, for each frame of this video poses are generated using openpose [13]. The generated pose is the input for DCGAN and the original frame is the expected output from the DCGAN. Using this pair of input and output images, we trained our DCGAN (as shown in Figure 15.2).

Apart from the introduction, this paper consists of five other segments: Segment 2 analyzes the related work made in the field related to motion transfer learning. The methodology is showcased in Segment 3. The results and analysis have been performed in Segment 5. In Segment 6, the conclusion has been drawn along with the future scope. The last segment contains the list of references used in this paper.

15.2   Related Work

Generative Adversarial Networks belong to the set of generative models, that is, they are able to produce new content. For example, a human face generator, which generates faces

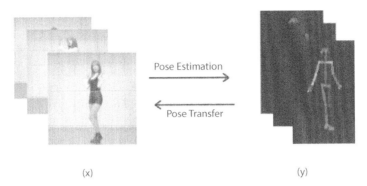

(x)   (y)

Figure 15.2 Our technique makes correspondences by recognizing presents in video outlines (Video to Pose) and afterward figures out how to create pictures of the objective subject from the assessed present (Pose to Video).

of humans who may not even exists. Speaking in mathematical terms, GAN are basically generating some random data and we try to model our network in such a way that it produces data from a specific class, which were human faces in a human face generator. Inside GAN there are two networks which are working, one is generator and other is discriminator, they both are neural networks. What a generator does is, it takes some random input and generates an output. The discriminator takes the output of the generator as input and tells whether it is real or fake. So speaking about training, the generator tries to fool the discriminator by producing an image, which is close to real, and discriminator tries to find out whether the image is real or fake. So there is a fight kind of going between generator and discriminator and this fight eventually increases the performance of both generator and discriminator, and eventually our generator is trained.

Pose generative image modeling from DCGAN is a relatively new approach for automatic image generation, although, various different techniques have been used for motion transfer video to video translation. The approach in Ref. [1] renders subject images in various different motions using multi-view fitted 3D models. A novel approach for rendering video-realistic interactive character animation from a database of 4D actor performance captured in a multiple camera studio is proposed in Ref. [2]. The approach successfully reconstructs captured dynamic shape appearance of human-like character motion.

A MoCoGAN proposed framework is depicted in Ref. [3] which generates a sequence of video frames consisting of content and motion part. Hence, allowing them to generate videos with either different motion of different content. In Ref. [4], an RNN architecture with forward kinematics layer is proposed which translates input motion into target characters with different skeleton figures. A video based cloning technique using deep generative networks is proposed in Ref. [5]. Another similar approach is presented in Ref. [6] which also focuses on spatiotemporal constraints for effective retargeting. Ref. [7] uses a novel motion descriptor based on optical flow for retargeting.

Detecting and generating poses is a crucial step in the process of motion translation. A Deep neural network based approach for high precision pose estimation [8]. Approaches in Refs. [9, 10] employ adversarial networks for human pose estimation and generating 3D pose annotations. An open source full body estimation for 2D pose estimated in presented in Refs. [11, 13]. An end to end trainable GAN is used in Ref. [12] which focuses on fitting 3D poses to 2D images.

In recent works, multiple generative networks such as human synthesis net and fusion net are used for enhancing realism into video to video translation [14]. Other works include feeding medium quality controlled 3D models for synthesizing human character images [15]. With the recent development in the field of multiple different types of GANs, polished unsupervised image generation is possible. CycleGAN introduces a cycle consistency loss by coupling inverse mapping between target and source domains, cycle consistency maintained by mapping F and G functions, $F(G(x)) \approx x$ and $G(F(y)) \approx y$ in X and Y domains, cycle consistency loss along with adversarial loss is used [16].

High resolution condition GAN is used in Ref. [17] which uses a multi scale generator and discriminator and incorporates object instance segmentation, technique presented in the paper allows users to interact with object appearance. Another approach uses a DiscoGAN to learn cross domain relations while preserving identity and orientations. The DiscoGAN present in the paper doesn't use extra annotated supervision [18]. CoGAN or Coupled GAN uses marginal samples to generate joint distribution [22]. GAC-GAN is used for appearance controlled movement translation. GAC-GAN uses ACGAN loss and shadow extraction modules and is used for generating new appearances from video records. Two types of GANs are used in making GAC-GAN, layout GAN and appearance GAN. Layout GAN helps in describing motion in videos at pixel level [23]. SimGAN or simulated and unsupervised learning GAN doesn't use random noisy vectors but actually uses synthetic images which is later refined while preserving the annotation information, this type of GAN also uses adversarial loss while training the refiner network [24]. Pix2Pix is another type of conditional GAN used for image to image translations, this type of GAN uses UNet architecture which contains two both encoder, decoder network, the discriminator used here is PatchGAN architecture also known as Markovian discriminator [25].

Xu et al. [21] uses multi-see catches of an objective subject performing straightforward movements to make a database of pictures and movement translation through a fitted 3D skeleton and relating surface work for the objective. Work by Casas et al. utilize 4D Video Textures [20] to minimalistic ally store a layered surface portrayal of an examined target individual and utilize their transiently intelligible work and information portrayal to render video of the objective subject performing novel movements. Interestingly, our methodology investigates movement transfer between 2D video subjects. What's more, stay away from information adjustment and lifting into 3D space.

A UNet-like architecture is used in Pose Guided Person Generation Network for synthesizing arbitrary but blurry results which are later refined for generating high quality images. The technique proposed in the paper contains two major steps for synthesizing such images, pose integration stage consists of generator G1 and pose mask loss, in the second stage image refinement, a generator G2 is used which is completely tested on Deep fashion dataset [19].

15.3   Methodology

Step 1: Preprocessing and cleaning of the input Video
Step 2: Pose Detection and Estimation from all frames of the video
Step 3: Training DCGAN to generate various poses for input image
Step 4. Combining images generated from DCGAN to form the augmented video.

15.3.1   Pre-Processing

In the first step of our approach, the source video is split into multiple frames first. We follow this by removing unwanted noise from our split images using bilateral filters. It is highly effective in noise removal while keeping edges sharp. But the operation is slower compared to other filters. Gaussian filter takes the neighborhood around the pixel and finds its Gaussian weighted average. This Gaussian filter is a function of space alone, that is, nearby pixels are considered while filtering. It doesn't consider whether pixels have almost the same intensity. It doesn't consider whether a pixel is an edge pixel or not. So it blurs the edges also, which we don't want to do since sharp edges around the image, helps in detecting and estimating poses accurately. Some starting and ending frames of the video are removed from the dataset because it contains static noise which contains excessive noise and less movement.

15.3.2   Pose Detection and Estimation

In the second step of our approach, we need to generate the poses of the detected people from the multiple preprocessed frames of the video. The procedure of pose detection is divided into 4 major steps, at first a DCGAN model is created, this model is designed to predict the heatmaps of the areas detected/estimated poses with input as the video frame having source person. Using the heatmap generated from the above model, body parts are extracted, peak values from the heatmap are used to link the body parts.

For pose estimation, a DCGAN is used to generate the pose of the source person from the image. Two major stages of pose generation and estimation is pose integration and image refinement. A U-Net like generator and discriminator is used in the above mentioned stages and the source image and target image is inputted to generate the estimated pose [19]. The architecture used is mentioned in Figure 15.3.

15.4   Pose to Video Translation

This is performed using a conditional GAN whose input is the generated pose from the previous step along with the random Noise. In this step generator tries to fool the discriminator, and discriminator tries to figure out whether the image is fake or real, And during

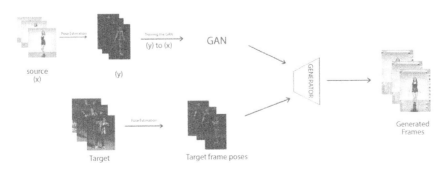

Figure 15.3 Architecture.

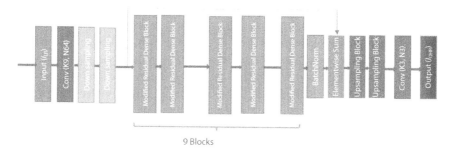

Figure 15.4 Generator Network Architecture.

this fight between generator and the discriminator accuracy of the models increases which in end results into two independent models and these can be used to either generate the target image or to check whether an image is real or fake.

The loss function used is a combination of Adversarial and Content loss which is a modification of the Perceptual Loss function. The Adversarial loss gives a weight of 10^{-3} to the discriminator loss, but in our implementation, the weight of this loss is increased to 10^{-2}. The generator network architecture is shown in Figure 15.4.

15.5   Results and Analysis

The DCGAN modal proposed has been trained on 19,675 images of single dancer Youtube video and a total of 19,000 iterations were performed. The final discriminator loss is 0.0003 and the generator loss is 5.8206. The graph of discriminator loss and generator loss is plotted for every iteration as shown in Figures 15.5 and 15.6. As shown in the figure, the decrease in losses indicates that the model is making better and optimized results. In every iteration, we use these losses to train the model better and further improve accuracy and decrease losses.

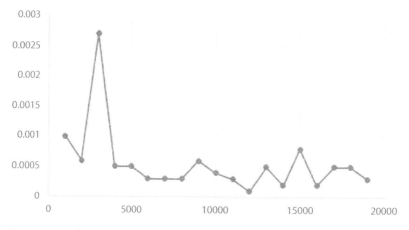

Figure 15.5 Discriminator loss.

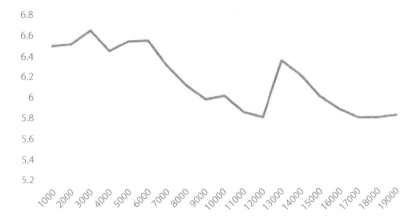

Figure 15.6 Generator loss.

Discriminator Loss is determined using the adversarial Loss function that is

$$Loss_{adv}(G,D_y,X) = \frac{1}{m}\sum_{i=1}^{m}(1-D_y(G(x_i)))^2$$

$$Loss_{adv}(F,D_x,Y) = \frac{1}{m}\sum_{i=1}^{m}(1-D_x(F(y_i)))^2$$

Let's consider the generator loss which is the generator's main motive is to maximize this functionality. In other words, it tries to make discriminators wrong every time and try to increase the probability of getting discriminators wrong.

D(x) is the Discriminator's output for a real instance.

G(z) is the generator's output.

D(G(z)) is the Discriminator output for a fake instance.

The output of Discriminator D does not have to be between 1 and 0.

Discriminator Loss tells us about how well he is able to recognize the real and fake images and as the loss decreases our generator accuracy of generating the image increases. But since this is an iterative process discriminator also has been improving their results as a generator, so the result gets benefited from this, and our images will become more realistic as the iterations/epochs increases.

The final results for the generated frames and alongside the original video are shown in Figure 15.6.

The Loss is consist of two losses that is adversarial loss and the cyclic loss,

Adversarial Loss is as follows

$$Loss_{adv}(G,D_yX) = \frac{1}{m} * \sum(1-D_y(G(x_i)))^2$$

$$Loss_{adv}(F,D_x,Y) = \frac{1}{m} * \sum(1-D_x(F(y_i)))^2$$

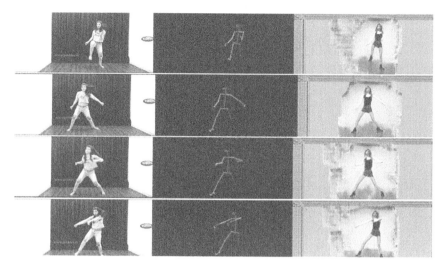

Figure 15.7 Generated results.

and Cyclic Loss is as follows,

$$Loss_{cyc}(G,F,X,Y) = \frac{1}{m}\sum_{i=1}^{m}[F(G(x_i))-x_i]+[G(F(y_i))-y_i]$$

So here in Figure 15.6, we can see generator loss is continuously decreasing but the rate is less that means our generator is struggling to confuse our discriminator because the generator is also learning at the same time.

The combination loss will be,

$$Loss_{full} = Loss_{adv} + \lambda Loss_{cyc}$$

Here the value of λ is taken as 100, to somewhat equalize the impact of generator and discriminator both.

As shown in Figure 15.7 the frame in the first column is the motion we are willing to transfer to our target image and column in the second frame is the estimated pose and the third and last columns are the motion transfer from the source object to the target image.

As we can see we are able to transform the images to particular pose well but still there's an issue with the image quality (Figure 15.8).

15.6   Conclusion and Future Scope

Our proposed approach was able to produce high quality results of the generated images from the source video with the discriminator loss of 0.0003 and generator loss 5.8206. One can also use densePose network to generate the pose of the source image and then use the generated poses to train the generator, this method is expected to give better results as the pose generated by densePose [27] converts whole body as compared to stick image generated by openPose.

Figure 15.8 Original image and generated image.

One of the use cases of this framework is to create a synchronized motion dance video of multiple different subjects. Having trained models for multiple subjects, we can use the source video to generate the motion of all target persons. Second use case of this system can be to use discriminator to check whether the image is "fake" or "real". One can also use a separate face GAN to generate better facial expressions which would result in more realistic video of the target person.

Trained discriminator can also be used to detect whether an image is real or fake as it was trained to determine if the pose is generated accurately and realistic, this can be very useful in forensic science for detecting image morphing or modifications done on an image.

Background augmentation using BAGAN [26] can be used for effectively adding background to the proposed model which lacks in the background and spits out gray background as shown in Figure 15.6. The advantage of using background GAN would help in augmenting various backgrounds for synchronized dancing videos.

References

1. Cheung, G.K.M., Baker, S., Hodgins, J., Kanade, T., Markerless human motion transfer, in: *3D Data Processing, Visualization and Transmission, 2004. 3DPVT 2004, Proceedings. 2nd International Symposium on*, IEEE, pp. 373–378, 2004.
2. Casas, D., Volino, M., Collomosse, J., 4D Video Textures for Interactive Character Appearance. *Comput. Graphics Forum (Proceedings of EUROGRAPHICS)*, 33, 2, 371–380, 2014.
3. Tulyakov, S., Liu, M., Yang, X., Kautz, J., Mocogan: Decomposing motion and content for video generation. *IEEE Conference on Computer Vision and Pattern Recognition (CVPR)*, 2018.
4. Villegas, R., Yang, J., Ceylan, D., Lee, H., Neural kinematic networks for unsupervised motion retargeting, in: *The IEEE Conference on Computer Vision and Pattern Recognition (CVPR)*, June 2018.
5. Aberman, K., Shi, M., Liao, J., Liscbinski, D., Chen, B., Deep video-based performance cloning, in: *Computer Graphics Forum*, vol. 38, pp. 219–233, Wiley Online Library, John Wiley & Sons Ltd ,America 2019.
6. Bansal, A., Ma, S., Ramanan, D., Sheikh, Y., Recycle-GAN: Unsupervised video retargeting, in: *ECCV*, 2018.
7. Efros, A., Berg, A., Mori, G., Malik, J., Recognizing action at a distance, in: *IEEE International Conference on Computer Vision*, Nice, France, pp. 726–733, 2003.
8. Toshev, A. and Szegedy, C., Deeppose: Human pose estimation *via* deep neural networks, in: *CVPR*, 2014.

9. Chou, C., Chien, J., Chen, H., Self Adversarial Training for Human Pose Estimation. *2018 Asia-Pacific Signal and Information Processing Association Annual Summit and Conference (APSIPA ASC)*, Honolulu, HI, USA, pp. 17–30, 2018.

10. Yang, W., Ouyang, W., Wang, X., Ren, J., Li, H., Wang, X., 3D Human Pose Estimation in the Wild by Adversarial Learning. *2018 IEEE/CVF Conference on Computer Vision and Pattern Recognition*, Salt Lake City, UT, pp. 5255–5264, 2018.

11. Hidalgo, G., Sheikh, Y., Kitani, K.M., Bansal, A., Sanabria, R., Xiang, D., Li, X., Idrees, H., *OpenPose: Whole-Body Pose Estimation*, 2019. https://www.ri.cmu.edu/wp-content/uploads/2019/05/MSThesis Gines Hidalgo latest compressed.pdf

12. Chen, X., Song, J., Hilliges, O., Unpaired Pose Guided Human Image Generation, *ArXiv* abs/1901.02284, 31 Jan 2019.

13. Cao, Z., Hidalgo Martinez, G., Simon, T., Wei, S.-E., Sheikh, Y., OpenPose: Realtime Multi-Person 2D Pose Estimation using Part Affinity Fields. *IEEE Trans. Pattern Anal. Mach. Intell.*, 2018. arXiv preprint arXiv:1812.08008.

14. Zhou, Y., Wang, Z., Fang, C., Bui, T., Berg, T., Dance dance generation: Motion transfer for internet videos, *arXiv* preprint arXiv:1904.00129, 2019.

15. Liu, L., Xu, W., Zollhofer, M., Kim, H., Bernard, F., Habermann, M., Wang, W., Theobalt, C., Neural rendering and reenactment of human actor videos. *ACM Trans. Graph.*, 38, 5, 139:1–139:14, October 2019.

16. Zhu, J.-Y., Park, T., Isola, P., Efros, A.A., Unpaired Image-to-Image Translation using Cycle-Consistent Adversarial Networks, in: *IEEE International Conference on Computer Vision (ICCV)*, 2017.

17. Wang, T.-C., Liu, M.-Y., Zhu, J.-Y., Tao, A., Kautz, J., Catanzaro, B., High-Resolution Image Synthesis and Semantic Manipulation with Conditional GANs, in: *CVPR*, 2018.

18. Kim, T., Cha, M., Kim, H., Lee, J.K., Kim, J., Learning to discover cross-domain relations with generative adversarial networks, in: *Proceedings of the 34th International Conference on Machine Learning - Volume 70 (ICML'17)*, D. Precup and Y. W. Teh (Eds.), vol. 70 JMLR.org, pp. 1857–1865, 2017.

19. Ma, L., Jia, X., Sun, Q., Schiele, B., Tuytelaars, T., Van Gool, L., Pose Guided Person Image Generation, 2017.

20. Xu, F., Liu, C.S., Bharaj, G., Tompkin, J., Dai, Q., Seidel, H.-P., Kautz, J., Theobalt, Video-based characters: creating new human performances from a multi-view video database, in: *ACM Transactions with Graphics (TOG)*, vol. 30, p. 32, ACM, New York 2011.

21. Casas, D., Volino, M., Collomosse, J., Hilton, A., 4D Video Textures for Interactive Character Appearance. *Comput. Graphics Forum*, 33, 371–380, 2014.

22. Liu, Y. and Tuzel, O., Coupled generative adversarial networks, in: *NIPS*, 2016.

23. Wei, D., Xu, X., Shen, H., Huang, K., GAC-GAN: A General Method for Appearance-Controllable Human Video Motion Transfer, in IEEE Transactions on Multimedia, doi: 10.1109/TMM.2020.3011290, 2020.

24. Shrivastava, A., Pfister, T., Tuzel, O., Susskind, J., Wang, W., Webb, Russel., Learning from Simulated and Unsupervised Images through Adversarial Training, July 2016.

25. Isola, P., Zhou, J.-Y., Zhu, T., Efros, A., Image-to-Image Translation with Conditional Adversarial Networks, Nov 2018.

26. Ma, Y., Liu, K., Guan, Z., Xu, X., Qian, X., Bao, H., Background Augmentation Generative Adversarial Networks (BAGANs): Effective Data Generation Based on GAN-Augmented 3D Synthesizing, Symmetry. 10. 734. 10.3390/sym10120734, December 2018.

27. Guler, R.A., Neverova, N., Kokkinos, I., DensePose: Dense Human Pose Estimation In The Wild, Feb 2018.

Twin Question Pair Classification

Ashish Sharma, Sachin Sourav Jha*, Sahil Arora, Shubham Garg and Sandeep Tayal

Department of Computer Science and Engineering, Maharaja Agrasen Institute of Technology, Rohini, Delhi, India

Abstract

Everyone must be aware of Quora, the site which is used by everyone. Be it a student, a teacher, a professional, or anyone, this site has something for everyone as it can help in solving queries related to every subject. You just need to post your query and you can rest assured that several fellow users would be putting their hands up to resolve your query. There is a problem though, sometimes multiple users can have similar queries but they fail to realize that a similar question has already been posted on the forum. So sometimes, a situation can arise where several users have submitted a similar query. The users who answer the question might not be aware that there are different versions of the question, so they end up missing the other versions. In this research paper, the aim is to classify a question pair if they are similar or not. To do this, we have used a dataset given by Quora on Kaggle. That dataset contained 4 lakh entries which helped us in training our models and get the desired results from it. In this research paper, we have used the knowledge of Natural Language Processing and different classification and boosting algorithms to see which is more helpful. Then we have compared the accuracy of various models to come to figure out which algorithm is most suitable for the task. The same has been done with the help of several graphs and tables to point out the difference in the accuracy of different algorithms. Before applying any algorithm it was important to clean and pre-process the data. Once that was done, we just applied techniques like Count Vectorizer with xG Gradient Boosting, TF-IDF Vectorizer with xG Gradient Boosting, Logistic Regression, and Random Forest.

Keywords: Machine learning, twin questions, quora, random forest, logistic regression, xG boost, count vectorizer, bag of words

16.1 Introduction

Quora is a great platform to find answers to your problems. In that platform, you can post your problems and a helpful community would be more than happy to solve your queries. There is a problem when multiple people ask similar questions differently. In that case, the users are forced to check answers to each question. Here it is important to find an algorithm which can detect similar questions [23].

**Corresponding author*: Sachinsourav.maitcse@gmail.com

Namita Gupta, Prasenjit Chatterjee and Tanupriya Choudhury (eds.) Smart and Sustainable Intelligent Systems, (215–228)
© 2021 Scrivener Publishing LLC

In this project, we have tried to prepare a machine learning [25] model which can help us in resolving the issue of duplicacy. Our algorithm will use the concept of NLP (Natural Language Processing), and pattern recognition to access similarities and judge if we can merge this question.

Natural language processing [12] (NLP) is the branch of artificial intelligence gives the computer the ability to understand human language and speech. The problem with the computer is that it can only understand precise words and sentences but we normally don't use precise language to communicate with others. Hence we need to convert our text into a form which can be understood by the computer. The processing of the natural language into a form which can be understood by computer is known as Natural Language Processing. Needless, to say we used NLP a lot to tackle our problem.

We had to work hard as we had to learn a few algorithms and had to Google a lot to get ideas about the project. While constant searching we learned about this competition where we had to create a model to find duplicacy [19] in the questions on Quora. We went one step ahead as we tried to implement this idea on various social media platforms which might make the experience even better for the users.

In the beginning, we learned that logistic regression can be a good idea to implement but it didn't give us very good results as the accuracy was less than 80%. Complex algorithms like xG boosting with Count Vectorizer and TF-IDF Vectorizer gave much better results.

The best results were given by the Random Forest algorithm which gave us an accuracy of 83%. In the given paper, we have compared the results of different algorithms which will help us to decide the best algorithm to sort our problem.

16.2   Literature Survey

The concept of the problem involves, that we use pattern recognition and decision trees-based models. Our survey includes the study of various techniques programmers have used, in order to improve the accuracy, better-trained models and better predictions.

The algorithms vary from regression to random forest and deep learning models like LSTM.

Some of our studied papers include:

16.2.1   Duplicate Quora Questions Detection by Lei Guo, Chong Li & Haiming Tian

They used two approaches to solve this problem. The main idea of both approaches was to first perform feature extraction of all questions and then train and predict. In the first approach, they vectorize all words based on Google's Word2Vec model but there is a problem in this method that two words with different word appearances could have very similar vector representation this loss is compensated by TF-IDF weights [20]. In the second approach, they used LSTM (long short term memory) recurrent neural network. LSTM has a special input requirement, to fulfill that requirement, they assigned a unique ID to every word based on its frequency of occurrence in the dataset. The weight thus assigned is based on the word2vec model. To put it simply, the whole approach was based on Keras deep learning library. They used a different classification method for the first approach like Decision Tree, Random Forest, KNN, and SVM. As the KNN method gives the least mean square error, so they finally choose to use the KNN model the second approach a simple built-in evaluation function was there so no classification method was there.

Accuracy Score: 77% using LSTM.

16.2.2 Natural Language Understanding with the Quora Question Pairs Dataset by Lakshay Sharma, Laura Graesser, Nikita Nangia, Utku Evci

In this paper, they explored Natural Language Understanding (NLU) and tried several algorithms to check to get the best accuracy. They used various machine learning algorithms including the linear, tree-based, and even neural network models. They started with building linear models, three in number, they tried 3 combinations of the n-gram. In all the 3 combinations they used logistic regression only with stochastic gradient descent, they tested unigram features, bigram features, and trigram features, trigram gave the best results [21]. Now they used support vector machine but the RBF kernel SVM was taking much time with lesser accuracy so they used only linear kernel SVM. For improving accuracy they tried varying penalty term c, whose optimal value (i.e. 0.19) gave the best results for SVM with trigram features. They also tried plane sentence embedding to try for accuracy in linear models. Then came Tree-based models but with a challenge that features in linear based models cannot be extracted as it is for trees as the tree-based models use decision splitting, so they added some misc features in the dataset and removed punctuation. They then finally tested 5 different neural networks namely CBOW, LSTM, BiLSTM, LSTM with word-by-word attention and BiLSTM with word-by-word attention. After trying so many algorithms they got the best accuracy from the continuous bags of words, neural network models. Apart from this hit and trial they also conducted error analysis to improve the results.

Accuracy Score: 83% using Continuous Bags of Words Model.

16.2.3 Duplicate Detection in Programming Question Answering Communities by Wei Emma Zhang and Quan Z. Sheng, Macquarie University

This model is an improvement to an existing model of developing a two-stage "ranking-classification" detection method. Initially, they had done some preprocessing tailored to the programming related questions [18, 22]. In the first stage of duplicate detection, they had selected candidate questions by giving ranking to all historical questions and selecting top-ranked ones. For this, they used 3 ranking algorithms and the main thing is that ranking among candidates is not important only those question needs to be selected that are possible duplicate and asked frequently. In the second stage of the same previous technique is followed by some advancement training of classifiers.

The generated three types of features for each question pair (vector similarity, relevance, association) Different classification techniques are used like KNN, Naive Bayes. Ada Boosting, Logistic regression, Random Forest, etc. with every feature and recorded the performance.

Accuracy Score: 88% using Ada Boosting algorithm.

16.2.4   Exploring Deep Learning in Semantic Question Matching by Arpan Poudel and Ashwin Dhakal [1]

They used data splitting in the ratio of 9:1 which gave them a test set of 10% & training set of 90%. Their 10% test set data is of 40,429, it symbolizes they used a dataset of around 4 lakh. They tried to extract more information about the dataset using the bags of words model and Google news vectors. They tried six different supervised machine learning algorithms but didn't get great results. So they made an artificial neural network design consisting of five hidden layers and 15 best parameters. Then they used batch sizes of 32 and 16 epochs to train their model and got much better results.

Accuracy Score: 81% using Random Forest.

From the above literature surveys, we noticed that accuracy in the range of 80s is par. Most research papers managed to get an accuracy of more than 80% and they achieved it with varying methods. Boosting and Random Forest was very popular among the programmers to tackle this problem.

16.3   Methods Applied for Training

16.3.1   Count Vectorizer

Count Vectorizer is an extension of the Bags of Words model [30]. The Bags of Words model is the latest method to extract features from the text in ML [17]. In the Count vectorizer technique, all the words are counted and the frequency for every word is calculated. Then the correlation among different sentences is found.

All the given sentences and paragraphs can be converted into a map of words with their frequencies, which can be represented as. For example:

"It was the best time to invest in the stock market",
"How to invest in stock market",
"How should I learn ML",
"What to do, so as to become expert ML",
"it" = 1 , "was" = 1 , "the" = 1 , "best" = 1 , "time" = 1, "stock" = 2, "market"=2
    "How" = 2 , "invest" = 2 , "in" = 2 , "should" = 1 , "learn" = 1 "what" = 1
"to" =4, "do"=1, "so"=1, "as" =1, "become"=1, "expert"=1, "ML" =2

Count Vectorizer's technique is based on Frequency, i.e. where we count the occurrences of words. and further process our dataset.

In our dataset of four lakh entries, the Count Vectorizer converted this whole dataset into lists instead of words. Those lists contained the frequencies of the words in that particular, and those frequencies served the purpose of telling if the two questions were similar or not.

Working:
    Step 1: We need to collect the data [26].
    Here you can see a small part of the dataset.
    "It was the best time to invest in stock market",

"How to invest in stock market",
"How should I learn ML",
"What to do, so as to become expert ML",

Step 2: Design the Vocabulary
We will convert our sentences into our vocabulary
The unique words given are:

"it"	"should"	"was"	"learn"
"best"	"What"	"the"	"ML"
"to"	"so"	"time"	"do"
"in"	"expert"	"invest"	"as"
"stocks"	"become"	"How"	"stock"
"in"	"market"		

We can see that there are 30 words but they are comprised of just 22 different words.

Step 3: We then need to create document vectors.
Now that we have map ready, we will assign a weight to each word.
Our aim for this step is to turn our sentences into vectors so that we can use them as i/o in our algorithm.
The vocabulary has 22 words, so we can use a fixed-length document-representation of different scoring words.
As we have our vocabulary prepared, so every word has to be given suitable weights or score the word.
Some additional simple scoring methods include:

1. Counts. Counting each word's occurrence in our dataset.
2. Frequencies calculation.

16.3.2   TF-IDF Vectorizer

This method is very important in information retrieval or text mining as it can be used to measure the importance of a certain word. Different words have different importance [16] so if two questions have words of less importance it won't make an impact on the outlook and vice versa.

As mentioned above, Count Vectorizer gives a matrix in terms of a number of occurrences of a certain word. On the other hand, the TF-IDF Vectorizer [5] gives a normalized score on the basis of the weight of the word.

Let us two important formulas of this concept:
Inverse document frequency is mathematically represented as
IDF = Log [(Number of documents) / (Number of documents containing the word)]
TF = (Number of repetitions of a word in a document) / (# of words in a document)

Working:

    Step 1: Tokenize the sentences, which mean that we will just convert the sentences to the words. Then we will calculate the frequency of words in each sentence.

    Step 2: Calculate the term frequency and make the matrix.

TF = (Number of repetitions of a word in a document) / (# of words in a document)

Similarly, generate the Inverse Document Frequency (IDF) and make the matrix

IDF =Log [(Number of documents) / (Number of documents containing the word)] [27]

    Step 3: TF-IDF is the name given because it accounts for the scores generated by both TF and IDF as we multiply both. Then the scores are calculated and given to the words.

    Step 4: Then the sentence scores are generated and the questions are compared to check if they are similar or different.

16.3.3 XG Boosting

In the University of Washington, this algorithm [14] was developed as a research project. While artificial neural networks have the ability to give the best results for complex text and data, this XG Boosting technique (Figure 16.1) is brilliant when it comes to medium-sized text.

    The algorithm is different from other algorithms due to these things:

1. XG Boost can support a lot of applications as it can be used to solve regression, classification, and ranking problems.
2. It is a very portable algorithm as it can be used in Windows, Linux and even Mac, which makes it very useful.
3. Another benefit of this algorithm is to support a number of languages like Java, C++., Python and even more.

Working:

    Step 1: Clean and pre-process the text.

    Step 2: Use Count Vectorizer and TF-IDF Vectorizer as an extension of bags of words model.

    Step 3: Apply xG boost [24] with the given specifications to get the best results.
        max_depth = 50.
        n_estimators = 80
        objective = 'binary:logistic' eta = 0.3

Figure 16.1 Evolution of XG boosting.

Actually, xG Boosting [13] has emerged as the best algorithm (Figure 16.2), especially in terms of time taken by it.

Logistic Regression is one of the most famous models in machine learning. The function is named after the core function which is the building block of the technique i.e. Logistic function. This function is also known as the sigmoid function and it is shown as:

$$1 / (1 + e^\wedge\text{-value})$$

This is a special function because it gives the result between zero and one, no matter how big the value is.

When we draw the graph for the given function it is something shaped like 'S' (Figure 16.3).

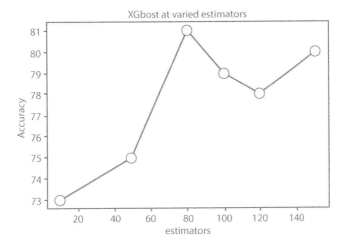

Figure 16.2 XGboost at varied estimator.

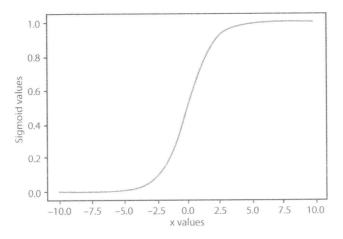

Figure 16.3 Graph of logistic regression.

This is an awesome system for binary classification problems like our problem. In our problem, we need to tell if the two questions are similar or not, hence logistic regression [8] is the perfect solution to our query.

We need to ensure that there is no overfitting [4], which can make it difficult for them to fit new data.

Working:

Step 1: First, we need to pre-process and clean the data.

Step 2: Then we need to create the train and test data set. We divided it in 4:1 ratio, after multiple trials with other ratios.

Step 3: Call Logistic Regression Library (Figure 16.5).

Step 4: Fit test and train data in the regression.

Step 5: Get the prediction (Figure 16.4).

16.3.4 Random Forest Classifier

Random Forest is another system for binary classification problems like our problem. As the name suggests, it consists of a number of decision trees that give the answer if something belongs to class zero or one. Basically, Decision Trees are the building blocks of the

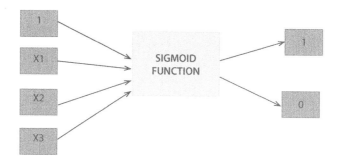

Figure 16.4 Sigmoid Function.

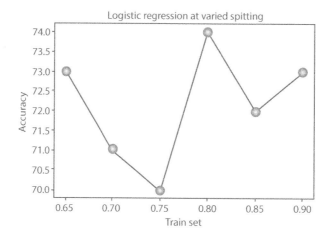

Figure 16.5 Logistic regression at varied data splitting.

random forest [7]. It also uses ensemble learning [3, 15]. When a group of a number of uncorrelated trees is asked to give a decision, they are very likely to give the right decision. So when a lot of trees are together, the decision is given on the basis of the votes of all the members.

Working:

Step 1: The text is clean.

Step 2: The Random Classifier library is called.

Step 3: We try a different number of trees, like 50, 100, 150, etc. but we got the optimal result for 125 (Figure 16.6).

Step 4: Finally, the answer is given on the basis of votes of all the given trees.

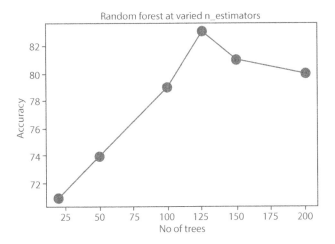

Figure 16.6 Random forest graph with different no. of trees.

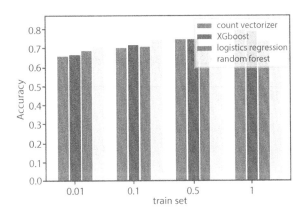

Figure 16.7 Comparison of all models at various data sampling rates.

Comparison of Models Used (Figure 16.7)

Model	Precision	Recall	Accuracy
XGB	0.80	0.80	0.79
Logistic regression	0.75	0.73	0.74
SGDC	0.73	0.75	0.74
Random forest	0.81	0.82	0.83

16.4   Proposed Methodology

16.4.1   Data Collection

We got the dataset [11] from Kaggle, where we trained our model to perfect it. This project aims at making easier and better for everyone involved with Quora and other websites modeled on this giant. We collected lots of data labeled by humans as duplicate or non-duplicate. As the data provided to us was labeled we tried to supervise learning algorithms to tackle this problem.

16.4.2   Data Analysis

We first analyzed the data to get an idea if the data was imbalanced or not. If it was imbalanced our focus would have been to precision and recall rather than accuracy but we checked the labels and found out that the data was very balanced. So we moved to the next step which was cleaning and pre-processing of the data.

16.4.3   Data Cleaning and Pre-Processing

Data cleaning [9] is one of the important steps in machine learning algorithms. A lot of time needs to be spent on data cleaning because arranging the data in the desired form is important to apply algorithms on it. This involves removing or correcting incorrect data so it can be useful to us. Some problems with the data which need to process by data cleaning techniques are redundancy, inconsistency, inappropriate data, and missing data.

Data required some preprocessing [2, 10]

- Remove repeating whitespace characters (spaces, tabs, line breaks). Convert tabs and line breaks to spaces.
- Remove stopwords. These include the most commonly occurring words in a language, like "the," "on," "is," etc.
- Convert all text to required cases.
- Replace short forms to full forms like to have.
- Convert US English to standard English.
- Put correct punctuations and articles.

16.4.4   Embedding

Embedding maps words in a text document to number space (these number-space representations are called word vectors). We have to use Fast text embedding [6]. The Fast text model for English is pre-trained on Common Crawl and Wikipedia text. The fast text represents each word as a set of sub-words or character n-grams. For example, the word "fishing" is represented, assuming a subword length of 3 (trigram), as follows: {'fishing', 'fis', 'ish', 'shi', 'hin', 'in').

16.4.5   Feature Extraction

We tried the bags of words model where we mapped the words with their frequencies in the dataset. For that, we used both count vectorizer, which creates a map of words with their respective frequencies, while processing a sentence these maps are used to assign values to sentences and TF-IDF vectorizer, which also creates a map, but it assigns weights to words that are inversely proportional to their occurrence in the set, now these weights are mapped with the input sentences to calculate values for sentences, and used for similarity processing. Using these we got much more information about our datasets, and we were ready to use this information in our algorithms.

16.4.6   Data Splitting

We divided our data set into the test and training set and tried a number of different algorithms to see which gets better results. It is important to find a good balance between training and test set because if our training set is too less, the model won't learn much. Similarly, if we take too much data in training set, we will have to face over fitting, hence finding balance is the key.

16.4.7   Modeling

XG Boosting was one of the models picked by us, and after a lot of hit and trial, we got the best results after using 50 as the value of max depth and 80 as the number of estimators.

Logistic Regression is a very popular classifier for such problems but it didn't fare well so we moved onto the random forest where we got the best results.

16.5   Observations

We have achieved an accuracy of around 83% with the Random forest classifier after the training of the data on a sample of 4 lakh entries. As explained in Figure 16.1 the evolution of XG boosting techniques, so we used them to our model, leaving us with an accuracy of varying from 71–80% for varying estimators as given in Figure 16.2.

From Figure 16.5 we can infer that logistic regression increased with the increase in the share of the test set. It varied from 67–74% depending on the share of the test set.

Finally, in Figure 16.6 we can see the relation between a number of trees and accuracy in the random forest. We got the best results at 125 trees where the accuracy peaked at 83%.

In Figure 16.7, we compared all the models together, plotting them in the same graph. Random Forest consistently gave the best performance.

16.6　Conclusion

Our goal was to specify if the two questions are similar by looking at the two questions. To solve this complex problem we used a dataset provided by Quora. We trained various machine learning algorithms which had four lakh entries, so we can tell if two questions are similar are not.

After doing the required cleaning and data-preprocessing, we applied various algorithms. First, we applied Logistic regression which gave us poor results. So we tried xG boosting with Count Vectorizer and TF-IDF Vectorizer which gave us an accuracy over 80%.

The best results were achieved with Random Forest with 125 trees, so we got an accuracy of 83% which is quite good. In the future, we would like to apply deep learning techniques with various weights to get even better results.

References

1. Dhakal, A., Poudel, A., Pandey, S., Gaire, S., Baral, H.P., Exploring Deep Learning in Semantic Question Matching. *2018 IEEE 3rd International Conference on Computing, Communication and Security (ICCCS)*, 2018.
2. Alasadi, S., Review of Data Preprocessing Techniques in Data Mining. *J. Eng. Appl. Sci.*, 12, 4102–4107, 2017.
3. Polikar, R., Ensemble Learning, in: *Ensemble Machine Learning*, pp. 1–34, 2012.
4. Campillo-Gimenez, B., Jouini, W., Bayat, S., Cuggia, M., Improving case-based reasoning systems by combining k-nearest neighbor algorithm with logistic regression in the prediction of patients' registration on the renal transplant waiting list. *PLoS One*, 8, 9, e71991, 2013.
5. Jing, L.-P., Huang, H.-K., Shi, H.-B., Improved feature selection approach TFIDF in text mining. *Proceedings: International Conference on Machine Learning and Cybernetics*.
6. Wieting, J., Bansal, M., Gimpel, K., Livescu, K., Towards Universal paraphrastic sentence embeddings, *arXiv* preprintarXiv:1511.08198, Conference paper:ICLR 2016, pp. 1, 2015.
7. *Classification: Theory—Decision Trees and Random Forest*, Web article, 2018.
8. Application of Logistic Regression with Different Sampling Models, in: *Applied Logistic Regression*, pp. 203–222, 2005.
9. Exploratory Data Mining and Data Cleaning: An Overview, *Exploratory Data Mining and Data Cleaning Wiley Series in Probability and Statistics*, pp. 1–16, New Jersey, Wiley, 2003.
10. Hari, R. and Puce, A., Data Acquisition and Preprocessing, in: *MEG-EEG Primer*, pp. 89–97, 2017.
11. Phan, X.H., Horiguchi, S., Ho, T.B., Automated data extraction from the web with conditional models. *Int. J. Bus. Intell. Data Min.*, 1, 2, 194, 2005.
12. Nerbonne, J., *Natural Language Processing in Computer-Assisted Language Learning*, Oxford Handbooks Online, Oxford, 2012.
13. Network Intrusion Detection System using XG Boost. *Int. J. Eng. Adv. Technol. Regular Issue*, 9, 1, 4070–4073, 2019.
14. Chakravarthy, D.G. and Kannimuthu, S., Extreme Gradient Boost Classification Based Interesting User Patterns Discovery for Web Service Composition. *Mobile Netw. Appl.*, 6, 4, 2019.

15. Pachange, S., Joglekar, B., Kulkarni, P., An ensemble classifier approach for disease diagnosis using Random Forest. *2015 Annual IEEE India Conference (INDICON)*, 2015.
16. Medved', M. and Horák, A., Sentence and Word Embedding Employed in Open Question-Answering. *Proceedings of the 10th International Conference on Agents and Artificial Intelligence*, 2018.
17. Feng, Y. and Zhang, Y., Deep Web query interface schema matching based on matching degree and semantic similarity. *J. Comput. Appl.*, 32, 6, 1688–1691, 2013.
18. Zhang, W.E., Sheng, Q.Z., Lau, J.H., Abebe, E., Ruan, W., Duplicate Detection in Programming Question Answering Communities. *ACM Trans. Internet Technol.*, 18, 3, 1–21, 2018.
19. Silva, R.F.G., Paixao, K.V., Maia, M.D.A., Duplicate Question Detection in Stack Overflow: A Reproducibility Study, *Evolution and Reengineering (SANER 2018)*, 25, 3–6, 2018.
20. Guo, L., Li, C., Tian, H., *Duplicate quora question detection*, Semantic Scholar, online, 2013.
21. Sharma, L., Graesser, L., Nangia, N., Evci, U., Natural Language Understanding with the Quora Question Pairs Dataset, 2017.
22. Zhang, W.E., Sheng, Q.Z., Lau, J.H., Abebe, E., Ruan, W., Duplicate Detection in Programming Question Answering Communities, *ACM Trans. Internet Technol.*, 3–17, 18, 2018.
23. Quora Insincere Questions Classification. [Online]. Available:https://kaggle.com/c/quora-insincere-questions-classification.[Accessed: 29-Sep-2019].
24. Brownlee, J., *Loss and Loss Functions for Training Deep Learning neural networks, machinelearningmastery.com*, 28-Jan-2019, [Online]. Available:https://machinelearningmastery.com/loss-and-loss-functions-fortraining-deep-learning-neural-networks/.International Journal of Scientific & Engineering Research Volume 10, Issue 7, July-2019 2004 IJSER © 2019http://www.ijser.org IJSER.
25. Eremenko, K. and de Ponteves, H., *Machine Learning A-Z (Python & R In Data Science Course)*, Udemy, [Online]. Available: https://www.udemy.com/machinelearning/. [Accessed: 22-Oct-2019].
26. D.D.J.D. Scientist, *Machine Learning Mastery, Machine Learning Mastery*. [Online]. Available: https://machinelearningmastery.com/. [Accessed: Oct-Nov-2019].
27. Probability and Statistics Topic Index, Statistics How To. [Online]. Available: http://www.statisticshowto.com/correlation-matrix. [Accessed: 21-Sep-2019].
28. *Project Jupyter*, Project Jupyter, [Online]. Available: http://jupyter.org/. [Accessed: 13-Oct-2019].
29. *Python Programming Tutorials*, Python Programming Tutorials, [Online]. Available: https://pythonprogramming.net/. [Accessed: 15-Oct-2019].
30. D'Souza, J., An Introduction to Bag-of-Words in NLP, Medium, 04-Apr-2018. [Online]. Available: https://medium.com/greyatom/an-introduction-to-bag-of-words-in-nlp-ac967d43b428. [Accessed: 13-Oct-2019].

Exploration of Pixel-Based and Object-Based Change Detection Techniques by Analyzing ALOS PALSAR and LANDSAT Data

Amit Kumar Shakya[1*], **Ayushman Ramola**[1] and **Anurag Vidyarthi**[2]

[1]Sant Longowal Institute of Engineering and Technology, Sangrur, India
[2]Graphic Era (Deemed to be University), Dehardun, India

Abstract

Land use/Land cover classification is essential from the point of Earth explorations and scientific investigation. Earlier, the land-use and land cover changes are monitored with the assistance of the pixel-based approach, and now objects based approaches have taken their place. In the pixel-based approach, image pixels are examined to monitor the changes developed in land use and land cover. The newly developed method in the field of remote sensing is object-based change detection (OBCD) techniques. These approaches have entirely changed the study of remotely sensing and satellite image processing. The pixel-based approach made a comparison based on changing pixels between two or a series of images. In contrast, the object-based approach constitutes the formation of objects (classes), *e.g.*, water, urban, agriculture, soil, etc., between two images and making a comparison between them. One of the important accept of these techniques is how accurately they provide us information about the changes in the nearby surrounding. This paper begins with the development of traditional pixel-based methods and ends with the evolution of the latest object-based change detection techniques. LANDSAT and PALSAR images are used to represent the changes developed in the land use/ land cover using pixel-based and object-based approaches.

Keywords: Remote sensing, satellite image processing, pixel-based change detection, object-based change detection, LANDSAT, PALSAR

17.1 Introduction

In the field of remote sensing (RS), change assessment is an essential area of examination. Changes developed in the Earth surface occurs due to both natural and human-made interference on the Earth's surface. Deforestation, nuclear chemical accidents, urbanization, overpopulation, etc. are some man-made interference while landslides, avalanche, cyclones, floods, droughts, earthquakes, volcanic eruptions, wildfires, etc. are some natural disasters caused due to excessive human interference [1, 2]. These changes affect the land-use (LU) and

---

[*]Corresponding author: xlamitshakya.gate2014@ieee.og

Namita Gupta, Prasenjit Chatterjee and Tanupriya Choudhury (eds.) Smart and Sustainable Intelligent Systems, (229–244)

land-cover (LC) at a varying rate from place to place. Hansen *et al.* [3] presented an investigation of global warming using pale climate data and explained there adverse impacts on young people, future generations, and Mother Nature. Wan [4] developed a novel "phase correlation decomposition" model to analyze the joint effect of various illumination factors affecting the satellite images. They used a pixel-based approach in their investigation. National Aeronautics and Space Administration (NASA) [5] used the image differencing (ID) technique to quantify the amount of urban land cover changes from April 1973 to April 1975 for Austin, Texas. Marinelli *et al.* [6] developed a novel change detection technique based on pixel selection for hyper spectral satellite images. The objective of their research work is to improve the pixel quality in each band resulting in the overall improvement of the image quality. Cao *et al.* [7] developed a novel change detection method based upon "conditional random field (CRF)." In their advanced process, they have improved the image quality by enhancing the pixel intensity. Their method also acts as an alternative for noise reduction because their proposed CRF automatically removes noise from the image. Zhang *et al.* [8] developed a scale based algorithm for obtaining changes from the satellite images. In their experiment, they used very high resolution (VHR) satellite images. Their developed algorithm work on the fusion of both pixel-based and object-based techniques the result produced by them are shown on SPOT 5 and GF 1 images. Bruzzone *et al.* [9] discussed a problem related to the unsupervised classification, which gets developed by different images. To overcome these problems, they developed two methods based on Bayes theorem and Markov random field. Feng *et al.* [10] used the scale factor to establish an improvement in the image analysis. They have taken multiple images and perform various image processing operations like stacking, segmentation, and correlation on the image to improve its quality. Their proposed method outperforms different existing techniques of image classification and analysis. Dymond *et al.* [11] studied the strength of the means of RS in forest management and ecology. They observed that the phonological information in satellite images and vegetation indices have independently improved the classification. They used two techniques for classification, i.e., ID and Tasseled Cap classification, and concluded that phonological changes of forest were accurately observed by combining both theme thods. Ramachandra *et al.* [12] used the ID technique to detect changes and to obtain the histogram for the difference image for developing a Geographic Resources Decision Support System for analyzing LU and LC. Cheng *et al.* [13] located locations of landslides and then used the multi-temporal ID technique to obtain a difference image band ratio, which was used to calculate the grey level threshold for change detection. In Ref. [14] scientist reviewed various binary methods of CD and concluded that the ID gives better results than image rationing when moist forest area is under investigation. Brewer *et al.* [15] analyse the field under fire and evaluate the behavior of the pre-fire area and compare them with the post-fire area. They concluded that the results produced from the ID method are more acceptable when compared with Normalized Burn Ratio (NDR) NDR/4 and NDR/5 methods. Nordberg [16] used the ID technique to obtain three change images, i.e., change the image in brightness ΔB, greenness ΔG, and wetness ΔW. Finally, all three different images were added up together to obtain a single difference image and the normalized difference vegetation indices (NDVI), which proves to be the most efficient method. Lin *et al.* [17] used the ID technique to observe and quantifies the rate of recovery in the vegetation caused due to the landslide caused by an earthquake in the state of Taiwan. Zhang [18] used the image ratio technique to obtain superior accuracy for further JPEG compression. Kim [19] used the image regression technique to get an excellent resolution in high-resolution images. Ma *et al.* [20] used vegetation differencing techniques to monitor the content of dust in the region of Change River. Besides this, more information about various other pre-classification change detection techniques can be obtained from Refs. [21, 22]. Object-based change detection techniques are beneficial, and they are used these days extensively in the field of remote sensing [23]. Detailed information about these techniques can be obtained from Ref. [24]. Yang *et al.* [25] used a hyper spectral remote sensing approach to improve the performance of the classifier, which is used to classify satellite images. The organization of this paper is as follows: in Section 17.2, details about various pixel-based and object-based change detection techniques are presented. In Section 17.3 experimental result is presented. Finally in Section 17.4, concluding remarks about the research work are explained.

17.2 Classification of Pixel-Based and Object-Based Change Detection Methods

The change detection methods for image classification are divided into two broad categories pixel-based change detection methods and object-based change detection methods. Pixel-based methods are used in early times, and object-based have gained popularity these days. In a pixel-based change detection image, pixels are analyzed as a whole based on window size to analyze image texture. In object-based change detection method, image is classified based on classes formed in a model for investigation. These classes are samples in the form of water, agriculture, tall vegetation, short vegetation, dry soil, wet soil, forest, mountains, etc. Here we have investigated both methods mathematically and practically. Some standard pixel-based change detection method includes image differencing [26], image ratio, image regression, vegetation index differencing, principal component analysis [27], etc., the object-based method includes minimum distance classification (MDC), maximum likelihood classification (MLC), spectral angle mapper (SAM), spectral angle divergence, parallelepiped classification, support vector machine (SVM), and artificial neural network [28]. Nowadays deep learning approach is also gaining popularity.

Pixel-based image classification techniques provide information about image features based on pixel counts. These pixel values are also known as digital numbers (DN). They are used to analyze the texture of the image. Detail information about some pixel-based change detection like image ratio, model differencing, image regression, vegetation index differencing is presented as follows.

17.2.1 Image Ratio

In this approach of change detection, two images of different time intervals are rationed to obtain an output image, which is having various features value. Let the images at different time interval are I_1 and I_2 having (p, q) pixel position. Then the ratio of both the images is defined as $I_{Ratio}(p, q)$, which is expressed by Equation (17.1).

$$I_{Ratio}(p,q) = \frac{I_1(p,q)}{I_2(p,q)} \tag{17.1}$$

The range of the image ratio is $I_{Ratio} \in (0, \infty)$, if $I_{Ratio} = 1$ than the normalized value of $I_{Ratio}(p, q)$ is obtained by the Equation (17.2).

$$I_{Ratio}(p,q) = arc \tan \frac{I_1(p,q)}{I_2(p,q)} - \frac{\pi}{4} \qquad (17.2)$$

The ratio of two images in different time intervals is defined within the range $\left[\frac{-\pi}{4}, \frac{\pi}{4} \right]$. Image ratio of two different multispectral images is considered as a new method for change detection. This method provides information about the developed changes directly and easily to the users.

17.2.2   Image Differencing

In this approach, multi-temporal images belonging to the same geographical area from the same satellite and sensors taken at two different time intervals are subtracted from each other to obtain a new model, which is known as a "difference image." As the name suggests in this approach, images of two different time intervals are subtracted from each other. This method is based on a simple mathematical procedure in which subtraction is performed to obtain the output image.

Equation (17.3) expresses the mathematical expression to obtain a difference image from two multitemporal images.

$$I_{diff}(p, q)[Newly\ developed\ image] = I_1(p, q) - I_2(p, q) \qquad (17.3)$$

Here I_1 and I_2 are the images obtained at the time t_1 and time t_2 respectively, (p, q) are the coordinates belonging to pixels position, I_{diff} represents the intensity difference between the images. Assume that the change due to LC is less as compared to other factors, than we expect that the difference developed in the land cover is distributed mainly around the mean value. For the zero mean difference distribution, the mathematical expression is expressed by Equation (17.4).

$$(\bar{I}_2(p,q)) = \frac{\sigma_1}{\sigma_2}(I_2(p,q) - \mu_2) + \mu_1 \qquad (17.4)$$

Where $\bar{I}_2$ is the image represented in the normalized form of I_2, μ_1, σ_1 and μ_2, σ_2 are the mean and standard deviation (SD) respectively of (initial image) I_1 and (final image) I_2. After performing the image normalization, the mean and SD of the two satellite images are equalized.

Thus the difference image developed will have a value equivalent to zero, which is expressed by the Equation (17.5).

$$I_{diff}(p,q) = |I_1(p,q) - \bar{I}_2(p,q)| \qquad (17.5)$$

17.2.3   Image Regression

It is defined as the procedure to estimate the relationship between the dependent variable and the independent variables present in an image. One of the purest forms of image regression is linear image regression. Mathematically image regression can be understood from Equation (17.6) where the mathematical operation is performed to obtain regression between image pixels.

$$\overline{I}_2(p,q) = a \times I_1(p,q) + b \tag{17.6}$$

To obtain the value of a and b, we define square error between the measured data and the predicted data. The sum of the squared error is represented by the Equation (17.7).

$$e^2 = (I_2(p,q) - \overline{I}_2(p,q))^2 = (I_2(p,q) - a\, I_1(p,q) - b)^2 \tag{17.7}$$

The sum of the squares error when calculated from First to N pixels is expressed by the Equation (17.8).

$$S = \sum_{n=1}^{N} e^2 = \sum_{n=1}^{N} (I_2(p_n,q_n) - aI_1(p_n,q_n) - b)^2 \tag{17.8}$$

Calculating the partial derivative of $w.r.t\, b$ and is expressed by the Equation (17.9).

$$\frac{\partial s}{\partial b} = -2 \sum_{n=1}^{N} (I_2(p_n,q_n) - aI_1(p_n,q_n) - b) \tag{17.9}$$

17.2.4   Vegetation Index Differencing

The vegetation index is a unique feature of satellite remote sensing through which vegetation of an area is monitored through different temporal features investigation. It mainly works through analyzing the photosynthesis area of the agricultural fields. It is further divided into "Normalized difference vegetation index (NDVI), Soil adjusted vegetation index (SAVI), and Enhanced vegetation index (EVI)."A mathematical expression representing the Normalised difference vegetation index is expressed by Equation (17.10), which is the ratio of the difference and summation of Near Infrared and Red band, respectively.

In the map (Figure 17.1), the "Negative values of NDVI (values approaching −1) correspond to water. Values close to zero (−0.1 to 0.1) generally correspond to barren areas of rock, sand, or snow. Lastly, low, positive values represent shrub and grassland (approximately 0.2 to 0.4), while high values indicate temperate and tropical rainforests (values approaching 1)". The pictorial representation of the NDVI technique for the green plant and non-green plant is shown the Figure 17.2. For green plants, 50% of the near-infrared rays are reflected, and only 8% of the visible light is reflected. In the non-green plant, 40%

Figure 17.1 Global soil moisture map indicating different levels is moisture [29].

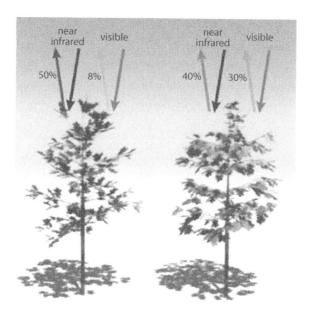

Figure 17.2 Normalized difference vegetation index (NDVI) representation of the green and non-green plant.

of the near-infrared rays are revealed, and 30% of the visible light is reflected. Thus from the NDVI technique, we can conclude that green plants absorb more visible light as compared with the less green plant. Therefore NDVI technique can also be used to measure the amount of greenness in the plants and trees.

$$\text{NDVI} = \frac{(\text{NIR} - Red)}{(\text{NIR} + Red)} \quad\quad (17.10)$$

Here NIR is near-infrared, and Red is the red channel present in the plant. The range of NDVI is [− 1, 1]. If the NDVI is close to 1, then it indicates that the area is highly "green." NDVI values close to negative (−1) indicate no vegetation. In some cases, they are also considered as water.

Study of change detection techniques through "Object-based change detection methodology."

"Object-based change detection" or OBCD is used to classify the image into small and different objects these objects are created with a set of pixels under consideration, like water, bare soil, agricultural, deserts, etc. There are several image classification techniques, and here we are presenting a summary of Minimum distance classification (MDC), Maximum likelihood classification (MLC), Spectral angle mapper (SAM) and Support vector machine (SVM).

17.2.5   Minimum Distance Classification

This technique is used to classify unknown image data. In this approach, the distance between the pixel of interest and sample pixel (class) is reduced. The length can be expressed as a parameter for similarity, so the minimum distance is identified by the maximum similarity. This is represented by Equation (17.11).

$$d_{x_{tp}\mu_c} = \sqrt{\left(x_{tp}^2 - \mu_c^2\right)} \qquad (17.11)$$

Where (x_{tp}) is the test pixel.
(μ_c) = mean value of the cluster, class, or object.

17.2.6   Maximum Likelihood Classification

It is considered as an essential method for satellite image analysis in which pixels of images are classified with maximum likelihood with the corresponding data. The mathematical expression representing the development of the maximum likely hood between the image pixels is described in Equation (17.12).

$$L_p(x) = \frac{1}{(2\pi)^{n/2} \sum k^{\frac{1}{2}}} \exp\left[-\frac{1}{2(x-\mu_p) \sum_p^{-1} (x-\mu_p)^{-1}} \right] \qquad (17.12)$$

Where x = data of the image in n band
$Lp(x)$ = likelihood of object class x belonging to class p
μ_p = mean vector representation of class k
$\sum_p$ = representation of the variance matrix and covariance matrix

17.2.7   Spectral Angle Mapper (SAM)

In SAM, a particular spectrum of the area under consideration is compared with another spectrum *i.e.*, with a reference spectrum. The function of this object-based change detection

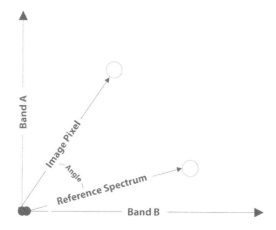

Figure 17.3 Spectral angle mapper.

technique is to calculate the similarity between the two different images. The SAM classifier is represented by Figure 17.3.

17.2.8   Support Vector Machine

The support vector machine is a type of supervised learning algorithm for data analysis and study using a machine learning approach. It is used for image classification into objects and regression data analysis purposes. SVM can effectively perform nonlinear image regression as well as linear image regression based upon Kernal principals. In the SVM algorithm, there is a hyperplane that separates two different supporting vectors, *i.e.*, support vector 1 and support vector 2. The pixels are two classified in two different categories, which lie at one side and the other side of the hyperplane [30]. These pixels are represented by the yellow and blue colors in Figure 17.4. This algorithm was developed by "Hava Siegelmann" and "Vladimir Vapnik," the primary objective while developing these algorithms was to support computer vision and pattern reorganization. Still, later this algorithm becomes quite useful in image analysis and satellite remote sensing applications. Today this algorithm is quite helpful for soil moisture retrievals, image classification, and several other satellite application purposes.

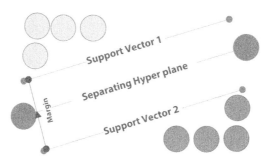

Figure 17.4 Support vector machine hyper loop diagram.

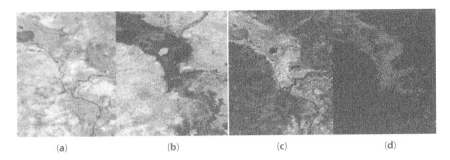

Figure 17.5 Cambodia flood LANDSAT data (a) pre-flood (b) post-flood (c) image differencing (d) image.

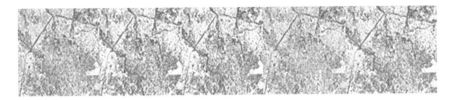

Figure 17.6 PALSAR data (Roorkee) (a) first band, (b) second band, (c) third band, (d) fourth band, (e) band fused PALSAR data.

17.3   Experimental Results

Here we are presenting the results of visual image representation obtained after applying the image differencing and image ratio change detection technique. Here we have taken two false-color pre- and post-flood satellite images of River Mekong, Cambodia, shown in Figure 17.5(a) and (b) respectively obtained from NASA Earth Observatory [29]. Pixel-based change detection image differencing and image ratio results are shown in Figure 17.5(c) and (d), respectively. The image differencing and image ratio is performed using Matlab software.

Here we have observed that the image differencing is useful for providing a better visual interpretation of the image, but such useful information is not retrieved in the image ratio. Now we have taken PALSAR data and classified the PALSAR data through object-based change detection using ENVI 4.8 software. The four different bands of PALSAR data are represented in Figure 17.6(a–d). All the bands are stacked together using the "layer stacking technique" available in ENVI 4.8, the resultant image obtained from as a band fused PALSAR data is shown in Figure 17.6(e).

Similarly, through object-based change detection techniques, PALSAR data are classified in various classes. The rate of classification can be obtained through "user accuracy, producer accuracy, omission error and commission error," respectively, which can provide other information about the rate of classification.

17.3.1   Omission Error

This error occurs when numbers of pixels are removed from the correct class and get added to some different categories under consideration.

17.3.2   Commission Error

This error occurs when numbers of pixels are unintentionally added to a class under consideration.

17.3.3   User Accuracy

It is the accuracy created from the point of the map maker. The mathematical expression of the user's skill is expressed by Equation (17.13).

$$User\ Accuracy = 100\% - ommision\ error \qquad (17.13)$$

17.3.4   Producer Accuracy

It is defined as the accuracy which is derived from the map user. The mathematical expression of the producer's accuracy is expressed by Equation (17.14).

$$Producer\ Accuracy = 100\% - Commission\ error \qquad (17.14)$$

17.3.5   Overall Accuracy

It is defined as the ratio of the total number of pixels that are correctly classified to the total number of pixels present in an image. The mathematical expression of the overall accuracy is expressed by Equation (17.15).

$$Overall\ Accuracy = \frac{Correctly\ classified\ pixels}{Total\ image\ pixels} \qquad (17.15)$$

Now the classification of the PALSAR data is performed. Four different classes are created, *i.e.*, water, soil, agriculture, and urban. The detailed data is shown in Figure 17.7, where blue represents water, black represents soil, green represents grass, and finally, urban is represented by orange color. Image classification results of OBCD algorithms Minimum distance classification, Maximum likelihood classification, SAM, and SVM results are shown in Figure 17.7(a), (b), (c) and (d) respectively.

The four classification matrix of the object-based change detection algorithm is presented. For different classification techniques, producer accuracy, user accuracy, omission error, and commission error are calculated and tabulated in Tables 17.1–17.4.

The result of these classification techniques suggests that all the algorithms behave distinctly and produced different results under different conditions. A comparative analysis of the classification features for class urban, water, bare soil, and vegetation is presented in Figures 17.8, 17.9, 17.10, 17.11, respectively.

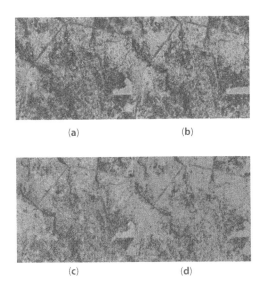

(a)   (b)

(c)   (d)

Figure 17.7 PALSAR data classification through (a) minimum distance classification, (b) maximum likelihood classification, (c) spectral angle mapper (SAM), (d) support vector machine (Data Courtesy: Japanese Aerospace Exploration Agency JAXA).

Table 17.1 Statistics derived through minimum distance classification.

S. No.	Classes	Producer Accuracy	User Accuracy	Omission Error	Commission Error
1	Urban	74.00	89.12	26.55	09.88
2	Water	88.00	61.54	14.35	40.52
3	Bare Soil	97.00	86.00	06.00	15.64
4	Vegetation	81.88	96.00	18.55	03.11

Table 17.2 Statistics derived through maximum likelihood classification.

S. No.	Classes	Producer Accuracy	User Accuracy	Omission Error	Commission Error
1	Urban	84.00	84.56	16.12	11..48
2	Water	76.00	67.55	20.14	31.00
3	Bare Soil	81.00	87.99	23.44	12.88
4	Vegetation	82.54	80.54	16.38	18.65

Table 17.3 Statistics derived through spectral angle mapper.

S. No.	Classes	Producer Accuracy	User Accuracy	Omission Error	Commission Error
1	Urban	87.56	67.15	39.54	31.66
2	Water	12.00	36.84	87.22	66.67
3	Bare Soil	54.66	92.66	48.22	54.99
4	Vegetation	62.00	70.11	14.52	27.88

Table 17.4 Statistics derived through support vector machine.

S. No.	Classes	Producer Accuracy	User Accuracy	Omission Error	Commission Error
1	Urban	99.00	65.54	01.24	34.00
2	Water	98.00	83.05	02.54	16.94
3	Bare Soil	77.54	97.84	18.54	16.95
4	Vegetation	76.74	92.00	24.38	02.20

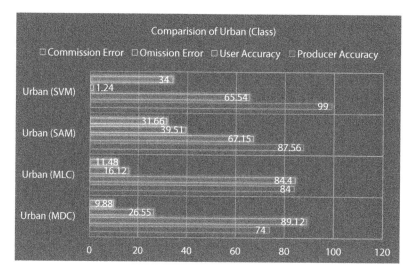

Figure 17.8 Comparative analysis of class 'Urban.'

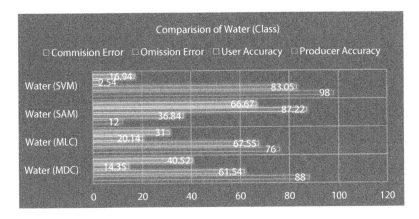

Figure 17.9 Comparative analysis of class 'Water.'

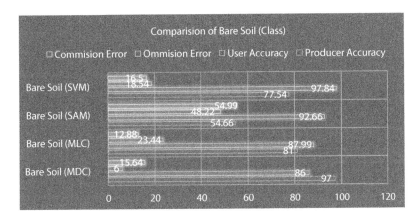

Figure 17.10 Comparative analysis of class 'Bare Soil.'

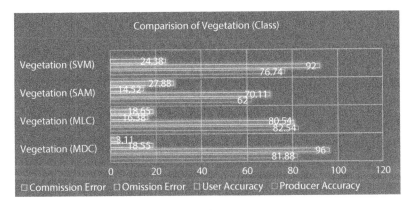

Figure 17.11 Comparative analysis of class 'Vegetation.'

17.4   Conclusion

Change detection techniques are quite useful for image interpretation and visualization purposes. Pixel-based and object-based both provide useful image information for image interpretation and understanding. A pixel-based approach is an old approach for image interpretation, whereas the object-based approach is the current approach. Both the methods and their combination are very effectively used in remote sensing applications. In the future, we can observe the combination of both pixel-based and object-based change detection approach for image interpretation. Researchers and scientists are already working in this area.

Acknowledgment

The authors are thankful for the National Aeronautics and Space Administration (NASA), NASA Earth Observatory for the satellite image of Cambodia used in Figures 17. 5(a) and (b) respectively and Japanese Aerospace Exploration Agency (JAXA) for the PALSAR data of Roorkee, India, used in Figure 17.6. Authors are also thankful to Dr. Rishi Prakash, Associate Professor, Graphic Era (Deemed to be University) for allowing the use of PALSAR data who holds the ownership of the PALSAR data.

References

1. Asokan, A. and Anitha, J., Change detection techniques for remote sensing applications: A survey. *Earth Sci. Inf.*, 12, 1, 143–160, 2019.
2. Shakya, A.K., Ramola, A., Kandwal, A., Prakash, R., Change Over Time in Grey Levels of Multispectral Landsat 5TM/8OLI Satellite Images, in: *Lecture Notes in Electrical Engineering*, pp. 30–356, Mesra, Ranchi, Springer, Singapore, 2019.
3. Hansen, J., Kharecha, P., Sato, M., Masson-Delmotte, V., Ackerman, F., Beerling, D.J., *et al.*, Assessing "Dangerous Climate Change": Required Reduction of Carbon Emissions to Protect Young People, Future Generations and Nature. *PLoS ONE*, 8(12): e81648, 2013, https://doi.org/10.1371/journal.pone.0081648
4. Wan, X., Liu, J.G., Li, S., Yan, H., Phase Correlation Decomposition: The Impact of Illumination Variation for Robust Subpixel Remotely Sensed Image Matching. *IEEE Trans. Geosci. Remote Sens.*, 57, 9, 6710–6725, September 2019.
5. C.S. Corporation, *Landsat image differencing as an automated landcover change detection technique*, NASA Center for Aerospace Information (CASI), Greenbelt, Maryland, August 1978.
6. Marinelli, D., Bovolo, F., Bruzzone, L., A Novel Change Detection Method for Multitemporal Hyperspectral Images Based on Binary Hyperspectral Change Vectors. *IEEE Trans. Geosci. Remote Sens.*, 57, 7, 4913–4928, 2019.
7. Cao, G., Zhou, L., Li, Y., A new change-detection method in high-resolution remote sensing images based on a conditional random field model. *Int. J. Remote Sens.*, 37, 5, 1173–1189, 2016.
8. Zhang, Y., Peng, D., Huang, X., Object-Based Change Detection for VHR Images Based on Multiscale Uncertainty Analysis. *IEEE Geosci. Remote Sens. Lett.*, 15, 1, 13–17, March 2018.
9. Bruzzone, L. and Prieto, D.F., Automatic analysis of the difference image for unsupervised change detection. *IEEE Trans. Geosci. Remote Sens.*, 38, 3, 1171–1182, May 2000.

10. Feng, W., Sui, H., Tu, J., Huang, W., Xu, C., Sun, K., A Novel Change Detection Approach for Multi-Temporal High-Resolution Remote Sensing Images Based on Rotation Forest and Coarse-to-Fine Uncertainty Analyses. *Remote Sens.*, 10, 7, 1–22, 2018.

11. Dymond, C.C., Mladenoff, D.J., Radeloff, V.C., Phenological differences in Tasseled Cap indices improve deciduous forest classification. *Elsevier: Remote Sens. Environ.*, 80, 460–472, 2002.

12. Ramachandra, T.V. and Kumar, U., Geographic resources decision support system for land use, land cover dynamics analysis, in: *Proceedings of the FOSS/GRASS Users Conference*, Bangkok, Thailand, 2004.

13. Cheng, K., Wei, C., Chang, S., Locating landslides using multi-temporal satellite images. *Elsevier: Adv. Space Res.*, 33, 296–301, 17 April 2004.

14. Lu, D., Mausel, P., Batistella, M., Moran, E., Land cover binary change detection method for use in the moist tropical region of the Amazon: A Comparative Study. *Int. J. Remote Sens.*, 26, 1, 101–114, 10 January 2005.

15. Brewer, C.K., Winne, J.C., Redmond, R.L., Opitz, D.W., Mangrich, M.V., Classifying and mapping wildfire severity: A comparison of methods. *Photogramm. Eng. Remote Sensing*, 71, 11, 1311–1320, November 2005.

16. Nordberg, M.L. and Evertson, J., Vegetation index differencing and linear regression for change detection in a Swedish mountain range using Landsat TM and ETM+ imagery. *Land Degrad. Dev.*, 16, 139–149, 23 August 2005.

17. Lin, W.-T., Chou, W.-C., Lin, C.-Y., Huang, P.-H., Tsai, J.-S., Vegetation recovery monitoring and assessment at landslides caused by the earthquake in Central Taiwan. *For. Ecol. Manage.*, 210, 55–66, 2005.

18. Zhang, D., Yin, T., Yang, G., Xu, M., Li, L., Sun, X., Detecting image seam carving with low scaling ratio using multi-scale spatial and spectral entropies. *J. Vis. Commun. Image Represent.*, 48, 1, 281–291, October 2017.

19. Kim, K.I. and Kwon, Y., Single-Image Super-Resolution Using Sparse Regression and Natural Image Prior. *IEEE Trans. Pattern Anal. Mach. Intell.*, 32, 6, 1127–1133, June 2010.

20. Ma, B., Pu, R., Wu, L., Zhang, S., Vegetation Index Differencing for Estimating Foliar Dust in an Ultra-Low-Grade Magnetite Mining Area Using Landsat Imagery. *IEEE Access*, 5, 8825–8834, May 2017.

21. Shakya, A.K., Ramola, A., Kandwal, A., Mittal, P., Prakash, R., Morphological Change Detection in Terror Camps of Area 1 and 2 by Pre-and Post-strike Through MOAB: A, in: *Advances in Communication, Devices, and Networking*, pp. 253–263, Sikkim, Springer, Singapore, 2019.

22. Shakya, A.K., Ramola, A., Kandwal, A., Mittal, P., Prakash, R., Morphological Change Detection in Terror Camps of Area 3 and 4 by Pre-and Post-strike Through MOAB: B, in: *Advances in Communication, Devices, and Networking*, pp. 265–275, Sikkim, Springer, Singapore, 2019.

23. Shakya, A.K., Ramola, A., Kandwal, A., Prakash, R., Comparison of supervised classification techniques with ALOS PALSAR sensor for Roorkee region of Uttarakhand, India. *Int. Arch. Photogramm. Remote Sens. Spat. Inf. Sci.*, 1, 639–701, November 2018.

24. Ma, B., Pu, R., Wu, L., Zhang, S., Vegetation Index Differencing for Estimating Foliar Dust in an Ultra-Low-Grade Magnetite Mining Area Using Landsat Imagery. *IEEE Access*, 5, 8825–8834, May 2017.

25. Yang, M., Li, C., Guan, J., Yan, X., A Supervised-Learning-Norm Distance Metric for Hyperspectral Remote Sensing Image Classification. *IEEE Geosci. Remote Sens. Lett.*, 15, 9, 1432–1436, September 2018.

26. Shakya, A.K., Prakash, R., Ramola, A., Pandey, D.C., Change Detection from Pre and PostUrbanisation LANDSAT 5 TM Multispectral Images, in: *IEEE, International Conference on Innovations in Control, Communication and Information Systems (ICICCI)*, Noida, 2017.

27. Shakya, A.K., Ramola, A., Kandwal, A., Estimating Change Percentage in Texture Developed by the Water Turndown of Bolivia's Lake Poopo, in: *IEEE, International Conference on Automation and Computational Engineering (ICACE)*, Noida, 2018.

28. Ramola, A., Shakya, A.K., Pham, D.V., Study of statistical methods for texture analysis and their modern evolutions. *Eng. Rep.*, e12149, 2, 4, 1–24, 2020.

29. Przyborski, P. and Levy, R., *Normalized Difference Vegetation Index (NDVI)*, 30 August 2002, [Online]. Available: https://earthobservatory.nasa.gov/features/MeasuringVegetation/measuring_vegetation_2.php. [Accessed 26 January 2020]. NASA Earth Observatory, Paul Przyborski and Robert Levy, https://earthobservatory.nasa.gov/features/MeasuringVegetation/measuring_vegetation_2.php

30. Al-Yaseen, W.L., Othman, Z.A., AhmadNazri, M.Z., Multi-level hybrid support vector machine and extreme learning machine based on modified K-means for intrusion detection system. *Expert Syst. Appl.*, 67, 1, 296–303, 2017.

Tracing Bad Code Smells Behavior Using Machine Learning with Software Metrics

Aakanshi Gupta[1], Bharti Suri[2] and Lakshay Lamba[1*]

[1]*Amity School of Engineering and Technology, GGS Indraprastha University, New Delhi, India*
[2]*University School of ICT, GGS Indraprastha University, New Delhi, India*

Abstract

The inappropriate symptoms in the code design pattern which are developed by the developers at the software development phase are termed as bad code smells. Bad code smells concur to deep rooted and serious issues in the software during maintenance phase. Using a various combination of object-oriented metrics; bad smell detection tools and techniques provide different results in many ways. In this study, four different machine learning algorithms namely J48, JRip, Random Forest and Naive Bayes, have been considered to detect three types of bad smells God Class, Long Method and Feature Envy. The prime attribute to extract the bad smells features is software metrics. These metrics names are: Lines of Code, Depth of Inheritance, Coupling between objects and many others that have been put to identify the quality of code at different levels. The results demonstrated that the machine learning algorithms achieved high accuracy with the validation method of 10-fold cross-validation. The bad smell detection through machine learning can come up with efficiency up to 90% and more in a few test cases.

Keywords: Bad code smells, machine learning, object oriented metrics, software engineering, sampling, JRip, coupling, data mining, supervised learning

18.1 Introduction

Bad Code smells are the block of codes that violates design principles and negatively impacts quality of the code. The term code smell was initially popularized by Kent Beck in late 1990s [1] which he quoted it as 'A code smell is a hint that something has gone wrong somewhere in your code, use the smell to track down the problem.' Later the usage of the term increased when Martin Fowler [1] brought it into consideration in some of his books. Beck and Fowler informally described 22 bad code smells and associated them with different refactoring techniques that can be applied to improve the quality of the software design.

Corresponding author: lakshaylamba123@gmail.com

Namita Gupta, Prasenjit Chatterjee and Tanupriya Choudhury (eds.) Smart and Sustainable Intelligent Systems, (245–258)
© 2021 Scrivener Publishing LLC

Bad code smells are not usually bugs, the evidence whether code smells are actually harmful is not very concrete. In the last decade, the term is considerably brought under discussion, yet it still remains a topic of debate if code smells are useful conceptualizations of code equality issues from a developer's perspective. Some studies [18, 19, 23] depict that code smells do not effect change effort or developers do not really refactor code to check bad code smells. Software engineers are also aware of these code smells but are not really concerned with their impact, given the low refactoring activity. On the contrary, an empirical study [27] provide industrially based evidence of refactoring the code for removing code smells that increases the development productivity and improves code quality factors. In this way literature provides us with different results, therefore we are not able to achieve a fully grown knowledge of the impact of bad code smells on software code designs. For all these reasons a better targeted code smell detection technique is required.

The remedy, provides the application of supervised machine learning techniques for the detection of bad code smells. The application of supervised learning for bad code smell detection requires formalized datasets, which includes the selection of data to be analysed and algorithms to be used in the experimentation. For this purpose a large set of object-oriented metrics [4–6] covering various aspects of software design, have been calculated on java source codes. Metrics are considered as independent variables in the machine learning approach [7, 28]. This procedure uses stratified sampling process on 14 java projects, accompanied by the set of pre-existing bad code smell detection tools [20]. This methodology ensures the existence of a particular smell at a particular instance. The selected instances are used to train the machine learning algorithms to perform experiments. The main contributions of this paper are:

- Determining that application of machine learning can provide an accuracy of greater than 90%.
- Comparing different ML algorithms and selecting the best amongst them for a particular smell detection.
- Providing code smell detection rules.
- Validating the results using 10-Fold Cross Validation technique.

The classification process is performed on 3 bad code smells: God Class, Long Method and Feature Envy (Table 18.1) using four different machine learning algorithms. The experiments carried out with the help of machine learning techniques obtained high performances, regardless of the type of smell.

This paper is organized through following sections: Section 18.2 presents the related work and motivation. Section 18.3 introduces the methodology based on machine learning

Table 18.1 Brief description about considered smells.

Bad Code Smell	Annotation
God Class	A class which performs too many functions.
Long Method	A method which contains too much lines of code.
Feature Envy	A method which refers to other classes more than its own.

techniques. Section 18.4 describes the result analysis and validation using statistical parameters and graphs. Section 18.5 discusses the validity threats, limitation of the work and conclusion.

18.2   Related Work and Motivation

The concept of bad smell is given by Martin Fowler *et al.* [1] who state it as, parts of code which disobeys the object oriented principle. He also proposed an informal explanation of 23 bad code smells. There are numerous studies which scrutinize the evolution of bad code smells. Tufano *et al.* [23] analyzed about the results of code smells generation that when there is an update in the code there may arise a smell. Gupta *et al.* [3] presented a systematic literature review about the detection technique in the code smell and a survey on the most studied code smell, code clone [2]. Chatzigeorgiou *et al.* [6] investigated two open source system for evolution of 3 bad smells by examining past versions of the code and stated that these problems exits right from the beginning of the software. Peters *et al.* [19] considered a bad smells to be symptom of anti-pattern and determined its lifespan by mining the software repository. Tahmid *et al.* [22] identified code smells clusters in three steps: detection of smells, extraction of their relationship and generation of graphs and finally found the smelly clusters.

Determining the type of code smell is an important task. Fontana *et al.* [9] considered that code smells are structure characteristics of software and analyzed four code smell detectors on six versions of one open source system. Fontana *et al.* [10] also detected code smells with machine learning and compared the results obtained by different algorithms. Gupta *et al.* [12] proposed a bad smell prediction model using the concept of entropies. Lessman *et al.* [14] strived for the software quality improvement and classified the models from the code attributes to enable a timely identification of fault prone modules. Khomh *et al.* [13] proposed a Bayesian approach for the detection of anti-patterns and generate a model on two open source projects, they also calibrated their model using machine learning techniques to offer an improved detection technique. Maiga *et al.* [15] introduced a support vector machine approach for detection of anti-patterns called as SVM-Detect and with a high accuracy. Palomba *et al.* [18] proposed an approach to detect 5 bad smells using change history information mined from versioning systems and identified that these results cannot be identified solely based on code analysis. Wieman *et al.* [24] describe an approach called as anti-pattern scanner for examining and scanning the problems in the software systems. Moha *et al.* [27] proposed a standalone automatic code smell detection tool which is used to detect bad code smells specifically for java source code.

Mantyla *et al.* [16] grouped the code smells into categories and subjectively evaluate the software evolvability using cod smells. Paiva *et al.* [17] evaluated and compared four bad smells detection tools for three code smells and presented that the evaluated tools found various levels of accuracy in different contexts. A good quality software is considered as the one which is efficient, consistent and easy to maintain. But there are several factors which causes hindrance to quality of a software. Code smells are considered to be one of most common one as they decrease code readability, increases complexity and consumes more computer memory which makes a software vulnerable [29] to bugs and errors. Bad code smells also resists future developments resulting in high maintenance cost. In today's world, things just happen within a click, therefore a software should be coded in such a way that it minimizes the flaws which can damage its functionality. That is why the motivation to improve the quality of a software is never ending. The primary aim is to improve code characteristics by improving four main aspects of the code which are: efficiency, readability, testability and maintainability. Many times bad code smells occur unintentionally in a software code, which might be because of bad design practices or lack of experience. Therefore we need to understand the behavior of code smells.

18.3   Methodology

To apply machine learning for the detection of bad code smells, one needs a formalized datasets. Application of machine learning requires the proper selection of data to be used in experimentation. Figure 18.1 illustrates the steps involved for entire M-L process implemented in the research.

The research proceeds with a collection of 14 open source software systems on which experiments are performed. Next is to extract object-oriented code metrics from these source codes. Following this phase, static code analysis tools are used to detect the presence of a bad smell in the code. These extracted bad code smells are then associated with code metrics. Finally, the selection of candidates is done by stratified sampling process. Using this approach, all three bad smells datasets are created on which the experiment is performed and different machine learning algorithms (J48, JRip, Naive Bayes and Random forest) are applied to train the model.

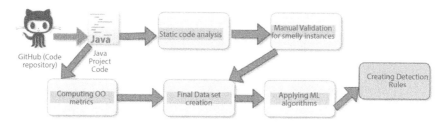

Figure 18.1 Workflow for machine learning algorithms implementation.

18.3.1   Data Collection

The proposed code smell detection system uses 14 project code repositories which are written in java language. These java codes are downloaded from GitHub repository. The reason for the selection of these systems is that they are easily compilable to correctly compute the metrics values. Table 18.2 proposes the summary of projects characteristics that are considered in the research.

We extracted large set of object oriented metrics which are considered as independent variable in the machine learning approach. These metrics are computed on all 14 Java systems. The selected matrices are at class, method, package and project level; the set of metrics is composed of according the quality dimensions of the code, i.e., size, complexity, count

Table 18.2 Summary of selected projects with their characteristics.

Selected Systems	Lines of code	Number of classes	Number of Functions	Number of Files
Android-Universal-Image-Loader-master	7,218	140	815	88
bigbluebutton-master	94,536	1,422	9,539	1,140
Bukkit-master	32,560	791	5,022	731
clojure-master	40,402	802	4,171	173
dropwizard-master	50,067	1,288	5,446	877
jfreechart-1.0.19	144,343	1,093	11,875	1,017
JHotDraw5.3-master	14,873	275	2,316	197
junit4-master	29,964	1,440	4,157	450
libgdx-master	275,286	3,958	46,925	2,325
metrics-4.1-development	19,017	402	2,059	251
netty-4.1	250,832	4,447	28,187	2,369
nokogiri-master	12,920	155	1,209	88
okhttp-master	57,088	768	5,553	307
presto-master	557,315	6,552	49,272	4,806

and inheritance. All metrics have been computed through Scitools Understand (version 5.0). Understand is an IDE (Integrated Development Environment) that can extract wide range of metrics and can generate customized reports.

18.3.2   Static Code Analysis

To detect the hints of a bad smell in a code, static analysis of the code is being performed. The term static code analysis refers to a method of computer program debugging, carried out at the implementation phase of a software development life-cycle, to ensure that quality of the code meets the software standards. Machine learning application needs a well formalized training dataset i.e. the label must specify if a certain part of the code (class or method) is effected by a particular type of bad code smell or not. This phase of the experiment is required to create an organized datasets; so that M-L algorithms do not have randomly distributed instances. Table 18.3 illustrates the chosen metrics; classified under 4 quality dimensions of object oriented software.

Following this idea, we considered two static code analysis tools as shown in Table 18.4, PMD and JDeodorant which acts as experts in formulating an organized dataset [15, 17, 24]. The reason for considering these tools is that they were freely available and could generate reports in different formats.

Table 18.3 Metrics Selection.

Size	Complexity	Count	Inheritance
AvgLineCode	Cyclomatic	CountDeclMethodAll	MaxInheritanceTree
CountLineCode	SumCyclomatic	CountDeclClass	PercentLackOfCohesion
AvgLineBlank	AvgCyclomatic	CountClassCoupled	
	MaxCyclomatic	CountClassDerived	
		CountInput	
		CountOutput	
		CountClassBase	
		CountDeclFunction	
		CountDeclClassMethod	

Table 18.4 Bad code Smells and detection tools.

Smells	Tools
God Class	PMD
Long Method	PMD, Jdeodorant
Feature Envy	PMD, Jdeodorant

18.3.3   Sampling

Sampling refers to the selection of a subset, also known as statistical sample, from within the group to estimate the characteristics of whole group. As stated earlier that supervised learning requires large organized datasets. Formation of such large datasets requires a lot of human resources and efforts. To overcome this situation, stratified sampling process is used based on the hints provided by static code analysis tools. Stratified sampling provides with greater precision than a simple random sample of the same size, increasing the chance of creating a dataset depicting different application domains. It also increases the speed to formalize the dataset and hence decreasing its costs. Firstly, each dataset element is annotated with two values; the name of the project containing it and a variable N which reports the number of tools reporting a positive evaluation i.e. indicating that they considered the element affected by a smell. Each dataset elements are then grouped and an instance 'I' is evaluated and added to the training set [10].

The final training set is normalized in size, by randomly excluding some of the negative instances (if needed) forming a balanced training dataset containing approximately 1/3 positive instances (i.e. smelly instances) and 2/3 of negative instances (non- smelly). The reason for less proportion of positive instances is that usually a very small fraction of a code is effected by that smell. In the end we obtained three balanced datasets, one for each bad code smell, which composed of 450 instances in total.

18.3.4 Machine Learning Approach

The main focus was to calculate that how much effective are machine learning algorithms for the detection of bad code smells. This proceeds in two stages: First, by creating datasets for each type of bad code smells (i.e. God class, Long Method, Feature Envy) with the help of static code analysis tools and by means of stratified sampling process. Second, by selecting suitable machine learning algorithms (which in our case are: J48, JRip, Random Forest and Naive Bayes) and examining them on generated datasets by means 10-fold cross validation process [21]. In each dataset created, different columns represent different object oriented Metrics which are classified under 4 quality dimensions. In addition, there exists a Boolean feature which represents the label (true or false) that specifies whether the instance is effected by a bad code smell or not. The machine learning algorithms were implemented with the help of WEKA (version 3.8.3) tool [25]. Weka supports several data mining tasks including data analysis, predictive modelling, visualization and various other attributes. A short summary of selected algorithms is provided in the Table 18.5.

The listed classifiers produces human readable models which helps in finding the best algorithm for the detection of each type of bad code smell. These results are validated with the help of cross validation technique and several standard performance measures such as: F-Measure, Area under ROC, Precision, etc.

18.4 Result Analysis and Manual Validation

The analysis performed on java projects with the help of static code analysis tools had verified results. The percentage of smelly instances in each project for specific smell type is the result of static analysis and manual validation performed on each project. The results of performance accuracy of each algorithm against every bad code smell are depicted in Table 18.9. For each algorithm the percentage accuracy is mentioned. Accuracy is the proportion of correctly classified instances in the positive and negative class. Simulated results show that JRip and J48 produced best results in terms of accuracy for detecting all three types of smells, whereas Random Forest and Nave Bayes also produced high performance.

For God Class, J48 and JRip nearly produced same accuracy (Table 18.6), with JRip being more accurate amongst the two with Random Forest and Nave Bayes being the third and fourth best algorithms. JRip and J48 again proved to better in terms of accuracy for detecting Long Method and Feature Envy with almost 98% accuracy as shown in the Figure 18.3

Table 18.5 Short summary of selected ML algorithms.

Classifier	Description
J48	Implements C4.5 decision tree and predicts the target variable of new dataset record.
JRip	Implements a propositional rule learner and produce propositional rules for classification.
Random Forest	Builds classification trees as a forest of random decision trees.
Nave Bayes	Simple probabilistic classifier based on applying Bayes' theorem.

(and Table 18.9). The cross-validation results on all three types of bad code smells have very high accuracy values that almost vary between 90 and 99%. The search for the best algorithm for individual type of bad code smell has been evaluated through various performance evaluators to compare the experimented results. Tables 18.6, 18.7, and 18.8 depict the values of these performance evaluators. Pictorial representation of these values is also provided in the form of bar graphs (Figure 18.2). A short explanation of these evaluators is provided in the paper.

TP Rate: The True Positive Rate determines the number of instances predicted positive that is actually positive. It is also known as sensitivity.

FP Rate: False Positive Rate determines the number of instances predicted positive that are actually negative.

Precision: Precision is also referred to as positive predicted value. It determines the fractions of predicted positives that are actually that are actually positive.

$$Precision = TP / TP + FP \tag{18.1}$$

Where FP is the false-positive rate.

Recall: Recall determines what fraction of those instances that are actually positive were predicted positive.

$$Recall = TP / TP + FN \tag{18.2}$$

Where FN is the false-negative rate.

F-measure: It is a measure of a test accuracy and is defined as the weighted harmonic mean of the precision and recall of the test.

Table 18.6 Statistical analysis for God Class.

Classifier	TP Rate	FP Rate	Precision	Recall	F-Measure	ROC-Area
Naïve Bayes	0.933	0.086	0.933	0.933	0.933	0.968
JRip	0.987	0.013	0.987	0.987	0.987	0.978
J48	0.984	0.014	0.985	0.984	0.984	0.975
Random Forest	0.978	0.031	0.978	0.978	0.978	0.992

Table 18.7 Statistical analysis for long method.

Classifier	TP Rate	FP Rate	Precision	Recall	F-Measure	ROC-Area
Naïve Bayes	0.92	0.106	0.921	0.92	0.92	0.975
JRip	0.991	0.017	0.991	0.991	0.991	0.983
J48	0.989	0.018	0.989	0.989	0.989	0.996
Random Forest	0.964	0.083	0.966	0.964	0.964	0.996

Table 18.8 Statistical analysis for Feature Envy.

Classifier	TP Rate	FP Rate	Precision	Recall	F-Measure	ROC-Area
Naïve Bayes	0.813	0.31	0.821	0.813	0.801	0.958
JRip	0.976	0.031	0.976	0.976	0.976	0.977
J48	0.973	0.026	0.974	0.973	0.973	0.976
Random Forest	0.964	0.052	0.964	0.964	0.964	0.994

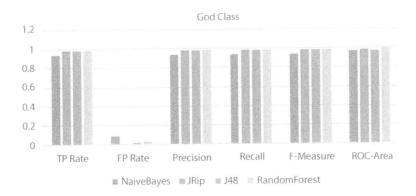

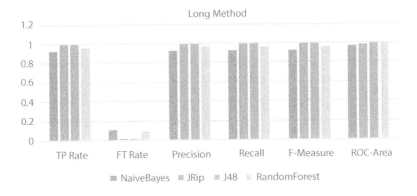

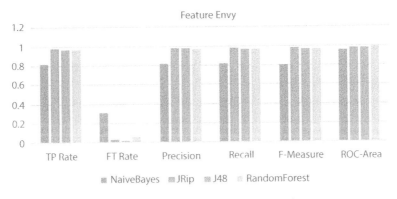

Figure 18.2 Machine learning algorithms performance for respective smells.

Table 18.9 Accuracy in percentage of ML algorithms.

Classifier	God Class	Long Method	Feature Envy
Naïve Bayes	93.33	92	81.33
JRip	98.66	99.11	97.55
J48	98.44	98.99	97.33
Random Forest	97.77	96.44	96.44

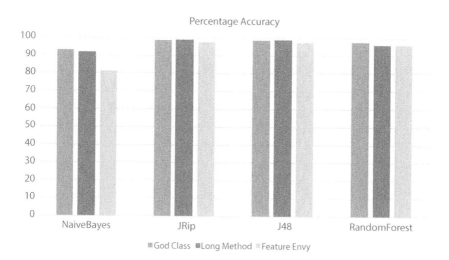

Figure 18.3 Accuracy in percentage for each ML algorithm.

$$F\text{-}measure = 2 * Precision * Recall \,/\, Precision + Recall \qquad (18.3)$$

ROC-Area: Receiver operating Characteristic is a plot of true positive rate against the false positive rate at various threshold points.

The graphs given in Figure 18.2 depict the performance of machine learning algorithms for respective smells. J48 and JRip proved to be the top performing algorithms for each type of bad code smell. All type of performance evaluators appears to be the best amongst these two algorithms. It might not be wrong to conclude that all the algorithms have high performances regardless of the type of bad code smell.

In view of the obtained result, it will be correct to conclude that all the algorithms obtained high performances under various performance evaluators. About 97% of true positive rate indicates that most the instances were correctly classified. High values of F-measure and ROC-Area signifies high test accuracy. For detection of God Class smell, J48 and JRip produced simple detection rules. J48 detects that whenever the value of SumCyclomatic metric exceeds the value 47, it becomes a candidate for God Class type of Bad Code Smell. JRip also produced rules almost similar to that of J48 as shown in the Table 18.10.

Table 18.10 Extracted Rules from the ML Algorithms.

Bad Code Smells	Rules by J48	Rules by Jrip
God Class	SumCyclomatic >47	SumCyclomatic >= 48
Long Method	CountLineCode >79 and Cyclomatic >9	CountLineCode >= 80 and Cyclomatic >= 10
Feature Envy	PerecntLackOfCohesion >50 and CountClassCoupled >5	PercentLackOfCohesion >=50 and CountClassCoupled >= 5

18.5   Threats, Limitation and Conclusion

One of the most important threats to internal validity is related decide whether a particular instance is smelly instance or not. Though there are several tools which detect the presence of a smell in a code but they do not guarantee the level of impact that how much those instances could affect the system. Moreover, manually validating the smelly candidates can also not guarantee the threat of an instance to the system. Several factors such as experience of the developer, depth of knowledge in object oriented programming and human error can also count in effecting the internal validity of the experiment. Threats to external validity majorly depend upon how much the selected systems are reliable. We cannot guarantee their correctness as these systems are open source. Sampling criteria could also cause a distortion in building the training set because the selection criterion is partly random. The experiment has some limitations as well. First possible limitation could be the manual validation process. This process is undertaken by students not the domain experts, which possibly can add up to introduction of errors in dataset formation. Second, we are not sure about the amount of data required for training the machine learning algorithms.

This paper presents a methodology for bad smells (God class, Long method and Feature envy) detection using machine learning algorithms. We apply four machine learning algorithms, Naive Bayes, JRip, J48 and Random forest with almost 98% accuracy on the 14 projects dataset. Many statistical parameters like precision, recall and f-measure have been calculated for validating the obtained results. In the end we conclude that the experiments performed for the detection of bad code smells under supervised machine learning techniques obtained very healthy results.

References

1. Fowler, M., Beck, K., Brant, J., Opdyke, W., Roberts, D., *Refactoring: improving the design of existing code*, Addison-Wesley Professional, Reading, Massachusetts, 1999.
2. Gupta, A. and Suri, B., A survey on code clone, its behavior and applications, in: *Networking Communication and Data Knowledge Engineering- Proceedings of ICRACCCS-2016*, Springer, pp. 27–39, 2016.
3. Gupta, A., Suri, B., Misra, S., A systematic literature review: Code bad smells in java source code, in: *International Conference on Computational Science and Its Applications*, Springer, pp. 665–682, 2017.

4. Aggarwal, K.K., Singh, Y., Kaur, A., Malhotra, R., Empirical study of object-oriented metrics. *J. Object Technol.*, 5, 8, 149–17, 2006.

5. Bansiya, J. and Davis, C.G., A hierarchical model for object-oriented design quality assessment. *IEEE Trans. Software Eng.*, 28, 1, 4–17, 2002.

6. Chatzigeorgiou, A. and Manakos, A., Investigating the evolution of bad smells in objectoriented code, in: *International Conference on the Quality of Information and Communications Technology*, IEEE, pp. 106–115, 2010.

7. Chidamber, S.R. and Kemerer, C.F., A metrics suite for object oriented design. *IEEE Trans. Software Eng.*, 20, 6, 476–493, 1994.

8. Deligiannis, I., Stamelos, I., Angelis, L., Roumeliotis, M., Shepperd, M., A controlled experiment investigation of an object-oriented design heuristic for maintainability. *J. Syst. Softw.*, 72, 2, 129–143, 2014.

9. Fontana, F.A., Braione, P., Zanoni, M., Automatic detection of bad smells in code: An experimental assessment. *J. Object Technol.*, 11, 2, 5–1, 2012.

10. Fontana, F.A., Mantyla, M.V., Zanoni, M., Marino, A., Comparing and experimenting machine learning techniques for code smell detection. *Empir. Softw. Eng.*, 21, 3, 1143–1191, 2016.

11. Fontana, F.A., Zanoni, M., Marino, A., Mantyla, M.V., Code smell detection: Towards a machine learning-based approach, in: *Software Maintenance (ICSM), 2013 29th IEEE International Conference on*, IEEE, pp. 396–399, 2013.

12. Gupta, A., Suri, B., Kumar, V., Misra, S., Blazauskas, T., Damasevicius, R., Software code smell prediction model using shannon, renyi and tsallis entropies. *Entropy*, 20, 5, 372, 2018.

13. Khomh, F., Vaucher, S., Gueheneuc, Y.-G., Sahraoui, H., Bdtex: A gqm-based bayesian approach for the detection of antipatterns. *J. Syst. Softw.*, 84, 4, 559–572, 2011.

14. Lessmann, S., Baesens, B., Mues, C., Pietsch, S., Benchmarking classification models for software defect prediction: A proposed framework and novel findings. *IEEE Trans. Software Eng.*, 34, 4, 485–496, 2008.

15. Maiga, A., Ali, N., Bhattacharya, N., Sabane, A., Gueheneuc, Y.-G., Antoniol, G., Aimeur, E., Support vector machines for anti-pattern detection, in: *Automated Software Engineering (ASE), 2012 Proceedings of the 27th IEEE/ACM International Conference on*, IEEE, pp. 278–281, 2012.

16. Mantyla, M.V. and Lassenius, C., Subjective evaluation of software evolvability using code smells: An empirical study. *Empir. Softw. Eng.*, 11, 3, 395–431, 2006.

17. Paiva, T., Damasceno, A., Figueiredo, E., SantAnna, C., On the evaluation of code smells and detection tools. *J. Softw. Eng. Res. Dev.*, 5, 1, 7, 2017.

18. Palomba, F., Bavota, G., Di Penta, M., Oliveto, R., De Lucia, A., Poshyvanyk, D., Detecting bad smells in source code using change history information, in: *Proceedings of the 28th IEEE/ACM International Conference on Automated Software Engineering*, IEEE Press, pp. 268–278, 2013.

19. Peters, R. and Zaidman, A., Evaluating the lifespan of code smells using software repository mining, in: *Software Maintenance and Reengineering (CSMR), 2012 16th European Conference on*, IEEE, pp. 411–416, 2012.

20. Sangeetha, M. and Sengottuvelan, P., Systematic exhortation of code smell detection using jsmell for java source code, in: *Inventive Systems and Control (ICISC), 2017 International Conference on*, IEEE, pp. 1–5, 2017.

21. Stone, M., Cross-validatory choice and assessment of statistical predictions. *J. R. Stat. Soc. Series B (Methodol.)*, 36.2, 111–147, 1974.

22. Tahmid, A., Nahar, N., Sakib, K., Understanding the evolution of code smells by observing code smell clusters, in: *Software Analysis, Evolution, and Reengineering (SANER), 2016 IEEE 23rd International Conference on*, vol. 4, IEEE, pp. 8–11, 2016.

23. Tufano, M., Palomba, F., Bavota, G., Oliveto, R., Di Penta, M., De Lucia, A., Poshyvanyk, D., When and why your code starts to smell bad (and whether the smells go away). *IEEE Trans. Software Eng.*, 43, 11, 1063–1088, 2017.

24. Wieman, R., *Anti-pattern scanner: An approach to detect anti-patterns and design violations*, Delft University of Technology, 2011.

25. Hall, M., Frank, E., Holmes, G., Pfahringer, B., Reutemann, P., Witten, I.H., The weka data mining software: an update. *ACM SIGKDD Explor. Newsl.*, 11, 1, 10–18, 2009.

26. Moha, N., Gueheneuc, Y.-G., Duchien, A.-F. *et al.*, Decor: A method for the specification and detection of code and design smells. *IEEE Trans. Software Eng. (TSE)*, 36, 1, 20–36, 2010.

27. Moser, R., Abrahamsson, P., Pedrycz, W., Sillitti, A., Succi, G., A case study on the impact of refactoring on quality and productivity in an agile team, in: *Balancing Agility and Formalism in Software Engineering*, pp. 252–266, Springer, Berlin, Heidelberg, 2008.

28. Wang, L. and Alexander, C.A., Machine learning in big data. *Int. J. Math. Eng. Manag. Sci.*, 1, 2, 52–61, 2016.

29. Bhatt, N., Anand, A., Sarma, Y., Venkata, S., Kumar, V., *Modeling and characterizing software vulnerabilities*, IJMEMS, India, 2017.

A Survey on Various Negation Handling Techniques in Sentiment Analysis

Sarita Bansal Garg[1]* and V.V. Subrahmanyam[2]

[1]*Maharaja Agrasen Institute of Management Studies, Delhi, India*
[2]*School of Computer and Information Sciences, IGNOU, New Delhi, India*

Abstract

Sentiment Analysis or opinion mining alludes to the way toward deciding sentiments or feelings communicated in content about a subject. But this sentiment changes with the presence of other constructs in the sentence. Negation is one such construct which either flips the sentiment or increase or decrease the intensity of the sentiment. This paper is an attempt to study the work done by the different researchers for identification of the negation cues and their scope. Paper is organized according to the different feature selection methods employed and how different researchers contributed to this. Various algorithms proposed by the researchers were presented. We have also identified the shortcomings of the various studies which form the basis for further development using other techniques like deep learning.

Keywords: Deep learning, natural language processing, sentiment analysis, negation handling, feature selection techniques, semantic based, syntactic based, syntactic rules

19.1 Introduction

Sentiment Analysis or opinion mining alludes to the way toward deciding sentiments or feelings communicated in content about a subject. It is a wide research territory which is at the crossing point where we use various areas of text analysis, natural language processing, computational linguistics and biometrics to first identify, extract, quantify and study its affective states and subjective information. Generally speaking, sentiment analysis focuses on determining the attitude of a person with respect to some topic, event or product or the overall contextual polarity or emotional reaction towards it. This analysis of sentiments can be done at the three levels: at the document level, at the sentence level and at the aspect level. At the document level, the whole document is classified as positive, negative or neutral irrespective of the features addressed in the document. For sentence level analysis, all the sentences of the documents are analyzed individually and

Corresponding author: saritabansal2607@gmail.com

Namita Gupta, Prasenjit Chatterjee and Tanupriya Choudhury (eds.) Smart and Sustainable Intelligent Systems, (259–280)
© 2021 Scrivener Publishing LLC

categorized as positive, negative or neutral. Last one is the phrase level or aspect level which is very important as it can categorize the sentiments based on the features specified in the sentence because maximum times it happens that for example any product is good based on certain features and bad on other features just like phone's battery life vs weight of the phone. For this first different features need to be identified in the sentence and then analyzed individually based on these features. A good sentiment analysis is that which is aspect based as true sentiments about any product can be found out feature wise and can be used for product comparisons.

Negative utterances are a core feature of every system of human communication. The study of negation has played a pivotal role in the investigation of formal and natural linguistic systems, from Aristotle and Plato to logicians, contemporary linguists, and psychologists. Negations includes words like no, not, shouldn't, etc. [1]. They are significant phonetics since they influence the polarities of different words. The expression of negation is widely varied, with regard to the form of negation itself (as an adverb, a suffix, a prefix, or even a verb) and to the conditions on the occurrence of negative polarity items. So, the study of negations plays a very important role in sentiment analysis as they affect the polarities of other words. At the point when a negation occurs in a sentence it is likely to determine the sequence of words which are influenced by the negation. The scope of negation refers to the number of words it affects and might be limited only to the next word after a negation or may extend up to different words following negation. For example, in sentence "this restaurant is not nice but its food is good", the scope of negation is just constrained to the word following after negation. Then again, in another sentence "nobody serves us for a long time", the scope of negation is until the end of the sentence. Different models demonstrate that the extent of nullification isn't fixed and changes depending on various etymology highlights, for example, conjunctions, accentuation stamps and grammatical feature (POS) of invalidation and so on. Also, the nearness of a negation term does not imply that all words in the sentence conveying polarities will be inverted [2]. In any case, the greater part of the current assumption investigation frameworks utilized customary techniques, (for example, static window [3, 4] and strategy dependent on punctuation marks [5]) to manage this complex phonetic marvel.

Various forms of negation are there and they are explicit (those with explicit clues like not, no etc.), implicit (without occurrence of any negation word), diminishers (e.g., not very good—instead of inverting the polarity, it diminish the polarity of good), morphological (where basic word modified by either prefix like *non*, *un*, etc. or by suffix like *less*, etc.) [6] and other restrained linguistic patterns. A reasonable refinement should be made while deciding the extent of various kinds of negation terms viably in light of the fact that they influence polarities in various ways. Researches till date focused mainly on the explicit negations or morphological negations where a pre-defined list of negation was considered. These researches were nowhere to be general.

Our goal in conducting this survey is to study the existing researches in the area of negation handling and tries to identify their shortcomings or drawbacks. This would be further used in trying to devising a method for sentiment analysis which would be general and consider all types of negations.

19.2   Methods for Negation Identification

Feature Selection plays a very important role in the task of sentiment analysis. The success or failure of any sentiment analysis task depends on how you have selected the features for the purpose. For Negation Handling, it is important to know the sequence in which the negation cue appears and how it is linked with the neighboring words. Different feature selection methods can be categorized in the following ways:

19.2.1   Bag of Words

It was a popular method used for feature representation in classifiers. Here the document/sentence is represented as a term frequency vector where each word occurring in the document/sentence was represented by a word and its presence or no of times it was occurring (term frequency) irrespective of its position or order. Ref. [5] used this popular method of feature representation in their experiment. Here, the authors used the BOW representation to identify the negated terms and explicitly negate the term with each word occurring after that till the punctuation mark, making each word negatively polarized.

Example: I do not NOT_like Not_this Not_new Not_Samsung Not_Phone

Here, two distinct features indicate a plain occurrence and a negated occurrence of a word. Therefore, these two examples view the same word as two things that are completely different. Since all the terms here are treated as independent entities and are subject to this alteration of the negation regardless of whether or not it is a polar expression. The spectrum of negation cannot therefore be adequately modeled. Not only is this linguistically incorrect, but it also raises the high dimensional feature space with more sparse features (because most words in a corpus will only be negated once or twice and dimension are directly dependent on the size of the vocabulary). Also, it doesn't consider or cater to co-occurrence statistics between the words and assume all words to be independent of each other. But, for the identification of scope of negation terms this should not be so, as negated term may be applicable on the other co-occurring words

19.2.2   Contextual Valence Shifters

Every POS whether it is a noun or an adjective has an attitude (valence) associated with it, whether it is a positive attitude word or an negative attitude word. Valence shifters or Sentiment shifter or Polarity shifters are the words or phrases which can flip or modify the sentiment orientations of texts or phrases. These are the complex linguistic structures that include explicit specified negations, contrasts, intensifiers and diminishers, etc. For this a valence calculation method is proposed which need to be incorporated for determining the polarity of the sentiment words and the overall sentiment of the review [7]. As a notation, positively valence words were marked as +2 in the lexicon whereas −2 for negatively valence words. Based on their assumption they stated that a simple "not" can flip the valence of a term whereas intensifiers both negative and positive can weaken or strengthen the base valence of the term and in turn the polarity of the whole sentence e.g., Shyam is good at cricket versus Shyam is not good at cricket.

good ⎮2 combined with not, not good −2, Suspicious −2, deeply suspicious −3 Efficient +2, rather efficient +1

In Ref. [8], the effect of valence shifters is examined using the movie reviews. Three types of valence shifters are examined: negations, intensifiers and diminishers. General Inquirer is used for the identification purpose. Xerox Parser is used to determine which negation/intensifiers/diminishers apply to which term known as scope of negation term. Two methods are used in this. Term counting method and support vector machine. When the training data or the labeled data is not available then the term counting method can be used to directly measure the effect of valence shifters. SVM can more effectively classify in terms of accuracy but difficult to incorporate the effect of valence shifters as some level of effect is already included in it. Experiments showed that combining the term counting method and Support Vector Machine method helps in achieving much better results. But the main limitation observed here was that the process here is some but subjective. Experiments showed that adding specific bigrams with SVM helped in improving the results. But which bigrams to add and which to include is totally subjective. Also, the positive and negative terms which were used may not be totally positive or totally negative. They must be given weights before the consideration and similarly, overstatements and understatements must be weighted.

Knowing the prior polarity of the subjective expressions is a very important feature which can be incorporated to calculate the polarity of the sentences. To implement this, Ref. [9] developed a lexicon and tag the 8000 subjectivity clues with their prior polarity i.e. positive, negative, neutral, both. First experiment was conducted for a simple classifier which gave the accuracy of 47% assuming that the polarity of the clue instance was same as the prior polarity of the instance in the lexicon. Two-step method was proposed where the contextual polarity was being considered and then the polarity was estimated. 28 features divided across 5 categories (Word Features, Modification Features, Sentence Features, Structure Features and Document Features) were considered for first step to determine whether the clause was neutral or polar. 28-feature classifier gives an accuracy of 75.9% as compared to the simple classifier. In the second step, polar clues were classified as positive, negative, neutral and both. Classifier with two classes of features i.e. Word Features and Negated Polarity Features containing in total 10 features achieved an accuracy of 65.7%. With the generation of lexicon for prior polarity of the sentiment phrases, this approach tested for various combinations of features. They achieved very good results which need to be incorporated in wider level of reviews and sentences to identify the overall sentiments. Accuracy achieved was very low in comparison to the efforts devoted to generate the results.

19.2.3 Semantic Relations

Semantic relationships are the associations that exists between the meanings of words (semantic relationships at word level), between the meanings of phrases, or between the meanings of sentences (semantic relationships at phrase or sentence level). In simple words it can be defined as any relationship which can exist between two or more words based on the meaning of the words.

The Principle of Compositionality states that the meaning of a composite phrase relies upon the meaning of its components and on the syntactic rules by which they are combined. In Ref. [10], using this principle, the authors attempted to cover the gap between the learning-based methods and expression-level polarity classification and proposed a new learning-based method. This approach was founded on compositional semantics which incorporated structural inference into the learning procedure. Here, new insights for content—word negators (e.g., eliminated) which can negate the polarity of surrounding words or constituents similar to function-word negators (e.g., not, never) were explored. They suggested a simple two-step process in which the polarities of the constituents of the expression were evaluated in the first step, followed by the application of a simple set of inference rules to recurrently combine them. They compared learning and non-learning based approaches to polarity classification at the expression-level (with and without compositional semantics) and stated that the simple heuristics which are based on compositional semantics perform much better (89.7% in accuracy) then other rational heuristics not incorporating compositional semantics (87.7%).Compared to simple learning-based approaches that did not integrate compositional semantics (89.1%), their performance is much higher. And, when these heuristic rules integrating compositional semantics are paired with approaches based on learning, much better performance has been achieved (90.7%). But experiments showed that the expression-level classification accuracy decreased uniformly as we further attempted to integrate the potentially disambiguating context. The success of experiment here all depends on the correct and complete specification of inference rules for the data. This required a lot of human effort. Instead of manually annotating all the inference rules, the approach must be automatic and compositional inference rules must be learned from the data itself.

So far, shallow parsing features such as part-of-speech tagging was used which helped in extracting frequent adjectives and noun or noun phrases as opinion words and represented the different features of the product. Instead of POS tagging, however if linguistic structure of high level like adjective–adverb–noun phrase of the sentence was considered then it can help in providing much better understanding of the semantic meaning of user's opinions and contribute in the task of sentiment analysis. In Ref. [11], a parse and paraphrase based model was suggested to identify and classify semantically elated phrases in review texts, taking quantifiers (modifying adverbs) and qualifiers (negations) into considerations. To identify and extract these words, a lexicalized probabilistic syntactic grammar is used in the suggested approach. To assess the strength of sentiment in adjectives and quantifiers/qualifiers including negations on a numerical score, a cumulative linear offset model was introduced and implemented. Here the focus was on feature based analysis and based on unigram statistics, only high frequency adjectives and nouns were selected. Linguistic structures helped in successfully predicting the scope of reference of the negation over the correct constituent of a sentence and created proper association between negation and its modified words which was hard to predict from syntactic point of view. Instead of using any lexicon, user ratings along with the reviews were used for calculating the sentiment score of clauses and hence for the reviews. Experiments proved that the suggested method performed substantially better than a neighbor baseline models. However, the success of the model was directly depending on the correct specification of the syntactic grammar and generation rules for the identification and extraction of adverb–adjective–noun phrases. The author here was solely focusing on these phrases for the sentiment analysis.

19.2.4   Relations and Dependency-Based or Syntactic-Based

In English grammar, structure of a sentence refers to the arrangement of words, phrases and clauses in a sentence and syntax or syntactic structure refers to the meaning of a sentence because of this structure of sentence. This structure of a sentence is governed by the grammatical rules of that language. A syntactic dependency is a relation between two words in a sentence with one word being the governor and the other being the dependent of the relation. Syntactic dependencies often form a tree. In most of the published work on negation detection, lexical approaches were used. These approaches make use of syntactical structural information of a sentence which can be retrieved from parse trees generated through NLP parsing. These methods seemed to be effective and reliable but determining the scope of negation was still a big challenge for many. The scope of negations could be determined reliably when a negated term is close to the negated signal, but when they are far apart and separated with multiple words the results were totally unsatisfactorily. In Ref. [12], a novel approach to deal with it was devised with special focus on the clinical radiology reports. A classification scheme which was based on the negation signal's syntactical categories and their corresponding natural language phrase patterns was specified. This scheme helped in locating negated concepts which lies both in close proximity to negation signals and also for those which are at a distance from them. Instead of using a Unified Medical Language System, a grammar based classification scheme was derived because of antonymous form of representation in them. Each grammar rule was further translated into a structural rule to help NDM extract negated phrases within a parse tree generated for each sentence from the clinical reports. This approach identified negated phrases with sensitivity of 92.6% and 99.87% specificity. But the limitation of this study was that only the complete negations were considered and partial negations like "probably not" along with the negations within a word like "non-tender" and "colorless" were ignored.

In Ref. [13], authors assumed that sentimental terms and the negation terms were either individual word or multi word phrases. They provided with the non-trivial method of computing the scope of the negation terms and hence the polarity of the sentence was determined. This was then compared with the other techniques. In the proposed technique, parse tree and typed dependencies which were generated by a parser were used and then special rules were framed for the identification of the negation scope. When this proposed method was clubbed with the Decision Tree Method, for automatically determining the polarity of the candidate scope the overall accuracy of 88.4% was achieved. One main limitation of this paper was that they limit the analysis to a set of negative terms which they listed in the paper.

Till now researches were focused on rule based systems. Ref. [14] proposed a machine learning system which detected the scope of negation but here the focus was biomedical texts. BioScope Corpus's three sub_corpora representing different text types were used here for the experiments. The system worked in two phases. In the first phase, authors focused on the identification of negation terms whereas in the second phase the scope of the identified negation terms were determined. GENIA tagger and the standard format of the 2006 CoNLL Shared Task were used for processing and representation of the selected text from the corpus. The task of scope finding was modeled as two consecutive classification tasks. In the first task, the token of the sentence was classified based on its presence at the beginning, inside or outside of the negation signal (for multiword negation terms).In the second classification task, the tokens of a sentence were classified as being the first element, the last or neither of the scope (for scope of the negation term).For the identification of negation signals, IGTREE on TiMBL platform was used as classifier. The classifier was parameterized by using gain ration for feature weighting. For scope finding, three-classifier (memory-based learning as implemented in TiMBL, SVM and CRF) were used for predicting and CRF meta learner, a fourth classifier used the predictions to predict the scope class. Proposed method produced good results with error reduction upto 32%. But this method was tested using the biomedical texts and need to be tested for general domain corpora.

The effort needed to resolve the issue of negation handling is very high as compared to the number of negated sentences encountered in any text/review for sentiment analysis and is said to be insignificant. So, in Ref. [15] authors experimented towards finding an automatic approach for handling the syntactic negation for sentiment analysis. It used the polarity and intensity of the words along with the dependencies, relation of words with other words within the sentence and the structure of the sentence. It showed a mixed and combined approach to lexical and syntactic analysis for sentiments. A number of existing lexical and syntactic analysis resources like SentiWordNet [16], WordNet [17] etc., were used in the suggested approach for sentiment analysis. Two main components of the framework were the syntactic parser and the sentiment analyzer. Syntactic parser dealt with identification and classification part whereas polarity was determined by sentiment analyser. The syntactic parser used Penn Tree Bank parser and Stanford parser. It identifies the negation and POS that are involved in the identified negation. This was further used by the sentiment analyzer for polarity calculation. It also identifies the semantics involved in a sentence. The words in a sentence, their meanings, alternative words, polarity of each word and intensity associated with each word were basic elements used by it for sentiment identification. In order to calculate the polarity of a sentence, some rules were defined on the basis of POS. Most negation words were classified as adverbs, suffix, prefix or verbs. The nouns were used to determine the meaning of another noun. The scope of negation was identified by the dependency tree indicating how it was interacting with other words in the sentence and whether it was a single word or a phrase/clause within a sentence. The negation was handled in each phrase accordingly. The intensity of polarity will not exceed ($\pm$) 1, where + is for positive and − is for negative polarity. The rule for calculating the intensity of a sentence was defined. Proposed method was compared with 5 human annotators and using Pearson product-moment correlation coefficient (r), there is strong correlation between the results produced by them. Results were very promising but the dataset considered here was very small and consist only of 55 sentences.

In Ref. [18], a framework for automatic detection of negation effect on consumer reviews was proposed. The main focus here was to identify those sentences or cues which looks like positive but actually negative in sense. The framework had five main components i.e. Pre-processing, Syntactic Parser, Dependency Table, Rules for Negation and Classification. Stanford Parser plays the important role here. It helps in POS tagging which in turn helps in identifying and developing dependency table. Precision, Recall and Accuracy are the three metrics which were used for calculation or check the effectiveness of developed algorithm. Without considering negation, it gives a precision of 79%, Recall of 76% and Accuracy of 88%. While negation is taken into consideration, precision is 84.87%, Recall is 84.81%, Accuracy is 91.8%. Even if the suggested algorithm gives very promising results, the main limitation of this is that it was majorly tested and verified on mobiles and laptops only. The dependency table which was developed considered these two domains only and it needs to be checked and verified for other domains too. So, this method is said to be very genre specific.

Authors of Ref. [19] proposed a method for negation scope detection for basically three types of negations. They listed the words for syntactic class of negations along with the diminishers and morphological types for negations. The proposed method used three linguistic features (conjunction analysis, punctuation marks and heuristics based on POS of negation terms) along with the static window. They deal and proposed for each type of negation listed and gave heuristic for some exceptions which can occur. They experimented and tested the method using 1,000 randomly selected compound sentences contacting negations from review sites like Amazon, Ebay and Cnet. Results indicated that the proposed method outperformed all the other existing classifiers. The main limitation of the proposed method was that it focused on the analysis of sentiments at the sentence level where the reviews or the sentiments are not limited to single sentence and can go up to many sentences depicting different sentiments in different sentences and on different aspects. So, this method needs to be extended for analysis of sentiments along with the negation at the small scale document level.

Natural languages are very complex and there is a lot of variety in human expressions. This altogether makes the estimation of sentiments of a sentence all the more difficult. Complex structures of the sentences or reviews can only be interpreted correctly if we consider the context in which they appears along with what other words are present along with them. In [20], authors incorporated the Word Sense Disambiguation (WSD) algorithm [21] with a proposed negation handling technique. Two datasets were used here. First one was a corpus of tweets about the movie American Snipper and second one is a multi-set dataset which consists of tweets about a variety of topics. Both the datasets are uniformly distributed and were annotated. After the initial preprocessing (tokenization, POS tagging, lemmatization) of data, WSD was applied to determine the sentiments of the polysemous words. In the Negation Handling algorithm, first the sentences were parsed using a statistical dependency parser i.e. Stanford Parser to analyze the typed dependencies i.e. their grammatical structure and separate clauses. Depth-First Search (DFS) strategy was employed to find the negation words on the generated dependency-based parse trees. Sentiment scores were calculated using the rules mentioned by the authors. Experiments showed that for the American Sniper dataset, accuracy of 67% was achieved as compared to 59% accuracy for the standard lexicon based approach and for the multi-set dataset accuracy was of 62.57% in comparison to 56.36% accuracy for the standard approach. Even if the proposed approach showed improvement in the accuracy, still the achieved accuracy was very low and need to be improved by considering more features like the influence of different conjunctions or the use of punctuation marks or giving weights to the words according to their POS tags.

19.3   Word Embedding

A Word Embedding is a learned representation for text where words that have the same meaning have a similar representation. Here, the individual words are represented as real-valued vectors in a predefined vector space. Each word is mapped to one vector and the vector values are learned in a way that resembles a neural network, and hence the technique is often used in the field of deep learning. One-hot, GloVE, Word2Vec, etc. are some of the word embedding used popularly with the Deep Learning for various NLP applications. Where one-hot encoding gives us very sparse representation of words, GloVE and Word2Vec gives dense representation and can be used in the case of transfer learning.

In Ref. [22], neither word embedding nor deep learning were used by the authors but still we kept their research in this category as they used very similar representation in their research. Here, they used TF-IDF to represent different words or reviews in their database. TF-IDF stands for Term Frequency-Inverse Document Frequency. It is a very common algorithm and is generally used for transforming the text into a meaningful representation of numbers just like word embedding. It is a very popular technique or algorithm used for extracting features in NLP applications and most popular application is the page/document ranking in the search results. TF-IDF is an occurrence based numeric representation of text. More is the importance of a word in the document, higher is its TF-IDF score.

The main objective of the authors in Ref. [22] is to compute the document level sentiment analysis. But for this analysis document's score was based upon the underlying entity or aspect scores. To calculate the aspect scores, the document was classified into multiple classes with multiple aspects. This research was applied to calculate the faculty performance by applying sentiment analysis on the faculty's feedback by the students. Different aspects on which the faculty performance was calculated were taken up from the NAAC accreditation criteria such as, knowledge, communication, presentation and regularity of the faculty. This research can be thought of as divided into two parts. Where the first part deals with extraction of sentences containing features or aspects under consideration, second part calculates the polarity of opinions for that particular feature. Negations cannot be handled at the document level. They must be handled at the entity level. For this, bi-gram feature was used and the negation word and the sentiment bearing word for negation were replaced by its anonym word. The TF-IDF value of the negating feature was replaced by the anonym feature TF-IDF value. The dataset used here consists of 5,000 student feedback comments about the faculty performance. First the data was preprocessed and then for every entity set, each and every feature was represented in numerical format as a feature vector by computing its TF_IDF value. Naïve Bayes (NB) and Support Vector Machine (SVM) classifiers were used of the classification purpose. Experiments showed that the SVM (81%) performed better than NB algorithm (72.8%) and provided better accuracy at the entity level than the document level. But the main disadvantage for this study was that it consider only four pre-specified features or aspects and if student gave his/her feedback for the faculty for some other criteria that was not considered here. Features considered in this study were taken from NAAC accreditation

Table 19.1 Comparative Study of Research According to the Feature Selection Method. (*Continued*)

Researcher Name & Year	Feature used	Dataset	Model Used	Result	Limitation/ Shortcoming
Theresa Wilson, Janyce Wiebe & Paul Hoffmann, 2005	Semantic Based	Multi Perspective Question Answering (MPQA) Opinion Corpus	BoosTexter AdaBoost. HM machine learning algorithm with 5,000 rounds of boosting.	75.9% of accuracy for Neutral-Polar Classification. 65.7% of accuracy for Polarity classification.	Algorithm still needs to be incorporate at wider level of reviews and sentences for sentiment calculation.
Yang Huang, Henry J. Lowe, 2007	Syntactic Based	1,000 radiology reports (500 reports as training set and 132 randomly selected reports as testing set)	Hybrid approach (Parsing + negation grammer)	Sensitivity (recall) of 92.6%. Precision of 98.6%.	Only complete and explicit negations were considered. Experiments were based on the radiology reports and not tested on the general domain.

(*Continued*)

Table 19.1 Comparative Study of Research According to the Feature Selection Method. (*Continued*)

Researcher Name & Year	Feature used	Dataset	Model Used	Result	Limitation/ Shortcoming
Yejin Choi & Claire Cardie, 2008	Compositional Semantics (Both Syntactic and Semantic)	Polarity Lexicon: Lexicon of Ref. [9] expanded using the General Inquirer Dictionary. Negator Lexicon: Seed Words, General Inquirer & WordNet. Multi-Perspective Question Answering (MPQA) Corpus	Rule based along with SVM	Simple heuristics which were based on the compositional semantics (89.7%) outperform both the other reasonable heuristics (87.7%) and other simple learning-based methods which did not incorporate compositional semantics (89.1%) in terms of accuracy whereas when learning methods were combined with the heuristic rules based methods incorporating compositional semantics performance further improved (90.7%)	The process must be automatic and compositional rules must be learned from the data itself.

(Continued)

Table 19.1 Comparative Study of Research According to the Feature Selection Method. (*Continued*)

Researcher Name & Year	Feature used	Dataset	Model Used	Result	Limitation/ Shortcoming
Lifeng Jia, Clement Yu & Weiyi Meng, 2009	Syntactic based	1,000 sentences randomly sampled from rateitall. com and TREC blogosphere review collection	Rule based	Proposed method gives an overall accuracy of 88.4% when compared with different heuristics of scope calculation. Similarly considering Mean Average Precision (MAP) for comparing the retrieval effectiveness on TREC collection gives an improvement of 10.4% for positive documents and 7.4% for negative documents in comparison to methods given by other researchers.	Created a list of negative terms and only this list was considered for the experiment.

(Continued)

Table 19.1 Comparative Study of Research According to the Feature Selection Method. (*Continued*)

Researcher Name & Year	Feature used	Dataset	Model Used	Result	Limitation/ Shortcoming
Roser Morante, Walter Daelemans, 2009	Syntactic based	BioScope's three subcorpora based on clinical free-texts, biological full papers and paper abstracts.	Supervised Machine Learning System (IGTREE as implemented in TiMBL). For scope finding, three classifier (memory-based learning as implemented in TiMBL, SVM and CRF) were used for predicting and a fourth classifier i.e. CRF metalearner was used to predict the scope class using these predictions.	Precision of 81.76% for Abstracts, 72.21% for papers and 86.38% for clinical reports. Recall of 83.45% for abstracts, 69.72% for papers and 82.14% for clinical reports.	Method was tested using the Bio-Medical corpus and need to be tested for general domain corpora.

(Continued)

Table 19.1 Comparative Study of Research According to the Feature Selection Method. (*Continued*)

Researcher Name & Year	Feature used	Dataset	Model Used	Result	Limitation/ Shortcoming
Jingjing Liu, Stephanie Seneff, 2009	Semantic Based	137,569 reviews were collected from an online Restaurant evaluation site on 24,043 restaurants located in 9 cities of U.S.	Rule based	Proposed method gives a recall of 49.7% and precision of 52.9% which increases to 54.1 and 51.4% respectively when combined with baseline method for sentiment scoring.	Focus here was only on the adverb–adjective–noun phrase and rules specified were only related to these phrases. Not much improvement in the results.
Amna Asmi, Tanko Ishaya, 2012	Syntactic Based	55 sentences	Rule based (framework was proposed which includes syntactic parser and sentiment analyzer)	Strong correlation between the proposed system and human annotators.	Very small corpora of 55 sentences only.

(*Continued*)

Table 19.1 Comparative Study of Research According to the Feature Selection Method. (*Continued*)

Researcher Name & Year	Feature used	Dataset	Model Used	Result	Limitation/ Shortcoming
Wareesa Sharif, Noor AzahSamsudin, Mustafa Mat Deris, Rashid Naseem, 2016	Syntactic Based	Customers Reviews	Rule based (framework was proposed which includes syntactic parser, generating dependency table and polarity calculator)	Without considering negation, it gives a Precision of 79%, Recall of 76% and Accuracy of 88%. While negation is taken into consideration, Precision is 84.87%, Recall is 84.81%, Accuracy is 91.8%.	Very domain specific, only two genres were considered and need to be tested on other genres.
Claudia Diamantini, Alex Mircoli, Domenico Potena, 2016	Syntactic Based	100 Tweets about the Movie American Sniper containing 33 negative tweets, 32 neutral/ objective tweets and 35 positive tweets). 497 tweets about different topics (177 negative tweets, 139 neutral/ objective tweets and 181 positive tweets)	Word Sense Disambiguation (WSD) + Negation Handling Technique (algorithm) based on Dependency Parser	Gives the accuracy of 67% for American nipper dataset and 62.57% for Multiset dataset which is 8% and approx. 7% more than the standard approach respectively.	Very low accuracy and need to be improved by considering more features.

(Continued)

Table 19.1 Comparative Study of Research According to the Feature Selection Method. (*Continued*)

Researcher Name & Year	Feature used	Dataset	Model Used	Result	Limitation/ Shortcoming
Umar Farooq, Hasan Mansoor, Antoine Nongaillard, Yacine Ouzrout, Muhammad Abdul Qadir, 2017	Syntactic Based	Randomly selected 1,000 compound sentences from the review sites like Amazon, Ebay and Cnet which contains at least one negation.	Rule based	Accuracy of 83.3%	Specific to sentence level depicting single sentiment so need to be extended.
N. D. Valakunde, M.S. Patwardhan, 2013	TF-IDF	5,000 student feedback comments about faculty performance for last 8 years collected from the institute where this study was conducted	Naïve Bayes (NB) algorithm and Support Vector Machine (SVM)	For the direct document level, NB gave 65.10 % accuracy and SVM gave 67.23% accuracy whereas for aspect based document level sentiment analysis, NB gave 72.80% accuracy and SVM gave 81.00% accuracy.	For the study, features/aspects considered for aspect level sentiment analysis were predefined and were based on a specific country's accreditation process and cannot be applied universally.

(*Continued*)

Table 19.1 Comparative Study of Research According to the Feature Selection Method. (*Continued*)

Researcher Name & Year	Feature used	Dataset	Model Used	Result	Limitation/ Shortcoming
Federico Fancellu, Adam Lopez & Bonnie Webber, 2016	Word-Embedding	Synthetic test set of negative sentences extracted from Simple English Wikipedia was created and annotated.	Feed-forward neural network, Bi-directional LSTM	For scope detection task considering cue information, universal POS and word embedding: Simple Feed Forward give a approx Precision of 89.93, Recall of 77.15 and F1 score of 83.05. Bi directional LSTM gave a Precision of 92.6, Recall of 85.13 and F1 score of 88.72.	Experiment need to be incorporated with the polarity calculation.
Dipesh Gautam, Nabin Maharjan, Rajendra Banjade, Lasang Jimba Tamang, Vasile Rus, 2018	One-hot-encoding and word2vec word embedding	Annotated dialogues from DeepTutor Dialogues	Deep Learning Method using LSTM	M4 has the highest F-1 scores for the detection of focus (.839), scope (.857) and cue (.995) when one-hot-encoding is used for input sequences based on 10-folds cross validation. For word embeddings also, M4 exhibited best F-1 score.	Dialogues were used for the identification of negation cues and results were not incorporated to calculate the sentiments.

19.4 Conclusion

In this paper, we have presented various Negation Identification methods like Bag of Words, Contextual Valence Shifters, Semantic Relations, Relations and Dependency Based or Syntactic Based and Word Embedding methods. We have identified the need for the development of new techniques or some fusion methods which will handle the negation in sentiment analysis. This paper also gives an exploratory comparative study of the contributions made by various researchers with an inclination towards Feature Selection Methods they had used. Various feature selection methods like Unigrams, Bigrams, PoS Tagging, Syntactic based, Word Embedding, Compositional Semantics etc. were used. Pros and cons of all the methods were discussed and the whole summary is placed in a tabular form at the end. Also, in this study we had summarizes various models and datasets used by researchers in their work. It is identified that using machine learning for negation handling in sentiment analysis gives very promising results. But, it needs structured data and lots of human efforts and time is devoted for proper extraction of features in ML methods, specifying inference rules or developing lexicons.

The other solution suggested is using Deep Learning which saves the effort that one need to do in manual extraction of features for the sentiment analysis. Deep Learning is just an extension of Neural Network where many hidden layers of neurons are used in between the input and output layers of the network. Neural Networks were designed to mimic the human brain neurons and is a field of Artificial Intelligence. The working is also similar and you need activation and optimization algorithms to make it work for the forward and back propagation. This has a big advantage over Machine Learning. In this it doesn't require structured data and it learns and extracts different features needed automatically by passing the data through different layers. Also, Deep Learning has a special category of models known as sequence models which can be specifically used for sequence data in Natural Language Processing. Recursive Neural Network, Recurrent Neural Network, GRU, LSTM are some of the example of sequence models. But, there are various other factors on which the success of Deep Neural Networks depends, like deciding how deep the network should be, how many units in each layer etc. along with the problem of over fitting or under fitting of models, values of different hyper parameters like learning rate, regularization parameters, etc. Also, there is need of a proper labeled data base which gives the sentiment scores considering all types of negations. Most popular dataset which was used by many researchers is the IMDB dataset. But, for our research we would be focusing on Stanford Sentiment Treebank as it is the dataset which considers negations also while assigning the sentiment scores to the movie reviews. Deep Learning would automatically identify and learn these constructs. Some researchers addressed the issue of sentiment analysis using deep learning and some addressed the issue of identification of negation cues, scope and their focus by applying Deep Learning. Our main focus would be on the combining of above two research directions and try to develop a model which would incorporate all the features of Natural Language and can be used for effective sentiment analysis. For this broadly various types of sequence models along with other models (like CNN) would be explored and implemented. CNN models are generally used for processing image data but its application in the field of NLP cannot be ignored. So, we need to explore the combination of various models to test the effectiveness of the models for the task in hand.

References

1. Horn, L.R. and Kato, Y., *Introduction: Negation and polarity at the millennium, in negation and polarity, syntactic and semantic perspective*, pp. 1–19, Oxford University Press, Oxford, 2000.

2. Jia, L., Yu, C., Meng, W., The effect of negation on sentiment analysis and retrieval effectiveness, in: *Proceedings of the 18th ACM Conference on Information and Knowledge Management*, pp. 1827–1830, 2009.

3. Hogenboom, A., Van Iterson, P., Heerschop, B., Frasincar, F., Kaymak, U., Determining negation scope and strength in sentiment analysis. *Proceedings of IEEE International Conference on Systems, Man and Cybernatics*, pp. 2589–2594, 2011.

4. Wilson, T., Wiebe, J., Hoffmann, P., Recognizing contextual polarity: an exploration of features for phrase-level sentiment analysis. *Comput. Linguist.*, 35, 3, 399–433, 2009.

5. Pang, B., Lee, L., Vaithyanathan, S., Thumbs up?: Sentiment classification using machine learning techniques, in: *Proceedings of the ACL-02 Conference on Empirical Methods in Natural Language Processing*, vol. 10, pp. 79–86, 2002.

6. Givon, T., *English Grammar: A Function Based Introduction*, John Benjamins Publishing, Amsterdam/Philadelphia, 1993.

7. Polanyi, L. and Zaenen, A., Context valence shifters, in: *Proceedings of the AAAI Spring Symposium on Exploring Attitude and Affect in Text*, pp. 1–10, 2004.

8. Kennedy, A. and Inkpen, D., Sentiment classification of movie reviews using contextual valence shifters. *Comput. Intell.*, 22, 2, 110–125, 2006.

9. Wilson, T., Wiebe, J., Hoffmann, P., Recognizing contextual polarity in phrase-level sentiment analysis, in: *Proceedings of Human Technology Conference and Conference on Empirical Methods in Natural Language Processing*, pp. 347–354, 2005.

10. Choi, Y. and Cardie, C., Learning with compositional semantics as structural inference for sub sentential sentiment analysis, in: *Proceedings of the Conference on Empirical Methods in Natural Language Processing*, Association for Computational Linguistics, pp. 793–801, 2008.

11. Liu, J. and Seneff, S., Review sentiment scoring *via a* parse-and-paraphrase paradigm, in: *Proceedings of the 2009 Conference on Empirical Methods in Natural Language Processing*, vol. 1, Association for Computational Linguistics, pp. 161–169, 2009.

12. Huang, Y. and Lowe, H.J., A novel hybrid approach to automated negation detection in clinical radiology reports. *J. Am. Med. Inform. Assoc.*, 14, 3, 304–311, 2007.

13. Jia, L., Yu, C., Meng, W., The effect of negation on sentiment analysis and retrieval effectiveness, in: *Proceedings of the 18th ACM Conference on Information and Knowledge Management*, pp. 1827–1830, 2009.

14. Morante, R. and Daelemans, W., A meta learning approach to processing the scope of negation, in: *Proceedings of the Thirteenth Conference on Computational Natural Language Learning*, Association for Computational Linguistics, pp. 21–29, 2009.

15. Asmi, A. and Ishaya, T., Negation identification and calculation in sentiment analysis, in: *the Second International Conference on Advances in Information Mining and Management*, pp. 1–7, 2012.

16. Miller, G.A., WordNet: A lexical database for English. *Commun. ACM*, 38, 11, 39–41, 1995.

17. Penn_Treebank, *The Penn Treebank Project [WWW]*, available from http://www.cis.upenn.edu/~treebank/, University of Pennsylvania, Philadelphia, 1992.

18. Sharif, W., Samsudin, N.A., Deris, M.M., Naseem, R., Effect of negation in sentiment analysis, in: *Sixth International Conference on Innovative Computing Technology (INTECH)*, IEEE, pp. 718–723, 2016.

19. Farooq, U., Mansoor, H., Nongaillard, A., Quzrout, Y., Qadir, M.A., Negation handling in sentiment analysis at sentence level. *JCP*, 12, 5, 470–478, 2017.

20. Diamantini, C., Mircoli, A., Potena, D., Negation handling technique for sentiment analysis, in: *Proceedings of International Conference on Collaboration Technologies and Systems (CTS)*, IEEE, pp. 188–195, 2016.

21. Valakunde, N.D. and Patwardhan, M.S., Multi aspect and multi-class based document sentiment analysis of educational data catering accreditation process, in: *International Conference on Cloud & Ubiquitous Computing & Emerging Technologies*, IEEE, pp. 188–192, 2013.

22. Diamantini, C., Potena, D., Sabelli, A., Storti, E., Semantic disambiguation in a social information discovery system, in: *Proceedings of the Collaboration Technologies and Systems (CTS)*, pp. 326–333, 2015.

23. Fancellu, F., Lopez, A., Webber, B., Neural networks for negation scope detection, in: *Proceedings of the 54th Annual Meeting of the Association for Computational Linguistics*, vol. 1, pp. 495–504, 2016.

24. Gautam, D., Maharjan, N., Banjade, R., Tamang, J.L., Rus, V., Long short term memory based models for negation handling in tutorial dialogues, in: *the Thirty-First International Flairs Conference*, 2018.

20

Mobile-Based Bilingual Speech Corpus

Nivedita Palia[1]*, Deepali Kamthania[1] and Ashish Pahwa[2]

[1]School of Information Technology, Vivekananda Institute of Professional Studies, Delhi, India
[2]Data Science Novuse Internet Pvt. Ltd., Gurgaon, India

Abstract

In the context of speech processing, there is a massive significance of corpus which provides the credibility of all the experimental conclusions carried out with it. Bilingual speech corpus is a multi-speaker speech corpus that is primarily oriented in Hindi and the English language. The present study describes the methodology and experimental setup used for the generation and development of bilingual speech corpus. Continuous and spontaneous (discrete) speech samples from both languages are collected on different mobile phones in a real-time environment, unlike studio environments. A brief comparative study of 18 readily available multilingual speech corpus developed for Indian languages is made against the proposed corpus. An annotation scheme is discussed which helps us later to carry out further study how the recognition rate varies on the basis of language, device, text, and utterance.

Keywords: Bilingual speech corpus, Pangram, Speaker recognition system (SRS), Hindi, English, GoldWave, Utterance, Wave file

20.1 Introduction

Human has always been attracted for designing a machine which depicts human behavior having the ability to speak and responding naturally to spoken language [1]. For the development of such systems speech corpus is a prerequisite [2]. The speech signal conveys many levels of information to the listener. At the initial stage, speech conveys a message via words. But at higher stages speech conveys information about the language being spoken and the emotion, gender and the identity of the speaker [3]. The task of the Speech recognition system is to recognize what is spoken while on the other hand, the goal of Speaker recognition systems is to identify who is speaking [4].

India is the land of different languages. The constitution of India has approved 22 languages. According to the 2011 census, there have been more than 19,569 mother tongues spoken by Indians [5]. The Constitution of India designates the official language of the Government of India as Hindi written in the Devanagari script in 1950, while English was declared as an associate official language in 1965 [6].

---
*Corresponding author: nivedita134@gmail.com

Namita Gupta, Prasenjit Chatterjee and Tanupriya Choudhury (eds.) Smart and Sustainable Intelligent Systems, (281–294)
© 2021 Scrivener Publishing LLC

Hindi belongs to the Indo-Aryan branch of the Indo-European family of languages [7]. It is spoken mainly in the states of Bihar, Chhattisgarh, Delhi, Haryana, Himachal Pradesh, Jharkhand, Madhya Pradesh, Rajasthan, Uttarakhand and Uttar Pradesh in India as shown in the Indian Language map given below in Figure 20.1. According to the census of 2011 [5], it has 48 officially recognized dialects and it is spoken by approximately 43.63% of the Indian population.

Most of the speech corpus developed using only the English language and very few works have been done for the Hindi language [9, 10]. Viewing this scenario on the foot-print of Linguistic Data Consortium, University of Pennsylvania Central Institute of Indian Languages, Mysore started developing the repository of Indian languages, Linguistic Data Consortium for Indian Languages. The already developed Indian language speech corpus is domain-specific (such as defence, agriculture, etc.) and has not available for experiment purposes. In this paper, an attempt has been made to develop a Mobile Speech Corpus for Indian languages.

Further, the paper is organized as follows: In Section 20.2 a brief overview and comparative study of the multilingual Indian speech databases are presented. Experimental setup and methodology used for the development of bilingual speech corpora are discussed in Section 20.3 followed by a detailed description of bilingual speech corpora in Section 20.4. In Section 20.5 concluding remarks and future work are stated.

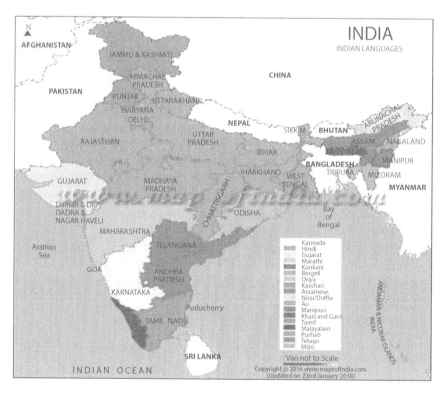

Figure 20.1 Indian language map. ▨▨▨▨ shows Hindi spoken states [8].

20.2 Overview of Multilingual Speech Corpus for Indian Languages

In this section, a detailed comparison of 18 readily available multilingual Indian speech corpus is presented. According to information collected, out of these 18 speech corpora, 10 speech corpus include Hindi and English as a language of recording along with other native languages. Among the 10 corpora, only four have been recorded using the mobile phone as one of the recording devices. Two of them have an in-room environment. Table 20.1 shows a detailed comparative study of 18 readily available multilingual speech corpora for the Indian language. It has been observed that only one database (6) has been developed for speaker recognition purposes while other databases have been developed under the controlled condition for a specific purpose.

On the basis of the study of various speech corpus discussed above an ideal speech corpus constitute the following parameters.

- Adequate speech samples from a large number of speakers in order to validate the performance of the developed system.
- Speech samples from all possible dialects in order to check different pronunciation in a different language [28].
- Speech samples from speakers belonging to the different age groups to study the age effect on pronunciation [28].
- The ratio of males is to females speakers should be approximately 1:1 [29].
- Speech Samples from speakers belonging to different educational backgrounds to track the effects speaking fluency, intelligence level, speaker's experience, Lombard effect, etc. [30–32].
- Phonetically rich text for recording [33–35].
- Data should be recorded in a different acoustic environment to develop a more realistic SRS [28].
- Different recording devices should be used to track the effect of channel effects on the performance of SRS [36–38].
- To analyses, the effect of intersession variability on the performance of the SRS speech sample should be collected in different session at different time span [3, 39].

The purpose of this work is to develop a speech corpus in a realistic environment for the Indian language. A speech sample from Hindi and the English language has been recorded using two different mobile phones in-room environment. Speakers belonging to the different dialectal background have been selected to record a pangram and spontaneous text in both languages. In the coming section, the detailed methodology and brief description of the bilingual mobile speech corpus have been discussed.

20.3 Methodology for Speech Corpus Development

In this section, various steps involved in the creation of bilingual speech corpus are discussed. Figure 20.2 shows the stepwise procedure used in the development of bilingual speech corpus.

Table 20.1 Comparative study of readily available multilingual speech corpora for Indian language.

S. No.	Database developed by	Recording Environment	No. of Speakers	Text	Specification	Languages	Recording Devices	Application
1.	CDAC, NODIA [11, 12]	Noise Free & Echo Cancelled	Not known	Sentences and words	44.1 kHz, 16 bit & stereo mode	Hindi, Marathi, & Punjabi	Not Known	Speech Synthesis
2.	CDAC and ELDA, France [13]	Passenger in moving vehicles, Public Places, Home, office environment, etc.	Hindi as 1st language: 2,000, Hindi as the second language: 1,800, Indian English: 1,800, Mandarin: 800, Korean: 1,000	Sentences and words	8 bit, 8 kHz, A-law speech files	Hindi: by first & second-language speakers, Indian English, Mandarin, & Korean	Mobile	Automated telephone services.
3.	EMILLE/CIIL [10, 14]	Not Known	Not Known	Not Known	Not Known	14 different Indian languages (Assamese, Bengali, Gujarati, Hindi, Kannada, Kashmiri, Malayalam, Marathi, Oriya, Punjabi, Sinhala, Tamil, Telugu & Urdu)	Not Known	Text translation
4.	Utkal University, Bhubaneswar [15, 16]	Laboratory Environment	Not Known	Monosyllable, Bisyllable, Trisyllable & some of the Polysyllable	16 kHz (16 bit), mono channel	Hindi, Odiya, Bengali, and Telugu.	Noise Cancellation Microphone	Text to speech synthesis

(Continued)

Table 20.1 Comparative study of readily available multilingual speech corpora for Indian language. (*Continued*)

S. No.	Database developed by	Recording Environment	No. of Speakers	Text	Specification	Languages	Recording Devices	Application
5.	IIT, Kharagpur [15]	Studio Environment	92	News bulletin broadcast	Not known	Hindi, Telugu, Tamil, & Kannada	Microphone	General-purpose.
6.	IIT, Guwahati [17, 18]	Hostels and labs	Phases 1&2: 100, Phase 3: 200, Phase 4: 470 (collected in 3 parts	Reading and conversational	16 kHz, 8 kHz for mobile	Hindi, English and one favorite language.	Mobiles, microphone, recorder	General purpose
7.	KIIT, Gurgoan [19]	Office environment	100	Sentences	16 kHz	Hindi and Indian English	Mobile, microphone	Mobile-based speech recognition.
8.	LDC-IL [20]	Not Known	Not Known	Not known	Not known	In 22 different Indian languages	Not Known s	General Purpose
9.	IIT, Hyderabad [21]	Professional studio	4–5	Sentences	Not known	Bengali, Hindi, Kannada, Malayalam, Marathi, Tamil and Telugu	Microphone and Laptop	General-purpose.
10.	Rajiv Gandhi University, Arunachal Pradesh [22]	Laboratory	200	Sentences	16 kHz (16 bit) mono-channel	4 native languages of AP, Hindi, and English	Microphones and digital recorders.	speaker verification
11.	IIT, Hyderabad [15, 23]	Noise-free environment	15	Sentences	Not known	Telugu, Hindi, and English	Laptop and microphone	Speech to speech synthesis

(Continued)

Table 20.1 Comparative study of readily available multilingual speech corpora for Indian language. (*Continued*)

S. No.	Database developed by	Recording Environment	No. of Speakers	Text	Specification	Languages	Recording Devices	Application
12.	CFSL, Chandigarh [24]	Office environment	Not known	Isolated and contextual	Not known	Hindi and English	Recorders	Speaker Identification
13.	ICS, Hyderabad [24]	Not known	Not known	Not known	Not known	Telugu and Hindi	Not known	Interactive Voice Response System.
14.	CFSL, Chandigarh [25]	Office environment	100	Sentences and isolated words	Not known	10 different Indian languages	Microphone, mobile, recorder and landline telephone	Speaker identification
15.	CDAC NODIA and DRDO [26]	normal office, noisy office, and in moving car	30 speakers	Sentences and isolated words	16 kHz (16 bit) in mono mode	Hindi, Bengali, and Manipuri	Not known	General-purpose
16.	CFSL, Chandigarh [24]	Laboratory	80	Isolated and contextual	22kHz, 16 bit	Hindi, English, Punjabi, and Kannada	Recorder	Speaker identification
17.	C-DAC, Kolkata [24]	Professionals studio	Not known	Words and sentences	22,050 Hz 16-bit PCM mono	Bengali, Assamese, and Manipuri	Not known	speech synthesis system
18.	IIIT Hyderabad and HP lab Bangalore[27]	Noisy environment	559	Sentences	Not known	Marathi, Tamil, and Telugu	Mobile phones and landlines	General-purpose

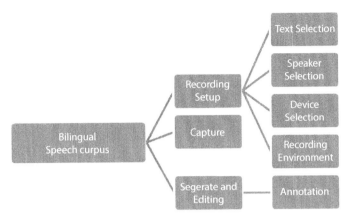

Figure 20.2 Research model to create bilingual speech corpus.

20.3.1   Recording Setup

The first step to create the speech corpus is to decide in which condition speech corpus to be developed. What speaker has to speak and on which device and what is the population of the corpus. Details about all these prerequisites required to develop a bilingual speech corpus have been elaborated in this section.

20.3.1.1   Text Selection

The first step followed in the creation of a bilingual speech is the selection of phonetically rich text. The selected text should be minimum in size as well as it consists of enough occurrence of each type of sounds to record all types of co-articulation effect [27]. For this purpose a pangram in Hindi and English languages shown in Figures 20.3 and 20.4 has been used as a recorded text. The existing Hindi pangram does not contain all consonants of the Hindi language [40]. The referred Hindi pangram has been designed for the first time which consists of all consonants letters of the Hindi language.

घोर, बलशाली, जुझारू, ज्ञानी, ढोंगी तथा ऋषियों को बड़ी त्रासदी देने वाले दुष्ट राक्षस रावण का राज्य खण्डित करने वाले भगवान श्रीराम का जन्म अयोध्या में महाराज दशरथ के जेष्ठ पुत्र के रूप में बड़े दृढ़ यज्ञ में छदम खीर चखने के फलस्वरूप हुआ था।

Figure 20.3 Hindi Pangram.

The Quick Brown Fox Jumps over a Lazy Dog.

Figure 20.4 English Pangram.

Table 20.2 Speaker Classifications.

Attribute	Specification
Gender	Male: 31 Female: 29
Age	20–40 years
Qualification	Undergraduate/Graduate
Dialectal background	Haryanvi (6) Khari Boli (42) Rajasthani (4) Pahari (4) & Bhojpuri (6)

Speaker Id: _____   Date: _____   Time: _____

Personal Information

1. Name:
2. Date of Birth:
3. Gender: Male/Female
4. Qualification:
5. Place of schooling:
6. Place of stay for last 5 years:
7. Stammering:
8. Any Diseases:
   Linguistic Background
7. Mother Tongue:
8. Languaged you can speak:
9. Language you can read or write:
10. Linguistic Background of Mother:
11. Linguistic Backgound of Father:
   Contact
12. E-mail:
13. Contact Number:
14. Address:
   Official
14. Recording Device Details:
15. Recording Environment:
16. Recording Text:
17. Files Name:
18. Recorded by:

Figure 20.5 Speaker information form.

20.3.1.2   Speaker Selection

The speech samples have been recorded from 60 speakers who were comfortable in speaking and reading both Hindi and English language. The speakers who belong to different dialectal backgrounds were chosen. All speakers were in the age group of 20–40 years and qualified for their school education. Each speaker recorded his introduction followed by two utterances of each pangram in both languages. The ratio of the male speakers to the female speakers is approximately 1:1. Table 20.2 shows the exact number of male and female speakers. The speaker's information including physiological characteristics such as gender, age, place of residence, qualifications etc. have been collected using speaker form as shown in Figure 20.5.

20.3.1.3   Device Selection

For recording purposes, two mobile phones of different make have been selected for studying the impact of different devices on speech samples. The quality of the speech samples is based on sampling frequency. The sampling frequency of speech samples for Device 1

Table 20.3 Technical specification of the recording devices.

Device/Sensor	Device 1	Device 2
Make/Model	*Samsung Galaxy S4 Verizon 4 Glte*	*Sony Xperio Tipo*
Sampling rate	44.1 kHz	16 kHz
Recording format	.wav	.wav

Figure 20.6 A snapshot of data recording in-room environment.

(Samsung) is 44.1 kHz and 16 kHz for Device 2 (Sony). Table 20.3 shows the technical specification of the devices.

20.3.1.4 *Recording Environment*

The speech samples have been recorded at Vivekananda Institute of Professional Studies in the classroom with an electric fan and air conditioner switched off. The data were collected simultaneously in both mobiles as shown in Figure 20.6. The mobile phones have been kept at a distance of 15 inch. from the speaker's mouths. Further after recording session, the speech waves have been transmitted to the system.

20.3.2 Capturing

For the proper analysis of the recognition system, the speech data should include all formants, noise patterns, silences, co-articulation effects, etc. Speech samples of speakers are captured using a voice recorder in the mobile phone in offline mode and then transfer to the system for further processing. Figure 20.7 shows the waveform of speaker 1 for device 1.

20.3.3 Segregation and Editing

Segregating the voiced region from the silence/unvoiced portion of the captured signal and removing unwanted speech samples is required for the development of a reliable SRS.

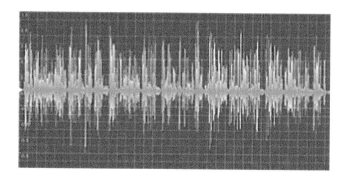

Figure 20.7 Represent speaker1_device 1.wav (Specification: 16 bits, 44.1 kHz and mono channel).

The segregation and editing of speech samples have been done using the GoldWave toolbox to remove the silence between two speech samples. An individual speech sample of each device has been segregated into 6 wave files as shown in Figure 20.8 and saved as per naming schema is given below.

20.3.3.1   Annotation

After the segregation of the wave files, each individual speaker file for each device has been stored into six individual files as shown in Figure 20.9. The naming scheme followed to store the speech files has given below in Table 20.4.

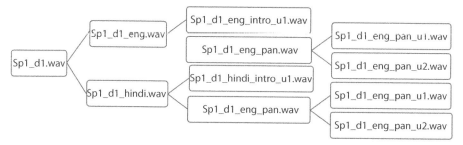

Figure 20.8 Hierarchical representation of annotation for speaker1_device1.wav (Specification: 16 bits, 44.1 kHz and mono channel).

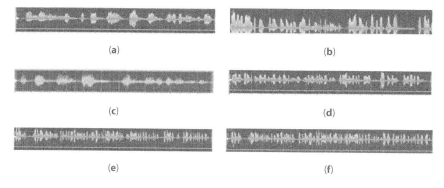

Figure 20.9 Segregated wave files of speaker 1 for device 1. (a) sp1_d1_eng_intro_u1.wav (b) sp1_d1_eng_pan_u1.wav (c) sp1_d1_eng_pan_u2.wav (d) sp1_d1_hindi_intro_u1.wav (e) sp1_d1_hindi_pan_u1.wav (f) sp1_d1_hindi_pan_u2.wav.

Table 20.4 Specification of naming scheme for the given format: SpeakerId_DeviceId_Language_TypeOf Text_UtteranceId.

Fields	Range
Speaker id	*Sp1–Sp60*
Device id	*D1—Samsung & D2—Sony*
Language	*eng—English & hindi—Hindi*
Text	*intro—introduction & pan—pangram*
Utterance id	*u1—utterance1 & u2—utterance 2*

20.4   Description of Bilingual Speech Corpus

The important features of bilingual speech corpus have been summarized below in Table 20.5. The corpus has been developed from non-paid speakers in the uncontrolled environment as per the availability of the speaker and their natural way of communication has not been altered.

Table 20.5 Brief description of bilingual speech corpus.

Attributes	Description
Number of speakers	60 (31 Male and 29 Female)
Data types	Speech
Type of speech	Reading & Spontaneous
Sampling rate	44.1 kHz and 16 kHz
Sampling format	16 bits resolution
Speech duration	1 min
Device	Mobile phone voice recorder
Number of devices	20 (Samsung Galaxy S4verizon 4 Glte and Sony Xperiatipo)
Text	Pangram and introduction
Language	Hindi & English
Application	Text-independent, Text-dependent speaker recognition
Utterance	2 (pangram), 1 (introduction)
Acoustic environment	Room environment
File format	.wav
Number of files for each speaker	12(6 per device)
Total Number of files	720

20.5   Conclusion and Future Scope

In this paper, the methodology and experimental setup for the development of the bilingual mobile speech corpus for Hindi and the English language have been presented. Ideal parameters of speech corpus are discussed along with the comparative study of the readily available multilingual speech corpus for Indian languages. The speech samples of 60 speakers have been recorded in parallel using two different mobile phones in-room environment. The developed corpus has one hour of the speech sample. The individual speech sample is one minute per device with a sampling rate of 44.1 kHz (D1) and 16 kHz (D2) and 16 bits. The developed speech corpus can also be used for other speech processing systems. Further efforts should be in the direction of developing a larger corpus and to develop an SRS.

References

1. Jung, B.H. and Rabiner, L.R., Automatic Speech Recognition- A Brief History of the Technology Development, in: *Encyclopaedia of Language and Linguistics*, K. Brown (Ed.), Elsevier, Oxford, United Kingdom 2004.
2. Nivedita, Ahmed, P., Dev, A., Agrawal, S.S., Hindi Speech Corpora: A Review, in: *International Conference on Asian Spoken Language Research and Evaluation*, O-COCOSDA/CASLRE, India, 2013.
3. Reynolds, D.A., An Overview of Automatic Speaker Recognition Technology, in: *IEEE International Conference on Acoustics Speech and Signal Processing*, vol. 4, pp. 4072–4075, 1999.
4. Ertas, F., Fundamentals of Speaker Recognition. *J. Eng. Sci.*, 6, 2–3, 185–193, 2000.
5. http://www.censusindia.gov.in/2011Census/C-16_25062018_NEW.pdf
6. *Constitutional Provisions: Official Language Related Part-17 of the Constitution of India*, Department of Official Language, Government of India, New Delhi, India, July 2015.
7. http://hindinideshalaya.nic.in/
8. http://www.mapsofindia.com/
9. https://www.ldc.upenn.edu/
10. http://www.elda.org/en/
11. http://www.cdacnoida.in/snlp/stechnology/speech_corpora.asp.
12. Arora, K., Arora, S., Verma, K., Agrawal, S.S., Automatic extraction of phonetically rich sentences from large text corpus of Indian languages. *INTERSPEECH-ICSLP*, Jeju, Korea, 2004.
13. Sanders, E., LILA: Cellular telephone speech database from Asia, in: *Proceeding of LREC*, 2008.
14. Xiao, Z., McEnery, T., Baker, P., Hardie, A., Developing Asian language corpora: standards and practice, in: *4th Workshop on Asian Language Resources*, Sanya, China, 2004.
15. Shrishrimal, P.P., Deshmukh, R.R., Waghmare, V.B., Indian language speech database: A review. *Int. J. Comput. Appl.*, 47, 5, 17–21, 2012.
16. Mohanty, S., Syllable based Indian language text to speech system. *Int. J. Adv. Eng. Technol.*, 1, 2, 138–143, 2011.
17. http://www.iitg.ac.in/eee/emstlab/SRdatabase/introduction.php.
18. Haris, B.C., Pradhan, G., Misra, A., Multi-variability speech database for robust speaker recognition. *National Conference on Communications (NCC)*, pp. 1–5, 2011.
19. Agrawal, S.S., Sinha, S., Singh, P., Olsen, J., Development of text and speech database for Hindi and Indian English specific to mobile communication environment, in: *Proceeding of International Conference on The Language Resources and Evaluation Conference, LREC*, Istanbul, Turkey, pp. 3415–3421, 2012.

20. http://www.ldcil.org/resourcesSpeechCorp.aspx

21. Prahallad, K., The IIIT-H Indic speech database, in: *Proceeding of Interspeech*, Portland, USA, 2012.

22. Bhattacharjee, U. and Sarmah, K., Development of speech corpus of speaker verification research in multilingual environment. *Int. J. Soft Comput. Eng.*, 2, 6, 443–446, 2013.

23. Arora, S., Saxena, B., Arora, K., Agrawal, S.S., Hindi ASR for travel domain, in: *Proceedings of OCOCOSDA*, Kathmandu, Nepal, 2010.

24. Agarwal, S.S., Samudravijaya, K., Arora, K., Recent advances of speech database development activities for Indian languages. *International Symposium on Chinese Spoken Language Processing*, 2006.

25. Sharma, S., Jain, S.K., Sharma, R.M., Agarwal, S.S., Present scenario of forensic speaker identification in India, in: *Proceeding of O-COCOSDA*, Nepal, 2010.

26. http://www.cdacnoida.in/snlp/stechnology/corpora_DRDO.asp

27. Anumanchipalli, G., Chitturi, R., Joshi, S., Kumar, R., Singh, S.P., Sitaram, R.M., Kishore, S.P., Development of Indian Language Speech Databases for Large Vocabulary Speech Recognition Systems, in: *Proceedings of International Conference on Speech and Computer (SPECOM)*, Patras, Greece, 2005.

28. Patil, H.A. and Basu, T.K., Development of speech corpora for speaker recognition and evaluation in Indian languages. *Int. J. Speech Technol.*, Springer, 11, 17–32, 2009.

29. Doddington, G.R., Przybocki, M.A., Martin, A.F., Reynolds, D.A., The NIST speaker recognition evaluation overview: methodology systems, results, perspective. *Speech Commun.*, 31, 2–3, 225–254, 2000.

30. Kersta, L.G., Voiceprint-identification infallibility. *J. Acoust. Soc. Am.*, 38, 1978, 1962.

31. Lombard, E., Le signe de l'élévation de la voix. *Annales de Maladies Oreille, Larynx, Nez, Pharynx*, 37, 101–119, 1997.

32. Junqua, J.C., Fincke, S., Field, K., The Lombard effect: a reflex to better communicate with other in noise, in: *Proceedings of International Conference on Acoustics, Speech, and Signal Processing, ICASSP'99*, vol. 4, pp. 2083–2086, 1999.

33. Sambur, M.R., Selection of acoustic features for speaker identification. *IEEE Trans. Acoust. Speech Signal Process.*, 23, 176–182, 1975.

34. Su, L.S., Li, K.P., Fu, K.S., Identification of speakers by use of nasal co-articulation. *J. Acoust. Soc. Am.*, 56, 1876–1882, 1974.

35. Wolf, J.J., Efficient acoustic parameters for speaker recognition. *J. Acoust. Soc. Am.*, 51, 2030–2043, 1972.

36. Norton, R., The evolving biometric marketplace to 2006. *Biom. Technol. Today*, 10, 9, 7–8, 2002.

37. Reynolds, D.A., The effects of handset variability on speaker recognition performance: Experiment on the Switchboard corpus, in: *Proceedings of International Conference on Acoustics, Speech, and Signal Processing, ICASSP'96*, pp. 113–116, 1996.

38. Reynolds, D.A., HTIMIT and LLHDB: Speech corpora for the study of handset transducer effects, in: *Proceedings of International Conference on Acoustics, Speech, and Signal Processing, ICASSP'97*, Munich, Germany, pp. 1535–1538, 1997.

39. Gish, H. and Schmidt, M., Text-independent speaker identification. *IEEE Signal Process. Mag.*, 11, 4, 18–32, 1994.

40. http://clagnut.com/blog/2380/#Hindi

21

Intrusion Detection using Nature-Inspired Algorithms and Automated Machine Learning

Vasudev Awatramani* and Pooja Gupta

Maharaja Agrasen Institute of Technology, New Delhi, India

Abstract

With the surge of awareness and strategies against threats in space of the modern digital environ-ment, machine learning is rapidly coming up as a fitting solution to many of the malign threats. Such systems are proficient to detect whether an application is under attack from a malicious entity. In this work, the methodology focuses on building an Intelligent Intrusion Detection System uti-lizing a blend of Nature Inspired Heuristics and Automated Machine Learning. The study applies Evolutionary Algorithms for feature selection as well as Hyperparameter Optimization. Moreover, the research explores Bayesian Search for Neural Architecture Search to estimate the ideal archi-tecture of an artificial neural network (ANN). By employing the following techniques, the work achieves a near state of the detection rate of 98.5%.

Keywords: Architecture search, hyperparameter optimization, deep learning, automated machine learning, intrusion detection, information security, nature inspired algorithms, feature engineering

21.1 Introduction

Security in computer networks is one of the prominent concerns in cyber security, dis-tinctly in present times as the network usage is expanding exponentially due to increased use of handheld devices. Consequently, the development of robust transmission protocols and practices are always necessitated. Yet, such versatility can often leave backdoors and loopholes to vulnerabilities from malicious entities. Intrusion Detection Systems (IDS) are such applications that detect malign threats over oblivious network users without jeopar-dizing the safety of the host as well as the network.

An IDS is a listen-only device and serves as a passive preventive mechanism to recognize exploiting advances on the web. At any instance, a web server caters to numerous clients and consequently produces substantial traffic. Each of these network connections can be outlined to a combination of sharp attributes. Hence, movement across the network can

---

**Corresponding author*: vasudev.w13@gmail.com

Namita Gupta, Prasenjit Chatterjee and Tanupriya Choudhury (eds.) Smart and Sustainable Intelligent Systems, (295–306)
© 2021 Scrivener Publishing LLC

be orderly recorded and employed to examine trends in case of deviations from innocuous behavior. The IDS monitors traffic and communicates its verdicts to an administrator or an automated procedure that practices action to counter the exposed mal-intent from imperilling the integrity of the network.

Accounts of interactions between users and the network are accessible in abundance. Hence, Intelligent Systems can be devised that can efficiently monitor transmissions. The proposed approach focuses on the utilization of Nature Inspired Met heuristics as a mechanism for feature extraction and Automated Machine Learning for applying customized and tailored decision-making policies. For the stated purpose, the methodology employs NSL-KDD [1] dataset as its source of transmission records over the web.

The NSL-KDD is a revised variant of the KDD'99 cup [2], a tabular dataset formulated for the International Knowledge Discovery and Data Mining Tools Competition. The goal of the competition was to design an intrusion detector having predictive capabilities of differentiating between intrusions or attacks, and normal associations. The dataset comprises records of the internet traffic seen by a simplistic intrusion detection network having 43 fields. Out of these, 41 are trainable characteristics referring to the transmission input and the two are target features, 'Label' that describes transmission as normal or attack and 'Score' that represents the austerity of the given threat. Within the dataset there are 4 distinct categories of attacks: Probe, Remote to Local (R2L), Denial of Service (DoS), and User to Root (U2R).

A brief description of these attacks is as follows:

1. DOS: Denial of service drains the victim's computation resources rendering it incapable to handle genuine requests. Percentage of Packets with errors is a significant feature in tracking such attacks.
2. Probing: Its intention is to obtain information about the remote victim Attacks include Ip Sweep and Port Scanning
3. U2R: In User-to-Root, an attacker uses a standard account to login into a victim system and tries to gain root/administrator privileges by abusing some vulnerability. Xterm and Rootkit are typical examples of such malign activities.
4. R2L: stands for Remote-to-Local, the intruder penetrate a remote machine and gains local access of the victim machine.

There are 39 distinct attacks that can be broadly classified into 4 categories of DoS, Probe, U2R and R2L as described in Table 21.1. However, these categories do not have a balanced representation in the dataset, leading to difficulty in classification. Figure 21.1 represents the distribution of the categories, it may be noted that U2R is not completely absent but has very insignificant representation as compared to other attacks.

Since, the distribution of each is not uniform; the approach needs to be robust enough to account for such a challenge. It is known, many machine learning algorithms are affected by such heterogeneity, especially linear classifiers that effectively return the majority class as their prediction for any given input. Therefore, to work past this obstacle tree based classifiers such as Decision Trees, Random Forests and Gradient Boosted Trees are suitable as they are not affected. Furthermore, Deep Learning models are also immune to this predicament

Table 21.1 Types of Attacks described in the dataset.

DoS	Probe	U2R	R2L
neptune	mscan	xterm	ftp_write
mailbomb	nmap	SQL attack	guess_password
pod	ipsweep	rootkit	httptunnel
processtable	saint	perl	imap
worm	portsweep	ps	multihop
teardrop	satan	loadmodule	phf
processtable		buffer overflow	sendmail
udpstrom			spy
apache2			snmp Guess
			xlock
			xsnoop
			warezmaster
			warezclient

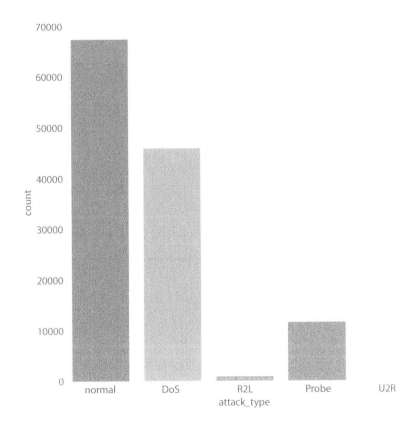

Figure 21.1 Distribution of attack types.

unless the data is severely imbalanced such as in Fraud Detection, where around 95% of the samples may belong to the Non-Fraudulent case and fraudulent samples are sparse.

Feature Engineering is one of the most undervalued aspects of any machine learning pipeline. Mining and Identifying relevant features promote better data quality, which results in a powerful intelligent system. In this dataset, there are a number of features such as duration of a transmission, having high variance, and hence, lacks the presence of sharp boundaries that can help identify a presence of any attack.

However, there appear to be certain features that dictate the presence of specific attacks, for instance the Number of Source Bytes for each of the Labels as shown in Figure 21.2 indicates that a higher number is likely the system is under Probe Attack.

Consequently, such features can sometimes be helpful. Such as, observed from Figure 21.3, it can be easily inferred that ICMP protocol is most insecure and vulnerable. Likewise, UDP does seem to be secure when the network is susceptible to R2L.

Such deductions though miniscule, are true even in real world sense, ICMP is infamous for numerous reasons such as reconnaissance attacks by adversaries against a given target, and therefore, ICMP packets are blocked and are widely blocked in networks.

21.2   Related Work

This section covers some of the prior work and their notable contributions in the development of Intrusion Detection systems utilizing the NSL-KDD dataset. Dhanabal *et al.* [3] performed a comprehensive study on NSL-KDD dataset and its variations by testing them against various classifiers such as J48, SVM and Naive Bayes. Moreover, the authors focused on minimal attribute selection, employing only normalized attributes as inputs for classification. By studying the correlation among the features, they narrowed to 6 features out of 41, and were able to attain a detection rate of 99.8% with the J48 algorithm. Ingre *et al.* [4]

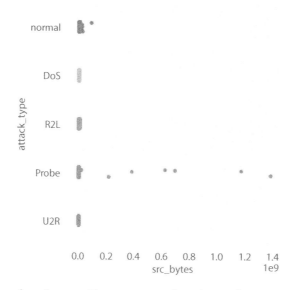

Figure 21.2 Distribution of attack types with respect to number of source bytes.

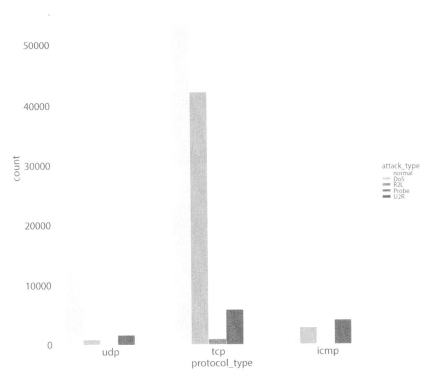

Figure 21.3 Distribution of attack types with respect to protocol of connection.

were one of the first researchers to employ Artificial Neural Networks for detecting intrusion through NSL-KDD. They applied feature reduction techniques as proposed by Bajaj *et al.* [5] that identified attributes which were redundant or had little effect on the classification process. Using a reduced vector of 29 attributes, followed by Z-Score Normalization, Ingre *et al.* achieved a binary detection accuracy of 81.2% and classification accuracy of 79.9% applying a minimalistic neural network consisting of only 2 hidden layers and no non-linear activations. Aggarwal *et al.* [6] analyzed KDD-NSL with WEKA and observed a reduced False Alarm Rate (FAR), hence an enhanced Detection Rate. Their work revolved around combination of 4 broad categories of the attributes Basic, Host, Traffic and Content. A set of 15 permutations of these attributes were formulated and fed to Random Tree Algorithm in WEKA. Rule-Based Classification has also been explored on NSL-KDD, with Wutyi *et al.* [7] employing Hidden-Semi Markov Models. They applied a blend of self-defined as well as algorithm-generated heuristics for different types of attacks. Furthermore, they claimed that the dataset contained a mislabeled defect between R2L and U2R. Popular Analytics and Data Mining techniques have also been explored over NSL-KDD. Meryem *et al.* [8] applied a MapReduce based pipeline for intrusion detection. They proposed a system involving unsupervised clustering algorithms such as K-Means and a supervised instance-based model such as K-NN trained over NSL-KDD.

Some of the methodologies focused on algorithms for feature manipulation as their primary research purpose. Hota *et al.* [9] studied NSL-KDD proposed an approach that heavily relied on extraction of suitable features from the dataset. They appropriated various feature selection methods such as Correlation Analysis, Info Gain, Correlation, RelieF algorithms and Symmetrical Uncertainty. These modified features were fed to tree-based classifiers achieving more than 99% accuracy such that the reduced input vector consisted of 11 attributes only. Other studies such as that of Benaddi *et al.* [10] applied statistical feature compression techniques such as Principal Component Analysis (PCA), followed by Fuzzy Clustering. The reduced attribute representations were used by K-Nearest Neighbor (KNN) algorithm as a detection of attacks but achieved comparatively lower performance of 53%.

In recent years, studies have also included the application of modern Deep Learning for IDS development. Ding *et al.* [11], investigated Convolutional Neural Network as a deep representation learning approach and produced enhanced detection rate of 96.73% over other constructs such Deep Belief Networks (DBNs), Long Short Term Memory Units (LSTM). Gurung *et al.* [12] employed Sparse-Autoencoders as an unsupervised feature representation and Logistic Regression Classifier, attaining a precision score of 84.6% and recall score of 92.8%.

21.3 Methodology

The proposed approach intends to study a blend of Nature-Inspired Algorithms (NIAs) and Deep Learning (DL) methods. The application of NIA is for feature representation such that a feature vector for further processing factors is produced which a fitting and concise erudition is. Furthermore, the methodology employs NIAs as a parameter optimizer for DL models as well. Such utilization of NIAs is an illustration of Automated Machine Learning and compared with popular Automated Methods such as Bayesian Search.

21.3.1 Nature Inspired Algorithms for Feature Selection

Feature selection is a dimensionality compression technique employed to eliminate impertinent characteristics. Furthermore, it enhances the classification accuracy. Feature selection procedures achieve a unique representation of generalized features from the original feature vector. In recent years, NIAs have been attracting a considerable amount of attention due to their novel feature selection methods and approaches.

The study utilizes Bat Algorithm (BA) for feature selection in combination with conventional Machine Learning Algorithm.

BA was proposed by Xin-She Yang [13] based on echolocation behaviour of bats for intricate optimization problems. Parameter control and frequency tuning are some of the characteristics of BA that surpass its counterparts such as Genetic Algorithms, and Harmony Search. BA proves to give good results for many optimizations such as non-linear tasks studied by Kiełkowicz *et al.* [14] used BA. Whereas Abatari *et al.* [15] proposed a BA inspired method to solve the Optimal Power Flow (OPF) problem.

    a) Microbats use sonar, called echolocation to detect prey, and evade hindrances. These bats emit a very loud noise pulse and attend to the echoes that reflect from the neighboring objects.

        1. Each virtual bat in the swarm travels randomly with a velocity V_i at position X_i with a varying frequency or wavelength and loudness A_i.

2.   Loudness can range from maximum possible value A_0 to a minimum value.
3.   The bat explores and locates its prey by alternating frequency, loudness and pulse emission rate R.
4.   The search of the fittest solution continues until specified halt criteria are sufficed.
5.   The process involves a frequency-tuning method to regulate the dynamic response of swarms of bats to determine the best position in the space.

BA has certain distinguished benefits over other metaheuristic algorithms such as:

- Automatically zooming into a region of a search space where promising solutions have been found.
- BA manages parameter control, which can vary the values of parameters (Loudness and Pulse Rate) on run time as the iterations proceed to provide smooth switching from exploration to exploitation when the fittest solution is nearing.

By employing BA, we are able to represent input feature of shape (41), as a vector of shape (22).

21.3.2   Automated Machine Learning

The achievement of machine learning in a broad spectrum of applications has driven to a tremendous need for machine learning systems that can be used off the shelf by non-experts. To be serviceable in practice, such methods need to automatically determine a suitable algorithm and feature pre-processing actions for a new dataset at hand, and also establish their several hyperparameters. Novel works have been raised to produce a domain of Automated Machine Learning such as Neural Architecture Search (NAS) [16]. Studies like NASNet [16] (custom-built network architecture for given Image Recognition dataset) utilize many procedures to automate the learning process. These include Reinforcement Learning [17], Bayesian Optimization [18], Evolutionary Heuristics [19] and Random Search [20].

Automated Machine Learning strives to enhance the contemporary approach of building ML applications by self-regulation. ML specialists can benefit from AutoML by automating tiresome actions such as feature engineering, architecture search, hyperparameter optimization and model selection.

The study employs two AutoML policies:

1. Architecture Search following Bayesian Search
2. Hyperparameter Optimization of Deep Learning Network utilizing Particle Swarm Optimization.

21.3.3   Architecture Search using Bayesian Search

Bayesian search discovers the state that satisfies an objective function by formulating a probability model based on the prior evaluation. This probability model known as *substitute* or *surrogate* is more flexible to compute than the objective, so the subsequent input values to evaluate are selected by applying a criterion to the surrogate. The primary notion behind is to curb fallacious evaluations of the target function by picking the subsequent input states based on those that have yielded a profitable outcome in the past.

The suggested method is inspired by Jin *et al.* [21] that explores the search space by modifying the neural architectures supervised by Bayesian optimization (BO) algorithm.

In the context of NAS, the prescribed BO algorithm iteratively loops over the following steps:

1. Update: Develop a Gaussian process model with randomly produced architectures and their performance.
2. Synthesis: Produce subsequent architectures optimized by an established procurement function.
3. Observation: Capture metrics of performance by training the produced architecture.

However, there are 3 major hurdles with the above approach

1. Sustaining intermediate output vector shape consistency when altering new architectures.
2. BO to guide network alteration for optimization of the acquisition function in tree-structured space.
3. Altering traditional Gaussian Process is based on Euclidean Distances whereas NAS is depicted in terms of tree structures.

These challenges have been addressed by Jin *et al.* in their work. Employing their prescribed methods the study achieves an accuracy of 96.1%. In Figure 21.4, it can be observed that optimization tries to tweak around with order of Activation and Dropout Layers when formulating new architectures. Moreover, if we observe the first architecture, it has two consecutive Rectified Linear Units, which is needless. However, for both architectures, the intermediate Hidden Layers had the same number of hidden units (64 units).It might be noted that though, the above procedure is computationally expensive and time-consuming, taking around 100 trials to reach the optimal architecture. Also, NAS considers the entire 41 features from the dataset as its input. Therefore, there might be some effect on the performance if feature engineering is carried out prior to feeding the inputs to Generated Network.

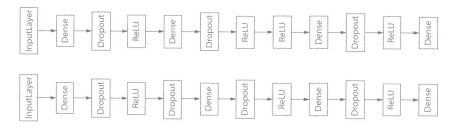

Figure 21.4 Examples of model architectures as produced by NAS using bayesian search.

21.3.4   Hyperparameter Optimization Through Particle Swarm Optimization (HPO-PSO)

For the NAS produced architecture, the study intends to optimize Deep Neural Network (DNN) hyperparameters viz. learning rate. Learning rate is an essential Hyperparameter in DNN that decides the step size at subsequent epochs while advancing toward the minima of the given loss function. It must be noted that the optimizer used for training the network is Stochastic Gradient Descent with a fixed momentum value that can also be optimized. Particle swarm optimization (PSO) is a population-based optimization methodology formulated by Kennedy *et al.* [22], motivated by the social mannerism of flocking of birds.

PSO simulates the behavior of bird flocking in the following situation:

1. A flock of birds randomly seeks food in an area. Moreover, is only one food source in the search space.
2. However, all the birds do not know the location of food. Yet they are able to determine the food's location in subsequent iterations.
3. Therefore, the flock follows the bird which is nearest to the food as its best strategy.

The learning rate produced from PSO is 0.5738×10^{-2}. Figure 21.5 represents loss over changing learning rate over 100 iterations. It can be observed that PSO does not alter the nature of training of the model. PSO only provides an optimum value of the hyperparameter learning rate such that the network can converge to the state of minimum loss faster. For the first 20 epochs, the loss of the model follows the same trend in both cases PSO-Optimized and Unoptimized. However, with PSO the model has already converged to the supposed minimum loss before 20 iterations, whereas the Unoptimized system consumes more than 80 epochs to achieve this. Nevertheless, the performance is still better observed with PSO-Optimized hyperparameters.

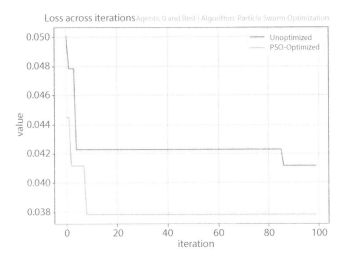

Figure 21.5 Loss function across the iterations.

Table 21.2 Accuracy over discussed techniques.

Model	Detection Accuracy
Bat algorithm & traditional random forest	97
Bayesian optimization NAS	96.1
PSO-HPO network	98.5

21.4 Results

A comparison has been drawn between the proposed methods. It can be noted from Table 21.2, that the application of Bat Algorithm not only proves to be an effective feature reduction but enhances the performance of the detection system as well. Though the deep learning architecture produced by NAS is not as proficient as expected, there is an improvement observed when combined with PSO-HPO.

A pipeline involving Combination of Bat Features and NAS was also studied but produced comparatively lower performance of 92.8% possibly due to data hungry nature of DNNs.

21.5 Conclusion

In this work, a novel scope of Evolutionary Algorithms and Automated Machine Learning was examined. These methods are not only nascent in designing of Intelligent Cyber security systems and are still in embryonic stages in the field of Intelligent Systems. The study achieves a near state-of-the-art detection accuracy over the NSL-KDD dataset. Our future work shall concern with automating the design of Deep Neural Networks as well as pre-processing tasks with the application of Reinforcement Learning and Combinatorial Optimizations, instead of discussing Evolutionary and Search methods. Moreover, later study shall also focus on making such auto-generated models more efficient in terms of computation by compression [23] and pruning [24] techniques.

Apart from the described approaches, Sequence classifiers are also getting popular for session security of a client over a network. The activity of a client such the requests it makes or the route that a given packet follows, are mapped to a sequence of fixed or even variable length and fed to Recurrent architectures such Bi-directional LSTMs or GRUs. Though not possible with NSL-KDD, research in such a blend of Machine Learning and Cyber security can produce phenomenal results.

References

1. Tavallaee, M., Bagheri, E., Lu, W., Ghorbani, A., A Detailed Analysis of the KDD CUP 99 Data Set. Submitted to *Second IEEE Symposium on Computational Intelligence for Security and Defense Applications (CISDA)*, 2009.
2. Tavallaee, Bagheri, Lu, Ghorbani, A Detailed Analysis of the KDD CUP 99 Data Set. *Proceedings of the 2009 IEEE Symposium on Computational Intelligence in Security and Defense Applications (CISDA 2009)*, 2009.

3. Roshni R., Mol, Dr. C. Immaculate Mary, Intrusion Detection System from Machine Learning Perspective, *Int. J. Eng. Res. Technol. (IJERT)*, ICATCT, 8, 03, 2020.

4. Ingre, B. and Yadav, A., Performance analysis of NSL-KDD dataset using ANN. *2015 International Conference on Signal Processing and Communication Engineering Systems*, Guntur, pp. 92–96, 2015.

5. Bajaj, and Arora, Improving the Intrusion Detection using Discriminative Machine Learning Approach and Improve the Time Complexity by Data Mining Feature Selection Methods. *Int. J. Comput. Appl.*, 76, 1, 5–11, August 2013.

6. Aggarwal, and Sharma, S.K., Analysis of KDD Dataset Attributes—Class wise for Intrusion Detection. *Procedia Comput. Sci.*, 57, 842–851, 2015.

7. Wutyi, K.S. and Thwin, M.M.S., Heuristic Rules for Attack Detection Charged by NSL KDD Dataset, in: *Genetic and Evolutionary Computing*, vol. 387, Advances in Intelligent Systems and Computing, Springer, Cham, 2016.

8. Amar, M., Samira, D., Ouahidi, B., Lemoudden, M., A novel approach in detecting intrusions using NSLKDD database and MapReduce programming. *Procedia Comput. Sci.*, 110, 230–235, 2017.

9. Hota, S. and A.K., Decision Tree Techniques Applied on NSL-KDD Data and Its Comparison with Various Feature Selection Techniques, in: *Advanced Computing, Networking and Informatics*, vol. 1, pp. 205–211, 2014.

10. Ding, and Zhai, Intrusion Detection System for NSL-KDD Dataset Using Convolutional Neural Networks. *Proceedings of the 2018 2nd International Conference on Computer Science and Artificial Intelligence—CSAI '18*, 2018.

11. Gurung, S., Ghose, M.K., Subedi, A., Deep Learning Approach on Network Intrusion Detection System using NSL-KDD Dataset. *Int. J. Comput. Netw. Inf. Secur. (IJCNIS)*, 11, 3, 8–14, 2019.

12. Benaddi, Ibrahimi, Benslimane, Improving the Intrusion Detection System for NSL-KDD Dataset based on PCA-Fuzzy Clustering-KNN. *6th International Conference on Wireless Networks and Mobile Communications (WINCOM)*, 2018.

13. Yang, X.S., A New Metaheuristic Bat-Inspired Algorithm, in: *Nature Inspired Cooperative Strategies for Optimization (NICSO 2010). Studies in Computational Intelligence*. González J.R., Pelta D.A., Cruz C., Terrazas G., Krasnogor N. (eds.), vol 284. Springer, Berlin, Heidelberg. https://doi.org/10.1007/978-3-642-12538-6_6.

14. Grela, D. and Kiełkowicz, K., Modified Bat Algorithm for nonlinear optimization. *Int. J. Comput. Sci. Netw. Secur.*, 16, 10, 46–50, 2016.

15. Abatari, H., Seyf Abad, M., Seifi, H., Application of Bat Optimization Algorithm in Optimal Power Flow. *Electrical Engineering (ICEE) 2016 24th Iranian Conference on 2016*, 2016.

16. Zoph, B. *et al.*, Learning Transferable Architectures for Scalable Image Recognition. *2018 IEEE/CVF Conference on Computer Vision and Pattern Recognition*, pp. 8697–8710, 2017.

17. Zoph, B. and Le, Q.V., Neural Architecture Search with Reinforcement Learning, *ArXiv*, 2016, abs/1611.01578.

18. Archetti, F. and Candelieri, A., Automated Machine Learning and Bayesian Optimization, in: *Bayesian Optimization and Data Science. Springer Briefs in Optimization*, Springer, Cham, 2019.

19. Liang, J., Meyerson, E., Hodjat, B., Fink, D., Mutch, K., Miikkulainen, R., Evolutionary neural AutoML for deep learning, in: *Proceedings of the Genetic and Evolutionary Computation Conference (GECCO '19)*. Association for Computing Machinery, New York, NY, USA, 401–409, 2019.

20. Bergstra, and Bengio, Random Search for Hyper-Parameter Optimization. *J. Mach. Learn. Res.*, 13, 10, 281–305, 2012.

21. Jin, H., Song, Q., Hu, X., Auto-Keras: An Efficient Neural Architecture Search System, in: *Proceedings of the 25th ACM SIGKDD International Conference on Knowledge Discovery & Data Mining (KDD '19)*. Association for Computing Machinery, New York, NY, USA, 1946–1956, 2019.

22. Kennedy, and Eberhart, Particle swarm optimization. *Proceedings of ICNN'95—International Conference on Neural Networks*, Perth, WA, Australia, vol. 4, pp. 1942–1948, 1995.

23. Choudhary, T., Mishra, V., Goswami, A. *et al*. A comprehensive survey on model compression and acceleration. *Artif. Intell. Rev.*, 53, 5113–5155, 2020. https://doi.org/10.1007/s10462-020-09816-7.

24. He, Y., Zhang, X., Sun, J., Channel Pruning for Accelerating Very Deep Neural Networks. *2017 IEEE International Conference on Computer Vision (ICCV)*, 2017.

Part 3
SECURITY AND BLOCKCHAIN

22

Distributed Ownership Model for Non-Fungible Tokens

Jaspreet Singh* and Prashant Singh†

Bharati Vidyapeeth's College of Engineering, Delhi, India

Abstract

Digital assets direct monetary value. Although, maintaining its integrity, ownership and transparency is a huge challenge. It includes fraud, tampering, duplication and more. So, blockchain provides integrity and allows trustless transactions without any central authority. Currently, Non-Fungible Tokens (NFTs) are used to create such digital assets providing the uniqueness in each asset, although its real-life valuation is not that simple to create a marketplace. This paper presents the concept of distributed ownership of any digital asset (NFT) amongst many people in the form of percentage shares. We name the token as distributed NFT (dNFT). It holds the properties of NFTs as well as it can be traded in the form of percentage shares as in real world. Each digital asset in this model is validated by the validators who act as a trust entity in the system. Hence, it is authentic, verifiable and acts as real market place for all types of digital assets.

Keywords: Distributed ownership, digital assets, blockchain, smart contract, non-fungible tokens

22.1 Introduction

All the Cryptographic digital assets, just like physical assets, have many properties such as fungibility, semi-fungibility and non-fungibility. In terms of economics, fungibility refers to the interchangeability or equivalence of each unit of a commodity with other units of the same commodity. Hence, Fungible Tokens (FTs) work fine for the tokens that tends to have currency-like properties rather than being something unique and valuable itself. It is an essential feature of any currency for the means of exchange and store of value. Bitcoin, Ether, EOS, etc. are examples of Fungible tokens. On the other hand, the non-fungible tokens are special type of tokens that represent a unique asset. They represent scarce physical property, like crypto kitties, artwork, crafts, virtual house, etc. Hence, they are non-interchangeable, unique and indivisible tokens. The other type of tokens is Semi-Fungible Tokens (SFTs) [1]. These tokens are 1 of any 'n' number of tokens with a serial number or slightly different metadata. This paper focuses on dNFT which can be considered in between of NFTs and FTs also having properties of SFTs.

Corresponding author: jaspreets.2020@gmail.com
†*Corresponding author*: prashant.singh11097@gmail.com

Namita Gupta, Prasenjit Chatterjee and Tanupriya Choudhury (eds.) Smart and Sustainable Intelligent Systems, (309–322)
© 2021 Scrivener Publishing LLC

So, the power of blockchain to spread digital information can help in prospering other industries as well like theatre, music industry, e-books, videography, etc., where piracy and illegal use of content are damaging the industry. Hence, proliferation of digital information can be proved invaluable to the content creators in these industries. Therefore, support in creation, storage and distribution of digital information should reflect that value and safeguard the rights and interests of its true owners. This signifies the value of providing the true ownership on blockchain to such digital assets along with creating a marketplace. But, Non-Fungible Tokens (NFTs) in itself are indivisible in nature thus, its ownership is absolute or none at all.

This paper presents an alternative approach, which addresses this problem by providing a distributed ownership model architecture. This proposes that one need not necessarily purchase the complete ownership of a non-fungible token rather can acquire a certain percentage of ownership of the token. Such a token may be called as dNFT (distributed Non-Fungible Token). In particular, it can be thought of partnership of any digital asset like ownership of houses wherein multiple owners exist for a particular house which is unique. So, each unique house here can be sought of as the Non-Fungible Token (NFT) with distributed stakes (or) rights.

22.2   Background

Blockchain technology is the most important concept for providing distributed trust and the concept of ownership on blockchain has become popular in recent times to provide scalability and real-time use cases for blockchain.

22.2.1   Blockchain Technology

A blockchain is an incorruptible digital ledger of economic transactions that stores various data in an append-only fashion, preventing modification of previously stored data hence ensuring integrity and a time-stamped series of immutable records of data that is managed in a decentralized way. Generally, there exist permissioned and permission less blockchains. The former incorporates centralization features into the protocol, partially including the trust, hence only peers approved by a single entity may join the consensus (e.g., Hyperledger). In contrast, the permission less blockchains are decentralized and trustless, hence any peer may join the consensus protocol immediately (e.g. Ethereum). Blockchains are also classified according to the in-band investment: Proof-of-Work, Proof-of-Stake, Delegated Proof of Stake and many more.

In Proof of Work mechanism, nodes in the network (miners) work to solve a computationally hard cryptographic puzzle repetitively consisting of the mathematical function (e.g. Bitcoin) [2]. Committing a fraudulent transaction on the blockchain will require the party to have over half of the total hash rate of the entire network that is extremely hard to attack. In Proof of Stake (PoS) mechanism, on other hand replaces miners with validators where they lock up some of their coins as stake. A group of validators takes turns proposing and voting on the next block, and the weight of each validator's vote depends on the size of their stakes on system. When the validators discover a block which they think can be added to the blockchain, they validate it by placing a bet on it. The validators get reward proportionate to their bets. Delegated Proof-of-Stake (DPoS) is a more efficient PoS mechanism. DPoS uses a reputation system and real-time voting to achieve consensus. Community members vote for super representatives to secure their network and these representatives will be rewarded by validating transactions for the next block (e.g. EOS blockchain).

22.2.2   Ownership

With blockchain technology, all ownership of digital assets can be recorded in a trustless environment whether it is bought, sold, leased, or transferred as the owner sees fit.

Non-Fungible Tokens are supposed to grant ownership of digital assets to people the same way they have ownership of tangible property in the real world. NFTs are protected copyrights, because they are an expression of an idea recorded. However, the NFTs so far created are simply a continuance of the current system of licenses and indisputable title to property [3, 4]. One can buy and sell the whole NFT's ownership at once by bidding for its price.

22.3   Proposed Architecture

In order to deal with the problem of NFTs being owned by single entity, a distributed ownership architecture is proposed. A hierarchical approach for the category, token name and their percentage holdings is implemented. Category is at the top-most hierarchy which tells us about what marketplace it is holding. This can be used to group various tokens of a similar class.

22.3.1   Overview

Multiple stakeholders exist for everything in the real world, whose ownership tends to be acceded, be it a house, music, photography, research work, gaming or sharing. Subsequently, each NFT creation should have some physical significance, value and probability.

Decentraland is one such example where non-fungible ERC721 LAND tokens are present. It is a virtual reality platform powered by the Ethereum blockchain that allows users to create, experience, and monetize content and applications. In this virtual world, users purchase plots of land that they can later navigate, build upon, and monetize. MANA is an ERC20 token that must be burned to acquire LAND tokens. Here, the LAND is an NFT that cannot be distribute or shared. There is no scope of buying high valued NFT and share it currently. Figure 22.1 shows that there has been a constant demand for Decentraland in past one year.

Other than distributed ownership of Land, following examples are mentioned below that show that there is an extensive requirement of fractional ownership in various industries.

- 2.5 million new scientific papers are published each year
- The global art market represents approximately USD 50 billion worldwide.
- Almost 5 billion videos are watched on YouTube every single day.
- 24,000 songs are uploaded every day and 1 million tracks in six weeks.

Another important aspect to highlight here is that all of the aforementioned cases entail significantly high transaction speed (TPS) and verifiability. So, EOS blockchain (or any

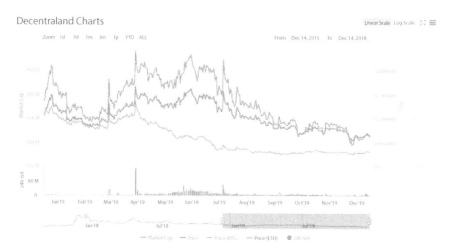

Figure 22.1 Decentraland price trends.

other Delegated Proof of Stake consensus blockchain) over Ethereum blockchain becomes a prominent choice. This also ensures faster transaction speed.

Every creation of NFT by owner needs to be verified by trusted validators in the real-world. They need to select 1 validator from trusted validators list and one is chosen by contract randomly by some random number generation. It may be generated off chain. The user data is encrypted by their unique information (e-mail, name, phone, etc.) using chosen validator's key and the json document is signed. The hash is shared on blockchain and once both of the validators verify the creation, it is alive for buying, selling and transferring functions.

22.3.2   Implementation

The paper describes the implementation in EOSIO blockchain. The constant "assets" is declared for the 100% total current supply of any unique token. Though they can be burnt but cannot be minted. These are initialized as 100 PER as the current supply. PER is the token symbol referring percentage, whenever new token is created by anyone under some category. 10 PER of token VT-A means 10% ownership of VT-A. Hence, multiple accounts can have the ownership on same token without the token itself being fungible. Also, it is not a compulsion that 100 PER needs to be issued at once. One can issue any x PER to accounts where x ≤100. The reward or the royalty can be distributed by the issuer or creator to their share-holders. PER hereby acts as a stable token for that NFT token asset. In order to uniquely identify each NFT, dnftID is used that gets auto-incremented with the creation of every new token. This is also done to ensure that we don't always need to add the category and token name in all the tables. We can point to them by just their unique category ids hence saving the RAM at large. Note that On EOSIO blockchains, the RAM is used for permanent storage. The data is accessed very quickly every time they are called upon providing a permanent means of storage.

In Figure 22.2, Alice has 100 PERs of VT-A, 70 PERs of VT-B while Bob has 30 PERs of VT-B and 40 PERs of VT-C. Note, the total issued supply of VT-C is only 40% so it may be that the issuer has got only 40% rights so he cannot distribute more than that. Similarly, this leads to not only an easy to use global market space for such scenarios. Like for any video, VT can be the category where one can create their unique token.

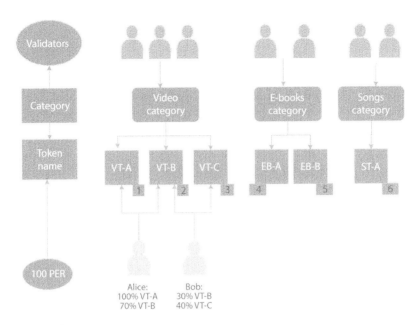

Figure 22.2 Token architecture.

To ensure that these holdings can be tradable, anyone having PER at any token can list them for sale at the contract by paying for the RAM. The lists table is updated by token's dnftID, seller, holdings and price Per Percent. Their PERs are transferred to the contract's account to ensure safety. The sale listing can be cancelled any time before it being sold and RAM allocation can be freed up. The RAM payer, in this case, was kept seller himself to limit the fake multiple small sales i.e., for 10× of PER at the same token, one does not make 10 sale listings of x PER each as that would waste the RAM unnecessarily.

22.3.3   Rationale for Smart Contract

The rationale for calling of functions created in smart contract for blockchains using EOSIO (e.g. EOS, Telos, WAX, Contentos or some other DPoS blockchain).

- "setconfigation" function is called by contract account specifying the version that helps external contracts parse functions and tables. The marketplaces, exchanges and other reliant contracts will be able to view this info using the following code. Thus, NFT holds its value and is known by its standard.
- Contract account adds the validators account for categories like videos, music, eBooks, photography, etc. "addvalidator" function is called for adding new categories for the marketplace. Distributing the power to actual authority that is present in real world is the main aim of this.
- Anyone can create the NFT under some particular category by calling "create" function. The creator's email id is verified to both validators along with the original JSON file, listing their creation and the legal binding agreement (if needed for some high valued NFT in real world).

- Two validators validate the creation after taking fees offered.
- Validators validate using "validate" function. This process will be automated after verifying the JSON through the email. Out of two validators, one is chosen by the creator of NFT (as per the popularity and submission of fees), the other one is chosen randomly. This ensures all validators are motivated to be in the system as well as be competitive for rewards.
- After validated creation of NFT by both validators, NFT creator can issue ownership of NFTs to different accounts. Issuing NFT can be done by calling function "issue". It is for the fact that various stakeholders may exist before selling the rights truly.
- All current owners of NFT can list for sale of their ownership at fixed rate (using "listsale" function) or choose the bidding mechanism (using "start-bid" function).
- Investors can buy the ownership using "transfer" function by sending EOS to the contract with the memo as: "saleID, seller" to validate and transfer the crypto like EOS [5, 6].
- Sale listing or bidding may be closed by seller before expiration. Bidding is realized as unsuccessful if that happens. For the successful bidding, highest bidder receives the ownership shares. Functions for them are "closesale" and "closebid" respectively.
- "burn" function needs to be called by creator in case of non-validation to release RAM or when anyone wants to burn their ownership shares.
- In case any validator is found suspicious, "delvalidator" function is called by contract account. Validator account no longer can validate any further NFTs.

22.3.4   Smart Contract Tables

Tables in EOS blockchain are used to store data which is immutable in nature. The data is stored in RAM and can be fetched very fast. Singletons tables are used to store contract state. They consist of single row in a table. Multi-index table consists of multiple rows generally having a primary key and the scope. Following tables are required to define a distributed NFT on blockchain.

- Singleton Table "tokenconfigs"
    - standard: default name of standard for which NFTs uphold the value.
    - version: versions of contract can be upgraded.
- Multi-Index Table "categories"
    - category: category of Non Fungible Token.
    - validatorID: vector of all the validator IDs.
- Singleton Table "uids"
    - dnftID: last ID alloted to NFT.
    - validatorID: last ID alloted to validator.
- Multi-Index Table "accounts"
    - dnftID: Unique ID of NFT.
    - amount: PERs or percentage rights of NFT.

- Multi-Index Table "owners"
  - owner: Lists the owners of NFT provided as scope.
- Multi-Index Table "dnftstats"
  - burnable: bool that tells if NFT is burnable or not.
  - issuer: issuer or creator's account name.
  - tokenName: Unique NFT token name.
  - dnftID: Unique ID of NFT.
  - currentSupply: Current supply of NFT's ownership percentage.
  - baseURI: Base URI for NFT.
  - originHash: sha256 hash of the details of creator.
  - span: Time span or validity of NFT.
  - validated: bool value, is true if NFT is verified by both validators.
  - validatedBy: account names of both validators.
- Multi-Index Table "lists"
  - saleID: unique saleID of the sellings of rights.
  - tokenName: Unique NFT token name.
  - category: category name of NFT.
  - seller: Seller account name.
  - perPercentAmt: Cost of 1 percent of NFT.
  - percentShare: Total percentages on sale.
  - expiration: Expiration date and time of the sale.
- Multi-Index Table "bids"
  - saleID: unique saleID of the sellings of rights.
  - tokenName: Unique NFT token name.
  - category: category name of NFT.
  - seller: Seller account name.
  - percentShare: Total percentages on sale.
  - basePrice: Base price for the bidding.
  - currentBid: Current highest bid in the current time.
  - currentBidder: Account name of current bidder.
  - expiration: Expiration date and time of the bid.
- Multi-Index Table "validators"
  - validatorID: unique ID for each validator.
  - validator: Validator's account name.
  - email: email-id of validator.
  - categories: list of all categories allowed to validate.

The NFTs created by the owner(s) can be sold on blockchain as per their wish in decentralized and faster way. The price at which rights are sold is directly transferred to the account of owner with no middle-men. It can be verified through above tables.

22.4   Use-Cases

Different use-cases can exist for the distributed NFT architecture requiring partial ownership. Some of them are listed below:

- *Music and Videography*: Crowd funding the music rights ownership using dNFT. The content creators can crowd-source the music before it is released and based on the performance in past, bidding or listing for the percentage shares could be done.
- *Photography*: Multiple stakeholders exist for photography for instance, the photographer and its staff. After selling it on daft powered blockchain system, the reward is distributed as per the shareholdings.
- *Real estate*: Multiple owners may exist for one particular house. The real-estate builders require money to invest that they take as booking charges of flats. The whole system can be made more transparent and validated.
- *E-books and Research works*: The research materials and E-books can have many sellers and publications. Managing and automating the system of collection of them.
- *Gaming industry*: Virtual assets like houses, cars, weapons, etc. This can be shared with multiple users in gaming platform.
- *Sharing platform*: GPUs and memory space can be shared with many users and directly the fee is charged as per their share and sent directly to owner.

Hence, wherever there is a scope of sharing the ownership, NFTs can be distributed. NFT standards popular in EOS blockchain that use typical NFT and SFT architecture are dgoods and Simple Assets [7, 8].

22.4.1   Transaction Volume

Transaction volume refers to the total number of transactions processed from, to or through the services and platform by provider during some particular time period. These are value of transactions sent on chain. The transaction on blockchain needs to be confirmed and in past times, it was noted that due to the *CryptoKitties* game accounts for over 10% of network traffic on Ethereum. As traffic increases, transactions become more expensive to execute quickly. Digital assets like videos, songs even require large number of transactions. Hence, if transaction volume can be limited it is a better option.

Figure 22.3 shows the recent increase in demand of NFTs in comparison to cryptocurrency Ethereum trades. People are getting aware of non-fungible tokens and the market for NFTs is booming on blockchain. The game of Crypto kitties is the standard example that can be quoted to show the demand for NFTs. Other small yet interesting fighting games are also getting popular on both Ethereum and EOS blockchains.

Present scenarios use various different smart contracts to be deployed for each type of category like music, video, research work, etc. for each type of NFT to be in market with standard ERC-721. With dNFT, focus is brought down to this number multifold with all transactions being done with same smart contract that creates a standard for the marketplace where trading and rewarding can be under same tree. The transactions volume is also sought to go down without compromising with the increasing demand by the introduction of batch transfers for the NFT rights directly while issuance. It also helps in saving the CPU cycles.

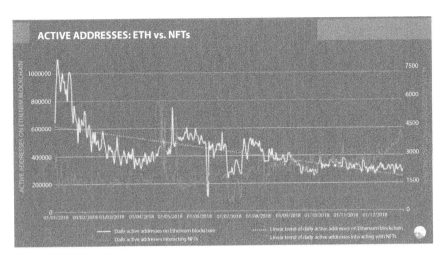

Figure 22.3 Transaction Volume.

22.4.2   Comparison Between NFT Tokens

Non fungible tokens (NFTs) and Semi fungible tokens (SFTs) are the popular tokens used to evaluate some unique asset. Both of them are derived of some special features and different in use cases. The comparison between NFTs, SFTs and Distributed Non Fungible Tokens (proposed in the paper) is discussed in the Table 22.1. The table explains the key differences between them on the basis of concept, use cases and their popular standards.

Table 22.1 Comparison between NFT, SFT and dNFT.

NFT	SFT	dNFT
Non fungible tokens are unique tokens and indivisible in nature representing unique assets.	Semi fungible tokens are to issue a run or batch of items that are for all intents and purposes the same.	dNFT allow distributed ownership of NFT representing digital assets that can have multiple stakeholders.
Use cases include scarce physical properties like artwork, cryptokitties, etc. owned by a single owner.	Use cases include physical items that are 1 of n with a serial number or slightly different metadata like concert tickets, 3D game assets etc. owned by single owner.	Use cases allow partial ownership in the form of real percentage, say x percent ownership of NFT like e-books, songs, videos, etc. allowing multiple ownership.
The most popular standard for such tokens is ERC721.	The most popular standard for such tokens is *dgoods*, *SimpleAssets* on EOSIO blockchains and ERC-1155.	dNFT standard focuses on this use case issuing 100 PERs (stable coins) against any particular NFT item like Video-A.

22.5   Example Usage

This section shows our studies on category Videos considering each unique video as a distributed NFT.

22.5.1   Current Scenario

YouTube is a centralized platform one of Google's subsidiaries. It is the most famous video streaming platform. At YouTube, there is no way where one can buy ownership on any video. There are content creators who are looking for funds instantly but are bound to wait for videos to reach their target before they can make money and invest on future videos. Since, investment is the predominant factor to create videos, creators face the challenge to reach the mass and sponsors. Currently, there is no way where one can host pre-crowd funding round, get the investments by selling ownership of videos. There are various cases like educational videos, web series etc. where creators can upload one chapter (or a demo/trailer/story gist) for crowd funding and sell the ownership of playlists. There is also no transparent manner where monetization of videos occurs.

There is a wide diversity in the types of videos and their contents. For small content creators ranging from singers to comedians, all require interaction with mass public. Currently, comedians get the publicity from videos they upload on YouTube. Based on it, they get chance to host live shows in real world. Top categories among 1,000 popular channels divided by categories are

1. Music
2. Gaming
3. Comedy
4. Entertainment
5. How To and Style.

22.5.2   Solution by Distributed NFT

A decentralized video streaming platform is developed with higher profits for both content creators as well as the public. Users come on the platform, buy percentage shares of the videos on offerings available by owners as per the rates applied (via crowd sale) or via bidding mechanism. This ownership is of Video Token, considering Video as one of the categories described in the Distributed NFT architecture model.

1. There are various reasons why content creators would like to be part of this system:
   a. Many stakeholders are involved in video creation. The distribution of funds in the transparent and trustless manner can be done through the system auto matically as per the rights owned.
   b. The videos are dynamic and there are risk factors involved with every new content. Even if the video is of same owner, various playlists or each video's investment very different.

Figure 22.4 Videos and their dynamic view.

    c. Trends for the video can't be predicted and are very instinctive as shown in Figure 22.4. The study shows that for same YouTube channel, there is a vast difference in its views and response by public. It may range from 10 million views in a week to only 50k views in a year.

2. There are various reasons why public and sponsors would like to buy the ownership of videos:

    a. Videos are the free source of income for the investor and it keeps on trending over good amount of time. The good content generates revenue over long period of time.

    b. With the reasonable rates, investors are tempted to buy some percent of ownership on videos of small and talented creators seeing their promos during pre-crowd funding.

    c. For large creators, bidding models is there, which can earn them lot of money beforehand for investments. Typical example for this would be web-series creation.

    d. The revenue generated through advertisement may decrease with time but is lifetime. It's like the same case as pension for public vs superannuation for creators.

3. Monetization of videos is in a transparent way. The unsigned users are can also be provided with liquid wallet so that transparent track of performance of video can be there. The factors that will determine the revenue generation of the videos are:

    a. Popularity of video

    b. Number of views of video in time period after it has been published.

4. The revenue generation for the system happens through:

    a. Advertisement policies

    b. Premium ad-free models

c. Premium Members model
d. Cryptocurrency coin of the platform, the use of which provides user with special benefits.

22.6   Results

The whole system of distributed ownership for verified and authentic videos is made that has power and transparency to all. Content creators can start pre-crowd funding rounds for their NFTs in return of its ownership and use the investments to create more. Figure 22.5 describes the business model canvas where value proposition, cost structure and revenue streams. It clearly indicates that Investors are bound to get long term benefits and content creators receive instant profits.

For EOSIO blockchains, the results were monitored and RAM usage is used for every creation and listing of the digital asset. It also depends on how much data is stored in the metadata fields like memo for transfer function. If considered empty, each digital asset may take up to 0.4–0.5 kB of RAM. Except the create action, for all other actions RAM payer may be configured to the contract. Overall, for users it was seen to be completely free to create and list their authentic NFTs after validation through minimal fees. The selling of rights is transparent and verifiable with both public and private offerings configured. The aim of viewing the percentage ownership as stable token "PER" was validated thoroughly by every owner in real world.

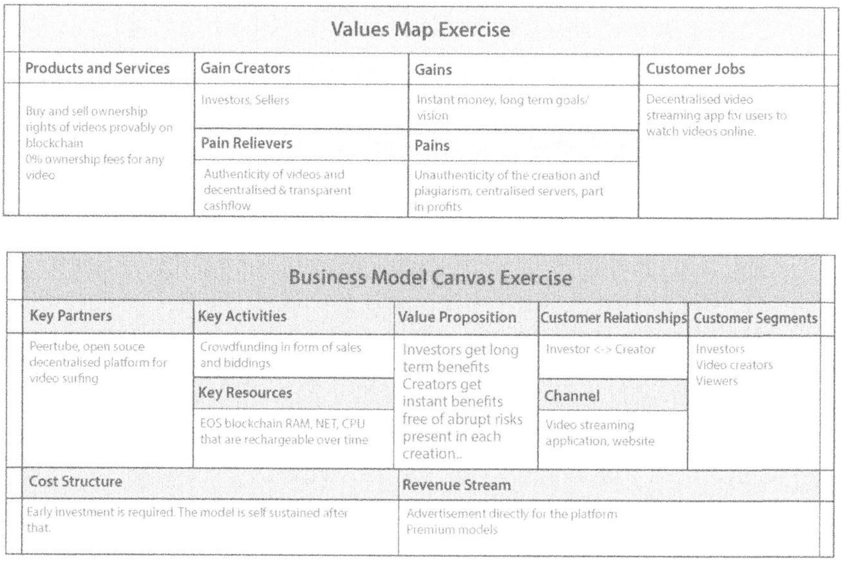

Values Map Exercise			
Products and Services	**Gain Creators**	**Gains**	**Customer Jobs**
Buy and sell ownership rights of videos provably on blockchain 0% ownership fees for any video	Investors, Sellers	Instant money, long term goals/ vision	Decentralised video streaming app for users to watch videos online.
	Pain Relievers	**Pains**	
	Authenticity of videos and decentralised & transparent cashflow	Unauthenticity of the creation and plagiarism, centralised servers, part in profits	

Business Model Canvas Exercise				
Key Partners	**Key Activities**	**Value Proposition**	**Customer Relationships**	**Customer Segments**
Peertube, open souce decentralised platform for video surfing	Crowdfunding in form of sales and biddings	Investors get long term benefits Creators get instant benefits free of abrupt risks present in each creation..	Investor <-> Creator	Investors Video creators Viewers
	Key Resources		**Channel**	
	EOS blockchain RAM, NET, CPU that are rechargeable over time		Video streaming application, website	
Cost Structure		**Revenue Stream**		
Early investment is required. The model is self sustained after that.		Advertisement directly for the platform Premium models		

Figure 22.5 Business Model Canvas.

22.7   Conclusion and Future Work

In this paper, we have successfully demonstrated that dNFTs i.e. Distributed Non-Fungible Tokens are the NFT tokens that meets following points:

1. Verifiable creation of NFT by validator on blockchain.
2. Allow fractional ownership in the form of percentages of NFT ownable by anyone.
3. Allows real world marketplace on blockchain.
4. Real percent ownership can be considered in the form of "PER" stable tokens on blockchain.

This paper was more focused on DPoS blockchains, same concept can be applied to other blockchains like Ethereum. The research was carried out on EOSIO blockchains for the reason that digital assets are more suited when transactions are considered gasless due to the abundance of transactions in these scenarios. The choice of blockchain and future work will be performed keeping the main aim of Meta transactions and cheap (or free) for users to be on the platform.

References

1. FriesenMark, R.W. and Klizas, M.C., *User interface for semi-fungible trading*, U.S. patent US7509283, January 31st, 2006.
2. Gervais, A., Karame, G.O., Wust, K., Glykantzis, V., Ritzdorf, H., Capkun, S., On the security and performance of proof of work blockchains. *ACM SIGSAC Conference*, 2016.
3. Lin, I.C. and Liao, T.C., A Survey of Blockchain Security Issues and Challenges. *IJ Netw. Secur.*, 19, 5, 653–659, 2017.
4. Pillai, B., Biswas, K., Muthukkumarasamy, V., Blockchain Interoperable Digital Objects. *International Conference on Blockchain*, 2019.
5. Rohr, J. and Wright, A., *Blockchain Based Token Sales, Initial Coin Offering, and the Democratization of Public Capital Markets*, technology@hastingslawjournal.org, 70, 2, Feb 9th, 2019.
6. Bal, M. and Ner, C., NFTracer, A Non-Fungible Token Tracking Proof-of-Concept Using Hyperledger Fabric, arXiv:1905.04795v1 [cs.DB], May 12th, 2019.
7. Dgoods, https://dgoods.org, December 5th, 2019.
8. Simple Assets, https://simpleassets.io, December 5th, 2019.

Comparative Analysis of Various Platforms of Blockchain

Nitin Mittal*, Srishty Pal, Anjali Joshi, Ashish Sharma, Sandeep Tayal and Yogesh Sharma

CSE Department, Maharaja Agrasen Institute of Technology, Delhi, India

Abstract

Blockchain is the newest and fastest growing technology which has gained much popularity in recent years. Due to the increasing number of users of blockchain, there are already many blockchain projects or applications that have been created and more new blockchain applications will be introduced in the near future. But the problem arises, how to choose the suitable platform for a given technology. It has always been the greatest challenge to determine the platform in a particular area. There is a need for a comparison analysis to find out the best suitable platform for a given blockchain project. This research includes the comparison of 5 most popular blockchain platforms on the basis of 21 different attributes concluded with a summary of different platforms and some suggestions for most commonly and widely used blockchain platforms.

Keywords: Consensus, smart-contract, ledger, ether, cryptocurrency, genesis, consortium, proof-of-work

23.1   Introduction to Blockchain

Hard copy documents or even centralized digital documents can be altered easily so in order to prevent this, Stuart Haber and W. Scott Stornerra introduced a document which has a timestamp on it so that unauthorized alterations cannot be done [6]. Further this work was continued by a person named Satoshi Nakamoto in 2008 where he introduced the concept of Hash Value into those blocks and algorithms to reduce the rate of adding blocks to the chain [7]. However, this technique was first implemented in 2009, when it was used as an asset for cryptocurrency which was Bitcoin [7]. Bitcoin is an online currency with a security network run by total strangers.

Trusting strangers may sound silly but this is a revolutionary concept, all based on blockchain, an open ledger that contains the history of all the transactions that have happened till date. Blockchains can be adopted to store any kind of digital information. All other models focus on locking people out but blockchain focuses on keeping everyone in which means that Blockchain can be the future of all secured digital transactions.

---

*Corresponding author: nitinmittal44066@gmail.com

Namita Gupta, Prasenjit Chatterjee and Tanupriya Choudhury (eds.) Smart and Sustainable Intelligent Systems, (323–340)
© 2021 Scrivener Publishing LLC

As the name suggests Blockchain is the chain of blocks which contains data in them [8]. Blockchain is the fastest growing technology and is not so complex what it looks like. Blockchain is a technology which supports digital currency. It is a decentralized, distributed and a public ledger. But what do these terms mean? Consider an example where your transaction gets failed due to reasons like insufficient funds or the problems in case of third party payment gateway. They charge you for the money transfer, also the data is saved at a central area which can be hacked easily, it is time consuming, so in order to overcome these problems, the concept of blockchain was introduced in which blocks are added after each transaction which is shared with all the participants in the network, making it decentralized and distributed network [9].

Figure 23.1 shows the basic architecture of a block chain containing different blocks which are connected to each other. Block chain is a sequence of blocks which are connected one after the other with the details of transactions that happened one after another in which the first block is called the genesis block as it is the very first block which does not have any parent block [6, 10, 11].

A block has different parts including the hash for its own block and its parent block which is created when a block is created. Hash is the information which differs blocks from each other [10]. Timestamp, which contains the time at which the transaction is done, details of the sender and receiver and other transaction details are also there.

As discussed by researchers, there are ways by which we can compare different Blockchain platforms and to use the one best suitable for related techniques [11–13]. This paper shows the comparative analysis of 5 different blockchain platforms with their advantages and drawbacks. Section 23.2 explains important terms of Blockchain, which make its defining features followed by the difference between bitcoin and blockchain as people get confused in these two terms in Section 23.3. Section 23.4 includes the brief information about different platforms that we are working on here and comparing it individually about its limitations. Section 23.5 includes the comparison of these various platforms in accordance with

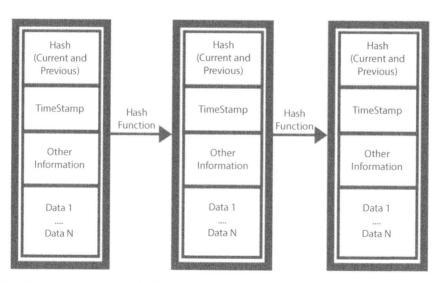

Figure 23.1 Blockchain Architecture [30].

different features they provide. The result of our comparative analysis and conclusion about which platform is suitable in which case is present in Section 23.6.

Depending on the type of transactions to be processed and how the data is to be accessed by different users in the network, blockchain is divided into three different types which are public blockchain, private blockchain and consortium blockchain. As the name suggest public blockchain is open which can be seen by everyone. To join these blockchain, no permission is required. This is the most open blockchain where user can see any data and can make any changes to the network which are legal. As it is a public blockchain, so it is accessed by large number of users and also any unknown user can join it. Examples of public blockchain are Ethereum and bitcoin. Private blockchain is not open for all the users but only limited authorized users are allowed to join the network. It is not public for all so it is made by any organization for its personal use. Not everyone can add any user in the network but only the one who creates it can add users to the network. Examples of these types of blockchains are Ripple and hyper ledger. Now we have consortium blockchain, which is the mixture of both public and private blockchain networks. So, how it can be both at the same time? Just like in public blockchain, anyone can join the network, similarly, here also anyone can join the network. Just like in private network that ownership of the network is in hand of some people only, similarly here also, ownership is in hand of some users, just like a work given for administration.

23.2   Important Terms of Blockchain

23.2.1   Decentralization

Many different systems have a centralized method which means that they have a centered authority which is having all the power but decentralization means that the power is shared among everyone in the blockchain link [9]. In this way it prevents failure as there is no central authority so malfunctioning of any one node will not affect the whole link [6].

23.2.2   Ledger

The sequence of blocks in a blockchain is called a ledger. A ledger is not editable which means that the data present in it cannot be altered or changed but only new data can be added to it. It is something which is shared among all the users to make the blockchain system distributed and public. In a centralized database, there is only one single point of failure, but a distributed ledger is something used to remove the central authority and make it distributed.

23.2.3   Consensus Algorithm

It is the work done by special nodes called minors to verify the transaction which is done in order to create a block and add it to the ledger [10, 14]. All the minors compete with each other to verify the transaction and find out the algorithm to add it to the ledger. The one who wins the race is awarded with some amount. This process of adding a new block in the chain is known as mining. Consensus Algorithm includes Proof of work (PoW), Proof of Stake (PoS), Delegate Proof of Stake (DPoS), Byzantine fault tolerance, etc. [8].

23.2.4   51% Attack

Consider that there are 100 users in a blockchain link and everyone is having their copy of ledger. For a User to manipulate the contents of a block he must be able manipulate the blocks of more than half of the user which is 51% [8]. Only then can he reverse the transaction or double spend his digital currency. In the early time this attack was easy and practical as the number of users was less but now the growth of users has expanded in large numbers that altering those blocks is not practical.

23.2.5   Merkle Tree

A block can contain one transaction or thousands of transactions. Each transaction is having a different hash which is not possible to store as it will need more space. So there is a need for only one hash for each block. In order to do that Merkle tree is introduced, where all the transactions are present in the lowest level and hash value is found for two transactions adjacently. If there are n transactions in the lower level, there will be n/2 hash values in the level above it. And so on, there will be only one hash value at the uppermost level. Merkle tree is actually a binary tree so what If there are an odd number of hash values at any level, then the last hash value is repeated to make it even in number.

23.2.6   Cryptography

Cryptography is the only technique which is making blockchain more secure by providing privacy to the data which is present in the blockchain network. Cryptography consists of two things: Security and authenticity. Former is to prevent the users to access the data that are unauthorized whereas the latter is to save any data in the network to get updated or changed. There are many different ways by which blockchain network can be provided with privacy and security using cryptography for example, Hashing techniques, Public & private key, digital signatures which are the advantages of blockchain network but all these techniques have 4 common things, these are the basics things which is essential for a network to be secure and private and these are: Authentication, Integrity, Confidentiality and Non-Repudiation [15].

23.2.7   Smart Contract

It is the term that was first used by Nick Szabo in 1997, 12 years before bitcoin was introduced. The purpose of introducing it was that he thought that keeping records of contract on paper was old and also not fast and secure. So he wanted to convert it to all online and digital form. Smart contracts hold the same meaning as contracts but as a soft copy which is distributed to all other members in the link. It is a small program code that is stored inside a block which gets implemented only when the particular goal has been reached [16]. If the goal is not reached then it reverses the transaction and helps in keeping a third party out of the other two or more users. With this technique no one is in control of the money as everything is distributed means that the output of the contract is validated by everyone on the network. Smart contracts are immutable meaning, if smart contract is created or the code is created, it cannot be altered by anyone, if changed, then everyone in the link will get to know about it.

23.3   Bitcoin or Blockchain

It is often confusing what blockchain and bitcoin is and how they are related to each other. Whenever it comes to bitcoin, people think of unauthorized money or the way by which money is earned against the law. Just like car runs on the technology of moving tires similarly bitcoin is a car whereas blockchain are tires which help bitcoin to run [17]. Having a central authority between two users which acts as a medium for transaction often cost people transaction fees, in order to prevent that, in 2009, bitcoin was launched which was not real money but just a virtual money or say, digital money holding some value, on the other hand, Blockchain is the technology which is the core component of Bitcoin as it works on that technology of storing the bitcoin transactions in an open ledger which is distributed to everyone present in the link [7, 18]. We can think that blockchain is the operating system where bitcoin is an execution of blockchain technology. Whenever a transaction is done, a block is created which includes the senders address, receivers address and the amount which is sent, now this block is verified by other users in the link and after verification it is added to the ledger. Bitcoins are not real money, they are just virtual money which is given value to it by the users using it.

23.3.1   Primary Key and Public Key

Consider that a user hack your account and use it to send money to himself by creating a block and then distributing it. So, how can this be prevented, the solution is cryptography, hence, bitcoin is called cryptocurrency. There are two keys that are linked to a bitcoin wallet, a private key and a public key. Private key is the key which is used to create your digital signature and also the transaction entry itself. This is the reason that if someone tries to change the data of a block or a transaction then that signature is also changed, which is used to verify that it is original and not altered. But how will other people verify that the data is not altered, this is done by the public key, which is used to verify that it is the same signature. If it is a match then the transaction is verified [8].

23.3.2   Workflow of Bitcoin

Thousands of transactions are going on simultaneously in the bitcoin network with everyone having the distributed open ledger. All the minors are working on the verification of the transaction and ready to add them to the ledger but which transaction will be added first and which will not is the challenge. This is overcome by a competition. Each minor has to solve a computationally difficult math problem and that transaction will be added which is solved at the earliest by any minor or end users (nodes). This process is also known as Proof of Work that comes under Consensus Algorithm. These puzzles are complex in nature and can only be solved by brute force which requires a lot of time and computational power so they are really expensive. The reason people are interested in solving these problems and maintaining the blockchain is the incentives they get on solving these problems. The minor who's entry gets added to the ledger is rewarded with some amount of bitcoins which keeps them motivated [19].

23.4   Platforms of Blockchain

With the fastest growing users of Blockchain, Different blockchain developers require different features to implement their application development of Blockchain. For this, different blockchain Platforms are introduced that have a common base technology of blockchain but having different key features which makes them suitable for different applications [12]. With the rapid growth the list of platforms are increasing day by day. The first platform which was introduced to the real world was Bitcoin in January 2009. This was the time when blockchain came into action. This section includes the overview of five different popular Blockchain platforms on the basis of features like consensus algorithm, overview, speed, scalability, etc.

23.4.1   Ethereum

It is a Blockchain-based distribution which is public and an open source, designed to implement features on the concept of World computer [20]. It is used for financial exchanges and many different digital contracts. It is a decentralized blockchain platform which has unique features of Smart contract, Decentralized Autonomous Organizations (DAO), smart Property and also including Cryptocurrency [21].

23.4.1.1   History

The second generation of blockchain which came after Bitcoin and helped people to look blockchain not only as bitcoin but far beyond it was introduced by Vitalik Buterin, who made it live by July 2015 [21]. He introduced the concept of Ethereum Virtual machine (EVM) which made Ethereum the first virtual machine to be implemented in Blockchain, which is the result of a more simple scripting language which was Turing Complete [19].

23.4.1.2   Ethereum and Bitcoin

As bitcoin was used only for financial exchanges, Ethereum is used for both money and documents transactions [22]. Due to its EVM capability, Ethereum can do more than 15 transactions per second and add a block in ledger around 12–15 s whereas bitcoin can add a block in around 10 min, slowing the transactions to 3–4 transactions per second. The system known as initial coin investment system (ICO) is used as coin release method in Ethereum whereas mining is done in bitcoin. After solving the consensus algorithm, the users are rewarded with 5 Ethers and in bitcoin, users are rewarded with 12.5 bitcoins [17, 18, 21].

23.4.1.3   Gas and Ether

Ethereum Blockchain has its own value of token which is Ether, also known as ETH. It is used to pay transaction fees and computational services fees. Ether, in practical terms, does not hold any value [8, 21]. It cannot be considered as a currency used for transactions directly but it works as a gas for the Ethereum blockchain. Gas is basically present inside the Ethereum virtual machine which is the transaction fees you pay. The value of Ether is changed day by day but the transaction cost remains the same so to overcome this gas is introduced which remains same for the transaction but the value of gas as per ether changes frequently. It is necessary for the user to give a good amount of gas for the transaction otherwise the miners will not find it necessary to work on it and to add it to the blockchain network.

23.4.1.4   Workflow

In order to get into the Ethereum Blockchain and use its features like smart contracts, it is necessary to have clients. Most of the clients are developed by the Ethereum foundation only but some of them are developed by a community of many programmers. Ethereum works on the concept of Decentralized Autonomous Organization (DAO) which means that it exists entirely on blockchain and also it is governed by its protocol. The languages on which the Ethereum smart contracts are coded are Serpent, solidity, LLL. Ethash Algorithm, also known as memory intensive consensus mechanism is used for mining purposes. This comes under proof of work mechanism, so it has two limitations, one is that due to high computations it requires high energy consumption and the other one is that due to open and decentralization, smart contracts can be accessed by everyone in the network which makes it more prone to 51% attack. To overcome this, developers are trying to make it ASIC resistant which means that it is immune to mining and making it unappealing [23]. In coming years, the ethash algorithm will be converted from proof of work to proof of stake, limiting the number of minors by only allowing them to contribute at cost of a certain stake. If in a network, few machines are not working properly or are down then also it maintains a stable state and also has a fault tolerance. Presently, this platform of blockchain, Ethereum is used widely in many applications and due to this, it will keep its popularity for a very long time.

23.4.2   Hyperledger

Hyperledger (Umbrella project) is the multi project open source platform that means anyone can use that platform and download it which is controlled by open source Foundation of Linux, which helped connect different industries from blockchain [24]. The Hyperledger was started in December, 2015 by some technical members from different sectors and all of them have an only aim is to make blockchain as a technology which is more accessible to the users. Later in May, 2016 Brian Behlendorf was appointed as the executive director of the project [19]. Every individual can create a personal blockchain by using hyper ledger as a software and many companies also started using hyper ledger for their business in order to improve the business. People all over the world can come and help hyper ledger get developed as a Software and platform.

23.4.2.1   Purpose of Introducing Hyperledger

Other platforms like Bitcoin or Ethereum focused on business to customers (B2C) where everything was public and open to others but what about business to business (B2B), which means that in these platforms it was impossible to add those transactions which are not meant to be shared with everyone just like in business of two companies, it is not accepted to be followed by a third company [20]. Businesses are unique in their own way. With this idea, developers thought of hyper ledger as a software which everyone can use to create one's own personalized blockchain services, with different techniques in their own ways and in these 3–4 years, it has gained a large amount of members from banking, technology, supply chain, etc.

23.4.2.2   Features

Hyperledger is a consortium blockchain network, also known as permissioned network with different levels of permission by leveraging trust, not everyone can join the network on its own, there is a membership service provider (MSP) where members can enrol in a particular network. As compared to different platforms, it does not have any cryptocurrency but based on need, a user can create one for itself, also it has smart contracts which are written in chain code. The language in which the hyper ledger open source project is written is Golang and java. Just like tools are required to make a car, similarly, there are hyper ledger tools that are required to create a blockchain app, like hyper ledger composes, hyper ledger quilt, hyper ledger explore, hyper ledger cello. It has different frameworks including iroha, sawtooth, fabric, Indy, Burrow out of which fabric is the most popular and highly used framework [20, 25, 26].

23.4.2.3   PBFT

Hyperledger allows developers to choose whether they require a consensus mechanism at all. When they two choose to opt for a consensus mechanism, an algorithm called Practical Byzantine fault tolerance (PBFT) is used which is also used in other blockchain platforms like stellar [26]. PBFT works in the following way, each node on the network maintains an internal state regarding ongoing specific information or status of the network. When the node receives a message, they use the message with the previous state to run a competition. This competition in return helps the node to arrive at a decision regarding the validity of the message. After reaching its individual decision about the message, it shares it with all the other nodes in the network. A consensus decision is determined based on the total decisions submitted by all the nodes. The key difference between Proof of Work and PBFT is that in proof of work only one node which solves the problem at first shouts out the answer unlike PBFT which requires all the participating nodes in the consensus to return a decision [14].

23.4.2.4   Framework Use Cases

Hyperledger framework has different use cases like Hyperledger Iroha is used when there is need for development of mobile applications, when Ethereum smart contract blockchain platform is permissioned then it is known as Hyperledger Burrow, Hyperledger Fabric is used when there is a need for development of applications with modular architecture [19, 20]. For running distributed ledgers, modular platforms are utilized by Hyperledger Sawtooth.

23.4.3   R3 Corda

R3 is a private enterprise blockchain technology company which leads 300 firms working together to build distributed applications for usage across industries such as financial services , healthcare, insurance and digital assets. R3 company was founded in 2014 by David E Rutter. Corda is one of the developments introduced by R3 [27].

23.4.3.1   *History*

Corda was first introduced in April 2016 and in November 2016 Corda goes to open source after one year in September 2017 Cordacon, R3 flagship conference launches where cordacon brings 800+ industry leaders, technologists to look at the key mode in blockchain and the latest application built on Corda [28]. In October 2017, Corda 1 brings API stability and then Corda 2 is launched in 2017. After that corda 3 brings wire stability and corda 4 also releases with 1,800+ commits.

23.4.3.2   *Purpose*

Corda is an open source blockchain platform specially designed for the financial sector [28]. It is a distributed ledger technology and isn't a blockchain. The main purpose of this is to remove the costly friction in business transactions by avoiding business intermediaries [29]. It only focuses on the finance domain. Corda enables a business transaction directly and with strict privacy using smart contracts. As a private platform it allows business and individuals to transact privately where two or more participants can share only necessary information without broadcasting the transaction or details across the entire network. Counting the numbers of industrial transactions which happens daily will go to billions. There is different version of corda which helps to share information between two different applications of corda which coexist on the same network. Corda is not tied to any particular consensus algorithm and it doesn't have its own cryptocurrency. Today, the corda network is a publicly available internet of corda nodes operated by 300 participants across the global ecosystem [30].

23.4.3.3   *Corda vs Bitcoin*

As a bitcoin are processed on their own public blockchain technology called bitcoin network which is slightly focused on running a program that detail transaction using the bitcoin cryptocurrency whereas the corda is a private distributed network and focussed on to assured the identity of transaction as it is enable business to transact directly and strict privacy using smart contract. In Corda, applications developed by independent developers are interoperable. As bitcoin is a public platform so it can any member can access the details of the network but corda has a strict privacy to transact the details across the entire network.

Corda has a Kotlin and java programming language for smart contracts whereas bitcoin has Script and manuscript language for contracts and as our developers found coding smart contracts in Kotlin to be more productive than coding in script [30].

23.4.3.4   Consensus

Corda are put in using the transaction which employed the existing state object and produce the new state object [31]. In Corda, there are two aspects of consensus which are validity consensus in this, the transaction is accepted by the contracts of each input and output state. This is checked by each signer before they sign the transaction. When verifying the proposed transaction party may not try every transaction in the transaction chain that they need to be verified, it is to verify any missing transaction. And another one is Uniqueness Consensus which is the transaction is only checked by a notary service. In this consensus, the requirement that none of the transaction can be employed which is already in the other transaction. So, by implementing the same logic and code, transactions can be validated by each member separately. However two perfectly validated transactions can possibly exist simultaneously.

23.4.4   Stellar

23.4.4.1   History

Stellar is an open source protocol for payments which has the feature of transferring any type of currency from one to another. It is a non-profit organization which is maintained by stellar development foundation in the year 2014 by Jed McCaleb and Joyce Kim [32, 33]. Consider that someone wants to send money from India to US, both have different currencies which are Indian Rupees and US Dollar respectively, both will need different organizations linked between them to convert the money to respective currencies and then transferring them. This cost a large amount of transaction fees and also due to the third party inclusion, it ensured less security, to overcome this, stellar was introduced. Stellar was designed to reduce that amount which was about 9–10% of the money transferred and helped everyone to work on a single network for all financial transaction systems.

23.4.4.2   Assets and Anchors

Assets are any currency which holds value in real world like bitcoin, Euros, etc. To commerce these assets, stellar platform is used. Just like in other platforms, smart contracts are needed to circulate an asset, stellar doesn't need any smart contract for their assets. As stellar is an open source network software, due to this, it is more secure and very much easier to use. Assets are the things that act as an energy source for stellar. There are 3 different assets in stellar network which are Lumens, Non-anchored and anchored assets. Lumens are the local currencies which act as a medium currency between all other types of assets in the decentralized network. Non- anchored assets are the virtual currencies which do not hold any value in real world but these are created on the network for smooth flow. They cannot be redeemed or collateralized. Anchored assets are the currencies that hold real value with them and are not virtually created on the network but they are connected to the network by an anchoring entity. They can be redeemed. We can give a name bridge to anchors as they connect outside currencies. Taking the deposit and then giving the credit in return of that deposit in the stellar wallet of that account address and giving back the assets after receiving the credits which is termed as honour withdraws, all these things are done by anchors [26].

23.4.4.3   *Features*

Stellar has some key features [34]. A stellar platform is a multi- currency network, any currency, asset or a token can be issued directly inside of a stellar network. The transactions happening in the stellar network get confirmed in less than 5 s. The fee required for the transaction is quite nominal as only a cent will be paid for 10,000 transactions. In the stellar platform the participant has the choice of choosing the participant they trust on the network out of several members present in the network. The Stellar platform is much faster as it can process thousands of transactions in a second. The cryptocurrency of stellar network is Lumens (XLM) (Brett Roberts, 2018). The XLM are the native asset of the Stellar network. XLM is responsible for the real time transfer of the value in the network and it acts as a bridge currency between the digital-fiat assets that are issued by the Anchors. Stellar Decentralized Ledger can be thought of as a database that can store more than just account balances and payments. Another use case for this database is storing the offers to buy and sell the assets. All these offers represent a global order book called Decentralized Exchange (DEX) [33].

23.4.4.4   *Stellar Consensus*

There are two types of consensus algorithms used in stellar networks, one is called Local Consensus or Quorum Slice and another is called Global Consensus or Quorum [35]. It can be said that when there is enough of local consensus it would be a Global Consensus or in other words, a quorum arises when there is enough of Quorum Slice in the network. In a stellar consensus mechanism, it is not necessary in global consensus that every participant agrees with everyone in the network but simply agreeing with the neighbor is enough for everyone. This consensus is similar to Byzantine algorithm with a flexibility trust, low latency and asymptotic security.

23.4.5   Multichain

23.4.5.1   *History*

People from different sectors grew a lot of interest in blockchain and its applications. Apart from different open source platforms of blockchain, there is another kind of platform known as multi chain platform [36]. Multichain chain was introduced in 2015. Many organizations have a private financial transaction of which access to it cannot be given to everyone, to develop this type of private blockchain, multichain is used. Multichain technology provides an API and a command line interface which helps in setting up multichain. Due to an increasing number of users, it gained interest in data-oriented applications.

23.4.5.2 Features

To ensure complete stability and control over the transaction, the blockchain ledger is shared with all the users in the blockchain environment. But in multichain network two or more users create their own network of blockchain, where transactions happening in this network cannot be accessible by any other third party user, unless permission is given to that user. For example, there is only one single blockchain network for bitcoin whereas in only one year, there are more than 10 different applications on multi chain out of which solutions in the pharmaceutical industry gained interest very rapidly. Multichain is designed to make sure about transfer and custody of digital assets [13].

23.4.5.3 Consensus Algorithm for Multichain

Proof of work consensus algorithm is used to do mining in multichain blockchain but using it in a network it optional [13]. As, multichain network is a private blockchain network, nodes or miners has to have a valid permission to mine multichain blocks. Due to this, the transaction cost in multichain technology is very low as compared to other platforms.

Just like two people are physically connected while shaking their hands, similarly, handshaking in multichain network is a process in which the nodes in the blockchain network connect and communicate with each other. The nodes present in the blockchain identify each other with the IP address and the list of permissions a node has. With this each node can send messages to other nodes, however the P2P connection aborts if the process is not delivering any satisfying results.

23.4.5.4 Smart Filters

With time, multichain has developed very much and many versions of it have been introduced. Smart filters were introduced in Multichain version 2.0 [37]. They are the rules and regulations which are used to check the validity of the transaction. There are two types of smart filters which are transaction smart filter and stream smart filter. The difference between the two filters is that in transaction smart filters, input, output and meta data is examined, whereas in stream filters, on and off chain data are validated. But they both can be written in JavaScript.

23.5 Blockchain Platforms and Comparative Analysis

With the advancement in Blockchain, different blockchain platforms are being introduced and the existing ones are upgraded, adding new features to them. Based on the 5 different platforms studied above, comparison between them is done on the basis of different attributes or key characteristics like aim, currency, consensus, smart contract, development, hash function, speed, security, scalability, etc. which gives the basis to choose the right platform for blockchain development. The Comparative analysis of blockchain platforms shows in Table 23.1.

Table 23.1 Comparative analysis of platforms.

Platform Features	Ethereum	Hyperledger	R3 Corda	Stellar	Multichain
Operation mode	Public	Consortium	Private	private	Private
Year of starting	2015	2015	2014	2014	2015
Aim	Become global decentralized supercomputer	Platform for enterprises to create their own permissioned blockchain	Developing an enterprise-grade distributed ledger platform for business across a variety of industries	Develop software for everyone to work on a single network for all financial transaction systems.	designed to make sure about transfer and custody of digital assets.
Governance	Ethereum Developers	Linux Foundation	R3	Steller development foundation	Open Source
Currency	Ether (ETH) Cryptocurrency	No native Cryptocurrency but can be made using chain code	No native cryptocurrency	Lumens (XLM)	Native currency
Consensus	Proof of work, proof of state (Ethash)	PBFT (Practical Byzantine Fault tolerance)	Notary nodes can run several consensus algorithm	FBA (Federated byzantine agreement)	Proof of Work
Project	https://ethereum.org/	https://www.hyperledger.org	https://www.corda.net	http://stellar.org	https://www.multichain.com

(Continued)

Table 23.1 Comparative analysis of platforms. (Continued)

Platform Features	Ethereum	Hyperledger	R3 Corda	Stellar	Multichain
Smart contracts	yes	yes	yes	No, but combine transactions with various constraints	Smart filter
Development language	Golang + Python	Golang + Java	Kotlin + Java	Metron	C++/JavaScript
Hash function	Keccak256	SHA3 SHAKE256	SHA-256	SHA-256	SHA3-256
Stateless/stateful	stateful	stateful	stateful	stateful	stateless
Secondary storage	Level DB, Rocks DB	Rocks DB	H2Database	Rocks DB	Level DB
In memory ds	Trie	Merkle Tree	Merkle Tree	Stellar tree	Merkle Tree
Transactions per second	7–12	20,000+	15–1,678	3,000+	500–1,000
Purpose	B2C (Business to Customer)	B2B (Business to Business)	B2B	B2B	B2B
Availability of API access	Yes	No	Yes	Yes	Yes

(Continued)

Table 23.1 Comparative analysis of platforms. (*Continued*)

Platform Features	Ethereum	Hyperledger	R3 Corda	Stellar	Multichain
Availability of SDK	Yes	Yes	Yes	Yes	Yes
Smart contracts implementation	Solidity	Chain code	Kotlin	Multiple SDK available	JavaScript
Scalability	No	No	Yes	Yes	No
Privacy feature	No	Yes	Yes	Yes	Yes
Trust model	Untrusted	Semi trusted	Trusted	semi trusted	Trusted

23.6   Conclusion

Different research papers include the overview of blockchain, platforms of blockchain, they also included the application of blockchain on how blockchain is used in different sectors of the world. With the feature of transparency and security, blockchain has seen most of the people attracting towards it. Blockchain has brought a new level of trust and confidence. On the knowledge of previously published research papers, section one is concluded with the overview of blockchain followed by its key features. From Section 3, we conclude that blockchain and bitcoin are not the same, infact, bitcoin technology is the technology that runs on blockchain technology. Different blockchain projects, with different technologies and different features, there is a need to choose the best platform for that application. These platforms provide any organization an environment for using different technologies as per their requirement. On the basis of different key features, these 5 different platforms are compared to each other to help developers to choose the best one. Comparison of these platforms is a race which brings out the best in them. Developers can compare different platforms on the basis of the above table. For example, Ethereum is an untrusted platform which cannot be used for business organizations, a stellar platform is the platform which does not have its own smart contract, but it uses the transactions and applies rules on them to create a smart contract for them. R3 Corda and Stellar are the two platforms which are highly scalable. Generally from the given table, it can be concluded that blockchain Platform Ethereum is the best suitable platform as it is the most basic platform which is running from a very long time. This platform does not have a lot of features but it makes the basis of any blockchain platform. We can say that other platforms are Ethereum platforms only, which have some extra features in them. Blockchain is immutable, blockchain is tamper-proof, blockchain is trustworthy, blockchain is fully secure and blockchain reduces risk factor. All these are the unique features that people are still not aware of. Blockchain platforms are upgrading themselves at a very fast rate to include new features to them, there are already very unique features in different blockchain platforms and it would be interesting to find out how far these platforms will evolve and show their best in them.

References

1. State of blockchain 2016: Blockchain funding overtakes bitcoin, January 2020. [Online]. Available: http://www.coindesk.com/state-of- blockchain-q1-2016/.
2. Bitcoin mining pools. January 2020 [Online]. Available: https://www.buybitcoinworldwide.com/mining/pools/.
3. Szabo, N., *The idea of smart contracts*, Satoshi Nakamoto Institute, https://www.bitstein.org/ 1997.
4. Castro, M. and Liskov, B., Practical byzantine fault tolerance. *Proceedings of the Third Symposium on Operating Systems Design and Implementation*, vol. 99, pp. 173–186, 1999.
5. Wood, G., Ethereum: A secure decentralised generalised transactionledger, *Ethereum Project Yellow Paper*, EIP - 150 Revision, 1–32, 2014.
6. Blockchain, Wikipedia. January 2020 [Online]. Available: https://en.wikipedia.org/wiki/Blockchain.
7. Nakamoto, S., *Bitcoin: A Peer-to-peer Electronic cash system*, Cryptography Mailing list, metzdowd.com, 2009, [Online]. Available: Https://Bitcoin.org/bitcoin.pdf.
8. Reiff, N., 1 Blockchain Explained, December 2019. [Online]. Available: https://www.investopedia.com/terms/b/blockchain.asp.

9. Rosic, A., *What is blockchain technology? A step-by-step Guide for beginner*, January 2020, [Online]. Available: https://blockgeeks.com/guides/what-is-blockchain-technology/.

10. Zheng, Z., Xie, S., Dai, H., Chen, X., Wang, H., An Overview of Blockchain Technology: Architecture, Consensus, and Future Trends, in: *IEEE 6th International Congress on Big Data*, 2017.

11. Dennis, R., Owen, G., Rep on the block: A next generation reputation system based on the blockchain, in: *The 10th International Conference for Internet Technology and Secured Transactions (ICITST-2015)*, 2015.

12. Ivanov, A., *et al.*, *Technical comparison aspects of leading blockchain-based platforms on key characteristics*, Scientific notes of NaUKMA, *Computer Science*, Volume 1, 2018.

13. Kuo, T-T., Rojas, H.Z., Ohno-Machado, L., Comparison of blockchain platforms: a systematic review and healthcare examples. *J. Am. Med. Inform. Assoc.*, 26, 5, 462–478, 2019.

14. H.W. *et al.*, Blockchain Contract: A Complete Consensus using Blockchain, in: *IEEE 4th Global Conference on Consumer Electronics (GCCE)*, 2015.

15. Kessler, G.C., *An Overview of Cryptography*, Handbook on Local Area Networks, Auerbach, 2019.

16. Sharma, Y., Balamurugan, B., A survey on privacy preserving methods of electronic medical record using blockchain. *J. Mech. Contin. Math. Sci.*, 15, 2, 32–47, 2020.

17. Hurlburt, G.F., Bojanova, I., Bitcoin: Benefit or Curse?, in: *IT Pro*, 2014.

18. Bitcoin, [Online]. Available: http://Bitcoin.org.

19. Macdonald, M., Liu-Thorrold, L., Julein, R., The Blockchain: A Comparison of Platforms and Their Uses Beyond Bitcoin, in: *COMS4507—Advanced Computer and Network Security*.

20. Prerna, HyperLedger vs Ethereum - which blockchain platform will benefit your business? 22 May 2019. [Online]. Available: https://www.edureka.co/blog/hyperledger-vs-ethereum/.

21. Ethereum, January 2020 [Online]. Available: http://ethereum.org.

22. Vyas, A., Nadkar, L., Shah, S., Critical connection of Blockchain Development Platforms. *Int. J. Innov. Technol. Explor. Eng. (IJITEE)*, VIII, 380–385, 2019.

23. Ma, J., Asic Resistant. February 2020 [Online]. Available: https://www.binance.vision/glossary/asic-resistant.

24. Hyperledger, January 2020 [Online]. Available: http://hyperledger.org.

25. Hyperledger Fabric, January 2020 [Online]. Available: http://github.com/hyperledger/fabric.

26. Miguel Castro, B.L., Practical Byzantine Fault tolerance, in: *Third Symposium on Operating Systems Design and Implementation*, New Orleans, USA, 1999.

27. Corda R3 [Online]. Available: https://docs.corda.net/releases/release-M1.0/data-model.html.

28. Github Platform. December 2019 [Online]. Available: https://github.com/corda/corda.

29. Brown, R.G., *The Corda Platform: An Introduction*, R3CEV, https://www.r3.com/reports/the-corda-platform-an-introduction-whitepaper/, 2018.

30. R3 Corda, December 2019 [Online]. Available: https://docs.corda.net/key-concepts-consensus.html.

31. Shrivas, M.K. and Yeboah, D.T., The Disruptive Blockchain: Types, Platforms and Applications. *5th Texila World Conference for Scholars (TWCS)*, 2018.

32. Stellar, January 2020, [Online]. Available: https://en.wikipedia.org/wiki/Stellar_(payment_network).

33. Lemenants, S., 2019. [Online]. Available: https://www.lumenauts.com/lessons/assets-and-anchors.

34. Assets and Anchors, February 2020, [Online]. Available: https://www.lumenauts.com/lessons/assets-and-anchors.

35. Mazieres, D., 2017, *The Stellar Consensus Protocol: A Federated Model for Internet-level Consensus*, Stellar Development Foundation. http://www.scs.stanford.edu/17au-cs244b/notes/scp.pdf

36. Greenspan, D.G., Multichain.com, Coin Science, 2, 5–10, 2015, [Online]. Available: https://www.multichain.com/download/MultiChain-White-Paper.pdf.

37. Greenspan, G., Multichain 2.0, 2019, [Online]. Available: https://www.multichain.com/blog/.

38. Vujicic, D., *et al.*, Blockchain technology, bitcoin, and Ethereum: A brief overview, in: *17th International Symposium INFOTEH-JAHORINA (INFOTEH)*, 2019.

39. Chinmay Saraf, S.S., Blockchain platforms: A compendium, in: *IEEE International Conference on Innovative Research and Development (ICIRD)*, 2018.

40. Blockchain Platform for the Enterprise, January 2020. [Online]. Available: https://hyperledger-fabric.readthedocs.io/en/release-1.4/security_model.html.

41. [Online]. Available: https://blockgeeks.com/guides/different-blockchains/.

42. Joshi, A.P., Han, M., Wang, Y., A survey on security and privacy issues of blockchain technology. *Math. Found. Comput.*, 1, 121–147, 2018.

43. Zhang, A.a.L.X., Towards secure and privacy-preserving data sharing in e-health systems *via* consortium blockchain. *J. Med. Syst.*, 42, 8, 140, 2018.

44. Rui Zhang, R.X., Security and Privacy on Blockchain. *ACM Comput. Surv.*, 1, 1, 1–35, 2019.

45. Licheng Wang, X.S., Cryptographic primitives in blockchains. *J. Netw. Comput. Appl.*, 1, 43–58, 2019.

46. Nabil El Ioini, C.P., A Review of Distributed Ledger Technologies. *OTM 2018 Conferences— Cloud and Trusted Computing (C&TC 2018)*, 2018.

47. Gareth, P.E.P., Understanding Modern Banking Ledgers through Blockchain Technologies: Future of Transaction Processing and Smart Contracts on the Internet of Money. *SSRN Electron. J.*, November, 1, 1–33, 2015.

48. Taylor, T.D.-K. and Paul, J., A systematic literature review of blockchain cyber security. *Digit. Commun. Netw.*, 6, 147–156, 2019.

49. Mazieres, D., *The stellar consensus protocol: A federated model for internet-level consensus*, Stellar Development Foundation, 2017.

50. Sirer, E.G., Eyal, I., Majority is not enough: Bitcoin mining is vulnerable. *Proceedings of International Conference on Financial Cryptography and Data Security*, Berlin, Heidelberg, pp. 436–454, 2014.

51. Scheuermann, F., Tschorsch, F., Bitcoin and beyond: A technical survey on decentralized digital currencies. *IEEE Commun. Surv. Tut.*, 18, 3, 2084–2123, 2016.

52. Möser, M., Anonymity of bitcoin transactions: An analysis of mixing services. *Proceedings of Münster Bitcoin Conference*, Münster, Germany, pp. 17–18, 2013.

53. Sasson, E. B., *et al.*, Zerocash: Decentralized anonymous payments from bitcoin. *Proceedings of 2014 IEEE Symposium on Security and Privacy (SP)*, San Jose, CA, USA, pp. 459–474, 2014.

54. Kraft, D., Difficulty control for blockchain-based consensus systems. *Peer-to-Peer Netw. Appl.*, 9, 2, 397–413, 2016.

55. Chen, W. *et al.*, A Survey of Blockchain Applications in Different Domains. *International Conference on Blockchain Technology and Applications (ICBTA)*, 2018.

56. Bonneau, J. *et al.*, SoK: Research perspectives and challenges for bitcoin and cryptocurrencies. *IEEE Symposium on Security and Privacy (SP)*, pp. 104–121, 2015.

57. Buterin, V., White Paper, A Next-Generation Smart Contract and Decentralized Application Platform. 2013, [Online]. https://ethereum.org/en/whitepaper/.

58. Nadal, S.K.a.S., Ppcoin: Peer-to-peer crypto-currency with proof-of-stake, Self Published paper, vol. 19, 2012.

59. Development of electronic money and its impact on the central bank role and monetary policy, *Issues in Informing Science and Information Technology*, vol. 6, pp. 339–349, 2009, https://www.bartleby.com/essay/Electronic-Money-and-Its-Impact-on-Central-P3LXLLYVJ.

60. Barber, S., Boyen, X., Shi, E., Uzun, E., Bitter to better how to make bitcoin a better currency, in: *Financial cryptography and data security*, pp. 399–414, Springer, Germany, 2012.

61. Böhme, R., Christin, N., Edelman, B., Moore, T., Bitcoin: Economics, Technology, and Governance. *J. Econ. Perspect.*, 29, 213–238, 2015.

Smart Garbage Monitoring System

Akshita Goel and Amita Goel*

Department of Information Technology, Maharaja Agrasen Institute of Technology, Delhi, India

Abstract

There has been a rapid growth in the pace of environmental development in the past few years on the worldview scale. Now, using emerging technologies and a sustainable approach, the theory of smart cities is earning impetus all around the globe. And so a smart city would be imperfect without an intelligent waste management system. The paper elucidates the application of "Smart Bin" in managing a priority-based garbage collection and monitoring system. This techno-powered dustbin is an improvement of a regular dustbin by raising it to be an intelligent product using IoT. The network of sensors enabled bin provides an automatic open and close facility and clear differentiating audio alert for the color-coded bins. With a finer approach to categorization and segregation, it facilitates successful waste treatment. Real-time analysis of the trash in bin is done based on the basis of several physical parameters on the cloud platform –Thinkspeak at the interval of 15 seconds. SMS alert is sent to the municipal authority with the live location when the bin is overflowing or the level of gas has reached the threshold limit. A comparison of real-time data with actual data is done to show the accuracy of the model. Through this paper, we aim to show that the installation of smart bins will contribute towards an enhanced waste management system that will create a circular economy coupled with evolving production and consumption behavior while minimizing the environmental impact.

Keywords: Smart dustbin, logics, embedded sensors, waste management, internet of things (IOT), analytics, GSM module, GPS

24.1 Introduction

While the world is in a phase of development, there is one stinking dilemma that needs to be managed well is Garbage! In day-to-day life, we come across the photos of trash canisters being flooded and all the trash spilling out. Any kind of unmanaged waste poses a significant threat to the environment and public health as it acts as a breeding base for insects, rodents, mosquitoes or other disease vectors. A major challenge in the urban areas is the task of trash collection like in India and for the vast majority of other nations as well. Thus, a framework must be constructed which can annihilate this issue or at least reduce the menace caused by it. Proper waste management techniques are very crucial to control the garbage menace which has spread everywhere. The proposed research presents one of

---

Corresponding author: amitagoel@mait.ac.in

Namita Gupta, Prasenjit Chatterjee and Tanupriya Choudhury (eds.) Smart and Sustainable Intelligent Systems, (341–354)

the most adept approaches to maintain our surrounding conditions healthy and clean. The concept of smart city is still a novel concept in developing country like India, in spite of the fact that it has gotten a great deal of consideration in recent years when our Prime Minister gave the idea of constructing 100 smart urban cities. As the number of smart cities in the country goes up, the responsibilities accompanying them also increase. The primary need of a healthy and clean way of life starts with cleanliness and this in turn starts with a bin. The community will get its garbage disposed of properly only if the bins are arranged well and the garbage is gathered well. The main problem in the current waste administration framework is the unfortunate status of trash bins.

In this paper, we have attempted to re-design the simple yet essential part of the urban waste administration framework, which is the Garbage bin. It is a viable alternative to the conventional method of waste management—door-to-door, community dustbins collection and transportation via sloping channel system. The novel idea of Smart Dustbin will make a bigger impact in educational institutions, healthcare centers, tourist spots and pilgrimage sites where the volumes of waste generation are increasing day by day showing a red alert over pollution.

The Internet of Things is a field wherein encompassing devices are inter-linked through wireless and wired systems without client intercession. In the understanding of IoT, devices communicate and trade information to offer progressed and intelligent types of assistance for the users. Attributable to the latest advances in cellular devices furnished with different rationales, logics sensors and correspondence modules, in conjunction with wireless communication network technology innovations, for example, Bluetooth, Wi-Fi (wireless fidelity) and telecommunication standards like LTE, the IoT has established a significant scholarly momentum.

The manual waste collection system has drawbacks like insufficient information regarding the time and place of collection when the bins are overflowed. In such a scenario, the trucks might visit the place when the dustbin has not yet been filled. There is an absence of a legitimate garbage monitoring framework to pursue all activities of waste collection and disposal. This paper demonstrates powerful answer to deal with the trash. This system is implemented using logics, sensors and Arduino UNO microcontroller. The information related to every dustbin can be checked with the assistance of an analytics platform. The sensors, logics, microcontrollers and IoT module ensures that the clearing of trash bins is maintained by signaling the trash levels and henceforth acknowledge the individuals not to spill the waste outside of the trash bin. When they attempt to spill it out of the dustbin, the hand movements are sensed through motion detectors and an appropriate audio message to the user is played creating the awareness about the color coded dustbin for easy waste segregation. This facilitates a categorization of waste which in turns solves the problem of waste treatment. This framework similarly detects the bogus reports and henceforth can reduce the flaw in the daily execution of waste management. When either the amount of the garbage or the amount of poisonous or both reaches a certain threshold level in the bin, SMS alerts pop-ups to the android phone of the concerned authority stating the garbage specification and GPS tracked live location. This brings down the number of trips that a garbage van taken to collect the garbage. This process also helps to maintain the cleanliness in the surroundings and reduce the spread of diseases caused by garbage. The accuracy of the model is carried out through a comparison chart which shows the deviation of the automated bin from the regular one. The prime goal of the model is to plan, design, create and execute automated waste monitoring framework.

24.2 Literature Review

The Internet of Things (IoT) is a contemporary communication paradigm that envisages the upcoming future in which the devices of day-to-day life will be furnished with logics, micro-controllers, sensors, transceivers for digital communication, and appropriate IoT protocol stacks that will make trouble-free communication with one another and with the users, turning into an indispensable part of the Internet [1]. The idea of IoT, hence, targets making the Internet even more pervasive and omnipresent. Besides, by enabling quick access and interaction with a wide range of day-to-day gadgets and devices for instance, smart home devices, vehicles, visualization and monitoring sensors, surveillance system, displays and so on, the IoT will open the gates to many new applications that make use of the potentially enormous amount and variety of data produced by these devices to provide new services to residents, companies, and public administrations. With the advancement comes problem like costing, storage, auto-scaling, high availability, development speed and more.

The collection of waste is a visible and pivotal municipal service that demands huge loop expenditures. Waste collection issues are, however, the most cumbersome operational issues to decipher. IoT-Based Smart Garbage System For Efficient Food Waste Management System [2], authors give a detailed study on the optimization of municipality vehicle routes and schedules for adequately gathering waste in parts of Eastern Finland. In the paper titled Smart Waste Management using Internet-of-Things by Chitluri Sai, Bhupathi Rayudu, Radhika, Raju Anitha [3] idea of intelligent bin is being proposed, which notifies on overflowing of bin and appoint a kept up person for the same. The reported person will send the information from his web application to the waste administration authority through SMS. In this endeavor, a strain check is carried to know the heist of the generated record. It will aid in avoiding the situation of overflowing and maintain cleanliness.

In Exploring Arduino: Tools and Techniques for Engineering Wizardry [4] describes different capabilities of the Arduino, while interfacing with external hardwares like sensors, protocols, etc. In GSM and GPS Based Garbage and Waste Collection Bin Overflow Management System for Kitwe City Council [5] Ngosa, Shadrick and their mates designed a SMS alert based notification system using microcontroller Arduino Mega 2560 microcontroller that sends the overflow information of the dustbin to the concerned authority. The research work particularly focuses on the Kitwe City Council in Zambia as it faced numerous difficulties with regards to garbage collection in markets, business sectors, public places, and other open spots. Trash bins stand uncollected for a prolonged time, placing marketers' lives in danger due to cholera outbreak, particularly in monsoon season. Arduino Documentation [6, 7] describes about the inbuilt functions and programming variability of the microcontroller.

The Global Positioning System (GPS) comprises of a system of 24 dynamic satellites (and 8 spares) found nearly 20,000 km over the Earth's surface. They orbit the globe once every 12 h to provide worldwide information about position, time and speed with direction [8, 9]. The Global System for Mobile communication (GSM) is a universally acknowledged norm for telecommunication. GPS recognizes sites on the Earth by estimating the range from the satellites, while the GSM utilizes narrowband time division multiple access (TDMA) for offering content and voice-based application over cellular networks [10].

Our research work includes GPS and GSM empowered system through ground-primarily based stations and satellites to track the height of trash within smart dustbin. Auditing is accomplished by using a distance sensor or ultrasonic sensor which actuates the GSM module if the level of trash in the bin hits the defined maximum value. In this situation, the module informs the municipal authority for waste collection through a short message service (SMS). Simultaneously, the GPS receiver delivers the approximate positioning of the bin for waste removal and disposal.

IoT Based Waste Management System for Smart Cities [11] summarized the execution of a real-time garbage level tracking framework in smart bins using a level sensor. *Garbage and Street Light Monitoring System using Internet of Things* [12] Prof. R.M. Sahu and his students incorporate both waste and street light monitoring which avoids mishaps amid night. The research work is helping to reduce power usage and manpower. In *Smart Garbage Monitoring System for Waste Management* [13] Muhammad Rahim and co-authors deal with the height of the garbage in the bin. They labeled the heights with 3 predefined values and used leds to detect the accuracy of the model. The alerts of the height of the waste present in the bin are sent to the cleaning authorities through SMS. Research work of P.L., Kola Vaishnavi, Swathi titling *Innovative Smart Dustbin with an Android Applications using IOT* [14] gives a comprehensive overview of displaying the physical conditions such as moisture, temperature and gas of the waste on a mobile application in real time.

ThinkSpeak Documentation [15] illustrates how to integrate the code with the ThinkSpeak platform. It is imperative that data delivered to the control system is stored and retained both in the cloud and database for which a data warehouse infrastructure must be developed. It is to qualify for deeper analyzes of the data gathered with the passing years. It leads to a thorough description of waste generation trends, so as to establish explicit resource allocation predictions. Moreover, data analytics is performed on excel once the data on ThinkSpeak is imported to excel for visualization and analysis [16].

The primary goal of *Greenbin* [17] is to efficiently segregate garbage at origin itself so that each waste component could generate some useful power. Authors describes that the goal is achieved by using Sensors like odor sensor, capacitive-based humidity sensor, inductive based metal sensor and gas sensor. Based on the analysis of Arkady Zaslavsky's study on *The Internet of Things: Challenges and State-of-the-Art Solutions in Internet-Scale Sensor Information Management and Mobile Analytics* [18], we gained an understanding of the scopes and insights for the management of mobile monitoring and sensor data which can assist in the segregation of data from various dustbins. In *Top-k Query Based Dynamic Scheduling for IoT Enabled Small City Waste Collection* [19], Theodoros and fellow mates demonstrated a comprehensive concept of dynamic scheduling needed for waste disposal and the Top-k query leading to the criterion of bin cleaning operation by prioritizing.

24.3   System Design

During the implementation, the hardwares connected to the bin are shown in Block diagram as shown in Figure 24.1(a). There are multiple sensors used for different purposes. Microcontroller Arduino UNO is soldered on the half lid of the bin. MCU is connected to GPS, GSM Module, Esp8266/Wifi module, servo motor and sensors. Ultrasonic sensors also called as level or distance sensors are soldered on the circular body of the bin. Two

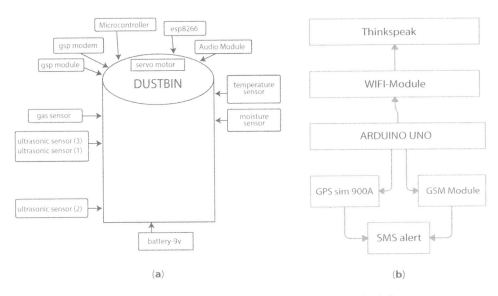

Figure 24.1 (a) Block diagram of integration of hardwares on dustbin. (b) Block diagram at reception part.

ultrasonic sensors on the upper body finds the level of the gas and garbage filled and the third fitted near the bottom detects the presence of a human being within the range to perform automatic open and close functionality. Gas sensors measure the amount (in volume) of gas present in the bin. Temperature sensor measures the temperature and moisture sensor reports the moisture content in the bin. Audio module plays the recorded audio clip on the on-off action by microcontroller signals. The 9v battery works as the power source for the model.

Block diagram of the micro-controller at reception part for the data flow is given in the Figure 24.1(b). Here, the micro-controller is connected to GPS and GSM which sends the SMS notifications on the overflow condition. While the Wifi module works all the time to move the real time data of the bin to the cloud at the interval of 15 s.

24.4   System Specifications

24.4.1   Components

1. Microcontroller-Arduino UNO
2. LCD display
3. ESP8266-NodeMCU
4. ISD1820 Audio module
5. Servo motor-9g
6. Breadboard, PCB
7. Ultrasonic Sensors/Distance sensors (3)
8. Soldering Iron, wire
9. Voltage regulator
10. Moisture Sensor

11. Temperature Sensor (RTD)
12. MTQ-3 Gas sensor
13. GSM
14. GPS
15. Jumper wires
16. 9v Battery

24.4.2   Simulation Tool

Arduino IDE [7] is an open source software to simulate the program. It is freely available on its home website. Anyone can download Arduino IDE from www.arduino.cc. It compiles the Arduino program in it and then by using USB cable we can dump program to micro-controller.

24.4.3   Analytics Tool

ThingSpeak [15] is cloud platform and API for storing and retrieving data from hardware and perform visualization and analysis.

24.5   Circuit Diagram

The circuit diagram for the hardware connections are given in Figures 24.2 and 24.3. ATMega328P is a 14 input/output pins micro-controller. Every Arduino board requires a way to be connected to a power supply. The Arduino UNO is connected and powered from the computer's USB cable, or from a wall power supply terminated in a barrel jack. The board has 5 pins A0 through A5 for analog input. These pins reads the signal from an analog sensor such as the moisture sensor, temperature sensor, and gas sensor and translating it into a digital value that the microprocessor can read. In 14 digital I/O pins (15) of which

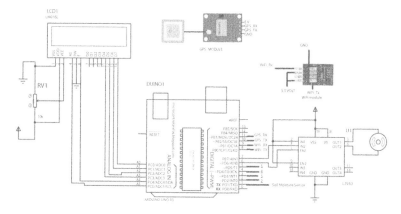

Figure 24.2 Ultrasonic pin numbers to be connected to micro-controller.

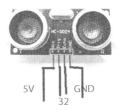

Figure 24.3 Hardware integration to micro-controller.

6 give PWM (Pulse Width Modulation) output. These pins can be set to act as digital input pins to read logic values (0 or 1) or as digital output pins to drive various modules such as LEDs, relays, etc. The marked pins can be used for PWM generation. Pin 0 is connected to the MTQ-3 gas sensor, pin 1 is connected to soil moisture sensor. Pins 10, 11 are connected to the GPS module. GPS module is also connected to GSM module. Pins 8, 9 serve as the transmitting and receiving pin for the Wi-Fi module or esp8266. The driver motor is attached to digital pins 7, 8. Audio module is attached to OUT1, OUT2 of driver motor. On your board, TX (transmit) and RX (receive) appear in two places. The pins responsible for serial communication are indicated at the digital pins 0 and 1. The TX led flashes with different speeds while sending the serial data. Flashing speed depends on the board's baud rate. RX flashes during the process of receiving. There are wires in servo motor which attach to the outside world. The white wire is called the control wire, one wire is connected to power supply (+5 V) and one is for ground.

24.6   Proposed Approach

The Arduino is used as a micro-controller. Ultrasonic sensor (1) identifies the amount of garbage in dustbin. Ultrasonic sensor (2) detects the presence of a human at a distance which helps in automatic open/close of the dustbin using servo motor. If any of the sensors don't detect the level then it doesn't send the information to the cloud. The humidity sensor is designed to calculate the moisture value inside the bin. The temperature sensor is been used to find the temperature inside the dustbin. Moisture sensor helps to analyze whether the trash disposed of in the bin is dry or wet. This will further help in easy waste segregation by the authorities. Gas sensor is required to sense the presence of poisonous gases which causes bad odor. The gas sensor is integrated with the distance sensor to find the volume of gas in terms of level (in cm) in the bin. The Arduino uno powers all the Sensors, esp8266, GPS Modem and GSM Module using the 5 V pin. When the level is detected by all the three ultrasonic sensors then it sends the signal to the Arduino Controller for further process. As the Signal is received by Arduino then it activates ESP8266 which is the wifi module to deliver the data to the cloud platform. The microchip of the IoT module (wifi module) is fitted on the bin.

To increase awareness among the people about the concept of blue and green bins, the audio will be played every time the lid of the bin is opened. The audio instructs the people about the type of bin they are using so that they contribute in keeping the surroundings clean. Audio clippings saying—"This dustbin is for dry waste only. Don't throw wet waste in it. Thank you". GSM module is used for signal transmission (send and receive SMS). GPS module is used for location tracking in terms of longitude and latitude. GSM module sends the alert message to the person when threshold value of gas and garbage height is reached. This is a strategic approach to promote the concept of using intelligent bin among people.

The LCD display is used for the system testing. Audio is been played when the ultrasonic sensor detects the presence on a person near dustbin and plays audio as well as open and closes the bin. A duration of 7 s is set to keep the bin open and close Think speak is the real-time IOT analytics virtual cloud that shows the track and information of the bins at every time interval. As esp8266 is activated then it sends all the real-time data regarding specified parameters of garbage in bin to the cloud in every 15 s for the tracking by concerned people.

GSM is a digital, circuit switched network for telephony system and it is used for sending the SMS alert. GPS is a satellite based navigation that works all over the world in every weather pattern, 24 h a day without any charges. The GPS modem sends the latitude and longitude position attached to the SMS which helps to track the current position of the trash bin. The slave part is located in the dustbin and the master unit is installed in the control room. If the trash amount exceeds the defined values, an indication is provided by the ultrasonic sensor to the micro-controller and via GSM; SMS will be delivered to the control room reporting the cleaning authority that the bin is full. When the SMS is received at the control room in the master unit, it will specify the location of bin as well. GPS SIM908 module is capable of using dual UART, only a single UART is used in this board. By connecting with the Arduino Uno, the GPS engine is switched ON through AT commands and similarly GSM is controlled through same UART by AT commands. Individual antennas are provided for both GSM and GPS. A STUB antenna is provided for GSM and an external Magnetic PATCH antenna is for GPS. The Modem has default bate rate as 9,600. On reaching the defined threshold value of the garbage fill level in the smart bin, GSM and GPS Modules along with Ultrasonic sensor are simulated all at once which sends the SMS alerts to concerned authority regarding the overflow of bin. Then the authority will send a van by informing the van driver to replace the fully filled dustbin by a blank dustbin. When the blank dustbin is kept at that place then it's utilized by the general people go through the waste in that dustbin.

Analysis of the collected real time data on the cloud platform—ThinkSpeak [15] with the actual data is conducted to check the accuracy of the model with logic and sensors. An accuracy test is conducted by importing the values displayed on ThinkSpeak [15] to the excel sheets and then comparing the actual values to find the results of deviation. The excel data collected can further be used to carry data analytics on the type and volume of garbage collected in the bins in the particular area. This analysis will help to diminish the impact of global waste generated each day.

24.7   Implementation

The hardware components are gathered as per their specifications. Then they are tested using led. The connections are made to the micro-controller as per Figures 24.2, 24.4(a), and (b). A cylindrical structure for the bin is Cut out and a Circular disc made of Cardboard is used as its Lid. A double sided tape or packing tapes are used to secure everything. A Shaft is drawn, and the IR module identified by hand is mounted to the

Figure 24.4 (a) Side view of the model. (b) Top view of the model.

top of the shaft. The shaft's other end must be connected to the bin's side of (walls). The garbage monitoring IR module is attached inside it with double sided tapes. GSM module is simulated with the mobile number to which it will send the alert messages. While simulating, SIM card should be inserted in the slot of the module because the module needs the cellular network to send the location data to the server as well as for the purpose of sending the short messages. The code is written for the functionalities of each hardware component for their interfacing with the controller. Arduino IDE is used as the simulating tool to debug and run the code.

The username and password of the wifi connection are attached to the code to deliver the data of the sensors to the cloud. Arduino IDE is an open source software mainly used for writing, uploading and compiling the C++ code into the Arduino Module. It is readily available for operating systems like Windows, MAC and Linux. It runs on the Java Platform which comes with numerous inbuilt functions, declarations and commands and play a crucial role for editing, debugging, testing and compiling the code. The environment allows either C or C++ as coding language. If the code works perfectly then it is uploaded to the controller. Connections are checked again if not working then the potentiometer is rotated slowly as long the LED glows. Then slowly it is rotated keeping hands over it so as to adjust the distance as per the requirement. It is just a work of calibration of potentiometer.

Setup an account on ThinkSpeak and create channel. Include its unique API key and channel id in the code. The ultrasonic sensor (1), (3) detects the level of garbage by measuring the distance and sends it to the cloud. The level sensor measures the time taken from when the signal is transmitted to when it is received. Then the distance 'd' (in cm) is measured using following formula:

$$d = (s \times t) \div 100$$

$$d = (340 \times t) \div 100$$

$$D = d \div 2$$

Where the speed of sound in air in meters per second is denoted by s, t is the time taken in seconds for the signal to travel from the transmitter to the sensor's receiver. The calculated distance can be converted from meters into centimeters by dividing it by 100.

The ultrasonic transmit the signal with the speed of 340 m/s. Now, Supply 5-7V power to the circuit. Once the system is set ON, Arduino starts identifying for any object near the distance Sensor. If the distance Sensor identifies any object like a foot or hand for example, Arduino will calculate its distance and if it less than or equal to a certain predefined entered value (threshold value), it will signal the Servo Motor and with the help of the extended arm, it will instruct the lid to open. The servo is used to rotate the bin's lid. The servo has an angled mounting shaft with controls. Unlike ordinary motors, certain specified angles can be set to move it. The shaft can be configured to rotate between 0 and 180°. In our framework, 0° is defined as a closed lid and 180 as an open lid. The control IC inside it takes care of the positioning of the motor. All the data will be sent to the cloud platform at every interval of every 15 s and a graph will be traced out to show the real time statistics of the bin as shown in Figures 24.5 and 24.6. Using audio module will create awareness among the

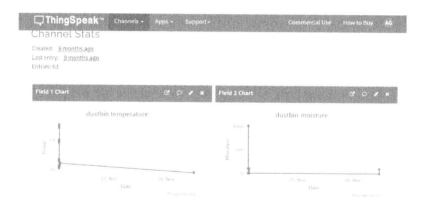

Figure 24.5 Real-time temperature and moisture graph on ThinkSpeak.

Figure 24.6 Real-time waste level and gas level data on ThinkSpeak.

people regarding the usage of color coded bin for different biomedical waste. It is of utmost importance to remove the waste in a proper, safe manner. Color coding helps disposal companies differentiate between different wastes and easily sort them into categories as all waste doesn't go to same landfills. Some wastes undergo the process of recycling and reuse.

After certain pre-defined time, the lid will automatically be closed. On reaching the defined threshold value, SMS is delivered to the device as shown in Figure 24.7. The result of the height of filled waste is validated by comparing the collected data and actual data to find if the sensor values are approximate accurate as shown in Figure 24.8.

Figure 24.7 Real time SMS alert on overflow condition.

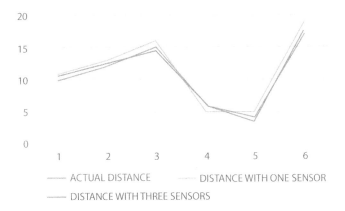

Figure 24.8 Accuracy chart.

24.8   Result

This research work is secured for categorizing waste, systematic disposal, careful and timely collection and successful recycling. It is an interrelated arrangement for the current garbage disposal issue. Microcontroller based intelligent dustbin defeats the problems related to the currently existing waste management system. It will help to designate a relative set of intelligent dustbins to a defined number of households on account to their encountered waste amount. The dustbin will be automated using a servo motor. The dustbin will be opened only when the user is administered in the range specified in the code of microcontroller. The lid will remain opened till some pre-defined time value and then close automatically. Other sensors send the real time data to the cloud and is also reported on the bin using LCD display during system testing. An audio message played every time the lid opens will help to encourage the use of color coded bins-blue and green bins for easy segregation. The physical conditions of the bin are mapped in the interval of every 15 s on the analytics platform. This data is simultaneously imported to the excel sheet for further data visualization and data insights. An alert message in form of SMS is sent to concerned authority when the bin is full with the live location of the bin for easy tracking. An accuracy chart is plotted to find the deviation of the true data values with the sensor values. This data is then carefully studied to draw insightful conclusions and suggest the further scope of improvement in the research work.

24.9   Conclusion

In this paper we analyzed and conducted a fundamental research on the existing solutions for waste management system and then proposed a model that ensures the waste disposal is carried out in more optimal way. The value exists in the concept that real-time monitoring of the garbage management ecosystem facilitates the collection and removal of waste in reasonable time and avoids toxic waste from environmental degradation. Manual garbage management lacks a proper strategy to monitor garbage and collect them in a viable time plan, therefore, the framework designed will impact the individuals to intelligently manage their waste. The model precludes the irregular cleaning of the dustbins by sending alarms in form overflow information to the concerned individual at periodic intervals thus keeping a vigilant check on the performance of the concerned department. This is evident from the accuracy chart shown in Figure 24.8 that the accuracy of the model is approximately 85%. Using advanced Arduino controller along with a Wi-Fi module, GSM and GPS empowered system improves the efficiency of the entire system of waste collection, segregation and disposal by diminishing the need for human intervention. Also, this model will prove as an asset for physically challenged and aged people. The audio feature puts a special focus on the blind people who are unable to distinguish between the colored bins.

24.10   Future Scope

Today, most likely the waste collected ends up to one of the landfills around the city where non-biodegradable waste mixes up with recyclable and reusable material leading to a turmoil condition. These fetid grounds are the mounting symbol of trash mayhem. The smart dustbin is essentially improvised to a great extent by switching to automated segregation of the produced waste into biodegradable and non-biodegradable waste, in order to overcome a major problem that hampers the solid waste management system. With further improvement, a specialized mechanism to drive out animals and birds from feeding and contaminating the surrounding areas can be implemented. Hence, these strategies can minimize the involved human cost and reduce the overall cost of waste management system worldwide supported by the separation of different waste at the placement location itself and also to a large extent by minimizing the spread of emissions. Outdoor smart bin will create more impact if the circuiting is made water proof while indoor bins will create more impact if their operation is controlled through mobile app commands thus transforming them into robotic bins. With the advent of new technologies like Augmented Reality, 3D view of the dustbin from inside out will help for easy identification of the waste. The system should target on scaling up the productivity and dissolving the call for human interaction during the entire waste management cycle. Advances in route planning and optimization [20] enable the waste gathering mechanism to be incorporated with real-time data that have been made accessible to the municipal authority on the cloud. A user-access control could be established at the nodes to curtail security attacks such as DDOS, Drive-by-attack, Sniffing, phishing, replay attack, MitM and other attacks on the system [21]. Signal/image processing, cryptography algorithms, and proper authentication and authorization, as opposed to conventional techniques should be proposed to avoid security bugs and threats which may emerge during the course of the development and application of the system. The possible future work involves introducing a fog architecture approach [22] to add a benefit to the framework's networking and connectivity and processing capabilities nearer to the end-user, and improvising the inter linking of these resources with remote IoT hardware components.

References

1. Atzori, L., Lera, A., Radhika, J., Anitha, R., The internet of things: A survey. *Comput. Networks*, Elseveir B.V., 54, 15, 2787–2805, 2010.
2. Hong, I., Park, S., Lee, B., Lee, J., Jeong, D., Park, S., IOT based Smart Garbage system for efficient food waste management, Hindawi Publishing Corporation. *Sci. World J.*, 2014, 13, 2014.
3. Srikanth, C.S., Rayudu, T.B., Radhika, J., Anitha, R., Smart Waste Management using Internet-of-Things. *IJITEE*, 8, 2518–2522, 2019.
4. Blum, J., *Exploring Arduino: Tools and Techniques for Engineering Wizardry*, John Wiley & Sons, Inc, 10475 Crosspoint Boulevard Indianapolis, IN 46256, p. 384, Wiley, 2013.
5. Willie, N., Lucy, K., Shadrick, K., Victor, P.D., John, S., GSM and GPS Based Garbage and Waste Collection Bin Overflow Management System for Kitwe City Council. *IJERT*, 7, 55–61, 2018.
6. Arduino Uno Datasheet, https://datasheet.octopart.com/A000066-Arduino-datasheet-38879526.pdf.
7. Arduino documentation, https://www.arduino.cc/.
8. Nasa science—How GPS works? Official U.S. government information about the Global Positioning System (GPS), https://spaceplace.nasa.gov/gps/en/.
9. What is GPS, Official U. S. government information about Global Positioning System (GPS), https://www.gps.gov/systems/gps/.

10. GMS documentation by The International Engineering Consortium, 19, http://www.uky.edu/~jclark/mas355/GSM.PDF.

11. Prakash, V., Prabhu, IoT based waste management system for smart cities. *IJIRCCE*, 4, 1267–1274, 2016.

12. Sahu, R.M., Godase, A., Shinde, P., Garbage and Street Light Monitoring System using Internet of Things. *IJIREEICE*, 4, 107–109, 2016.

13. Yusof, N.M., Jidin, A.Z., Rahim, M.I., Smart Garbage Monitoring System for Waste Management. *MATEC Web of Conferences*, vol. 97, 301–305, p. 01098, 2017.

14. Mamatha, S., Vishwas, P.L., Vaishnavi, K.K., Swathi, V., Vittal, S., Innovative Smart Dustbin with an Android Applications using IOT. *IJRASET*, 7, 301–305, 2019.

15. ThinkSpeak integration with microcontroller, https://community.thingspeak.com/documentation%20…/.

16. ThinkSpeak, https://www.mathworks.com/help/thingspeak/channel-data-import.html.

17. Anitha, V., Gomathi Nayaki, P., Ramya, K., Rajkamal, R., Kayalvizhi, E., A novelapproach for waste segregation at source level for effective generation ofelectricity—GREENBIN. *ICSEMR*, Chennai, India, 2014.

18. Zaslavsky, A. and Georgakopoulos, D., Internet of Things: Challenges and state-of-the art solutions in Internet-scale Sensor Information Management and Mobile analytics. *16th IEEE Conference*, p. 3, 2015.

19. Anagnostopoulos, T.T., Medvedev, A., Zaslavsky, A., Khoruzhnicov, S., Top-k Query based Dynamic Scheduling for IoTenabled Smart City Waste Collection. *16th IEEE Conference on Mobile Data Management*, 2015.

20. Yu, L., Kong, D., Shao, X., Yan, X., A Path Planning and Navigation Control System Design for Driverless Electric Bus. *IEEE Access*, 6, 53960, 2018.

21. Condry, M.W. and Nelson, C.B., Using Smart Edge IoT Devices for Safer, Rapid. *IEEE Proc.*, 104, 938, 2016.

22. Oteafy, S.M.A. and Hassanein, H.S., IoT in the Fog: A Roadmap for Data-Centric IoT Development. *IEEE Commun. Mag.*, 56, 157, 2018.

Study of Various Intrusion Detection Systems: A Survey

Minakshi Chauhan and Mohit Agarwal*

Department of Information Technology, KIET Group of Institutions, Delhi, NCR, Ghaziabad, India

Abstract

Nowadays, Internet-based technologies are extensively being used to transfer, store and process the information. The massive growth of information over the Internet offers a rich environment to the attackers and intruders to expand the attack surface. In Information and System Security, intrusion detection is the act of detecting such actions that attempt to compromise the security of computer systems; Confidentiality, Integrity or Availability of a computer resource. Intrusion Detection is the process of observing and analyzing the activities happening in a computer system to identify any security violating activities. In this paper, the structure of IDS, different types of intrusion detection techniques and various types of attacks have been presented. This paper also presents the comparative study of various intrusion detection systems based on techniques used, various parameters of detection performance and their use in different domains.

Keywords: Intrusion, host-based, network-based, anomaly-based intrusion detection, attacks, data mining techniques

25.1 Introduction

Intrusion Detection (ID) can be defined as monitoring and analyzing the events occurring in a computer system and therefore, detecting those events which may cause security violations [1, 2]. Over the years, system security has become prominent and has been getting attention of researchers. Many researchers have coined the security technologies such as Cryptography, Access Control, Intrusion Detection, Authentication, and Firewalls to solve the various security violation problems [3]. However, intrusion detection is not yet a perfect technology. When an unauthorized user attempts to take an unauthorized access to the information, a resource or a system that user is not legally permitted to take. Then this unauthorized action is called intrusion and that user is called intruder. The intruder may be from outside or inside in the system, who exceeds his limited authority to gain unauthorized access to the system for the purpose of misusing that system. Intrusion detection identifies that intruder and his unauthorized actions to use or misuse the system and further prevents

Corresponding author: rs.mohitag@gmail.com

Namita Gupta, Prasenjit Chatterjee and Tanupriya Choudhury (eds.) Smart and Sustainable Intelligent Systems, (355–372)

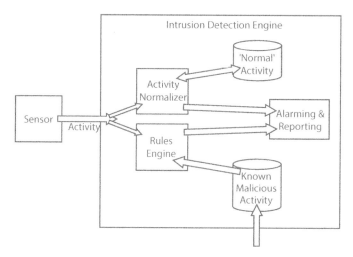

Figure 25.1 Components of IDS.

such actions happening in the future. The Intrusion Detection System (IDS) is a full-fledged system consisting of software and hardware providing the functionality of intrusion detection either on an individual host or a network of connected hosts. The self-evident reason for doing intrusion detection is to detect suspicious activity on computer systems or networks which may cause harm through security policies violations [4]. In the subsequent sections, the general structure of IDS, different categories of attacks, different intrusion detection techniques and some recent IDS based on data mining and machine learning techniques have been discussed.

25.2 Structure of IDS

The general structure of IDS consists of the modules such as Sensor, Activity Analyzer, Rules Engine, Normal Activity Database, Known Malicious Activity Database and Alarming & Reporting as shown in Figure 25.1. The information in form of data packets, host activity, application activity or sensor data is provided to the activity normalizer and the rules engine. The rules engine searches the patterns from the known malicious activity database which maintains the signatures of all the already occurred malicious activities. The activity normalizer analyzes data statistically according to the normal activity baseline. It also constantly adjusts the baseline in normal activity database as the usage changes over time to make computer systems or network more dynamic. In case of any suspicious activity, both the activity normalizer and the rules engine trigger the alarming and reporting [5].

25.3 Intrusion Detection Systems

Broadly, intrusion detection solutions fall into two types according to their positioning within the computer system. These are host-based IDS and network-based IDS.

25.3.1   Host-Based IDS (HIDS)

This method works on an individual host on which it gets installed and detects the intrusions from the activities occurred on that host. It checks the data such as the records of various activities of host; system logs files, audit operation system record files, and rule patterns, etc. [6]. This system detects the malicious activities from the data originated on the host itself. This method works well on the insider attack that does not include network traffic [7].

Advantages:

- Since HIDS monitors only the host, it can determine the intrusion more accurately.
- It does not need to install extra hardware or software because everything is on the host.
- Encrypted messages are not serious problem because they received in the host and can be decrypted more easily.

Disadvantages:

- Takes more time to report attacks.
- It should be installed on each host.
- Due to being on the host, it consumes host resources.

25.3.2   Network-Based IDS (NIDS)

The Network based IDS examines the network packets for the detection or presence of attacks and anomalies from network traffic. NIDS monitors the external malicious activities on the network of many connected hosts. This method is able to detect the malicious activities caused by the external intruders but having problem from inside threats. NIDS generally consists of one or more network-based sensors as network interfaces set to promiscuous mode which monitor and filter all network traffic going through the network segment and protect multiple hosts connected to that segment. The alerts are generated when suspicious traffic has been detected [4].

Advantages:

- It analyzes the network packets to detect attacks.
- Not installed on each and every Host.
- This system can check several hosts at the same time.

Disadvantages:

- "Insider attack" is the serious threat in this type.
- It requires some extra dedicated hardware.
- It can work only for network attacks.
- Analyzing encrypted message is a challenging task.
- Detection from high speed networks is also challenging.

25.3.3 Types of Network-Based Detection Technique

There are three main types of network-based detection technique: Signature-based (or Pattern-matching) Intrusion Detection Systems (SIDS), Anomaly-based Intrusion Detection Systems (AIDS), and Hybrid Intrusion Detection Systems (Hybrid IDS).

25.3.3.1 *Signature-Based (or Pattern-Matching) Intrusion Detection Systems (SIDS)*

Signature based ID System simply looks and matches a signature or pattern of the packet or data with the already existed patterns or signatures of the previously defined or happened activities. Therefore, SIDS or pattern matching method finds the previously happened attacks named as "Known Attacks". This method matches the intrusion signature with the previously existed signature in the signature database, reports an attack and triggers an alarm if match found. SIDS works better for known attacks but fails to detect zero-day attacks due to the unavailability of new intrusion signature in the database. Signature-based (or Pattern-matching) Intrusion Detection sometimes is also known as knowledge-based detection [8].

25.3.3.2 *Anomaly-Based Intrusion Detection Systems (AIDS)*

AIDS overcomes the limitation that is inability to detect zero-day attacks by observing the user unusual behavior which does not match to the defined standard user behavior. Anomaly can be defined as the deviation between the observed user behavior and defined standard behavior. AIDS does not rely on any previously maintained signature database [9]. It detects the intrusions malicious activities by identifying the uncommon behavior of users. The problem with this method is due to inability to identifying undesirable behavior, it can generate high false alarm. Many researchers presented the methods to reduce the false alarming. Anomaly detection has many applications in different fields such as medical malpractices, identifying anomalous behavior of moving objects, unusual behavior of users on social media platform and credit fraud [10].

25.3.3.3 *Hybrid Intrusion Detection System*

The Hybrid IDS integrates the fundamental concepts of both the systems SIDS and AIDS; and overcomes their problems; SIDS is unable to detect zero-day attacks and AIDS can generate large number of the false alarms [11]. A Hybrid IDS has components like Data Acquisition Module, Analyzer, Signature Database, Anomaly Detector, Signature Generator, and Counter-measure module as shown in Figure 25.2. Data acquisition module consists of multiple sensors. A sensor can be located either on an individual host in Host based systems or a network segment in network-based systems to read each packet passing through it. The Signature database stores a set of signature or rules. Data storage is used to capture and stores the packets if they arrive at a high speed. Next, the Analyzer module compares the arrived packets with the signatures or rules kept in Signature database using some pattern-matching algorithm. If no match is found, then it informs to Anomaly detector. The Anomaly Detector investigates for any irregularity using some pattern finding technique. Then it sends a message to signature generator module that creates new signature and writes that new created signature in Signature Database. If the Analyzer finds any match, then it informs Counter-measure

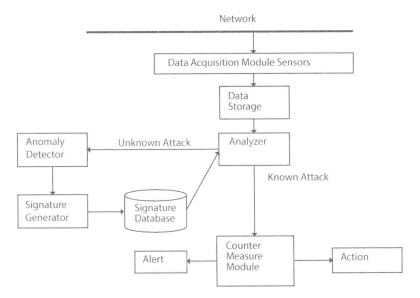

Figure 25.2 Architecture of a Hybrid IDS [11].

module in case of known attack and makes an entry in log file. The counter measure module takes appropriate actions and sends alerts defined by the security policies set by the administrator. Several authors have opted this model to implement the IDS with the objective of improved accuracy, less memory need, and less false positives and negatives [12, 13].

25.4 Types of Attacks

Any attacker can perform the different types of attacks on the computer system resources or network which can harm or corrupt that system. Those attacks can be categorized as follows:

- Confidentiality—In this category of attack, any attacker attempts to gain access to the information for which he is not authorized [14].
- Integrity—In this type of attack, any attacker attempts to affect the system state, or any data residing on or passing through the system.
- Availability—n this category of attack, any attacker tries to prevent an authorized user from accessing a service or resource [6].
- Control—In this type of attack, any attacker tries to gain or steal authorized user's credentials further to have attacks on confidentiality, integrity, and/or availability.

Apart from these broad categories of attacks, many researchers specifically mentioned and tested their proposed approaches on the following attacks:

- Denial-of-Service: the attacker prevents the authorized user to access a service. Example: the attacker can make computational and memory resources busy so that the legitimate user cannot access those resources.

- R2L (Remote to Local): Any unauthorized user or attacker tries to get an access to the remote system by sending a message over the network or using a legitimate user account on that remote system.
- U2R (User to Root): Any unauthorized user or attacker tries to get a remote unauthorized access to the root by using a legitimate or a valid user account.
- Probe: Any unauthorized user or attacker tries to gather information about networks so that violations can be made in future.

25.5 Recent Improved Solutions to Intrusion Detection

With advancement of recent technologies like Cloud services, IOT devices, the Intrusion Detection System (IDS) has become a prominent technology to detect anomalies and attacks in the network. Many researchers have integrated IDS with data mining [15, 16], fuzzy logic [17], neural networks [18], machine learning and optimization techniques [19] to improve the methods of detecting anomalies and attacks with the objectives of improving the accuracy of detections. The information security is main concern with the advanced technologies like IoT [20] and Cloud computing [21]. With the increased usage of IoT networks and clouds in different domains, these have become more vulnerable targets for intruders and attackers. Many researchers have proposed different methods and approaches to detect malicious actions of intruders and found the need of security in cloud and IOT to be implemented on the layers as well as protocol levels in the service models. Many IDS based on statistical methods, knowledge based methods and machine learning techniques have been studied and presented in Table 25.1 according to the algorithms used and the results produced with their detection performance. The exiting AIDS techniques can be categorized as the following:

1. Based on Statistical methods
2. Based on machine learning methods and Data mining techniques
3. Knowledge based
4. Evolutionary methods
5. Based on Statistical methods

IDS based on the statistical methods uses a distribution model for normal behavior profile to detect potential intrusions based on statistical metrics such as mean, median, standard deviations and mode of packets. Statistical IDS generally uses one of the following models; Univariate, multivariate [22], and time series model. In univariate technique based IDS statistical normal profile is created based on only one measure of behaviors in computer systems for identifying abnormalities in each individual metric. While, the Multivariate technique considers more than one measures to specify the relationships between variables including multiple data variables which can be correlated. The multivariate statistical IDs face challenges to estimate correlations and distributions for high-dimensional data. Any time series data can be defined as a series of observations made over a certain time interval. A new observation can be considered as abnormal if it is not occurring at that time interval [23]. Researchers used any occurred abrupt variation in time series data for detecting network abnormalities [24].

25.5.1   Based on Data Mining and Machine Learning Methods

Machine learning process is used to infer the knowledge from huge amount of data by applying a set of rules, methods, or complex "transfer functions" to find out unusual data patterns and predict abnormal behavior of user profiles. Several researchers have applied machine learning techniques in the area of AIDS such as clustering, neural networks, association rules, decision trees, genetic algorithms, and nearest neighbor methods [25, 26] with the aim of improving accuracy and reducing the requirement of human interventions. Machine learning algorithms can be classified into supervised, unsupervised and semi-supervised techniques which are extensively being used in building AIDS and finding patterns.

25.5.2   Knowledge-Based

An expert system based approach requires creating a knowledge base consisting genuine traffic profile with the help of human knowledge and detects any action different from this defined profile as intrusion. This technique helps in reducing false positive alarms but requires the regular update of knowledge base regarding the normal expected behavior of traffic profile. This group of techniques include Finite state machine [27], Description Language [28], Expert System [29] and Signature analysis-based IDS [30].

25.5.3   Evolutionary Methods and Optimization Techniques

This group of techniques makes use of nature inspired algorithms such as ACO, PSO, Genetic Algorithm and Evolutionary computing, etc. to improve the accuracy. These evolutionary approaches based on the principle of evolution and concept of fitness methods are used for classification and feature selection in the intrusion detection systems [31, 32].

25.6   Analysis of Exiting IDS Based on Technique Used

The comparative analysis of various existing IDS has been presented in Table 25.1. The comparison was done on the basis of parameters Algorithm used, techniques followed and detection performance including the accuracy of model proposed, false positive rate, false negative rate, and false alarm rate. The brief description of the research work given in Table 25.1 has been discussed as follows.

In Ref. [22], the authors described an IDS using Multivariate statistical analysis and tested the model using Both the Hotelling's T^2 test statistic and the chi-squared distance test X^2 test statistic measure. The measures consider the distance of an observation from the multivariate mean. This method produced reduced false alarm rate.

In Ref. [29] the authors proposed a hybrid IDS and follow the detection technique based on misuse concept. The model takes less time for the training and testing processes of the model with producing detection rate of 99.1% (for known attacks) and detection rate of 30.5% (for unknown attacks) and false positive rate 1.2%. The authors concluded that decision tree performs well for known attacks but not for unknown attacks.

Table 25.1 Comparison of various IDS methods.

S. No.	Paper	Year	Description	Technique used	Detection Performance (Accuracy %)
1	[22]	2002	Multivariate statistical analysis	Statistical	Detection Rate = 92 False Alarm Rate = 0
2	[33]	2005	SVM, ANN	Machine Learning	Detection Rate = 100 False Positive Rate = 8.53
3	[34]	2008	Used AdaBoost algorithm.	Machine Learning	Detection rate = 90.738% False Alarm Rate = 3.428%
4	[35]	2011	SVM-based IDS with BIRCH algorithm	Machine Learning	Accuracy = 95.72% False Positive Rate = 0.73%
5	[36]	2013	Random Tree classification	Data Mining technique	Accuracy = 97.49%
6	[37]	2013	SMO Classifier	Machine Learning	Accuracy = 97.36 False Alarm Rate = 0
7	[38]	2013	C4.5	Data Mining technique	Detection Rate = 99.55
8	[39]	2014	Extreme learning machines	Machine Learning	Detection Rate = 100 False Alarm Rate = 0.6
9	[40]	2014	Linear Genetic Programming and Bees Algorithm, SVM	Machine Learning	Detection Rate = 96.7% False Alarm Rate = 12.2%
10	[15]	2014	EDADT (Efficient Data Adapted Decision Tree), hybrid PSO, C4.5	Machine Learning, Optimization Techniques	Accuracy = 98.12 False Alarm Rate = 0.18
11	[41]	2015	SVM, Bee Colony Algorithm	Machine Learning, Optimization Techniques	Average Accuracy = 88.46
12	[42]	2015	Online Sequential Extreme Learning Machine	Machine Learning	Accuracy = 97.71% False Positive Rate = 1.81%

(Continued)

Table 25.1 Comparison of various IDS methods. (*Continued*)

S. No.	Paper	Year	Description	Technique used	Detection Performance (Accuracy %)
13	[43]	2015	A multi-objective PSO algorithm for feature selection.	Optimization Techniques	Detection Rate = 98.9 False Alarm Rate = 2.0%
14	[44]	2016	K- Nearest Neighbor technique and K-Means Algorithms	Data Mining technique	Detection Rate = 91.86 False Positive Rate = 0.78 Accuracy = 93.29
15	[45]	2016	SVM, ELM, Modified K-means Technique	Machine Learning	Accuracy = 95.75 Detection Rate = 95.17 False Alarm Rate = 1.87
16	[46]	2016	SVM-KNN-PSO	Machine Learning, Optimization Technique	Accuracy = 91.67
17	[47]	2018	SVM	Machine Learning	Accuracy = 99.98
18	[48]	2018	MLP and Payload Classifier	Machine Learning	Accuracy = 89
19	[49]	2018	ABC and AdaBoost algorithms	Machine Learning, Optimization Technique	Detection Rate = 99.4 Accuracy = 97.5 False Positive Rate = 0.04
20	[50]	2018	SVM+ Naïve Bayes + C5 classifier	Machine Learning	Accuracy = 99.82

In Ref. [33], the researchers used SVM and ANN (Artificial Neural Network) on DARPA 98 and concluded as SVM performs better than ANN. In this paper the detection rate flows between 40 and 100% and false positive rate flows from = 8.53 to 39.25.

In Ref. [34], the authors used AdaBoost, one of the machine learning algorithms to lower the computational complexity of the model to detect the anomalous behavior and reduce false alarm rate. The authors opted this algorithm because it is fast, good for correcting misclassification, simple to implement and works for heterogeneous (categorical and continuous type of data) datasets for IDS.

In Ref. [35], the researchers used SVM with hierarchical clustering for better in detection of DoS and Probe attacks. The work used balanced iterative reducing and clustering (BIRCH) algorithm using clustering hierarchies on KDD CUP 99 dataset for intrusion detection with Accuracy of 95.72% and false positive rate of 0.73%.

In Ref. [36], the authors presented the comparison of different classifiers Alternating Decision Tree, C4.5, NBTree, RandomTree, RandomForest, and REPTree classifier on NSL-KDD data set. The comparison shows that Random Tree classifier with discretization and feature selection method produced the highest accuracy over the other methods/classifiers mentioned and reduced false alarm rate but long execution time.

The authors presented a signature based model using machine learning and optimized techniques [37]. This paper also describes the building a dataset by capturing real time traffic and use of various classifiers including SMO classifier (Sequential Minimal Optimization). The comparison was performed on the parameters as the accuracy, false alarm rate and hit rate measures. On The basis of measures the researchers concluded that random forest, RIPPER rule learner and C4.5 decision tree performed best.

In Ref. [38], the authors compared various classifiers SVM, ANN, KNN, Naïve Bayes and Decision tree on NSL-KDD dataset for intrusion detection to detect anomaly based on parameters such as true positive and false positives. On the basis on comparison performed, the authors found that C4.5 algorithm has improved accuracy and efficient data sampling into subsets. C4.5 classifier shows the good performance for real time classification.

This paper presented a semantic based approach using extreme learning machine [39]. Extreme learning machine is one of the popular machine learning algorithms which further provides easy semantic feature addition in detection. The model was tested on KDD98 data set and ADFA Linux Data Set and by performing semantic analysis of system calls.

In Ref. [40], the authors presented a model using Linear Genetic Programming (LGP) and Bees Algorithm (BA) algorithms and SVM. The LGP-BA (Linear Genetic Programming and Bees Algorithm) used to select features and the SVM for categorization of the selected features. The authors concluded that SVM works better than others and produces better performance in terms of accuracy and efficiency.

This paper presents a hybrid model using machine learning algorithm SVM for classifying attacks and optimization technique Bee Colony for optimal clustering purpose to improve IDS performance [41]. The model was performed on KDD99 dataset. The model produced average accuracy of 88.46% for different attacks.

This paper presents a model using Online Sequential Extreme Learning Machine based technique and tests the technique on NSL KDD dataset and Kyoto University benchmark dataset based on the parameters false positive rate, true positive rate, false negative rate and true negative rate, precision test time and F1 score [42]. The authors claimed for better accuracy, low detection time and reduced false positive rate.

Ref. [43] proposed a model using optimization technique MPSO algorithm (Multi-objective PSO) algorithm for feature selection with discretization this model was applicable for both discrete and continuous data. This method is highly robust and efficient for real-time attacks detection. The authors concluded that this method produces high detection rate, low false positive rate and quick response.

The authors in Ref. [44] presented a hybrid approach based on data mining techniques K- Nearest Neighbor technique (K-NN) and K-Means Algorithms. The proposed approach was tested on KDD and Kyoto University data with real time detection. The proposed approach was compared with the other methods and validated for effective anomalies detection in networks and for producing reduced False Positive Rate.

In Ref. [45], the authors presented a multi-level Hybrid IDS using SVM and ELM and also used a modified version of K-means Technique to achieve better efficiency and improved accuracy in detection method. The proposed IDS was tested on KDD Cup 1999 for different types of attack under known and new attacks category.

In this paper [46], the authors presented an IDS based on SVM-KNN-PSO including LUS (Local Unimodal Sampling as Meta-optimizer), and WMA (Weighted Majority Algorithm) to obtain improved classification accuracy and ensemble type of classifier to produce better accuracy than WMA. The classifiers were compared on the basis of elapsed time and classification accuracy.

Ref. [47] presented a new dataset called Bot-IoT consisting of labeled IoT related traffic and other network traffic. The work includes the application of three classifiers namely support vector machine, a recurring neural network and a long short-term classifiers. The performance of these mentioned classifier for best 10 selected features were observed on the basis of parameters as accuracy, precision, recall, testing time and fall out. The author claimed that SVM achieved highest recall and fall out.

Memory RNN (LSTM-RNN) Highest accuracy and improved detection rate on Bot-IoT. In Ref. [48] the authors proposed an IDS using MLP and Payload Classifier for improved detection accuracy. The MLP (Multi-layer Perceptron). MLP showed accuracy of 94.5%. The proposed model obtained accuracy of 95.2% when combined with payload classifier. Fisher algorithm was used for feature selection.

Ref. [49] presented a hybrid and reliable approach based on machine learning AdaBoost and optimized technique artificial bee colony along with the taxonomy of anomaly based IDS. The method was tested to the benchmark dataset multi-class NSL-KDD. The proposed approach was compared with the others based on the parameters such as detection rate, false positive rate, feature selection method, as well as the time and space requirements of different methods. The authors concluded that method shows increased accuracy, improved detection rate, and speedup detection time.

Ref. [50] presented an IDS using C5 algorithm and provided the comparison with other classifiers C4.5, SVM and Naïve Bayes. C5 outperforms over the other classifiers and produces the detection accuracy of 99.82% evaluated on NSL-KDD dataset.

25.7   Analysis of Existing IDS in Different Domains

Now days, increased use of Internet promoted the various new Internet based emerging technologies like Web applications, Internet of Things, Cloud Computing and Wireless Sensor Networks etc. Along with the internet, these technologies are being used extensively. Hence, the protection of the user information in these different domains becomes a necessity. Intrusion system provides a mechanism to protect the user data in these different

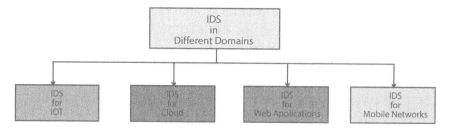

Figure 25.3 IDS in different domains.

domains. Further, we have discussed some exiting IDS in the domains IOT, Cloud, Web Applications and WSN respectively as shown in Figure 25.3.

25.7.1 IDS for IoT

IoT is an emerging technology which is growing at rapid pace and connects millions of autonomous devices over the Internet. Hence it provides a huge space for intruders to compromise the security, confidentiality and integrity. In IoT environment, an intrusion detection system has two modes to operate; standalone system or collaborative system. The former mode considers only local traffic patterns within the network domain while the later one observes the collective behavior of different nodes across different domains. The solution for different nodes from different domains forming a collaborative network can be grouped in two types as centralized and distributed. In centralized settings the any detected malicious activities are reported to a centralized system. In the distributed also called decentralized settings, alert information from each service provider is shared and processed in a completely distributed fashion. Ref. [51] proposed IDS based on dimension reduction using PCA (Principle Component Analysis) and reduced feature selection using Linear Discriminate Analysis along with KNN and Naive Bayes classifiers to detect multiple attacks in IOT environment. Dimension reduction and reduced feature selection techniques helped to reduce the complexity of the proposed model. Ref. [52] proposed a client based and three layered security IDS system to detect anomalous behavior of intruders. This model provided increased the level of security but subsequently increased overheads. In first module i.e. Process whitelist Module, a whitelist is prepared, all the running process are compared with this list to filter the malicious process. At the second module, called PBM (Process Behavior Module) monitors each parameter of the running process and applies a trained ML classifier to separate the malicious behavior. In the next module SBM monitors the processes according to the process-issued system call. Although the machine learning techniques work better but increase the cost from first module to third module. This model has given detection performance with a detection rate of 79.09% at the first layer. The second layer gives a detection rate of 97.02% and false positive rate of 2.97%. The third module shows the highest performance with a detection rate of 100% and 0 false positives at third layer. Ref. [53] designed a blockchain-based IDS named CIoTA, an extension of EMM (extensible Markov model), to perform distributed and collaborative anomaly detection having incremental update capabilities via self-attestation and consensus among IoT devices. This model was tested self-built

IOT simulation platform consisting IOT devices with limited resources. Ref. [54] discussed the detailed IoT architecture and the associated security vulnerabilities with their design and implementation of intrusion detection systems for IoT according to the future requirements.

Ref. [55] presented an IDS for Internet of Vehicles based on tree based algorithms DT (Decision Tree, Random Forest, Extra Tree, and XGBoost, and other ML classifiers based on Detection rate, FAR, Accuracy and F1 score showing that tree based algorithms works better than KNN and SVM classifiers.

25.7.2   IDS in Cloud Computing Environment

Cloud computing is a fast growing emerging technology providing different services to the users on demand basis creating and contributing to cost effective and effortless environment. IDS in cloud environment can be categorized as host based IDS, Network based IDS, Distributed IDS and VM/Hypervisor based systems [56]. The author also classified cloud network attacks as insider and outsider of the cloud network attacks. With this categorization cloud networks mainly gets affected by attacks such as Denial of service (DOS), User to root, Port scanning and backdoor channel attacks. In Ref. [32] the authors proposed an IDS having two phases; first for feature selection using CS-PSO algorithm and second phase for classifying the malicious activities using Logistic Regression, AdaBoost and Random Forest over the cloud, and tested the method on NSL-KDD dataset. The proposed approach shows high classification accuracy. Ref. [57] presented a novel cluster based Collaborative IDS Framework for Cloud using machine learning techniques to improve the detection accuracy. The framework was divided into two units; detection and correlation unit. The correlation unit must be the part of at least one cluster. Due to collaboration between NIDSs, knowledge base remains up-to-date and coordinated attacks against can be prevented.

25.7.3   IDS in Web Applications

With the exponential growth in the usage of web based activities, the space for attacks and vulnerabilities have been increased. So the detection of the attacks, analysis of the incoming request and identification of the potential threats has become a necessity. Ref. [58] defined some required characteristics of the web based applications and web traffic required to create a detection architecture for web; Communication Protocol (HTTP/HTTPS), Web Request, Multiple Users with Multiple Roles, Continuous Changes, Dynamicity, Heterogeneity, Bot Requests with the security measures such as Input Validation, output Validation, Access Control, Session Verification, Bot Detection with their Web vulnerabilities. Ref. [59] provided the different existing intrusion detection response systems according to the different network attacks. Timely appropriate response for the occurred attack is required for the better network performance. Ref. [60] proposed an approach of anomaly detection based on the syntactic context of the network payload to increase the accuracy at application layer as the detection from a plain byte sequence of payload is difficult to identify the potential threats. Ref. [61] provided an automated method for identification of harmful or suspicious requests among peer web servers based on the statistical techniques. To increase the network performance and throughput affected by the various attacks, IDS must response properly.

25.7.4   IDS for WSN (Wireless Sensor Network)

A wireless sensor network is a network of autonomous sensor nodes having capabilities of processing of the sensed data and transmitting the result with limited resources and power consumption. The applications for WSN are being created and used at a large scale. Hence, WSN security becomes a big concern. In Ref. [62] the authors outlined some security issues, challenges and IDS approaches in respect of WSN security.

Ref. [63] provided the details of IDS for the Mobile Ad Hoc Networks (MANET), WSN and Cyber-Physical Systems (CPS) with the associated vulnerabilities along with some research directions for IoT domain. Ref. [64] proposed IDS with eight major components, namely the network trace dataset, data pre-processing module, Allen's interval algebra module, feature selection module, classification module. In Ref. [65] the author proposed an approach using spatial partitioned negative selection algorithm taken from immune biological system. This proposed IDS protects the sensor data along with the power consumption, resource constrained and time effectiveness. The authors compared the proposed IDS with other IDS on the basis of detection rate and false alarm rate. Ref. [66] proposed fuzzy based intrusion detection architecture. Feature selection and classification are two important aspects for building the IDS. The authors used dynamic recursive feature selection algorithm for optimal feature selection and fuzzy rules for classification. The fuzzy rules were used to classify the types of intruder into definite, medium probable and high probable intruders.

25.8   Conclusion

An exponential growth in the usage of the internet across all the popular domains enables the sharing of the available resources, accessing the services lying at the ends and massive transfer of the data and information. Most of the mentioned features are quite vulnerable for the threats from the external agencies and thus provoke the need for the safeguarding the existing information and system from unauthorized access. Intrusion Detection System (IDS) as discussed in above sections can play a significant role in identifying an unauthorized computer system activity which may challenge the integrity of the existing network security. Through this paper, we present an underlying structure of the IDS, various attacks, and survey of various intrusion detection techniques with their solutions based on statistical, data mining, machine learning and neural network techniques. It can be clearly observed from the comparative study of various IDS techniques that the researchers are extensively using the data mining and machine learning techniques in order to address the challenges such as zero-day-attacks detection in case of Host based ID systems, false alarm generation rate in case of Anomaly based ID systems and improvement of attack detection accuracy.

References

1. Anderson, James P. *Computer security threat monitoring and surveillance.* Technical Report, James P. Anderson Company, 1980.
2. Bace, R.G., *Intrusion detection.* Sams Publishing, 2000.

3. Allen, J., Christie, A., Fithen, W., McHugh, J., Pickel, J., Stoner, E., State of the practice of intrusion detection technologies. No. CMU/SEI-99-TR-028. CARNEGIE-MELLON UNIV PITTSBURGH PA SOFTWARE ENGINEERING INST, 2000.

4. Denning, D.E., An intrusion-detection model. *IEEE Trans. Software Eng.*, 2, 222, 1987.

5. Axelsson, S., *Research in intrusion-detection systems: A survey*, Technical report 98-17, p. 120, Department of Computer Engineering, Chalmers University of Technology, 1998.

6. Bace, R., *An introduction to intrusion detection and assessment for system and network security management*. ICSA Intrusion Detection Systems Consortium Technical Report, 1999.

7. Creech, G. and Hu, J., A semantic approach to host-based intrusion detection systems using contiguous and discontiguous system call patterns. *IEEE Trans. Comput.*, 63, 807, 2013.

8. Kumar, V. and Sangwan, O.P., Signature based intrusion detection system using SNORT. *Int. J. Comput. Appl. Inf. Technol.*, 1, 35, 2012.

9. Alazab, A., Hobbs, M., Abawajy, J., Alazab, M., Using feature selection for intrusion detection system, in: *2012 International Symposium on Communications and Information Technologies (ISCIT)*, IEEE, p. 296, 2012.

10. Khraisat, A., Gondal, I., Vamplew, P., Kamruzzaman, J., Survey of intrusion detection systems: techniques, datasets and challenges. *Cybersecurity*, 2, 20, 2019.

11. Patel, K.K. and Buddhadev, B.V., An architecture of hybrid intrusion detection system. *Int. J. Inf. Netw. Secur.*, 2, 197, 2013.

12. Karim, H.A.R.A., Handa, S.S., Murthy, M.R., A Methodical Approach to Implement Intrusion Detection System in Hybrid Network. *Int. J. Eng. Sci.*, 4817–4820, 2017.

13. Singh, DM., Harbi, N., Zahidur Rahman, M., Combining Naive Bayes and Decision Tree for Adaptive Intrusion Detection. International journal of Network Security & Its Applications [Internet]. *Academy and Industry Research Collaboration Center (AIRCC)*, 25, 2, 2, 12–25, 2010. Available from: http://dx.doi.org/10.5121/ijnsa.2010.2202

14. Proctor, P.E., *Practical Intrusion Detection Handbook*, Prentice Hall PTR, 2000.

15. Nadiammai, G.V. and Hemalatha, M., Effective approach toward Intrusion Detection System using data mining techniques. *Egypt. Inform. J.*, 15, 37, 2014.

16. Ektefa, M., Memar, S., Sidi, F., Affendey, L.S., Intrusion detection using data mining techniques, in: *2010 International Conference on Information Retrieval & Knowledge Management (CAMP)*, IEEE, p. 200, 2010.

17. Bridges, S.M. and Vaughn, R.B., Fuzzy data mining and genetic algorithms applied to intrusion detection, in: *Proceedings of 12th Annual Canadian Information Technology Security Symposium*, p. 109, 2000.

18. Mukkamala, S., Janoski, G., Sung, A., May. Intrusion detection using neural networks and support vector machines, in: *Proceedings of the 2002 International Joint Conference on Neural Networks, IJCNN'02*, vol. 2, IEEE, p. 1702, 2002.

19. Satpute, K., Agrawal, S., Agrawal, J., Sharma, S., A survey on anomaly detection in network intrusion detection system using particle swarm optimization based machine learning techniques, in: *Proceedings of the International Conference on Frontiers of Intelligent Computing: Theory and Applications (FICTA)*, Springer, p. 141, 2013.

20. Tabassum, A., Erbad, A., Guizani, M., A Survey on Recent Approaches in Intrusion Detection System in IoTs, in: *2019 15th International Wireless Communications & Mobile Computing Conference (IWCMC)*, IEEE, p. 1190, 2019.

21. Sari, A., A review of anomaly detection systems in cloud networks and survey of cloud security measures in cloud storage applications. *J. Inf. Secur.*, 6, 142, 2015.

22. Ye, N., Emran, S.M., Chen, Q., Vilbert, S., Multivariate statistical analysis of audit trails for host-based intrusion detection. *IEEE Trans. Comput.*, 51, 810, 2002.

23. Viinikka, J., Debar, H., Mé, L., Lehikoinen, A., Tarvainen, M., Processing intrusion detection alert aggregates with time series modeling. *Inform. Fusion*, 10, 312, 2009.

24. Qingtao, W. and Zhiqing, S., Network anomaly detection using time series analysis, in: *Joint International Conference on Autonomic and Autonomous Systems and International Conference on Networking and Services—(ICASISNS'05)*, p. 42, 2005.

25. Kshetri, N. and Voas, J., Hacking power grids: A current problem. *Computer*, 50, 91, 2017.

26. Xiao, L., Wan, X., Lu, X., Zhang, Y., Wu, D., IoT security techniques based on machine learning: How do IoT devices use AI to enhance security? *IEEE Signal Process. Mag.*, 35, 41, 2018.

27. Walkinshaw, N., Taylor, R., Derrick, J., Inferring extended finite state machine models from software executions. *Empir. Softw. Eng.*, 21, 811, 2016.

28. Laarouchi, Y., Kaâniche, M., Nicomette, V., Studnia, I., Alata, E., A language-based intrusion detection approach for automotive embedded networks. International Journal of Embedded Systems [Internet]. Inderscience Publishers; 10, 1, 1, 2018. Available from: http://dx.doi.org/10.1504/ijes.2018.10010488

29. Kim, G., Lee, S., Kim, S., A Novel Hybrid Intrusion Detection Method Integrating Anomaly Detection with Misuse Detection. *Expert Syst. Appl.*, 41, 1690, 2014.

30. Kenkre, P.S., Pai, A., Colaco, L., Real time intrusion detection and prevention system, in: *Proceedings of the 3rd International Conference on Frontiers of Intelligent Computing: Theory and Applications (FICTA) 2014*, Springer, p. 405, 2015.

31. Murray, S.N., Walsh, B.P., Kelliher, D., O'Sullivan, D.T.J., Multi-variable optimization of thermal energy efficiency retrofitting of buildings using static modelling and genetic algorithms–A case study. *Build. Environ.*, 75, 98, 2014.

32. Ghosh, P., Karmakar, A., Sharma, J., Phadikar, S., CS-PSO based Intrusion Detection System in Cloud Environment. Emerging Technologies in Data Mining and Information Security [Internet]. Springer Singapore, 261–9, 2018. Available from: http://dx.doi.org/10.1007/978-981-13-1951-8_24

33. Chen, W.H., Hsu, S.H., Shen, H.P., Application of SVM and ANN for intrusion detection. *Comput. Oper. Res.*, 32, 2617, 2005.

34. Hu, W., Hu, W., Maybank, S., Adaboost-based algorithm for network intrusion detection. *IEEE Trans. Syst. Man Cybern. Part B (Cybern.)*, 38, 577, 2008.

35. Horng, S.J., Su, M.Y., Chen, Y.H., Kao, T.W., Chen, R.J., Lai, J.L., Perkasa, C.D., A novel intrusion detection system based on hierarchical clustering and support vector machines. *Expert Syst. Appl.*, 38, 306, 2011.

36. Thaseen, S. and Kumar, C.A., February. An analysis of supervised tree based classifiers for intrusion detection system, in: *2013 international conference on pattern recognition, informatics and Mobile engineering*, IEEE, p. 294, 2013.

37. Shafi, K. and Abbass, H.A., Evaluation of an adaptive genetic-based signature extraction system for network intrusion detection. *Pattern Anal. Appl.*, 16, 549, 2013.

38. Adebowale, A., Idowu, S.A., Amarachi, A., Comparative study of selected data mining algorithms used for intrusion detection. *Int. J. Soft Comput. Eng. (IJSCE)*, 3, 237, 2013.

39. Creech, G. and Hu, J., A semantic approach to host-based intrusion detection systems using contiguousand discontiguous system call patterns. *IEEE Trans. Comput.*, 63, 807, 2013.

40. Hasani, S.R., Othman, Z.A., Kahaki, S.M.M., Hybrid feature selection algorithm for intrusion detection system. *J. Comput. Sci.*, 10, 1015, 2014.

41. Gupta, M. and Shrivastava, S.K., Intrusion detection system based on svm and bee colony. *Int. J. Comput. Appl.*, 111, 27–32, 2015.

42. Singh, R., Kumar, H., Singla, R.K., An intrusion detection system using network traffic profiling and online sequential extreme learning machine. *Expert Syst. Appl.*, 42, 8609, 20152015.

43. Sujitha, B. and Kavitha, V., Layered approach for intrusion detection using multiobjective particle swarm optimization. *Int. J. Appl. Eng. Res.*, 10, 31999, 2015.

44. Guo, C., Ping, Y., Liu, N., Luo, S.S., A two-level hybrid approach for intrusion detection. *Neurocomputing*, 214, 391, 2016.

45. Al-Yaseen, W.L., Othman, Z.A., Nazri, M.Z.A., Multi-level hybrid support vector machine and extreme learning machine based on modified K-means for intrusion detection system. *Expert Syst. Appl.*, 67, 296, 2017.

46. Aburomman, A.A. and Reaz, M.B.I., A novel SVM-kNN-PSO ensemble method for intrusion detection system. *Appl. Soft. Comput.*, 38, 360, 2016.

47. Koroniotis, N., Moustafa, N., Sitnikova, E., Turnbull, B., Towards the development of realistic botnet dataset in the internet of things for network forensic analytics: Bot-IoT dataset. *Future Gener. Comput. Syst.*, 100, 779, 2019.

48. Ustebay, S., Turgut, Z., Aydin, M.A., Intrusion detection system with recursive feature elimination by using random forest and deep learning classifier, in: *2018 international congress on big data, deep learning and fighting cyber terrorism (IBIGDELFT)*, IEEE, p. 71, 2018.

49. Mazini, M., Shirazi, B., Mahdavi, I., Anomaly network-based intrusion detection system using a reliable hybrid artificial bee colony and AdaBoost algorithms. *J. King Saud Univ.-Comp. Info. Sci.*, 31, 541–553, 2019.

50. Khraisat, A., Gondal, I., Vamplew, P., An anomaly intrusion detection system using C5 decision tree classifier, in: *Pacific-Asia Conference on Knowledge Discovery and Data Mining*, Springer, p. 149, 2018.

51. Pajouh, H.H., Javidan, R., Khayami, R., Ali, D., Choo, K.K.R., A two-layer dimension reduction and two-tier classification model for anomaly-based intrusion detection in IoT backbone networks. *IEEE Trans. Emerging Top. Comput.*, 7, 2, 314–323, 2016.

52. Mudgerikar, A., Sharma, P., Bertino, E., E-Spion: A System-Level Intrusion Detection System for IoT Devices, in: *Proceedings of the 2019 ACM Asia Conference on Computer and Communications Security*, p. 493, 2019.

53. Golomb, T., Mirsky, Y., Elovici, Y., CIoTA: Collaborative Anomaly Detection via Blockchain. *Proceedings 2018 Workshop on Decentralized IoT Security and Standards [Internet]*. Internet Society. 2018. Available from: http://dx.doi.org/10.14722/diss.2018.23003

54. Elrawy, M.F., Awad, A.I., Hamed, H.F., Intrusion detection systems for IoT-based smart environments: a survey. *J. Cloud Comput.*, 7, 21, 2018.

55. Fu, W., Xin, X., Guo, P., Zhou, Z., A practical intrusion detection system for Internet of vehicles. *China Commun.*, 13, 263, 2016.

56. Chiba, Z., Abghour, N., Moussaid, K., El Omri, A., Rida, M., A survey of intrusion detection systems for cloud computing environment, in: *2016 International Conference on Engineering & MIS (ICEMIS)*, IEEE, p. 1, 2016.

57. Singh, D., Patel, D., Borisaniya, B., Modi, C., Collaborative ids framework for cloud. *Int. J. Netw. Secur.*, 18, 699, 2016.

58. Agarwal, N. and Hussain, S.Z., A Closer Look at Intrusion Detection System for Web Applications. *Security and Communication Networks [Internet]*. Hindawi Limited, 2018, 1–27, 2018. Available from: http://dx.doi.org/10.1155/2018/9601357

59. Anwar, S., Mohamad Zain, J., Zolkipli, M.F., Inayat, Z., Khan, S., Anthony, B., Chang, V., From intrusion detection to an intrusion response system: fundamentals, requirements, and future directions. *Algorithms*, 10, 39, 2017.

60. Duessel, P., Gehl, C., Flegel, U., Dietrich, S., Meier, M., Detecting zero-day attacks using context-aware anomaly detection at the application-layer. *Int. J. Inf. Secur.*, 16, 475, 2017.

61. Zachara, M., Identification of Possible Attack Attempts Against Web Applications Utilizing Collective Assessment of Suspicious Requests. *Transactions on Computational Collective Intelligence XXII [Internet]*. Springer Berlin Heidelberg, 45–59, 2016. Available from: http://dx.doi.org/10.1007/978-3-662-49619-0_3

62. Ghosal, A. and Halder, S., Intrusion Detection in Wireless Sensor Networks: Issues, Challenges and Approaches. *Wireless Networks and Security [Internet]*. Springer Berlin Heidelberg, 329–67, 2013. Available from: http://dx.doi.org/10.1007/978-3-642-36169-2_10

63. Khan, Z.A. and Herrmann, P., Recent Advancements in Intrusion Detection Systems for the Internet of Things. *Security and Communication Networks* [Internet]. Hindawi Limited, 2019, 1–19, 2019. Available from: http://dx.doi.org/10.1155/2019/4301409

64. Selvakumar, K., Karuppiah, M., SaiRamesh, L., Islam, S.H., Hassan, M.M., Fortino, G., Choo, K.K.R., Intelligent temporal classification and fuzzy rough set-based feature selection algorithm for intrusion detection system in WSNs. *Inf. Sci.*, 497, 77, 2019.

65. Zhang, R. and Xiao, X., Intrusion Detection in Wireless Sensor Networks with an Improved NSA Based on Space Division. *Journal of Sensors* [Internet]. Hindawi Limited, 2019, 1–20, 2019. Available from: http://dx.doi.org/10.1155/2019/5451263

66. Nancy, P., Muthurajkumar, S., Ganapathy, S., Kumar, S.S., Selvi, M., Arputharaj, K., Intrusion detection using dynamic feature selection and fuzzy temporal decision tree classification for wireless sensor networks. *IET Commun.*, 14, 888, 2020.

Part 4

COMMUNICATION AND NETWORKS

26

Green Communication Technology Management for Sustainability in Organization

Shivangi Sahay[1] and Anju Bharti[2]*

[1]ECE Branch, B. Tech, IGDTUW, Kashmere Gate, New Delhi, India
[2]Department of Management, Maharaja Agrasen Institute of Technology, GGSIP University, Delhi, India

Abstract

Green communication technologies nowadays are being preferred and implemented in the organization. The adoption of the green communication technology will help in businesses. It will help in two ways, in reducing power consumption and lowering the operating costs of organizations. Green communication technologies are important for monitoring speed and energy in different organizations. This technology will also help in calculating estimated savings according to the power consumed in the process.

A tremendous growth was observed in market of green communication. This growth was recognized due to increasing demand for green communication technology in telecom and IT industry for better energy efficiency. The demands for all intelligent management of the power systems and renewable energy sources have suddenly risen up. To add to this, the government regulation also mandating the utilization of green communication technologies in order to reduce electronic waste from obsolete computing equipment. It is helping in driving the market for green communication. There is a requirement of the green technology for the development of the modern world. The focus is to make development in communication technology as green as possible.

Keywords: Green, communication, computing, technology, system, environment, global warming, sustainability

26.1   Introduction

Today, when we are facing global warming, the main issue for all enterprise is to take up the environmental issues to adopt environmentally-sound practices in all fields. Energy productivity can be improved by adopting Information Communication Technology (ICT). It will also maintain dynamic economy with high quality of life. ICT has created some demands about meeting software & hardware requirements. There is enhancement of needs in hardware related to software systems causing production of more powerful systems. The footprints are created day by day by these powerful systems. Precautionary measures have to be taken to reduce footprints by avoiding global warming [1]. The company must meet

*Corresponding author: anjubhartidr@gmail.com

Namita Gupta, Prasenjit Chatterjee and Tanupriya Choudhury (eds.) Smart and Sustainable Intelligent Systems, (375–386)

its requirements using high engineering and green approach solution ways to avoid carbon footprints.

Green communication market has been growing substantially in recent years. It has now become mandatory according to government regulations to reduce electronic waste as obsolete computing equipment. This is one of the reasons behind mandating the utilization of green communication technologies in order to form the market for green communication.

Information Communication Technology (ICT) improves overall energy productivity. Society has gained a lot by ICT system. It uses less energy needed to design, manufacture, and distribute the ICT devices and equipment. It increases the operating efficiency of the ICT technologies after online installation. It also optimizes the performance of other energy using systems [1].

In years to come, 5G would be the next evolution of cellular technology as per the user demand. But this technology will consume more energy resulting in release of more CO2. So, the future needs green communication for sustainability (Figure 26.1).

"Communication technology has important role to play in everyday life. The real world tasks are controlled by machines and computers mostly. All this is possible due to advancement in information and communication technology [2]." Green communications is energy-efficient communications and minimizes resource use whenever possible in all branches of communications.

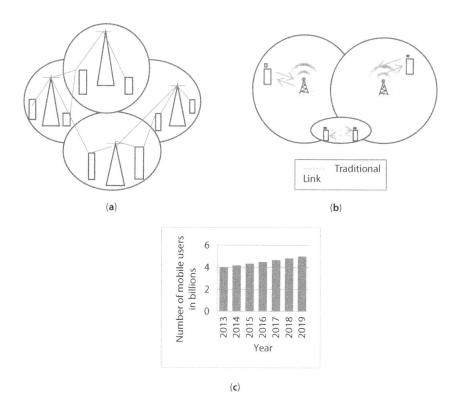

Figure 26.1 Estimate of mobile phone users worldwide, Statista, 2017, EAI. Endorsed Transactions on Energy Web and Information Technology.

Following are Green Networking Strategy:

- To Implement virtualization.
- To Practice server consolidation.
- To save energy, must upgrade older equipment for newer one.
- To Employ systems management for increasing efficiency.
- Green networking can be used in telecommuting, remote administration and videoconferencing.

Green communications extends to all branches of communications, including Radio Communications—for example:

Green computing or green technology is greener way of using computers and related resources. Green technology is about practicing energy-efficient central processing units, servers and peripherals. It would also reduce resource consumption with proper disposing off of electronic waste.

A green data center is a source for storage, management, and dissemination of data which is designed for maximum energy efficiency saving environment from e-pollution. Cellular networks have concerns regarding energy efficiency. They have to maintain not only the profitability but also to reduce environmental effects. There is no doubt that the authorities are continuously exploring future technologies to bring improvements in the network infrastructure.

ICT progressiveness is driving innovation productivity and growth in organizations. It has grown to 8.7% of global GDP by 2020 [3]. ICT create environmental problems. As electric grids contribute greenhouse gas emissions in the environment so it faces a great challenge. "There are several environmental problems during production and disposal of IT hardware" [4]. ICT enables entirely new energy efficient processes and reduces impacts on environment. ICT is so energy-efficient that it can save energy consumption of ICT itself [5] (Table 26.1).

Corporate needs to have a robust strategy as service providers to survive long in the environment. For example, Dell, HP, and Intel have established Green IT around the data

Table 26.1 Carbon footprint in ICT sectors (in Megatones of CO_2) (Source: Bronk *et al.*, 2010).

	2009	2015	2020
Data Centers PCs	121.30	229.87	369.48
	126.69	222.41	516.55
Mobile Gaming Consoles	1.54	3.74	6.58
	11.23	26.04	40.22
Carbon Conversion Number (CCN)	1.3	1.265	1.23
Total	260.77	482.06	932.84

center. Accenture, Deloitte and EDS, etc. are pioneering in efforts to improve environmental responsibility in a holistic way.

26.2   Sustainability of Green ICT

One of the objectives of communication technologies would be to sustain technology saving the environment. Sustainability relates to economic, environmental, and social impact of organizations. Green IT can be considered for sustainability in organization. 'Green' and 'sustainability' concept are linked to each other. Green means to be energy efficient and environmental friendly. "Sustainable means planning and investing in a technology infrastructure in such a way that serves the needs of today while conserving resources and saving money for the future generations" [6]. Green IT will provide effective results achieving sustainability [7]. It focuses on energy efficiency and utilization of equipment [8].

The corporate are trying hard to make Information technology sustainable. "Green IT" term is being promoted by computer manufacturers for making communication greener. "All the electronic devices (IT) accounts for 2% release of human greenhouse gas worldwide" [9].

Following are the issues in Green IT:

- To find ways for replacing personal computers with less no. of energy efficient clients
- Energy efficient chips and disk drives need to be designed
- Multiple operating systems can run on one server by using Virtualization software
- Data centers may consume less energy
- Data centers may be powered using renewable energy sources
- Reducing electronic waste from obsolete computing equipment
- Promoting telecommuting and remote computer administration for reducing transportation emissions.

26.3   Going Green and Sustainability

'Going green' principles must be accepted and cultivated amongst employees of organization to become sustainable. It will help organizations to become more efficient, competitive and profitable [10]. The industries are benefitted financially after accepting environment friendly methods.

ICT/Green ICT is application within the field of environmental sustainability as per the International Federation of Global & Green ICT. They are acting as integrating and enabling technologies for the economy and they profoundly affect society. Though, changes in ICT used globally have worsened the situation of environment but have supported environmental sustainability activities.

'Going green' is related to sustainability and used interchangeably sometimes. Green includes improving process without harming the environment. Process may include creating a product being made entirely out of recycled materials. Sustainability is known for its holistic approach considering all production process and logistics of the system. Sustainability and green to have positive impact on organization [11]:

1. Motivating new Customers to Increase Sales
   Consumers have awareness and are conscious of the environment. So, the company practicing green and sustainable will be in much demand and will strengthen company's reputation. Green manufacturing standards may bring in government contracts.
2. Reducing Energy-Related Costs
   Machinery which can run through solar energy and wind energy are energy efficient and will help greatly in reducing monthly bills. Corporates involved in recycling and going paperless will also save on supply costs improving bottom-line. Annual savings can be managed by improvements in consumption of energy and water by the manufacturers.
3. Tax Incentives Earnings
   Company involved in sustainable improvements may save taxes as per rules and earn benefits.
4. Motivating Workforce Morale and Innovations
   Identifying and implementing green and sustainable initiatives by employees is a collaborative effort. This culture of teamwork will influence in a positive way engaging them in work for sustainability. Working towards achieving sustainability will bring innovation in the organization.
5. Impact on Society
   By implementing changes in the organization will help in reducing carbon footprint thereby reducing toxins in the environment. This process of sustainability will enhance profitability. In this way, the organization may help future generations providing improved air and water quality, fewer landfills and more renewable energy sources for the society.

26.4   ICT: Green and Sustainability

Environmental problems can be managed using e-mobile innovation ensuring the sustainable environmental management [12]. ICT can take care of following areas [13]:

a) ICT field to be energy efficient
b) Smart Cities to be sustainable
c) Buildings to be Energy Efficient
d) Smart Grids Installation
e) Taking care of Water Management
f) Managing Climate Change

All the above components are the best example of development of green technologies. The overall objectives can be fulfilled if we are able to convert cities into smart cities maintaining sustainability. It would help in improving the quality of life of the people. It would also take care of their cultural, economical and overall healthy and safe social growth in this dynamic environment [14]. Smart city incorporates information and communication technologies to enhance the quality and performance of urban services such as energy, transportation and utilities in such a way that it reduces resource consumption, wastage and overall costs.

26.5   Benefits: Green IT Practices

Green IT practices can provide financial benefits in businesses. There are various benefits of Green IT according to Ref. [7]. The most important one is to help in reducing power consumption so it lowers down the cost. The other benefits include providing energy efficiency. After observing these benefits, the government has also prioritized rules and regulations in the market considering the importance of climate change.

Going green for the planet by the business will differentiate from the competition. The positive impact can be made for customers who care about the climate, and can save money [15].

Green IT would be able to remove the negative impact of IT operations on the environment by designing, manufacturing, operating and disposing of computer-related products. Green IT practices would also reduce the use of harmful materials. And will add to maximize energy efficiency as well as promote the biodegradability of products. Green IT have other components to enhance sustainability like redesigning of data centers and green networking, virtualization, and cloud computing.

- Cloud Computing
  Cloud computing is newer process of saving energy. It is about outsourcing the programs and functions of one's own computer to service providers over the internet. It is a mean of sharing storage capacity with others. Even a mobile can handle large volumes of data. 'Digital sharing' is also used for handling large data.
- Green Cloud
  Green cloud also provides environmental benefits to the society in the form of information technology (IT) services which is delivered over the Internet.

Saving Environment by Using IT
Green IT minimizes greenhouse emissions with help of computer systems and operating data centers. Green IT can be followed in various ways [4]:

- PCs to reduce energy consumption
- Enabling power management features
- To turn off the systems when not in use
- Saving energy by using screensavers
- Use of Thin-client computers
- Greening of Data Centers
- Every possible way of conservation of energy
- Eco-friendly design
- Virtualization.

Virtual Strategy can be utilized for reducing consumption by data center. Data centers are able to consolidate their physical server infrastructure by hosting multiple virtual servers on more powerful servers. In this manner it consumes less electricity simplifying the data center.

26.6   Management Perspective: Green IT

Corporates are finding newer ways of IT operations so that they consume less energy. Because of the rise in environmental problems, enterprises are increasingly going green in its process. The most effective way is to adopt the Green IT by the companies. The organizations are finding opportunities to accept and improve their practices to be sustainable [16]. If the corporates adopts Green IT, they would not only be cutting cost but also be sharing knowledge, building capabilities, forming alliances, and positioning their resources in young minds.

There is an opportunity in new market for the companies to maintain the environment providing Green IT services. Green IT means "Consulting services that help enterprise IT organizations reduce their companies' environmental impact by assessing, planning, and implementing initiatives that make the procurement, operation and disposal of IT assets more environmentally responsible" [16].

Following are the approaches to green the Information Technology for enterprises [4]:

- Tactical incremental approaches are the measures where organizations accepts green goals in existing IT infrastructure. It will help in minimizing cost reducing energy consumption [17].
- Strategic Approach refers to develop green IT as well as cost efficiency. It motivates for reducing carbon footprint and considers other factors also such as branding of products as well as image creation and marketing of products.
- Deep green approach is all about afforestation, reforestation, buying carbon credits, or using solar or wind energy [1]. Green approach will improve the highlighted strategic approach.

26.7   Biodegradable Device Components

Recently, Carbon based organic technologies were supposed to address the energy and cost inefficiency issues raised by their inorganic counterparts. The Organic electronics based on conjugated polymers or small molecules as the core semiconductor element in the 1970s and early 1980s, entered the research field holding the high promise of delivering low-cost and energy-efficient materials and devices. The stability of organic semiconductors is facing hurdles in their development regarding their performance as solid competitors of the inorganic counterparts despite intense effort of the scientific community. That's why the large-scale immediate replacement of hard core inorganic components with organic counterparts is not immediately foreseen. Carbon based materials has a considerable advantage over the inorganic counterparts due to their 'soft' nature which makes them flexible, highly conformable and even imperceptibly thin electronic devices.

'Green' materials have been accepted as an emerging concept within the carbon-based class to achieve far more ambitious goals, for example, integration of electronics into living tissue with the aim of achieving biochemical monitoring, diagnostic, or even drug delivery tasks; or generating human and environmentally benign technologies. To achieve the ambitious goal of sustainability, new ways in the field of technology/electronics would be accepted and those will be the "Green" materials and "green" technologies [18]. Following will be the outcomes:

(i)   These are highly abundant and having low cost
(ii) These are economically feasible and avoid the usage of toxic solvents for the fabrication of electronic grade materials and do not generate toxic waste requiring expensive handling and disposal.

In addition, the synthesized electronic grade materials should ensure

(iii) processing routes should be of low cost in practical devices and
(iv) it should render electronics that feature biodegradability in mild degradation conditions at the end of their life cycle

'Green' materials and technologies are now in the stage of emerging concepts. So, a 'Green' organic material by means of 'green' technologies remains truly challenging at this time.

Scientists are often inspired by the apparent simplicity and by the true complexity of nature and trying to find out the solution of unfolding environmental disaster in order to achieve the technological sustainability [18]. The objective is to find out similar kind of object as the nature has provided for creating a novel class of engineered materials able to deliver complex functions, e.g. reproducing the photosynthesis process by means of a synthetic-leaf; fabricating artificial compound eyes with the aid of 3D biomimetic polymers; self-assembled peptide sequences that found applications in electronics; designing super-hydrophobic (lotus effect), and super-adhesive (gecko effect) [18]. There is abundance of materials that nature has provided us as the extremely efficient energy consumption engine that we could use for infinite inspirations.

Recently, it has been found that a cross-disciplinary research field currently is emerging as 'organic bioelectronics, where biocompatible materials are implemented in various electronic devices interfaced with living tissue.' Scientists from various branches contribute to the success of this emerging area of research by designing novel biocompatible (active or passive) materials and conceiving device and circuit layouts.

- Organic Bioelectronics
  'Organic bioelectronics' has been projected as a complementary technology for the immediate future, generating electronic interfaces in emerging fields and new markets, thus decreasing the need for conventional electronics requirement in those emerging areas [18]. Among the successful demonstrations of organic bioelectronics one can enumerate ultra-thin electronic platforms for self-sustaining bioelectronics components for various applications. The organic bioelectronics field may prove to be the suitable host for welcoming

natural and nature-inspired organic materials and a perfect trampoline for achieving the ambitious goal of "green" and sustainable electronics future [18].

- Transient electronics

  There is an emerging technology called as Transient electronics (or biodegradable electronics) whose key characteristic is an ability to dissolve, resorb, or physically disappear in physiological environments in a controlled manner. These potential applications usage may be for eco-friendly sensors, temporary biomedical implants, including data-secure hardware. These biodegradable electronics built with water-soluble, biocompatible active and passive materials can provide multifunctional operations for diagnostic and therapeutic purposes, such as monitoring intracranial pressure, identifying neural networks, assisting wound healing process, etc. [19].

  As we know, different technology applied in electronics has made tremendous impacts on human society and has been widely used in almost every field, including telecommunication, entertainment, and healthcare, to name a few. An emerging type of device that possesses 'transient' function is gaining increasing attention recently [20]. Devices made out of biodegradable materials have capability to completely or partially dissolve, resorb or physically disappear after functioning in environmental or physiological conditions at controlled rates, and are termed as 'transient electronics', or 'biodegradable electronics' for biomedical or eco-friendly applications. For green electronics, introducing biodegradability to consumer electronics would be much better for the environment. Otherwise, the normal equipment, monitors etc. might alleviate landfill and environmental issues will be caused by electronic waste (E-waste is produced more than 50 million tons each year) [21, 22]. These elimination is further associated with costs and risks resulting from recycling operations. There is one more advantage of transient devices that it is capable of self-destruction that protect information from unauthorized access which can be used as data-secure hardware.

  There are certain materials like monocrystalline silicon nano membranes (mono-Si NMs), studies have showed that it can dissolve in physiological environments with rates ranging from a few nanometers to more than 100 nm per day [23] depending on the types of aqueous solutions. So, the degradable inorganic dielectrics, together with metals, polymer substrates, and dissolvable Silicon Nano Membranes enable fully biodegradable electronics with superior operation characteristics compatible with semiconductor foundry process [23, 24]. To adapt the sensitive nature of biodegradable materials to device integration, Novel fabrication techniques have been developed, preventing materials destruction by solvent, temperature, or water.

  A variety of fully biodegradable devices in physiological solutions have been demonstrated, including thermal therapy device [20], intracranial pressure sensor (ICP), electrocorticography (ECoG), recording systems [19], radio frequency (RF) electronics , batteries [27], drug delivery systems, etc.

- Wooden: Paper/Silk Chip

  Portable electronics are made up of typically made of non-renewable, non-biodegradable and potentially toxic materials. If these are being discarded, this would create an alarming situation for the environment. A team of University of Wisconsin-Madison researchers have made an effort to lessen the environmental burden of electronic devices, and they collaborated with researchers in the Madison-based U.S. Department of Agriculture Forest Products Laboratory (FPL) to develop a surprising solution and made a semiconductor chip made almost entirely of wood.

The research team, led by UW-Madison electrical and computer engineering professor Zhenqiang "Jack" Ma, described the new device in a paper published on May 26, 2015 by the journal 'Nature Communications' [25].

The Project leader Zhiyong Cai, for an engineering composite science research group at FPL, has been developing sustainable nanomaterials since 2009. He said "If a big tree cut down to the individual fiber, the most common product is paper where the dimension of the fiber is in the micron stage." "But if the same could be further broken down to the nano scale then at that scale very strong and transparent CNF paper could be made by this material" [26].

Almost the same kind of experiment was done with paper being the oldest and most familiar 'substrate' materials of natural origin by Vladu M *et al.* (2012). Paper is made from plant-derived cellulose and is the cheapest biodegradable substrate material. It enables large-area printing of 'use-and-throw' devices. The arrays of OFETs and OFET circuits have been printed on paper, demonstrating flexible devices with performance on-par with more traditional substrates [18].

According to VladuM *et al.* (2012), another natural material they have come across is the silk. Silk has polypeptide polymer and consist of two main proteins: fibroin and sericin. The protein Fibroin is made up primarily of repeating units of glycine, serine, and alanine that afford interchain hydrogen bonding, providing the mechanical robustness of silk fibers. This material combines many advantages for biodegradable or biomedical applications [18].

By the above facts, it has been found that numerous materials with a bio-origin have been identified as suitable substrates for the fabrication of organic electronics that can help in making green technology quite sustainable. Many of these materials demonstrate excellent insulating properties, which combined with the ease of their process ability make them suitable as gate electrode insulators for various applications. These materials will enable several functionalities for example in case of low-cost, non-toxicity, biodegradability, and often biocompatibility and bioresorbability for biomedical applications.

26.8   Conclusion

The environment problem has to be taken on a serious note. So, protection of environment and climate change is the priority to be discussed in international arena. Throughout the world wide, the incidence of natural disaster has increased. There is an evidence of ecological imbalance. It has indirectly affected water and food supply, public health, industry, agriculture and infrastructure. Green IT can help in further deterioration of the environment. As the mankind cannot stop its growth and technology for its better-ment. So, the role of ICT would be in improving energy efficiency. Today, the lifetime of electronics is becoming shorter, because of the newer technology keep pouring in shorter duration. It is creating an ecological problem. Some kind of initiatives must be taken to address the issue of electronic waste with biodegradable organic electronic materi-als. The advantages of dumping organic materials must be discussed that how these are biodegradable in nature which is safe and nontoxic. These types of upcoming materials may lead to fully biodegradable and even biocompatible/biometabolizable electronics for many low-cost applications. There is a need to give more emphasis on renewable sources. The mankind must ensure the reliability of energy supplies and services to promote green products and sustainable production.

Climate change is a problem as many businesses got affected around the world. The decision-makers are trying to help in solving this problem by implementation of a number of sustainable and eco-friendly technologies or projects. The United Nations is providing international platform to discuss and implementation of strategy over mini-mizing global climate change. Green ICT is being acknowledged and being considered for designing new technology and other systems to reduce impact on environment. The environmental impacts has to be reduced which may come from the data center, portable devices, printers, or any other category of ICT. Now, the organizations must develop an improved and practical framework in different sectors fighting with the big challenge of managing sustainability.

References

1. Ozturk, A., Umit, K., Medeni, I.T., Ucuncu, B., Caylan, M., Akba, F., Medeni, T.D., Green ICT (Information and CommunicationTechnologies): A Review of Academic and Practitioner Perspectives. *Int. J. eBusiness eGovernment Stud.*, 3, 1, 31, 2011.

2. Malik, N.A. and Ur Rehman, M., Green Communications: Techniques and Challenges. *EAI Endorsed Trans. Energy Web Inf. Technol.*, University of Bedfordshire, Luton LU1 3JU, United Kingdom, 4, 14, 1, 2017.

3. Stern, N., The climate group, *Science of Climate Change Bill Hare Potsdam Institute for Climate Impact Research Breaking the Climate Deadlock, IPCC Synthesis Report*, https://www.theclimategroup.org Tokyo on June 27th 2008.

4. Murugesan, S., Harnessing Green IT: Principles and Practices. *IT Prof.*, 10, 24–33, 2008, http://dx.doi.org/10.1109/MITP.2008.10.

5. Laitner, J. A., GeSI, Global e-sustainability Initiative, *SMARTer2030, ICT Solutions for 21st Century Challenges*, Belgium, 2015.

6. Pollock, C. and Pretty, J., *Pastures new*, https://www.newscientist.com, 21st April 2007.

7. van Osch, W. and Avital, M., From Green IT to Sustainable Innovation. *AMCIS2010 Proceedings*, Paper 490, 2010, http://aisel.aisnet.org/amcis2010/490.

8. Watson, *et al.*, *Setting Priorities in Energy Innovation Policy: Lessons for the UK*, A joint proj-ect of the Science, Technology and Public Policy Program and the Environment and Natural Resources Program Belfer Center for Science and International Affairs, http://seg.fsu.edu/ p, p. 2, 2008.

9. Le Blanc, D., Global Action Plan, *Creating sustainable communities*, Dublin, Annual report, 2016 http://globalactionplan.ie/wp-content/uploads/2017/10/2016-GAP-Report-Final-small.pdf, 2016.

10. www.nist.gov/blogs/manufacturing-innovation-blog/five-benefits-embracing-sustainability-and-green-manufacturing.

11. Lagas, B., *Five Benefits of Embracing Sustainability and Green Manufacturing*, September 10, 2015, https://www.qualitydigest.com/.

12. Green Press Initiative, *The Georgetown Journal of International Affairs Annual Report*, http://press.georgetown.edu/, 19, 65, 2008.

13. Ernst and Young, Issue 7, June 2011 Quarterly newsletter, in: *Corporate Responsibility*, 2011.

14. Casini, M., *2nd International Conference on Green Energy Technology (ICGET 2017)*, IOP Publishing, IOP Conf. Series: Earth and Environmental Science 83, 2017, 012014 Green Technology for Smart Cities, 2017.

15. https://www.theguardian.com/environment/2018/oct/08/climate-change-what-you-can-do-campaigning-installing-insulation-solar-panels.

16. Mines, C., *The Dawn of Green IT Services*, Forrester Research, Inc, Cambridge, MA, 2008.

17. Bronk, C., Lingamneni, A., Palem, K., *Innovation for sustainability in information and communication technologies (ICT)*, Internal report, Rice University, https://www.ece.rice.edu/, 2010.

18. Irimia-Vladu, M., Głowacki, E.D., Voss, G., Bauer, S., Serdar Sariciftci, N., Green and biodegradable electronics. *Mater. Today*, 15, 7–8, 340–346, July–August 2012, https://doi.org/10.1016/S1369-7021(12)70139-6.

19. Li, R., Wang, L., Kong, D., Yin, L., Recent progress on biodegradable materials and transient electronics, https://doi.org/10.1016/j.bioactmat, *Science Direct*, 3, 3, 322–333, 2018.

20. Hwang, S.W., Tao, H., Kim, D.H., Cheng, H., Song, J.K., Rill, E., Brenckle, M.A., Panilaitis, B., Won, S.M., Kim, Y.S., Song, Y.M., Yu, K.J., Ameen, A., Li, R., Su, Y., Yang, M., Kaplan, D.L., Zakin, M.R., Slepian, M.J., Huang, Y., Omenetto, F.G., Rogers, J.A., A Physically Transient Form of Silicon Electronics. *Science*, 337, 1640, 2012.

21. Jamshidi, R., Çinar, S., Chen, Y., Hashemi, N., Montazam, R., Transient bioelectronics: Electronic properties of silver microparticle-based circuits on polymeric substrates subjected to mechanical load. *J. Polym. Sci. Part B Polym. Phys.*, 53, 1603, 2015.

22. Tanskanen, P., Management and Recycling of Electronic Waste. *Acta Mater.*, 61, 1001, 2013.

23. Hwang, S.-W., Park, G., Edwards, C., Corbin, E.A., Kang, S.-K., Cheng, H., Song, J.-K., Kim, J.-H., Yu, S., Ng, J., Lee, J.E., Kim, J., Yee, C., Bhaduri, B., Su, Y., Omennetto, F.G., Huang, Y., Bashir, R., Goddard, L., Popescu, G., Lee, K.-M., Rogers, J.A., Dissolution Chemistry and Biocompatibility of Single-Crystalline Silicon Nanomembranes and Associated Materials for Transient Electronics. *ACS Nano*, 8, 5843, 2014.

24. Yin, L., Farimani, A.B., Min, K., Vishal, N., Lam, J., Lee, Y.K., Aluru, N.R., Rogers, J.A., Electrically Tunable Selective Reflection of Light from Ultraviolet to Visible and Infrared by Heliconical Cholesterics. *Adv. Mater.*, 27, 1857, 2015.

25. Zhenqiang, "Jack" Ma, High-performance green flexible electronics based on biodegradable cellulose nanofibril paper *J. Nature Communications*.

26. Cai, Z., *New kind of wood chip: Biodegradable computer chips made from wood*, University of Wisconsin-Madison, https://www.sciencedaily.com/, May 26, 2015.

27. Yin, L., Huang, X., Xu, H., Zhang, Y., Lam, J., Cheng, J., Rogers, J.A., Materials, designs, and operational characteristics for fully biodegradable primary batteries. *Adv. Mater.*, 26, 3879, 2014.

27

A Means of Futuristic Communication: A Review

Vivek*, Deepika Kukreja and Deepak Kumar Sharma

Netaji Subhas University of Technology, Dwarka, New Delhi, India

Abstract

Current communications over the Internet are either human–human or human–machine. Internet of Things (IoT) is a concept of machine to machine (M2M) communication in which real-world objects with embedded technologies are connected over the Internet and communicate with each other or with the external environment. This paper studies the concept of IoT with its integration with cloud, edge and fog computing; challenges associated with it and its applications. The security of such an environment established using aforementioned technologies is paramount; the things referred here are all energy constrained hand-held devices. The resource pool for such environment is limited hence should be wisely allocated. The paper provides a review of futuristic communication technologies, discusses their challenges, provides analysis and compares the different computing techniques in terms of connectivity, security, energy conservation, delay-energy trade-off, resource scheduling, etc.

Keywords: Blockchain, Internet of Things, genetic algorithm, offloading, privacy, task scheduling, vehicular fog services, zigbee

27.1 Introduction

27.1.1 Internet of Things

IoT is a system of computation, mechanical and digital devices, real-world objects with a unique identifier and can transmit the data over a network without the need for interaction between humans or human–machine communication.

27.1.1.1 Characteristics of IoT

- Inter-connectivity: Any object with infrastructure for communication can be interconnected.
- Heterogeneity: The devices are based on different hardware and network technologies. The devices interact with other devices or services using different networks.

---

*Corresponding author: vivekwish1007@gmail.com

Namita Gupta, Prasenjit Chatterjee and Tanupriya Choudhury (eds.) Smart and Sustainable Intelligent Systems, (387–400)

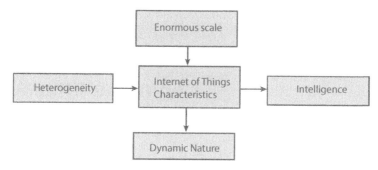

Figure 27.1 IoT Characteristics.

- Dynamic Nature: The state of devices, its location, and speed change dynamically.
- Enormous scale: The number of devices that communicate with each other is larger in number than devices connected to the Internet.

Figure 27.1 describes the characteristics of IoT.

27.1.1.2   Different Forms of IoT

- Internet of Everything (IoE): IoE describes the situation where a large number of things viz. objects, people, devices embedded with sensors, connected using either public or private network communicate using some standard protocols.
- Industrial IoT (IIoT): IIoT describes use cases from manufacturing or utilities. The term is also applicable in smart cities and smart grids.
- Consumer IoT (CIoT): CIoT refers to millions of personal items like wearables, smart-phones and smart appliances that are connected over the internet for enabling the sharing of data.

27.1.1.3   IoT Applications

IoT applications include fields of farming for increased growth of fruits and vegetables and prevention of wastage of resources, transportation services for better traffic control, in emergencies to provide a swift response, manufacturing industries for asset profitability and safety of workers and maintenance of machines.

Figure 27.2 shows various application areas of IoT: smart cities, homes, for transportation systems and manufacturing industries.

27.1.1.4   Challenges in IoT

- Security: With the increase in several devices the vulnerabilities of connected devices increases due to the below standard design of devices.
- Signaling: For the collection and transmission of data between devices, signaling is necessary. There can be communication between devices and server or between devices.

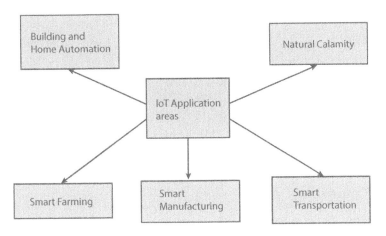

Figure 27.2 Application of IoT.

- Presence Detection: Presence detection enables the tracking of devices and fixing any issue in the network.
- Privacy: To protect the individual's information from disclosure in the IoT environment. Privacy satisfies the properties of authenticity, trustworthiness, and confidentiality.
- Standards: Absence of guidelines and documentation can hamper control and coordination by IoT devices.
- Trained Workforce Requirements: IoT usage requires a group of people who know about technologies included.
- Scalability: The ability of a framework, system, or procedure to deal with an expanding amount of load or its capability to increment in size to accommodate growth.
- Heterogeneous nature of devices: Heterogeneity means allowing the platform to communicate with different types of devices using multiple protocols.
- Energy-efficient transmission of data and resource management: Method to increase energy efficiency and network capacity.
- IoT Connectivity: With smart devices transmitting and receiving data between them, the minimum rate of battery consumption is required. Bandwidth and data consumption are also other issues that concern IoT connectivity.

27.1.2 IoT and Cloud Computing

IoT generates a huge amount of data for which processing and storage cannot be done at end devices due to its limited/no computation and storage capacity, therefore cloud computing platforms can be used for this purpose. Two main approaches for convergence of IoT and Cloud [1] are (i) Integration of IoT functions and technologies into Cloud and (ii) Integrating Cloud techniques into IoT.

27.1.2.1   Issues With IoT Cloud Platforms

1. Distance: As the distance between end nodes and the cloud can be large, therefore cloud platform is not suitable for delay-sensitive applications.
2. Security Threats:
   a. Privacy of location and identity
   b. Node compromise and layer addition/removal attack
   c. Semi trusted cloud security.

27.1.3   Fog Computing

The fog computing paradigm stretches the functionality of the cloud towards the nodes close to the IoT nodes, these devices (fog nodes) can be deployed at any place: on an industrial facility floor, on power shaft, near to a railway line, on a vehicle-top. A fog node is a device with computational capacity, storage facility, and network connection. Figure 27.3 shows the three-layered architecture of fog computing. The first layer consists of end-nodes with limited computation capability. The second layer is the fog layer, where the local processing of data is performed. The third layer is the cloud layer which acts as a final point for storage and processing of data.

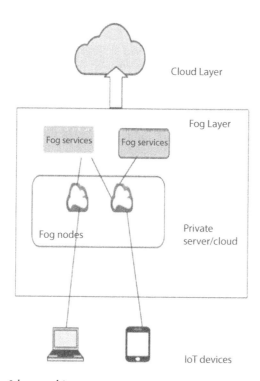

Figure 27.3 Fog computing 3-layer architecture.

27.1.3.1   Analysis of Data in Fog Computing

- The time-constrained data is forwarded to the node which is close to the IoT nodes. For example, in smart grid systems, nodes near to the grid sensors perform the process of detection of issues/faults.
- Data whose processing can be delayed several minutes is passed to nodes other than fog nodes known as aggregate nodes for analysis. In the Smart Grid scenario, each substation may act as an aggregate node.
- Data that does not have strict time constraints is forwarded to the cloud layer for processing and storage purposes [2].

27.1.4   Edge Computing

Mobile Edge Computing (MEC) is an architecture that provides services, cloud layer functions, and IT services at the edge of the mobile network and, in general, at the network edge. MEC allows the network to be shared and has computation capabilities virtually anywhere, and therefore reduce deployment time. They have centralized control and coordination of remote computer capabilities [3]. MEC allows the Base Station (BS) to deploy an edge computing server to provide mobile users with the computation and temporary storage services [4].

With the increasing number of IoT devices, fast processing and increase in adoption of cloud and increase of overhead on the network the need for deploying edge computing for IoT are also increasing.

27.1.5   Comparative Analysis of Cloud, Fog and Edge Computing

Table 27.1 discusses the differences between cloud, edge and fog computing when used along with IoT in terms of location of processing and storage capabilities.

The organization of the rest of the paper is as follows: the literature review is presented in Section 27.2 that includes various existing works in the field of IoT, its challenges and various integration of IoT with edge and fog computing and consequent issues. Section 27.3 discusses

Table 27.1 Cloud v/s fog v/s edge paradigm.

Comparison factor	Cloud Computing	Fog Computing	Edge Computing
Location of processing the data	Central cloud server which is located at a long distance from the source node	Tasks are allocated to the fog nodes or gateway that is present in the local area network.	The processing of data is done at the sensor or device not forwarded to any other node.
Processing and storage capabilities	Processing is better than fog and edge technologies and storage capacity of the cloud is greater than the edge and fog technology	Processing capability and storage capacity is lower than cloud and greater than edge computing.	Processing capability and storage capacity is lower than the cloud and fog.

various simulators available for IoT. Section 27.4 discusses some of the real-time testbeds. The paper is concluded in Section 27.5 that also recommends several future directions.

27.2   Literature Review

This section gives the existing works which have been done in the field of IoT. The work is divided into different classes namely for improving the security, energy efficiency and resource management for energy-constrained devices. Pooja Yadav *et al.* [5] analyze the present situation of IoT in India, the work examines security issues, surveys the hazard

Table 27.2   Work done for improving security in IoT.

Citation	Objectives/Issues	Proposed Method
[7]	Existing secure information aggregation algorithms don't permit dynamic gathering and data conglomeration in fog computing	A data aggregation scheme that preserves privacy and resists against collusion attack while developing data encryption, decryption and aggregation methods
[8]	The risk of privacy leakage is high. New trajectory-based privacy scheme is proposed	The proposed method uses the Trusted Third Party (TTP) server for protecting privacy based on location information to solve the issues of performance.
[9]	Intrusion Detection System (IDS) based on deep learning has fine detection accuracy but vulnerable and weakly stable to low-frequency attacks	An IDS based on Genetic Algorithm and Deep Belief Network (DBN) is presented
[10]	Previous algorithms used routing with multiple candidate forwarders in WSNs, but Denial of service has become an issue	Design a trust model based on statistical state information (SSI) to construct geographic opportunistic routing based on trust that improves the data delivery process reliability
[11]	Issue of parallel processing of Complex Event Processing (CEP) queries are adequately addressed	Genetic Algorithm used for finding the optimum scheme of the distribution of CEP operators on IoT network hosts
[12]	For homogeneous IoT devices, the existing algorithms perform data aggregation which do not work for data of hybridized devices	Data Aggregation that is lightweight and preserves the privacy is proposed to early filter false/malicious data injected at the network edge
[13]	Secure and efficient multi-factor authentication scheme for devices	The method using device capabilities and digital signatures is proposed, the devices will only be allowed if the authentication through multi-factor method is successful
[14]	Cross-data center authentication methods for the fast-moving vehicles accessing Vehicular fog services (VFS)	A lightweight anonymous authentication based on blockchain for distributed VFS is applied

factors from the Indian point of view. Emeakaroha *et al.* [6] research a cloud-based smart things information checking, assortment, and processing stage. Table 27.2 briefly presents the existing works that are done for dealing with various security issues related to IoT.

As energy is a vital resource for a network that is being made using energy-constrained devices. The work has also been done in the past for energy management as presented in Table 27.3.

Table 27.4 discusses the existing work done for resource utilization efficiency and off-loading of tasks.

Table 27.5 discusses the previous works done for issues related to signaling and IoT connectivity.

Table 27.6 discusses the previous works done for reducing the delay.

Table 27.3 Literature review for increasing the energy efficiency of an IoT.

Citation	Objectives/Issues	Proposed Method
[15]	The objective is to reduce energy consumption while maintaining QoS	combine QPSO (quantum PSO) with non-dominated sorting genetic algorithm(NSGA-II) to achieve joint QoS-Energy efficient scheduling algorithm
[16]	For adapting cloud infrastructure, high latency and unawareness about the location is an issue	The request is sent to fog node which checks the status of VMs and load balancing techniques like RR, throttle, Active VM is applied
[17]	The objective is the allocation of computing resources that are limited to Data Service Subscribers (DSSs) to achieve the performance that is optimal and stable	Stackelberg game is formulated to analyze pricing problems for all data service operators (DSOs).
[18]	Reduce energy consumption with minimum delay	(i) Collaborative task scheduling to achieve service delay and energy consumed in a balanced manner (ii) The algorithm proposed to balance energy-delay which uses the Lyapunov optimization.
[19]	A trade-off is adopted to achieve optimal energy consumption with delay threshold	Cloud-fog cooperative scheduling algorithm to reduce energy consumption
[20]	Preference similarity and real-world deployment environments are poorly addressed	Discovery of nodes based on both preference and movement pattern, improve the efficiency of search and to reduce overload

Table 27.4 IoT resource management/offloading.

Citation	Objectives/Issues	Proposed Method
[21]	As numbers of end-users increases, efficient load balancing method is required	Improved Particle Swarm Optimization with Levy Walk (IPSOLW) is proposed to balance the load of fog
[22]	As the number of applications being deployed increases, resource-constrained devices cannot fulfill the resource requirements	A resource allocation method that offloads computations to achieve energy efficiency and to reduce system cost
[23]	Communication latency, the delivery deadline, and service access frequency become an issue when the application is executed in a distributed manner	Forwarding strategy for latency aware modules is proposed that reallocates modules so that the number of computationally active fog nodes is optimum.
[24]	Higher delay, low availability of resources	A model that is based on multi-long short-term memory (LSTM) is designed to predict the traffic value that guides the offloading process. The method is improved by using the concept of cross-entropy so that the throughput of the system improves
[25]	When the application is executed in a distributed manner, utilization of resources needs to be done in an efficient manner	A method that maps modules in a way that ensures usage of resources in an efficient manner
[26]	The objective is to design a distributed algorithm that has less complexity for offloading tasks that are computation-intensive with the assumption that keeping the priority of tasks to be same	To achieve the efficient allocation of computation in distributed mode deferred acceptance method is proposed

27.3 IoT Simulators

Table 27.7 presents different simulators that are available for simulating IoT along with their features and properties.

27.4 IoT Test Beds

Table 27.8 mentions some of the real-time test beds available for IoT along with different characteristics.

Table 27.5 IoT Connectivity.

Citation	Objectives/Issues	Proposed Method
[27]	A distributed algorithm to develop an ad-hoc IoT network.	A Markov Decision Process (MDP) algorithm where each node finds out optimal connections while considering the trade-off between throughput and power consumed
[28]	Increase in scale of interconnected things impacts planning and operation of cellular networks because of various traffic models and high signaling overhead	Implement two effective M2M signaling reduction techniques. One involves removal of signaling that is unnecessary and other is based on the aggregation that is done over capillary networks
[29]	Previous algorithms support IoT connectivity in a limited way due to increased delay in access.	Random access is provided by multiple access methods based on sparse codes. This reduces the access delay and increases the number of IoT device that completes random access successfully
[30]	Reduction of orphan nodes (nodes that do not receive network address and cannot join the network) and improving ZigBee Networks' connectivity.	A method for a recommendation based on a method that uses nodes' weight for evaluating the impact of the transfer on the network.

Table 27.6 Existing works for minimizing delay in IoT.

Citation	Objectives/Issues	Proposed Method
[31]	Workload assignment in fog computing while maintaining minimum delay, cost, and energy.	The algorithm uses inter fog communication in addition to the fog-cloud and IoT-cloud communication to reduce the delay through load sharing.
[32]	Fog-IoT paradigm has issues of deadline, optimal utilization and handling of dynamic arrival of data as IoT systems are continuously evolving. In this paper, the study of the scheduling of workload for the worst-case delay and optimal utilization is done.	A dynamic scheduling algorithm to maximize the throughput and to guarantee delay in the worst case.
[33]	To improve delay, link and service quality, a method that optimizes both computing and radio resources is proposed.	To optimize the satisfaction of users, the problem of resource allocation is formulated as a nonlinear problem while considering delay, quality of transmission.

Table 27.7 Simulators for IoT.

Simulator	Scope	Language	Cyber attack Simulation	Target domain
iFogSim [34]	IoT	Java	No	Generic
IoTSim [35]	Big data analytics	Java	No	Generic
CupCarbon [36]	Network	Java/custom scripting	No	Smart city
Cooja [37]	Network	C/Java	Using custom extension	Focus on low power sensors
OMNet++ [38]	Network	C++	Using custom extension	Generic
NS3 [39]	Network	C++	Yes	Generic
QualNet [40]	Network	C/C++	Yes	Generic

Table 27.8 IoT test-beds.

Test bed	Scale	Environment Type	Device Type	Application
JOSE [41]	A large number of sensors	Out-door environment	Heterogeneous	Environment and structure monitoring
Smart Santander [42]	About 20,000 sensors	Real city	Heterogeneous	Development of smart cities
FIT IoT-Lab [43]	Less than 2,700 sensors	A lab environment	Heterogeneous	Analysis of algorithms

27.5 Conclusion and Future Scope

IoT is an upcoming communication technology that is based on the interaction between devices. In this paper, the concept of IoT, its features and areas of application are discussed. Integration of IoT with cloud, fog, and edge paradigms and issues associated with it are also studied. Analysis and comparison amongst different IoT based networks is presented. Different simulators and real-time test beds available for simulating IoT environments are discussed that would help the researchers to carry the work. Different research areas can be taken up to resolve the security challenges of IoT, resource management, task offloading, towards designing of energy-aware IoT techniques, routing, reducing the latency of such networks. Different optimization techniques can also be used to resolve the aforementioned issues.

References

1. Biswas, A. and Giaffreda, R., IoT and Cloud Convergence: Opportunities and Challenges. *IEEE World Forum on the Internet of Things (WF-IoT)*, South Korea, Seoul, pp. 375–376, 2014.

2. Fog Computing and the Internet of Things: Extend the Cloud to Where the Things Are, https://www.cisco.com/c/dam/en_us/solutions/trends/iot/docs/computing-overview.pdf, 2015.

3. McCann, J., Quinn, L., McGrath, S., O'Connell, E., Towards the Distributed Edge—IoT Review. *IEEE, 12th Int. Conf. on Sensing Tech. (ICST)*, China, pp. 263–267, 2018.

4. Ahmed, E. and Rehmani, M., Mobile Edge Computing: Opportunities, Solutions, and Challenges, Elsevier. *Future Gener. Comput. Syst.*, 70, 59, 2016.

5. Yadav, P., Mittal, A., Yadav, H., IoT: Challenges and Issues in Indian Perspective. *IEEE, 3rd Int. Conf. On Internet of Things: Smart Innovation and Usages (IoT-SIU)*, Bhimtal, Nainital, India, pp. 1–5, 2018.

6. Emeakaroh, V., Cafferkey, N., Healy, P., Morrison, J., A Cloud-Based IoT Data Gathering and Processing Platform. *3rd Int. Conf. on Future Internet of Things and Cloud*, Rome, Italy, pp. 50–57, 2015.

7. Xiaodong, S., Liehuang, Z., Chang, X., Kashif, S., Rongxing, L., A privacy-preserving data aggregation scheme for dynamic groups in fog computing, Elsevier. *Inf. Sci.*, 514, 118, 2020.

8. Lia, G., Yina, Y., Wua, J., Zhaoa, S., Lina, D., Trajectory Privacy Protection Method Based on Location Service in Fog Computing. *Procedia Comput. Sci.*, 147, 463, 2019.

9. Zhang, Y., Li, P., Wang, X., Intrusion Detection for IoT Based on Improved Genetic Algorithm and Deep Belief Network. *IEEE Access*, 7, 31711, 2019.

10. Kotenko, I. and Saenko, I., An Approach to aggregation of security events in Internet-of-things Networks based on genetic optimization. *Intl IEEE Conf. on Ubiquitous Int.& Comp., Adv. and Trusted Comp., Scalable Comp. and Comm., Cloud and Big Data Comp. Internet of People, and Smart World Congress (UIC/ATC/ScalCom/CBDCom/IoP/SmartWorld)*, Toulouse, France, pp. 657–664, 2016.

11. Lu, R., Heung, K., Ali, A., Ghorbani, A., A Lightweight Privacy-Preserving Data Aggregation Scheme for Fog Computing-Enhanced IoT. *IEEE Access*, 5, 3302, 2017.

12. Shen, S., Huang, L., Zhou, H., Yu, S., Fan, E., Cao, Q., Multistage Signaling Game-Based Optimal Detection Strategies for Suppressing Malware Diffusion in fog-Cloud-Based IoT Networks. *IEEE Internet Things*, 5, 1043, 2018.

13. Alizai, A., Tareen, N., Jadoon, I., Improved IoT Device Authentication Scheme Using Device Capability and Digital Signatures. *IEEE Int. Conf. on Applied and Engg. Mathematics (ICAEM)*, Taxila, Pakistan, pp. 115–119, 2018.

14. Yao, Chang, X., Mišić, J., Mišić, V., Li, L., BLA, Blockchain-Assisted Lightweight Anonymous Authentication for Distributed Vehicular Fog Services. *IEEE Internet Things*, 6, 3775, 2019.

15. Song, L., Chai, K., Chen, Y., Schormans, J., Loo, J., Vinel, A., QoS-Aware Energy-Efficient Cooperative Scheme for Cluster-based IoT Systems. *IEEE Syst.*, 11, 1447, 2017.

16. Hayat, B., Yousaf, S., Mehmood, M., Efficient Energy Utilization in Cloud Fog Environment. *Int. J. Adv. Comput. Sci. Appl.*, 10, 617, 2019.

17. Zhang, H., Xiao, Y., Bu, S., Niyato, D., Yu, F., Han, Z., Computing Resource allocation in three-tier IoT Fog Networks: A Joint optimization approach combining Stackelberg game and Matching. *IEEE Internet Things*, 4, 1204, 2017.

18. Yang, Y., Zhao, S., Zhang, W., Chen, Y., Wang, X., DEBTS: Delay Energy Balanced Task Scheduling in Homogeneous Fog Networks. *IEEE Internet Things*, 5, 2094, 2018.

19. Abedin, S.F., Bairagi, A.K., Munir, M.S., Tran, N.H., Hong, C.S., Fog Load Balancing for Massive Machine-Type Communications: A Game and Transport Theoretic Approach. *IEEE Access*, 7, 4204, 2019.

20. Li, Z., Chen, R., Liu, L., Li, G., Chen, Z., Liu, R., Gelong, L., Dynamic Resource Discovery Based on Preference and Movement Pattern Similarity for Large-Scale Social Internet of Things. *IEEE Internet Things*, 3, 581, 2015.

21. Khan, Z., Butt, A., Alghamdi, T., Fatima, A., Akbar, M., Ramzan, M., Nadeem, J., Energy Management in Smart Sectors Using Fog Based Environment and Meta-Heuristic Algorithms. *IEEE Access*, 7, 157254, 2019.

22. Li, Q., Zhao, J., Gong, Y., Zhang, Q., Energy-efficient computation offloading and resource allocation in fog computing for Internet of Everything. *China Commun.*, 16, 32, 2019.

23. Mahmud, R. and Buyya, K., Latency-Aware Application Module Management for Fog Computing Environments. *ACM Trans. Internet Techn. (TOIT)*, 9, 1, 2018.

24. Zhao, X., Yang, K., Chen, Q., Duo, D., Jiang, D., Xu, X., Xinzhuo, S., Deep-Learning based mobile data offloading in mobile edge computing, ScienceDirect. *Future Gener. Comput. Syst.*, 99, 346, 2019.

25. Taneja, M. and Davy, A., Resource aware placement of IoT application modules in fog-cloud computing paradigm. *IEEE Symp. on Int.Net. and Service Mgmt.*, Lisbon, Portugal, pp. 1222–1228, 2017.

26. Chiti, F., Fantacci, R., Picano, B., A Matching Theory Framework for Tasks Offloading in Fog Computing for IoT Systems. *IEEE Internet Things*, 5, 5089, 2018.

26. Kwon, H., Lee, J., Park, H., Intelligent IoT Connectivity: Deep Reinforcement Learning Approach. *IEEE Internet Things*, 20, 2782, 2019.

27. Kouzayha, N., Jaber, N., Dawy, N., Measurement-Based Signaling Management Strategies for Cellular IoT. *IEEE Internet Things*, 4, 1434, 2017.

29. Moon, S., Lee, H., Lee, J., SARA: Sparse Code Multiple Access-Applied Random Access for IoT Devices. *IEEE Internet Things*, 5, 3160, 2018.

30. Chang, H., A connectivity-increasing mechanism of ZigBee-based IoT devices for wireless multimedia sensor networks, Springer. *Multimedia Tools Appl.*, 78, 5137, 2019.

31. Yousefpour, A., Ishigaki, G., Gour, R., Jue, J., On Reducing IoT Service Delay *via* Fog Offloading. *IEEE Internet Things*, 5, 998, 2018.

32. Yiqin, D., Zhigang, C., Deyu, Z., Ming, Z., Workload scheduling toward worst-case delay and optimal utility for single-hop Fog-IoT architecture. *IET Commun.*, 12, 2164, 2018.

33. Gu, Y., Chang, Z., Pan, M., Song, L., Han, Z., Joint Radio and Computational Resource Allocation in IoT Fog Computing. *IEEE Trans. Veh. Technol.*, 67, 7475, 2018.

34. Gupta, H., Dastjerdi, A., Ghosh, S., Buyya, R., iFogSim: A toolkit for modeling and simulation of resource management techniques in the Internet of Things, edge and fog computing environments, Wiley. *J. Softw. Pract. Exper.*, 47, 1275, 2017.

35. Zeng, H., Garg, S., Strazdins, P., Jayaraman, P., Georgakopoulos, D., Ranjan, R., IOTSim: A simulator for analyzing IoT applications, Elsevier. *J. Syst. Archit.*, 72, 93, 2017.

36. Mehdi, K., Lounis, M., Bounceur, A., Kechadi, T., Cupcarbon: A multi-agent and discrete event wireless sensor network design and simulation tool. *Proc. 7th Int. ICST Conf. Simulat. Tools*, pp. 126–131, 2014.

37. Osterlind, F., Dunkels, A., Eriksson, A., Finne, N., Voigt, T., Cross-level sensor network simulation with Cooja. *Proc. 31st IEEE Conf. Local Comput. Netw.*, Tampa, FL, USA, pp. 641–648, 2006.

38. Varga, A. and Hornig, R., An overview of the OMNeT++ simulation environment. *Proc. 1st Int. Conf. Simulat. Tools Tech. Commun. Netw. Syst. Workshops*, pp. 1–10, 2008.

39. Henderson, T., Lacage, M., Riley, G., Dowell, C., Kopena, J., Network simulations with the ns-3 simulator. *SIGCOMM Demon*, vol. 14, 2008.

40. Jha, A., V., Appasani, B., Ghazali, A., N., Performance Evaluation of Network Layer Routing Protocols on Wireless Sensor Networks. *Int. Conf. on Comm. and Electronics Systems (ICCES)*, 1862–1865, 2019.

41. Teranishi, Y., Saito, Y., Murono, S., Nishiniga, N., JOSE: An open testbed for field trials of large-scale IoT services. *J. Natl. Inst. Inf. Commun. Technol.*, 62, 151, 2015.

42. Sanchez, L., Muñoz, L., Galache, J., Sotres, P., Santana, J., Gutierrez, V., Ramdhany, R., Gluhak, A., Krco, S., Theodoridis., E., Pfisterer, D., SmartSantander: IoT experimentation over a smart city testbed. *Elsevier Comput. Networks*, 61, 217, 2014.

43. Roziers, C., Chelius, G., Ducrocq, T., Fleury, E., Fraboulet, A., Gallais, A., Nathalie, M., Thomas, N., Vandaele, J., Using SensLAB as a First Class Scientific Tool for Large Scale Wireless Sensor work Experiments. *Int. Conf. on Research in Net.*, Springer, Berlin, Heidelberg, Germany, pp. 147–159, 2011.

28

Experimental Evaluation of Security and Privacy in GSM Network Using RTL-SDR

Hardik Manocha[1], Utkarsh Upadhyay[2]* and Deepika Kumar[1]†

[1]Bharati Vidyapeeth's College of Engineering, New Delhi, India
[2]Jamia Millia Islamia University, New Delhi, India

Abstract

With rapid development and growth in the telecommunication sector, there is a recognizable rise in adversary actions. These adversary actions (eavesdropping, keeping records, and storing personal data) can rupture the private communication protocols and can tamper with the privacy of a targeted person. The paper includes oversight of the importance of privacy in telecommunication systems, the cheap adversary actions taken to generate a social profile, targets a vulnerability in GSM mobile architecture using open source software and software-defined radio, and discusses the awareness of the existing vulnerabilities among the public. This paper also predicts the security awareness rating for colleges using ridge regression and binary classification.

Keywords: Privacy, RTL-SDR, GSM, Security, IMSI, ridge regression, machine learning, IMEI

28.1 Introduction

"Privacy is a fundamental human right recognized in the UN Declaration of Human Rights, the International Covenant on Civil and Political Rights and in many other international and regional treaties." Privacy predicates human ethics and other unique statures analogous to freedom of association and freedom of speech [1]. The publication of this report reflects the growing importance, diversity, and complexity of this fundamental right.

In modern times, privacy means a lot to us. Internet and the growth in the fields like machine learning can easily predict one's choices by running algorithms on the simplest and even the smallest kind of user data. Hence, even filling cookies form on a web browser makes you vulnerable to data stealing.

The advancement in the telecommunication sector may also lead to the unveiling of personal data. The following are a few instances of encroachment of data privacy in the telecommunication sector:

---
*Corresponding author: utkarshdhy@gmail.com
†Corresponding author: deepika.kumar@bharatividyapeeth.edu

Namita Gupta, Prasenjit Chatterjee and Tanupriya Choudhury (eds.) Smart and Sustainable Intelligent Systems, (401–412)
© 2021 Scrivener Publishing LLC

- Providing arbitrators with all the data that consumers share with the tele-communication firms within the compass of their utilities.
- Eavesdropping, storing customer private information.
- Use of customer's personal data for commercial and political objectives without customer compliance.

Due to the continuous growth in the telecommunication network and the development of various network applications, there has been a significant increase in the number of vulnerabilities that has surfaced with these advancements. Although now almost every country has upgraded its cellphone networks to 3G and 4G bands due to commercialization and popularization of smartphones and wireless technologies. Even then, in developing countries such as India, 2G is still used by millions of people. As technology changes rapidly, breaches and vulnerabilities also become wider. But due to the lack of awareness of GSM [2] technology and its vulnerabilities, the privacy of millions is at risk. This paper majorly focuses on how one's confidential details can be easily compromised and further used to tamper with the customer's privacy. Section 28.2 discusses the previous works that have been carried out by the researchers in the past years. Section 28.3 discusses the important sources of private information of the user which a SIM [3] carries. Sections 28.4 and 28.5 discuss about a vulnerability in GSM architecture, the instruments, and procedure which demonstrates the further exploitation of GSM. Section 28.6 shares the experimental results and analysis of the surveys and general security awareness. Section 28.7 concludes our paper.

28.2   Literature Review

In 2015, Ref. [4] examined the security protocols in GSM on proving the vulnerabilities in GSM using certain tools researchers. And the research concluded that people are not informed enough about the security protocols not being robust and secure. Thus on further research, in 2016, USRP 200 [5] was used to establish a fake BTS to exploit the vulnerabilities in GSM. This method proved to be costly but was successful in exploiting the security protocols, therefore enabling us to perform different adversarial attacks on the architecture once this protocol is breached. To make it cost-effective, In 2017, RTL-SDR [6] was used for the analysis of GSM interface as it proved to be a better receptor than USRP while being incredibly cheap, as concluded in 2015 [7] after an experimental study on RTL-SDR. This study proved that the same adversary actions could be performed in a budgeted manner. Also, in 2014 [8], research came out with a device, which was built after several surveys and evaluation of structural artifacts which promised to catch IMSI catchers. It can be easily implemented into the network providers system unlike the Stingray [9] which are relatively expensive and sold only law enforcement agencies. The research claimed that the device is cost-effective, installation-friendly, and if installed on the towers at a geographic location can give out the geo-location of the active IMSI catchers in use.

As per the literature, a research gap was found. That is if such adversary practices exist and GSM in itself is not so secure then why the same device isn't implemented yet and why is there a lack of awareness?

Therefore, in this paper, one of the GSM vulnerabilities is exploited and surveys are conducted on students and organizations giving us datasets to predict the "security awareness rating".

28.3   Privacy in Telecommunication

When it comes to privacy in telecommunications, IMEI and IMSI are the most confidential numbers to one's privacy that a SIM [3] carries.

IMSI (International Mobile Subscriber Identity) identifies the new user and checks the user's identification with the network provider. It is unique for every user's cellular network. It is reserved as a "64-bit field" which is commissioned by the mobile to the network. IMSI acquires details of a user's network locally as VLR (Visitor Location Register) or as HLR (Home Location Register). Each IMSI number, which is allotted uniquely to different users, authenticates that particular user, the local network of the user, and the user's country code. IMSI is first sent to the network tower as a 10-digit number, which contains all the information about the user. Now, for privacy concerns of a user, IMSI is not used anymore and another unique bit field is 'randomly' generated known as TMSI (Temporary Mobile Subscriber Identity) to prevent adversary attacks against IMSI while keeping the information carried by the IMSI hidden. The format of IMSI is shown in Figure 28.1.

IMSI is specifically used for [11]:

1. Determination and authentication of the home network of the user.
2. Authentication and identification of a user when intelligence specific to a user is exchanged between home and visitor networks.
3. Authentication and identification of a mobile network station for registration of the network station through a radio control path in wireless visited network.
4. Authentication of the mobile network station for authorizing on the radio control path.
5. Identification and authentication of the user to allow for billing and charging of visiting mobile users.

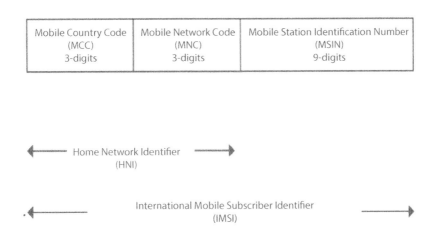

Figure 28.1 Format of IMSI [10].

A privacy flaw with the IMEI, which enables one to track user routine [12]:

- A unique identifier could be generated by an application on an installation on the phone. Nonetheless, an application can easily reveal if that particular application was ever installed on that particular mobile before during reinstallation with the help of IMEI. Cross-referencing of the mobile phone location retrieved through passive sniffing from a base station can be done with the information table of previously installed applications using IMEI.
- When a user changes his cell phone and inserts the old SIM card in his new phone, he can be tracked by the IMSI radiated on switching ON the phone.

IMSI can be paraphrased as the mobile phone's equivalent of a user's email ID. If the IMSI is sent to a server automatically by an application then it is of as much of a privacy and security issue as a website that sends the user's email ID to a remote server. If people find the latter as a privacy concern then this makes the former one a privacy concern too.

After the decisions of the PUCL v. Union of India in 1997, the interception of communication was considered unlawful unless carried out according to the prescribed guidelines [13]. However, the guidelines were only incorporated after the Telegraph Rules in 2007. Rule 419A discusses authority permissions and safeguards to be enforced while tapping communication. It also encompasses the need to renew the tapping permissions, and the flushing of existing data after two months.

28.4 A Take on User Privacy: GSM Exploitation

According to the latest reports, GSM today has more than 7 billion users globally. The increase in computational power and the emerging approach towards open source technology have led to devising multiple exploits to bypass the A5/1 A5/2 A5/3 [14] encryption algorithms that secure the GSM network.

Going down the hierarchical chain of these vulnerabilities, few are easier to exploit. Following invasion schemes require a deep understanding of the architecture and material gadgets to execute. Therefore it is safe to say that an adversary with the correct knowledge, and the required 'firepower' can cause critical damage to the infrastructure. Eavesdropping and man-in-the-middle attacks remain the two critical issues known for GSM security.

In the next segment, we will exploit a GSM vulnerability by passively sniffing network traffic through the air using RTL-SDR: inexpensive software-defined radio [7].

28.4.1 IMSI Catching

IMSI catching is one of the oldest attacks on the GSM infrastructure, which served the generation of IMSI capturing devices called "IMSI-Catchers", capable of sniffing IMSIs, both actively and passively.

28.4.1.1   Active Attacks

A fake BTS (Base Transceiver Station) [15] is set which will essentially act as a mobile tower posing between the target mobile phone and the services provider's real towers. This fake BTS will imitate the job of a real BTS and allow multiple mobile handsets to connect to it. The BTS can operate independently as a free node and order the connected devices to acknowledge themselves. This sort of eavesdropping is called as a Man-In-The-Middle Attack. Different radios are publically available on the market, which is capable of active IMSI catching [5, 16].

28.4.1.2   Soft Downgrade to GSM

The adversary can create an environment to forcefully switch to lower bands like GSM by exploiting the "TAU Reject and Attach Reject messages", the rogue BTS will acknowledge the connected devices that it is prohibited to access 3G and LTE services on a set provider [17–19]. The target mobile device will then only attempt to connect to GSM base stations. A combination of all such methods could set off a full staged MITM attack completely controlling the mobile network traffic [20].

28.4.2   Eavesdropping

IMSIs can also be sniffed through the air channel by intercepting mobile phone traffic and location tracking. With open-source modules like GR-GSM, it is possible to passively "catch" IMSI numbers that appear during transmission on a given ARFCN. This method cannot force mobile phones to reveal its IMSI (and IMEI) numbers through LAC change and forced re-authentication [21, 22].

Note: We have employed this method to gather IMSIs for research purposes only.

28.5   Experimental Setup

28.5.1   Hardware and Software

1. RTL-SDR [23]: It is a cheap software-defined radio that uses a DVB-T TV tuner dongle based on the RTL2832U chipset with a wide range of signal reception up to 2,100 MHz
2. GR-GSM: It is an open-source tool for analysis of GSM signals, based on the air-probe and libOsmocore libraries.

28.5.2   Implementation Algorithm and Procedure

1. Set up RTL-SDR to capture air packets (see Figure 28.2).
2. Use grgsm_livescan to gather the ARFCNs of nearby radio.
3. Start listening through grgsm_livemon on a particular ARFCN or frequency.
4. Run the script to dynamically decrypt the gathered IMSIs over the shared port.

Figure 28.2 Setup [Ubuntu Machine, RTL-SDR, test mobile devices with known IMSI].

5. Pipe the data into a capture file (.pcap).
6. Observe captured TMSI distributes according to mobile network code and country code respectively.

28.6   Results and Analysis

The following images (see Figures 28.3 and 28.4) show the captured TMSIs and IMSIs of different users, it also shows the mobile operator, area code and country code of these users respectively. Upon repeating the scans over the next 7 days, no change in the TMSI of our particular device was observed.

Disclaimer: We've hidden a section of the TMSI and IMSI number for privacy purposes. The below data set was recorded during a demo run over an interval of 10mins and was able to gather 450+ IMSIs.

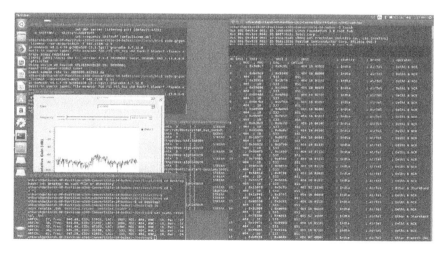

Figure 28.3 Live scanning and decoding over 940.211M frequency.

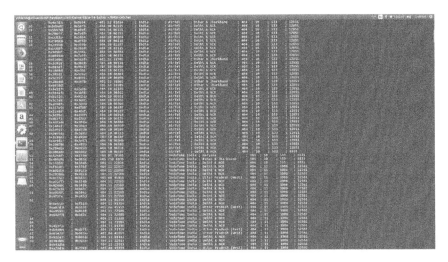

Figure 28.4 Captured IMSIs over 946.2M frequency.

A Pew Internet Project [24] survey determined that 85% of adults considered gravity to regulate access to their particular data. Information privacy (see Table 28.1) is also an important concern for an organization and major work nowadays happen on phone calls, and text messages which can be compromised by further exploitation of IMSI's and the study show that 85% of companies that responded in a survey experienced some sort of

Table 28.1 Analysis of Information Services [17].

Levels of Analysis	Topic Areas	
	Information Privacy Concern	Information Privacy & E-Business Impacts
Individual	36	28
Group	0	0
Organization	0	6
Societal	3	0
Individual + Organization	2	3
Individual + Societal	4	1
Organization + Societal	0	0
Individual + Organization + Societal	1	0
	46	38

privacy breach and 63% of the companies experienced multiple security breaches [25–27]. This shows that the privacy and information of a person and even an organization is always at risk. These breaches can be of any kind ranging from exploiting several modules present on the servers to the private information communicated through a cell phone. Due to the further advancement in technology like predicting useful information by training machine learning [28–30] algorithms on available data and performance prediction.

A survey was carried out for further research on awareness among the public and organizations. No organizations were part of this survey because most organizations are reluctant to share such data. The Survey was carried out with the help of Google forms, which contained the following (see Table 28.2) parameters and classified into two classes (Heard of it, Knows for sure) which was circulated in three engineering colleges in New Delhi, India.

This survey was further used for the prediction of security awareness in colleges based on the parameters (adversary Methods) from Table 28.2. We applied ridge regression and binary classification to predict the awareness ratings for each college. The following regression pseudo-code was used to predict our results:

    a.   Ridge Regression is used to generate the function which evaluates college on the given adversary parameters
    b.   Use the ratio of 'knows for sure' and 'heard' for each adversary method as a single feature.
    c.   Random Offset = 0.589 (Here Random Offset is added to represent the ratio better)
    d.   Formula for plotting <know/heard> ratio graph:
          data_arr[index] = RANDOM_OFFSET+row['knows']/row['heard']
    e.   Sum = {method<knows for sure>/method<heard> in all methods}
    f.   Dataset: Methods are divided based on the college.

This gave us the following prediction of ratings:

Figure 28.5 represents the 'knows/heard' ratio of all the adversary methods individually for a particular college. On the y-axis is the 'knows/heard' ratio and on the x-axis are the

Table 28.2 Data from the survey on security awareness.

Adversary Methods	College 1		College 2		College 3	
	Heard of it	Knows for sure	Heard of it	Knows for sure	Heard of it	Knows for sure
Call Eavesdropping	40	3	41	6	48	8
SMS Hijacking	29	2	34	3	31	2
Location Tracking	43	5	40	2	35	6
DOS attack	19	1	17	0	23	2
Cracking Encryption	11	0	16	0	19–	1

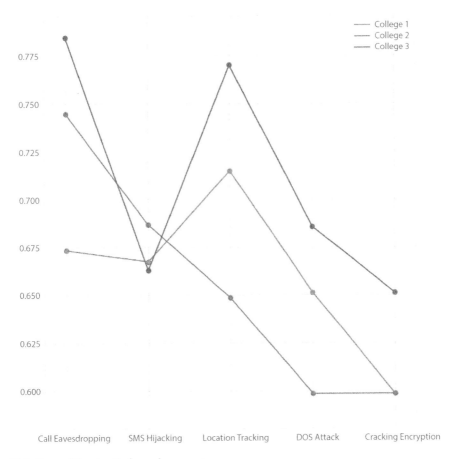

Figure 28.5 Knows/Heard ratio for each parameter.

adversary methods as parameters. This ratio helps in predicting the security awareness rating of each college. Here, from the data we can infer the following results:

1. For College 1 :
   a. Maximum ratio parameter: Location tracking
   b. Minimum ratio parameter: Cracking encryption
2. For College 2 :
   a. Maximum ratio parameter: Call eavesdropping
   b. Minimum ratio parameter: DOS attack
3. For College 3 :
   a. Maximum ratio parameter: Call eavesdropping
   b. Minimum ratio parameter: Cracking encryption.

These results show that people are more informed about call eavesdropping and are less informed about cracking encryption.

The bar graph (see Figure 28.6) represents the predicted security awareness rating of the 3 colleges (out of 10) on which the survey was conducted. We have taken inference

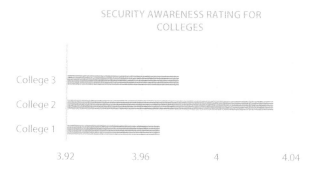

Figure 28.6 Security awareness rating for colleges.

from both the figures that less than half of the people who participated in the survey were unaware of the security concerns related to such a regularly used technology.

28.7   Conclusion

In this paper, we discuss the current telecommunication laws in India, which advocates the need to comprehensively include various methods to reduce adversary attacks. We have implemented a passive sniffing technique to capture TMSI's of multiple network users at different frequencies using low-cost Software Defined Radio capable of sniffing air traffic at lower GSM bands (900–1,800 MHz). Further conducted surveys on security awareness concerning various adversary methods, which on applying various learning models predict the security ratings, which further expose the ignorance and lack of understanding of such methods among the public.

References

1. International Human and Privacy Rights Protection Association, http://www.ihprpa.org/, 2015.
2. Yuchun, M., Yinghong, H., Kun, Z., Zhuang, L., General Application Research on GSM Module. *2011 International Conference on Internet Computing and Information Services*, Hong Kong, pp. 525–528, 2011.
3. Pradhan, Marimuthu, K., Niranchana, R., Vijayakumar, P., Secure Protocol for Subscriber Identity Module. *2017 Second International Conference on Recent Trends and Challenges in Computational Models (ICRTCCM)*, Tindivanam, pp. 358–362, 2017.
4. Pannu, M., Bird, R., Gill, B., Patel, K., Investigating vulnerabilities in GSM security. *2015 International Conference and Workshop on Computing and Communication (IEMCON)*, Vancouver, BC, pp. 1–7, 2015.
5. Dubey, A., Vohra, D., Vachhani, K., Rao, A., Demonstration of vulnerabilities in GSM security with USRP B200 and open-source penetration tools, in: *Communications (APCC), 2016 22nd Asia-Pacific Conference on*, 2016, August, IEEE, Chicago, pp. 496–501.
6. Aggrawal, K., Kamani, M., Vachhani, K., Analysis of GSM air interface using DVB-T receiver and GNU radio. *2017 International Conference on Trends in Electronics and Informatics (ICEI)*, Tirunelveli, pp. 635–640, 2017.

7. Vachhani, K. and Mallari, R.A., Experimental study on wide band FM receiver using GNURadio and RTL-SDR. *2015 International Conference on Advances in Computing, Communications and Informatics (ICACCI)*, Kochi, pp. 1810–1814, 2015.

8. Dabrowski, A., Pianta, N., Klepp, T., Mulazzani, M., Weippl, E., IMSI-catch me if you can: IMSI-catcher-catchers, in: *Proceedings of the 30th Annual Computer Security Applications Conference (ACSAC '14)*, ACM, New York, NY, USA, pp. 246–255, 2014.

9. Norrman, K., Näslund, M., Dubrova, E., Protecting IMSI and User Privacy in 5G Networks, in: *Proceedings of the 9th EAI International Conference on Mobile Multimedia Communications (MobiMedia '16)*. ICST (Institute for Computer Sciences, Social-Informatics and Telecommunications Engineering), ICST, Brussels, Belgium, Belgium, pp. 159–166, 2016.

10. Wikipedia. (2016, September). International mobile subscriber identity [Blog Post]. Retrieved from https://en.wikipedia.org/wiki/International_mobile_subscriber_identity

11. International Mobile Subscriber Identity (IMSI) Oversight Council (IOC), https://www.atis.org/01_committ_forums/IOC/Docs/IMSI-Guidelines-v15.pdf.

12. Thomas Pornin. (2014, January 26). What is the risk of leaking IMEI/IMSI numbers over a network [Blog Post]. Retrieved from https://security.stackexchange.com/questions/49343/what-is-the-risk-of-leaking-imei-imsi-numbers-over-a-network

13. Elonnai Hickok. (2010, November 22). Privacy and Telecommunications: Do We Have the Safeguards? [Blog Post]. Retrieved from https://cis-india.org/internet-governance/blog/privacy/privacy-telecommunications

14. Okunbor, D., A5-based GSM cryptosystem implementation and analysis. *2017 International Conference on Infocom Technologies and Unmanned Systems (Trends and Future Directions) (ICTUS)*, Dubai, pp. 1–1, 2017.

15. J Man Group Ltd. (2016, November 8). Active 4G LTE Vulnerability lets Hackers see texts, track locations and eavesdrop on conversations [Blog Post]. Retrieved from https://www.electron-icproducts.com/Active_4G_LTE_vulnerability_lets_hackers_see_texts_track_locations_and_eavesdrop_on_conversations.aspx#

16. Active GSM Monitoring System with IMSI Catcher and Decryption Unit, http://www.pki-electronic.com/products/interception-and-monitoring-systems/active-gsm-monitoring-system-with-imsi-catcher-and-decryption-unit/.

17. Hadžialić, M., Škrbić, M., Huseinović, K., Kočan, I., Mušović, J., Hebibović, A., Kasumagić, L., An approach to analyzing the security of GSM network, in: *Telecommunications Forum Telford (TELFOR), 2014 22nd*, 2014, November, IEEE, pp. 99–102.

18. Aissi, H., Chen, D.Q., Ravi, R., Downgrading to Minimize Connectivity, ArXiv, abs/1911.11229. 2019.

19. Lin, S., Zheng, B., Chen, F., Ji, F., Yu, H., Soft Demodulators Based on Deterministic SMC for Single-Carrier GSM in Broadband Channels. *IEEE J. Sel. Areas Commun.*, 37, 9, 1973–1985, 2019.

20. Cay, S., Ozeke, O., Ozcan, F., Aras, D., Topaloglu, S., To downgrade, or not to downgrade: That is the question. *EP Europace*, 20, 1, 217, 2018.

21. Park, S., Shaik, A., Borgaonkar, R., Seifert, J.-P., Anatomy of Commercial IMSI Catchers and Detectors, *In Proceedings of the 18th ACM Workshop on Privacy in the Electronic Society (WPES'19)*. 74–86, Association for Computing Machinery, New York, NY, USA, 2019.

22. Moon, J., Lee, S.H., Lee, H., Lee, I., Proactive Eavesdropping With Jamming and Eavesdropping Mode Selection. *IEEE Trans. Wireless Commun.*, 18, 7, 3726–3738, 2019.

23. Valerio, D., *Open source software-defined radio: A survey on GNUradio and its applications*, Technical Report FTW-TR-2008-002, Forschungszentrum Telekommunikation Wien, Vienna, 2008.

24. Belanger, F. and Crossler, R., Privacy in the Digital Age: A Review of Information Privacy Research in Information Systems. *MIS Quart.*, 35, 1017–1041, 2011, 10.2307/41409971.

25. Dan Swinhoe. (2020, April 17). The 15 biggest data breaches of the 21st century [Blog Post]. Retrieved from https://www.csoonline.com/article/2130877/the-biggest-data-breaches-of-the-21st-century.html

26. Dongre, S., Mishra, S., Romanowski, C., Buddhadev, M., Quantifying the Costs of Data Breaches, In: Staggs J., Shenoi S. (eds) *Critical Infrastructure Protection XIII. ICCIP 2019. IFIP Advances in Information and Communication Technology*, vol. 570, Springer, Cham, 2019, 10.1007/978-3-030-34647-8_1.

27. Pandey, A., *A history of data breaches. XRDS: Crossroads*, vol. 24, pp. 11–11, The ACM Magazine for Students, 2018.

28. Riihijarvi, J. and Mahonen, P., Machine Learning for Performance Prediction in Mobile Cellular Networks. *IEEE Comput. Intell. Mag.*, 13, 1, 51–60, Feb. 2018.

29. Mitola, J., *Cognitive radio: An integrated agent architecture for software defined radio*, Doctor of Technology, pp. 271–350, Royal Inst. Technol., 2000.

30. Pérez-Romero, J., Zalonis, A., Boukhatem, L., Kliks, A., Koutlia, K., Dimitriou, N., Kurda, R., On the Use of Radio Environment Maps for Interference Management in Heterogeneous Networks. *IEEE Commun. Mag.*, 53, 184–191, 2015.

29

A Novel Consumer-Oriented Trust Model in E-Commerce

Jyoti Malik* and Suresh Kumar

Ambedkar Institute of Advanced Communication Technologies & Research, Delhi, India

Abstract

Electronic commerce shortly abbreviated as E-Commerce basically provides a platform for buying and selling of products and also provides various types of services along with the transfer of money. Exponential growth of E-Commerce in size and investment on the large scale becomes important to study Trust factor associated with E-commerce. Trust is a state or willingness of a person to depend on some vendor for delivering services according to commitments and also having belief that vendor will use his personal data ethically along with the perception that internet is technically secure. In literature, we have found various case studies with different statistics of E-Commerce. We have categorized E-Commerce in different parameters like mobility, online services, B2C and hyperlocal, etc. and investment of US from 2013 to 2018 as a case study. In this paper, we have proposed a novel Consumer Oriented Trust Model in E-Commerce. Proposed model has divided into five levels with five components.

Keywords: E-Commerce trust, website credibility, trust intention, trust belief, disposition of trust

29.1 Introduction

E-Commerce basically provides a platform for buying and selling of products and also provides various types of services along with the transfer of money. Global E-Commerce size in retail is projected to US $27 trillion by the end of 2020 and the projection of Indian E-Commerce market is US $200 billion by 2026 [1].With the current trends, India is the highest revenue generating country in the world and projected to reach us $120 billion in 2017. A lot of India's big firms are looking for investment opportunities in this sector [2, 3]. 100% FDI allowed in B2B E-Commerce, 100% FDI under automate route is permitted in market model in E-Commerce [4]. Because of ongoing digital transformation in the country along with the government initiatives, it is estimated that India's Internet usage base will be 829 million by the end of 2021 [5]. In this paper, Section 29.2 describes the literature survey. Section 29.3 presents the Trust pyramid with characteristics of virtual Trust and the scenarios of three different cases of Trust building are explained. Categorization of

---

*Corresponding author: jyotimalikk992@gmail.com

Namita Gupta, Prasenjit Chatterjee and Tanupriya Choudhury (eds.) Smart and Sustainable Intelligent Systems, (413–426)
© 2021 Scrivener Publishing LLC

E-Commerce in different spheres and investment in last five years are mentioned in Section 29.4. Lastly in Section 29.5, we have proposed novel pyramid based customer oriented Trust model in E-Commerce.

29.2   Literature Surveys

The main objective of any business model is to have plan for successful business operation and relates it to existing products or services. In literature, we have found various E-Commerce models namely: B2C, B2B, C2C, C2B, B2G, and C2G [6, 7]. In India, the major developments in the E-Commerce sector are firstly focused on the development of digital infrastructure by launching various Digital India Programs. It also makes efforts to lower the data tariff, availability of cheaper smart phones by increasing the market competition and also launches programs to increase the digital literacy [8]. Secondly, India becomes the second largest online market with internet usage of 430 million. Factor fueling the digital economy for the last decade are sustained growth in disposable income, making availability of affordable smart phones, lower the mobile data tariff, improving the digital literacy, rise of internet penetration, creation of digital payment acceptance infrastructure and continuous support from the government [9, 10]. With the development on such a large scale, one factor that bothers the most is establishment of Trust between customer and E-Commerce.

Sometimes, the Trust is established very easily but in some cases, customer thinks twice before sharing its detail with the website because of lacking of trust between website and customer [17, 25]. In order to establish the Trust initially credibility of website is an important factor. Website credibility is about designing the website to make it appear Trustworthy and knowledgeable. A credible website makes people-Trust what it felt comfortable that it is worth spending their money. Now it is important to define Trust. McKnight [11], Kim [12] and Suresh [25] all defined the nature of Trust as interrelated and multidimensional. Thus, Trust is a state or willingness of a person to depend on some vendor for delivering services according to commitments and also having belief that vendor will use his personal data ethically along with the perception about the internet that it is secure technically. HinnaKristinna [13], Kyangyongohk [14] and Wasfi Al Rawabdeh [15] stated that different type of Trust has different implications to different consumer behavior. Initially, the Trust is basically in two unfamiliar Trustees and make a relationship between two unfamiliar actors who do not develop credibility towards each other and also not having affective bonds and meaningful information regarding each other. The domain of initial Trust domain contains the time period during which a Trustee visit and explore a website first time. Trust plays a major role in overcoming risk and insecurity perceptions. Lakshmi Lyer [16] stated that Trust makes consumer confident and comfortable, which led to share of their personal information, making purchases and considering the advice of different usages as present in terms of reviews and rating.

Multidisciplinary and Multidimensional nature of Trust has validated multidimensional and multidisciplinary modal of Trust in E-Commerce. This model includes four constructs-Trusting beliefs, Institution based Trust, Trusting intentions, Disposition of Trust. In general, Trust is divided into two sub categories, one is Identification based Trust and other is Calculus based Trust. Calculus based Trust is totally assumption based Trust where the vendor assumes the customer against his/her item based on the rewards given for their words and deeds in terms of not selling. This type of Trust is more appears in market where interaction is Virtual. Identification based Trust is based on the relationship between the two, desire and interaction with each other [8]. In this type of Trust mutual interaction and understanding, respect for each other values and desires are the reasons for building up of Trust. Here, once the people understand each other interest and develop mutual understanding, respect each other, then identification based Trust is developed which is also known as mutual trust. Trust categorization based on analysis: On the basis of analysis Trust can be named as perception based Trust or network based Trust. The perceptive business Trust or network based Trust is building among the people who have similar interest and needs among them. Trust is shown only in the uncertain environment where the risk factor must be present. Trustier is going to recognize vulnerabilities to some extend and risk is accepted by the Trustier.

As risk is always present in ecommerce in the form of vulnerabilities; therefore vendors of ecommerce can behave in unpredictable manner. Both buyers and customers are having uncertainty regarding the risk or (vulnerabilities) at the time of using ecommerce sites for purchase, sending information making online transaction [18]. Any relationship of Trust is built between two parties one is Trustee and another is Trustier. In the virtual environment that is online system, Trustee is basically an E-Commerce website and Trustier is a customer who makes order, purchase something online, making transaction online, etc. on the ecommerce website that is with Trustee. Here the relationship between the Trustier and Trustee is virtual in nature. The Trustee works in accordance with the Trustier as a result Trust is built up between them. Trust is completely a subjective matter in both virtual and real environment [19, 20]. It is directly related to environment and personal factors as role of Trust is calculated differently in different scenario among different person according to various environment and personal attitude. Behaviors of Trust in terms of action basically depend on the type of risk or vulnerability occur [16]. It may be lead to cancellation of transaction, discontinuous of online services by the customer in case Trust is abandoned, distrust occur [21].

29.3   Trust Pyramid

Figure 29.1 shows the baseline relevance and initial Trust refers to the bottom level or level 1 is which needs to be established. Interest and preference represents the Level 2 consists of over other options. After establishment of initial Trust, Trust established in terms of interest to go further forward into the website start making preferences over the other options. Level 3 is mentioned by personal information Trust where user is ready to share its personal information such as name, e-mail contact number etc. At level 4 is referred by the most sensitive part of E-Commerce Trust environment where Trust is established with sensitive and financial information as customer is ready to disclose its banking information such as credit card number, CVC, account number etc. Lastly the top level of Trust pyramid is mentioned by Level 5 where Trust is established completely and user is willing to commit to an ongoing relationship. Therefore, people have different kinds of needs at each level of commitment in order to establish Trust. Once the user needs are fulfilled then he will be in the position to trust more and reached to the next level by addressing the demands.

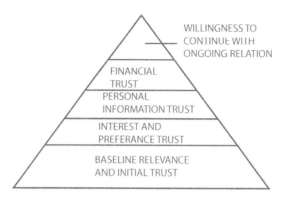

Figure 29.1 Trust pyramid 1.

29.3.1   Trust Scenarios

In this part, we are presenting three different cases of trust scenarios. Case 1: It shows the ideal condition of step by step establishment of trust by going through different level if the user is new or user does not have initial trust (Figure 29.2).

Case 2: In some cases, a login wall appears and asks a new user his/her name and phone number or some personal information before accessing the website. It does not give time to the new user to establish initial Trust or comfort compulsion to give personal information by registering to the website and the site is straight forwarded to level 3. These sites do not address levels 1 and 2 Trust establishment at all. Here various types of questions arise from the site of new user such as—Is it better than other website or options? Does it seem to have my interest? All these type of questions from the user must be address outside the login wall by using any tagline that describe website or its contents or some social proofs or images that determine the very well usage of the site by different user or that indicate its popularity. In this case all these proof help to build Trust levels 1 and 2 to some extend but not completely. If this user does not know anything about the website, a pressure is always exists on the website for addressing trust as shown in Figure 29.3.

Case 3: In this case, the website assume that a user is already at level 3 and forced him to registered either through e-mails or some other way but actually the user is at level 1

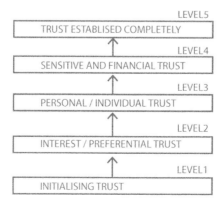

Figure 29.2 Case 1.

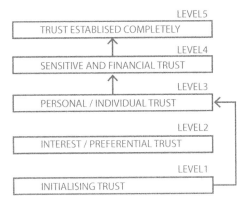

Figure 29.3 Case 2.

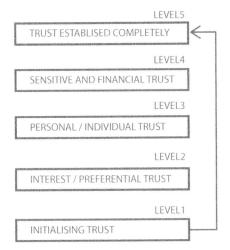

Figure 29.4 Case 3.

and till now no Trust is establish yet. At the screen, a scrolling window is displayed which asks to enter personal information. This scrolling window cannot be closed by the user. In addition to make login or new registration various options are present on the wall either to register with Facebook, Google, or any other social account. As connecting through an existing account is level 5 requests and makes ensure that Trust is already established. It is shown in Figure 29.4.

29.3.2   Statistics of E-Commerce

India is the fastest growing E-Commerce market with expected market size to be US $200 billion by 2026. It is shown in Figure 29.5 below. Reason of triggered growth of E-Commerce is internet penetration to both urban and rural areas, low tariff because of the large competition at the operator level, cheaper smart phones availability to both urban and rural areas. It is also projected that Indian economy will be US $ 250 billion by 2020. It is shown in Figure 29.6.

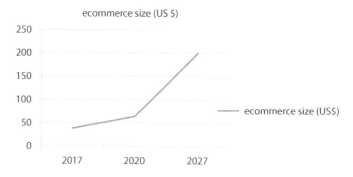

Figure 29.5 India ecommerce size.

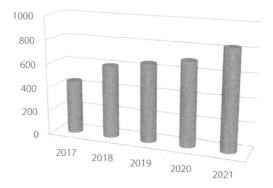

Figure 29.6 Internet estimate usage.

29.3.2.1   Case Study: Consumer Trust Violation

In 2016, personal information of nearly 57 million Uber users was breached by accessing data from company's third party cloud service. This hacking is done by 2 hacker and breach information such as name, driver licensed numbers. In March 2018, a bug was discovered in Google API .This bug allows third party developers to access the personal data of Google plus users. Google kept it secret instead of informing it to the user for nearly one year. A political consulting firm of Cambridge analytics make access to millions of Facebook data. This breach takes place due to the design flaws in a data mishap which affects 87 million Facebook users. Therefore, trusted companies such as Uber, Facebook, Google have lack of regulations and disclosure proving that users must take personal data security by their own.

29.4   Categorization of E-Commerce in Different Spheres

29.4.1   Hyperlocal

Hyperlocal ecommerce industry in India work on the basis of "near me" concept. Urban India has gradually embraced consumption and is increasing option for seamless services. Growing internet penetration, rise in the number of people using smart phones and increasing disposable incomes have acted as a catalyst for the hyperlocal sector while shopping customer behavior and expectations. Hyperlocal delivery has been primarily associated with grocery and food delivery services and e-pharmacy, etc. Company Zomata Media Pvt Ltd., Bundi Technology Private Limited (Swiggy), Naspers, Tiger Global, etc.

29.4.2   Travel and Hospitality

The journey of the ecommerce travel and hospitality industry in India began with IRCTC launching its first transaction website in early 2000 followed by the online ticketing website and hotel booking platforms, the tourism industry has accepted ecommerce as its mainstream and has changed the dynamics of the industry. Company: 1) Oravel Stags Private Limited (oyoroom. com), 2) Casa2 Stays Private Limited (Fabhotel.com), and 3) Yatra Online Private Limited.

29.4.3   Business to Customer (B2C)

It has availability of numerous choices in terms of brands, discounts, offers, reduced delivery time, personalization, cash on delivery, digital payment infrastructure and easy to return have been major factor for development of the B2C. Companies: Flipkart India, Paytm Ecommerce, Supermarket Grocery Suppliers Pvt Limited (Big Basket), Lenskart Solution Pvt Limited, Nykaa E-Retail Pivoted Limited.

29.4.4   Education Technology

Education technology ecommerce has tremendous potential in bridging the gap and it can be a game changer in disseminating of knowledge across the spectrum. This sector has also a key adapter of Deep Tech such as ALVR Analytics to allow for better content and value add. Companies: Think & Learn Private Limited (Biju), Sorting Hat Technologies Private Limited (Unacademy), Veduntu Innovations.

29.4.5   Payments and Wallets

The payment acceptance infrastructure has been significantly upgraded with new merchants accepting digital payments in both online and offline channel. Recent technologies advancement supported by the govt like UPI/BHIM and platforms like Google Pay, PhonePe, etc. promoted by private players have further given a boost to digital payment. As per RBI, payment software records robust growth in 2017–18 with volume and value growth at 44.6% and 11.9% respectively. Electronic transaction as a percentage of total volume of retail payment increased to 92.6% in 2017–18 from 88.4% in 2016–17. Companies: One 97Communication Limited (Paytm), One Mobikwik System Private Limited, Itzcash Card Limited, etc.

29.4.6   Business to Business (B2B)

B2B adds a significant value to the supply chain especially in the tiers 2 3 until where access to products, inventory holding and privacy is always a challenge. B2B segment is driven by consumer durables (mobile and mobile accessories), apparels, home furnishing. Companies: 1. Hiveloop Technology Private Limited (UDAAN), 2. 63Ideas Infolabs Private Limited (ninfacat), 3. 10i Commerce Services Private Limited.

29.4.7   Mobility

Mobility is being seen as a segment that can be an effective band sustainable solution to address the structural challenges in the transportation sector largely emanating from lack of infrastructure (roads, parking, etc.) and first (last mile connectivity) Companies: Ani Technologies Private Limited (OLACab), Zoomcar India Private Limited.

29.4.8   Financial Technology

Finance companies are offering cheaper, agile, environment and innovation banking and insurance solution through extensive use of automation and technology, as compared to their tradition peers. Companies: Edtechaces Marketing and Consulting Private Limited (Policy Bazaar), Zenlefin Private Limited (Capitor Float), Acko General Insurance Limited, Rubique Technologies India Private Limited.

29.4.9   Health Technology

With nearly 500 startups, Health sector in India provides technology further validation of companies stepping up to the challenge to improve healthcare across the board. Advanced health tech starts up are solving complicated problems like technology enabled monitory, Diagnosis and treatment it contain-aggregators, e-pharmacy, personal health fitness discovery, health information management, techno enabled diagnosis service and anomaly detection, telemedicine medical. Companies: Current Health Care Private Limited, Pacto Technologies Private Limited, Netmeds Market Place Private Limited, Bright Lifecare Private Limited (Healthkart).

29.4.10   Social Commerce

India has adapted well to social media channels like WhatsApp and Facebook where influence plays a major role in increasing followers. There has been evolution in the definition of the influences in our social circles from a mere one to one personal connection to a more social media based interactions which cater to style, fashion and utility of younger generation. Social commerce while initially driven primarily by Facebook and WhatsApp, have witnessed an advent of social ecommerce companies that are further enabling commerce by providing ease in product, end to end logistics, personalization, etc. Companies: Mohalla Tech Private Limited (Sharechat), TVF Media Labs Private Limited.

29.4.11   Gaming

India is one of the top five countries for mobile gaming in the world. Mobile gaming is expected to cross us $1 billion in market size $ by 2020.With the mobile gamer base set to become 300 million by then. The sector comprises of social gaming like Dream11, pubg, Clash of Clan. Companies: Dream11 Fantasy Private Limited, Nazara Technologies Limited, Head Infotech Private Limited, Sparskills Technologies Private Limited (9 stacks).

29.4.12   Logistics Technology

It provides logistics solution to the other ecommerce sectors. Companies: Zinka Logistics Solution Private Limited (Blackbuck), Diptab Ventures Private Limited (Letstransport.in).

29.4.13   Online Classified and Services

The Indian online classified industry has been a rapid growth amidst major structural changes, introduction of new categories offering, evolving business model, etc. companies like Quikr and OLX have historically dominated the online classified sector in India. But there has been an advent of focused vertical players. Especially in cars, property (job, etc.) that have change the paradigm significantly. Company: Girnar Software Private Limited (Cardekho), Droom Technologies, Quikar India Private Limited.

29.5   Categorization of E-Commerce in Different Spheres and Investment in Last Five Years

Table 29.1 below contains the investment in US $ from 2013 to 2018 in respective category of ecommerce.

Table 29.1 Investment in US $ from 2013 to 2018 in respective category of E-Commerce.

Category	2013	2014	2015	2016	2017	2018	Total
Hyperlocal	36.8	65.5	353.5	100.6	109.3	1637.0	2302.7
Travel and Hospitality	8.6	30.3	167.8	205.0	578	1025.8	2015.5
B2C	499	3041.2	1914	770	2586.2	1002.3	9812.7
Edtech	14.1	5.1	30.2	151.3	89	742.2	1031.9
Payments and Wallets	5.5	1.0	3.6	7.6	1425.4	564.0	2007.1
B2b	6	35.2	22.7	98	60.8	540.1	762.8
Mobility	7.2	269.8	939	38.5	1262.4	379.7	2896.6
Fintech	6.1	52.3	439.2	83.6	251.6	347.7	1180.5
Healthtech	6.1	52.3	439.2	83.6	251.6	347.7	1180.5
Social Commerce	0.1	57.7	169.2	44.1	18.1	100.2	389.4
Gaming	1.8	0	5.5	1	80.6	104.4	193.3
Logistic Tech	14.1	5.1	30.2	151.3	89	742.2	1031.9
Online Classified Services	22.4	245.0	487.5	206.3	141.6	236.0	1338.8

29.6   Proposed Model

29.6.1   Different Components of Web Trust Model

Our proposed model has divided in following five components:

- Institution Based Trust: Institution based Trust, a sociological dimension and based on the perception of the individual on the institution. Here the perception [22] is basically related to the structure characteristic such as safety, security of the internet which influences Trusting intention and belief of specific vendor.
- Trust Related Behaviors: It includes actions which show dependence on web vendor in terms of vulnerability and risk. It basically include Trust related behavior such as making any purchase, act on reviews or rating provided on the website and sharing personal information [23].
- Disposition to Trust: It is a general way to Trust on others and influences ones Trust intention and belief.
- Trusting Intention: Trusting Intentions are the intention to involve in Trust related behavior related to trustee. It contains two sub constructs namely subjective probability of dependence and Willingness to dependence. Subjective probability of dependence is the probability of dependence of one on other. Willingness to depend is basically the violation preparedness of making oneself vulnerable to the Trustee.
- Type of Trust Belief: Trusting beliefs is basically perception of specific web vendor attribute and shows the confidence towards the Trustee based on Trustier perception i.e. a web vendor must have attribute which is beneficial to the Trustier [24]. Basically, there are three types of Trusting belief namely:
  o Competence: It includes ability to do what Trustee need. It consists of competence, expertness, and dynamism.
  o Benevolence: It means motivation and carefulness of the Trustee to do what the Trustee needs and requirement. It consists of goodwill, benevolence, responsiveness.
  o Integrity: It includes promise and honestly of the Trustee. Figure 29.7 shown below contains clustering of Trust belief with control variables. It consists of integrity, morality, credibility, reliability, dependability [14].

29.6.2   A Novel Consumer-Oriented Trust Model

This model provides explanation of different factor external or control variables and different Trust belief act on each level of Trust pyramid which help in establishment of Trust at each level. Figure 29.8 shows Schematic Architecture of Customer Oriented Trust Model. Various levels of this model are described as below:

A. Level 1: At level 1 various factor contribute towards the initial establishment of Trust.
   i.   Prior Baseline web experience (of customer)

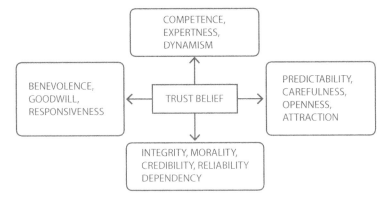

Figure 29.7 Trust belief.

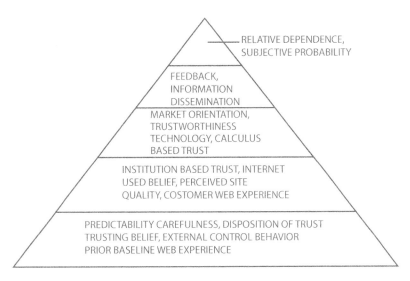

Figure 29.8 Schematic architecture of customer oriented trust pyramid model.

   ii. Disposition of Trust: Disposition of Trust consist of Faith in humanity in term of Benevolence, competence, integrity.
   iii. External control Behavior: External control behavior like education, income, communication, internet, exchange of different information on different platform contributes towards the establishment of Trust.
   iv. Trusting Belief: There are three type of Trust belief contribute towards:
       • Competence belief: expertness, competence, dynamism.
       • Benevolence: responsiveness goodwill, benevolence
       • Integrity: Reliability, Morality, credibility, dependency, integrity Carefulness, Predictability, attraction and Openness are also the factor contribute at level 1.

B. Level 2: At level 2 various factor contribute towards the establishment of trust.
   i. Institution based Trust: It includes situational Normality of General i.e. Benevolence, competence, Integrity. Institution based Trust, a sociological

dimension and based on the perception of the individual on the institution and basically related to the structure characteristics such as safety, security of the internet which influences Trusting intention and belief of specific vendor

   ii.   Internet usage belief

   iii.   Perceive site quality in terms of timeliness, usefulness, advance

   iv.   Situational assurance

   v.   Customers web experience in terms of length, frequency, self-perceived experience

C. Level 3: At level 3, three factors contribute towards the development of Trust.

   i.   Market orientation: Coordination, information dissemination and gathering, responsiveness

   ii.   Technology Trustworthiness -Reliability, Security, privacy

   iii.   Calculus based Trust

D. Level 4: Various factors contribute at this level.

   i.   Trust with Sensitive (financial information)

   ii.   Trust in terms of Risk (financial, social, time, performance risk, psychological)

   iii.   Trustworthiness in term of feedback, information dissemination.

E. Level 5: At this level factor contribute towards the establishment of Trust.

   i.   Relative dependence: It is a form of dependence on web vendor, Trust mechanism (nature of relationship) is dynamic and there is willingness to commit for ongoing relationship.

   ii.   Subjectivity: probability of depending on others advice, take into consideration other reviews, advice, provide personal information, making purchase.

29.7   Conclusion

E-Commerce has changed the way of buying and selling the products. Different E-commerce model made it possible. With exponential growth of E-Commerce and investment on the large scale, it becomes important to study the Trust factor associated with E-Commerce. In this paper, we have described level of trust pyramid along with different scenarios. Further, we have proposed consumer based model describing various factor contributing towards establishment of trust in E-commerce. In future, we will apply Consumer Oriented Trust Model for Business to Customer type of E-Commerce. Moreover, we are working on mathematical trust model for different popular websites to compute trust mathematically.

References

1. Http://statista.com/topics/2454/ecommerce-in-india.
2. Eugine Franco, C. and BulomineRegi, S., Advantages and challenges of E-Commerce customers and business in Indian perspective. *Int. J. Res.-Granthaalayah*, 4, 3, 7–13, March 2016.

3. Shahjee, R., The Impact of electronic commerce on business organization. *Sch. Res. J. Interdiscip. Stud.*, 4/27, 3130–3140, 2016.

4. Http://dipp.gov.in/publication/fdi-statistics.

5. Http://statista.com/topics/2157/internet-usage-in-india.

6. Tamilarasi, R. and Elamathi, N., E-Commerce Business. *Int. J. Eng. Technol. Manag. Res.*, 4, 10, 33–41, 2017.

7. Kumar, N., Ecommerce in India: An Analysis of Present Status, Challenges and Opportunities. *Int. J. Manag. Stud.*, V, 2, 3, 90–95, April 2018.

8. Roy, S. and Telang, A., Myntra: An Online Ecommerce Retailer to a Mobile Commerce Player. *Int. J. Appl. Eng. Res.*, 13, 2499–2503, 2018.

9. Kaushal, T., Growth and emerging trend of Ecommerce in India. *Int. J. Sci. Eng.*, 3, 1, 25–31, 2018.

10. Nagesga, N.S., Entrepreneurship and Innovation in Ecommerce. *Int. J. Eng. Technol. Sci. Res.*, 5, 1, 618–624, 2018.

11. McKnight, D.H., Choudhury, V., Kacma, Developing and Validating Trust Measures for E-Commerce: An integrative typology. *Inf. Syst. Res.*, 13, 3, 334–339, 2002.

12. Kim, D.J., A Study of the Multilevel and Dynamic Nature of Trust in E-Commerce From A Cross Stage Perceptive. *Int. J. Electron. Comm.*, 19, 11–64, 2014.

13. Paakki, H., Framework for Consumer Related Trust Issues in E-commerce, in: *Frontier of E-Business Research*, 2004.

14. Kyungyoungohk, and Kim, M., Who is leading China's E-Commerce Industry? The antecedents and Consequences of E-Worm focusing on one person media. *J. Theor. Appl. Inf. Technol.*, 96, 5, 18–40, 2018.

15. Wasfi, A., Zeglat, D., Alzawahreh, A., The importance of Trust and Security Issues In Ecommerce Adoption in Arab World. *Eur. J. Econ. Finance Adm. Sci.*, 52, 1, 172–178, 2012.

16. Salam, A.F., Lakshmilyer, Palvia, P., Singh, R., Trust in E-Commerce. *Commun. ACM*, 48, 2, 73–77, 2005.

17. Sfrerianto, S., Saragih, M.H., Nugraha, B., E-Commerce Recommender for Usage Bandwidth Hotel. *Int. J. Electr. Eng. Comput. Sci.*, 9, 1, 227–233, 2018.

18. Roozbeh, and Hajati, Z., Trust in E-Commerce. *Int. J. Innov. Appl. Stud.*, 10, 3, 917–922, 2015.

19. Viot, C., Subjective Knowledge Product Attributes and Consideration set: The wine case. *Int. J. Wine Bus. Res.*, 24, 3, 219–248, 2012.

20. Wang, S., Zhang, L., Ma, N., Wang S., An Evaluation Approach of Subjective Trust Based on Cloud Model, in: . *J. Softw. Eng. Appl.*, I, 44–52, 2008.

21. Alarcon, G.M., Lyons, J.B., Christense, J.C. *et al.*, The Effect of Prospensity to Trust and Perceptions of Trustworthiness on Trust Behaviour in Dyads. *Behav. Res. Methods*, 6, 1, 0014–0016, 2018.

22. Charishma, K. and Krishna, Sk G., Connecting-OSN media to E-commerce for Cold Start Product Recommendation using MICRO login Information. *Int. J. Innov. Technol.*, 6, 1, 0014–0016, 2018.

23. Patil, M.T. and Rao, M.Y., Building a Template for Intuitive Virtual Ecommerce Shopping Site in India. *Int. J. Inf. Technol. Comput. Sci.*, 10, 2, 44–59, 2018.

24. Corbitt, B.J. and Thanasankit, T., Trust and E-Commerce—A Study of Consumer Perception. *Electron. Commer. Appl.*, 6, 102–105, 2003.

25. Kumar, S. and Chaudhary, N., A Novel Trust Scheme in Semantic Web, in: *Springer Proceedings of ICT4SD 2018, Information and Communication Technology for Sustainable Development. Advances in Intelligent Systems and Computing*, vol. 933, pp. 103–110.

30

Data Mining Approaches for Profitable Business Decisions

Harshita Belwal*, Sandeep Tayal, Yogesh Sharma and Ashish Sharma

CSE Department, Maharaja Agrasen Institute of Technology, Delhi, India

Abstract

Data mining is a technique using huge data sets which are processed for discovering unsuspected relationships and patterns among the data. This will result in the knowledge which is acquired by processing the patterns of information. Further that knowledge is used to formulate a profitable business approach. Hence, we would be able to predict appropriate and right facts to the desired person at the apparent time so that recommended decisions can be taken faster. To accomplish this task, we have various data mining methods and machine learning programs that can be used to collect the data, then structuring the data, and then finally converting it into some useful information. That information can be used for making profitable business management decisions, this is business intelligence.

Keywords: Data mining, Business Intelligence, Machine Learning, Data Mining Technique, Profitable business approach, Data Warehouse, Data Structuring, Business Management Decisions

30.1 Introduction to Data Mining and Business Intelligence

Data mining is a branch of computer science in which methods from stats, database theory, data science, and machine learning are blended.

To have any Data Mining approach from a business view, our foremost requirement is to understand the Business and establish the goals which need to be fulfilled. Data sets are acquired and checked if they are in accordance with our requirements or not. In the next step, Data is prepared and transformed, which results in the final updated data set. Mathematical models are used to bring light on the patterns in the data sets. The identified patterns are evaluated following business objectives. Data mining techniques like Classification, Clustering, Prediction, Regression etcetera are being used extensively for this task.

Data mining is booming up in the modern era because the power of the database had been realized by the researchers. The database is simply formed by accumulating all the

---

Corresponding author: belwalharshita@yahoo.in

Namita Gupta, Prasenjit Chatterjee and Tanupriya Choudhury (eds.) Smart and Sustainable Intelligent Systems, (427–442)

statistics. In the recent scenario, many companies have been using data mining to formulate their business strategy. Companies like Amazon, Walmart, Starbucks, Netflix, etc. have been investing in this lucrative business strategy and hence also attracting other firms [1].

Business Intelligence [BI] is a tremendously Wide-Reaching and convoluted domain that includes managing performance, analytics, predictive modeling, data mining, etc. BI completely revolves around transforming the proliferated information into a tidy organized form [2].

BI will allow navigating to the desired data on our own, without any external dependency. Due to this, the organizations would no longer have to search their way through analyzing the complex data in spreadsheets manually, instead of that, BI systems can be used by the employees to request the desired information.

By using BI methods and software on the retail market, anyone can generate a logical review of huge data sets containing information of the customers. This will authorize the manager to see their customers' loyalty towards their brand along with their demands [3]. All this will aid in predicting the preferences and habits of a segment of customers. This will create new opportunities for providing better service and encourage the use of targeted advertising marketing campaigns like instant shipment, deal coupons of products related to customer's interests, etc. So basically, the analyzers can recognize and know the customers more efficiently, based on their historical transactions and their actions, further that information can be used to increase turnover or differentiate their dedicated brand from others by providing better and unique services.

In the next sections of this paper, there will be an overview of data mining techniques and BI, followed by the comparative study of attributes of the various data mining techniques used in BI along with some applications of data mining in business.

30.2   Outline of Data Mining and BI

Data mining is a well-flourishing statistical and machine learning technique that is useful for predicting the data. Using this we can extract interesting information or patterns from large databases, for example in product marketing, a marketing manager must find a particular section of a population which is going to react for their product, so to accomplish that task he needs to recognize the whole population and then use the correct approach to classify the population. Similarly, in predictive modeling, few ways can be used to interact with the customers by using different channels like direct marketing, print advertising, etc. [4]. An analyst would select an optimal channel through which they can send their message to the customers by using data mining. Apart from these usages, data mining is also used for budgeting, detecting fraud, and inconsistencies—which may lead to a loss in the subsequent time. The sole purpose of using data mining in business is to understand their customers and business most effectively.

Data mining has many techniques among which, Decision Tree Technique is very popular because of two reasons, it can do both investigative analysis and predictive modeling, moreover, it can be represented in the structure of a tree. At present data mining is being used in many different industries, starting from E-Commerce to Crime agencies [5].

Nowadays it is all about the database and its analysis. Data mining and BI are inseparable today as together they act as a tool which can accelerate the growth of any firm. It is the need of the hour to find the information which is not yet known about business, company, and customers. It is quite difficult to look for a hidden relationship in the data stored in the data warehouses. BI gives insights into a company. BI uses various data mining algorithms to fulfill this task. BI is an integration of a procedure, technologies, and tools which are used to turn data into information. Information is modeled into knowledge and that knowledge further formulated into moneymaking plans, which leads to rewarding business action. Figure 30.1 is depicting the above-stated approach by pictorial representation. Typical BI applications are Customer Segmentation, Customer profitability, Fraud Detection, target marketing, etcetera which will be discussed in the coming sections.

The data warehouse is the center of every organization where the data is stored for the analysis from the business view. Figure 30.2 represents the pictorial representation of BI Architecture in brief. Data Sources stores the data in raw form on which various actions could be performed. By organizing, summarizing, regularizing the data along with some other actions upon it, the Data present in the Data sources is used by the technical staff for building the data warehouse. Various business users like analysts in a firm can work

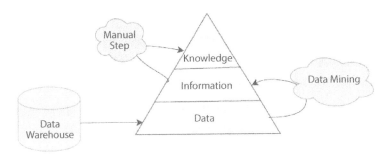

Figure 30.1 Integration of data mining and BI.

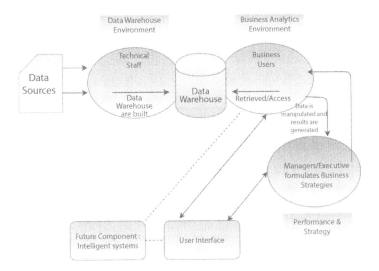

Figure 30.2 BI Architecture.

on the data present in the data warehouse. The user interfaces like dashboard/portals are used to view the processes or results which are derived from the data reflecting the ongoing trend. The Data Mining algorithms basically work in Intelligent systems on their own. They directly work on the data in the data warehouse and also deliver the results so that analysts can analyze it. Finally, the results of the data mining algorithms go to the managers/executives in an organization and then they formulate strategies to deal with trends shown by data. Thus, they take profitable decisions for their business [6, 7].

30.2.1 CRISP-DM

CRISP is a Data mining model that is very popular because it comes up with a structured approach for drafting a data-mining scheme to work with. CRISP-DM is an acronym for the Cross industry standard process for data mining [8]. Figure 30.3 shows the 6 phases of the CRISP model. In the first stage, which is a Business understanding phase, the goal is to recognize the problem which needs to be resolved from the business perspective. In the succeeding second stage, that is the Data understanding phase, the actual data is acquired and the task is to figure out whether the strengths and limitations of the data are matching with the problem or not. Basically, in the second stage, the data is acquired, then described, then explored, and then finally it is verified. In the third stage, that is Data Preparation, the data is prepared in sync with the Analytical Technology's requirement which includes, converting data into a tabular format, filling up the mislaid or absent values, transforming data to non-identical types, and scaling numerical values. The fourth stage of this model is the Modeling phase, in which a modeling technique is first selected than tests are generated to check the model robustness, and then finally the model is built and assessed. In the Fifth stage that is the Evaluation Stage, the results are studied. In the Deployment stage, the outcome of Data Mining is put into usefulness [9, 10].

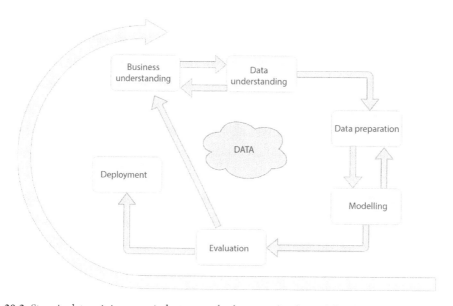

Figure 30.3 Steps in data mining cross industry standard process for data mining (CRISP-DM).

30.3   Leading Techniques used for Data Mining in BI

Data mining is a very effective process in which the main aim is to extract knowledge from a large amount of data by using various techniques. Another phrase for data mining is Knowledge Discovery from Data. The need for data mining comes from evolution in the size of the database. Over time the size of the Database is getting larger with the advancements in technologies, due to which the manual analysis of the data is not possible. This creates the need for automatic data analysis for which Data mining is being used. Statistics, Artificial Intelligence, and Machine learning are the Data Mining technologies that form its foundation.

Various Data mining techniques have been formulated to fulfill different needs. The task is to choose the most suitable technique which meets the requirements of the firm [11]. Following are some major Data mining Techniques:

30.3.1   Classification Analysis

In this method, we are forecasting a certain consequence based on the input and to anticipate that result, the algorithm runs on a training set, which contains the group of attributes and their respective results. The algorithm attempts to find out the relationship present between attributes that would make it possible to foresee what is next to come [12]. So basically it is a very convoluted data mining technique in which we collect the attributes into observable categories and then use them to conclude. Induction tress and Neural Networks are some classification techniques. Classification of Emails into legitimate or spam can be considered as an example of this technique [13].

30.3.2   Clustering

Using this approach, we are aiming to put similar objects together in a solitary cluster and dissimilar objects together in an additional cluster. In this technique, the researchers don't have any prior knowledge which means the number of unknown clusters is yet to be discovered. Partitioning and Hierarchical clustering are the main categories of clustering. In the former one, the data objects are dissected into subsets or groups in a way such that each data object is present in exactly one group or cluster, while in the later one hierarchical trees are made organizing the set of nested clusters [14, 15]. Density based, Grid based, Model based are some other popular categories of clustering. Identifying the similar web usage patterns, or segmenting the Customer's Database based on similar buying patterns are some examples of this technique [16].

30.3.3   Regression Analysis

It is a statistical procedure maneuvering which we can estimate the relationship between variables, which helps in understanding the changes in the characteristic value of the dependent variable. Mostly it is used for predictions. There are two kinds of Regression analysis, that is a simple regression analysis and multiple regression analysis. In Simple regression, a single quantitative and independent variable X is manipulated to foresee the other Quantitative, and dependent, variable Y. In Multiple Regression more than one quantitative and qualitative variable $X_{1....}$ X_N is used to foresee a quantitative and dependent variable Y. Linear Regression, Regression tree, Lasso Regression, and Multivariate Regression are some popularly known regression algorithms. For instance, the regression model can be used to foresee the worth of a property which can be traced based on its location, facilities, and other features [17].

30.3.4   Anomaly Detection

Through anomaly detection, we want to identify the unusual cases within our data, which seems to be homogenous. This technique can be used to detect frauds, Intrusions in the network, and other events that are of great significance. It is a sort of Classification. In this technique, only a single class is shown on the training data so it is carried out as one-class classification. Its model can be utilized to foresee whether a data point is a classic for a specified distribution or not [18]. An unusual data point can be regarded as an outlier or as an example of a previously obscured class. Support Vector Machine, Bayesian Network, and Neural Network etcetera are some techniques for Anomaly Detection.

30.3.5   Induction Rule

In this technique, based on data from the past, future actions and behaviors can be predicted. A model is created based on rule induction which is of if/then/else type. Generally, the rule induction models are derived from the decision trees, which have decision branches. We have various rule induction algorithms like MLEM2, LEM2, etc. [19].

30.3.6   Summarization

By using this technique we can produce a compact representation of the data set which is rigorously studied to interpret correct results. Tabulation of mean, standard deviation is some summarizing methods that are used for analyzing data, visualizing data, and for generating automated reports. In this technique, we are compressing the data sets into a smaller group of patterns while clasping on to the maximal to the point information. There are different data summarization techniques in data mining which are Frequency histograms, Quantile plot, Quantile–Quantile plot, Scatter Plot, and Local Regression curve [20].

30.3.7   Sequential Patterns

In this technique, we work on the given set of sequence and we try to find the complete set of frequent subsequences and abnormalities in the sequence. Our algorithm requires to be efficient, scalable, being able to find a complete set, and incorporating various user-specific constraints kinds. Sequence pattern mining is a data mining technique that has a much broader application in customer retention, targeted marketing, stocks, and markets etcetera. Most importantly it has applications in bioinformatics, fraud detection, healthcare also. The Challenge of the sequence pattern mining is that a huge number of possible sequential patterns are hidden in the database which has to be discovered by using a suitable algorithm [21, 22].

30.3.8   Decision Tree

It is used to generate the rules which are simple to interpret and understand. ID3 is an example of a decision tree algorithm. The Decision tree methods are established on conditional probabilities, just like Naïve Bayes [23]. Decision tree algorithm generates rules, unlike Naïve Bayes here the rules are the conditional statements that can effortlessly be elucidated by the people, and further, it can be used easily within a database to pinpoint the set of records. Decision trees are constructed by representing graphically all the possible solutions to a decision based on certain conditions. There are three different kinds of nodes in the decision tree, that is, the root, branch, and leaf nodes. The root node represents the main question, the branch nodes are the intermediate nodes, using which the main question will be answered and leaf nodes represent the solutions. Information gain and Entropy are the two factors using which Decision trees are created. Information Gain is the measure of how much information has been provided by the answer to a specific question and entropy is a measure of how much uncertainty is there in the information. An increase in information gain will lead to a decrease in the entropy [24]. The models made by Decision Tree Algorithms are more accurate and understandable with comparatively little user intervention. It is a fast algorithm in terms of both builds and applies time.

30.3.9   Neural Networks

In this technique, the information is gathered by drawing out the existing patterns in the database. This is done by using the artificial neural network. Artificial Neural networks simulate the neural network in humans. In humans, the neurons are used as a medium to feel sensory input. Similarly, the artificial neural network acts as a conduit for the input of data, which is processed by the complex mathematical equation. So neural networks imitate the human brain by studying the data sets and implementing learning to generalize patterns for classification and predictions. Artificial Neural networks can be understood as a network of many interconnected neurons, which are inspired by logical neurons. They are capable of performing some specific tasks like clustering, classification, etc. The basic model of an Artificial neural network comprises inputs, weights, summarization unit and threshold unit to get the output. There are three distinct layers in the network, namely input, hidden and output layer. Here the input layer will contain all the inputs. The succeeding hidden layer provides nonlinearity to the network and it processes input and weights, finally, the output layer is present which will have the output. Neural Networks are non-linear statistical data modeling tools [25, 26]. Many Data Warehousing organizations are gathering data from datasets by using Neural networks as a tool for Data Mining. Feedforward Neural Network and Recurrent Neural Network are the Neural Network topologies. A neural network needs to be trained so that the application produces correct output for a particular input. Supervised Learning and Unsupervised Learning are the two ways using which the neural networks can be trained [27].

30.3.10   Association Rule Mining

In Data Mining it is useful for examining and speculating the behavior of the customer. As the set of items present in a transaction is known as market basket so this mining technique is also known as Market basket analysis. It is majorly used in retail sector Association rules to help in uncovering the interrelation among the unrelated data in a relational database [28]. An example of an association rule would be if any buyer purchases a loaf of bread, then he or she is most likely to buy butter also, this expresses, how the items are connected and how they lean to group with each other. Such facts can be used for formulating marketing strategies. This technique has two parameters, support, and confidence, which are used for measuring the strength of a rule. Support measures the frequency of association of items and the confidence shows the strength of association [7]. There are three types of an association rule, that is Single Dimensional, Multi-Dimensional, and Hybrid Association rules. Apriori Algorithm, Eclat Algorithm, and F.P Growth Algorithm are some popular algorithms of this technique.

30.4   Some Implementations of Data Mining in Business

30.4.1   Banking and Finance

It can be used to predict qualified applications for loan/credit card approval, by studying the old customers. Bank will be evaluating the risk, which is there in an individual's loan application. It is one of the most foremost interest of the banks for their longevity in the highly competitive market and for their benefit. Data mining will do the analysis of loan prediction for the right criteria of the loaner, the loaner that can pay the loan with the interest and will give benefit to the bank itself. A large amount of data needs to process and analyzed for knowledge extracting and thus enable the support for loan prediction and decision making [29].

30.4.2   Relationship Management

Identify customers who can be targeted to make new relations. It is a procedure used for foretelling the customer behavior and selecting actions to influence that behavior which would be for the well being and sake of the company. Various services like helpline support or warranty claims, etc. proves to be useful to hold the customer with the brand. The ultimate aim is to discover, allure, and acquire brand new clients, along with nurturing the old ones. In the process, it also focuses on turning down the figure invested for marketing and client service to maximize the net gain. Healthy customer relations will always result in a strong and healthy attachment between the customer and the dedicated brand of the organization. By maneuvering data mining techniques for having these healthy customer relations, many corporations are using this application in their businesses [30].

30.4.3   Targeted Marketing

The right segment of the crowd can be identified which will be correct responders to promotions. By using data mining the companies can study the existing strategies and can also develop a new strategy to increase their growth rate. Companies formulate the strategy for targetting the particular section of the population and thus booming their product in the market [31].

30.4.4   Fraud Detection

Financial affairs or transactions are deliberately studied and from the series of recorded incidents, we try to recognize the deceitful incidents. This is happening because non-cash transactions are increasing. So to prevent this from happening the retailers and banks take necessary steps to detect fraud before its occurrence. Companies have a wealth of transactional and historical fraud data. In a real-world scenario, credit card companies use this technology to identify whether the transactions taken on a credit card are possible or not. By using algorithms, the candidates who can do fraud can be identified and thus the companies can look over them. Fraud tends to occur in patterns and thus by using data mining techniques, the data is processed and the variables which lead to fraud are identified and thus frauds can be prevented from happening [32].

30.4.5   Manufacturing and Production

Its always better to prepare for what is next to come. The productivity of a plant in an enterprise can be analyzed by the management through the reports generated by suitable data mining technique and thus the management can check whether the efficiency goals are being satisfied or not. Whenever a product is launched in the market, companies use data mining techniques to identify the failure and the success rate of their product so that they can automatically do the necessary adjustments when the process parameter changes [33].

30.4.6   Market Basket Analysis

Retail industries are trending with globalization. Data is being collected by everyone during the movement of retail stocks. In terms of parameters like support and confidence, it is analyzed by the analyst whether the purchase of one item is leading to the purchase of another item or not. Market Basket analysis helps to formulate a strategy for allotment of self space, building up a store, and making the promotional strategy of various events and sales [34].

30.4.7   Propensity to Buy

Customers are identified, who are willing to buy and have the money to purchase the manufactured product. It helps in targeting the right customers at the right time. The profitability of the campaigns can be increased by focussing on the customers which are most likely to buy a particular product instead of focussing on the wrong group of customers [35].

30.4.8   Customer Profitability

The main concern is to understand the demand of the customers. Here it means that understanding whether the customer is willing to buy a good quality product whose price is higher in comparison to a cheaper product with low quality. This is a kind of trade-off situation among price and quality. Moreover, this study could give different results for different segments of the population so strategies have to formulated accordingly [36].

30.4.9   Customer Attrition and Channel Optimization

Customer attrition helps in understanding that whether customers are leaving or not. Their behavior could be studied and hence the necessary actions could be taken by the organization to engage the customers with them so that the loss of high-value customers can be prevented in comparison to lower value customers [37].

In channel optimization, the goal is to connect with the customers using a favorable medium. By using Data mining algorithms, the best channels are identified and then used by the organization to get their products to the customers [38].

30.5   Tabulated Attributes of Popular Data Mining Technique

With the advancement in Data mining, different techniques are being used as per the requirement for making profitable business decisions. Based on different Data mining techniques that were introduced in the above sections, a comparison, below is drawn in Table 30.1, showing different attributes of different various Data Mining Techniques, which are being used by firms to take remunerative decisions for their businesses.

The attributes used in the table are briefly explained in the following section.

30.5.1   Classification Analysis

Accuracy rate—Percentage of correct Predictions.

Precision—It is part of accurately calculated affirmative observations among total predicted affirmative observations.

Recall—It is the fraction of accurately interpreted affirmative observation among the total affirmative observations in the class.

F Measure—It is calculated by taking mean harmonically of the Precision and Recall columns.

ROC Area—It shows the predictive representation of the considered classification algorithms.

RMSE—It is the root mean squared error deviation. It is determined by taking the square root of the mean square error. RMSE generally signifies the difference in the estimated and actual value [12].

30.5.2   Clustering

Distance Measures—It indicates the closeness of the group of points in a cluster. $D(x,y)$.

Distance measure axioms—$D(x, x) = 0$; $D(x, y) = D(y, x)$; $D(x, y) \leq D(x, z) + D(z, y)$

Simple Matching Coefficients—Invariant, if the binary variable is symmetric

Jaccard Coefficient—Non-invariant if the binary variable is asymmetric

Nominal variable— >2 states $d(i,j) = (p - u)/p$ Here u denotes number of matches and p denotes number of variables.

Table 30.1 Attributes of Popular Data Mining Techniques in BI.

Techniques	Attributes						
Classification Analysis	Accuracy rate	Precision	Recall	F measure	ROC Area	RMSE (Root Mean Squared Error Deviation)	
Clustering	Distance Measures	Standardization/ Normalization	Simple Matching Coefficients	Jaccard Coefficient	Nominal variable	Ordinal Variable	Ratio Variable
Anomaly or Outlier Detection	Volume	Edge entropy	Graph entropy	Edge Weight Ratio	Average Outward/ Inward Edge Weight		
Regression Analysis	Dependent (Response) Variable	Population Y-Intercept	Population Slopes	Independent (Explanatory) Variables	Random error		
Induction Rule	Criterion	Sample ratio	Pureness	Minimal prune benefit			
Summarization	Transaction Data Set (T)	Current summary (S_c)	Candidate Set (C_c)	Scoring Parameter (k_s)	Increment Parameter	Best Candidate (C_{best})	
Sequential patterns	Item set	Sequence	Event	Length			
Decision tree	Gain Ratio	Gini Index	Entropy	Interpretation	Information Gain	Purity	
Neural Networks	Summer	Threshold Unit	Weight of Connection	Input	Bias	Output	
Association Rule Learning	Support	Confidence					

Ordinal Variable—Order is Important. Example Rank

Ratio Variable—Positive measurement on a nonlinear scale, approximately at an exponential scale such as Ae^{BT} or A^{-BT} [16].

30.5.3   Anomaly or Outlier Detection

Volume—For recognizing abnormality related to an unusually large network.

Edge Entropy—Change in volume of data as well as the change in their underlying classification.

Graph Entropy—This attribute seizes the behavior in which a malware commence communication.

Edge Weight Ratio—Spam messages are checked on the edge.

Average Outward/Inward Edge Weight—Surrounding includes the server which is involved in the anomaly [39].

30.5.4   Regression Analysis

$$Y = \beta_0 X_1 + \beta_1 X_1 + \beta_2 X_2 \ldots\ldots + \beta_p X_p + \varepsilon$$

Dependent (Response) Variable—Y

Population Y-Intercept—β_0 represents the slope

Population Slope—$\beta_1, \beta_2 \ldots \beta_p$. β_1 represents the expected change in the average value of y as a result of one unit change in x.

Independent (Explanatory) Variables—$X_1, X_2 \ldots X_p$

Random error—ε represents the approximate value of y when the value of x is zero [40].

30.5.5   Induction Rule

Criterion—The algorithm follows the greedy approach, so there is a need for a criterion that can evaluate the effect of the addition of a new conjunct on the rule.

Sample ratio—It is the proportion of data used for tutoring in the example set.

Pureness—It denotes the minimum proportion of accuracy desired in the classification rule.

Minimal Prune Benefit—It denotes the percentage rise in the prune metric needed at the minimum [19].

30.5.6   Summarization

For the select-best algorithm Transaction Data Set, Current summary (S_c), Candidate Set (C_c), Scoring Parameter (k_s), Increment Parameter act as an input parameter.

The best Candidate (C_{best}) acts as an output parameter for the best candidate method [41].

30.5.7   Sequential Pattern

Item Set—It contains sequential patterns.

Sequence—It is the sequence of ordered elements.

Event—Consists of a set of items.

Length—It shows the number of instances of items in a sequence [7].

30.5.8   Decision Tree

Gain Ratio—It is an attribute-based on entropy. It is used to calculate information or disorder.

Gini Index—It is another measure for analyzing purity or impurity. Gini impurity is referred to as 1 minus the sum of the squares of the class probabilities of a dataset.

Entropy—$H(S) = -p(+)Log2\ p(+) - p(-)Log2\ p(-)$ bits. Here S is a Subset of training Examples and $p(+)$ / $p(-)$ is the percentage of positive/negative examples in S.

Interpretation—Assume item X belongs to S than interpretation tells us the number of bits required to tell if X is positive or negative.

Information Gain—It shows the decline in entropy, after the splitting of data set on an attribute.

Purity—In pure set (3 yes/3 No), this indicates that there is complete Certainty. In Impure set (4 Yes/0 No), this indicates that there completely uncertainty [42].

30.5.9   Neural Networks

$$Summer = \sum_{i=1}^{n} Xi * Wi + b$$

Threshold Unit—It is used to measure the output of the Neuron. It is a transfer function that works in the output layer.

Weight of Connection—(Wi) It changes input data within the hidden layers of the network.

Input—It denotes the input of the neural network.

Bias—(b) It is an attribute which needed to modulate the output along with the weighted sum of the input.

Output—Neural is a group of neuronal units. Grouping of these units may lead to n Number of Decisions that are based on the input [26].

30.5.10   Association Rule Learning

$$A \geq B$$

Support—It displays the probability of transactions which accommodates both A and B

Confidence—It displays the probability that a transaction accommodating A also contains B [7].

30.6   Conclusion

The goal of BI is to achieve finer conclusions rapidly. To achieve this BI uses different suitable methods and programs of data mining to gather and construct the data, and transform it into information and maneuver that information to enhance business-related decisions. BI takes the large amount of data brought into being by businesses and transforms it into meaningful information on which actions could be taken. BI enables the manager to sail to the desired data on their own and discover whatever they need without depending on the others. Moreover, through the use of BI methods and software, the managers are entitled by having the capability to run analytical reports on enormous data sets of customer information. This will give the potentiality to recognize or even predict the independent customer's or segment's needs, preferences, and habits, moreover this enables the anticipation of new chances to sell, conveying finer services, and even come up with targeted marketing campaigns.

Businesses are growing rapidly by integrating BI with data mining. The time demands to understand the value of a relationship with the customer. Data mining was earlier associated with Data warehouses, which is now being associated with Big Data. Data Mining is today revolving over the three steps, that is, Exploration, Modeling, and Deployment. There are various data mining techniques available for usage, so the challenge is to find the best-suited technique for a particular business requirement which will give expected best output and will contribute to the growth of the organization.

References

1. Indranil Bose, R.K.M., Business data mining—a machine learning perspective. *Inf. Manag.*, 39, 3, 211–225, 2001.
2. BI vs Data Mining: What's the Difference and How Can They Be Used?, 16 November 2018. [Online]. Available: https://datafloq.com/read/bi-data-mining-whats-the-difference-how-used/5698.
3. *Business intelligence*, Wikipedia, United States, 2 December 2019. [Online]. Available: https://en.wikipedia.org/wiki/Business_intelligence.
4. *Data mining*, Wikipedia, United States, 5 December 2019. [Online]. Available: https://en.wikipedia.org/wiki/Data_mining.
5. Peter, A., Data Mining And Its Relevance To Business, 30 November 2018. [Online]. Available: https://analyticstraining.com/data-mining-and-its-relevance-to-business/.
6. Durcevic, S., *The Role Of Data Warehousing In Your Business Intelligence Architecture*, DataPine, Berlin, Germany, 29 May 2019. [Online]. Available: https://www.datapine.com/blog/data-warehousing-and-business-intelligence-architecture/.
7. Data Mining Overview, Association Rule Mining (16.12.10). TIB AV-PORTAL, 8 December 2019. [Online]. Available: https://av.tib.eu/media/333.
8. [Online]. Available: https://st3.ning.com/topology/rest/1.0/file/get/2808314343?profile=original.
9. *Cross-industry standard process for data mining*, Wikipedia, United States, 11 December 2019. [Online]. Available: https://en.wikipedia.org/wiki/Cross-industry_standard_process_for_data_mining.
10. Data Mining Tutorial: Process, Techniques, Tools, Examples, 14 December 2019. [Online]. Available: https://www.guru99.com/data-mining-tutorial.html.

11. Alton, L., The 7 Most Important Data Mining Techniques, 22 December 2017. [Online]. Available: https://www.datasciencecentral.com/profiles/blogs/the-7-most-important-data-mining-techniques.

12. Ünal, D., and Begüm, Ç., Comparison of Data Mining Classification Algorithms Determining the Default Risk. *Hindawi*, 2019, 8, 03 February 2019.

13. Data Mining Concepts—Classification, 15 December 2019. [Online]. Available: https://docs.oracle.com/database/121/DMCON/GUID-3D51EC47-E686-4468-8F49-A27B5F8E8FE4.htm#DMCON004.

14. Clustering Techniques, 16 December 2019. [Online]. Available: http://user.it.uu.se/~kostis/Teaching/DM-05/Slides/clustering1.pdf.

15. Data Mining—Clustering, 17 December 2019. [Online]. Available: https://docs.oracle.com/database/121/DMCON/GUID-7FB17270-54F6-4898-A4F9-319CD94B450B.htm#DMCON008.

16. Data Mining—Clustering, 20 December 2019. [Online]. Available: http://www.cs.put.poznan.pl/jstefanowski/sed/DM-7clusteringnew.pdf.

17. Data Mining Concepts—Regression, 22 December 2019. [Online]. Available: https://docs.oracle.com/database/121/DMCON/GUID-51A08CFC-1487-4887-AB47-794C50D67358.htm#DMCON005.

18. Data Mining Concepts—Anomaly Detection, 23 December 2019. [Online]. https://docs.oracle.com/database/121/DMCON/GUID-D9D23B6C-5215-4E37-80E3-F2460D82A533.htm#DMCON006.

19. *Rule Induction*, Elsevier's Science Direct, Amsterdam, Netherlands, 25 December 2019. [Online]. Available: https://www.sciencedirect.com/topics/computer-science/rule-induction.

20. *Explain data discretization and summarization*, Ques10, Mumbai, Maharashtra, 2016, [Online]. Available: https://www.ques10.com/p/160/explain-data-discretization-and-summarization/.

21. Sequence Pattern Mining & Time Series, 03 January 2011. [Online]. Available: https://av.tib.eu/media/329?hl=sequence+pattern+mining.

22. *Regression analysis*, Wikipedia, United States, 20 December 2019. [Online]. Available: https://en.wikipedia.org/wiki/Regression_analysis.

23. Data Mining Concepts—Decision Tree, 21 December 2019. [Online]. Available: https://docs.oracle.com/database/121/DMCON/GUID-14DE1A88-220F-44F0-9AC8-77CA844D4A63.htm#DMCON019.

24. From a Single Decision Tree to a Random Forest, 21 December 2019. 2019, [Online]. Available: https://www.knime.com/blog/from-a-single-decision-tree-to-a-random-forest.

25. Patrizio, A., Top 15 Data Mining Techniques for Business Success, 22 February 2019. [Online]. Available: https://www.datamation.com/big-data/data-mining-techniques.html.

26. Gill, N.S., *Artificial Neural Networks Applications and Algorithms*, Xenonstack, Chandigarh, India, 01 March 2019. [Online]. Available: https://www.xenonstack.com/blog/artificial-neural-network-applications/.

27. Yashpal Singh, S.C., Neural Networks in Data Mining. *J. Theor. Appl. Inf. Technol.*, 5, 6, 2010.

28. Data Mining Concepts—Association, 21 December 2019. [Online]. Available: https://docs.oracle.com/database/121/DMCON/GUID-491998B3-B92B-4F84-8A79-94780B8AFD0C.htm#DMCON009.

29. Benati, M., Data Mining in Banks and Financial Institutions, 08 November 2011. [Online]. Available: https://www.rightpoint.com/thought/2011/11/08/data-mining-in-banks-and-financial-institutions.

30. Chua, F., How Data Mining Helps Improve Customer Relationship Management Process, 2 May 2018. [Online]. Available: http://customerthink.com/how-data-mining-helps-improve-customer-relationship-management-process/.

31. How Data Mining Can Help Advertisers Hit Their Targets, 09 March 2017. [Online]. Available: https://knowledge.wharton.upenn.edu/article/how-data-mining-can-help-advertisers/.

32. Wikipedia, Data analysis techniques for fraud detection, 7 December 2019. [Online]. Available: https://en.wikipedia.org/wiki/Data_analysis_techniques_for_fraud_detection.

33. Thelwell, R., 5 real life applications of Data Mining and Business Intelligence, 2 June 2015. [Online]. Available: https://www.matillion.com/resources/blog/5-real-life-applications-of-data-mining-and-business-intelligence/.

34. Data Mining Applications For Business Intelligence, 7 December 2019. [Online]. Available: https://www.egafutura.com/wiki-en/data-mining-applications.

35. Levin, Ö.A.a.D., *How to Use Predictive Purchase Behavior Modeling to Understand Consumers*, HubSpot, Cambridge, United States, 25 November 2015. [Online]. Available: https://blog.hubspot.com/agency/predictive-analytics-buy.

36. McNab, D., *What is Customer Profitability and Why Should We Measure It?*, Canadian Marketing Association, Toronto, 2 December 2019. [Online]. Available: https://www.the-cma.org/disciplines/analytics/archive/what-is-customer-profitability.

37. Marx, A., Customer retention analytics: 5 strategies to reduce churn with data, getthematic, 06 December 2018. [Online]. Available: https://getthematic.com/insights/5-ways-data-and-text-analytics-improve-customer-retention/.

38. Levey, R.H., Using Data to Channel-Optimize Marketing, Chief Marketer, 14 February 2012. [Online]. Available: https://www.chiefmarketer.com/using-data-to-channel-optimize-marketing/.

39. Anomaly Detection to Predict Credit Card Fraud, 06 June 2019. [Online]. Available: https://www.ukdiss.com/examples/predict-credit-card-fraud-anomaly-detection.php.

40. Machine Learning—Linear (Regression|Model), 24 December 2019. [Online]. Available: https://datacadamia.com/data_mining/linear_regression.

41. V. Chandola and V. Kumar, "Summarization - compressing data into an informative representation," *Fifth IEEE International Conference on Data Mining (ICDM'05)*, Houston, TX, pp. 8 pp.-, 2005, doi: 10.1109/ICDM.2005.137.

42. Decision tree learning, Wikipedia, 25 December 2019. [Online]. Available: https://en.wikipedia.org/wiki/Decision_tree_learning.

Part 5

LATEST TRENDS IN SUSTAINABLE COMPUTING TECHNIQUES

31

Survey on Data Deduplication Techniques for Securing Data in Cloud Computing Environment

Ashima Arya[1]*, Vikas Kuchhal[1]† and Karan Gulati[2]‡

[1]CSE Dept., B.M Institute of Engineering & Technology, Sonipat, India
[2]B.M Institute of Engineering & Technology, Sonipat, India

Abstract

In recent years, the growth of data is generated at a very high speed by number of consumers. Cloud Computing comes up with a solution of storing that data without expanding so much cost. Deduplication is finding the duplicate data when compared with one or more data base or data sets. This paper explained and categorizes data deduplication techniques applied on stored data in distributed computing condition to provide security when database size expands. In this study the authors elaborated the coordinating procedures of scrambled information and open difficulties for information deduplication.

Keywords: Techniques, cloud computing, cloud service provider, data deplication, security and challenges, features of cloud computing, threats and attacks

31.1   Cloud Computing

31.1.1   Introduction

Cloud computing is a computing technique used for the portage of hosted services via Internet [1]. Cloud computing depends on distributing quantify resources and hardware's rather than having personal devices or local servers to handle different types of applications offered by Cloud Service Providers(CSPs) [2]. Distributed computing has changed the manner in which figuring and programming administrations are conveyed to the clients as indicated by their necessities and prerequisites. Standard meaning of this processing system is characterized by The National Organization of Guidelines and as "a model that encourages convenient and dynamic access to an enormous pool of registering assets that can be shared, powerfully dispensed, and released absent a lot of administrative contribution or specialist co-ops help" [4].

---

*Corresponding author: ashiarya@gmail.com
†Corresponding author: vikas.kuchhal@gmail.com
‡Corresponding author: kgulati141@gmail.com

Namita Gupta, Prasenjit Chatterjee and Tanupriya Choudhury (eds.) Smart and Sustainable Intelligent Systems, (445–460)

Table 31.1 Characteristics of cloud computing.

S. No.	Features	Description
1	Self Service	The client can request any resource, platform or service according to their need in a pay go manner.
2	Pay-per-use	Services provided by the CSPs are priced per use way [3].
3	Elasticity	Services and resources are used and released according to the feasibility of the users [3].
4	Customization	Resources taken by the user must be highly customized i.e. allowing users to deploy specialized virtual appliances and privileged access to the virtual service [3].

31.1.2   Cloud Computing Features

The characteristics of cloud computing is described in Table 31.1.

31.1.3   Services Provided by Cloud Computing

There are few services provided by the Cloud to their clients according to their usage, resources, platform and data [6] shown in Table 31.2.

   a.   Software-as-a-Service (SaaS)
   b.   Platform-as-a-Service(PaaS)
   c.   Infrastructure-as-a-Service(IaaS)
   d.   Hardware-as-a-Service (HaaS)
   e.   Data-as-a-Service (DaaS).

Table 31.2 Services provided by cloud computing.

	Services	Description
1	Software-as-a-Service (SaaS)	In this type of model a user can access any software and application via internet using an interface.
2	Platform-as-a-Service (PaaS)	This model offers platforms for deployment of software and application created by users.
3	Infrastructure-as-a-Service (IaaS)	This model provides infrastructure such as computing, storing and networking to users.
4	Hardware-as-a-Service (HaaS)	These models allow users to access hardware resources.
5	Data-as-a-Service (DaaS)	This model will provide valid data to the authorized users.

Table 31.3 Types of clouds.

	Type	Description
1	Public	All the assets can be effectively accessible to the client by the cloud administration gave as pay-go way.
2	Private	As its name, only data is available to the particular organization and only that organization can maintain and control its data.
3	Hybrid	Features of public and private clouds are combined in this approach.

31.1.4 Types of Clouds Based on Deployment Model

On the basis of deployment model, cloud can be classified into three types as public, private or hybrid [7]. Table 31.3 shows the types of Clouds which are used by the clients according their requirements and needs.

31.1.5 Cloud Computing Security Challenges

31.1.5.1 Infrastructure-as-a-Service (IaaS)

CSP has the apparatus and in peril for housing, running conjointly, dealing with it. All through this model, customer pays on per-use premise. Properties and components of IaaS include

- Organization Level Getting
- Dynamic scaling
- Motorization of regulative assignments
- Utility enrolling organization and charging model
- Net connective
- Work space virtualization.

The virtualization risks and vulnerabilities that impact especially IaaS transport model are: Security dangers sourced from

a) Checking VMs from the administration reason in virtual condition is that the host machine will have the proposals that let the host to screen and talk with VM applications up running. During this way, it's increasingly more indispensable to thoroughly make sure about the host machines than making certain particular VMs. VM-level affirmation is huge in disseminated processing condition. The undertaking will co-discover applications with shifted trust levels on partner equivalent host and will protect VMs during a typical multi-inhabitant condition. This award dares to intensify the upsides of virtualization. VM-level protection licenses VMs to remain secure inside the blessing ground-breaking server ranches. Moreover, as VMs travel between differed things from on-premise virtual servers to non-open fogs to open fogs, and even between cloud sellers [25].

b) Correspondences among VMs and the information is this way the host stream between VMs shared virtual resources; very the host will screen the framework traffic of its own speed up VMs. This can concede significant features for attackers which they will use it like normal composing board which permits data to move among VMs and during this way the host using participating harmful program in VMs [22]. It isn't unremarkably seen as a bug or requirement at the reason once one will start attentive, change, or correspondence with a VM application. The host condition ought to be a great deal of thoroughly made certain worried than the individual VMs. The host will affect the VMs inside the related ways:

- The host will Start, shutdown, delay, and restart VMs.
- Checking and plan of benefits that are available to the VMs, these include: focal preparing unit, memory, plate, and framework utilization of VMs.
- Change the quantity of CPUs which includes memory and number of virtual plates, and collection of virtual compose interfaces that are available to a VM.
- Checking the applications that are running inside the VM.
- View, copy, and certainly adjust, data place away on the VM's virtual circles.

Security dangers sourced from other VM

a) Checking VMs from elective VM Checking VMs may manhandle security and assurance, by the new style of CPUs, incorporated with a memory protection feature, may thwart security and insurance encroachment. A major explanation behind hold virtualization is to disengage security mechanical assemblies from partner untrusted VM by moving them to a particular trusted in secure VM [20].

b) Correspondence between VMs one among the foremost fundamental strings that bargain mercantilism data between virtual machines is that the way by that it's sent. Sharing resources between VMs may strip security of each VM as partner model facilitated exertion using application key shared composing board that let mercantilism information between VMs, this situation misuse security and assurance. In like manner, a malicious VM will have opportunity to initiate to totally unique VMs through shared memory [25].

c) Renouncing of Organization (DoS): A DoS attack we have an inclination cost be partner making an endeavour to dismissal organizations that give to endorse customers to model though making an endeavor to actuate to site we see that feeling to over-troubling of the server with the requesting to instigate to the domain, we won't to initiate to the domain and watch erroneous conclusion. This occurs at the reason once the live of requesting which can be dealt with by a server outperforms its capacity, the DoS ambush stepping pulling a piece of fogs inconvenient to prevail in to the clients [20]. Use of a (IDS) one in all the valuable technique for obstruction against this kind of attacks.

Practical courses of action and methodology for slaughtering these ambushes or diminishing their belongings are recorded as follows:

1. Reliable framework division
2. Firewalls realizing

3. Traffic cryptography
4. Framework checking.

31.1.5.2   Platform-as-a-Service (PaaS)

PaaS is partner way to deal with rent instrumentation over the net, PaaS give capacity to oversee application while not presenting any stage or mechanical assemblies on their nearby machines, PaaS suggests giving stage layer resources along with working structure support and programming progression frameworks during which it will allow to create more elevated level organizations,

There are s differed ideal conditions from PaaS

- programming bundle working structure might be changed and refreshed a comparable scope of your time as might want.
- PaaS permit topographically sent groups to sharing information to make programming adventures.

31.1.5.3   Software-as-a-Service (SaaS)

SaaS in like manner alluded to as "programming for the asking" using SaaS supplier licenses partner application to customers either on demand through a participation or at no charge and this consider some segment of utility critical thinking model, where all advancement inside the cloud must be constrained to over web as organization. SaaS was essentially normally sent for bargains power robotization and purchaser Relationship the officials (CRM). By and by, it's become fundamental spot for a couple, business assignments, counting machine-controlled charging, invoicing, human quality the board, financials, report the officials, organization work space the administrators and collaboration. Software as an encourage applications square measure get to using internet browsers over the net [26]. Along these lines, internet browser security is fundamentally imperative. Data security officials should regarding |contemplate totally various ways for making sure about SaaS applications. web Organizations (WS) security, Extendable terminology (XML) encoding, Secure Connection Layer (SSL) and available options that square measure used in executing information protection transmitted over the net. The pro association needs to affirm their various customers don't manhandles assurance of different customers, similarly it's extraordinarily essential for buyer to validate that the correct wellbeing endeavours square measure began mean while it's difficult to actuate an affirmation that the machine will be open once required.

SaaS security hazard is aggregate up as:

- Check and endorsement
- Information mystery
- Availability
- Data security
- Information get to
- Information breaks
- Disposition the administrators and sign in technique.

Navneet Singh [19] arranged right rational responses for valuate the assurance threats in SaaS during which the shopper ought to be asked:

- What estimations are used for uncovering?
- What's the level of access controls?
- Is that the given information is successfully balanced inside the inside checking gadgets?
- Anyway crucial and essential the endeavor information is?

31.1.5.4   Hardware-as-a-Service (HaaS)

Equipment as an assistance (HaaS) alludes to oversaw administrations or matrix figuring, where registering power is rented from a local supplier. For each situation, the HaaS model is like other help based models, where clients lease, instead of procurement, a supplier's tech resources. Techopedia clarifies Equipment as a Help (HaaS). HaaS fills the accompanying needs in oversaw administrations:

It includes an agreement for the upkeep and organization of equipment frameworks. This sort of administration might be remote or on location, contingent upon the equipment arrangement necessities. It assists clients with overseeing equipment permitting necessities.

In aggregate registering situations, HaaS members frequently use Web Convention (IP) associations with use the figuring intensity of remote equipment. A client sends information to a supplier, and the supplier's equipment performs essential activities to the information and afterward sends back the outcomes. These sorts of understanding help singular organizations rent processing power, as opposed to put resources into extra on location equipment.

Probably the most well-known kinds of HaaS models are delegated distributed computing administrations, in which information stockpiling media and even dynamic processing equipment are segments of a remotely provisioned administration for clients [28].

31.1.5.5   Data-as-a-Service (DaaS)

Data as an encourage (DaaS) might be a data course of action and spread model during which information archives (checking content, pictures, sounds, and chronicles) are made open to customers over a framework, commonly the net. The model uses a cloud-based rudimentary advancement that underpins web organizations and SOA (organization sorted out designing). DaaS data is place away inside the cloud and is open through shifted contraptions. The organization moreover offloads the disadvantages of information the officials to the cloud supplier.

Data as an assistance (DaaS) might be a cloud approach wont to support the transparency of business-essential information in an inside and out arranged, guaranteed and moderate methods. DaaS relies on the standard that predefined, significant information will be given to customers to the soliciting, independent of any definitive or geographic separation among clients and providers.

DaaS executes reiteration and lessens associated utilizations by obliging basic information during a lone space, permitting information use and what's more change by shifted customers through a singular update reason. At first utilized in web mashups, the DaaS framework is normally utilized by business associations. DaaS thinks about, anyway needn't bother with, the unit of information worth and use from programming or stage worth and use. A few DaaS merchants, with totally unique assessing models, exist round the world [27].

31.2   Data Deduplication

31.2.1   Data Deduplication Introduction

The cloud computing provide facilities to manage resources, software and personal data with high reliability and security control [8]. Same data may be uploaded by the different users which may cause anomalous increase of data [9]. For this problem, technology comes up with a solution i.e. deduplication technique. This technique reduces the cloud space so that it can able to store more large datasets.

Deduplication of information might be a strategy utilized for "dispensing with excess documents or extra fine grain squares of information."

31.2.2   Key Design Criteria for Deduplication Techniques

From the survey of this study four key plan choices are recognized regular to all protected deduplication frameworks as information granularity, deduplication area, stockpiling engineering, and the cloud administration model.

31.2.2.1   Information Granularity

In data granularity, data is partitioned into different parts known as block for the elimination of duplicates [11]. Table 31.4 shows the different ways of partition such as

    a. File-level deduplication
    b. Block-level deduplication.

From the audit we have found that square level deduplication has a higher deduplication extent than record level deduplication and offers commonly low overhead in keeping up the metadata [12].

Table 31.4 Different Ways of Partition.

Partition	Description
File-level Deduplication	This methodology is considered as the essential technique. In this procedure hash work is utilized. Hash mark of the information accessible in a record are figured and contrasted with locate the copy information in a document.
Block-level Deduplication	Substance of a record is partitioned into squares and copy worth will be removed from each square. Two methodologies are utilized to separate records into hinders as a) Fixed-size piecing: A document is separated into equivalent fixed-size squares, and afterward hash calculation is applied to each square. b) Variable-size piecing: utilizes Rabin fingerprinting as a calculation to create hash marks.

Table 31.5 Deduplication Locations.

Location	Description
Server Side	Deduplication is done at the server side after receiving the data by CSP and eliminate from that data only.
Client Side	Deduplication is done by the client with the help of hash counts. A client at first figures a hash a motivating force for the data to be moved and sends it to the CSP before moving the genuine substance of the data. The CSP by then checks whether a comparable hash regard exists away.
Passage Side	Deduplication uses stockpiling passages to execute deduplication. The door performs deduplication alongside a CSP in the interest of the customer.

31.2.2.2   Deduplication Area

Data deduplication can be performed on three region destinations as the server side, client side, and section side [13]. These unmistakable region sides are explained in Table 31.5.

The benefit of Customer Side Deduplication is to diminish arrange transmission capacity utilization when contrasted with Server-Side deduplication [14].

31.2.2.3   System Architecture

Two cloud system architectures are used for secure deduplication

    a.   Single cloud system architecture
    b.   Multi cloud system architectures described in Table 31.6.

Single cloud system architecture is used by CSPs such as

    a.   Dropbox
    b.   Google Drive
    c.   Mozy.

Multi cloud system architecture is used by CSPs such as

    a.   RAIDer
    b.   CDStore.

Table 31.6 System Architecture.

System architecture	Description
Single Cloud System Architecture	It constructs a single CSP for storage.
Multi Cloud System Architecture	It constructs multiple CSPs for storage for dispersing the user's data.

Table 31.7 Duplicate Check Boundary.

Duplicate Check Boundary	Description
Intrauser	In this approach, the duplicate data is found out only when it has been outsourced in the cloud storage.
Interuser	In this methodology, copy information is discovered from all put away information over various information proprietors in the distributed storage.

The upside of this methodology over single cloud is one purpose of disappointment and seller lock-in [15]. The information is repeated and separated into various offers [16]. These offers are conveyed and handled by deletion codes like the Reed–Solomon code, as an essential unit for checking copies.

31.2.2.4   Duplicate Check Boundary

Another parameter for categorizing deduplication technique is duplicate check boundary. Two approaches are used for duplicate check boundary shown in Table 31.7 as

    a. Intrauser
    b. Interuser.

Intrauser deduplication approach is utilized where copies are probably going to be found among rehashed reinforcements made by a solitary client.

Interuser deduplication is useful where countless copies exists among information possessed by various clients in a similar association, for example, business records, VM pictures.

31.3   Literature Review

Supriya E. More and *Sharmila S. Gaikwad* distinguish consistent data frames and lessens them to one example to abstain from squandering volume inside the walled in area arrange. To brought ensure secure deduplication up in cloud, this examination paper plate secure deduplication for picture, content and video.

Jin Li, Xiaofeng Chen, Mingqiang Li, Jingwei Li, Patrick P.C. Lee, and *Wenjing Lou* endeavor to officially address the matter of accomplishing conservative and dependable key administration in secure deduplication. We watch out for first present a gauge approach inside which each client holds an independent key for encoding the focused keys and redistributing them to the cloud. Nonetheless, such a standard key administration topic produces a gigantic assortment of keys with the expanding assortment of clients and requirements clients to dedicatedly safeguard the ace keys.

Young-joo Shin, Dongyoung Koo, and *Junbeom Hur* examine current investigation on secure deduplication for cloud data in thought of the assault inevitabilities misused most by and large in distributed storage. On the possibility of arrangement of deduplication framework, we will in general investigate security dangers and assault projections from each inside and outside enemies.

Dr. G. Sushmitha Valli and *Harika Arete*: data pressure and deduplication are 2 crucial procedures used by cloud administration providers (CSPs) to improve usage of territory away media. data deduplication may result at document level or square level. Deduplication is likewise made at flexibly or the objective completion. Graceful deduplication expends extra procedure force and it gets inconvenient to deal with it with existing assets.

Dutch T. Meyer and *William J. Bolosky* gathered documenting framework content data from 857 PCs at Microsoft over a range of about a month. We tend to break down the data to see the overall viability of data deduplication, altogether considering entire record versus square level end of excess.

G. Prof. Mahesh utilization of distributed storage stage for capacity and procedure, there's a developing interest of some component or philosophy which can offer the capacity of taking out excess data and in this manner accomplishing higher zone and data measure necessities of capacity administrations.

Jan Stanek, *Alessandro Sorniotti*, and *Elli Androulaki*, present an extraordinary idea that separates data in accordance with their quality. bolstered this thought, we will in general style an encoding subject that ensures etymology security for less-voyaged data and gives more fragile security and higher stock piling and data measure points of interest for in style data. Along these lines, data deduplication might be successful for in style data, while semantically secure encoding ensures less-voyaged content.

Manish Reddy and *Dr. K. Rajendra Prasad* assessed various calculations and strategies on secure deduplication approaches through efficient and dependable procedures. The discovering show that a blend of made sure about deduplications approaches with expanded safety efforts would give uncommon security decisions to a thriving and solid de-duplication.

Mark W. Storer, *Kevin M. Greenan*, *Darrell D.E. Long* and *E.L. Miller* built up an answer that has every data security and zone strength in single-server stockpiling and disseminated stockpiling frameworks. Encoding keys are created during a reliable way from the lump information; in this way, indistinguishable pieces can perpetually encipher to a comparable cipher text. In addition, the keys cannot be found from the encoded piece data.

31.4　Assessment Rules of Secure Deduplication Plans

Secure deduplication plans region unit assessed as far as 2 variables:

(a) The security properties that each subject gives
(b) The framework overheads acquired on a CSP and a customer.

As to insurance threats, a secure deduplication subject is expected to fulfil the resulting security properties:

(1) Secrecy: the underlying information content redistributed to distributed storage mustn't be unveiled to anybody with the exception of the client UN organization possesses the data.
(2) Accessibility: The re-appropriated information ought to be available to clients UN organization own the data, even all through framework disappointment.

(3) Side-channel obstruction: In customer side deduplication frameworks, it should be impractical to discover any information concerning re-appropriated information by attentive deduplication traffic over the system.

(4) Ownership credibility: In customer side deduplication frameworks, exclusively a real shopper (or a client) UN organization has the underlying information should be confirmed as partner bona fide proprietor of the redistributed information inside the distributed storage.

(5) Information respectability: A shopper or CSP should be prepared to check that the re-appropriated data has not been changed or erased by enemies.

Applying secure deduplication could bring about some ineluctable costs for CSPs. Hence, each topic is furthermore assessed with pertinence execution and power inside the accompanying viewpoints [24]:

(1) Calculation overhead
(2) Stockpiling overhead
(3) Correspondence overhead.

31.5   Open Security Problems and Difficulties

Albeit broad analysis has tackled varied problems with relation to the protection, protection, also, unwavers quality during a cloud deduplication framework, there still keep intriguing and essential open analysis difficulties.

31.5.1   Data Ownership the Board

Because of restrictive the administrators and forswearing, expect that different customers have obligation regarding cipher text re-appropriated to conveyed capacity. As time sneaks past, numerous customers could request the CSP to eradicate or adjustment their information, and furthermore the CSP around then deletes the ownership information on the customers from the exclusive rundown for the relating information. The unacknowledged customers should then be whole from intending to the information place away inside the appropriated stockpiling once the undoing or adjustment request. On the other hand, when a customer moves information that starting at as of now exists inside the conveyed stockpiling, the purchaser got the opportunity to be blocked from accessing the information that was place away before the individual got exclusive by moving it. These dynamic exclusive changes could happen plenteous of the time during a modest cloud system, and during this way it got the chance to be intentionally discovered the best approach to keep one's eyes off from the assurance corruption of the cloud organization.

Notwithstanding, the past deduplication plans haven't had the decision to achieve secure access the board during a situation with a novel belonging adjustment in spite of its noteworthiness to make certain in regards to deduplication, in lightweight of the undeniable reality that the cryptography key in most existing secure deduplication plans is gathered deterministically and once during a while new once the fundamental key assurance [19]. During this implies, to that degree as denied customers keep the cryptography key, they'll get to the relating information inside the dispersed stockpiling at whatever point, regardless of the authenticity of their ownership. Thus, information restrictive the board and disavowal is one endeavouring open issue for secure deduplication.

31.5.2   Achieving Semantically Secure Deduplication

Semantically secure coding plans engage customers who care with respect to assurance to imprint their information on the client feature. Be that since it may, the honest utilization of semantics coding may make deduplication unconventional, as all free cipher texts territory unit most likely to be made from undefined records. During this way, pleasing deduplication and semantically secure coding could be an intense investigation reason. Metallic component could be a thriving course of action, anyway it's vulnerable to detached creature power ambushes on the hash of the information, eminently once the information is obvious, in light-weight of the very actuality that the coding is settled (i.e., not semantically secure).

One ground-breaking announce achieve semantically secure deduplication is to permit a basic up loader to figure his information with an aimlessly created coding key and circularize it just to buyers who share comparable information securely Unfortunately, a portion of the plans need the guide of at least one further outside KSs, that could be a strong notion that is depleting to satisfy in accommodating cloud structures also, zone unit even vulnerable to on-line creature power attacks [30].

31.5.3   POW in Decentralized Deduplication Structures

Redistributed information when deduplication is possibly advancing to be vulnerable against data hardship or lack of sanitization since information deduplication techniques keep just 1 copy of the information as antagonistic golf stroke away fluctuated copies. To deal with the obligation of re-appropriated data, a decentralized philosophy has been late focus of examination. Decentralized deduplication plans are applied to multicloud ability style, that unites shifted circulated capacity organizations into a single warehousing organization. Their work has fundamentally focused around considering settled IDAs that change data into shifted settled proposals with some reiteration and disperse the proposals over differed CSPs. These philosophies ensure re-appropriated data against information griminess to a chose degree and proceed with security from inside adversaries, along with the CSP. Be that since it may, they cannot be solidly applied to customer aspect deduplication structures in a very multi cloud style. A POW plan is required for customer feature deduplication to prevent outside enemies mounting spillage ambush or unapproved data access by using deduplication. The security of POW is frequently dependent upon the min-entropy of the decentralized information in a point of view on outside adversaries. when information with min-entropy k is dispersed into n shares, each gracefully has min-entropy ki with the tip objective that $ki \leq k$ what's extra, $I = n$ $i = 1$ $ki = k$. For adversaries, breaking the POW for each gracefully severally, which is a partition and-beat method, might be a store simpler than breaking it for the total particular data while not a second's postponement. Thusly, the best level of POW security for the re-appropriated data can't be guaranteed in a very multicloud designing. we must to boot address this issue to achieve efficiency gets using decentralized customer aspect deduplication structures while to boot making certain security and availability [16].

31.5.4   New Security Risks on Deduplication

Few new sorts of security risks which will be given to conveyed capacity frameworks once deduplication techniques are applied. Inside the underlying spot permit us to consider a situation any place deduplication are regularly capably sceptre or incapacitated for the inquiring. In such movable deduplication, a dispersed stockpiling system could be powerless against information spillage ambush by adversaries.

For the subsequent security chance, permit us to consider a disseminated stockpiling structure that supports unplanned see and make sq. activities. Handling deduplication to the ability any place each observe and create exercises are visit makes imperative execution defilement the shrouded reposition system. Around then, by abusing the introduction overhead of deduplication, these new sorts of attack haven't been thought of anyway inside the composition, and later we tend to make do with that these issues are similarly essential issues for secure deduplication as promising future work [31].

31.6   Conclusion

Data deduplication is a secure technique for data redundancy and maintaining the security of cloud data. In this paper, we have explained and categorize the deduplication techniques according to the key design criteria. This approach provides secure dedeuplication according to the cloud computing environment for diverse the range of threats.

References

1. Mei, L., Chan, W.K., Tse, T.H., A tale of clouds: Paradigm comparisons and some thoughts on research issues, in: *Asia-Pacific Services Computing Conference, AP-SCC*, IEEE, pp. 464–469, 2008.
2. Baliga, J., Ayre, R.W., Hinton, K., Tucker, R.S., Green cloud computing: Balancing energy in processing, storage, and transport. *Proc. IEEE*, 99, 1, 149–167, 2011.
3. Singh, A. and Hemalatha, M., Cloud computing for academic environment. *Int. J. Inf. Commun. Technol. Res.*, 97–101, 2012.
4. Rimal, B.P., Choi, E., Lumb, I., A taxonomy and survey of cloud computing systems. *INC, IMS and IDC*, vol. 9, pp. 44–51, 2009.
5. Wang, Z., Shuang, K., Yang, L., Yang, F., Energy-aware and revenue-enhancing Combinatorial Scheduling in Virtualized of Cloud Datacenter. *J. Converg. Inf. Technol.*, 7, 1, 62–70, 2012.
6. Teng, F., *Management of Data and Scheduling of Tasks on Architecture Distributees*, (Ph.D. thesis), 2011.
7. Takabi, H., Joshi, J.B., Ahn, G.J., Security and privacy challenges in cloud computing environments. *IEEE Secur. Priv.*, 8, 6, 24–31, 2010.
8. Marti, A., Dan, B., Ilya, M., Ananth, R., Gil, S., Message-locked encryption for lock-dependent messages, in: *Advances in Cryptology—CRYPTO 2013. Lecture Notes in Computer Science*, vol. 8042, pp. 374–391, Springer, 2013.

9. Hussam, A., Lonnie, P., Hakim, W., RACS: A case for cloud storage diversity, in: *Proceedings of the 1st ACM Symposium on Cloud Computing*, pp. 229–240, 2010.

10. Blasco, J., Di Pietro, R., Orfila, A., Sorniotti, A., A Tunable Proof Of Ownership Scheme For Deduplication Using Bloom Filters. *IEEE Conference on Communications and Network Security (CNS'14)*, pp. 481–489, 2014.

11. Deepak, R., Jagannathan, S.B., Cezary, D., Improving duplicate elimination in storage systems. *ACM Trans. Storage*, 2, 4, 424–448, 2006.

12. Broder, A.Z., Identifying and filtering near-duplicate documents, in: *Combinatorial Pattern Matching. Lecture Notes in Computer Science*, LNCS, vol. 1848, pp. 1–10, Springer, 2000, http://dx.doi.org/10.1007/3-540-45123-4_1.

13. Egorova, D. and Zhidchenko, V., Visual parallel programming as PaaS cloud service with graph-symbolic programming technology. *Proc. Inst. Syst. Program. RAS*, 3, 47–56, 2015.

14. Paulo, J. and José, P., A survey and classification of storage deduplication systems. *ACM Comput. Surv.*, 47, 1, 1–30, 2014, http://dx.doi.org/10.1145/2611778.

15. Dutch, T. and Bolosky, W.J., A study of practical deduplication. *ACM Trans. Storage*, 7, 4, 1–20, 2012.

16. Sharkey, S. and Zewari, H., Alt-POW: An alternative proof-of-work mechanism. *IEEE International Conference on Decentralized Applications and Infrastructures (DAPPCON)*, 2019.

17. Nesrine, K. and Maryline, L., A secure client side deduplication scheme in cloud storage environments. *6th International Conference on New Technologies, Mobility, and Security (NTMS'14)*, 2014.

18. Ibikunle, A., Cloud Computing Security Issues and Challenges. *Int. J. Comput. Netw. (IJCN)*, 3, 5, 2014.

19. Navneet Singh, P., Software as a Service (SaaS): Security issues and Solutions. *Int. J. Comput. Eng. Res. (IJCER)*, 04, 2250–3005, 2014.

20. Archana, K. and Patil, M.S., Secure data Deduplication with dynamic ownership management in cloud storage. *Int. J. Trend Sci. Res. Dev.*, 2, 4, 2273–2277, 2018.

21. Thulo, M.I. and Eloff, J.H.P., Towards optimized security-aware (O-sec) VM placement algorithms. *Proceedings of the 3rd International Conference on Information Systems Security and Privacy*, 2017.

22. Runge, L., Security and data integrity in a client-server environment. *Inf. Syst. Secur.*, 3, 1, 45–56, 1994.

23. VMS mean and minimum utilization VM selection algorithm for cloud Datacenter. *Int. J. Recent Technol. Eng.*, 8, 5S, 63–67, 2020.

24. Jayant, S., An analysis on security concerns and their possible solutions in cloud computing environment. *3rd International Conference on Role of Engineers as Entrepreneurs in Current Scenario—2014 (ICREECS-2014)*, 2014.

25. Stavrinides, G.L. and Karatza, E., Scheduling different types of applications in a SaaS cloud. *Proceedings of the Sixth International Symposium on Business Modeling and Software Design*, 2016.

26. Aftab, S., Afzal, H., Khalid, A., An approach for secure semantic data integration at data as a service (DaaS) layer. *Int. J. Inf. Educ. Technol.*, 5, 2, 124–130, 2015.

27. Stanik, A., Hovestadt, M., Kao, O., Hardware as a service (Haas): Physical and virtual hardware on demand. *4th IEEE International Conference on Cloud Computing Technology and Science Proceedings*, 2012.

28. Shahzad, A. and Hussain, M., Security issues and challenges of mobile cloud computing. *Int. J. Grid Distrib. Comput.*, 6, 6, 37–50, 2013.

29. Hemalatha, S., A secure access policies based data. Deduplication System. *Int. J. Res. Appl. Sci. Eng. Technol.*, 7, 3, 463–465, 2019.

30. Kaaniche, N. and Laurent, M., A secure client side Deduplication scheme in cloud storage environments. *2014 6th International Conference on New Technologies, Mobility and Security (NTMS)*, 2014.

32

Procedural Music Generation

Punya Aachman*, Piyush Aggarwal and Pushkar Goel

Maharaja Agrasen Institute of Technology, New Delhi, India

Abstract

This paper proposes an approach towards procedural generation of music which can be used by a person without any musical knowledge. This can be used to create recreational music according to a person's disposition. It can also be used in professional capacity to make music of different genres by content creators, game developers, animators and/or musicians to quickly create music loops, ambient/background sounds, gameplay music or even film scores with an interface providing control over each parameter to generate limitless variations. It takes inputs such as mood, intensity, pace and duration to create the music of desired effect. The proposed approach creates the required music with competent complexity and smooth timber. This can be verified with the results embedded in the paper. The future research can be focused on adding more variables for producing more complex music as well as making the process real time for easier understanding of the model.

Keywords: Procedural, music, generative, progression, phase, pattern, chords, orchestral

32.1 Introduction

Music has become instrumental in assisting and even dictating flow and mood of any event.

Its usage has become widespread and often acts as a key distinguishing feature which can resonate with the audience and amplify the intensity as well as the ambience of the affair. Hence a lot of effort, time and money is directed towards manual generation of musical score.

By utilizing the proposed approach, music can be generated without any professional help or music knowledge.

This thus enables a person to create music in accordance with their purpose by choosing the kind of effect and not to be bothered with the technical aspects of music generation.

It leads to lesser use of resources, time and efforts. It also allows them to focus only on the creative aspects and need not be concerned with the technical aspects. Abstraction of music generation is thereby facilitated by this, helping users to only focus on the type of music and not the proceedings for the job.

**Corresponding author*: aachman98@gmail.com

Namita Gupta, Prasenjit Chatterjee and Tanupriya Choudhury (eds.) Smart and Sustainable Intelligent Systems, (461–468)
© 2021 Scrivener Publishing LLC

This study aims to devise an approach to create music according to user's inputs by

(1) creating required MIDI file for the music and
(2) rendering the generated MIDI tracks using digital instruments.

32.2 Related Work

Procedural content generation [1] is used for creating content tailored to the user's needs and demands. Generation of content according to user mood has been researched for quite some time. The elementary research for this began with the study of semantics of emotions [2] which relates emotions to events, fields, agents and objects leading to developing emotional intelligence. The paper [3] worked toward building responses to emotions using four physiological signals, with a dataset which included data for eliciting and experiencing eight basic emotions over a period of time. Generation of music, in particular by a machine has been investigated for a long time with a popular early example being Mozarts's Musikalisches Würfelspiel (Musical Dice Game) [4] where musical segments are created according to the roll of dice. This approach looked into entropy changes for understanding tonal changes as well as studied the effect of possible distance in space in musical dice game.

Creating music according to the users' emotions have also been studied and various approaches have been suggested for that. In the last decade, creation of music according to emotion procedurally has been touted as the most successful approach. This can be used to create music according to the situation which is very useful for games [5] which is demonstrated by the paper illustrating use of different procedural approaches used in games like Legend of Zelda, Spore for better involvement of users. The research suggests that incorporating music according to the mood [6] can help in focusing as well as increased engagement of the user by changing pace or tone of the music according to the user's condition.

Procedurally generated music can be very diverse, ranging from producing elementary sound effects to eliminate repetition to inducing complex harmonies and melodies. Different approaches of procedural generation can be classified into two groups: transformational and generative algorithms [7]. Transformational algorithm changes the parameters of single note rather than general music disposition or data representations while generative algorithms works on changes in potential size of data or representation scheme.

There has been related work to our system like CHARM [8] representation which provides abstraction of musical data by using Abstract Data Types (ADT) to elicit the required mathematical properties from the abstract music encoding. There has also been work by Robertson [9] that discusses the limitations which lie in the same domain. There have been instances of creating music using evolutionary approach, like Loughran *et al.* [10] who developed a system which combined context free grammar with tonality driven functions to generate various piano melodies and Dahlsted's evolution of piano pieces [11]. Many other approaches can be studied in Evolutionary Computer music book [12] which provides insights for composers, by describing the process and components for creating innovative music and musicologist by studying the transmission and variations in music over time.

Many patents are also available for creating music such as a system which enables users to orchestrate a virtual concert [13] by using weighted exhaustive search to analyze and quantitatively assess various aspects of music like tone, harmony, pace and give scores to the piece generated by checking the requirements. There is also a system which enables users to create simple generative music [14] by assigning pitch and rhythm according to inputs provided by the user. However, these systems are unable to create a more natural music experience i.e. they lack incorporation of emotions. Our approach emphasises on procedural music generation with support for complex orchestral music and thus overcomes the prior limitations of this problem.

32.3   Experimental Setup

The experiment has been conducted on a machine with Intel® Core™ i5-6200U CPU at 2.8 GHz (4 logical CPUs) with a memory size of 8 GB. C++ has been used as the development language with Linux as the base operating system. The development environment consisted of Visual Studio Code editor and GCC (GNU Compiler Collection) as the compiler suite. An equivalent compiler suite is provided by minGW on Windows Operating System.

32.4   Methodology

The approach utilizes procedural techniques to reduce the program's disk footprint while significantly improving system performance. The inputs taken from the user (web-page or command line interface) are forwarded to the program in this very order: mood, intensity, pace, duration and seed value. Each input then contributes to the generation of an array of duration (of notes) which add up to the provided duration of the phase. Each phase can either have the same duration as the base phase or a different duration based on factors like intensity and mood.

B-Tree structure has been utilized in order to determine the duration of each phase and subdivide it by a power of two. Each subdivision is decided randomly based on the user input. More the pace, the more the subdivisions will be, hence the greater number of notes per phase as seen in Figure 32.1. This also enables us to create music pieces that don't sound rigid and create a more human renditioned version digitally.

For example, pattern[] = 8, 4, 4, 8, 2, 6.

The array of duration is then passed onto a random note generator which uses walker technique in noise generation as illustrated by Figure 32.2. The initial note is randomly chosen and then the progression is made by traversing the notes by a difference of one (or at max two) in either direction.

For example, walker[] = 6, 5, 4, 4, 5, 3 (with durations same as pattern[] array).

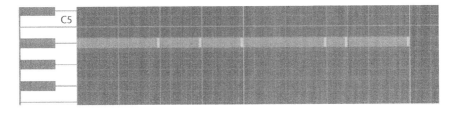

Figure 32.1 Total duration of phase (2 bars or 8 beats).

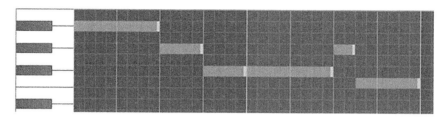

Figure 32.2 Notes generated (A# G# F# F# G# F).

On procuring the dominant note of the respective duration, the correct chord for each subdivision can be easily interpreted using the mappings provided in Table 32.1. Depending on the percent of mood factor, the chords are assigned on the principle of music theory and stored in a third array. The probability of selecting a major chord is likely to be higher in music with more cheerfulness (higher percentage of mood factor) and vice versa which is in compliance with the music theory.

For example, chord[] = 1, −2, 2, −1, −2, 1 shown by Figure 32.3.

A combination of these arrays forms a basic structure of sub-phase. Multiple subphases, in turn, can be connected in a tree structure with each leaf node having partial or complete variation (in either of the parameters: pace, duration, intensity, mood) to induce randomness, yet with a hint of repetition of familiar patterns as illustrated in Figure 32.4.

Any third-party application or a library capable of parsing a MIDI file can then be employed to render audible music in any format (wav, mp3, etc.). The generated file can then be passed back to a server which will provide the user with a simple and intuitive interface for visualising and playing the music.

Table 32.1 The Mappings used in the Procedural Music Generation.

Chord	Sa (Do)	Re (Re)	Ga (Mi)	Ma (Fa)	Pa (So)	Dha (La)	Ni (Ti)
Major	$C^{\sharp}$, $F^{\sharp}$	$G^{\sharp}$	$C^{\sharp}$	$F^{\sharp}$	$C^{\sharp}$,$G^{\sharp}$	$F^{\sharp}$	$G^{\sharp}$
Minor	$B^{\flat}m$	$E^{\flat}m$	$B^{\flat}m$, Fm	$E^{\flat}m$	Fm	$B^{\flat}m$, $E^{\flat}m$	Fm

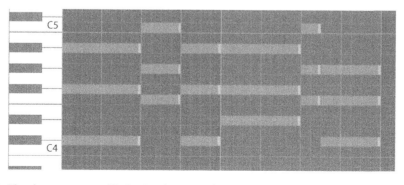

Figure 32.3 Chord representation (F# Fm F# Ebm Fm C#).

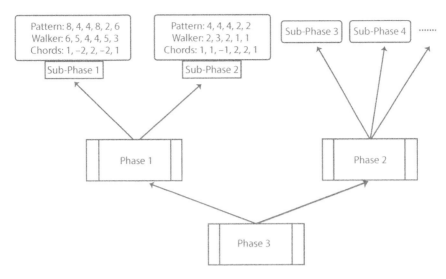

Figure 32.4 Music structure.

Alternatively, the MIDI file can be imported into a DAW of choice (LMMS *et al.*) for further manipulation like SFX, restructuring, and harmonization. The MIDI files can also act as a base template for composing digital music without the restriction of using orchestral instruments like violin, viola, cello, oboe and flute.

32.5   Result

Our approach successfully generates music according to the given inputs, as seen in Figures 32.5 and 32.6. The instruments used for creation of music are piano, violin (sustained and staccato), viola, cello, flute and harp. More instruments can be added to increase the complexity as well as aesthetic of the music generated.

Music sample 1 has a sad mood, high intensity and high pace while music sample 2 has a happy mood, low intensity and low pace. This can be interpreted with the sequencer and sheet music. Music sample 1 has more notes with shorter duration thus implying a higher pace than music sample 2. It has more minor chords than music sample 2 which can be seen by the music sheet thus signifying a sadder mood in compliance with music theory. The note velocity shown by the sequencer shows that music sample 1 is more intense than music sample 2.

Different music generated can be studied by using their corresponding sequencer and sheet music. Sequencer represents the notes of the music on piano and sheet music is a handwritten or printed form of musical notation that uses musical symbols to indicate the pitches (melodies), rhythms or chords of a song or instrumental musical piece. These, thus, can be used to provide quantitative differences between the different music generated.

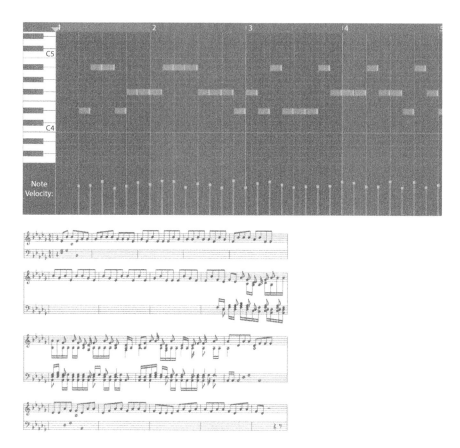

Figure 32.5 (a) LMMS piano roll (b) Sheet music of music sample 1.

Figure 32.6 (a) LMMS piano roll (b) Sheet music of music sample 2.

32.6   Conclusion

Through this study, we have proposed an approach for procedural music generation according to the user's inputs—mood, intensity, pace, duration.

Various modules are generated during the process of music creation with each result fed to the consecutive module for generating music according to our requirements.

The results of our work show that this approach can create orchestral music suitable for various real world use cases, with higher musical complexity than other approaches studied.

It is also shown that changes in inputs show a tangible change represented by sheet music and sequencer.

The complexity of the generated music can be further increased by including more instruments.

This will improve the texture while providing more possibilities for randomness to foster.

The same concept may be repurposed for real time music generation to ensure that changes to inputs are perceived immediately, allowing coverage of many diverse use cases.

Different approaches to generate patterns and melodies are also to be studied to ensure that finer music tailored to the user's requirements is created.

Our model can also be modified to generate distinct polyrhythmic music (5/4, 3/4) etc. depending on the problem at hand.

References

1. Blatz, M. and Korn O., A., Very Short History of Dynamic and Procedural Content Generation, in: *Game Dynamics*, O. Korn and N. Lee (Eds.), Springer, Cham, 2017.
2. Ortony, A., Clore, G.L., Collins, A., *The Cognitive Structure of Emotions*, Cambridge University Press, Cambridge, 1988.
3. Picard, R.W., Vyzas, E., Healey, J., Toward Machine Emotional Intelligence: Analysis of Affective Physiological State. *IEEE Trans. Pattern Anal. Mach. Intell.*, 23, 1175–1191, 2001.
4. Dawin, J.R., and Dimitri, V., Markov Chain Analysis of Musical Dice Games, In *Chaos, Complexity and Transport - Proceedings of the CCT '11*, Xavier L et al. (eds)., pp. 204–229, World Scientific Publishing Co. Pte. Ltd., 2012.
5. Collins, K., An Introduction to Procedural Music in Video Games. *Contemp. Music Rev.*, 28, 5–15, 2009.
6. Farnell, A., An introduction to procedural audio and its application in computer games, In: *Audio Mostly Conference*, v. 23, pp. 1–31, 2007.
7. Wooller, R., Brown, A.R., Miranda, E., Diederich, J., Berry, R., A framework for comparison of process in algorithmic music systems. *Generative Arts Practice 2005 – A Creativity & Cognition Symposium*, 2005.
8. Smaill, A., Wiggins, G., Harris, M., Hierarchical music representation for composition and analysis. *Comput. Hum.*, 27, 1, 7–17, 1993.
9. Robertson, J., de Quincey, A., Stapleford, T., Wiggins, G., Real-time music generation for a virtual environment. *Proceedings of ECAI-98 Workshop on AI/Alife and Entertainment*, Citeseer, 1998.
10. Loughran, R., McDermott, J., O'Neill, M., Tonality driven piano compositions with grammatical evolution. *IEEE Congress on Evolutionary Computation (CEC)*, IEEE, pp. 2168–2175, 2015.

11. Dahlstedt, P., Autonomous evolution of complete piano pieces and performances. *Proceedings of Music AL Workshop*, Citeseer, 2007.
12. Miranda, E.R. and Biles, A., *Evolutionary Computer Music*, Springer, London, 2007.
13. S.K. Meier and J.L. Briggs, System for real-time music composition and synthesis, US Patent 5,496,962, 1996.
14. A.P. Rigopulos and E.B. Egozy, Real-time music creation system, US Patent 5,627,335, 1997.

Detecting Photoshopped Faces Using Deep Learning

Siddharth Aggarwal* and Ajay Kumar Tiwari

Computer Science & Engineering Department, Maharaja Agrasen Institute of Technology, Delhi, India

Abstract

Since the beginning of the century, social media applications have given boost to many consumer-based technologies. These include revamp of cameras and better image editing techniques. Such techniques have become very common now and are used in everyday photography. Adding filters, removing background and changing features are the most common operations used. Here, we have come up with an approach that tackles photographs which have been morphed by using Photoshop alone using a neural network trained on real face images and their fake counterparts which have been manually generated by us using automation in Photoshop. We find our accuracy to be better than a human observer and also infer impressive scalability of such research.

Keywords: Adobe photoshop, artificial intelligence, convolutional neural networks, deep learning, filtering images, image processing, machine learning, morph detection

33.1 Introduction

From the past several years, social media like Twitter, Facebook, Instagram and SNS (Social Network Service) have been used by a large number of people and still the emerging of their use is increasing accordingly. They have become part of our lives. In particular, the development of smart devices such as smartphones has a remarkable role in uploading and downloading images to those social networks. With the advances of image editing techniques and user- friendly editing software, cheap rigged or manipulated image generation procedures have become broadly accessible. Out of all the editing techniques available, splicing, copy-move, and removal are the ones which are the easiest to use and access. Image splicing copies areas from a genuine image and pastes them to other images, copy-move copies and pastes sections within the same image, and removal eliminates regions from a real image. Because of this, making out the difference between the real images and the fake ones is highly problematic. The emerging research focusing on this topic—image forensics—is of great importance because it seeks to prevent attackers from using their tampered images for unscrupulous business or political purposes.

---

*Corresponding author: aggarwal.siddharth1@gmail.com

Namita Gupta, Prasenjit Chatterjee and Tanupriya Choudhury (eds.) Smart and Sustainable Intelligent Systems, (469–480)

In recent times, there is significant ease in finding cheap and user-friendly methods, particularly software applications, using which anyone in the world can accumulate and transform a large amount of visual data, be it in image format or video format. With all this positive advancement, there is also a negativity associated. As the dealing in the data of people has increased in the dark web, many people have become interested to use fake data and sell it off to companies as real data. Such fake data often requires visual data to accentuate on the validity of the data, because, certainly names, addresses and even the entire biodata can be made up, but an image of a face cannot be invalid. It can indeed be counterfeit, but it adds more validity to the authenticity of the data.

When such is the scenario, researchers and scholars have always been inquisitive to dive deeper into the world of image forensics. To find an answer to the questions of dubious images, it has been paramount to figure out the working of software that aid in editing of images. There have been many applications that help in this process of image manipulation. Some are open source like Gimp, whereas many others are expensive programs like Adobe Photoshop and Corel PaintShop that have an exorbitant amount of sophisticated features which have been built on the foundation of machine learning and artificial intelligence. Such techniques have added to the ease of their use. For instance, in Photoshop, if a user uploads an image of their face, the software can detect all the features of the face like the forehead, left and right eye, nose, mouth, teeth and even cheeks and chin. All these features can then be easily changed by dragging a linear scale bar which can therefore make a brand new face from an existing one. In some cases, this feature just adds beauty to the existing face and in other case, the new face is not similar to the original one in any sense. Many developers use these features to create filters and effects on faces of users on social media platforms like Instagram and Snapchat which can add an element of humor (by widening the length or breadth of the face) and sometimes beauty (by using blurring or sharpening of features that portray the false but prettified image).

Here, to try to solve a small issue in a large pool of issues, we have come up with an approach that deals with photos that have been morphed using Photoshop. According to a survey [11], around 3 in 4 people edit their images before uploading them to social media platforms. Photoshop is one of the most widely used image manipulation software in the industry which a layman can easily learn to use.

Its ease and ability to use make it the best choice for professionals from all industries. In this paper, we focus on one very sophisticated type of Photoshop feature—image adjustment using the Liquify filter. This is a state-of-the-art feature used for "beautification" and expression modification. Because of the high sophistication of this feature, it is hard to detect for humans which has made it a commonly used tool because its implications are widespread. We present a way using which these delicate changes become visible, alerting the viewer to the presence of modifications. Our suggested method is just one of such methods which can be and are already being used to discern the differences between real and fake images.

Our methodology involves using a Convolutional Neural Network which is carefully trained to sense warp alterations in images, particularly the faces. Like any exhaustive learning method, gathering adequate controlled training data was a challenging task. This is specifically correct for forensic purposes, as there is scarcity of datasets with huge amount of images which are manually replicated into fakes. To overcome this difficulty, make use of features in Photoshop to automatically generate fake training data that looks realistic. We first assemble a large dataset of scrapped real face pictures from diverse Internet sources. We then use the Face-Aware Liquify tool in Photoshop, which inhibits facial manipulation in high-level semantic operations, such as "increase nose width" and "reduce eye distance". By arbitrarily handling samples in this dataset, we obtain a training set that consists of the real images and their corresponding edited images which were generated through Photoshop. Next, training of our classification network on this dataset is done. Finally, we assess our methodology on a number of test cases, including images scraped from numerous places.

33.2   Related Literature

In determining the various operations to decipher the meaning of images and finding their accuracy, numerous people have found interesting problems and solutions that have grabbed international attention. From deciphering the various integral processes involved in capturing a colored image from a digital camera to understanding the implementation of images in high level programming languages, phenomenal researches have guided the field of image forensics throughout the past few decades. Chen *et al.* [12], in their renowned research used sensor noise to decode forgery in images. They also determined the role of compression of images as a major hindrance in detecting their manipulation. According to the research, the JPEG compression, the forged images are less accurately identified. This leads to new problems as almost all platforms, owing to the large amount of user data that they receive on a daily basis, have started using high level image compression. With compression, many features of the image are lost and that further complicates the task of image forensics. Other approaches that use camera techniques to identify manipulations, include research based on demosaicing artifacts and bispectral images. Median filtering [13] is another approach which has been reviewed by many scholars. With the advent of machine learning with the advance in hardware, there have been multiple researches using the advantages of neural networks and other machine learning techniques to detect fake images from real ones. Convolutional Neural Networks have been famously used in the past few years with images and speech to manipulate them and detect various abstractions in them. Graphics Processing Units (GPU) have made it easier to implement CNNs because of their highly parallel structure. Using the various hyperparameters in CNN and pre-trained models many robust approaches to tackle image forgery have been achieved. Cheng *et al.*, proposed rotation invariant approaches to achieve more than 13% increase in detection accuracy against forged images. They also showed dramatic improvement and significant robustness against JPEG compression.

Although the improvements in image forensics have been remarkable, there have also been advent in techniques like Generative Adaptive Networks [14] that have introduced a whole new field of fakes called "deep fakes". This has also shifted the focus of many researches who now focus on determining deep fakes from real images. Many scholars now focus on creating a large database of fake images and videos from this complex yet efficient methodology of using GANs. Thus, creation of a large fake dataset is done almost automatically once the network has been set up. This has led to a decrease in the number of studies in the field of image forensics that use dataset that has been self-created or handcrafted for the sole procedure of demarcating the difference in features that the features of a image editing software can bring.

Recent research has also paid due emphasis on the ability of image processing techniques to reduce noise from images. This has helped in better detection of images with compression applied to them. Although such methods still remain highly complicated and require many levels of pre-processing and adequate training. With high level architecture of neural networks used with high performance hardware, significant achievements have been recorded in such ad-hoc techniques.

33.3   Dataset Generation

To start with, a dataset of millions of images, Open Images is used. Using the Open Image downloader a large number of images are downloaded in the class of Human Face. To obtain other high resolution images, Flickr is scrapped to download portraits with human faces. Next, two datasets of real images: one from Open Image and other from Flickr are fed to Photoshop to generate a large, automatically generated set of manipulated images for training by FAL tool randomly for evaluation (Table 33.1). To obtain a diverse dataset of faces, we aggregate images from a variety of sources. Flickr is an image hosting website which has around 4 million images uploaded on the platform daily. The images are uploaded by the users can be of varied subjects. There are many groups and galleries which are made by users to upload a particular class of images. For our project, we were concerned with the human face class and we wanted images of high quality which have high resolution and close up shoots of the faces. These images are mainly described as portraits which include a clear subject in the foreground against a background which is kept less important while shooting the images. Using the Application Programming Interface provided by Flickr, we were able to scrape a gallery which contained around three hundred thousand images of human faces. There are many pools of clips created just for people to upload their images of face, this is primarily done to capture the brilliance of the cameras, as it is generally considered a specialty of a camera to be able to capture the details of something in foreground when it is in front of some background. When human faces are captured alongside touristic backgrounds, the camera's ability of capturing portraits is tested as a result. Although all these images contained human faces, we filtered them in the next step to ensure that the face in the image was clear and identifiable to our neural network.

Table 33.1 Dataset details.

	OpenImage	Flickr
Unmanipulated images	55,000	45,000
Manipulated images	55,000	45,000
Total Images	1,10,000	90,000

The process begins with scraping Flickr and taking images from the well renowned dataset Open Images. Although, Open Images is itself a dataset created by picking images from Flickr with the label of "human face", we also scrape Flickr specially for high resolution images. To separate the faces, we use the OpenCV library in python and crop the face region only. Altogether, the face dataset ended up comprising around 69,000 images from Open Images and around 116,000 Flickr portrait photos. To pre-process the images, we converted the image of a standard size where each image has dimension of at least 400 pixels on the shortest side.

Dataset was also generated keeping in mind that a pre-trained model might give better results than a non-trained one. Thus, we considered that faces, being a large proportion of training datasets used in training models which are used as the pre-trained standards already have some knowledge of a human face. Although this did not lead to a designing of an imperfect image with less identifiable parts of a face, it made us create a few images with high probability of wrong classification using modifications such as inverse and color balance shifting.

We use a pre-trained neural network with the OpenCV library which helps us in preprocessing images and preparing them for classification in the dataset. Using a pre-trained model has definite advantage over using a newly built model from scratch. The pre-trained models are generally trained on large image datasets such as Open Images or Image Net which increase the granularity of the features which the model starts to understand. This has been also studied in the articles by leading researchers on the topic of Transfer Learning with the capability to provide machine learning models better understanding of the image domain. This network, by using a threshold probabilistic model to determine if the image contains faces in them, filters them out and removes the images not useful for the training data. Additionally, each image is cropped and the shorter side is made equal of 400 px to obtain a consistent input data for training of the network.

33.3.1   Generating Dataset of Fake Images

Our objective is to construct a dataset of automatically distorted pictures that, when used for the task of training, makes a generality for artist-produced counterfeits. There are many tools available to create such images in Photoshop. But there are few that are as fast and automatic as the tool which we have used. The modifications that can be made by this tool in a couple of seconds can take an expert designer many minutes to bring about. Thus, unsurprisingly, we make use of the Face-Aware Liquid (FAL) tool in Adobe Photoshop to create several kinds of facial manipulations (Figure 33.1).

The FAL represents manipulations using sixteen parameters, which adjust a high quantity of semantics (e.g., nose width, eye distance, chin height, etc.). As shown in Figures 33.2 and 33.3, the tool can be used to forge images by creating delicate and convincing manipulations, such as making the face evenly proportioned or adding a smile. We arbitrarily sample the FAL parameter space. We randomly modify each image from its real face dataset one time. Using Photoshop for the generation fake images was a new approach which has still to be completely discovered. Many Image Processing Models generate fake images dataset using the Generative Adaptive Networks (GANs). As our use case was different we fed the data to photoshop to convert true images into unreal ones. Although editing was done in

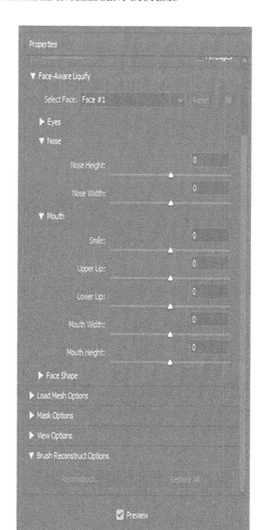

Figure 33.1 Screen Capture of FAL when a face image was used as an input and the filter of Liquify was applied to it in Adobe Photoshop.

all these images, the amount of data changed was subtle enough to go unnoticed by any human observer. An example of this is shown below. Although Figure 33.3 is the original image and Figure 33.2 is the manipulated image, the difference between the two is not very striking. This is because only a certain number of dimensions have been altered and that too with such precision that it does not change the meaning of the image or misrepresent the data which the image was supposed to represent. This is done to ensure that the faces are still able to be detected properly in the images. The aim is not to detect photoshopped images but rather photoshopped faces in general for which the image after being altered has to still look like a face. There are other image altering operations available in the software of photoshop to manipulate the images in such a way that changes their many properties

Figure 33.2 Original Image.

Figure 33.3 Manipulated Image.

including their color space or even their backgrounds and foregrounds. But the Liquify operation for the Face has led us to make such images which are just stretched or shrinked versions of the original images from a certain number of spaces where the meaning of the image is not lost. It is important to note that here we are not depending on many compression techniques like JPEG compression to hamper our detection. Instead we are using many medium and some high quality images to infer the behavior of the Convolutional Neural Network on such a randomized dataset of good quality features in the training and testing dataset. Our dataset also has a unique property that differentiates our research from other methodologies that have been used by scholars. Our dataset contains only faces, that is, there is no other body part and very minimal attention on the background of the image. It is ensured that the maximum region of the input image is occupied by an image of a face and all its features are easily extractable. In other words, it is confirmed that all the images that have a face have an unobstructed image of a face that is not being hidden (completely or partially) by an accessory or garment. In the initial step of refining the dataset, all such images were discarded such as the ones containing faces with sunglasses on that obstruct the detection of eyes. This was done to ensure that maximum features can be studied and taken into account while the process uncovers the mechanics of differentiating real and fake graphics. There is also a benefit of using smaller images when there is only one component to emphasize on. For instance, instead of just the face, had it been the entire body, a larger image would have been required to gather information about the features. But for just one facet, it easier to capture all information in a comparatively less dimensional image. All in all, data we have used for training has 95K images which were made using photoshop.

33.4   Methodolody

Our aim is to find out if or not the image has been retouched by Adobe Photoshop. Basically we want to know the answer to the question—"has this image been photoshopped?" For this we use a neural network. A neural network in computers takes inspiration from the functioning of the human brain. The decision for using a CNN based neural network came from figuring out the types of differences in the two classes, i.e., the real and the fake images. The difference is mostly in terms of pixels being stretched and present over a shorter area in some images and wider area in other. For our purpose, these patterns comprised a list of regions or pixels where the image can be compared. Based on the pixel intensity, their relative position, the network can classify it in two groups. We train a binary classifier by making use of a type of CNN which was developed by He *et al.* in 2015: Residual Neural Network (ResNet-50). It is found that with trivial output feature map obtained at the termination of the network, the accuracy is reduced in semantic dissection. In FCN, it also shows that when $32\times$ up sampling is needed, we can only get a very rough segmentation results. Thus, a larger output feature map is desired. A naive approach is to simply remove subsampling (striding) steps in the network in order to increase the resolution of feature map. However, this also reduces the receptive field which impacts the amount of context. It is important to note that such a decrease in receptive field cannot be accepted despite of the fact that it provides higher resolution. This is why, dilated convolutions are used. Owing to this, the receptive field of the higher layers in the network becomes higher which attributes its reduction in the lower layers because of eliminating sub-sampling. And it is found that using dilated convolution can also help for image classification task in this paper.

Depiction of the software used We started the dataset generation using Python programming language along with web scrapping libraries like requests, Beautiful Soup, selenium and others which were useful for the task of automation and downloading of photographs from the desired sources. Open Images is a dataset of around 9 million hyperlinks that direct to the pages of images that have suitable labels given to them traversing over 6,000 different classifications. The pictures are extremely miscellaneous. What is more is that they frequently comprise of complex scenes with several objects (8.4 per image on average). It was released by Google back in the year of 2016. There have been 4 versions of Open Images and the fifth one was recently released. The fifth version of Open Images was used in this project. PyTorch was used as the machine learning library for the task completion. PyTorch is an open-source framework which is extensively used in companies and academic institutes for the purpose of project development and advanced research. It gives the users two main features which were useful for this task as well. First is that it provides ability for Tensor computing along with the access to the Graphics Processing Units. Second was the provision of deep neural networks which were seamlessly built for the purpose of being directly reused. For instance, the architectures of many convolutional neural networks like the ResNet-50 are pre built in PyTorch which can be used with the invocation of a function. For the purpose of identifying faces in the downloaded images, we also made use of the OpenCV library which is again an open source computer vision library which is aimed at real time computer vision. Using the OpenCV support for Pytorch, we were able to use the deep learning methods to find faces in images and crop them to remove additional data. We also deleted the images which did not contain any face so that the training is done only on the right type of data. Similarly, this data cleaning procedure was repeated to ignore all the images that have mentions of only partial face or a face covered with anything that interrupted our network to fully capture all of its characteristics. To do this, a program that checks for all visible aspects of an image was created. It passed an image only if it checked all the boxes for identified eyes, nose, cheeks, chin, forehead, etc. Many images which despite of being completely decipherable to humans were discarded to make the process a bit less tedious.

33.4.1 Details of the Training Procedure

We initialized the network of the ResNet-50 network. We use the Stochastic Gradient Descent Loss function. Here, 'stochastic' means anything that is associated with a random possibility or probability. Therefore, in Stochastic Gradient Descent, the samples are chosen arbitrarily rather than choosing the whole dataset for each iteration. Rather, we use a "batch" size in which we store the number of images that we use to find the best gradient for the entire dataset in every iteration. The difference between the general Gradient Descent optimization, like Batch Gradient Descent and Stochastic Gradient Descent is that the batch in the general gradient descent is taken to be the whole dataset (Table 33.2). Although, using the whole dataset is really convenient for getting to the minima in a less noisy or less random manner, but for a huge dataset like ours, it isn't conceivable. This difficulty is solved by using Stochastic Gradient Descent. In SGD, batch size of one is used in every iteration to find the gradient for the whole dataset in each iteration.

The sample is randomly shuffled and selected for performing the iteration. Another thing which is indispensable is the mini-batch size hyperparameter. This parameter was fine-tuned after much inspections and trials. Finally, we have used mini- batch size of 32 the images, and initial learning rate is kept at 10^{-4} which is reduced by 10 when the loss graph starts to flatten. The model was trained for 100 epochs amounting to around 300k iterations. The choice for the number of iterations was made by following articles from other researches done which use a similar sample space.

Table 33.2 Training details.

Learning Rate	10^{-4}
Loss function	Stochastic Gradient Descent
Epochs	100

Convolutional networks make use of two important operations which allow them to maintain the spatial dimensions of an image. These are the striding operation and the pooling operation. Any other type of deep learning architecture does not preserve the spatial dimensions of the data as the CNN does. In fact, CNN can be thought of as automatic feature extractors from the image. If an algorithm used incorporates pixel vector, a lot of special information is bound to be lost, especially the spatial interaction between pixels. Whereas, in CNN, adjacent pixel information is precisely used while down sampling the image. This was important in our task as we wanted the network to figure out the small and subtle changes that were present in the two classes of images. There was not a categorical difference as they both contained images of human faces but a more peculiar difference that involved differences in the values of the interaction between the pixels of the image.

33.5   Results

According to the training, our model returns a probability about if the image is morphed or not Table 33.3.

Thus, for an input image if a probability returned is over 0.5, it is edited according to the model, otherwise it is not.

	Edited or not?	**Probability output**
Figure 33.2.	Not photoshopped	0.028
Figure 33.3.	Photoshopped	0.998

The above output shows the result for a manipulated image using the Face Aware Liquify tool in Photoshop. As we can see, the probability that the image is retouched is about 0.99, which is way over the threshold value of 0.5.

Table 33.3 Result format.

Probability	**Inference**
>0.5	Morphed
≤0.5	Not Morphed

33.6   Conclusion

The model described here is successfully able to detect facial manipulations created by the Face Aware Liquify tool most of the time. This approach of training a Neural Network to do this task with an entirely automatically created dataset throws light on the future possibilities and prospects that this strategy can solve. It can be realized by looking at the example figures above, that the model significantly outperforms humans in detecting morphed images. Using Convolutional Neural Networks in the field of Image forensics can give information about a whole gamut of meddling that was done with the image.

33.7   Future Scope

In further implementations, the circumference of the problem can be increased many folds. Firstly, the question of detecting the changes just in the face can now be taken to include other parts of the body. Second, from detecting just changes in humans, we can increase our scope to cover more things and objects which are commonly meddled with such as in fashion industry for creating duplicates of original goods.

References

1. Wang, S.Y., Wang, O., Owens, A., Zhang, R., Efros, A.A., Detecting photoshopped faces by scripting photoshop, in: *Proceedings of the IEEE International Conference on Computer Vision*, pp. 10072–10081, 2019, https://arxiv.org/pdf/1906.05856.pdf
2. LeCun, Y., Bengio, Y., Hinton, G., Deep learning. *Nature*, 521, 7553, 436–444, 2015.
3. Detecting Photoshopped Faces by Scripting Photoshop, https://peterwang512.github.io/FALdetector
4. Walt, S.v.d., Colbert, S.C., Varoquaux, G., The numpy array: a structure for efficient numerical computation. *Comput. Sci. Eng.*, 13, 2, 22–30, 2011.
5. https://suchir.io/posts/passenger-screening-algorithm-challenge-writeup.html.
6. He, K., Zhang, X., Ren, S., Sun, J., Deep Residual Learning for Image Recognition, 2016.
7. He, K., Zhang, X., Ren, S. and Sun, J., Deep residual learning for image recognition, in: *Proceedings of the IEEE conference on computer vision and pattern recognition*, pp. 770-778, 2016.
8. Chan, C., Ginosar, S., Zhou, T., Efros, A.A., Everybody dance now, in: *Proceedings of the IEEE International Conference on Computer Vision*, pp. 5933–95942, 2019. https://blog.init.ai/residual-neural-networks-are-an-exciting-area-of-deep-learning-research-acf14f4912e9
9. Sun, L., Resnet on tiny imagenet. Submitted on, 14. Vancouver, 2016.
10. Bondi, L., Lameri, S., Güera, D., Bestagini, P., Delp, E.J., Tubaro, S., Tampering detection and localization through clustering of camera-based CNN features, in: *2017 IEEE Conference on Computer Vision and Pattern Recognition Workshops (CVPRW)*, IEEE, pp. 1855–1864, 2017.
11. https://fstoppers.com/mobile/68-percent-adults-edit-their-selfies-sharing-them-anyone-95417.
12. Chen, M., Fridrich, J., Goljan, M., Lukas, J., Determining Image Origin and Integrity Using Sensor Noise. *IEEE Trans. Inf. Forensics Secur.*, 3, 1, 74–90, March 2008.
13. Kirchner, M. and Fridrich, J., On detection of median filtering in images. *Proc. SPIE, Electronic Imaging, Media Forensics and Security XII*, San Jose, CA, January 17–21, pp. 10-1–10-12, 2010.
14. Goodfellow, I.J., Pouget-Abadie, J., Mirza, M., Xu, B., Warde-Farley, D., Ozair, S., Courville, A., Bengio, Y., Generative adversarial networks. arXiv preprint arXiv:1406.2661, 2017.

34

A Review of SQL Injection Attack and Various Detection Approaches

Neha Bhateja[1]*, Dr. Sunil Sikka[1] and Dr. Anshu Malhotra[2]

[1]Amity University Haryana, Gurgaon, India
[2]The NorthCap University, Gurgaon, India

Abstract

In today's world, many of our interactions are with Web applications, HTML5 based hybrid mobile applications and IoT devices. These applications and devices have a database at the back-end which can contain sensitive information. The information might contain personal details as well as information which are not meant to be altered illicitly. Hackers are always looking to penetrate into the databases to gather information which can later be used for illegal purposes. Such breaches can cause harm to the individual as well as the organization responsible for managing that data. One such method is to use SQL injection attacks (SQLIAs). It enables the hacker to create SQL queries which can be used to alter or retrieve the state of the database. The paper is based on a review of various SQL injection approaches with the methods available to counter these attacks.

Keywords: SQL injection, SQL vulnerabilities, database security, input validation, SQLIA, SQL injection types

34.1 Introduction

With the advancement in technology, complexity of web applications is growing day by day. Previously, we used to have simple, static web applications serving static pages to the user. This changed to web applications interacting with databases and serving pages generated at run-time containing on demand data and visualizations [1]. With service oriented architecture (SOA) evolution, this has further moved to creating web services which interact with data and serve the required information. These web services can be accessed via web applications, mobile applications and also IoT devices.

According to a report published by Akamai [17], a US-based cloud service provider; majority of attacks are still SQLi attacks. During a period of November 2017 to March 219, 65% of the attacks they captured were of SQL injection. As the web application complexity is growing day by day, attackers are finding new patterns to create malicious queries which

---

*Corresponding author: bhateja.neha@gmail.com

Namita Gupta, Prasenjit Chatterjee and Tanupriya Choudhury (eds.) Smart and Sustainable Intelligent Systems, (481–490)
© 2021 Scrivener Publishing LLC

are hard to identify. This makes SQL injection an ever growing problem for application developers. Pattern matching used to be the go to approach for SQLi detection and prevention, but now only relying on it is opening the gates of your database to hackers.

The latest OWASP Top 10 [18] still features SQL injection attack at the top stop as the biggest risk for web application security.

Figure 34.1 below represents the basic architecture of a web applications and labels the SQL injectable layers.

There are broadly 2 main components in a Web application:

1. Client Side: This is known as front-end of web application. It typically represents a user/client sitting on his computer with a browser which is displaying the capabilities in which a user can interact with the application. For Example, this could be an online application for a job, an E-commerce website, etc. The main purpose of client side is to show users the functionalities, collect input from the user and display the outcome of the intended action.

   It is mainly written in HTML, CSS, JavaScript. Recent development in technologies has also introduced some frame words for creating the web experience using Angular, ReactJs, BackboneJs, etc.

2. Server Side: This is also called the back-end of the application. As the client cannot see this side of the application hence the name back-end is given. This component mainly consists of 2 layers

   a. Application Server with application logic: This layer consists of code written mainly in languages, but not limited to Java, Ruby on Rails, Python, etc. It contains the core business logic of the application. It also contains any third party API calls and interactions which might be required to serve user the expected output.

   b. Database layer: It is also called as persistent layer where all the data is persisted. It represents a database such as Oracle, Db2, etc. to store the data related to the application.

The application logic layer and database layer interact with each other to save and get the data as and when required.

In the above diagram, an HTTP request sends by the client to the Web server. The request can contain headers as well as form data, request parameters or query parameters. If this records are not sanitized before sending to the web server, we have opened a possible

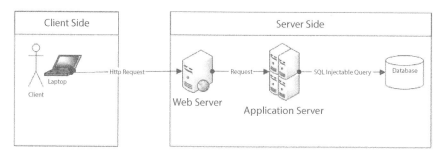

Figure 34.1 SQL attack in client-server.

loophole in our application to be SQL injectable. Web server then serves the request and it can send it to a database server or web service (which in turn connects with database). Ideally, SQL injection checks should be performed at layers before querying the database. The query could contain malicious inputs which may corrupt the data, serve the data to unauthorized users, give the hacker administrative rights, etc.

34.2   SQL Injection Attack and Its Types

SQL injection is a method through the attacker or the malicious person gain unauthorized access to database to obtain information for malicious purposes. The attacker can use the simple SQL queries like SELECT, INSERT, UPDATE and MODIFY and reconstruct them and then execute the malicious code as an input string on the web applications. These SQL injectable code can bypass the authentication and authorization process (or say, firewall) of the web applications and attacker gain unauthorized permission to access the database.

SQL injection is performed by different ways [1, 11]. Figure 34.2 represents the types of SQL Injection attacks.

- Tautologies: Injection of such kind of statements that always return true result after execution of WHERE statements. It is used to extract the data from database via bypassing the authentication.
- Illegal/Logically incorrect Queries: An error message generated by a web server contains important information for debugging. The attacker intentionally executes the incorrect queries find the vulnerable parameters from the error message.
- Union Query: An attacker injects incorrect query in the correct query with the help of UNION operator to extract the information. If the structure (data type and number of column) of both incorrect and original query is same, then Union query is executed.
- Piggy-backed queries: the attacker insert an additional statement in form of query with the actual query by using the ';'. The database server thus receives multiple queries to execute.
- Stored Procedure: Stored procedure are mainly used in databases due to their faster execution and better validations. They use the same execution plan whenever invoked. Attacks of this form occur when a dynamic query along with concatenation of parameters is done and sent to a stored procedure for execution.
- Blind Injection: It is also known as Inferential injection. Blind injection is performed by querying database with true of false questions and occurs when the application is built to show generic errors of the details of any database error.

Figure 34.2 Types of SQL attack [11].

Table 34.1 Types of SQL attacks [1, 11].

Types	Method
Tautologies	Performed by manipulating the SQL queries.
Illegal/Logically incorrect Queries	Performed by manipulating the SQL
Union Query	Performed by manipulating the existing SQL and injecting the vulnerable code
Piggy-backed queries	Performed by injecting the code into the correct query
Stored Procedure	Performed by injecting the code
Blind Injection:	Performed by injecting the code in form of true , false questions.
Alternate Encoding	Performed by manipulating the SQL

- Alternate Encoding: It is an alternate way to gain access to the database by using alternate encodings like ASCII, Hexadecimal instead of using plain single quote. This attack uses the fact that multiple encodings may represent the same character in different ways. It becomes harder to identify the character and thus detect and prevent SQLiA.

Table 34.1 represents in brief the ways in which SQL Injection attacks are performed. Using SQL injection, the assailant can
  - Abstract the useful information
  - Insert, delete or modify the data
  - Identify the database schema, version and type.
  - Bypass authentication.
  - Lock or delete the tables and provide denial of service information to the authorized users.
  - Execute the remote commands which are used by the administrators.

34.3 Literature Survey

Huang *et al.* [2] used black box approach and proposed WAVES i.e. Web Application Vulnerability and error scanner. It is a dynamic analysis process. The entry points of input data are determined by applying reverse engineering process and then vulnerable points are determined by using the malicious code.

Limitation: unable to detect all types of SQL attacks.

Bisht *et al.* [3] suggested a tool CANDID i.e. CANdidate evaluation for discovering intent dynamically. The idea behind using this tool is to perform the mining on the structure of programmer query and then compared it with the structure of user's query to perform prevention from SQL injection attack. This tool works on the web applications that are based on JAVA.

Gould *et al.* [4] proposed a JDBC checker analysis tool. This tool is implemented in JAVA, and is used to locate the precision of query strings that are dynamically generated.

Limitation: the scope of the tool is limited because unable to detect the general forms of SQL injection attack.

Lambert *et al.* [5] proposed a technique named, Query Tokenization to identify the SQL injection. Query Parser approach is used in this proposed work. Firstly, the tokenization process is performed on both original and user input query string and represented these tokens in two arrays. Then the length of these two arrays are compared to detect the SQL injection attacks occurs or not.

McClure [6] designed an object model, SQL DOM i.e. SQL Domain Object Model. This is used to identify faults in the code by generating SQL queries through group of classes associated to database schema instead of manipulation of the strings.

Limitation: this model is unable to detect the stored procedures.

Romil *et al.* [7] used an approach based on machine learning i.e. Support Vector Machine to detect the SQL injection attack. Through various parameters authors check the performance of used approach like accuracy, True Negative Rate (TNR), False Positive Rate (FPR), True Positive Rate (TPR) and observed 96.4 % detection of SQL injection attack.

Valeur *et al.* [8, 11] proposed Intrusion detection system (IDS). this machine learning approach is used to detect the attack performed on the database of the web applications. the behavior of web applications is identified by the configuration of various models and then detect the SQL vulnerabilities in web applications.

Weakness: the accuracy of the detection is based on value of trained data set.

Limitation: the detection of all types of attacks are not feasible.

Halfond *et al.* [9] proposed a model based technique i.e. AMNESIA used for analysis and monitoring the SQL attack. Firstly, analysis is performed on web application code and a model is generated based on the features of the queries and then monitoring is done by comparing the users input code with the model to identify the malicious code and non-malicious code.

Limitation: the success rate of this model based technique depends on correctness of the model which is created at time of analysis.

Cova *et al.* [10] developed a prototype which is based on PHP language, known as SWADDLER. This tool deals with the internal states of web application to detect the vulnerabilities by getting the information about the relationship between the application's entry point and inner state of application.

Huang *et al.* [12] proposed a tool WebSSARI i.e. Web Application Security by Static Analysis and Runtime Inspection, which perform the static analysis upon untrusted data according to some predefined functions. This tool works on the input data that passed through these predefined filters.

Limitation: the predefined functions that are used to perform analysis are not accurately defined.

Ali *et al.* [13] proposed MYSQLInjection, scanning tool used to do penetration testing on Web applications to detect the attack of SQL injection. The tool works on the PHP websites to detect SQL attack by using various variables and features to reveal the attack.

Limitation: this tool works only on PHP websites and unable to detect the attack on the Java Server Pages and Active Server Pages.

Martin *et al.* [14] proposed a tool SecuriFly, in which instead of characters, the string is track against the tainted data and then the input query string is sanitized.

Limitations: this tool is unable to detect the vulnerability on all type of input user's data and unable to identify the malicious code attack on the numeric fields.

Wassermann *et al.* [15] proposed a framework to achieve static analysis to validating the security properties of web applications. This framework is capable to detect only tautology attack instead of all other attacks.

Roichman *et al.* [16] proposed a practical solution method i.e. DIWeDa for detection of vulnerability in web database by classify the behavior of SQL queries that are releases at a session not at transaction or statement level. Authors used a classifier i.e. SQL session content anomaly intrusion to detect the known attacks as well as some complex attacks.

Limitation: the method is unable to detect each kind of attacks.

Srinivas *et al.* [19] proposed an algorithm Random4 used to provide prevention from SQL injection attack. This proposed algorithm is framed using the concept of cryptography using Randomization. With Random4 the user's input is converted into the cypher text and cypher keys are stored in database to compare it with the user input.

Shanmughaneethi *et al.* [20] proposed a method SBSQLID, known as Service Based SQL Injection Detection to detect the vulnerabilities of SQL attack. This proposed method works in three steps. Firstly, the user input is validated and passed for pattern matching. Then syntactic structure is verified with the help of query analyzer and in third step, database server generates an error message.

Pinzón *et al.* [21] presented a multiagent architecture which uses the hierarchical strategy together with distributed strategy to discover and restrict SQL injection attack by performing the classification and visualization on the gathered data. The identification of attacks is performed by using the neural projection and the clustering techniques.

Buehrer *et al.* [22] proposed a technique using the method of comparison. At run time they compare the parse tree of original SQL statement before any user input is included in it with that formed after input parameters are included. They proposed that their approach is easy to implement by the developers, but it adds a 3 ms overhead.

Nguyen-Tuong [23] proposed a fully automated approach for SQL injection detection. They proposed to check only the output that is coming from unreliable resources by scanning only some specific parts of the commands.

Bockermann *et al.* [24] proposed an approach based on machine learning techniques. The authors proposed to use the parse tree structure of the input SQL statements and apply clustering or outlier detection methods for checking any vulnerability at the database transaction level.

Dussel *et al.* [25] proposed to use the application layer context for anomaly based injection detection. The author proposed to check the payload at the application layer and applies a protocol analyzer. The authors tested their method and saw an improvement of 49% in accuracy of intrusion detection.

Kim, M.Y. *et al.* [26] proposed method using SVM classification to identify the SQL injection attacks being performed on database level. It uses the concept of feature vectors by converting the input query string into n-dimensional features vector and then semantic and syntax features are extracted where one to one mapping is done between the string value with the numeric features value.

Jang, Y.S., *et al.* [27] proposed a tool to protect java based web applications from SQLIA. the technique analyzed the size of the input query entered by the user and then compare the it with the actual query size to detect the attack.

Wang Y., *et al.* [28] propose that instead of the classical signature based algorithm for SQL injection detection they used a hybrid approach for SQL queries with program tracing method. They used hashing mechanism and represented the SQL queries as tree structure.

34.4   Summary

Table 34.2 represents a summary of the existing SQL Injection Detection methods.

Table 34.2 Existing SQL Injection Detection Methods [2, 3, 6–9, 12].

Tool/Method	Description
WAVES	Web Application Vulnerability and error scanner. It is a dynamic analysis process.
CANDID	CANdidate evaluation for discovering intent dynamically. This tool works on the web applications that are based on JAVA.
JDBC	JDBC checker analysis tool is implemented in JAVA, and is used to locate the precision of query strings that are dynamically generated.
Query Tokenization	Query Tokenization technique is used to identify the SQL injection. Query Parser approach is used in this proposed work.
SQL DOM	SQL Domain Object Model is used to identify faults in the code by generating SQL queries through group of classes associated to database schema instead of manipulation of the strings.
SVM	Support Vector Machine is a machine learning approach that is used to detect the SQL injection attack.
IDS	Intrusion detection system is a machine learning approach is used to detect the attack performed on the database of the web applications.
AMNESIA	analysis and monitoring the SQL attack. Firstly, analysis is performed on web application code and a model is generated based on the features of the queries and then monitoring is done by comparing the users input code with the model to identify the malicious code and non-malicious code
SWADDLER	This tool is based on PHP language and deals with the internal states of web application to detect the vulnerabilities by getting the information about the relationship between the application's entry point and inner state of application.
WebSSARI	Web application Security by Static Analysis and Runtime Inspection, which perform the static analysis upon untrusted data according to some predefined functions.
MYSQL Injection	This is a scanning tool used to do penetration testing on Web applications to detect the attack of SQL injection.
SecuriFly	The string is track against the tainted data and then the input query string is sanitized.
DIWeDa	Detection of vulnerability in web database by classify the behavior of SQL queries that are releases at a session not at transaction or statement level.
Random4	It is used to provide prevention from SQL injection attack. This proposed algorithm is framed using the concept of cryptography using Randomization.
SBSQLID	Service Based SQL Injection Detection to detect the vulnerabilities of SQL attack.

34.5   Conclusion

To conclude, SQLiA is one of the earliest known forms of database attacks but it still remains at the top due to the ever growing complexity of web applications and databases. With the advent of Service oriented architecture and micro services, these have open new fronts to tackle SQL injection attack. Multiple solutions have been provided via various authors to prevent and detect SQL injection attack, although no one guarantees a full range of capabilities with respect to the types of attacks. In future, the focus should be on creating such tools which can cater to multiple variations of SQL injection attack and also adapt themselves to new attacks being introduced into the web applications.

References

1. Tajpour, A., Ibrahim, S., Masrom, M., SQL Injection Detection and Prevention Techniques. *Int. J. Adv. Comput. Technol.*, 3, 82–91, 2011, 10.4156/ijact.vol3.issue7.11.
2. Huang, Y., Huang, S., Lin, T., Tasi, C., Web application security assessment by fault injection and behavior monitoring, in: *Proceedings of the 12th International Conference on World Wide Web*, pp. 148–159, 2003.
3. Bisht, P., Madhusudan, P., Venkatakrishnan, V.N., CANDID: Dynamic Candidate Evaluations for Automatic Prevention of SQL Injection Attacks. *ACM Trans. Inf. Syst. Secur.*, 13, 2, 1–39, 2010.
4. Gould, C., Su, Z., Devanbu, P., JDBC Checker, A Static Analysis Tool for SQL/JDBC Applications, in: *Proceedings of the 26th International Conference on Software Engineering (ICSE04) Formal Demos*, ACM, pp. 697–698, 2004.
5. Ntagwabira, L. and Kang, S.L., Use of Query tokenization to detect and prevent SQL injection attacks, *2010 3rd International Conference on Computer Science and Information Technology*, Chengdu, pp. 438-440, 2010
6. McClure, R.A. and Kruger, I.H., SQL DOM: compile time checking of dynamic SQL statements, in: *Proceedings of the 27th International Conference on Software Engineering*, pp. 88–96, 2005.
7. Romil, R. and Shailendra, R., SQL injection attack detection using SVM. *Int. J. Comput. Appl.*, 42, 1–4, 2012.
8. Valeur, F., Mutz, D., Vigna, G., A learning-based approach to the detection of SQL attacks, in: *Proceedings of the 2nd International Conference on Detection of Intrusions and Malware, and Vulnerability Assessment (DIMVA)*, Vienna, Austria, pp. 123–140, 2005.
9. Halfond, W.G. and Orso, A., AMNESIA: Analysis and Monitoring for NEutralizing SQL-Injection Attacks, in: *Proceedings of the IEEE and ACM International Conference on Automated Software Engineering (ASE 2005)*, Long Beach, CA, USA, Nov 2005.
10. Cova, M. and Balzarotti, D., Swaddler: An Approach for the Anomaly-based Detection of State Violations in Web Applications. *Recent Advances in Intrusion Detection, Proceedings*, vol. 4637, pp. 63–86, 2007.
11. Lee, I., Jeong, S., Yeo, S., Moon, J., A novel method for SQL injection attack detection based on removing SQL query attribute values. *Math. Comput. Modell.*, 55, 58–6, Elsevier, 2012.
12. Huang, Y., Yu, F., Hang, C., Tsai, C.H., Lee, D.T., Kuo, S.Y., Securing Web Application Code by Static Analysis and Runtime Protection, in: *Proceedings of the 12th International World Wide Web Conference (www 04)*, May 2004.

13. Bashah Mat Ali, A., Yaseen Ibrahim Shakhatreh, A., Syazwan Abdullah, M., Alostad, J., SQL-injection vulnerability scanning tool for automatic creation of SQL-injection attacks. *Procedia Comput. Sci.*, 3, 453–458, 2011.

14. Martin, M., Livshits, B., Lam, M.S., Finding Application Errors and Security Flaws Using PQL: A Program Query Language. *ACM SIGPLAN Notices*, 40, 10, 365–383, 2005.

15. Wassermann, G. and Su, Z., An Analysis Framework for Security in Web Applications, in: *Proceedings of the FSE Workshop on Specification and Verification of Component-Based Systems*, pp. 70–78, 2004.

16. Roichman A., Gudes, E., DIWeDa - Detecting Intrusions in Web Databases, in: *Data and Applications Security XXII. DBSec 2008*. Atluri V. (ed.), Lecture Notes in Computer Science, vol. 5094. Springer, Berlin, Heidelberg. https://doi.org/10.1007/978-3-540-70567-3_24

17. https://www.akamai.com/uk/en/multimedia/documents/state-of-the-internet/soti-security-web-attacks-and-gaming-abuse-report-2019.pdf.

18. https://www.owasp.org/index.php/Category : OWASP_Top_Ten_Project.

19. Srinivas, A., Narayan, G., Ram, S., Random4: An Application Specific Randomized Encryption Algorithm to prevent SQL injection, in Trust, Security and Privacy in Computing and Communications (TrustCom). *2012 IEEE 11th International Conference*, 25–27 June 2012, pp. 1327–133.

20. Shanmughaneethi, V., EmilinShyni, C., Swamynathan, S., SBSQLID: Securing Web Applications with Service Based SQL Injection Detection. *2009 International Conference on Advances in Computing, Control, and Telecommunication Technologies*, IEEE, 2009, 978-0-7695-3915-7/09.

21. Pinzón, C.I., Paz, J.F.D., Herrero, Á., Corchado, E., Bajo, J., Corchado, J.M., idMAS-SQL: Intrusion Detection Based on MAS to Detect and Block SQL injection through data mining. *Inf. Sci.*, 231, 15–31, 2013.

22. Buehrer, G., Weide, B.W., Sivilotti, P.A.G., Using parse tree validation to prevent SQL injection attacks, in: *Proc. of SEM*, ACM, New York, pp. 106–113, 2005.

23. Nguyen-Tuong, A., Guarnieri, S., Green, D., Shirley, J., Evans, D., Automatically hardening web applications using precise tainting, in: *Proceedings of IFIP Security 2005*, May 2005, Springer.

24. Bockermann, C., Apel, M., Meier, M., Learning SQL for Database Intrusion Detection Using Context-Sensitive Modelling (Extended Abstract), in: *DIMVA 2009. LNCS*, vol. 5587, U. Flegel and D. Bruschi (Eds.), pp. 196–205, Springer, Heidelberg, 2009.

25. Dussel, P., Gehl, C., Laskov, P., Rieck, K., Incorporation of Application Layer Protocol Syntax into Anomaly Detection, in: *ICISS 2008. LNCS*, vol. 5352, R. Sekar and A.K. Pujari (Eds.), pp. 188–202, Springer, Heidelberg, 2008.

26. Kim, M.Y. and Lee, D.H., Data-mining based SQL injection attack detection using internal query trees. *Expert Syst. Appl.*, 41, 11, 5416–430, 2014, https://doi.org/10.1016/j.eswa.2014.02.041.

27. Jang, Y.S. and Choi, J.Y., Detecting SQL injection attacks using query result size. *Comput. Secur.*, 44, 104–118, 2014, https://doi.org/10.1016/j.cose.2014.04.007.

28. Wang, Y. and Li Z., S.Q.L., Injection Detection *via* Program Tracing and Machine Learning, in: *Internet and Distributed Computing Systems, IDCS 2012. Lecture Notes in Computer Science*, vol. 7646, Y. Xiang, M. Pathan, X. Tao, H. Wang (Eds.), Springer, Berlin, Heidelberg, 2012.

35

Futuristic Communication Technologies

**Sanika Singh[1]*, Aman Anand[2], Shubham Sharma[3], Tanupriya Choudhury[4]
and Saurabh Mukherjee[5]**

[1]Department of Computer Science, ABES Engineering College, Ghaziabad, India
[2]Department of Computer Science and Engineering, Sharda University, Greater Noida, India
*[3]Department of Electronics and Communication Engineering, Sharda University,
Greater Noida, India*
[4]Department of Computer Science and Engineering, UPES, Dehradun, India
[5]Department of Computer Science and Engineering, Banasthali Vidyapith, Jaipur, India

Abstract

As everyone is eye witnessing in revolutionary generation where there is more need of smartness rather than anything else. And due to this the most important part of anyone's life is communication. As there is development in each and every field like Space technology, military, etc. each and every place communication is necessary. And now enhancement in communication technology is increasing day-by-day. Its promising by network developers that in near future we are going to shift ourselves to telepathy.

But, till this time we have shifted ourselves from wired to wireless, Bluetooth to WiFi, Infrared to Zigbee, etc. We are replacing the world with the slower mode of communication to much faster and reliable way to communicate to the world. We have replaced some wired communication to shift to Fiber Optical Communication.

But, this time it's the need of world to deal with Smart Energy Generation also as we are using Solar energy, wind energy and the sensors to communicate through devices which we use are of eco-friendly in nature. So, in this Futuristic Communication technology we are going to discuss about our shifting towards the evolving technology in the world and much more about the Smart Energy Communication and Ubiquitous Communication and also how Green technology sustainably affect our environment and our life.

Keywords: Wi-Fi, Li-Fi, Zigbee, LAN, PNT, PSTN, GPRS, UHF, RADAR, VLC, ITS

35.1 Introduction

Communication (or conveying information) is taken from the Latin word "Communicare" which can be interpreted as "to share or make communication (or convey information)". Basically, Communication is the act or process of using words, signals, sound, signs, etc. to

---

**Corresponding author*: sanikasingh39@gmail.com

Namita Gupta, Prasenjit Chatterjee and Tanupriya Choudhury (eds.) Smart and Sustainable Intelligent Systems, (491–510)
© 2021 Scrivener Publishing LLC

demonstrate our ideas, thoughts, etc. to someone else. But formally, it is a type of message which is given to an individual or group via letter, telephone, etc. or the way of sending information to the individual by the use of technology.

The branch of knowledge that deals with transmitting information or communicating is not an inborn unsatisfactory artefact. Similarly, all the devices that people want to use too much, it is unsatisfactory only when we won't be able to make use of a satisfactory measure of moderation over it. The art of Communication technology has the ability to seep into the society on a large intense level than it was pre-existing, which would mean vicious outcome. It is necessary that inspiration must be brought to the situation of restricting our association with our communication or transmission technology so, that it does not accumulatively destroy us.

Today in this modern era, Communication technology is also known as information technology which makes reference to all equipment , programs which are used to process and communicate information. Presently an individual communicates through e-mail, Telephoto (faxes), radio telephones, conferencing calls, etc. As the time passes, more enhanced and developing technologies will alter our way of communication and it will be totally up to us to welcome them or not. The art of technology communication is evolving at a breathtaking pace and in near future approximately after 50 years, we'll be able to share our thoughts directly to machines via electric signals or someone else's brain.

Nowadays, as there is enhancement in technology wired communication is getting replaced by many emerging wireless communication technologies. The emergence of wireless technology has brought a revolution in the field of communication, which produces many new ideas and uses to society. In this era, everyone is predicting unique solutions in the wireless field that helps to explore many new things. Wireless technology is the brand new technical term used to describe the affair related to telecommunication, where the electromagnetic waves transfer signals over the communication path.

As we have discussed so far we come across to know that a communication medium is diversified into two different categories which are most prominent part of communication models, and they are classified as follows:

a. Wired medium: Wired communication defines the way to the transfer of information or data over a Circuit (or pre-defined path)-based communication technology.
   E.g.: Cables, Ethernet Cables, Optical Fibre Cables, etc.
b. Wireless medium: Wireless communication defines the way to the transfer of data (raw facts and figures) or information without the application of any physical (or wired) medium. In wireless transmission air is mostly used as a medium through which all the signals propagate.
   E.g.: WiFi, LiFi, GiFi, Bluetooth, Zigbee, etc.

Hence, now the time comes when we have to switch over advanced versions of communication technologies and research those media for its proper and efficient working.

35.2   Types of Communication Medium

35.2.1   Wired Medium

Wired medium of communication systems consist of systems where data is sent through the wires. Wired or physical mode of communicating technologies are considered as the most secured among all different modes of data transmission aids. They are comparatively impervious to unfavourable atmospheric conditions in contrast to wireless (non-physical media) solution.

Most of the digital telecommunications now-a-days depend on the application of optical fiber transmission of information as a way of supplying clear indication for both inbound (incoming) and outbound (outgoing) transmissions. Optical Fiber is able of coordinating far more signals than the former cables used in history, while still continuing the coherence of the messages over longer range.

An example of wired (circuit-based) communications is Phone line Network Transceiver (PNT) used in home, which is connected to the local PNT's and can be switch through physical medium (wires) that functions from the home to the switch.

Web access from computer systems is also a common example of current-time wired (physical media) communications. In fact, telephone firm often employ the same wiring or circuit to provide both LAN solutions and basic telephone (PNT) services to home as well as business professionals.

35.3   Types of Wired Connections

a. Co-axial Cable: Co-axial cables have a cylindrical wire running down in the mid of enclosed sheath which is insulating in nature. Enclosing the wire, which is conducting in nature, behaves as a protection and a return path for the transmission of signals. Such type of cables are extremely impervious to noise due to protection of non-braided spiral binding of polymer (Figure 35.1).

b. Fiber Optic Cable: Such types of cables have longer and narrow fiber of glass through which light pulses transfer information. These cables support high data rates (Figure 35.2).

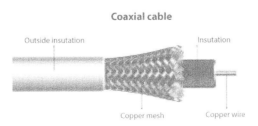

Coaxial cable

Outside insutation   Insutation

Copper mesh   Copper wire

Figure 35.1 Co-axial cable.

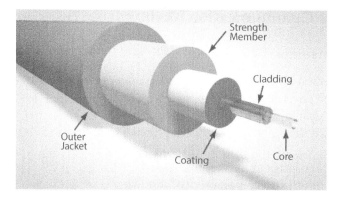

Figure 35.2 Optical fiber cable.

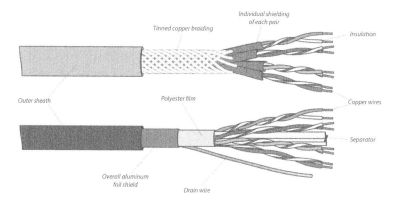

Figure 35.3 Twisted pair cable.

    c. Twisted pairs: These are paired wires which are twisted together. The twist decrease noise on the wires by canceling out, the amount of electromagnetic interference from the environment among transmitter and receiver (Figure 35.3).

35.3.1   Implementation of Wired (Physical Mode) Technology

Physical mode of communication technology has a number of benefits:

- It supports audio communication by using a circuit switching technique which is also known as PSTN—Public Switched Telephone Network.
- A telephone is used to perform a meeting or conference between two or more people who are set apart or isolated by an extent.

35.3.2   Limitations of Wired Technology

- Macrobending
- Attenuation
- Microbending

35.4   Wireless Communication

Wireless communication technology is rapidly expanding to impart the flexibility (contortion) and mobility in our day-to-day life. The use of cable restriction is one of the advantages of using wireless mode of communicating devices rather than wired communication. Other benefits include the dynamic emergence, cheaper and secured deployment.

In the current scenario, wireless mode of communication systems become an important part of different types of wireless devices, which gives user permission to communicate or transfer even from remotely operated areas. Wireless transmission can be happen through Radio Frequency (RF), Microwave Radiation and Infrared Radiation (IR) to provide user with high speed network zone. Technology like Bluetooth (BT), Wireless Fidelity (WiFi), GPS (Global Positioning System) and GPRS (General Packet Radio Service) uses RF to communicate between two distinct points whereas IR uses infrared (IR) waves for transmission of data from one point to another.

35.4.1   Types of Wireless Technology

    a. Wi-Fi (Wireless-Fidelity): Wi-Fi is a low power consuming wireless devices, which is used by numerous computing devices such as palmtops, laptops, etc. In this system, router routes as a transmission hub without the use of any physical material or wirelessly. These networks allow end user to join only when they are within the defined range of a router. Wi-Fi is very often used in networking applications that uses mobility and transferability wirelessly. These networks required to preserved with passwords, with a motive of security, otherwise it will be used by other users (Figure 35.4).

    b. Bluetooth Technology: The Bluetooth technology functions to permit us to create a connection with various electronic computing devices wirelessly [20]

Figure 35.4 Wireless-Fidelity (WiFi).

(air-medium) to a set-up for the transfer of data and information. Smart phones are linked to wireless earphones, mouse, bluetooth keyboard. By using these bluetooth devices the data can also be transmitted from one to another device. This transmission has numerous functions and it is applied regularly in the wireless world (Figure 35.5).

c. Satellite Communication: Satellite which is derived from Latin word "Satelles", which means to follows after a significant personality. Hence, satellite transmission is one of the self-contained wireless technologies. It is extensively roll out all over the earth to allow us to be interacted almost every nook and corner of the planet earth. When a beam of modulated microwave (signal) is transmit near the satellites then, it amplifies or modulates the microwave signal and transfers back to the receiver which is situated on the superficial part of the planet earth. These types of transmission carries two main elements like the space segments and the ground segments. The ground segment contains fixed and mobile transfer of information, reception and auxialry equipment and the space segments which are mainly comprises of the satellite itself (Figure 35.6).

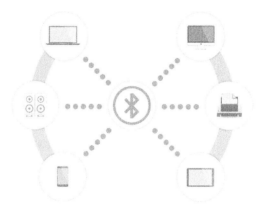

Figure 35.5 Bluetooth.

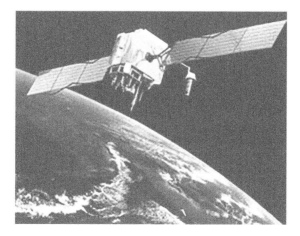

Figure 35.6 Satellite communications.

35.4.2   Applications of Wireless Technology

1. Security Surveillance Systems
2. TV Remote Control
3. Wireless Fidelity
4. Smart phones
5. Bluetooth Mouse, Keyboard, etc.

35.4.3   Limitations of Wireless Technology

- It is very important to protect the wireless network technique so that the information or data won't be able to be misused by any unauthorized users
- An unauthorized or prohibited person can easily crack the wireless zone of signals which is spreading through the air media.

35.5   Optical Fiber Communication

An optical fiber technology can be defined as a dielectric (non-conductor) waveguides, which operate at Optical Frequencies (OF). The apparatus or a tube, if bent, twisted or if terminated to emit energy, is called a waveguide, commonly. The electromagnetic, microwave or frequency wave energy transmits through it in the form of light. The light propagates, along a waveguide can be expressed in form of a set of guided (like wired media) electromagnetic waves, called as *modes* of the waveguide.

35.5.1   Types of Optical Fiber Communication

1. Step Index Fiber: The refractive index (ratio of velocity of light in vacuum to the speed in core) of the core is uniform throughout and undergoes a sudden

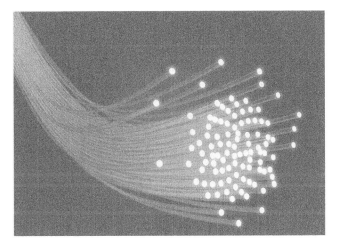

Figure 35.7 Optical fiber transmission of data.

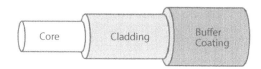

Figure 35.8 Parts of an optical fiber.

change (or step) at the cladding (middle part of optical fiber) boundary (Figure 35.7 and Figure 35.8).

2. Graded Index Fiber: The core refractive index is designed to differ as a function of the symmetrical distance from the centre of the fiber.

35.5.2   Applications of Optical Fiber Communication

a. Used in telephone systems.
b. Used in CCTV cameras for surveillance systems.
c. Used for connecting emergency groups like fire, police, and other emergency services.
d. Used in maintaining disciplines or to monitor individuals in hospitals, schools, and traffic management systems.

35.5.3   Limitations of Optical Fiber Communication

a. Though fiber optic cables last longer, the installation cost is high.
b. They are breakable if not encapsulated in a polymer sheath. Hence, more shielding is needed than copper ones.
c. The number of repeaters is to be multiplied with distance.

35.6   Radar Communication

RADAR acronyms for Radio Detection and Ranging System. It is basically an electromagnetic set-up which is used in the detection of the site or location and distance of a body from the site where the RADAR is positioned. It works by emitting energy into space or vacuum and monitors the echo or reflected wave from the body. It is deployed in the UHF—Ultra High Frequency and Microwave domain.

The RADAR system mainly contains a transmitter (transmit signals) which generates an electromagnetic signal or wave which is emitted into space or vacuum by an antenna. When this wave or electromagnetic signal strikes anybody, it gets reflected or re-emitted in different directions. This echo signal is acquired by the radar antenna which delivers it to the receiving end where receiver is present, where it is computed to calculate the geographical statistics or positioning of the body. The range is calculated by—"time taken by the signal to travel from the RADAR to the target and back". The object's location is signified in angle, from the direction of max amplitude (length or width) of echo waves, the antenna points to Figure 35.9.

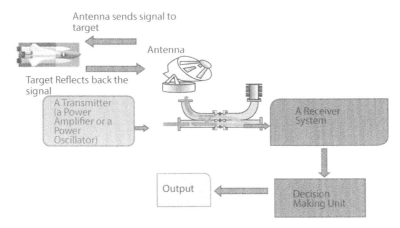

Figure 35.9 Working of RADAR.

35.6.1   Types of Radar Communication

a.   Pulsed RADAR: Pulsed RADAR sends high power and high rate of occurrence of pulses towards the selected object. It then halts for the echo signal or wave from the chosen body before another pulse is to be transferred. The range and resolution of the RADAR hang on the Pulse Repetition Frequencies (PRF). This is based on Doppler shift method.

The principle of RADAR detection of moving objects by the use of the Doppler shift functions on the fact that echo waves from immobilized bodies are in same phase and so, get cancelled while 511 echo waves from mobile body will have some difference or there is any change in phase [2].

b.   Continuous Wave RADAR: The Continuous Wave RADAR doesn't measures the range or reach of the selected object but rather the rate of change of range by calculating the Doppler shift of the signal which returns. In a CW RADAR electromagnetic radiation is radiated in place of pulses (Figure 35.10). It is generally used for speed measurement.

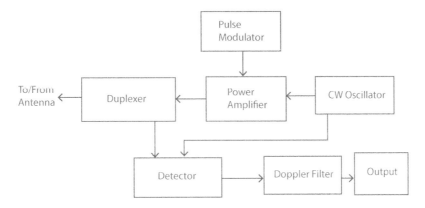

Figure 35.10 Pulsed RADAR.

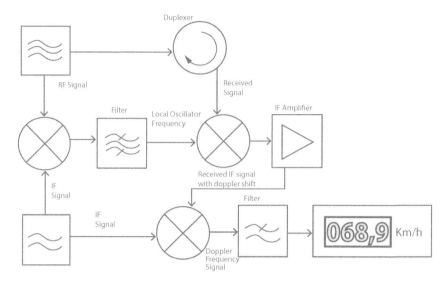

Figure 35.11 Continuous wave RADAR.

35.6.2   Applications of RADAR Communication

a.   Within air defense, this is applied for target or enemy detection, recognition and ammunition control (directing the ammune materials to keep an eye on targets).
b.   By ATC near airport area.
c.   The Air Surveillance RADAR is used for detecting and displaying the aircraft position in the airport terminals (Figure 35.11).
d.   Remote Sensing Ground.
e.   Traffic Control.
f.   To guide or provide path to the space vehicles for secured arrival on moon.

35.6.3   Limitations of RADAR Communication

a.   It cannot differentiate and resolve numerous targets which are very adjacent like our eye.
b.   It cannot recognize the color of targets.
c.   Targets are not visible which are under the water body and are present in depth.
d.   Targets are not visible which are positioned behind some conducting sheets.
e.   It is also not possible to recognize short distance targets.

35.7   Green Communication Technology, Its Management and Its Sustainability

Green technology has pull out a large amount of recognition with the evolution of the modern era. Similarly, with the evolution in communication technology the enterprises and researchers are focused to convert this communicating technology as green as feasible.

In cellular technology, the transformation of 5G (5th Generation) is the succeeding step to accomplish the user needs and it will be accessible to the users in 2020. This will enhance the energy utilization, which will result in excess radiation of CO_2.

Here, we will deal with varied strategy for the green communication technology and they are given below:

1. D2D—Device-to-Device communication
2. MIMO—Massive Multiple-Input Multiple-Output Systems
3. HetNets—Heterogeneous networks
4. GIOT—Green Internet of Things.

Mainly, the real world responsibilities are carried out by machines, automated devices and computers. All this is possible because of evolution in ICT sector i.e., information and communication technology. In air medium, or using wireless communication technology, data rate is boosted abruptly due to evolution and advancement in the electronic and communication technology at a larger rate.

The today's generation of mobile technology, i.e., 4-G, is now very much congested and overlaying issues like capacity shortage, bandwidth shortage, intervention and low data rates. 5G (5th Generation), that would be functioning by 2020, is scanned as the best possible way to solve these issues [12, 16].

It is presumed that the 5G will have the bandwidth and frequency of 1,000 times greater than that of 4G. Also, 5G communication would be able to serve vast number of gadgets [10, 11].

Higher data rates and fast speed web access will be a common requirement for these connecting gadgets. This would results in the radiation of viscous greenhouse gases. The devices which are energy efficient is used to control power consumption in cellular communication technologies and reduction in the emission CO_2 are one of the most prominent features of Green Transmission Technologies [22].

The development of 5G has a substantial desire for having green communications. Some of the technologies used for green communication used in 5G are defined below [4]:

- Device-to-Device (D2D) communication is a radio access technical advancement which provides users the potential to commune directly when they are closer to each other, without traversing congestion through the network infrastructure. Spectral and energy efficiencies of the network can be multiplied through these technologies. In D2D communications, the person can commune straight, which cause emission (offloading) of the network congestion at starting base stations [8]. Limited energy will be imbibe which results in reducing level of CO_2 emissions and other harmful radiations like RF (Radio Frequency) or EMI(Electro Magnetic) radiations [1, 5–7, 19].
- Massive MIMO Multi user: Multiple Input Multiple Output technology is on developing phase. In such set-up, a central station having numerous antennas at the same time assists a numerous amount of users having single-antenna device. The massive MIMO technology has several features like enhanced energy production, powerful immature, enhanced throughput, latency or discontinuation reduction and larger capacity gains. In massive MIMO, the

antennas selection plays a very important role. To manage the consumption of power at the central stations, the antennas or transreceiver should be omnidirectional (accessible in each and every direction) so, that it will produce energy efficiently. Charging or muting the antennas in no load or zero load condition will saveabout 50% of the power [3, 18].

> Challenges:
  - Energy Efficiency: The energy efficiency is a major dispute of concern for next generations of wireless or air media technologies because of the computational complexities of evolved technology and growth in size of central station location for transmitting of high data rates.

    The requirement of supplying demanded larger data rates and acute applications in wireless technology need larger amount of energy that is evolving rapidly. The higher energy consumptions has significantly impact globally. So, it is essential to develop high energy efficient technology which enables green communication for safer environment.
  - Spectral or Bandwidth Efficiency: The one of the most important and complex design limitation of a designing engineer for any transmission systems was the network bandwidth or frequency as well as throughput in terms of higher efficiency. Hence, network frequency and QOS (Quality of Service) are one of the most frameworks that make communication to play a very important role in the present scenario.
> Advantages Of Green Technology
  - Tax Relaxation Systems
  - Life Time value
  - Environmental Benefits

35.8   Space Air Ground Integrated Communication

Space air ground integrated communications system is an integration of numerous satellites in space, ground communication systems and aerial networks. It is an emerging way of communication and extensive research has been going on it for several years.

This technology faces several problems because of improper resources in the given network segments. Therefore, it is very necessary to handle each and every network segment properly and make sure they work seamlessly and simultaneously [17].

This integrated communication technology has several nodes for communication such as vehicle nodes, mobile users, drones, etc. These nodes are very much prone to security breaches and cyber-attacks as well.

> Security Issues: This technology faces security issues because of low latency and high network speed requirements. If any of the nodes are attacked then entire communication is under threat. Thus, Blockchain technology is often used to sort out this problem. Blockchain technology is decentralized, so this proves to be a plus point in communication.
> Key Technologies

In the upcoming years, the channel can be modernized as a mobile terminal, which will be furnished with respective sensors. Numerous and complex data resources, the channel require to exchange environmental information with other channels, boundary infrastructure, and boundary control centres through these sensors

- Traditional Structure: Divided into three parts, vehicle nodes, small—area management nodes and road side units. This structure is a central or consolidated one and is authenticated by negotiator. Cross-border identification information transmission can be done in two ways, first is to shift from a security spot to adjacent security spot. Second could be that channels transfer information from security domains A to B which is directed by numerous certificate authorities.
- Hash-based Structure: This structure is different from the previous one as it is distributed and decentralized. Certificate authorities are responsible only for vehicle node registration for the first time they join space–air–ground communication. In this structure, the management node of security domain of A calls protection supervisor, which adds the trans-boundary identity information of a channel to the blockchain, the protection supervisor of other node contemporizes the account to obtain the identity information of a channel.

35.9 Ubiquitous Communication

The way of intensifying computing environment by developing many gadgets which are present in all over the physical surroundings, but developing them effectively is not visible to the common mass.

The present scenario of 21st century may be one of the most fascinating scenarios in the past to be alive. We are seeing a remarkable abundance of interchange in societies around the each and every corner of the world in a very limited time period. The initiation of the most of this transposition is because of new emerging technology and the Internet or web access. In the last decade, we have seen every facet of the life of an individual and firms to undergo through many developmental phases and unpredictability. The telecommunication and Internet Technology have developed drastically during the past decade, laying a strong foundation for the next upcoming generation of the Ubiquitous Internet access, omnipresent (which is present everywhere) web technology and ultimate autonomous information or data on internet. Past, proved that one have to must look ahead and receive the futuristic vision as possible scenario of tomorrow's realms. Nowadays, technology such as Television, web access, Cell Phones, Traffic lights, polaroid cameras are most important part of our day-to-day life.

As wide spreading computing systems or Ubiquitous System are able of fetching, organizing and transmitting data, they can transform to the data conditions and activities, which means, a network which can gain knowledge about its surrounding and improve the individual experience and feature of life not only for an individual but also for human to other living beings.

As Mark Weiser has said and tries to develop a Universal Computing Environment (UCE) that hides:

a.   Computing Gadgets
b.   Device
c.   Resource
d.   Technologies.

Calculating or computing everywhere may be implanted on wearable handpicked devices which helps in communicating transparently to give varied service to the individual gadgets mostly having low power consumption and very short-range wireless transmission capability no gadgets which utilizes multiple on-board sensors to collect information about adjoining environment.

 ➢ The vow of ubiquitous computing:
    A life in which our attempts are effectively, though sophisticated, assisted by computing devices the idealistic imagination to be painted by the ubiquitous or wide spreading computing movement which stand in sharp contrast to what we are seeing when we take up our computing gadgets per day.
 ➢ Privacy and Challenges:
    In a fully network world with ubiquitous or widespread, sensor-fitted devices or gadgets some privacy and security factors happen to the people in this surrounding will be anxious about their privacy as, there is the capability of total monitoring must be in knowledge of the client and it must be transformed into the system architecture.

35.10   Network Planning, Management, Security

Network Planning:
Network planning & design: it's a repetitive task, encompassing topological design, network-synthesis, and network-realization, and its aim is to make sure that a new telecommunication network or service meets the need and requirements of the subscribers and operators. The procedure can be customized as per new network or service.
   This process begins with acquiring of external information that contains:

 •   Projection of how the new network and services will operate.
 •   The economic information regarding cost.
 •   The technical details of the network capabilities.

Planning a new network services involves implementing new system across the first four layers of the Reference Model (OSI).

Network planning process steps:

 •   Topological designs: On this stage we determine the place of the components and interconnect between them. Graph Theory is used to optimize the methods used in this stage. These techniques involve determining the cost of transmission, switching, and thereby determining the most conducive way of the connection matrix and location of switch and concentrator [9].

- Network Synthesis: This stage deals with the size of components used, on the basis of performance criteria such as the Grade of Service. The method is called as "Nonlinear Optimization", that involves determining the topology, transmission cost, etc., and using this information to calculate routing plan, also the size of every component.
- Network Realization: This process deals with finding methods to meet capacity requirements, and ensure authenticity within the network. The method used is said to be "Multicommodity Flow Optimization", and determines all information relating to demands, costs and reliability, and then using this information to calculate an actual physical circuit plan.

Network Management:
N/W management is a process of managing a network from fault and performance using different tools and technologies to keep up with the business requirements. The goal of network management is to achieve an error free network.

Network Management domains:

- Performance Management: To analyze, measure, report, and control the performance like utilization & throughput of various network components are the major goal of performance management. These components include individual devices such as links, routers, and hosts as well as the end to end abstractions like a path through the network.
- Faults Management: The objective of this process is to detect, and responding to fault condition into network. This technique is used to manage quick handling of the failures such as link failures, host failures, or router hardware problems, these problems are also known as a transient network failures. SNMP protocol plays a major role in fault management.
- Configurations Management: Tracing of the devices that are on the managed network, the hardware and software configurations are allowed under Configuration managements.
- Security Management: The main objective of security management is to control network resource access according to some well-defined policy. The key distribution centers are a component of network management. The use of firewall to monitor and control external access point to one's network is other crucial component.

Network Security:
It is the process of taking preventative measures to protect the networking infrastructure from unauthorized access, malfunction, modification, misuse, destruction, to create a secure platform for computers, users, and programs to perform their permitted critical functions within a secure environment [21].

Network Securities comprises of:
- Protection: Configuration of system and network should be done as correctly as possible.
- Detection: We must be able to identify when the configuration has changed or when some network traffic indicates a problem.
- Reaction: After identifying problems immediately, we must respond to them and return to a safe state as rapidly as possible.

Network Security Methods:
- Anti-malware: Viruses, worms, and Trojan attempts to spread across a network, and can lie low on infected machines for days or weeks. The security efforts should do the best to avoid initial threats and also avoid root causes that are making way to the network.
- Behavioral analytics: We should have knowledge about how normal network behavior looks like so that you can spot abnormalities or breaches when they arise.
- Data loss preventions: We Humans are inevitably the weakest security link. We need to implement technologies and processes to ensure that staffers don't deliberately or inadvertently send sensitive data outside the network.
- E-mail security: Phishing is one of the most common ways attackers gain access to a network. Email security tools are capable to block both incoming attacks and outbound messages having sensitive data.
- Firewall: In the network security world, we define the rules to permit or deny traffic at the border between your network and the internet, establishing barrier between the trusted zone and the wildest outside.

35.11   Cognitive Radio Communication

A cognitive Radio is basically a software radio or intelligent radio system that can be controlled. This system can be programmed and designed dynamically. It makes use of the best Wireless channels available in the proximity in order to avoid congestion and user interference. The channels available in the vicinity are automatically detected. The system then alters its communication reception specification accordingly to permit considerable simultaneous air media communication in provided spectrum band at a particular area.

The Spectrum assigned isn't fully utilized. Some portion go completely unused. Cognitive radio provides a potential solution to the tedious problem. A cognitive radio smartly detects whether a part of spectrum is applicable or not. Afterwards, it uses it for the time being without causing any sort of intervention with the transmission of other users. This optimizes the utilization of available radio frequency (RF) spectrum.

Cognitive sensor networks are positioned over a numerous amount of sensors for intuitive and autonomous acquiring of localized and presided information or data of the environment which we are noticing. Example of bio-inspired sensing and networking is monitoring of gene expression in feedback to variation in cell-population density (i.e., quorum sensing).

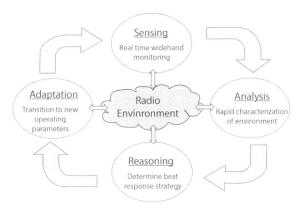

Figure 35.12 Modes of cognitive radio communication.

35.12   Types of Cognitive Radio Communication

- Full Cognitive Radio: It can be programmed to use best wireless channels available in the neighbourhood. It takes into consideration all the parameters about which the network moves (Figure 35.12).
- Spectrum Sensing Cognitive Radio: With the increase in the use of cognitive radio, the area of spectrum the area of spectrum sensing is becoming essential. It is done to use spectrum in an efficient manner.
  - Self-Spectrum Sensing: Here, the cognitive radio acts solitarily. The radio will design its pattern or configure itself on the basis of the waves it detect.
  - Cooperative Spectrum Sensing: Sensing is done by distinct radios which is present in the range of a cognitive radio network. The Overall network is adjusted automatically.

35.13   Next Generation Communications and Applications

Next generation communication technology is also known as advanced communication technologies. It refers to the enhancement of communication technologies. With increasing technological advancement in internet and other technologies the communication technology has evolved immensely. Next Generation communication technology provides more services such as high speed, high resolution image, a good quality of video as compared to the conventional communication technology. Major applications of Next Generation Communication Technologies are:

a. High speed communication is crucial in any organization and also for our personal use.
b. It serves a variety of applications such as: Automobiles, Health Care, Aerospace and Defense, Automation, Telecommunication, etc.

It is expected that next generation communication devices market will register a CAGR over 20% during 2020–2025.

The market for the next generation communication device is segmented by a 5G visible light communication or LiFi, wireless sensor, wsw and defense automation and geography. Visible Light Communication (VLC) is used in acts related to vehicle and transportation. It can include LBS (Light Based Sensor) Vehicle-to-Vehicle, We-to-We communication and Intelligent Transportation System (ITS). Visible communication or LiFi reduces the use of conventional wireless technology such as infrared, bluetooth and wifi which emit harmful RF and EMI waves [13–15].

5G provides better mobile experience for smart phone user and will also meet the growing demands of mobile communication in future acts.

35.14 Smart Energy Management

Energy and electricity have been a major concern for the society and the world at large. Resources are becoming scarce day-by-day due to the continuous use of resources by humans and because of this the cost of electricity is increasing. It is important for the society to utilize energy in an efficient way. One way of doing so is by installing an Energy Management System.

Smart Energy Management system will show every detail about the energy consumption thus helping us to carry out energy efficient technology will in turn save energy.

In short, Smart Energy Management helps us to diagnose possible energy doses and the current problems in new residential or commercial areas. Some of these smart energy systems are simple such as solar panels.

Smart energy management is about operating, producing and stockpiling electricity more effectively, economically and which are imperishable for the network of grid, and for particular operators.

It involves upgrading our energy communication system by giving us smart control and transmittive information technology to provide clients and network operators access as per their energy demands and budgets.

Smart Energy Management techniques cater for two main primary groups:

1. Client-owned behind-the-meter energy resources
2. Utility and Grid-based resource.

Energy techniques include:

End-to-end Smart Energy project conveyance, microgrids or microbended networks, scattered energy sources, smart network service, energy organization, and data analysis data optimization. This technique enables businessman and grid operators to reliably transmit to a several-directional power network that includes renewables or non-conventional and other smart generation tools and technologies.

Different types of Smart Energy Management:

1. For Home: In order to reduce the electricity bill people is started to shift towards smart Energy Management solutions. These include installation of energy saving home appliances such as: AC, microwave Washing Machines, and dryers. Insulating walls to control temperatures also way.

Using motion sensitive electronic devices is also being done to save energy.

2. For Business: Their aim is to Conserve energy on a large scale like homes businesses can install motion sensitive devices that turn off when no motion is detected. They can also use better insulation, etc. They also use power saving bulbs instead of fluorescent bulbs.

References

1. Panwar, N., Sharma, S., Singh, A.K., A Survey on 5G: The Next Generation of Mobile Communication, *Phys. Commun.*, 18, 2, 64–84, 2016.
2. https://5g-ppp.eu/wp-content/uploads/2015/07/5G-Infrastructure-Association-5G-PPP-overview_EuCNC-2015.
3. https://www.ngmn.org/wp-content/uploads/NGMN_5G_White_Paper_V1_0.pdf, 2015.
4. Andrews, J.G. *et al.*, What Will 5G Be?, *IEEE Journal on Selected Areas in Communications*, 32, 6, 1065–1082, 2014.
5. https://www.gsma.com/futurenetworks/wp-content/uploads/2015/01/Understanding-5G-Perspectives-on-future-technological-advancements-in-mobile.pdf, 2014.
6. Agiwal, M., Roy, A., Saxena, N., Next Generation 5G Wireless Networks: A Comprehensive Survey. *IEEE Commun. Surv. Tutor.* 18, 3, 1617–1655, 2016.
7. Qiao, J., Shen, X.S., Mark, J.W., Shen, Q., He, Y., Lei, L., Enabling Device-to-Device Communications in Millimeter-Wave 5G Cellular Networks. *IEEE Commun. Mag.*, 53, 1, 209–215, 2015.
8. Wei, L., Hu, R.Q., Qian, Y., Wu, G., Energy Efficiency and Spectrum Efficiency of Multihop Device-to-Device Communications Underlying Cellular Networks. *IEEE Trans. Veh. Technol.*, 65, 1, 367–380, 2016.
9. Dabbagn, M., Hu, B., Guizani, M., Rayes, A., Software-Defined Networking Security: Pros and Cons. *IEEE Commun.*, 53, 6, 73–79, 2015.
10. Zhang, J., Xie, W., Yang, F., An Architecture for 5G Mobile Network based on SDN and NFV. *6th International Conference on Wireless, Mobile and Multi-Media* (ICWMMN2015), pp. 87–92, 2015.
11. 5G security recommendations package #2: network slicing, NGMN Alliance, April, 2016.
12. 5G Security, *Ericsson white paper*, June, 2015.
13. The Road to 5G: Drivers, Applications, Requirements and Technical Development, GSA, November, 2015. https://www.huawei.com/minisite/5g/img/GSA_the_Road_to_5G.pdf, 2015.
14. https://www.qualcomm.com/media/documents/files/qualcomm-5g-vision-presentation.pdf, 2016.
15. https://www.huawei.com/minisite/5g/img/5G_Security_Whitepaper_en.pdf,2015.
16. Vij, S. and Jain, A., "5G: Evolution of a secure mobile technology", *3rd International Conference on Computing for Sustainable Global Development (INDIACom)*, pp. 2192–2196, 2015.
17. Cao, J., Ma, M., Li, H., Zhang, Y., Luo, Z., A Survey on Security Aspects for LTE and LTE-A Networks. *IEEE J. Mag.*, 16, 1, 283–302, 2014.
18. Zhan nications in LTE-Advanced Networks. *IEEE Trans. Veh.* Technol., 65, 4, 2659–2672, 2016.
19. Wang, M.J., Yan, Z., Niemi, V., UAKA-D2D: Universal Authentication and Key Agreement Protocol in D2D Communications. *Mobile Netw. Appl.*, 22, 3, 510–525, 2017. https://www.ngmn.org/publications/5g-security-recommendations-package-1.html.
20. Security challenges and opportunities for 5G mobile networks, NOKIA, 2017. https://www.ngmn.org/publications/5g-security-recommendations-package-1.html

21. Liyanage, M., Abro, A.B., Ylianttila, M., Gurtov, A., Opportunities and Challenges of Software-Defined Mobile Networks in Network Security. *IEEE Secur. Privacy,* 14, 4, 34–44, 2016.

22. Vassilakis, V.G., Moscholios, I.D., Alzahrani, On the security of software-defined next-generation cellular networks. *IEICE Information and Communication Technology Forum (ICTF),* pp. 61–65, 2016.

36

An Approach for Load Balancing Through Genetic Algorithm

Mahendra Pratap Yadav*, Harishchandra A. Akarte and Dharmendra Kumar Yadav

Computer Science and Engineering Department, MNNIT Allahabad, Prayagraj, India

Abstract

As the total of Internet users is rising widely, cloud service providers are facing various problems. A few of the most challenging cases faced by the cloud service provider is to provide services to end-user efficiently within the stipulated time. The cause of the problem is the huge request for the resources by the client at a precise time. For a system administrator, the most challenging task to enhance the system's performance more quickly and efficiently so that it can provide better services to the end-users. The demand for services is increasing and decreasing very frequently. To meet the expectations of end-user cloud providers uses several load-balancing techniques that help providers in distributing incoming traffic over various virtual machines for resource allocations. In this article, we have used a popular optimization technique: the genetic algorithm to manage the incoming traffics. The work has been compared with different other techniques like weighted round-robin, random, and round-robin algorithms, and then it has been found that the genetic algorithm offers better performance in terms of optimizing the uses of resources. It also minimizes the average response time which prevents the machine gets overloaded.

Keywords: Cloud computing, services, load balancing, virtualization, virtual machine, genetic algorithm

36.1 Introduction

Cloud computing is one of the most popular and new paradigms in the world of computing, which is used for extending and sharing pools of system resources over the Internet with minimal management effort and minimum time possible. It also provides cost reduction in establishing IT infrastructure to not only start-up companies but also to small and medium rms. In cloud computing resources are shared with the end user similar to public utility services such as power, water, telephone, etc. to provide services them. The resources shared by the cloud provider with the end user act as a service, and these service are classified commonly into three classes viz: Software-as-a-Service (SaaS) to run the client services, Platform-as-a-Service (PaaS) to come up with the application software and Infrastructure-as-a service (IaaS)

---

*Corresponding author: 2015rcs51@mnnit.ac; pratap2020@gmail.com

Namita Gupta, Prasenjit Chatterjee and Tanupriya Choudhury (eds.) Smart and Sustainable Intelligent Systems, (511–524)
© 2021 Scrivener Publishing LLC

for hosting the client application. Cloud providers use various deployment models to provide these services to end-user. Cloud deployment models have classified into four types, which are known as public to access any one at anywhere, private for specific person (e.g. militant or various security organization), hybrid (e.g. the public and private combining both) and community cloud for same types of organization [17, 18]. Cloud service providers used these service models for the end user to provide services. When the demand for any services increases, the cloud providers manage these demands with a load balancer. Load balancing is a powerful technique used by cloud provider to distribute the incoming traffic e.g. workloads over several computing machine, such as personal computers, cluster of virtual machines, or different data centers that consist of virtual machine, CPUs, or storage devices for their needs [14, 15]. The primary motive of load balancing algorithms is how to optimize resources use by the client as well as organization for their own benefits, curtail the overall average response time of the serving system and also prevent the overloading/under loading of any particular machine due to the huge incoming traffic at the peak demanding time. One should take care of the load balancer that it will not lead to a single point of failure. There are various scheduling algorithms utilized by the cloud provides. These scheduling algorithms are known as load-balancing methods, which are used by different load balancers to find out which back-end server will be used for sending the ongoing incoming request that is received. Some basic algorithms for load balancing are first-come first-serve (FCFS) and round robin (RR), weighted round robin (WRR) [16, 20]. The exponential growths of internet users as well as cloud clients have resulted as an expansion in the availability of the services as well as computing resource over the cloud. If the number of cloud user increases, so the service providers need to handle the massive request generated by that end-users. Due to that, one of the primary challenges then comes to improve the system performance better or same than the existing whenever such an outburst appears [13]. Hence, in cloud computing, most of the critical problems are still need to be explored. One of these problems is the load balancing due to the fluctuating workload to access the cloud services. The demand for services is increasing and decreasing very frequently. To meet the expectations of end-user cloud providers uses several load-balancing techniques that help providers in distributing incoming traffic over various virtual machines for resource allocations. In this paper, we have used a popular optimization technique such as the genetic algorithm to manage the incoming traffics. The proposed approach compared with the traditional load balancing techniques like weighted round robin, round robin, and random algorithms and show that the genetic algorithm gives better resources utilization and also minimizes the average response time which prevents the machine gets overloaded.

This article comprises of the following research contribution: In Section 36.2 we have discussed the motivation towards the proposed work. In Section 36.3 we discussed the background and related technology that can be used as in this article. In Section 36.4 we performed literature review which is related with the proposed work. In Section 36.5 we discussed the proposed solution. In Section 36.6 we discussed and presented the experimental setup and result analysis and in the last section we conclude the article in Section 36.7.

36.2 Motivation

When client hosts an application over a data center, the hosted application demand has been increased or decreased along with the time. The popularity of hosted application for users may increase or decrease the workload in the virtual machine. Different types of applications have various kinds of clients and they have their own different kinds of requirements. Therefore, to manage the diverse types of traffic workload with adequate computing resources to fulfill workload at collapse and peak demand time provisioning can be expensive. Alternatively, retaining least computing resources may not fulfill the requirement at that time when the workload is at the peak, and it can cause poor performance (e.g. more response time and less throughput) and violation of SLA constraints. To manage the dynamic traffic is very effectively for the resources utilization and less response time and maximum throughput.

36.3   Background and Related Technology

Cloud providers provide the services to the client according to the fluctuating workload with the help of some types of decisions and conditions. They use different auto-scaling mechanisms to full the client's demands at the right moment. Here we discuss various concepts and techniques that are used in this article

36.3.1   Load Balancing

It is a technique used by the cloud providers for distributing the incoming traffic from the task nodes among the several servers in the given environment ensuring that the system is neither overloaded nor idle. A good load-balancing algorithm is that which assures each and every node in the network performs more or less the same amount of work. A good load balancer (Figure 36.1) uses various load-balancing algorithms for maintaining the quality of services. Also a load-balancing algorithm is used to reduce the overhead and increase the throughput.

The primary task of any load-balancing algorithm is how to perform mapping of jobs in cloud domain to the free, which improves the overall response time along with efficient resource utilization [13]. So it is important aspect of cloud network that are used by the

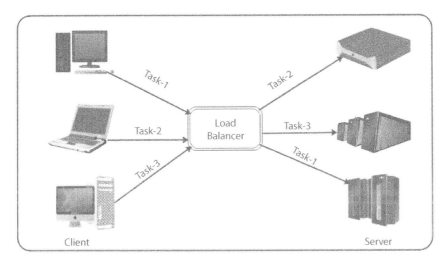

Figure 36.1 Load balancer.

service providers of cloud to provide the various services to end user. Load balancing technique is one of the essential property of cloud computing. As because it's not possible to predict in future how many number of incoming requests per second traffic comes in the cloud domain because of the active changing behavior of the cloud users. The primary contribution of the load balance at different layer that use various load–balancing algorithms in the cloud domain to allocate the incoming traffics load over various nodes to satisfy the user demands from the customer's point of view and to provide efficient computing resource utilization form providers point view [20].

36.3.2   Load Balancing Metrics

There are various terminologies that are used in load-balancing approach for managing the incoming traffic, which are discussed as follows:

a. Throughput (T): It is used to measure how many number of processes (Np) executed with in per unit time (t).

$$T = Np / t \qquad (36.1)$$

b. Response Time (R_t): It calculates the overall time that is required the system for serving and allocating the task. Let A_i and P_i be the arrival time and assignment time of the ith request respectively.

$$R_t = P_i - A_i \qquad (36.2)$$

c. Makespan: The time needed to calculate the maximum time to completion of all the tasks, which is allocated to the system.

d. Scalability (S(x)): Scalability of the system/model is to define the ability of the serving system to sustain better under any conditions. That means the surviving capability of the system to maintain at that peak level when the number of incoming traffics workload or size of task handle by the system is increased. Scalability means it is combination of the elasticity and automation. The linear scalability with slope λ can be defined as:

$$S(x) = \lambda * x \qquad (36.3)$$

e. Migration Time (M_t): This metric is used measure the how much amount of time requires for transferring a process form an overload machine to an ideal or under loaded machine.

f. Degree of Imbalance (Dim): It is used for measuring the system imbalance between among VMs. Let T_i be the time when the ith processing node becomes free.

$$Dim = \max_{1 \leq i \leq m}(T_i) - \max_{1 \leq i \leq m}(T_i) \qquad (36.4)$$

g. Fault Tolerance: It is a technique that can be used by load balancer when a fault occurs either software or hardware on the system, the system performs all the services without interruption. It determines the performance of an algorithm, which is used to manage the system failure, is a fault occurs on a node or links.

h. Energy Consumption (E_c): Energy consumption is used to calculate how much amount of energy exhausted by all nodes to perform the operation. Load-balancing is also used to prevent the serving system over-heating. Let C_i be the amount of energy consumed by i^{th} node respectively.

$$E_C = \sum_{i=1}^{N} (C_i) \tag{36.5}$$

i. Carbon Emission (C_e): The load balancing algorithms are very useful for reducing the carbon production generated by all resources. A machine, which is overloaded, generates more carbon in comparison with the under loaded machine. Carbon emission is used to measure the amount of carbon generated by all resources. Let R_i be the amount of carbon produced by i^{th} resource respectively.

$$C_e = \sum_{i=1}^{N} (R_i) \tag{36.6}$$

36.3.3 Classification of Load Balancing Algorithms

The load balancers use the different types of load balancing approaches to distribute the incoming traffic among nodes. These approaches are performed the load-balancing based on the system state or a process who initiated for transferring the task [18]. The details classification [21] of load balancing approaches are shown in Figure 36.2. In this article we have briefly discussed into two types which are based on the system state and also discussed below:

a. Static Algorithm: For a homogeneous and reliable environment, cloud providers as well as academia's are used the static load balancing algorithms to provide the services to end users and performed their experiment respectively. It is used to transfer the incoming traffic in the equal fashion among all the available servers. Static load balancing technique generally used average information of system behavior to transfer the incoming traffic over several among available servers. The transfer strategies are made independently for each and every system based on its actual present system state. The static load-balancing technique uses a basic understanding of the running applications along with analytical figures of the serving system to manage the incoming traffic load. There are diverse static load balancing algorithms that can be used by cloud providers as well as academia's namely

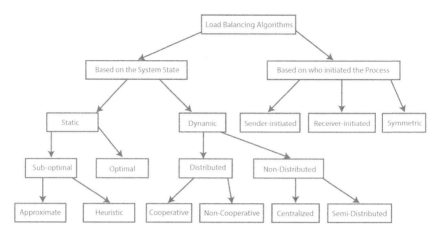

Figure 36.2 Classifications of load balancing algorithms.

    Round-Robin, Min–Min, Opportunistic Load Balancing (OLB), and Max–Min Algorithms [18].

  b. Dynamic Algorithm: For a heterogeneous environment, cloud providers as well as academia's are used the dynamic load balancing algorithms to provide the services to end users and performed their experiment respectively. This approach is helpful when we want to distribute the workload automatically without human intervention which is depended on the system present state to handle the incoming traffic. In this approach, it is distributed the incoming the traffic among various VMs on same data-center or other data-center dynamically at runtime. Unlike static load-balancing algorithms, the dynamic algorithms assign running processes effectively at run time when any one of VMs becomes under-loaded or over-loaded due to huge/less traffic. For distributed environment, there are two ways (e.g. distributed and non-distributed) to achieve the dynamic load balancing. In the dynamic approach they are used a queue to buffer the incoming traffic at the main host and dynamically allocate that traffic to remote hosts when they demanded for that. There are numerous dynamic load balancing algorithms that can be used by cloud providers as well as academia's namely Ant Colony Optimization (ACO), Throttled and Honey Bee Foraging [18].

36.4   Related Work

In this section, we have discussed those works which are related to the load balancing. Several researchers had contributed, and still, many researches are going on in the area of task scheduling just as load balancing for the cloud environments. Some of the authors use traditional scheduling approach similar to round robin, weighted round robin and FCFS for load balancing.

    The authors have proposed an algorithm in Ref. [1], which analyzes the performance of a system through the load balancing techniques in cloud environments. They say that they have been used various load-balancing algorithms to compare the system performance through different metrics such as response time, speed, throughput, complexity, etc. But, at last, they have concluded that all the reviewed algorithms would not be suitable for different area that is require for the load balancing.

A new algorithm has been proposed in Ref. [2], which uses the natural selection approach to select the appropriate node to transfer the task through the Genetic Algorithm approach. The proposed approach uses a fitness function. This fitness function defines in terms of cost of delay as well as execution of instruction. The delay cost is an estimated amount as a penalty that is pay to the customer by cloud service provider when the actual finishing of a job is more than the deadline time; which has been earlier advertised by the cloud service providers. The proposed load balancing technique is used to find a global optimum processor in cloud environment for scheduling jobs through load balancing technique. But they have considered only one parameter of Overall Average Response Time for comparison with other Algorithms. Also, they did not calculate fitness function after encoding chromosomes as binary strings.

In Ref. [11] Randles *et al.* have discussed another load balancing approach (e.g. Decentralized honeybee approach) which is based on the nature-inspired approach used in self-organization. The proposed approach performs the load balancing through the local server. The proposed approach enhances the system performance along with system diversity, but it faces another challenge, when the system size increases the throughput does not increase. The proposed approach is suitable in the situation where the varied population of different services are needed. The advantage of the said algorithm is that the performance of the serving system improves along with increased system diversity.

Zhang *et al.* have discussed in Ref. [6] about a new algorithm for managing the incoming traffic that is based on combination of both complex network theory and ant colony for federation of open cloud computing. The proposed approach uses an important characteristic namely scale-free of the complex network along with the small world to perform the load-balancing in better way. The proposed approach overcomes due to the heterogeneity of the system. It is adaptive for the dynamic cloud environment. The proposed approach excellent for scalability as well as fault tolerance hence it supports to improve the system performance.

Mesbahi *et al.* [7] have introduced a survey with the title "Load Balancing in Cloud Computing: A State of Art Survey". This article has explored the entire necessary requirement to develop and implement a suitable algorithm which will be performed the load-balancing for cloud environment. A new categorization of load balancing technique has been proposed in this article that evaluates load balancing based on appropriate metrics. They also concluded that modern load balancing approaches are also considered the energy saving with their pros and cons.

Vanisenko *et al.* [8] have presented another survey with the title "Survey of Major Load Balancing algorithm in distributed System". This survey categorized all the load balancing algorithms in the distributed application based on their suitability for diversified area such as cluster or grid or cloud system. This article also summarizes the comparative analysis of a system with different parameters (such as response time migration time, throughput, etc.) through different load-balancing algorithms.

Another survey has presented in the article [9] which has reviewed all load balancing problems, including Ant Colony Optimization (ACO), Particle Swarm Optimization (PSO), Genetic Algorithms (GA) and Artificial Bee Colony (ABC). The authors have also implementation of another load balancing algorithm namely Ant Lion Optimizer (ALO) for cloud computing environment, which was supposed to provide the consequences in load balancing.

36.5   Proposed Solution

The main intent of this article is for finding an appropriate remedy for the Load Balancing difficulty using Genetic Algorithm to optimize the usage of computing resources. Genetic Algorithm relies on operators namely: mutation, crossover and selection. Initially, a set of candidate solutions is used which is further evolved towards better solutions. The results are compared with different scheduling strategy such as FCFS (First-come First-serve), RR (Round Robin), WRR (Weighted Round Robin) and Random assignment. Various parameters are used for comparisons such as overall average response time and degree of imbalance between nodes. Certain cases like specific node failure have been handled separately. In case of failure of the node, all the pending tasks are reassigned to other nodes using Genetic algorithm.

36.5.1   Genetic Algorithm

At any moment the problem with load balancing can be found out even though the cloud computing is dynamic. The major problem is to match the N number of requests coming from the cloud users to the M numbers of processing nodes available in the cloud. Every processing node has some attributes like MIPS, cost of execution, and fail time of machine. MIPS indicates the number of millions of instructions that can be executed by the specified machine every second. Similarly, each request to be completed has attributes like the size of content, the title of the page, etc. The load balancer needs to allocate these N demands to the M number of processing nodes so that the net average response time will be minimized with keeping the degree of imbalance among nodes to a minimum [19]. A fitness function which evaluates fitness of the current solution is defined below.

Let A_i and P_i be the arrival time and assignment time of the ith request respectively. For minimizing the Average Response time the fitness function used is defined as

$$F_{response\ time} = \sum_{i=1}^{N}(P_i - A_i)/N \qquad (36.7)$$

Let T_i be the time when the ith processing node becomes free. For minimizing the degree of imbalance, the fitness function used is defined as:

$$F_{degree\ of\ Imbalance} = \max_{1 \le i \le m}(T_i) - \max_{1 \le i \le m}(T_i) \qquad (36.8)$$

a. Initial population generation: Random individuals have generated the population, which then leads to the evolution. In the primary step for generating the initial population through the functioning of the Genetic algorithm. The each and every member of this population used to encode a best possible solution of a problem. When the initial population created, each and every individual population is evaluated, based on that to assign a fitness value to that based on the fitness function.

b. Genetic Operators: Crossover and Mutation: The primary motive for doing mutation operation is for changing the genes of offspring and for increasing the variety of the population. This is the process of enabling GAs to come out of regional or substandard solutions for avoiding untimely convergence. Parent centric and mean centric operators are the two prime strategies of crossover development. The parent centric strategy causes offspring near every one of the parents whereas to mean centric produces offspring solutions adjacent to the centroid of the parents, which is in the neighborhood of a mean of the participating progenitors. A coin toss method is used for doing Crossover. The probability of mutation used is 0.5.

36.5.2 Flowchart of Proposed Strategy

Flowchart of proposed approach (Figure 36.3) and proposed algorithm (Algorithm 1) that the generation process is repeated till the end of a termination condition. The termination condition is either the chromosome with best fitness value is obtained or when the maximum number of iterations is exceeded.

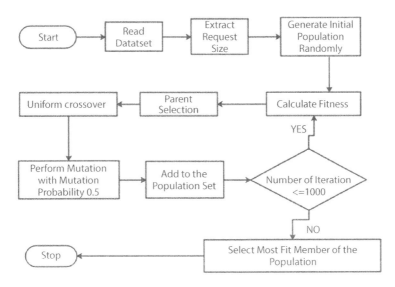

Figure 36.3 Flowchart of proposed approach.

Proposed Algorithm
Algorithm 1: Genetic Algorithm

I.   N ← number of requests
II.   M ← number of nodes
III.   i ← iterator
IV.   P ← initial population
V.   Require: N ≥ 0 and M ≥ 0
VI.   Ensure: fitness (P) ≥ 0
VII.   while i ≤ MAX ITERATIONS do
VIII.   p1 ← Parent 1 selected
IX.   p2 ← Parent 2 selected
X.   c1, c2 ← crossover (p1, p2)
XI.   mutate (c1)
XII.   mutate (c2)
XIII.   P.insert (c1)
XIV.   P.insert (c2)
XV.   Eliminate two least fit members
XVI.   end while
XVII.   return Fitness Value of most fit member

36.6   Experimental Setup and Results Analysis

In this segment we have discussed all the necessary steps that are used to implement proposed scenario.

36.6.1   Data Pre-Processing

For experimental purpose, in this article we have used a data-set which has been obtained from Wikipedia's page aspect statistics (https://dumps.wikimedia.org/other/pagecounts-raw/). We have considered the hourly requests for the month of January 2016 as our data set. The data set gives information as this article, the title of page recovered, the number of demands and the size of the content delivered. For the purpose of the algorithm we have filtered only the number of demands and the size of the content delivered.

36.6.2   Experimental Setup

Genetic algorithm is referred for finding the optimal assignment of incoming requests to various servers. A simulator is designed to compare the results of genetic algorithm with other standard algorithms like Round Robin, Weighted Round Robin and Random assignment. Netbeans IDE is used for designing the simulator. Initially the pre-processed data is loaded and VM specifications such as MIPS and cost are defined. The simulator provides the feature to assign the load according to the various algorithms including genetic algorithm. The results from various algorithms are compared on basis of two metrics. The two metrics are Average response time based and degree of imbalance based. The graphs are plotted for better visual analysis.

36.6.3 Result Analysis

From the experimental results which have been obtained from the simulator (i.e. cloudSim) are compared with respect to different parameters such as average response time and degree of imbalance. Table 36.1 shows the average response time for different algorithms for same and different VMs specification, which is visualized in the Figure 36.4 and the Figure 36.5 respectively. Table 36.2 shows the degree of imbalance for different algorithms for same and different VMs specification, which is visualized in the Figure 36.6 and the Figure 36.7 respectively. The results acquired from genetic algorithm are better than other standard

Table 36.1 Average response time for different algorithms.

Sr. No.	VM Specification	Round Robin	Random	WRR	Genetic
1	Same	2.1767	2.1739	2.1767	2.0165
2	Different	1.2608	1.2777	1.1171	0.9720

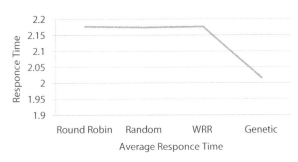

Figure 36.4 Graph for average response time for same VM.

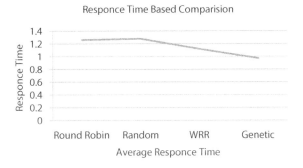

Figure 36.5 Graph for average response time for different VM.

Table 36.2 Degree of imbalance for deferent algorithms.

Sr. No.	VM Specification	Round Robin	Random	WRR	Genetic
1	Same	1.6461	3.0871	1.6461	0.8207
2	Different	4.2472	8.1426	1.7621	0.7812

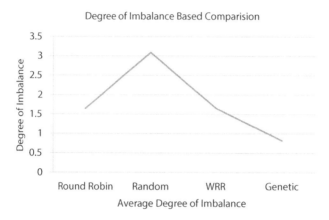

Figure 36.6 Graph for degree of imbalance for same VM.

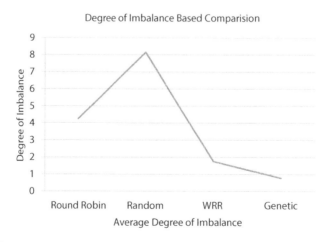

Fgure 36.7 Graph for degree of imbalance for deferent different VM.

algorithms for both of the metrics used (degree of imbalance and average response time). For VMs with similar specifications, Round Robin and Weighted Round Robin produce similar results. The genetic algorithm, round robin, weighted round robin and random assignment have been applied on hourly basis.

36.7   Conclusion

The paper dealt with the techniques to manage incoming traffic at peak-time. We have proposed an optimization algorithm for the balancing of load amid various virtual machines in cloud computing paradigm. To manage the incoming, the traffic is very efficient in term of service availability; to reduce the carbon emission and customers lost. Without an efficient approach cloud providers face very challenges such as service un-availability, more carbon emission, and minimum throughput, maximum response time. For optimization that purpose we have used one of the popular optimization technique i.e. genetic algorithms. This approach shows that it offers good efficiency and scalability of the system. The experimental outcome demonstrate that the prospective algorithm has given exceptional results among existing algorithms.

References

1. Kanakala, V.R.T. and Reddy, V.K., Performance Analysis of Load Balancing Techniques in Cloud Computing Environment, in: *2015 IEEE International Conference on Electrical, Computer and Communication Technologies (ICECCT)*, Coimbatore, pp. 1–6, 2015.

2. Dasgupta, K., Mandal, B., Dutta, P., Mondal, J.S., A Genetic Algorithm (GA) based Load Balancing Strategy for Cloud Computing. *Proc. Technol.*, 10, 340–7, 2013, https://www.science-direct.com/science/article/pii/S2212017313005318.

3. Randles, M., Lamb, D., Taleb-Bendiab, A., A ComparativeStudy into Distributed Load Balancing Algorithms for Cloud Computing, in: *2010 IEEE 24th International Conference on Advanced Information Networking and Applications Workshops, IEEE*, pp. 551–556 Apr 20, 2010.

4. Rajoriya, S., Load Balancing Techniques in Cloud Computing: An Overview. *Int. J. Sci. Res.*, 3, 2014, https://pdfs.semanticscholar.org/37f3/6f95e5ebd673df983597c443f39be63f67af.pdf.

5. Ghomi, E.J., Masoud Rahmani, A., Nasih Qader, N., Load balancing algorithms in cloud computing: A survey. *J. Netw. Comput. Appl.*, 88, 50–71, 2017. https://www.sciencedirect.com/science/article/pii/S1084804517301480.

6. Zhang, Z. and Zhang, X., A Load Balancing Mechanism Based on Ant Colony and Complex Network Theory in Open Cloud Computing Federation., in: *2010 The 2nd International Conference on Industrial Mechatronics and Automation May 30*, Vol. 2, pp. 240–243, 2010, *IEEE.* https://ieeexplore.ieee.org/document/5538385/.

7. Mesbahi, M. and Rahmani, A.M., Load Balancing inCloud Computing: A State of the Art Survey. *IJMECS*, 8, 3, 2016. http://www.mecspress.org/ijmecs/ijmecs-v8-n3/IJMECS-V8-N3-8.pdf.

8. Vanisenko, I.N. and Radivilova, T.A., Survey of major load balancing algorithms in distributed system, in: *2015 information technologies in innovation business conference (ITIB)*, Oct 7 *IEEE.* pp. 89–92, 2015. https://ieeexplore.ieee.org/document/7355061/.

9. Farrag, A. and Mahmoud, S.A., Intelligentcloud algorithms for load balancing problems: A survey. In 2015 IEEE Seventh International Conference on Intelligent Computing and Information Systems (ICICIS) *IEEE,* Dec 12, pp. 210–216, 2015, https://ieeexplore.ieee.org/document/7397223/.

10. Khan, S. and Sharma, N., Effective Scheduling Algorithm for Load balancing using Ant Colony Optimization in Cloud Computing. *IJARCSSE*, 2, 966–73, 2014. https://pdfs.semanticscholar.org/e2cc/4722d826943c99a3bdb5eb7dde8797 516a25.pdf.

11. Rajguru, A.A. and Apte, S.S., A comparative performance analysis of load balancing algorithms in distributed system using qualitative parameters. *Int. J. Recent Technol. Eng.*, 1.3, 175–179, 2012.

12. Palta, R. and Jeet, R., Load balancing in the cloud computing using virtual machine migration: A review. *Int. J. Appl. Innov. Eng. Manag. (IJAIEM)*, 3.5, 437–441, 2014.

13. Keshvadi, S. and Faghih, B., A multi-agent based load balancing system in IaaS cloud environment. *Int. Robot. Autom. J.*, 1, 1, 3, 2016.

14. Ghosh, S. and Banerjee, C., Priority based modified throttled algorithm in cloud computing. *2016 International Conference on Inventive Computation Technologies (ICICT)*, vol. 3, IEEE, 2016.

15. Domanal, S.G., Reddy, M., Ram, G., Load balancing in cloud environment using a novel hybrid scheduling algorithm. *2015 IEEE International Conference on Cloud Computing in Emerging Markets (CCEM)*, IEEE, 2015.

16. Ariharan, V. and Manakattu, S.S., Neighbour Aware Random Sampling (NARS) algorithm for load balancing in Cloud computing. *2015 IEEE International Conference on Electrical, Computer and Communication Technologies (ICECCT)*, IEEE, 2015.

17. Sotiriadis, S. *et al.*, The inter-cloud meta-scheduling (ICMS) framework. *2013 IEEE 27th International Conference on Advanced Information Networking and Applications (AINA)*, IEEE, 2013.

18. Ghomi, E.J., Rahmani, A.M., Qader, N., Nooruldeen, Load-balancing algorithms in cloud computing: A survey. *J. Netw. Comput. Appl.*, 88, 50–71, 2017.

19. Dasgupta, K. *et al.*, A genetic algorithm (ga) based load balancing strategy for cloud computing. *Procedia Technol.*, 10, 340–347, 2013.

20. Geethu Gopinath, P.P. and Vasudevan, S.K., An in-depth analysis and study of Load balancing techniques in the cloud computing environment. *Procedia Comput. Sci.*, 50, 427–432, 2015.

21. Singh, A., Juneja, D., Malhotra, M., Autonomous agent based load balancing algorithm in cloud computing. *Procedia Comput. Sci.*, 45, 832–841, 2015.

22. Dhinesh Babu, L.D. and Venkata Krishna, P., Honey bee behavior inspired load balancing of tasks in cloud computing environments. *Appl. Soft Comput.*, 13.5, 2292–2303, 2013.

Index

Printed and bound by CPI Group (UK) Ltd, Croydon, CR0 4YY